Perceiving
Events and Objects

Gunnar Johansson at the Department of Psychology, Uppsala University, during an interview with William Epstein in June 1992. (Photo: Lars Bäckström.)

Perceiving
Events and Objects

Edited by
Gunnar Jansson
Uppsala University, Sweden

Sten Sture Bergström
Umeå University, Sweden

William Epstein
University of Wisconsin-Madison

LEA **LAWRENCE ERLBAUM ASSOCIATES, PUBLISHERS**
1994 Hillsdale, New Jersey   Hove, UK

Lawrence Erlbaum Associates, Inc., Publishers
365 Broadway
Hillsdale, New Jersey 07642

Library of Congress Cataloging-in-Publication Data

Perceiving events and objects / edited by Gunnar Jansson, Sten Sture
   Bergström, William Epstein.
      p. cm.
   Proceedings of a symposium in honor of Gunnar Johansson, held
   Aug. 21-23, 1991, at Uppsala University.
   Includes bibliographical references and indexes.
   ISBN 0-8058-1555-4   22133402
   1. Visual perception--Congresses. 2. Johansson, Gunnar, 1911-
--Congresses. I. Jansson, Gunnar, 1932- . II. Bergström, Sten
Sture, 1930- . III. Epstein, William, 1931- . IV. Johansson,
Gunnar, 1911- .
   BF241.P394 1994
   152.14--dc20   94-8768
                                              CIP

Printed in the United States of America

10 9 8 7 6 5 4 3 2 1

Contents

VI

Applied Research

Commentaries on Selected Aspects of
Gunnar Johansson's Contributions

Vector Analysis

Perceptual Processing

Vection and Locomotion

Optic Sphere Theory

Concluding Remarks

Preface

In 1989, at the age of 78, Gunnar Johansson, together with his collaborator and former student Eric Börjesson, published a paper called "Towards a new theory of vision. Studies in wide-angle space perception" (*Ecological Psychology, 1*, 301–331). This was the first presentation of *the optic sphere theory.* The title chosen for that paper was neither modest nor incidental. The paper started intense discussions, at least among Swedish perceptionists.

Gunnar Johansson has had a long and productive career as an experimental psychologist in visual perception. Gunnar's doctoral dissertation, with David Katz as his mentor, introduced the perceptual vector analysis, which has inspired much research and discussion not only in Gunnar's own laboratory but worldwide. The dissertation opened the international window for Gunnar and brought him in contact with Gestaltists like Wolfgang Köhler and Hans Wallach and also with James Gibson. (Remember that this happened shortly after World War II, with all the isolation that meant!). Gunnar's later studies on vector analysis and depth perception, the first one when visiting James Gibson's laboratory, inspired a number of doctoral dissertations at Uppsala. And his more recent studies on the perception of biological motion became the starting point for many studies in several laboratories. But what about the optical sphere theory?

Since Gunnar does not like *Festschriften* we decided to celebrate his 80th birthday by arranging a symposium on the optic sphere theory. Gunnar agreed to this type of celebration on certain conditions: (a) there should be a small number of sophisticated contributors invited, and (b) those invited should read his theory and criticize it rather than act as devotees or present their own work. This is a very typical Gunnar Johansson reaction. He would never agree to a symposium just to celebrate himself. It has to contribute to the development of theory.

Some of the invited American scientists suggested, however, that the status of the vector analysis model after four decades should be discussed, so we talked Gunnar into accepting a discussion of "that old stuff" too.

The symposium was held at the Department of Psychology, Uppsala University, Uppsala, Sweden, August 21–23, 1991. To get acquainted with the optic sphere theory all the participants got a lot of written material, both published and unpublished, well in advance. The contributors to the symposium also exchanged preliminary versions of their contributions in order to optimize the conditions for good scientific discussions. At the end of the symposium the participants were excited enough to unanimously decide to collect their contributions in a book. It was also suggested that such a volume should include the main part of Gunnar's dissertation, "Configurations in Event Perception," which has been out of print for about 30 years. This means that the present volume contains some real classic stuff in event perception: Gunnar Johansson's dissertation abridged and commented on by himself. It also contains reprints of a collection of later papers by Gunnar, of course, both published and previously unpublished papers tracing newer developments of the optic sphere theory.

Instead of a formal biography of Gunnar this volume contains a transcript of an interview made by William Epstein in June 1992.

Reading the Johansson papers is a fascinating adventure since it illustrates the step-by-step development of an individual researcher and at the same time the development of his research area, visual perception.

Having read the Johansson papers the reader will certainly enjoy the attempt by William Epstein to trace Gunnar's 40-year-long trek from the land of Gestalt theory to the land of direct perception; that is the land of the special Johanssonian direct perception, which certainly includes perceptual processing, without becoming a land inhabited by Helmholtzians. This highly interesting analysis is followed by Gunnar's own comments.

Commentaries on selected aspects of Gunnar Johansson's contributions are presented under the subtitles *Applied Research, Vector Analysis, Perceptual Processing, Vection and Locomotion,* and *Optic Sphere Theory.* The volume ends with Gunnar Johansson's concluding comments, his Bibliography 1950–1993, and author and subject indexes.

Under the subtitle *Applied Research,* Kåre Rumar stresses Gunnar Johansson's pioneer work in Swedish human factors research, and Herschel Leibowitz takes an important implication of Gunnar's research on biological motion for the enhancement of nighttime pedestrian visibility as an example of the synergy between basic and applied research.

The power and simplicity of *vector analysis* methods is elegantly demonstrated by Jan Koenderink. Joseph Lappin stresses the simplicity and directness of the idea that perceived common and relative motions are aspects of the visual representation of the optical patterns rather than inferential reconstructions from retinal motions of individual points. His "hologram-like" model for local mechanisms carrying information about global structure through interference is really fascinating. It means that the common motion is described relative to an extrinsic frame of reference (like the retina), whereas relative motion is intrinsic to the pattern itself. This seems to be exactly what Johansson means when using the terms *common* and *relative motion.* Lappin also presents a series of empirical evidence for his ideas.

Runesson emphasizes that Gunnar Johansson's studies of biological motion mean an important swing from a proximal to a distal approach in studying perception, a swing that certainly seems important for Gibsonians. And Runesson demonstrates the advantages of a distal approach by his own pioneering research on kinematic specification of dynamics, the KSD-principle.

Sten Sture Bergström, in his contribution, makes an attempt to apply the Johansson analysis into common and relative components to the perception of illumination, color, and depth.

Under the subtitle *Perceptual Processing* we present contributions by Myron Braunstein, Julian Hochberg, and Gunnar Jansson. Gunnar Jansson discusses perceived bending motion, an area where he has collaborated with Gunnar Johansson. He stresses the principle of minimum object change that Jansson and Johansson introduced some 20 years ago and puts it in relation to the optic sphere theory. Myron Braunstein and Julian Hochberg, in their contributions, discuss Johansson's processing rules in a more general theoretical context. This part, then, discusses the most controversial parts of Gunnar Johansson's models of motion and depth perception; controversial because this part of his theory is where his agreements and disagreements with other theories are revealed. It is fascinating to follow these discussions of the status of Gunnar's "decoding principles" and "minimum principle" in relation to the Helmholtzian approach on one side and the Gibsonian direct perception on the other. If the "rules" that Hochberg asks for are of the type suggested by Gunnar and if they also are part of the "hardware," then how big is the difference between Gunnar's processing and Gibson's "tuning?" The reader has to judge for himself, but there is no doubt that these contributions raise a lot of highly interesting questions.

Under the subtitle *Vection and Locomotion* you will find two contributions, one by Richard Held and Herschel Leibowitz and the other by Claes von Hofsten and David Lee. They are very different and you have to stretch the title a little to have it cover both. Both focus on the relation between moving or stationary objects and a moving or stationary observer, but for very different reasons. Held and Leibowitz discuss Johansson's finding that a set of moving points in the visual periphery can induce perceived motion of the self. They discuss the ambiguity of such a situation and draw conclusions and put forth hypotheses about up-to-date issues like telepresence reported under certain conditions of teleoperation in robotics. von Hofsten and Lee on the other hand discuss the possibility of spatial scaling based on observer movement relative to moving or stationary objects in the environment. Their dialogue is very interesting and very basic for space perception and for the optic sphere theory.

The *Optic Sphere Theory*, finally, has been commented on in general theoretical terms in some of the chapters already mentioned, especially in those under the subtitle *Perceptual Processing*. But there are two contributions mainly discussing the optic sphere. Eric Börjesson discusses the optic sphere as a smart mechanism for determining slant and presents empirical evidence. James Todd in his paper examines the optic sphere theory and finds no advantage in Johansson and Börjesson's choice of a spherical projection surface. As a good exponent for the computationally oriented perceptionists he means that any projection surface will do, because there is always a mathematical relation between the different types of projection planes.

In his concluding remarks Gunnar responds to Todd's critique and offers a variety of observations stimulated by the preceding contributions.

Sten Sture Bergström

Acknowledgments

The editors are very much indebted to the contributors, especially to Gunnar Johansson, who has accepted a large amount of work, in particular by writing new contributions for this volume. Among the earlier work, the editing of an abridged version of his classical work from 1950, "Configurations in Event Perception," should be especially mentioned.

We appreciate assistance from Lars Bäckström concerning computer problems during the production of the book and from Sören Jansson who performed the computer work by first transforming the different contributions to a common format and then transforming this first version to the special camera-ready version. This work included revisions of many figures and tables. Lars Bäckström also served as a photographer during the interview with Gunnar Johansson (cf. p. II).

Acknowledgments of permission to reprint earlier published material is given in each case. Gunnar Johansson, as an author, has given a general permission to reprint his earlier papers.

The Swedish Council for Research in the Humanities and Social Sciences funded the symposium on which the book is based, as well as made the production of the camera-ready manuscript possible.

The editors

Contributors

Sten Sture Bergström, Department of Applied Psychology, Umeå University, Umeå, Sweden.

Erik Börjesson, Department of Psychology, Uppsala University, Uppsala, Sweden.

Myron L. Braunstein, School of Social Sciences, University of California, Irvine, California, USA.

William Epstein, Department of Psychology, University of Wisconsin, Madison, Wisconsin, USA.

James J. Gibson, Department of Psychology, Cornell University, Ithaca, New York, USA (deceased).

Richard Held, Department of Brain and Cognitive Sciences, Massachusetts Institute of Technology, Cambridge, Massachusetts, USA.

Julian Hochberg, Department of Psychology, Columbia University, New York, New York, USA.

Claes von Hofsten, Department of Psychology, Umeå University, Umeå, Sweden.

Gunnar Jansson, Department of Psychology, Uppsala University, Uppsala, Sweden.

Gunnar Johansson, Department of Psychology, Uppsala University, Uppsala, Sweden.

Jan Koenderink, Department of Physics and Astronomy, State University Utrecht, Utrecht, The Netherlands.

Joseph S. Lappin, Department of Psychology, Vanderbilt University, Nashville, Tennessee, USA.

David Lee, Department of Psychology, University of Edinburgh, Edinburgh, United Kingdom.

Herschel Leibowitz, Department of Psychology, Pennsylvania State University, University Park, Pennsylvania, USA.

Sheena Rogers, Department of Psychology, University of Wisconsin, Madison, Wisconsin, USA.

Kåre Rumar, Swedish Road and Traffic Research Institute, Linköping, Sweden.

Sverker Runeson, Department of Psychology, Uppsala University, Uppsala, Sweden.

James T. Todd, Department of Psychology, Ohio State University, Columbus, Ohio, USA.

RESOURCES FOR ECOLOGICAL PSYCHOLOGY

A Series of Volumes Edited by:
Robert E. Shaw, William M. Mace, and Michael T. Turvey

Reed/Jones • *Reasons for Realism: Selected Essays of James J. Gibson*

Warren/Shaw • *Persistence and Change*

Kugler/Turvey • *Information, Natural Law, and the Self-Assembly of Rhythmic Movement*

McCabe/Balzano • *Event Cognition: An Ecological Perspective*

Lombardo • *The Reciprocity of Perceiver and Environment: The Evolution of James J. Gibson's Ecological Psychology*

Alley • *Social and Applied Aspects of Perceiving Faces*

Warren/Wertheim • *Perception & Control of Self-Motion*

Thinès/Costall/Butterworth • *Michotte's Experimental Phenomenology of Perception*

Jansson/Bergström/Epstein • *Perceiving Events and Objects*

RESOURCES
for ECOLOGICAL PSYCHOLOGY

Edited by
Robert E. Shaw, William M. Mace, and Michael Turvey

This series of volumes is dedicated to furthering the development of psychology as a branch of ecological science. In its broadest sense, ecology is a multidisciplinary approach to the study of living systems, their environments, and the reciprocity that has evolved between the two. Traditionally, ecological science emphasizes the study of the biological bases of *energy* transactions between animals and their physical environments across cellular, organismic, and population scales. Ecological psychology complements this traditional focus by emphasizing the study of *information* transactions between living systems and their environments, especially as they pertain to perceiving situations of significance to planning and execution of purposes activated in an environment.

The late James J. Gibson used the term *ecological psychology* to emphasize this animal-environment mutuality for the study of problems of perception. He believed that analyzing the environment to be perceived was just as much a part of the psychologist's task as analyzing animals themselves, and hence that the "physical" concepts applied to the environment and the "biological" and "psychological" concepts applied to organisms would have to be tailored to one another in a larger system of mutual constraint. His early interest in the applied problems of landing airplanes and driving automobiles led him to pioneer the study of the perceptual guidance of action.

The work of Nicolai Bernstein in biomechanics and physiology presents a complementary approach to problems of the coordination and control of movement. His work suggests that action, too, cannot be studied without reference to the environment, and that physical and biological concepts must be developed together. The coupling of Gibson's ideas with those of Bernstein forms a natural basis for looking at the traditional psychological topics of perceiving, acting, and knowing as activities of ecosystems rather than isolated animals.

The purpose of this series is to form a useful collection, a resource, for people who wish to learn about ecological psychology and for those who wish to contribute to its development. The series will include original research, collected papers, reports of conferences and symposia, theoretical monographs, technical handbooks, and works from the many disciplines relevant to ecological psychology.

Series Dedication

To James J. Gibson, whose pioneering work in ecological psychology has opened new vistas in psychology and related sciences, we respectfully dedicate this series.

Biography

Gunnar Johansson: A Practical Theorist[†]

An Interview with William Epstein

(Edited by Sheena Rogers, University of Wisconsin-Madison)

Beginnings

William Epstein (*Bill*): Gunnar, why don't we start at the beginning, that is a good place to start the story. We thought that we would like to hear you comment on your early interest in philosophy while you were a student at Uppsala. What led you from a country store to philosophy?

Gunnar Johansson (*Gunnar*): I have to go back in time. I was born in a rural part of Uppland, Roslagen, 1911. I was in an elementary school for 6 years and then at the age of 12 I started to work in my father's country store, I think you call it a general store. My elder brother, who at that time also worked there, was very interested in literature and history and we had a little, rather qualified library in my home and I started reading these books early on. Among them I found an elementary book about the history of philosophy written by Hans Larsson, a well-known Swedish professor of philosophy. I think I was between 18 and 20 years old at that time. This book opened a new world for me and I began to buy more advanced books in the field. Thus it was Hans Larsson who initiated my engagement in philosophy. At the same time I tried to study by correspondence. Because I was working the whole time I devoted much of my spare time to these studies. Among other subjects, I studied German and English, but also biology, mathematics, and physics.

Bill: German philosophers?

Gunnar: Yes, right. German literature and also some philosophy. Oh, this is a long story...

Bill: Gunnar, may I ask: How did your parents react to this special interest that you had in philosophy?

[†] The interview was made at the Department of Psychology, Uppsala University, in June 1992. In addition to the main actors, Sten Sture Bergström and Gunnar Jansson took occasional part in the conversation. Alice Bergström made the transcription of the taped interview.

Gunnar (with a big laugh): They strongly supported my studies by correspondence. I think they did not know much about the specific subjects but they had a highly positive attitude to all types of studies.

Bill: How did you arrive at the decision to come to the university and devote yourself to philosophy in a formal way?

Gunnar: Earlier I had had some indirect contact with a *folkhögskola* (folk high-school). This is a special, still existing, Scandinavian kind of school for people who had not studied before. People from the countryside. I had some plan to be a teacher at such a school. For this position an academic exam in a number of subjects was needed. I started with philosophy but my candidate exam also included other subjects.

Bill: And so you came to the university attracted to philosophy. But at some point you must have lost the interest in philosophy or decided that empirical science was a better way to ask questions and get answers. How did that come about?

Gunnar: My studies in philosophy had a strong bias toward sensory psychology from an epistemological point of view and these studies evoked an interest in empirical studies of perception. For instance, during this period I read Gestalt psychology and also its critics. My exam also included the subject education, part of which included experimental psychology.

Gunnar Jansson (*GJa*): Had Karitz, the teacher, some effect on your choice? He was also interested in other sciences.

Gunnar: No, I don't think so. At least not in a direct way. But Karitz was interested in psychology and had close contact with science and medicine. In this respect he contrasted to the Uppsala school, engaged mainly in modern logic.

Bill: So then, you went from Uppsala to Stockholm and you began to work on empirical problems?

Gunnar: Not directly. Immediately after my licentiate exam in philosophy I was married and I worked for 3 years in Uppsala in vocational guidance. It was a very good position and interesting work. However, supported by my Karin, I decided to leave this safe life and go over to the adventure of research and study for a doctor's degree. As I have said, I was especially interested in Gestalt psychology and I knew that David Katz was professor at Stockholm. In consequence, I chose experimental work on perception with a theoretical aim as the subject for my dissertation and contacted Professor Katz.

Bill: Can you tell us a little bit about the origin of the experiments on event configurations? I don't know any other experiments that are really like those experiments. Maybe with the exception of Duncker's work on perceived motion.

Gunnar: During my preparatory studies of Gestalt psychology I had questioned the relevance of the Gestaltists' static analyses and noted that Wertheimer's law of common fate in fact represented a special category with just one member in his set of Gestalt laws. This special law was about perceptual organization of pictorial changes over time while all the other laws concerned perceptual configurations in static pictures. After reading Katz's book on Gestalt psychology I knew about his interest in the law of common fate. Therefore it was a matter of course to start with studies of this effect. I started my experimental studies by introducing different motions in different components of some typical, initially static, Gestalt-law patterns. Usually I projected a number of dark dots onto a vertical screen. The most important finding theoretically was the immediate and unavoidable perceptual splitting of the initially static Gestalt into two separate, moving Gestalts. Thus common motion was found to be the fundamental Gestalt-determining factor. From these studies grew my event perception concept and vector analysis studies.

Bill: But Katz himself never worked on motion to my knowledge.

Gunnar: No, he didn't, but he was very interested in this project. So, when he found that I could handle mechanical things, and that the apparatus I built were well adapted for my experiments, he strongly supported me. He also acted as a subject in many experiments.

Bill: But he didn't suggest the problem to you, did he?

Gunnar: No, not the event perception problem as such. Initially he just proposed the law of common fate. The broad event perception approach basically came from my experiments and my own stepwise theorizing.

Bill: And so now we have this long series of experiments, which, you told me the other day, lasted 3 years. Most people don't know about the experiments using intensity, or the experiments using touch, they know principally about the visual experiments. When I read the monograph recently I was impressed by the style. You would have some description of experiments and then there would be some theory, and more experiments and some theory. And, so even very early in 1950 when you were doing your doctoral dissertation you had an attitude towards the relationship between theory and data. Could you say something about that?

Gunnar: I am glad to hear that you have observed the special style of my old monograph. I observed the same thing when I recently worked on a précis of this monograph. I found it surprisingly dense and hard to compress. I think this style was a natural consequence of my experimental method. You see, at bottom I am a practical man. I deliberately established my research according to a "successive addressing of open questions to nature." Each experiment was designed to ask the following question: How does nature (the sense organ) react to this specific physical event? I knew that I was entering terra incognita and that therefore the traditional testing of earlier formulated hypotheses was improper. In fact, this method with open questions can be found in much of my later research.

Bill: My impression, Gunnar, is that you haven't changed in the 40 years since then. To work this way is part of your temperament and it showed up very early and has stayed with you all the way through. It is a particular personal style almost.

Gunnar: Probably, I never thought about that.

Bill: It seems so to me. After you completed your doctoral work you remained in Stockholm for 5, 6, 7 years?

Gunnar: Yes, I got my doctoral degree in the spring of 1950 and I stayed there in a docent position until 1956 when I was elected to professor at Uppsala University.

GJa: Assistant research professor is a common translation of docent.

Bill: The research that you did then, would that have been your own research or research in collaboration with other people?

Gunnar: No, I think I have been *en ensam varg* [a lone wolf].

Sten Sture Bergström (*SSB*): Yes, but Gunnar, wasn't it during that time you ran some experiments with a clinical application together with Dureman, Sälde, etc.?

Gunnar: Oh yes. Excuse me, I was wrong. I collaborated with Gösta Ekman and Hannes Eisler—and also with you Bill, during your Uppsala period. But in my research on event perception I think I have never had coworkers other than my students, my former students, and you, Bill.

Bill: You must have been doing clinical work with Dureman but psychophysics with Ekman?

Gunnar: Right!

GJa: Did you ever publish anything of what you did together with Gösta Ekman?

Gunnar: We had a very vivid discussion about modern psychophysics at that time and together we started an experimental project, an investigation concerning a hypothetical psychophysical difference between photopic and scotopic recording of brightness. I was responsible for the technical part of it and Gösta mainly for the psychophysical. However, before this project was ended I had moved to Uppsala and I do not remember its fate. Still, I remember that in its initial phase we found clear differences. I also remember that I sent you, Sten Sture, and Fredrik Backlund to Stockholm to help Gösta and Hannes recalibrate the rather complicated apparatus.

Bill: Did you study velocity perception?

Gunnar: Yes, I did. In fact I started my experimental work in Katz's laboratory with studies of velocity perception. This investigation was presented as qualification for my licentiate exam in education and psychology and published in *Acta Psychologica.* This exam was a necessary condition for starting studies for a doctors' degree in experimental psychology. After my dissertation I continued with studies of perception of velocity evoked by perceptual interaction (the perceptual combination of the velocities of two elements meeting on a common track). The perceived speed of two dots moving toward or away from each other on a vertical screen could be as high as twice the physical velocity of each one of them or still more.

Bill: And what sort of clinical work did you do with Dureman?

Gunnar: I did not really do clinical work. During my studies of perceived interaction of velocities, I had observed that a few of my subjects, whom I knew rather well, clearly deviated from the group. They seemed to react in a rather analytical way, producing far lower velocity ratings than the other subjects, and I got the impression that these subjects' recorded degree of velocity synthesis varied with their probable position on an analytical-synthetical personality scale. Especially the ratings from one of these subjects, who I regarded as a very intelligent person but also rather bizarre and maybe, to a certain degree, schizoid, who consistently produced ratings close to the ratings of the velocity of a single element.

I had told Dureman and Sälde about these observations and also demonstrated the phenomenon for them. They were at that time working on a broad project for diagnosing personality and they were curious whether this effect could, to some degree, vary with their clinical indications of analytical-synthetical personality trends.

SSB: They were making a test battery. A clinical test.

Gunnar: They found that the degree of this perceptual velocity effect had an astonishingly high correlation with the clinical analytic-synthetic ratings. May I just tell you an interesting real-life observation in this connection? You know that from my cottage at the Baltic Sea we have an open view over the water. When two boats meet a certain distance from the coast they seem to accelerate until they meet each other and then decelerate over the same distance.

Bill: You were one of the original ecological psychologists! You have confirmed this observation in everyday life. That's quite nice.

When you came to Uppsala as professor in 1957, did you find the department here with workshops and computers and experimental psychology laboratories? Is that what it was like when you came?

Gunnar: Sten Sture knows that there was nothing.

SSB: There was some space and rooms and some equipment—the old brass things from Leipzig.

Gunnar: Right, right. So you see, when I came here I started applied psychology. I had a project from SAAB, the Swedish aerocompany, for studying the characteristics of, what do you call them? Joysticks.

SSB: And aiming problems.

Gunnar: Yes, and the importance of fixation and such things. Sten Sture took part in this. Therefore, you see, I got a lot of money for buying equipment—and paying my assistants.

Bill: Gunnar, how did you come to these questions? I mean, you start out in a general store, go to philosophy, then you go to basic research on the perception of motion, and motion configuration, and events, and now you're studying joysticks. How does that happen? In the U.S. one doesn't see that very much. We tend to be very focused. It's very rare to find someone with this range of interest; there are exceptions, but it is still very rare. Did you choose to study these questions so that you could get money for your other research, or did you have a genuine interest in these questions?

Gunnar: I think I am rather broad-minded. Therefore I must answer: Both! You see this engagement was contracted before I left Stockholm. SAAB contacted me. They had found that I was probably the only researcher in Sweden who had a broad competence in perception of the type of interest to them. I accepted SAAB's proposal because of a real engagement in applied research but I must admit that, as the head of the Uppsala department, I had started that research without a personal engagement. As another sign of real interest in practical, useful research I will mention my many years of comprehensive research on traffic safety problems. Both Sten Sture and Gunnar worked as my assistants in this research. Finally, I can also tell you about two other experiences as an applied psychologist. While working on my dissertation I also fulfilled my military service as a psychologist. This work involved much study, especially of clinical psychology, which has later been of great value to me. Next, after my first year in Stockholm as docent, the University of Stockholm had no docent position vacant for me so now I had to find another temporary job. At that time there was a great shortage of manpower in Swedish industry, and as a consequence a very high degree of drifting. Because of my background I was engaged as an industrial psychologist with the task to create better relations between management and workers. In connection with this work I studied a number of books about relevant industrial psychology. I found this job very stimulating, but after a year the university could offer me a long-term position as a salaried docent and I could return to my research and teaching.

Bill: So now when you came here you really had to create shops and laboratories and equipment, and a part of that, or maybe most of it, was supported by funds that you had secured to do research on applied problems. Is that right?

Gunnar: Right. Practically all our equipment originated from applied projects. And after a few years the Uppsala laboratory was by far the best equipped in Scandinavia.

On Vector Analysis

GJa: How did you come to begin the vector analysis?

Gunnar: Oh, from my analyses of the experimental results. These results indicated some kind of vectorial relations between the element motions.

Bill: You know, Duncker, in his studies of induced motion, didn't have a formal vector analysis, but he did have an informal one. So that, for example, if you imagine that you have a stationary point which is surrounded by two frameworks and you move one of the frameworks, let's say the interior framework, to the left and the outer framework upwards, the perceived direction of the induced motion of the stationary point will be what a vector analysis would suppose.

Gunnar: Yes, I know. When I read Duncker's paper I appreciated it very much, especially because there I found my vector model confirmed in an unexpected way. When I read Duncker's paper my vector theory already had found its basic form. In my book I thoroughly discussed Duncker's finding. My vector theory began with an observation made during my initial experiments adding motion to some well known static Gestalts. Probably it will be of interest to you to hear about that. I will briefly describe the initial observations from which the theory of perceptual vector analysis was born. In the studies of common fate I had rear-projected a vertical-horizontal cross on a translucent screen. This Gestalt was built up by two sets of black dots specifying the vertical and horizontal lines of the cross. Each line could be given a vertical, horizontal, or diagonal motion to and fro, up and down, determined by a sine function. When both lines were given the same motion in the same direction, a rigid, moving cross was seen. However, when the direction of motion of one of these lines was changed, the initial configuration was immediately spoiled and instead two, independent, moving lines were seen. On one occasion I changed the phase angle between the vertical and horizontal dot lines by 90 degrees. This brought about an astonishing effect. I observed that the two dots just at the crossing of the two lines seemed to rotate in a complicated way, hard to specify. At first I thought there was something wrong with my apparatus but a control made clear that it worked in a perfect way and that the dots at the crossing in fact moved linearly on the screen. When I studied the geometrical relations between the motions of the two dots by varying the phase angle, for example, I realized that a vectorial interaction could explain it. The subsequent series of experiments represent a stepwise search for a general type of vectorial model for event perception.

Bill: So this was an unexpected discovery? Of course just making this surprising observation is no guarantee that one will see the significance of it, but you did.

On Köhler

Bill: Your mentioning of Gestalt psychology now leads me to ask about perhaps what must have been your first visit to the U.S. when you went to Cornell to attend the symposium on Gestalt theory. Did you meet Köhler there?

Gunnar: No. You see, Metzger, who was also invited, was to an extreme degree *persona non grata* for Köhler. Metzger had, during the Nazi time, written a book about Gestalt psychology and evidently for highly realistic, political reasons not mentioned Köhler's name in the book. So when Köhler heard that Metzger would take part in this symposium, he said no!

Bill: Oh, so then Köhler wouldn't come?

Gunnar: No, instead he sent his assistant at that time, Hans Wallach. From that conference Hans and I have been very good friends!

Bill: Yes, the two of you are very much alike. Hans was one of my teachers, and it's really owing to Hans that I developed an enthusiasm for perception. He was always so enthusiastic. He reminds me very much of you in that respect. So that was your first trip to the U.S. and maybe your first interaction with the international community?

Gunnar: Yes it was. However, Katz had many contacts and I think I met Köhler for the first time in Stockholm and after that Köhler visited me at the Uppsala laboratory rather often.

SSB: Yes, regularly. Every other year or so.

GJa: Köhler's second wife was Swedish.

Bill: What were your impressions of Köhler? Did you find him easy to get along with? Because he had a reputation of being, what's the word I want, being very formal.

Gunnar: Yes, in one respect he was of course but I had a good relationship with Köhler.

Bill: Did you talk about his work with him? His work on the electrical fields of the brain?

Gunnar: Yes, several times. Or to be more correct, Köhler talked to me about his theory and about the experimental support for this theory while I mostly only asked him about some, in my opinion, critical points. However, we also discussed my own research and in this respect Köhler showed a high degree of flexibility and expressed great appreciation.

SSB: I remember the first time I met him in Uppsala when I was a student. We were discussing his satiation theory, and Köhler was so enthusiastic that all of a sudden he shifted to German without noticing it. He spoke German for a while and went back to English and he never noticed these shifts.

Bill: Hans Wallach, too, would get very excited. Every so often he would get up from his chair and start walking up and down and talking all the time. Occasionally he'd forget himself and he would walk right outside the door and go walking down the hall. I stayed seated because I knew he would come back.

Earlier I characterized your style as taking an empirical step, a little theory, more empirical steps, a little more theory. But Köhler was very theoretically driven, interested in grand theory, although he had a strong empirical bent. What was your reaction to Köhler? Did you find his approach convincing? Did you press him? Did you criticize him?

Gunnar: It was not really possible to criticize Köhler, or to press him, only to express doubts. You see, Köhler was interesting in this respect. What he heard about our experiments, empirical results and so on, interested him very much because he tried to treat these results as support for the satiation theory. And you see, as a theory, I cannot think of anything more elegant in the history of psychology than Köhler's satiation theory. But I do not believe in its relevance. Already, when it was formulated, this theory was in conflict with what was known at the time about neural function of the sensory systems and, of course, this is far more clear today. I have always regarded the attempt to explain visual space perception as an electrochemical process in the animal brain volume conductor as very bizarre. However, I think that if we limit our demands on the theory to the presentation of a possible way to explain Köhler's satiation phenomena in volume-conductor terms I think it will be hard to refute it. However, I will also declare that I was very impressed with the person Köhler. He was a rather unique man. He was such a person of principle, so honest but also fearless and unshakable. I know this from what I know about his history but also from my personal contact with him. I think you know his history? And you know the risk he took? [Johansson is referring to Köhler's famous letter, written to a major German newspaper, setting out his objections to the Nazi government. Köhler was a professor at Berlin University at the time.]

Bill: Yes, I do know that.

Gunnar: The last time I met Köhler was when he got his honorary doctor's degree at our university. I think you remember that promotion, Sten Sture?

SSB: Yes, we were promoted at the same time.

Gunnar: Our collimator equipment and its possibilities to generate moving visual three-dimensional objects fascinated Köhler. An effect of this device is that you will see, monocularly, the optically generated object freely hanging and moving in an empty space. When I proposed that Köhler return to Uppsala in the autumn for an experimental collaboration on some problems common to both of us he seemed happy and accepted without much hesitation. A few weeks after his return to the U.S. I got a message about his sudden death.

Bill: I actually saw those effects in the old S:t Larsgatan laboratories. So you were going to collaborate with Köhler. What was going to be the question? Do you remember?

Gunnar: Yes, we talked about studies on perceptual object identity of moving and changing objects.

Bill: The studies that you reported in the changing form paper in 1964. When I came in 1966 I saw those displays. Have you been thinking about Gestalt theory now, 20 years after Köhler's death? Have you changed your mind?

Gunnar: No! My opinion of today about the classical Gestalt approach as a theory does not deviate much from my position in 1950. I still regard the Gestalt school as a highly important contribution to the understanding of visual perception. It introduced a new way of thinking but, in my opinion, at least in its classical form, it had severe limitations. I have already mentioned its anchorage in the analysis of pictures, initiated by the triumvirate Wertheimer, Koffka, and Köhler. However, I will also mention that later students of visual perception representing the Gestalt school have a far more open-minded attitude. I think this to a certain degree is due to the influence of Wolfgang Metzger. Metzger was certainly rooted in the classical school with its set of Gestalt laws, but I have found him totally free from dogmatism. His magnificent book *Gesetze des Sehens* (The Laws of Vision) published in three editions, the last in 1975 with nearly 700 pages, is a broad and highly impressive review of most kinds of experimental research on vision up to that year.

On Gibson

Bill: We mentioned a moment ago these experiments with changing shape that you did and published in 1964. They remind me a little bit of Gibson-style experimentation. Had you met James Gibson by then?

Gunnar: Oh yes! Gibson had invited me to stay for two semesters at Cornell for research and discussion, and the motion-and-change experiments were carried out there. [Johansson stayed at Cornell University with Gibson during 1961–1962, visited him again during a year spent as a fellow at the Center for

Advanced Studies in the Behavioral Sciences at Stanford University (1965–1966), and spent another semester at Cornell in 1971.]

Bill: Were you influenced by Gibson's thinking in planning these experiments on changing form and perceived depth in motion?

Gunnar: Yes, to some extent, in my choice of problem. Gibson and von Fieandt had carried out an interesting first study on changing form and got positive results with a rather primitive set-up. Both Gibson and myself regarded my project as a continuation of this study. However, Gibson did not take part in the planning and the experiments. He was overloaded with administrative tasks that year. In fact, we never planned or carried out any experiments together. Still, we often discussed the relations between our different theoretical approaches in a highly fruitful way.

Bill: So over the years you must have met Gibson often?

Gunnar: Yes, and Gibson visited Uppsala several times also.

Bill: Did you and Gibson interact easily? Did you find him to be congenial? Easy to work with, talk to? Because, like Köhler, he had very strong opinions.

SSB: The difference was that Gibson could turn down his hearing aid!

Gunnar: Gibson and I always discussed theoretical problems. As soon as we met we started and Jackie [Mrs. Gibson] had problems with us! I remember when we were flying together to some conference, we didn't remember leaving the plane because we were so engaged in our discussion!

Bill: What sort of influence do you attribute to Gibson's style of theorizing? Do you think of your own development as being parallel? Or a development that owes something to Gibson's work?

Gunnar: Both Gibson and myself were aware that we had our basic goal in common: working out a theory capable of explaining everyday visual perception. For an active perceiver this always means perception of physical change over time; motion of one's body relative to the environment and often motion of objects in the environment. In this respect, but I think only in this, we could be regarded as rather similar. Gibson's position was, as we know, developed during his military service as an applied psychologist. I myself regard my own position as self-evident for a person who, with a background of practical work and physical activity, has rather late been engaged in theorizing about the sensory processes that make such activity possible.

Next, you asked about relations between our styles of theorizing. There we differ very much. Gibson's 1950 approach was, as we know, the result of his dissatisfaction with the results of his attempts to put into practice in his applied military research traditional theories for analyzing visual perception. In this book he laid the basis for a theory far more close to real life. I myself had, regarding theoretical position, started from scratch with the objective of investigating the perception of events and, furthermore, my research was carried out in an analytical experimental style. The result was the theory of vector analysis in 1950. After this year, both of us successively elaborated our theories; Gibson in a rather radical way, resulting in a synthetical type of theory, and I along my initial analytical approach. For me, arguing with this difference in approach as a background was highly fruitful. We tested the relevance of our thinking on a colleague who strived along a different path toward the same goal. Therefore each of us always understood the other. These discussions gave me many valuable inspirations and widened my horizon. I also know that Gibson reacted in a similar way. But the difference between our theories was great for both of us.

GJa: I can think of one experiment that you did with sinusoidal distribution of light which you considered to be an application of Gibson's ideas, but he didn't think so.

Gunnar: Yes, that is true. And it is typical of our relationship. Often I would point out that my experimental results in fact supported his own theory but he would reply, "No, Gunnar, I don't mean it in that way!" Probably, in such cases, my own more analytical approach to our common problems was too alien to Gibson.

Bill: You started out with philosophy but have become very unphilosophical in your work. Köhler started out with physics, as you know, and was really very philosophical throughout. Köhler's book called *The Place of Value in a World of Facts*, is a philosophical treatise. And Gibson was really very philosophical, developing a new epistemology. It's been interesting to look at the three of you in this regard, and you stand out in leaving philosophy behind you, whereas Gibson became more and more philosophical. His 1979 book is very philosophical compared to the global psychophysics of the 1950 book. Did you argue philosophy with Gibson?

Gunnar: No! I think we never did.

GJa: Didn't you say that you liked the 1950 book much more than the other two books?

Gunnar: Yes, the 1950 book is my favorite. This book is so remarkable not only because of its content but because it opened a new era in the study of visual perception.

Bill: My own favorite is actually the 1966 book.

Gunnar: Oh yes! This is also a very good book. For my present theoretical work it is of great interest because it considered the interaction between the senses, then a totally new approach.

Bill: I·like that one particularly because it introduced an evolutionary ap-proach.

Gunnar: Yes, I agree. In my own theorizing I rather early on applied evolu-tion as a self-evident anchorage.

Bill: I thought you might like it especially.

GJa (to Bill): I think you had a seminar at Uppsala about Gibson's second book, but then you didn't like it too much.

Bill: There wasn't that much new in the way of theory of perception, but what was new was setting it in an evolutionary context. Because it always seems odd to me, theorizing about a function which is obviously so important in adap-tive behavior outside the context of evolution.

Gunnar: Gibson had great problems with his last book, it took a long time for him.

Bill: About 15 years.

Gunnar: Yes, and I read a lot of drafts.

Bill: Did you often comment on the book as he was writing it?

Gunnar: I think it was mainly in 1971 when I spent a semester at Cornell and we discussed his changed approach a lot. For instance, I remember that I pointed out that on the first page of my 1950 book I had declared that, in con-trast to retinal-image analyses, my studies were intended to investigate real-life perception and thus had an ecological aim. My research from the beginning must be said to have an ecological character in Gibson's sense of that term. I think Gibson mainly agreed. I also remember that at that time I pointed out that Gibson's concept of ecology lacked stringency.

On Biological Motion

Bill: So, let's turn now to the studies of biological motion. How did the studies of biological motion come about?

Gunnar: From my point of view the biological motion studies are just a continuation of my perceptual vector analysis research. I wanted to find out whether the vector analysis model was applicable to highly complicated motion patterns like those in everyday perception. Initially, I was thinking about approximately simulating animal and human motions in accordance with my established method. However, I soon found such simulation extremely complicated from a mathematical and mechanical point of view so I made direct recordings of simultaneous motions of the main joints of a real person. Some further considerations also told me that theoretically this method had a fundamental advantage: It yields an exact representation of possible vectorial interaction of the main bones in the human body while all pictorial information about the motions of these bones is lacking. Thus this method makes possible a rather perfect experimental arrangement with exact but severely reduced real-life representation. In the first studies I attached miniature flashlight bulbs to the leg and arm joints of an actor and filmed his motions in total darkness but later I substituted small patches of reflective tape for the lamps which reflected the light from a searchlight close to the movie camera.

GJa: The first figures appeared in the educational film with you and Maas?

Gunnar: No. After this first study, I think it was in the beginning of 1968, I worked for some time developing optimal technical conditions for such filming. After that, I made a film planned for public demonstration. I brought this film with me to the XIX International Congress in London in 1969 and showed it to Gibson and a few other colleagues, among them Hans Lukas Teuber.

GJa: Where have you hidden that one?

Gunnar: It is hidden in Japan! I also showed it at the XX Congress in Tokyo in 1972. Before I left I presented it to our mutual friend, Hayashi. Later, some Japanese colleagues of Hayashi used it in their research on biological motion. So I think it has done good service!

GJa: And that was made in 1968.

Gunnar: Yes, I think this is correct. And I will also tell you that early on I made a film with random alternating presentation of my own running style (once upon a time I was rather a good sprinter) and that of a female runner. The distance from camera to runner was adjusted to yield equal body size on the film.

Bill: Oh, gender discrimination!

Gunnar: Yes, and informal tests with some subjects indicated good capacity for discrimination. However, I never ran formal experiments. The film was planned just as a first test for a possible investigation of several similar types of visual discrimination, but these plans were not realized. I had too many eggs in my basket at that time. Later, instead, we have Cutting's and his coworkers' well known studies of the recognition of friends and gender from biological motion patterns.

Bill: Here is an anecdote: A couple of years ago I visited with my wife, Sheena, some friends of hers who have identical twin girls. They were maybe 2 years old, and everyone was saying how difficult it was to tell them apart. I had never met them before but I had no difficulty at all! As soon as they moved I saw that they were different. Everyone was startled but the mother said that in fact when one of them was an infant she had had some sort of problem with her hip. The consequence of that is that she generates a subtly different biological motion pattern than her sister!

Gunnar: Oh, how nice.

Bill: It's just a slight perturbation in the pattern.

Gunnar: But, you see, very small mechanical changes in the hip region will have a great effect. The motions in this region relative to the active center of gravity acts as a common component in the motion patterns both of the limbs and the head. You have given us a striking everyday example of the fantastic biological sensitivity to highly complicated biological motion patterns.

Bill: Once I made this observation, interestingly, then everybody could see it. And here is another anecdote. In the wintertime I run indoors on a track and there are a lot of other people running. I often make arrangements to meet a friend but we arrive separately so whoever comes first starts running, and the late arriver looks for the other person. With my eyes I can't identify my friend at a distance if he is stationary but as a soon he moves I can find him among all the other biological motion patterns on the track. My favorite in the Maas-Uppsala film is the dancing couple. I think that is just marvelous because you see how the 3D forms are articulated by the motion configurations and are never confused. The two partners in the dance remain perceptually articulated perfectly. It's very impressive. It's structure from motion long in advance of the interest in structure from motion that has developed lately. It's a favorite with the students in my introductory perception class. I think they'd be happy to watch that instead of hear me give a lecture any time. That work has received a great deal of attention. What are your impressions of the work that has followed? By people like Cutting and Berthenthal and the many other people have worked on biological motion.

SSB: And Sverker Runeson.

Gunnar: As you point out, my two source papers on biological motion 20 years ago have resulted in an astonishing, still ongoing, stream of studies. I think I have read a rather limited number of them and, therefore, it is not possible for me to offer an evaluation. However, the two authors you mentioned both have contributed in a highly substantial way. Cutting must be noted especially because he was the first one who, after the publication of my biological motion paper, continued with some frank and, for that time, shocking studies of the effect. Sten Sture also mentioned our own Sverker Runeson and I must admit that, for me personally, his studies of visual information about the dynamics of the human body by means of the biological motion effect stand out as the most impressive application. By using the method to reduce visual information he brilliantly demonstrated a then-unknown sensitivity to the dynamics of the human body. Simultaneously, and also in a highly substantial way, he contributed to the studies of biological motion as such.

It has astonished me that all the biological motion studies I have read are only variants of my initial patterns. I introduced the name biological motion because I considered the possibility of extending the research to studies of the perception of other animals and even of vegetation. Using a technique similar to the one by which I had produced the dancing couple I had tested this possibility by making a couple of short films with biological motion patterns from my Cocker spaniel and also from a flying seagull—with the usual positive results. Thus there exist a number of interesting problems of the recognition type not yet touched on. We can, for instance, study the effects of the following presentations, mentioning the perceiver first: man–animal, animal–man, animal–animal. I would be delighted to find some studies by biologists of that type. The biological motion effect is a most efficient demonstration and verification of the theory of perceptual vector analysis. Many students of this effect, however, neglect this theoretical background. They investigate the conditions under which the effect appears in a more or less distinct form, but do not pay attention to the underlying consequences for the theory of perception. Similarly, some handbooks on perception make use of the retinal image concept and still, in the same text, describe both the initial presentation of the perceptual vector analysis and the biological motion demonstration as an application of the vector analysis principles. I sometimes ask myself: How can theorists of today neglect the visual common

motion–relative motion effect and the fact that the optic flow through the lens
does not represent moving images but common and relative angular motions of
directed rays? Poor students!

Bill: Right, the implications of these phenomena for thinking about perception are not made clear. That may change now, Gunnar, because of the wide-
spread recognition that kinetic displays carry information that is not to be found
in static displays. I think that may change, but I think you are right, sometimes
it's included as just another...

SSB: Just another illusion.

On Teaching and Administering

Bill: We are seated here with two of your students, and a third one if I may
include myself, and that means you have been a teacher as well as a researcher. I
wonder whether you could reflect on your life as a teacher. If you had to do it
again would you rather not do any teaching at all? Has it been a source of satisfaction? Has it been rewarding?

SSB: Maybe you want Gunnar and me to leave.

Gunnar: No, no, you will hear. I think I have not been a good teacher. I am
not really engaged as a teacher.

GJa: Disagree!

Bill: You mean a classroom teacher?

Gunnar: Yes. But of course teaching research is very interesting. I like very
much to help students and colleagues in the planning of their projects and to
help them solve their experimental and technical problems. I do not know if I
am good in this respect but I am interested in it.

Bill: And it is satisfying?

Gunnar: Yes, just to see people understand what they have not grasped before. I have spent much time explaining.

Bill: When you say you have not been a good classroom teacher, let me offer
a comment about Hans Wallach. By the usual standards of classroom teaching
Hans Wallach just wouldn't pass and yet I've never had a more inspiring classroom teacher. Sometimes when he lectured he'd just be staring at the podium

never looking at the people in the class, and other times he'd get so involved in his thinking that instead of lecturing he'd be working things out in front of us. I imagine that some students would say he was a very bad teacher but when you look at the many people who were affected by his teaching you have to judge him to have been an extraordinary success. So sometimes one can't tell, Gunnar. To judge by your students you too have been an extraordinary success, probably in the classroom as well as in the laboratory. But I take it that teaching, at least laboratory teaching, has been an important part of your life and something you are glad to have done?

Gunnar: Yes! Oh yes! Of course. I am in contact with young, skillful people. I am very happy in one respect, the best happiness you can think about. I have had a number of students advancing and now, as you know, a large group of them have a very good international position, and I think this is something extraordinary. You have two of them here, and six of them have written articles in the symposium book—Sten Sture, Gunnar, Claes von Hofsten and Kåre Rumar.

SSB: ...Erik Börjesson and Sverker Runeson.

Bill: There is a student you had in the early 1970s whose work I recently re-read very carefully, Hans Marmolin?

Gunnar: Yes. Hans was bright. And I could mention several others also. Indeed, I had many very bright students.

Bill: Since you were the professor in the department did you also have to do administrative work?

Gunnar: Oh yes, a lot!

GJa: You loved it.

Gunnar: Oh, I strongly dislike it but, as you know, it is a necessary part of the professorship and I had to take this responsibility. After some years, however, this part of the job became more and more time-consuming. Besides the duties towards my own department and faculty I was engaged in a number of nationwide administrative activities. This took a lot of time and therefore, you see, I had to devote a great part of my spare time, nights, Saturdays and Sundays, to research. Sten Sture and Gunnar surely remember our programmatic experiments on car lighting over several years. Our nightly experiments at dark, military runways.

The Optic Sphere

Bill: Let's now turn to the optic sphere which you introduced a few years ago and again ask about the motivation for creating it. It is in one sense a culmination but it is also something entirely new, it's not just a continuation. No one, I think, could look at the 1950 event configuration book and anticipate the optic sphere theory.

Gunnar: To a certain extent I agree. My vector theory in the form given in the 1950 book was, in fact, the first computational theory.

Bill: That is a very good point. Yes, you are absolutely right.

Gunnar: The optic sphere theory is, instead, a theory deliberately freed from computational support. It is built on direct sensory recording of mechanical motions in the body. However, this theory also comprises the vector analysis effect because it can explain it in mechanical, noncomputational terms. Thus there exists a direct connection between these two theoretical approaches. But while the vector theory, strictly speaking, is descriptive, the new theory is explanatory.

You see, my findings of the rather unbelievable perceptual sensitivity to the biological motion effect for me successively evoked a feeling of dissatisfaction with the vector analysis theory in its initial form. The vector theory implicitly presupposed an automatic separation of common and relative motion components in the total optic flow by a so far unknown neural process. Also, if such processing could possibly be thought of as performed in the human brain, it still must be regarded as totally inconceivable in the primitive forms of chambered eyes like those of frogs and even mollusks like slugs and snails—early biological structures from which the human eye originates and which are anatomically similar to our eyes. Thus, I found that a new type of theory ought to be sought. A theory embracing the vector analysis model but also capable of explaining the visual perception of the environment without demanding neural computation. The optic sphere theory is the result of my many attempts to construct such a theory. What distinguishes this theory from other current theories is that it is uniquely mechanical. All optical information in the optic flow is received mechanically as recordings of angular changes of rays and no implicit neural computation is assumed. The theoretical background to this theory is the insight that evolution has produced a mechanical apparatus, the chambered eye, which automatically gives three-dimensional spatial information from focused light.

Bill: I admit that I did not recognize the original vector analysis as an early computational theory but it plainly is just that as you say. If I understand what you have just said, the optic sphere theory is a noncomputational theory. In that respect it stands apart from current so-called computational approaches. How do you think, if Gibson were alive, he might have reacted to this theory?

Gunnar: From my point of view a computational theory specifies a mathematical analog to the visual processing of optical information, while the optic sphere theory is dealing directly with mechanical motions in mechanical terms. In passing, it might be of some interest to observe that in my 1950 book I had already mentioned several times that the vector theory had a mechanical structure. It is hard to guess about Gibson's reactions. My theory embraces and makes use of many of Gibson's most important contributions to the understanding of visual space perception. I will mention, especially, his treatment of the senses as perceptual systems. A further development of this approach forms the basis for the optic sphere theory. We all know that, for Gibson, "direct perception" was a fundamental axiom for his theorizing. My mechanical theory verifies the soundness of this fundamental in the most immediate way. This aspect of the theory must have been of greatest importance for Gibson. I take for granted that he had severely criticized my "atomistical approach" with its ray concept, and had tried to substitute his own (rather diffuse) solid angle construction. Maybe my old friend finally would say that my theory is the next best ever presented! I myself regard my theory as in many respects being an effect and a continuation of both Gibson's and my own earlier work.

GJa: Do you think he would think the same?

Gunnar: To some extent, probably, yes.

Bill: There are real differences. It's not Gibson's theory, it's Gunnar's theory. It's different and I try to make that point in my essay in the volume. But it does have a family resemblance. In a family two brothers can be very different even though they are related.

Gunnar: But, you see, if you go to Gibson's theory it is also, to some extent, a noncomputational theory.

Bill: Yes, I think that is right. The word *computation* has become so frequent in usage that one doesn't know anymore what meaning to attach to the word noncomputational. We talk about computing perceptual representations. Cognition is computation, inference is computation. What is noncomputational? One doesn't know anymore.

Gunnar: I will point to the next step. I have described vision as a mechanical process but we also know that active visual perception is always steered by intentions. So you are something more than a mechanism, you see. In human vision you know that your perception of the environment is built up by a series of fixations, saccades, head and body movements. And each fixation point is intentionally chosen; it is chosen as an effect of your deliberate "hunting for information" using Gibson's term.

Bill: Aren't you worried about that, Gunnar?

Gunnar: I had to take this step, you see.

Bill: But it is very worrisome. I mean, how are you going to talk about intention in a...

Gunnar: No, I will not speak about intention in other ways than to accept that there is always a choice, an intentional choice. This belongs to life, you see, to every form of life.

GJa: What is the relation to attention?

Gunnar: Attention. At present this perhaps is a more convenient term.

Bill: I made some editorial changes in Gunnar's text, I changed it to attention.

Gunnar: To attention. Yes, I also use attention myself but, you see, attention is controlled by intention.

Bill: Yes, and that, of course you know, may land you in a great mess.

Gunnar: Yes, I do. And in some way it must be settled. You will find that not only visual perception but all biological activity is an effect of what we at present call intentionality. It is as if this term in some way were another term for active life: It belongs to the function of living cells down to amoebae and flowers. The problem of visual perception and intentionality must be considered seriously in its full breadth in the future. We must also observe that Gibson's "affordance" and "information hunting" concepts are, in fact, attempts in that direction, albeit so far very superficial attempts.

Bill: If I can offer a personal observation, Gunnar. Throughout your whole career as a scientist one thing that you have been very careful to do, always, is not to deny the facts. I think it was Köhler who had as rule for himself that, in his words, you should never falsify the phenomenal facts. So you are right. Intention is a fact of life and it is too bad that we don't know how to deal with it, but it remains a fact anyway. Since you always have accepted the discipline of facts, it is a very harsh discipline and makes a lot of trouble for you, you have to make a place for this fact and maybe you will do it in the next 20 years. We will hope so.

Gunnar: My productive time will soon be up and I think that I must leave this problem to the next two or three generations. I have thought about the relation between perception and intentionality but so far not found any other specific answer than that the problem seems to be erroneously set and has to be reformulated. In the optic sphere theory I stated that visual perception is the result of sensory interaction comprising the whole body. In this way it seems, at first, to be possible to explain visual information in everyday optic flow. Thinking in terms of activity in isolated sensory channels has blocked our understanding of vision. Maybe our thinking about the problems we now are touching at is blocked because of a similar restrictive and analytical attitude.

A Selection of Gunnar Johansson's Contributions

CONFIGURATIONS IN EVENT PERCEPTION

AN EXPERIMENTAL STUDY

INAUGURAL DISSERTATION

BY

GUNNAR JOHANSSON

FIL. LIC.

BY DUE PERMISSION
OF THE HUMANISTIC FACULTY OF STOCKHOLMS HÖGSKOLA
TO BE PUBLICLY DISCUSSED IN LECTURE ROOM B,
ON APRIL 15, 1950, AT 10:00 A.M.,
FOR THE DEGREE OF DOCTOR
OF PHILOSOPHY

UPPSALA 1950
ALMQVIST & WIKSELLS BOKTRYCKERI AB

Contents[†]

[†] This is a précis of the original text produced by Gunnar Johansson himself for this book. He has also interpolated occasional surveys of the contents on excluded sections. The headings of the contents presented here are those of the original book, but the page numbers refer to the present précis. An asterisk (*) indicates headings that are not included here. In the main body of the text, excluded sections are indicated by a dashed line. The added comments are written in italics and with larger margins. Notes are numbered consecutively as they appear in the present text. Experiments, figures, and tables are numbered as in the original text. Original citations in German have been translated into English.

Survey of the Contents

Our main concern has been to reproduce the initial theoretical and experimental background for the theory of visual vector analysis as developed in this book. However, we also have found that the mentioned, theoretically far-reaching approaches to event perception as such, as documented there, should be made clear. Owing to these intentions five sections can be identified in accordance with the following scheme.

Chapter I

In Chapter I, it is stressed that research on the perception of change over time, event perception, must be accepted as a crucial prerequisite for the understanding of real-life perception. Event perception is defined as the sensory recording of change over time in three respects, namely as perception of change of intensity of stimulation, change of quality of stimulation, and as spatial displacement, thus real motion. It is also said that most of the work will concern visual perception but that also event perception in the auditory and cutaneous senses will be paid attention to. Earlier studies of perception of real motion of relevance for our own work are described and analyzed.

This presentation of the project has here been reprinted in its full length, while the treatment of the earlier contributions has been strongly condensed. The section "An Excursus on Methodology," ending this chapter, has been reprinted in an abbreviated form.

Chapters II–V

Chapter II starts with a short introduction section about the author's engagement in the problem of motion configurations and about the technical requirements for the planned type of experiments. Most of the rest of the chapter consists of technical specifications of the apparatus used for producing dot motions on the display. Only the introduction and a few lines about the main structure of the apparatus are reprinted from this chapter.

In chapters III–V the author's experimental search for perceptual principles determining the visual event configurations is described, a search resulting in the development of the theory of visual vector analysis. These chapters are of great importance when it is a question of a deeper understanding of the theoretical and experimental fundaments of this theory. The description of how the theory was elaborated in the book is given in the form of a

*step-by-step progression of a series of 33 consecutive experi-
ments, interspaced by theoretical considerations. These experiments are tied together like links in a chain and the text is strict
and dense. Therefore, in order not to break up this chain, most of
these compact chapters have been reprinted word-for-word. Only
two experiments (nos. 8 and 24) and some minor parts of the dis-
courses have been excluded in the present version of the text.*

Chapters VI–VII

*Besides motion perception as mentioned in chapter I, two
other kinds of perceptual events are pointed out as objects for the
planned study, namely "change in stimulus intensity" and "change
of its quality." In chapters VI and VII these visual characteristics
are studied in the form of coordinated change of brightness and
color of spatially separated loci. The content of these chapters is
summarized.*

Chapters VIII–X

*In these chapters studies of corresponding effects of coordi-
nated change of "intensity" and "quality" in the auditory and cutaneous senses are described. Also these chapters are reproduced
in the form of summaries.*

Chapter XI

*In this last chapter the results of the project are summed up. It
is reprinted in abbreviated form.*

CHAPTER I

Framing of the Problem

We shall commence by drawing a distinction which is of fundamental importance for the present work.

A type of perception which implies unchangeableness, rest and constant forms, can be distinguished from a type where unceasing change is taking place.

As a typical example of the latter form of perception, let me take the view from my window at the present moment. Outside stands a weeping birch with its scanty foliage; its pliant branches moving rapidly backwards and forwards in the strong wind; each branch keeping its own peculiar rhythm. This is an example of unceasing motion, unceasing change. Motion is perhaps the most essential form of continual change that our perception gives us.

Let us also imagine that I had in front of me an instantaneous photograph of the tree, and was looking at it. That would furnish an example of the former type: perception of something that does not change. The same perceptual object is met with in both cases, but implies two radically different acts of perception. An essential condition for this difference is, without doubt, the different role played by the temporal factor in the two cases.

The difference between these two examples is not restricted to the fact that, in one case motion is perceived, and, in the other, rest. It is not the problem of motion perception itself that we are primarily referring to. What we wish to principally stress is rather the difference in the organization of a perceptual whole, which in both cases the stimuli constellation may give rise to. The birch, when completely at rest, acts as a closed, relatively undifferentiated unit. It is the diffuse exterior contours of the tree that dominate; and the various branches with their scanty leaves are very incompletely distinguished from each other. But the tree standing out there in the wind seems to be composed of a number of independent groups of leaves and branches, which there is no possibility of confusing or uniting, although they continually cross or half cover one another. And yet they do unite to form a unitary whole; a connection is felt to persist right down to the slowly moving trunk. *The motion has at the same time had a uniting and a segregating effect.*

Does the psychology of perception enable us to state why the tree in the photograph, this confusion of points and lines, appears as a closed whole; separated from its surroundings; and to explain the reason for the organization of the internal tree pattern?

In the well-known laws of configuration enunciated by Max Wertheimer, as well as in other formulations of the perceptual conformity which these express, we can find the possibilities for giving an explanation of the phenomenon in question. We need only mention the laws of similarity, proximity, and the good curve.

Can these, or other perceptual laws that have been studied, explain the different configurations which the birch in the wind gives rise to? Here, the answer has to be in the negative. No, not satisfactorily. A start has been made from several different quarters, but no definitive result has been reached.

This negative answer furnishes the programme for the present work, for it aims at contributing towards filling up the gap that has been alluded to. In the following pages we shall attempt to elucidate laws which regulate the perceptual configurations that are brought about by the interplay of continuous changes. Primarily we shall consider the configurations which are the result of several of these changes, whose carriers can be perceived as spatially separated, occurring simultaneously in the same perceptual field.

The example of the interplay of changes, which has been mentioned, has to do with motion, that is to say, with spatial changes. The investigation will not, however, be restricted only to this type of events, even though it may play a dominant part. There are other types of continuous changes which ought to be considered in this connection. As regards our example, we can point out, for instance, that the wind in the tree tops does not only cause an interplay of motions; it can also bring about a continuous changing of sensations of sound. We can hear the soughing of the wind; we can hear how it travels through a tree top or a grove of trees. In a similar way, we can also study the effect of gliding changes in lighting, etc.

Every continuous change of this kind, in the content of perception, we shall in the future term *event* (perceptual event). In cases where this is applicable, we shall distinguish between *part event,* when we refer to changes that take place in one or more elements within a larger group of these elements, and *event whole,* when interplay between all the elements is referred to. To the extent that these event wholes have a closed, organized form, synonymous terms such as event configuration, motion configuration, etc., will be employed.[1] The simplest part events that can form an event whole we shall call *event elements,* or when there is no risk of confusion, simply *elements.*

As the reader is aware, we do not possess any special sense for experiencing time, even though occasionally we may speak of a "time sense" (*Zeitsinn, sense du temps*) with reference to our ability to immediately experience time and to estimate duration of time, etc. But this experience of time is always connected with some special sensory material.

In this way, the same form of event, the same temporal succession, can be common for a number of events, composed of materials from quite different sensory fields. The same experience, for example, of regular sequence is ob-

---

[1] Cf. pp. 37–39.

served, whether a clock on a wall is heard ticking, or if only the pendulum is seen swinging.

In connection with these reflections, it can be asserted that, in an event, it is always a *material* that changes. The change in the material takes place in accordance with a certain time sequence, which is characteristic for the event in question. It can be represented graphically as a curve along a time axis. We shall call this time sequence *form* of event, or temporal form, and thus stress the special difference between *form* and *matter* that has been referred to.

Our perception gives rise to three principal forms of change: (1) change in stimulus intensity, (2) change of its quality, and (3) spatial changes (some form of displacement within the perceptual field). All these forms of change are well-known in connection with the senses of sight, hearing, and touch. It is very probable that, by means of suitable aids, motion can be demonstrated in other sensory fields, beside those mentioned, and the different forms would in that case be generally applicable for all senses. But in our argument, we shall nevertheless restrict ourselves to the three sensory fields mentioned above; because it is only here that the spatial change, motion, which phenomenally is perhaps the most essential form of change, has any practical significance.

Thus it is possible distinguish between three aspects of an event perception:

1. The material: the sensory material or the type of stimulation.
2. The dimension of change: intensity, quality, motion.
3. Temporal form of change: temporal curve.

From a methodological point of view, it is of great importance, when planning an investigation such as this, to have these different aspects of the event perception clearly in mind. This illuminates the situation of choice put into: the choice of variable factor or factors.

But the points of view with regard to the event perception that have been now considered allude to a single event. It has already been expressly pointed out that the main interest of our investigation is concerned with the configurations which may arise when several such events, which from a spatial point of view are separated, occur in the same perceptual field. In such groups of elements, we have also a spatial grouping factor to consider—and consequently still another variable factor: different positions of the event elements and differences in distance between them. And if the number of elements is changed, this may also alter the experimental results.

On Terminology

The psychological terminology in English relating to what we here have termed configurations and characteristics of configurations is rather indefinite.

Both the terms used and the meanings of the terms vary often from author to author, or at least from school to school.

On account of this, and as the author has no definite connection with any special school, it is expedient here, in the introduction, to give some definitions of the terms which we shall use in discussions concerning this field. We have used some of these terms undefined in the preceding section.

Let us begin with the term which has the widest range: *whole (event whole)*. Here we will make use of a definition given in Warren's dictionary:[2] *whole* is "that which, though possessed of parts or members or distinguishable aspects, yet possesses such a character as a unit that it may be treated without reference to the parts, members, or aspects."

In such cases where there is no possibility of seeing the parts, we also use the term *unit*.

It has proved expedient, when describing motion configurations, beside the generic term whole, to use also the particular terms *total whole* and *part whole* (or *part event*). By *part whole,* we have in view a relatively independent part of a larger whole, which in itself is composed of two or more members. The term *total whole* is used only in conjunction with the former term (part whole). It is a synonym for the general term *whole,* and is used only in order to avoid a confusion between *whole* and *part whole.* (Thus the two terms *part whole* and *total whole* are correlative terms.)

As a synonym for *part whole* we shall at times also make use of the term *group.* Consequently, this and other analogous terms—*grouping, group formation,* etc.—do not imply any theoretical connotation as differentiating between groups and wholes.

Another term which we shall often use is *organization.* It alludes to the arrangement or grouping of event elements or parts within a whole, which gives this whole its specific character.

Event configuration is a term which we have made use of already in the title of this book and in various contexts. Let us now try to express the definite meaning of this term in our own vocabulary. Firstly, we can say that it approximately coincides with the definition given for the term *whole.* But when using the term *configuration,* we wish to point out in a more pronounced manner, that we are dealing with an *organized* whole, a whole built up of parts between which there are mutual influences. Thus, also an event configuration is qualitatively something different from a mere constellation of separate events.

The reader will observe the contrast in significance between the two terms *configuration* and *constellation* as employed by us. The latter term is used primarily when speaking of the stimulus combination which gives rise to perceptual configuration. Thus it lacks the meaning of interconnection between the elements. This connection is a perceptual fact.

---

[2] Dictionary of Psychology, edited by Howard C. Warren, London, 1934.

Finally we wish to point out once again, that also when the prefix "event" is omitted, the terms now defined will primarily allude to combinations of events.

A Survey of Some Earlier Contributions to the Discussion
of our Problem

In this section of Chapter 1, earlier research, relevant for the aspects of event perception to be investigated, is reviewed. Six forerunners are mentioned, namely M. Wertheimer, D. Katz, E. Rubin, K. Duncker, A. Michotte, and W. Metzger. This part of the chapter can be summed up as follows:

__Max Wertheimer__. Wertheimer's "Law of Common Fate" as formulated in 1923[3] is described and analyzed. It is said that this Gestalt factor was described in very vague terms and that its interesting impulses never had been followed up by the Gestaltists. In his famous "Principles of Gestalt Psychology" Koffka (1935)[4] did not even allude to it. The conclusion is that "Wertheimer has stated the problem, but he has not solved it."

__David Katz__. Katz did not belong to the Gestalt group but his theoretical position was related to it. In his book "Gestalt Psychologie" Katz (1948)[5] has reformulated Wertheimer's "Common Fate" to a more limited and strict form and termed it "The Law of Common Motion." The author says that Katz' position in this respect played an important role as a starting point for his own research on motion perception.

__Edgar Rubin__. It is shown that Rubin early was interested in real motion perception. Especially a paper of Rubin (1927)[6] is paid special attention to. Rubin's work is said to have a close relation to the investigation to be described. Quotation: "Rubin demonstrated in greater detail, how a physically simple motion in perception can be dissociated into two separate motions a phenomenon he terms __motion analysis (Bewegungsanalyse)__. This phe-

---

[3] Max Wertheimer, "Untersuchungen zur Lehre von der Gestalt", *Psychol. Forschung* 4, 1923, pp. 301–350.

[4] Kurt Koffka, *Principles of gestalt psychologie*, New York, 1935.

[5] David Katz, *Gestaltpsychologie*, Basel, 1948, p. 33.

[6] E. Rubin, "Visuell wahrgenommene wirkliche Bewegungen", *Zeitschrift für Psychologie*, Abt. I, 103, 1927. (Republished in E. Rubin, *Experimenta psychologica*, Copenhagen, 1949.)

nomenon will occupy a central position in our own investigations. Rubin's contribution will then be considered more fully"

Karl Duncker. *The close relationship between Duncker's (1929)[7] paper "Über induzierte Bewegung" (About induced motion), and this project is pointed out.*

Albert Michotte. *It is shown that in spite of different problem areas there exist interesting technical relations between this project (Michotte, 1946)[8] and the author's.*

Wolfgang Metzger. *In 1934 and 1935 the Gestaltist Metzger[9] had published two papers on the perceptual effects of seeing the shadows of a number of vertical poles attached to a horizontal, slowly rotating turntable. These papers were described and evaluated with regard to this project, to which it was found to have close relations.*

An Excursus on Methodology

The present investigation is consciously and consistently based on a phenomenological description of the experiences that the various experimental situations involve. This method is almost self-evident in view of the task that we have outlined in the foregoing pages. Furthermore, it has been employed, to a more or less extensive degree, by all the investigators we have alluded to in our bibliography.

The phenomena which will be dealt with are of such a kind that what is primarily required is a *qualitative determination;* that is to say, a determination of the specific character of an experience that a certain stimuli constellation gives rise to. Consequently, exact quantitative measurements, as regards the experience in question, is not a matter of primary importance in the majority of cases. The *quantitative* determination of a certain quality, which can be obtained in the psychology of perception by the application of statistical methods, must be termed a subsequent stage, with regard to investigations of the type which is in question here. And it would be quite mistaken to attempt to determine the very quality of the perception by means of a procedure involving a consensus of opinion.

---

[7] Karl Duncker, "Über induzierte Bewegung," *Psychol. Forschung*, 12, 1929.

[8] A. Michotte, *La perception de le causalité*, Louvain et Paris, 1946.

[9] W. Metzger, "Beobachtungen über phänomenale Identität," *Psychol. Forschung*, 19, 1934. "Tiefenerscheinungen in optischen Bewegungsfeldern," *Psychol. Forschung*, 20, 1934–1935.

Instead we have to start by accepting an axiom of normality. That is to say, we postulate that in principle the perceptual apparatus functions in the same way for all (normal) individuals, regardless of the type of perception involved. It is this for all individuals' common mode of functioning with regard to a certain stimulation that we consider we obtain in the above-mentioned qualitative determination. As long as we are dealing with pronounced perceptual qualities, this determination is not affected by the fact that the ability to distinguish between qualities are very different among various individuals. By this ability, we mean the capacity to distinguish between fine shades of difference and to make refined observations in a certain field of perception. Thus, with the above-mentioned axiom as our point of departure, a form of experience which was judged to be compelling by a few observers may be considered as the natural form of experience with respect to the stimuli constellation in question for any normal individual whatsoever.

Consequently, in experiments of the type referred to, the question of the number of Os and the number of repetitions is not a statistical question. It is finally a matter of judgment for the experimenter, and what is decisive in each particular case is the character of the experiment.

The principles for the number of Os participating and for their selection, which the author, in agreement to the above indications, has adhered to for the present investigation are as follows:

A minimum number of from three to five trained Os whom the author knew to be capable of making a phenomenological description have taken part in every experiment. Besides, in the great majority of cases, a corresponding number of more or less inexperienced Os were also employed. In some experiments the number of Os participating in the experiment was further increased (to 10–20).

By this method of procedure, it has been found possible to state the differences in the reactions which could be presumed to be the consequence of different degrees of practice.

The author has, of course, carefully studied all the experimental situations, and has made comprehensive notes on his impressions. When expedient, these reports have been utilized in the preparation of the summary of the phenomenological description which accompanies every experiment. Thus, the author has himself acted as an O; the O with the most extensive training. But naturally, the author's conceptions have never been used for a *correction* of the description that is based on the rest of the experimental reports; in fact they have only been utilized, when this was necessary, for *supplementing* the latter. Whenever essential differences occur between the statements made, these differences have always been clearly indicated.

CHAPTER II

Introduction to the Investigation of Motion Configurations

The author started his work in the field of event perception by conducting investigations concerning the perception of motion, and it was while he was occupied with this research that the framing of the problems, which were outlined in the previous chapter, began gradually to take more definite shape. The priority of the study of motion is also due to other considerations. The present work will, from a quantitative point of view, be dominated by the study of constellations of motion, and the laws which govern event perceptions originating from such constellations. This is the case, even though as already indicated, only the sense of sight will be dealt with directly.

The question which is the fundamental theme of the entire investigation of motion is, in accordance with the foregoing: *Which are the factors that determine the genesis of motion configurations?*

We have already stated that when planning our work we found it expedient to distinguish between the temporal and material aspects of an event. This division has also proved decisive when conducting our investigation of motion. The material aspect is represented here by giving prominence to the spatial relations between the elements that are the carriers of the different motions.

Accordingly we shall have a series of experiments where mainly the temporal relations between the elements are varied. There will also be another series of experiments, where the spatial relations are the variable that form the center of interest.

The choice of the temporal form for the part events naturally in our case is very significant. Already at a very early stage, the author began to work with events which involve regular repetition, i.e., periodicity. Only when periodic repetitions take place, is the maximum configurational pregnance[10] attained.[11]

A fundamental form of course for periodic motion is undoubtedly the simple harmonic motion. Its curve of development—in ideal cases a pure sine curve—can be found in a number of motions that are important from a perceptual point of view. Wave motions of different kinds, pendulum movements, etc., are examples. It is also a component in circular motion, and may thus be seen, for example in the motion of a piston. Even in the movements of many living creatures (e.g., the flight of birds) traces of this type of motion can be found.

----

[10] We will use the term *pregnance (pregnant)* in accordance with a definition given by Woodworth—"a 'pregnant' figure is one which expresses some characteristic fully." (R. S. Woodworth, *Experimental Psychology,* New York, 1947, p. 645)

[11] This fact involves in itself very interesting problems.

Description of the Apparatus

The following considerations and requirements were of essential importance in the construction of an apparatus for the investigation of motion configurations: The apparatus must be capable of producing and setting in motion several objects whose motion is respectively independent. Freedom of choice with regard to the character of these different motions must not be too narrow; and one combination of motion must easily be converted into another when required. An important point was that the apparatus had to run without making any characteristic noise which could be recognized in connection with various motions. Finally, an indispensable requirement was that the apparatus should function with precision and should be capable of carrying out exact repetitions.

The final form of the apparatus embodying all these requirements may be described as follows:

Projection technique was employed. The movable objects were either pasted or drawn on a transparent celluloid disc, and projected with the required degree of magnification (or reduction) onto a translucent screen, where they could be seen by Os. Fig. 1 represents a schematic illustration of the projection system in question. Up to six different celluloid discs can be applied simultaneously, and each of these can be given a motion entirely independent of the others.

The motion of the various celluloid discs was accomplished by means of a system of levers and eccentric discs that converted a rotary motion into the type of motion required. The apparatus contained six such systems.

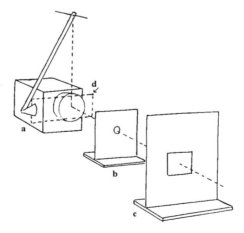

Fig. 1. (*a*) lantern box with condenser lens, (*b*) lens, (*c*) screen with a translucent window, (*d*) celluloid disc.

CHAPTER III

The Configurational Effect of Temporal Relations

On account of the possible variations which the apparatus is capable of producing, and because of the limitations based on the main principles that were mentioned earlier, the investigation of the possible role played by temporal relations as configurational factors in our combinations of motion can deal with two main groups of such relations: (1) frequency relations and (2) phase differences and phase sameness, in conjunction with the same frequency.

The latter group proved to be the more suitable when it was a question of gaining an insight, by means of systematic variations, into the laws that we are seeking. Consequently we shall, for the most part, concentrate on describing this group.

In Phase and Out of Phase Relations

We shall start by giving an account of some experiments of a more preliminary character. Their principal aim was to form a background for the subsequent experiments, by comparing the configurational character of the constellation of elements that we shall utilize at a later stage—both when at rest and when in motion. A secondary consideration, not without importance, was to familiarize Os with the experimental conditions, before they were expected to accomplish more exacting tasks.

Experiment 1. The objects whose interplay of motion is studied by us consist of four bright circular planes, which are projected on to the screen of the apparatus, which otherwise is not illuminated. They are all of the same diameter, about 3 mm, and are placed along a horizontal line, respectively 13 mm apart. The room in which the experiment was carried out was quite dimly lit; this makes the screen appear dark to Os, while the window seems to be a somewhat brighter surface (on account of light from the apparatus). Against this background the small circular planes appear bright white, with sharp outlines.

When in motion they have exactly the same vertical paths of motion, and since they are also in phase, their motion is identical. The grouping and the paths of motion are shown in full scale in Fig. 5.

As will be seen in the figure, the paths of motion are 10 mm long if they are measured from the upper edge of the upper turning point, to the lower edge of the lower turning point. In the figure, the four circles have been denoted by the letters *a, b, c, d* consecutively from left to right.

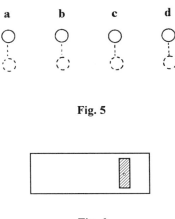

Fig. 5

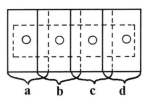

Fig. 6

Fig. 7

This method of notation will be consistently employed for all horizontal element sequences throughout this work.

From a technical point of view, the four bright circular planes, which we shall in future call *objects*, *elements*, or simply *points*, were prepared as follows: a black cardboard strip, about 10 mm wide, was pasted on each of the four celluloid discs, as shown in Fig. 6. In the cardboard strip a hole, 1.5 mm in diameter, was punched. The four celluloid discs were inserted into the apparatus in such a way that the cardboard strips partly cover one another, like fish scales. Fig. 7 illustrates this arrangement.

In front of the discs, a cardboard disc was placed as a screen. This disc is larger than the window of the screen attached to the apparatus. It was also fitted with a window, whose position is indicated in Fig. 7 by the rectangle, made up of dashed lines.

The result of this device is, of course, that the projection screen belonging to the apparatus is dark itself but has four bright points in a row.

The identical motion of the points was secured by all of the celluloid discs being driven by the same eccentric disc, and their levers being adjusted for exactly the same amplitude. The frequency was 0.7 c/sec.

This arrangement is as neutral as possible in respect of spatial relations. We have equal distances, the paths of motion have identical amplitudes and directions and their level of altitude is the same. It is set up in accordance with the principles we have formulated for the investigation of temporal factors. For the same reason, except for a few exceptional cases, this arrangement regarding the number of objects, spatial groupings, and paths of motion will be consistently adhered to throughout the chapter.

The instructions given to the observers requested them to record their impression of a more or less close affinity, connection, or "belonging-together" of the four elements.

Os started by looking at the screen when the four points on it were at rest, and then recording their impressions. The points were then set in motion, and Os were asked to make another report. This procedure was repeated several times. The distance between the screen and O was about 75–100 cm.

Fourteen Os took part in this, and the 6 following experiments described in this chapter. Four of these were acquainted with the psychology of perception, and had previously taken part in other experiments with the same apparatus. The remaining 10 had no experience at all of this kind.

The result of this first experiment showed a very satisfactory degree of unanimity. All Os described, more or less decidedly, the four points at rest as four relatively separate units without any marked connection. As soon as motion was introduced, all Os saw the points as a uniform line. "Four shining points on a rod which moves up and down," one of the Os stated, for example. Some of the Os pointed out, however, that they could see, when the sequence rest-motion was repeated, the points, even when at rest, as representing a stable line. They stressed, however, that the configuration was self-evident and inevitable only when motion set in.[12] The static constellation afforded more opportunity for the free play of the observational attitudes of the experimentees.

Neither when at rest nor when in motion was any tendency discernible on the part of the four elements to form groups or part wholes.

The experiment clearly demonstrates that a *series of elements with identically the same motion in perception form a configuration, and that this effect must be ascribed to the motion.* It is not found in the original stationary constellation of elements.

---

[12] It seems that this persevering configurational effect of motion has a rather short duration.

The result in itself is nothing new; our experiment has only confirmed what was already known. Wertheimer is referring to this configurational effect, when he speaks of "the factor of common fate," which we have mentioned previously. And we have also pointed out that David Katz has in a more striking fashion experimentally demonstrated the same phenomenon.

Our next task is to go a step farther and to investigate whether *identically* the same conditions regarding motion are necessary for the occurrence of the configurations in question. There are two factors in the three following experiments that we shall vary: the amplitude of the motion of the various elements, and their phase relations.

Experiment 2. This experiment and the next were supplementary to Experiment 1, and for this reason they have been included here, although it is a *spatial* factor, namely the amplitude of the motion, that was changed.

The four points are also in a row here. The left one is stationary, and the amplitude of the other three increases successively for every step taken towards the right. As in Experiment 1, all the elements have the same frequency and phase. Fig. 8 shows the length of the paths of motion and their respective position. (N. B. that on this account the velocity is different for all the elements.) The procedure and the instructions are a repetition of Experiment 1.

When at rest, the experiment naturally has the same row of points, as were present at the moment of rest in Experiment 1. But when the apparatus is started, however, it gives a different impression. The effect produced by this combination of motions on the observer is astonishing. There is a strikingly powerful and illusory impression of a connecting line between the points; or, as several of the Os have expressed it more concretely, it is a "rod" which oscillates about a fixed axle in the point to the left *(a)*. Os were unanimous in their reports. The following is a typical example: "a stick which is fastened at one end, and swings up and down with the other. "

The effect of uniformity is even more striking than in Experiment 1.

Experiment 3. In principle, this is a repetition of the previous experiment. The number of elements has been increased to six. The two exterior points (a and f) have no motion, and the amplitude of the rest is shown in Fig. 9.

Fig. 8   Fig. 9

The result of this experiment is, if possible, even more pregnant and self-evident than that of the previous one as regards the interconnection of the points. As indicated in Fig. 9 it gives the impression of a harmonically swinging line. We can imagine it, for example, as a swinging cord between two nodes when seen in profile. Several of the Os have experienced the motion as three-dimensional, and not of the kind that takes place on a surface. No less than three Os have compared it to "a swinging skipping rope," and this is perhaps the best way of expressing the experience of the combination in question. The impression of connection, of wholeness, simply forces itself on the observer in this way of perception. It is nearly as easy to say of a real swinging skipping rope with four knots that it is the four knots that move up and down, as to describe the impression of our experiment as four independent points which move in vertical paths.

What is the significance of these two experiments? In the first place, *that configuration can take place even if the elements have different amplitude, and consequently also different velocity.*

And secondly, that *differences in amplitude can be followed by a positive configurational effect.*

They can give rise to a configuration which is considerably stronger than that produced by the absolute equality of motion. The interconnection is much more striking.

Finally, we can state another fact. A combination of motion such as that in Experiment 3 can be experienced as a unitary motion on a surface; but it can also, even preferably, be perceived as a three-dimensional motion.

In his paper, "Tiefenerscheinungen in optischen Bewegungsfeldern," already mentioned in Chapter 1, W. Metzger has drawn attention to and investigated a very similar effect in connection with symmetrical combinations of motion elements. There Metzger gives the laws for such transpositions from two-dimensional motion combinations to a three-dimensional motion. We quote from Metzger's summary the following statement:

"Einheitlichkeit, Einfachheit, Symmetrie, Kontinuität und figurgerechter Aufbau *des Bewegungsgeschehens an figural einheitlichen Gebilden* sind die Prinzipien, die sich für das Entstehen von Tiefenerscheinungen in Bewegungsfeldern als massgeblich erwiesen haben."[13] (Uniformity, simplicity, symmetry, continuity and figurally correct structuring in figurally uniform structures are the principles that have been found to be determining for the occurrency of perception of depth in moving figural patterns.)

In the following chapters we will very frequently come across such three-dimensional effects. We can connect the actual case as well as the following with Metzger's results.

---

[13] Op. cit., p. 258

Experiment 4. Here we have once again the four original elements. They have the same amplitude, and as usual, the same frequency. On the other hand, a phase difference of 90° has been introduced between proximate elements. The four elements thus, in regard to phase differences, form the following series: 0°–90°–180°–270°.

Not even the radical difference between the motions of the elements, which this combination implies, is able to disrupt the line configuration. We continue to obtain a quite different character of a whole when in motion, than when at rest.

The configuration appears now, however, to have lost something of the self-evident character which was so typical of the previous combinations of motion. At least when requested to make a description several of the inexperienced Os hesitated. Two of them even stated that they were unable to detect any interconnection between the elements.

It has proved necessary, however, to treat the reports of inexperienced Os with great caution. We meet with here, the kind of difficulty that is often connected with this type of experiment: the difference between, especially in the case of inexperienced Os, a spontaneous experience and a conceptual description. One of the two Os who have just been mentioned as denying the existence of any interconnection between the elements, has given a spontaneous account which implies an inescapable configurational character. She stated that what she saw resembled a gliding snake, and that "it had a really horrible effect."

We are fully justified in ascribing greater value to the symbol than to the description.

Several of the other Os mention similar images which struck them as they watched the combination of motions. "Some sort of mechanism," "a revolving crank axle," "a wavy line." In every case it appears that there was a whole in motion. Thus the configurational character seems to be indubitable.

In the case of regular succession in phase difference between four elements, the greatest difference obtainable is 90°. The corresponding experiments with smaller phase differences (45°, 30°) were also carried out, and showed that analogous configuration occurs even under these conditions.

Consequently, we have the right to maintain *that all the elements of motion form a motion configuration, even if an arbitrary phase difference exists, provided that there is a regular succession with equally great phase angles between proximate elements.*

There is a qualification which has to be made, and which is due to our experimental arrangement: that our conclusions refer to elements seen against a stationary and homogeneous background. Numerous experiments with a chequered background have clearly demonstrated, however, that inhomogeneity of the background does not affect the experimental results. This applies to all temporal experiments.

This has brought us to the end of the four introductory experiments. They have both confirmed and further demonstrated how motion can act as a distinct configurational factor. We can also state that they have demonstrated two different types of organization principles in connection with a motion configuration.

A comparison between Experiments 1, 2, and 3 where all the elements are in phase, shows how relations between *amplitudes* is a decisive factor. We have there three different motion configurations and can state that their organization is determined by the amplitude relations.

Experiment 4 demonstrates an other type of organization factor. Here the amplitudes are equal and it is the *phase relations* which are decisive.

In accordance with the investigation principles already formulated, we shall in the present chapter concentrate on the last mentioned type of organization of motion configurations. Our task is now to see whether we can split up the simple type of motion whole given by both amplitude and phase sameness, by changes in phase relations. In this way we may hope to acquire knowledge of the laws that determine the genesis of motion configurations.

Phase Sameness and Phase Difference in the Same Series of Elements

What happens if between elements in the same group both phase sameness and phase difference exist? This is a question which the experiments in the preceding paragraph has inspired. There we dealt both with phase sameness and with phase differences, but only in separate experiments. We shall now take up this question, and propose to commence with the following experiment.

Experiment 5. The experimental conditions are the same as in Experiment 1, except that a phase difference of 180° between the elements *b* and *c* has been introduced. This means that *a* and *b* are in phase and also *c* and *d*.

The Os who had now gained some experience from the preceding experiments, in which all of them had taken part, were only required to freely describe what they were seeing. Only in a few cases, and then merely to emphasize the main purpose of the experiment, did the experimenter, during the course of an experiment, ask any questions. These referred to the observation of configurations, etc. On such occasions care was naturally taken to prevent, as far as possible, the questions becoming suggestive in effect. Also on the conclusion of the experiment, questions were sometimes put.

In order to obtain a clear view, and thereby to be in a position to discuss in a more differentiated manner some of the essential categories of the reports, the results in this section have been tabulated. The data of the reports have been classified in three categories of special interest. See the adjoining Table 1.

Table 1

Ob-server	Grouping	Total Whole	Compared to
KIS	*ab, cd*	no*	two cars racing in the dark on a hilly road
EI	*ab, cd*	yes	a weaving motion; two cars racing along a very uneven road.
MJ	*ab, cd*	yes	two cars closely following each other
POF	*ab, cd*	no*	an athlete lifting two dumb-bells
KJ	*ab, cd*	yes	a ribbon that is folded perpetually
W	(possibly *bc*)*	yes	a ribbon with two joints in the middle
US	*ab, cd*	yes*	a jointed line
DK	*ab, cd*	yes	a revolving mechanism*
EEJ	*ab, cd*	yes	a crank
RJ	*ab, cd*	yes	a kind of undulatory motion
EH	*ab, cd*	yes	blowing the bellows of a church organ
SN	*ab, cd*	-	-
RT	*ab, cd*	yes	-
S	*ab, cd*	yes	-

*data obtained after being questioned by the experimenter.

This combination of motion causes the four elements to divide into two groups. All Os, with one exception,[14] as is shown in the first column of the table, stated that a connection existed both between the elements a and b, and also between c and d.

This grouping is, almost without exception, what makes the greatest impression on an observer. It is in some sense completely self-evident. An experiment has been carried out in which Os had to concentrate on trying to produce some other group distribution; but that they should then really see the different groups simultaneously. This has, however, usually proved almost impossible, and the author's own experience confirms this. The grouping shown in the table is indubitably the only natural way of apprehending the combination in question.

The description is not, however, complete when the grouping has been determined. Usually, the two groups are not two isolated wholes adjacent to one another; but in their turn, unite to form a configuration, a kind of total whole. This embraces all the elements, and an interconnection between these persists even where the phase difference is introduced. It is as if we were dealing with a line with two folds or joints in the middle, to use an expression that was employed by several Os.

---

[14] See Table 1.

Fig. 10

The presence of this total whole is recorded in the second column of the table. To save space, it has been given in the form of answers to the question at the head of the table. In all cases not marked with an *, descriptions in this respect were given spontaneously.

In comparison with the distribution into groups, this encroaching total whole is of secondary importance for the majority of Os. The emphasis is laid in a striking way on the groups, and their interconnection, as a rule, only becomes apparent after the constellation of motion in question has been observed for some time. As will be seen from the table, two of our Os have not recorded any impression of this total whole during the course of the experiment. On the other hand, one O (W) only saw this total whole from the very outset.

The ordinary twofold configuration is illustrated in outline in Fig. 10. The primary connection in pairs is denoted here by an ordinary line, while the secondary connection between the groups is indicated by a dotted line. As is apparent, the positions indicated are those at the two turning points, and at the middle point of the path of motion.

Another characteristic phenomenon is the remarkably large number of images and associations regarding courses of motion, with which the Os were previously acquainted. These have been given in the third column of the table, and as will be noted, they are rather the rule than the exception. The Os usually say "it resembles...," and then comes the image which is often the central point of the whole description. We detected the same tendency even in the preliminary experiments, although the course there (with the exception, of Experiment 4) was much simpler, a rod with four light points, a swinging stick, a swinging skipping rope, etc.

We shall come across this tendency repeatedly in the following chapters, and consequently, we will refrain from commenting on this phenomenon until we have assembled more material (cf. p. 98).

In the experiments with group formations which we are now working with, as well as in the experiments with motion in general, from time to time a stray case arises which diverges in a more or less striking manner from the "normal" type of reaction. This shows how a subjective attitude can, at times even to a relatively high degree, affect the perception of motion.[15]

---

[15] Besides, there is the difficulty that has already been pointed out, concerning the inadequacy of some of the Os' statements, which are not, however, referred to here.

What happens if there exist both in phase and out of phase relations in the same group of elements? This is the question that we raised at the beginning of the section.

The answer is, in as far as we are entitled to draw conclusions from Experiment 5, that all the elements continue to form a whole, but that this consists of relatively independent groups. We have, in fact, obtained an organized motion configuration. Furthermore, our experimental results show that the organization is due to the temporal relations between the elements. It is the elements which are in phase that have formed such a group, while phase difference is characterized by dissociation between the groups.

This implies that being in phase in such a constellation continues to exercise a unifying function, while phase difference causes dissociation, but without the disruption of the total whole.

What actually takes place cannot of course be deduced from a single experiment of this type. It is the result of the whole series of experiments that may first enable us to answer this question. At the same time a troublesome duality must be cleared up, which up to the present seems to have vitiated the results. We saw that a phase difference (90° or less) in Experiment 4, gave rise to an integrating effect, while in Experiment 5, we have now found that a phase difference of 180° seems to cause in the first hand a disintegration. Can the phase difference, at one and the same time, have both an integrating and a disintegrating effect?

Another extremely important qualification must also be considered. Perhaps it is not the relations of motion in themselves that determine the distribution into groups that we have observed, but that the spatial relations are the cause of this. Let us look at Fig. 12. It shows the positions occupied by the elements of our combinations, just at the moment of turning.

This stationary pattern of points, displays a relatively distinct grouping *ab, cd.* Cannot this pattern, which is repeated at every turning, be the decisive factor that determines the group formation? If this is the case, then we are dealing with an application of well-known static configurational laws (proximity and a good curve).

Fig. 12

Experiments Where Being in Phase Conflicts with the Spatial Sequence

The discussion at the end of the last section showed that the points which particularly need to be elucidated are: (a) if the formation of groups always corresponds with being in and out of phase, and (b) if this is the case, the question whether the group formation can be deduced from these phase relations, from the *interplay of motions* that these give rise to, or if it is determined by static configurational factors.

We shall consider the problems by carrying out a regrouping of the phase relations.

A forming of pairs from four units can take place in three different ways. Besides the groups *ab, cd,* we can have *ad, bc* and *ac, bd.*

This redistribution of the four elements took place in the two experiments that will now be described.

Experiment 6. This experiment is a repetition of Experiment 5, except for the fact that it is *a* and *d* that form one of the groups that are in phase; and *b* and *c* constitute the other group. Thus from the point of view of being in phase, we have an inclosure grouping.

Table 2, which deals with the same categories of answers as did Table 1, gives a summary of the experimental results obtained from the reports on the experiment.

The first column of the table shows that the results in question concerning the division into groups are quite of a unanimous character. Os, without a single exception, saw two groups of connected elements, where *a* and *d* formed one group, and *b* and *c* the other.

In comparison with Experiment 5, the division into groups that was experienced has altered, so that even now it corresponds with the *distribution of phase sameness.*

For the majority of Os the inclosed group was the most conspicuous, and was the first to be mentioned. This condition, which may well be ascribed to the proximity of the elements to one another, did not affect the actual distribution of groups. This was usually accepted as being quite self-evident.

Also in the combination which we are now studying, there was an occurrence of a total whole (embracing both groups) analogous with the one which had been observed in Experiment 5. Here, as is indicated in column 2, all Os, with a single exception, experienced and noted a connecting band between the groups. This was perhaps still more pronounced in the combination now under discussion; for besides the higher frequency of the recorded observations of this phenomenon, two Os declared that this total whole was dominant.

Table 2

Ob-server	Group-ing	Total Whole	Compared to
EEJ	*bc, ad*	yes	a motor axle
DK	*bc, ad*	yes, pronounced	a kind of mechanism in 3-dimensional rotary motion
KJ	*bc, ad*	yes	a kind of revolving crank
POF	*bc, ad*	yes	a crank axle
RJ	*bc, ad*	yes, pronounced	1) gramophone regulator 2) a flying creature with shining eyes
EI	*bc, ad*	yes	the outer points are two movable arms
W	*ad, bc*	yes	a line with "fluttering" ends
US	*ad, bc*	yes	a line jointed in 2 places
KIS	*bc, ad*	yes	fluttering wings
RT	*bc, ad*	yes	-
SN	*ad, bc*	yes	-
MJ	*bc, ?*	no*	-
S	*bc, ad*	yes*	-
EH	*bc, ad*	yes	-

*Data given after being questioned by the experimenter.

When it is a question of the tendency to arouse associations with well-known courses of motion, we see that the experience gained in earlier experiments is repeated. Not less than 10 of the 14 Os had spontaneously suggested an image in their description of the phenomenon.

Experiment 7. This experiment represents the third possible way in which the elements can combine. It is thus a repetition of Experiment 5, only now the elements *a* and *c* are in phase, and so are *b* and *d*.

The results obtained by our 14 Os are given in Table 3. It will be easily seen that this is a repetition of the results of the two previous experiments.

Thus also here, a phenomenal grouping has taken place in accordance with the principle of being in phase. Also in this variant a total whole is observed in the same way as in the two former experiments. This phenomenon is recorded by the majority of Os, but not by all of them.

Also the tendency to arouse associations with other courses of motion, which Os had previously come into contact with, is observed.

Table 3

Ob-server	Grouping	Total Whole	Compared to
KIS	*ac,bd*	yes	a kind of mechanism
DK	*ac,bd*	yes, pronounced	reminds one of some motion connected with a locomotive
EEJ	*ac,bd*	yes	a motor axle*
RJ	*ac,bd*	yes, dominant	a crank axle
KJ	*ac,bd*	yes	a kind of turning or grinding motion
POF	*ac,bd*	yes, pronounced	transversal undulating motion
MJ	*ac,bd*	yes	some kind of joints between the points
US	*ac,bd*	yes	a flying creature*
RT	*ac,bd*	yes, but faint	-
W	*ac,bd* (*ab,cd)*	yes	-
SN	*ac,bd*	-	-
EH	*ac,bd*	-	-
S	*ac,bd*	yes*	-
EI	*ac,bd*	no*	-

*Data obtained after being questioned by the experimenter.

In addition to the experiments which have just been described, a considerable number have been carried out with five or six motion elements. The results of these are in agreement with those just described, in all respects that have been mentioned. Elements that are in phase form a group; the groups combine to form a total whole, and frequently an unsought for image arises when Os see a combination of motion of this character.

Experiments with a phase difference that is less than 180° have been carried out, and these have given the same results as far as the formation of groups is concerned.

The experiments which have been described in this section have afforded us material for answering the first of the two questions which were the immediate cause for the regrouping.

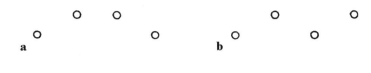

Fig. 15

We are in a position to state that the phenomenal formation of groups always corresponds with the relations of motion of the elements. The elements in phase have always formed a group, whatever position these elements may have had in the series of elements.

The above statement, nevertheless, does not forthwith permit us to draw the conclusion that it is the relations of motion, such as phase sameness and phase difference that give rise to the organization of the configurations perceived. The possibilities of affording an explanation which the purely spatial group formations seem to offer, and that were referred to in our second question and at the end of the previous section, will now have to be examined.

Let us now proceed to do this by consulting Fig. 15: (a) represents the respective position of the elements at the moment of turning, and when the phase distribution is *ad, bc* (Experiment 6), and (b) the same thing, but with the phase distribution *ac, bd* (Experiment 7).

We see that the regrouping as indicated in Experiments 6 and 7 quite excludes the possibility of the group formation being determined by static configurational factors. In (a), a tendency to see a continuous line is dominant in accordance with the law of the good curve, and every division into groups is artificial. If, nevertheless, it is desired to provoke a grouping, then in all probability *ab, cd* are the most likely groups (in accordance with the law of proximity, and the principle of symmetry). In (b), the groups *ab, cd* are most readily seen, and also here proximity and symmetrical factors play a part.

We are consequently justified in maintaining that it is not the usual static configurational factors that determine the group formation which we observed in our experiments. The spatial sequence, which on account of the law of proximity ought to have been the determining factor, was not able to take effect in our case, when it ran counter to the phase sameness.

Hence, we can, without further hesitation, take the next step: *The distribution into groups is determined by the phase relations with which we work.*

We make this statement for two reasons:

1. In a large number of experiments with different distribution of in phase and out of phase relations a formation of groups has taken place without exception. It was found that when elements were in phase, a primary connection between these elements was observed, whereas phase difference was accompanied by a separation between the groups.

2. The only thing that varied with regard to Experiments 1 and 4 was the apportionment of the phase relations between the various elements, and the spatial patterns that were determined by these relations.

We have succeeded in showing that it was not the spatial patterns that were decisive.

The Strength of Grouping as a Function of the Phase Angle

In the four preceding experiments we worked with 180° phase angle, i.e., the greatest possible difference. The present section will be devoted to an investigation of the significance of the magnitude of the phase angle for the intensity of the group formation.

Hence we are prompted to ask: What degree of phase difference is required to split up the original whole, consisting of all elements in phase with each other? In other words, where does the threshold of grouping lie? How are various phase differences related to one another?

Experiment 9. Os compared the intensity of grouping in a series of experiments with different phase angles between the in phase groups *ab*, *cd*. The following series of phase angles were employed: 180°, 90°, 45°, 20°, 10°, (5°). The frequency was, as usual, 0.7 c/sec.

In order to obtain as exact a graduation as possible, the Os were instructed to use a scale with five degrees: (1) very weak grouping, (2) fairly weak, (3) medium strength, (4) strong, and (5) an almost inevitable grouping. That is to say, a "rating method" was employed.

Table 4

O	Phase angle				
	180°	90°	45°	20°	10°
EI	4	4	2	1	0
MJ	5	5	3	1	0
US	4	5	2	1	0
RJ	5	5	3	1	0?

The grouping which was so weak that Os could detect it only by making a strenuous effort was taken as the subjective zero-point.

Each O was given time to acquaint himself thoroughly with this series before he had to make his rating. He had an opportunity of seeing it a sufficient number of times, both in descending and ascending series, and also a sequence taken at random. When the rating had to be carried out, the sequence was also taken at random.

Nothing but a ranking order between these various phase differences was aimed at with the aid of this rating scale. The use of the latter must be expected to vary considerably from O to O. The number of Os was also insufficient to permit more extensive conclusions being drawn. In the experiments carried out by four Os, however, the differences between Os' findings were surprisingly small. This is shown in Table 4 where the results are assembled.

According to the table, there is, in fact, no difference in strength between 180° and 90° phase difference (this is frequently confirmed in other experiments). Under 90° the strength seemed to diminish in proportion to the decrease of the phase angle. When a frequency of 0.7 c/sec. is employed, it is evident that a phase angle of 20° is approximately the line below which no real distribution into groups can take place. Os have, however, even when the phase angle was 10°, observed a difference, and usually, when they were put to the test, were able to distinguish different groups on making a definite effort. It cannot be said, however, that at this stage there was any real formation of groups with a normal perceptual attitude.

Experiment 10. The experiment was an entire repetition of Experiment 9, but with the phase combination *ad, bc.*

The results are given in Table 5.

Experiment 11: Here the third possible combination was tested. The experiment was a repetition of the two preceding ones, except for the fact that the phase combination was now *ac, bd.*

The results are given in Table 6.

Table 5

O	Phase angle				
	180°	90°	45°	20°	10°
EI	4	4	2	1	0
MJ	5	4	2	1	0
US	4	4	2	1	0
RJ	5	5	3	1	0

Table 6

0	Phase angle				
	180°	90°	45°	20°	10°
EI	4	4	2	1	0
MJ	4	4	3	1	0
US	5	4	2	1	0
RJ	5	5	3	1	0

If we now compare the three tables, we shall see that the results of the experiments described are in rather close agreement. The only difference is the tendency to experience the grouping of phase sameness somewhat more vividly in Experiment 9 (i.e., groups *ab, cd),* than in the other two experiments. The lower threshold has not been influenced by the regrouping.

Thus the three experiments taken together give definite answers to the two questions which were raised at the commencement of this section. We may summarize as follows:

A phase difference of about 20° forms the lower threshold for the formation of groups dependent on difference in phase, under the conditions regarding the spatial distance between the elements, the frequency, etc., which have been present in all the experiments so far.

Between the phase angles from 180° to 90° there is no actual difference with regard to the pregnance of grouping. In a successive series of diminishing phase differences, this pregnance appears thereafter to decrease progressively until the threshold value is reached.

It is not only the *pregnance* of organization that alters with the change of the phase angle. The character of the configuration is also changed. Especially revealing, in this respect, is the difference between the configuration at 180° phase difference and at 90°. The motion whole is, in the latter case, quite pliable, flexible, and supple in comparison with the more rigid, angular, and somewhat mechanical character of the motion whole connected with a phase angle of 180°. Consequently it was not only due to chance that the latter combination caused many of the Os primarily to think of mechanical contrivances, while the former (and perhaps still moreso when the phase difference was still less) awoke associations to movement of living creatures.

The Part Played by Frequency

In all the experiments which have been conducted up to the present we have worked with the same frequency of the periodic motions. This frequency was not chosen arbitrarily, but some of Os had to determine at a preliminary stage, which frequency suited them best. In this manner values of the period ranging between 1.2–1.8 sec was obtained, and they were able without much hesitation to make their choice.

It is of some interest to ascertain what influence other velocities (less favorable ones) have on the intensity of the formation of groups, and in the following experiments, it is this frequency which is common for all the elements, that is the variable factor.

Experiment 12. The experiment was carried out with three Os who took part in Experiments 9–11, and who were well-trained when it was a question of estimating the intensity relations between different group formations. The Os were requested with the aid of the scale mentioned on page 58 to estimate the intensity of the group formations in the series of constellations of motion that were shown them.

The series of values of period (always the same frequency for all four elements) tested was: 1 sec, 3 sec, 6 sec, and 18 sec. This series was repeated with 180°, 90°, and 45° phase angle between the groups of elements, and thus in reality, we have three experiments. For sake of clarity, these have been treated as a single experiment. The distribution of phase relations was in each case carried out in accordance with the scheme *ac, bd.*

The result of this experiment is shown in Table 7.

In accordance with the table this experiment showed that the configurational pregnance also became weaker as the frequency decreased. The table also clearly shows, however, that a small phase difference can, to a certain extent, be made up for by a higher frequency. On the other hand, when the frequency is

Table 7

O	180° phase angle				90° phase angle				45° phase angle			
	Length of period in sec				Length of period in sec				Length of period in sec			
	1	3	6	18	1	3	6	18	1	3	6	18
MJ	5	4	4	1	5	2	1	0	3	1	0.5	0
US	5	4	3	0	4	2	1	0	2	1	0	0
EI	4	4	3	0	4	3	1	0	3	2	1	0

very low, a direct phase opposition can produce a separation, where small differences are without effect.

The experimental results can be interpreted as indicating that it is the velocity of the changes in the respective relations in position between two elements, that is decisive with regard to the separating effect of phase difference.

Grouping at Various Phase Differences Within the
Same Series of Elements

Already during the discussion of the results of Experiment 5 we traced the troublesome duality of the way in which phase difference can function, and this has made itself felt in all the subsequent experiments.

We have found that one of the main principles in the series of elements, where both phase sameness and phase difference occur, is that being in phase has an integrating effect, while phase difference causes disintegration. From this point of departure, it may seem as if we had to deal with a kind of equality factor, which gives rise to a grouping in accordance with a principle of equality—inequality.

But apparently it is not as simple as that. We stated already on page 51 that in spite of phase difference, we must count with an integration that can span the cleavage that phase difference implies. The subsequent experiments demonstrated that this integration was not determined by spatial factors, but has to be ascribed to the interplay of motion itself. Thus the question connected with the above mentioned discussion becomes all the more obtrusive. Can phase difference function simultaneously as an integrating and disintegrating factor?

In order to obtain material for the continuation of our discussion, we shall conduct a few experiments with combinations of phase differences. Their purpose is to discover whether the primary whole, which being in phase always gives rise to, really has as its inevitable prerequisite such an equality.

Experiment 13. The four elements are, as usual, arranged in a horizontal line, and have the same frequency, 0.7 c/sec. No elements have the same phase; only various degrees of difference occur. It is both 45° and 135°. The distribution of these two phase differences is shown in the diagram in Fig. 16.

The result of this arrangement is very alluring. A separation into two groups is clearly evident, where *ab* is the one, and *cd* the other.

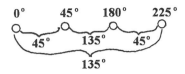

Fig. 16

The experiment was carried out with six Os, three of whom were well acquainted with experiments in phase differences, while the other three had only taken part in one of these experiments previously.

Five of these Os had without any hesitation indicated the above-mentioned groups *(ab, cd)*, and considered that they were distinctly visible. A highly qualified O (D. K.), when comparing this constellation of motion and the combination *ab, cd*, when there was phase sameness within the groups and a phase difference of 90° between the groups, pointed out that the most characteristic difference between these two motion configurations is that in the present experiment, the relationship between the part wholes and the total whole is equalized. The latter has, to a certain extent, relinquished its character of acting as a background, and is more conspicuous. At the same time the part wholes have lost something of their pregnance. This description corresponds with the author's own conception of the special trait of the phenomenon.

Another highly trained O (R. J.), has with the aid of the rating scale which was applied in Experiment 9, estimated the intensity of the formation of groups as grade 3; that is to say, he found that the formation of groups was of medium intensity.

Two of the Os stated that, in addition to the given groups *ab, cd,* they were able to see *bc* forming a group. The two remaining elements have then constituted a remainder without any real connection between them. This grouping, however, was stated to be quite secondary and unsatisfactory.

One inexperienced O stated that he only perceived a connection between all four elements; he was thus only able to see the total whole.

This total whole was mentioned spontaneously by all Os. It was compared by one O to a swimming fish ("a fish that remains stationary when swimming against a strong current"); and by another O it was compared to an undulatory motion ("a sea-wave"). The O who could only see the total whole compared it to a wavy line.

Our experiment has taught us a very important thing—which was quite unexpected in itself: *being in phase is not a prerequisite for grouping within a total whole.* Even a difference as large as 45° can give a group formation that is similar to the kind observed when the elements are in phase.

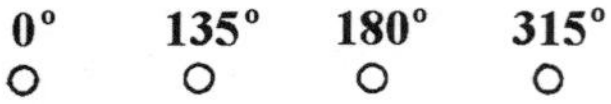

Fig. 17 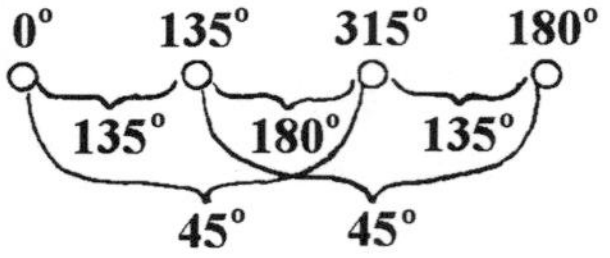   Fig. 18

In our experiment we have one phase angle that is 45°, and another that is 135°. We can state that the larger angle characterizes the difference between the groups, and the lesser occurs within the groups as a counterpart to the integration we have presumed to be due to being in phase.

A repetition of the experiment with a distribution of the phase relations in accordance with the two remaining possibilities enables us to determine whether this function of large and small phase angles is general.

> *Experiment 14.* The phase differences of 45° and 135° have been distributed in accordance with the diagram in Fig. 17. In general the experiment is a direct repetition of Experiment 13. The same six Os took part in it.

The result of the experiment was that distinct group formation *ad, bc* were reported. Furthermore, according to the reports, four of the Os found the inclosed group more conspicuous than the inclosing one.

The total whole is also clearly visible. It was compared by one of the Os to an "angular" undulatory motion, and by another O to a belt in flapping motion.

> *Experiment 15.* The phase differences have been distributed in accordance with the scheme in Fig. 18. In other respects, the same arrangement was employed as before. The same six Os also took part in this experiment.

The groups formed are now *ac, bd.* All Os saw this grouping, and considered that it was distinct. Both groups were of the same intensity.

The total whole also occurred, and was, inter alia, compared to a crank axle in motion. (cf. Table 3, column 4)

The last two experiments have confirmed that *the group formation* is *not dependent on phase sameness.* They have also demonstrated that the configuration of motion, as we assumed, is actually organized in accordance with the principle that a *smaller phase difference in contrast to a larger gives rise to a formation of groups.* Or keeping in mind that our material is still limited, we can say: a difference of 45° brought about a group formation, when it occurred together with

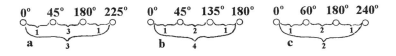

Fig. 19

a difference of 135°. In order to acquire fuller knowledge of the laws that govern the formation of groups in question, we shall examine another experiment.

Experiment 16. Os were permitted to see the following three combinations of phase differences in immediate succession: (1) 0°–45° 180° –225° (= Experiment 13); (2) 0°–45°–135°–180°; (3) 0°–60°–180°–240 ° (see Fig. 19). They were requested to state any group formations they might perceive, and to specify in which combination or combinations these were either most intense or most faint. Only three experienced Os took part in this experiment.

All Os stated without hesitation that the groups were *ab, cd* in all three cases. The three Os agreed that the first combination showed the most clear distribution. Between the remaining two, none of the Os was able to indicate any real difference. As motion configurations they also appeared to be so similar that one of the Os questioned whether any alteration had taken place.

An examination of the three phase combinations shows that in the first, the relation between the large and small phase differences was 1:3 (see Fig. 19). In the second combination the relations are, in the same respect, 1:2:4, and in the third 1:2.

The most pregnant distribution of groups occurred in the first combination. From this fact we are fully justified in maintaining that the intensity of the formation of groups is dependent on the relation between the magnitude of the integrating phase step and the magnitude of the next largest.

Thus it is not any absolute phase difference in itself which determines the intensity of the group formation, for example, in such a way that being in phase ought to produce the strongest connection, and that this should then successively decrease in a series where phase difference increased progressively: *It is on the contrary the relations between the small phase difference and the next largest which determines the intensity of the group formations.*

By also taking into consideration the results of Experiments 9–11 we can now state a principle which will cover all the group formations which we have met in the foregoing.

In every series of elements, where both phase sameness and phase difference occur, or where we find only varying degrees of phase differences, the elements which are in phase or have the least phase difference form a group. The inten-

sity of grouping is determined by the relation between the integrating phase step and the separating one.

Why Do These Effects Arise?

In the preceding part of this investigation we have determined the laws in accordance with which the various phase relations govern the organization of our motion configurations. It is naturally of fundamental importance to be able to formulate the connection between the occurrence of various phase relations on one hand, and different types of organization of our motion whole on the other hand; but that should not be our final goal. In order that we may be able to apply our result to the interplay of other forms of motion, we must inquire into the cause for the effects produced by various phase relations. We must now take the next step by formulating the following question: *Which factor or factors in the various phase relations bring about the effects in question?*

Faced with a question of this kind, we may, in view of the conditions of our experiments, point to two hypothetical factors: two factors, both of which vary regularly with phase differences, and which may be assumed to influence the organization of perception.

In connection with one of these, we can refer to Experiments 13–16. These experiments showed that a smaller phase angle in contrast to a larger determined the formation of the configuration. If we look upon the turnings of the elements as specially accentuated moments during motion, we have good grounds to assume that we are dealing with *a temporal proximity factor.* An ideal case of this temporal proximity would then be simultaneity, and a small time interval between the turnings of various elements would, in contrast to the larger intervals, also bring about integration. Accordingly it would be the relative degree of the temporal nearness, in analogy to the functioning of the spatial proximity factor, which was the determinant.

There is much to be said for supposing that such a pure succession-factor is at work here, and the author has made various attempts at isolating it from our next suppositional factor, in which the spatial aspect of the event is also present. The question has been formulated as follows: Can a temporal succession without being attached to motion give rise to a formation of groups corresponding to those found in Experiment 13?

In as far as this question can be answered by reference to event configurations when repeating the same stimulus with short duration, the reply would be in the affirmative.

The author has himself conducted some experiments of this nature, where short-durational flashes of light follow each other, for example, according to the scheme -- -- --. Wertheimer mentions a similar experiment in connection with the law of proximity;[16] and in his *Zeitpsychologie*, Benussi has described some experiments which coincide with our above question.[17]

The results were the same in all these cases: a group formation occurred, where the temporally most proximate signals united to form a group, and where the longer temporal distances between the groups were like vacant intervals.

It seems reasonable to interpret these experimental results so that the temporal succession between the accentuated moments, also in our motion configurations, are the active factors that cause integration and disintegration. For several reasons the author was inclined to accept this supposition. It must be pointed out, however, that the temporal proximity factors in question are different from the temporal proximity that occurs in our experiments where there are several continual part events which take place simultaneously. The attempts to produce an experimental situation, which would more directly correspond with the combinations of motion that have been studied, but without implying motion, and which should thus carry more weight as proof, produced an unexpected and interesting result, which will be considered in another chapter (Chapter VI).

The second of the hypothetical factors which is present in the phase relations is the *spatial* motion patterns that the phase relations which we have studied yield. These also vary in strict accordance with the phase differences. The larger the phase difference between two elements is on a scale from 0° to 180° phase angle, the greater and the relatively more rapid will the respective changes in position be. Can we find the active configurational factor in this series of different velocities in change of position?

It is too soon yet to try and bring this discussion to a conclusion. Only when we have conducted the series of experiments in the variation of spatial relations, which we have planned, will it be fitting to do so. A knowledge of the spatial relations of motion, and their effect on the configurations of motion, are of course necessary for an elucidation of the hypothetical configurational factor discussed.

---

[16] Op. cit., p. 308.
[17] V. Benussi, *Zeitpsychologie*, Heidelberg, 1913, pp. 99ff.

CHAPTER IV

Perceptual Dissociation of Systems of Reference

(Perception of Relative Motion)

Two Introductory Experiments

When setting out to investigate the role of the spatial factors in the genesis of motion configurations, it is quite natural to start, as did the author, to look for the essential spatial factors in the shape and direction of the different paths of motion.

As an introduction to this investigation, we shall therefore consider two of the experiments which were carried out at a preliminary stage, where the factors in question varied in the series of the four elements with which we worked in our temporal experiments.

Experiment 17. Four dark points, 3 mm in diameter, are projected onto a bright homogeneous background. They are arranged along a horizontal line, and the points are 12 mm apart, respectively. As in the previous experiments, the frequency is 0.7 c/sec. and the directions and lengths of the paths of motion are shown in Fig. 20.

As will be seen, *a* and *d* have sloping paths (30° inclination), while *b* and *c*, as usual, have vertical paths. All have the same frequency and phase, in order that no temporal factor should have any influence.

The question that the experiment attempts to answer may be stated as follows: Does a dissociation of the total whole occur if any element is given a direction in motion different from that of the others?

The result is an organization of the four elements which is self-evident for each O. One group is formed by *ad,* and another by *bc;* and both groups form together an event configuration. The phenomenological description is as follows: The line of points moves regularly up and down, and at the same time *a* and *d* move along the common line horizontally. It appears as if there was a kind of mechanism. *Because* the line moves vertically, *a* and *d,* which appear to be rigidly joined, are *forced to* move in a horizontal direction.

The result can prove quite astonishing for those who know the actual constellation of motions. What is seen is not a combination of *sloping* and vertical motion, but of *horizontal* and vertical motion.

Before we comment on these conditions, we shall first consider the following experiment.

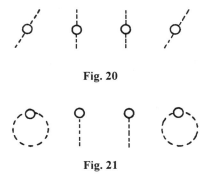

Fig. 20

Fig. 21

Experiment 18. The experiment is a repetition of Experiment 17, except for the motion of the elements *a* and *d*. These elements have now not only another direction of the paths of motion compared with the elements *b* and *c*, but the shape of their tracks is entirely different. In fact, their paths of motion are circular.

Fig. 21 shows the motion paths of the four elements. The revolution time for *a* and *d* is exactly the same as the periodicity for *b* and *c*. The elements *a* and *d* turn in the same direction.

The perceptual configuration which this combination of motion gives rise to is found to be very similar to the previous one. Also here, the entire line of points is seen to move vertically, while the two exterior points move horizontally, and this horizontal motion appears to be quite independent of the general vertical motion. This occurrence of two motions appears to be something quite self-evident for the observer. The two motions are actually *seen!* Even those who are aware of the actual circular motion of the exterior elements are unable visually to detect this, as long as the four elements are seen simultaneously. (If three of these are screened, then of course the circular motion of the fourth immediately becomes apparent.)

Both the total whole and the formation of groups occur in this combination of motion. A comparison of these two experiments shows that the only difference between them, from a phenomenal point of view, is that the temporal relations between the vertical and horizontal motions is different. In Experiment 17, the two motions reach their extreme positions simultaneously, while in Experiment 18, one motion culminates exactly in between two culminations of the other elements.

Both Experiments 17 and 18 have also been carried out with the two other possible element combinations, and the results obtained were in full agreement with those we are now commenting on. A separation into groups always takes place in connection with the presence of two different motions, and it is then the motions having similar paths which form the groups.

These experiments have clearly demonstrated one thing: Changes in the direction or shape of the paths of motion of some elements can cause a pregnant group formation. This takes place in such a way that the elements that have objectively equal paths of motion unite to form a part whole, without thereby disrupting their connection with the other elements.

But the experiments in question also have another significance. We do not see two groups of elements that are separated on account of different paths of motion. It is not, as might have been expected, that one group has vertical paths of motion, and the other group sloping or circular paths. No, we have been able to demonstrate that Os are compelled to see a vertical motion common to all elements, and simultaneously, an independent *horizontal* motion of a group of elements. The objective motion of the latter elements has in perception, been "dissociated" into two distinct motions.

We have also seen that two radically different paths of motion have given rise to very similar phenomenal combinations of motion. Both sloping and circular paths resulted in a horizontal motion as distinct from the common vertical motion.

This indicates that we must give up the supposition that we are able to determine from the objective shape or direction of the paths of motion the organization of the phenomenal motion whole. It is evident that, instead, we have to look for the group-forming factor that was active in Experiments 17 and 18, in the dissociation of the objective motion that we have experienced. Consequently it will be our task to seek for the laws that determine this dissociation. It is these laws, evidently, that give the relations between the physical motions and the perceptual phenomenon.

Dissociation of Systems of Reference

This phenomenon, which represents the perceptual disintegration of a physically simple and unitary motion into various components, has already been observed on several occasions.

Already in our introductory chapter we had occasion to allude to an article by **Edgar Rubin** on the perception of motion.[18] The latter is of fundamental importance to our present purpose. The phenomenon in question and its practical consequences were clearly demonstrated here for the first time. One can only regret that the author did not carry out the suggestions alluded to in the article and extend his investigations in this field. In its present condition, the article, in spite of the very considerable service it has rendered, is in the nature of a "vorläufige Mitteilung," (a preliminary report), as the subtitle suggests.

---

[18] Edgar Rubin: "Visuell wahrgenommene wirkliche Bewegungen." *Zeitschrift für Psychol.*, 103, 1927, pp. 384–392.

In it, Rubin treats the phenomenon we have observed by describing some experiments, and giving excellent examples from the experience of daily life. His experiment with the rolling wheel has already been referred to.

In his investigation of induced motion, **Karl Duncker** has demonstrated the same phenomenon by employing a stroboscopic technique.

Duncker discovered that induced motion could be produced by this technique, if there is a pronounced inclosure relation between the affected object (which objectively is at rest), and the influencing one. Duncker worked with a point inclosed in a square.

Duncker has also carried out a variant of Rubin's experiment with a rolling wheel.

In a study which represents a continuation of Duncker's work, **E. Oppenheimer** has observed the same phenomenon.[19] In this case, it is a vertical line that either increases or decreases, at the same time as it is displaced horizontally.

Like the other two investigators, **Hans Wallach**[20] has described, in a work which is closely connected with theirs, a case of *Systemtrennung* (system dissociation) that greatly resembles Oppenheimer's.

Finally, if we turn to **Michotte's** investigation of causality,[21] we shall find a corresponding observation there also.

---

[19] E. Oppenheimer, "Optische Versuche über Ruhe und Bewegung," *Psychol. Forschung,* 20, 1934–1935, p. 24.

[20] Hans Wallach, "Über visuell wahrgenommene Bewegungsrichtung," *Psychol. Forschung,* 20, 1934–1935, pp. 354–356.

[21] A. Michotte, *La perception de la causalité,* Louvain et Paris 1946, p. 68.

Lissajous-Combinations

In order that the reader may become acquainted with the event configurations that the phenomena of the dissociation of the systems of reference imply, we intend, in the following section, to give a comprehensive phenomenological description of a series of motion phenomena, which are very instructive in this respect. The special type of motion combinations that we are dealing with here incidentally represented the first contact the author had with the problem of the dissociation of systems of reference, and it proved rather difficult to analyze. It will to a considerable extent supply material for a following account of the laws of the dissociation of systems of reference.

The author has chosen to call these motion combinations Lissajous-combinations for the following reasons.

In physics there is a phenomenon known as Lissajous figures or Lissajous patterns. These form the curves that are the result of the combination of two simple harmonic motions at right angles to one another. They were called after the French physicist Lissajous (1822–1880), who produced such patterns with the aid of two tuning-forks, one placed vertically and the other horizontally. A beam of light is reflected from a small mirror attached to one limb of one of the tuning-forks, to a similar mirror on the next tuning-fork, and from there it is again reflected on to a screen. On this screen it describes the curves that have been referred to. If the two tuning-forks are exactly in tune, figures can be obtained such as a sloping line, an ellipse, a circle, and all the intermediate forms. The shape of the figure is determined by the phase relations of the oscillations of the tuning-forks. If the tuning-forks have not exactly the same frequency, this can result in the formation of different and constantly changing patterns.

In an apparatus which was constructed somewhat later, Eisenlohr's *Zweipendelapparat*, the same oscillation pattern in the form of apparent motion of a lead can be produced. Of course, Lissajous patterns can also be readily produced by means of a modern cathode ray oscillograph.[22]

The Lissajous figures have on several occasions proved of interest to the psychologists. They were probably first considered by **Ernst Mach**, who as a physicist was acquainted with these phenomena.

Benussi has in an interesting article on combinations of apparent movements, published in 1918, which we have already referred to, studied the effects of various phase relations between apparent motions at right angles to one an-

---

[22] See for example, Hoag; *Basic Radio*, 1946, pp. 173–175

other.[23] In 1930, **Weber** pointed out the three-dimensional apparent motions that a Lissajous figure can give rise to.[24]

From a technical point of view the sloping and circular paths which our apparatus produces are Lissajous figures with a very low oscillation frequency. They are as we know composed of two simple harmonic motions in one object with a spatial angle of 90° between the two components.

The author decided to call the motion combinations that we are about to study *Lissajous-combinations* because these give in the same perceptual field a simple harmonic vertical motion, and also a horizontal such motion. As opposed to the Lissajous *figures,* we have one carrier for each motion, and thus two objects in motion. (This is also the case with the Eisenlohr apparatus and with Benussi's combinations of apparent movements.)

Some Characteristic Lissajous-Combinations

(Phenomenological description)

We shall start our account of the Lissajous-combinations with the following experiment which deals with perhaps the simplest one of these combinations.

Experiment 19. Two dark points, about 3 mm in diameter move along rectilinear paths, against a homogeneous bright background. These paths are approximately 20 mm in length, and are at right angles to one another as depicted in Fig. 22. They have the same frequency, and the phase relations are such, that they reach the point *ab* simultaneously; here they for an instant fuse into a single point. From there they travel again to the peripheral turning points *a* and *b*, and then turn, and are once again fused at *ab,* etc.

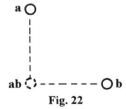

Fig. 22

[23] V. Benussi, "Über Scheinbewegungskombination," *Archiv für die gesamte Psychologie,* 37, 1918.

[24] Weber, "Apparent Movement in Lissajous Figures," *The American Journal of Psychology,* 42, 1930, pp. 647–649.

The frequency which was most often used in the experiments was 0.7 c/sec, but the phenomenon is not affected with regard to its organization even by quite considerable changes in this respect. The same applies as regards the length of the paths of motion.

No special instructions were given to Os with regard to fixation. They were permitted to freely look at the field, and were requested to describe the motions of the two points while the apparatus was working.

It was found that every observer experiences *sloping motions* of the two points. These seem to move along a common path; they meet at its middle point, turn, go back, etc. The sloping direction of the motions is quite coercive in its pregnance. The experiment was conducted with a large number of Os, and on several occasions the phenomenon was demonstrated before quite large audiences, but in this respect, the result was invariably the same.

Knowledge of the real direction of the paths of motion does not in any way influence the experience. Even when concentrating as much as possible, Os could not will themselves to see the two points simultaneously move in vertical and horizontal tracks. At best, it was possible to see a vertical and a sloping path, or a horizontal and a sloping one. This was done by strict fixation of one of the moving points, and then the "actual" motion path of this point became apparent.

In addition to the dominant sloping motion, an observant experimentee could also detect another motion; namely the movement of the whole system (the two points in sloping motion) in the opposite sloping direction. This common motion is not, however, at all so pregnant as the one firstmentioned. It is typically secondary in character. About 35% of Os did not notice it spontaneously. But on being questioned, all of them confirmed its presence without hesitation.

Our description, however, is not complete yet. For a number of Os (mostly the best observers), the experience of motion can suddenly change its character. Instead of a two-dimensional motion along a common path of motion for two separate elements; a three-dimensional motion is then seen in a stable body. "It becomes a rod with a bright knob at each end which twists around an inclined axle. It moves a quarter of a revolution forwards, and then a quarter of a revolution backwards; and at the same time, it rises and falls," one O stated. "It screws up and down a steeply inclined thread."

As has already been pointed out, only a *phenomenological description* of various Lissajous-combinations will be given in this section. We shall postpone for a time the analysis of the combination that has now been described and intend to turn at once to the description of a closely related motion pattern.

Experiment 20. The only change that is made with regard to Experiment 19 is that the paths of motion are readjusted, as shown in Fig. 23.

The paths cross and the two points meet at their point of intersection; for an instant they are fused, forming a single point, while passing one another. This passage is repeated once in each direction of motion.

Motion along a common sloping path is perceived also here. In another respect, we can distinguish between two variants; the phenomenon has a twofold significance which is of interest. The two points may be seen to approach each other along the common sloping path, then pass each other at the middle point of the path, turn simultaneously at the end of the common path, and again pass each other, etc. But the two points may also be seen to collide at the middle point, recoil violently, and then turn; again collide, recoil, etc. The latter variant is obviously a case of change of identity.[25]

A number of Os have, throughout the entire experiment, only seen one variant, while the others have experienced a repeated interchange between the two variants. This interchange has most frequently been so complete and so illusory, that it was thought to be brought about by technical means.

As an example of such an O's experience of the motion combination in question, a passage from one of the reports will be quoted. The O's comments during the course of the experiment were taken down verbatim. It is the report of an O who perceived the interchange as described, in a very pronounced manner.

> I can see two points that move towards each other along an inclined line. They meet, collide violently and recoil. No, now they pass, or penetrate each other. ... Now they recoil again. There are frequent changes, and I cannot make out any definite principle. Are you doing it at the back there? ... The points rise all the time in the other oblique direction in the course of meeting. It seems as if the line they follow is raised and lowered obliquely while they are in motion. ... Now they have entirely ceased to collide. That was curious.
>
> (R. W.)

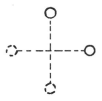

Fig. 23

---

[25] See Fig. 30 (p. 80).

Fig. 24

As this report has already shown, also in this combination, the secondary sloping motion of the entire common path of motion is present. This motion has been observed in the present experiment with about the same frequency as in the previous one.

Also in this experiment the trend to see a three-dimensional motion is observed. It appears here more readily than in the former combination, and most frequently it seems to be a quiet rotary motion. The two points become terminal points of a line which rotates about an inclined axle, which bisects the rod (see Fig. 24). During one half of the revolution, the rod ascends along the axle ("screws its way up"), while during the other half of the revolution it sinks back to its original level.

Os who have once seen this motion combination in this way show a marked tendency always to see it thus. This variant also seems to be more harmonious and restful than the other. It has a "meaning" in quite a different sense.

Experiment 21. This is a direct repetition of Experiment 20, except that the phase relations are changed. There is now a phase angle of 90° between the motion of the two elements. The result of this is that one point is at the point of intersection of the paths, when the other is at a turning point.

The experienced motion pattern is here quite different from the former ones. The dominant impression is of circular or whirling motions. Here also, it is impossible to see anything of the crossing of the two paths of motion, as given in the stimulus constellation.

The Os' descriptions can be summarized under three heads:

1. One point moves horizontally, while the other describes a circle round it.
2. One point moves along a vertical path, and the other describes a circle round it.
3. The two points whirl round each other or round a common center, in some kind of complex circular or whirling motion.

In all these cases it is a circular motion that makes the dominant impression.

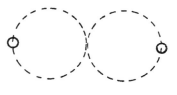

Fig. 25

Experiment 22. In this experiment the paths of motion have the same directions and positions as in Experiment 19, but the phase angle is the same as in Experiment 21: 90°.

Under ideal conditions, the result is a rectilinear and a circular path. Here, as in Experiment 21, it is the object on which is fixated that moves rectilinearly. Nothing corresponding to the whirling motion was observable here.

This description only applies, as was pointed out, to an ideal case and this is not often met with in practice. Actually, the path of motion of the object not fixated is nearly always described as a more or less pronounced egg-shaped ellipse.

Experiment 23. The two points move in circular paths in accordance with Fig. 25. Both motions, as usual, have the same frequency.

An O does not perceive circular motions; he only sees two points that approach each other along a horizontal line, fuse, separate again, etc. At the same time they execute a common vertical movement; the path of motion rises and falls.

As is seen from this, the motion pattern greatly resembles that produced in Experiment 19. The main difference is that the common path of motion has another orientation (horizontal instead of sloping).

Another point in which they differ is that the common motion is more independent, and more conspicuous in the present combination. This fact can be connected with the divergent phase relations (90°) that the two motions have here, as compared with those in Experiment 19.

At times, also in this experiment, a three-dimensional motion in the form of a rotation about a common center takes place.

Similar combinations between the motions of two points can, of course, be varied in a number of different ways. We shall, however, restrict ourselves to those now described, since already in these we meet with the principles for the organization of the perception of motion, which the combinations in question evince.

The experiments described were originally conducted with a large number of Os (15–25); furthermore, Experiments 20 and 21 have been carried out by means of a mass method with a total of 68 persons. All these experiments, together with some similar ones, have on several occasions also been demonstrated before interested persons, without a formal report being made. On all these occasions, the phenomenal motion pattern has always proved in accordance with the descriptions now given.

In all the experiments, after Os had described the perception of motion that the two points together had given rise to, they were shown the motion of each point isolated from that of the other, either by screening or removing it from the field. The result was invariably a description of the real motion.

The Motion Configuration and Its Parts

What is found the most remarkable by those who have had an opportunity of seeing these Lissajous-combinations is, without doubt, the radical changes that the motion of an element undergoes when the next element arises. The direction of motion is reversed: A rectilinear path becomes circular, a circular path becomes rectilinear, etc. And these effects have nothing to do with ignorance of the real motion paths on the part of the observer. They occur promptly and in a compelling manner, even if, in full view of the observer, the other element is repeatedly withdrawn or made to approach (which is easily accomplished with our apparatus).

Thus, from the field of motion perception, we have here an exemplification of the thesis that the whole is qualitatively something different from a summation of its component parts. And this is both so simple and revealing, and at the same time so striking and inevitable, that it does not permit any reservations being made. There is indeed a question if Gestalt Psychology, which has more energetically than any other branch of psychology proclaimed this thesis, ever produced in these respects a better exemplification.

But even if this in itself is of significant interest, yet for us it is not the primary consideration. We are not satisfied with noting discrepancies between stimulus and perception. Our question is concerned with the laws which make it possible, from a constellation of stimuli, to infer a perceptual configuration in this respect.

To commence with we shall subject the Lissajous-combinations that were described in the previous section to an analysis. This analysis is only concerned with the relations between real and phenomenal motion, inasmuch as we should try, in accordance with the principles of mechanics, to describe the real motion in a way that will best cover the phenomenal motion.[26]

---

[26] We have thus three descriptive categories: (1) real or physically given motion, (2) a mechanical transcript of this, and (3) the phenomenological description.

Analytical Description (Experiments 19, 20, and 23)

In an analysis, it proves expedient to distinguish clearly between the two-dimensional and the three-dimensional perceptual variants. Consequently, we shall adhere to this principle, and shall start with the former.

In this respect, the phenomenological descriptions of Experiments 19, 20, and 21 have shown that both elements in these experiments participated in motions in two directions, which were kept separate from one another. There is both the perceptually dominant motion, which consists in the motion of the elements from and to each other, and the motion that they execute conjointly which is secondary in relation to the former.

In other words, it is evident that in all these cases we are dealing with a form of system dissociation, a *motion analysis.* It is more complex, however, than that which we first observed in Experiments 17 and 18. Let us now choose Experiment 19 as our typical example, and we can start by examining it carefully.

Fig. 26 represents a kind of vector diagram of the *perception* of motion that is produced in this experiment. The two line vectors which are drawn from the points situated diagonally represent the primary motion of the points towards each other. The oval circumscribing these vectors signifies that they form a unit, with regard to the motion, which is represented by the vector arrow leading from the oval.

Fig. 27 represents a strictly mathematical vector diagram, indicating a division of the two physically given motions into their two components, which correspond with the perceptual motions. The continuous lines represent the given motions, vectors *bd,* respectively *cd* correspond to the primary perceptual motions while *be* and *cf* represent the secondary perceptual motions for each of the two objects.

This diagram shows what Rubin had demonstrated. The perceptual dissociation of the physically given motions is mathematically regular. The figure can be extended to represent two right-angled parallelograms of motion. We have here a regular dissociation of the motions given in stimulation into two components which are at right angles to each other.

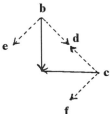

Fig. 26   **Fig. 27**

In view of the regularity which it has been shown to possess, the phenomenon can fittingly be described as motions relative to two different coordinate systems,[27] one fixed, and the other moving, in accordance with the principles for relative motion. The two equal vectors *be* and *cf* represent a motion relative to the fixed reference system. The motion of the moving reference system is taken to be identical with this motion. And relative to this moving system, the elements naturally only move to and from each other.

Experiment 20 as a two-dimensional motion phenomenon evinces in principle the same characteristics as Experiment 19. The respective changes in distance between the elements produce the primary motion; the motion relative to the moving reference system. The motion of this system is the common displacement relative to the background and surroundings, which is at right angles to the former motion. Figs. 28 and 29 are diagrams, similar to the ones employed by us in the analysis of Experiment 19. Thus Fig. 28 is a diagram of motion experience, and Fig. 29 a graphic dissociation of the physically given motions.

The recoil variant, with its change of identity just at the meeting point, can be graphically represented as shown in Fig. 30.

The perception of motion in Experiment 23 can be illustrated by Fig. 31 in accordance with the principles that regulated the two previous cases.

Consequently, this motion perception signifies that each of the two real circular motions is dissociated into two simple harmonic motions, with a phase angle of 90°; one of these is vertical and the other horizontal.

Common for the three experiments that have just been considered is that motions of stimulation are dissociated in each case into two components. As has already been pointed out, this is why they can be termed different cases of motion analysis.

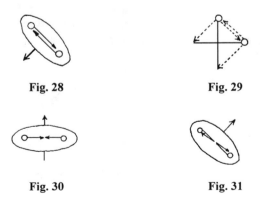

Fig. 28   Fig. 29

Fig. 30   Fig. 31

---

[27] This is principally the method used both by Rubin and Duncker.

Other Types of System Dissociation

We shall now consider the motion patterns in the shape of circular and whirling motions which result from a 90° phase difference between the elements. Consequently we intend to analyze Experiments 21 and 22.

In the latter experiments, as we know, phenomenally, the motion combinations exhibit altogether different characteristics from those which we studied in the preceding section.

The character of the motions are much more dependent on the observer's attitude than was the case in the experiments that were previously analyzed. In the phenomenological description we have distinguished between three different variants of experience,[28] and have established the fact that the choice between these is dependent on the fixation of the eyes.[29] That does not imply, however, that it is at all possible, in reality, to see the physically given motion pattern of the stimulus. In these experiments, we find instead, in the different perceptual variants, perhaps the most radical, not to speak of the most shocking, difference between stimulation and perception, that we have so far come across.

Our present task is also in these experiments to state the relations prevailing between stimulation and perception. We shall apply the same method as was employed in the foregoing section: Test the possibility of giving a mathematical description of the physically given motion constellation, in such a way that this description, in principle, corresponds with the phenomenological description.

As our point of departure, we repeat that the stimulation gives two simple harmonic motions with the same frequency and amplitude and the paths being at an angle of 90° in relation to each other. Also the phase angle is 90°. The perception implies either a rectilinear and a circular motion, or two complex circular or whirling motions.

Here we will seize that the experience always contains a more or less pure circular motion. As we have already indicated, a circular motion may be described in mechanics as the resultant of two simple harmonic motions, with the respective relations that we ascribed to the two motions in stimulation.

Thus our motion experiments give two motions, which, if they united in an element, would produce a circular motion. In the stimulus constellation, however, it is not one object that is the carrier of both the motions; but we have an object for each of the two motions. But an assumption which is highly probable is that we are dealing with the effect of a system dissociation, which brings about the union of the two motions in a single object. Therefore, we shall also

---

[28] From a functional point of view those may be reduced to two:

　　1. The phenomenon at pursuit eye movements (fixation of one object).

　　2. The phenomenon perceived when the eyes are in rest.

[29] To some extent, the fixation was also decisive in Experiments 20, 21 and 24; but here only *one* spontaneous attitude was stated, i.e., the balance between the elements.

here test more fully our method of describing the phenomenal motion, as the simultaneous perception of two different reference systems. It is of special importance in this case to distinguish between the three different descriptive categories that we are working with: (1) the one that is concerned with the physically given motion constellation, (2) various transcriptions of this constellation, in accordance with the principles of mechanics, (3) the phenomenological description. For the sake of keeping our concepts clear, we shall consistently term the first category *physical* description, and the second category *mechanical* description.

We shall commence with Experiment 21. Fig. 32 shows the physically given position of the two paths of motion. The position of the elements has been indicated for every 30° of the 360° period. If the points in the two paths of motion that have a phase angle of 90°, and where consequently the two objects are in the same moment are joined with a line, then it is found that all these lines are of the same length (see Fig. 33). That is to say, there is, in spite of the motion, always a constant distance between the two elements. Thus the continuous change in distance between the elements which was characteristic for the motion combinations that were analyzed in the previous section, and which gave rise to the motion we termed primary, does not occur here.

On the other hand, we find that the connecting line between the objects continuously alters its direction in relation to the vertical and horizontal axes.

We shall give two mechanical descriptions of the motion of this line:

1. We choose one of the two elements (e.g., b) as the system point in a moving frame of reference in which a is considered to move. The latter element then moves in a circular path with b at the center.

This is clear from the fact that the point a then is given two simple harmonic motions at right angles and with a phase difference of 90°. The course is illustrated in Fig. 34. There b is seen as a stationary reference point at the point of intersection of the two paths. Its movement along its path for every phase angle of 30° has been transferred to a motion of a in the opposite direction. Thus a acquires its original horizontal motion, and besides this, a simultaneous vertical motion. When a moves along its horizontal path to a_1, it has at the same time relative to b moved vertically a distance equal to the distance between b and b_1. Thus a occupies a position ab_1 relative to b. After the next time interval which corresponds to 30° a is found at ab_2, after a further 30° at ab_3, etc. In other words, we have, as is seen in the diagram, a circular motion relative to b, where the radius of the circle is equal to our connecting line, i.e., half the original path of motion.

2. The motion can also be said to represent a circulation of both the elements about the center point of the imaginary connecting line, and the simultaneous circulation of that point around the point of intersection of the paths of motion.

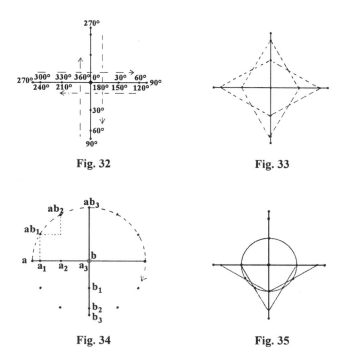

Fig. 32

Fig. 33

Fig. 34

Fig. 35

This course is shown in Fig. 35, where the center points of the connecting lines are indicated, and also connected with a circular line. The fact that (this can be seen in the figure) the line is rotated in relation to a fixed line, to the same extent (30°) for every time interval indicated, implies that according to this manner of description, the points move around their center point at constant velocity. In the same way it can be shown that also the circulation of the center point is constant in velocity, and that its periodicity is the same as that of the motion of the elements.

That is to say our description implies an absolute circulation of an imaginary center of motion, and a simultaneous circular motion of the two elements about this center. Thus we obtain one absolute and one relative motion.

It is evident that the former of these two descriptions coincides directly with the most usual of the perceptual variants in Experiment 21, the one that implies that one element moves along a rectilinear path and the other in a circle. We shall go into this more fully.

The rectilinear motion in perception corresponds directly with the physical motion of the same object. It is always with the physical motion the object that is followed with the eyes by pursuit movements which is carrier of this motion.

The other object executes a circular motion. This means that its motion is only seen in relation to the first mentioned element, a fact which is indicated by our corresponding mechanical description of the physical motion.

Thus the object is inevitably seen to execute the motion that it ought to execute, if it were seen by an observer situated on the object which has a rectilinear path. This proves conclusively that it is the motion of the element which is pursuit by the eyes that constitutes the frame of reference for the motion of the other object.

Our description makes it clear that also in this case, we are dealing with a separation in perception of two different reference systems.

It should be noticed in this connection that the motion of the element fixated has a double representation in perception. It both occurs as an independent motion of the object in question (relative to the background) and also acts as a component of the circular motion.

The type of system dissociation, which in accordance with Rubin, we have termed motion analysis, implies that the simple physical motion is in perception represented by two different motions of the same object. The system dissociation that we have now established is instead an example of how motions which from a physical point of view are separated, in perception fuse to form a unitary motion of one of the objects. It is undoubtedly most suitable to describe this form by the term *motion synthesis.*

We now turn to the perceptually complex variant which has been described as whirling motion. This is a variant that occurs when neither of the two objects is fixated; when we have no pursuit eye movement.

A careful phenomenological study of this variant shows that in its pure form, it has to be described as the circulation of the two elements round an invisible center; and at the same time a circular motion of the entire system. (Beside this pure form, there also occurs at times a kind of circular motion, which signifies that each object is always at the center of the other's motion. We shall commence by concentrating our attention on the pure form.)

Its phenomenological description given above coincides with our mechanical description No. 2.

We find both the rotation of the connecting line round its central point, and the circular motion of this point.

The motions relative to two different reference systems which the mechanical description No. 2 gives us are thus a reality in perception, although the system dissociation in this case has quite a different character, if it is compared with the variant that was first analyzed. There is no real carrier of the absolute motion in this case. It is an imaginary point that executes the motion in question—or, we can also say that the entire rotary system of two points is a carrier of this motion.

The latter fact is of importance with regard to the classification of the variant in question. That this is a case of system dissociation has already been estab-

lished. But does this signify a motion analysis, or a motion synthesis? With reference to what has been said above, it is without doubt most consistent to term
the combination in question a *motion analysis*. The collocation of the mechanical and phenomenological descriptions shows that the physical motion of each
element perceptually is divided into two motions, and that these two motions
can be perceived simultaneously. Primarily, the motion of the elements around
the common center of motion is perceived, and secondarily (very secondarily,
indeed), the rotation of the motion system is seen to take place round the point
of intersection of the physically given paths of motion. And the latter motion is
a common component of both elements.

This way of viewing the constellation, where perception really signifies two
different motions of the same element, is, however, as we have already remarked, less usual *in the pure form* (no O has spontaneously given a fully correct description). What Os often mean by whirling motion is probably that each
object, in a diffuse way, becomes the central point of the other's circular motion.
Our connecting line, as in the variant that was first analyzed, becomes the radius
instead of the diameter. In this way, there arise theoretically two separated movable systems, but they do not possess any constancy.

An alternation between different forms of experience can sometimes occur
in such a way as to cause one to think of the alternation between ambiguous
figures.

Analysis of Experiment 22

We shall now have no difficulty in turning to Experiment 22. The phenomenon described corresponds in principle with our motion synthesis variant, and
from a mechanical point of view, the combination can be described as a rectilinear absolute motion in one element, and a circular motion in the other, relative
to the former element.

The symmetry due to constant distance between the objects in Experiment
21 is not present in this motion constellation. In consequence, there is no possibility of a mechanical description of a double circular motion corresponding to
our mechanical description No. 2 in connection with Experiment 21. As we already know from the phenomenological description, the corresponding variant
was not present in perception. This is a good proof in addition to the preceding,
the motion configurations in our Lissajous-combinations in spite of radical differences from the stimulation, is nevertheless regular from a mechanical point of
view.

It was pointed out in the phenomenological description how the circular path
of motion was often replaced by an elliptic one. This is probably a sign that the

conflict which exists between the two systems of reference can be solved by a kind of compromise. The attachment of the circulating elements to the static background can assert its influence in this case, where the density of the field is less pronouned, and it shortens the motion component which is in conflict with the elements' relation to the background.

A Control Experiment

Experiments 21 and 22 have given us a rule which lays down that in motion synthesis, the phenomenal motion of one object is its real motion relative to the other object. In accordance with this rule, a phase angle of 45° between the motions of the two objects would result in an elliptical orbit of the influenced object. This fact is illustrated in Fig. 37. The figure is a diagram analogous to the diagram in Fig. 34, with the exception that the phase angle is 45°.

In connection with such a deduction, the following experiment is carried out as a control of the possibility of determining mathematically the course of the phenomenal motions.

Experiment 25. The experimental arrangement is the same as in Experiment 21, but the phase angle is now reduced to 45°. No special fixation was prescribed.

Three experienced Os took part in the experiment. All of them have described the path of one element as a straight line, and the path of the other as an ellipse in inclined position. The drawings of the elliptical orbit which Os have given are in principle equal to the ellipse obtained from the construction in Fig. 37 both according to form and direction. There was no description of any motion analysis in this experiment. (The three-dimensional variant is omitted.)

The result of this experiment is thus just what we had expected in accordance with the above-mentioned principle for motion synthesis. We can regard this as a proof of the adequacy of our method.

The Three-Dimensional Variant in our Lissajous-Combinations

Up to the present our examination of the Lissajous motions has been restricted to the ordinary two-dimensional perception. Before we are entitled to look upon our task as properly completed we must also consider the three-dimensional variant.

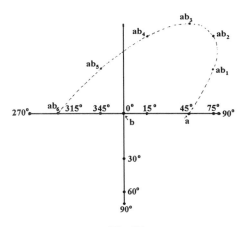

Fig. 37

In the Lissajous experiments which have been described, this latter variant was only present in experiments where motion analysis was observed.[30] It signified in such cases that the primary motions (motions relative to the movable coordinate system) are seen as the motion of a rigid body about a center of motion, a rotation of some kind. The secondary motion has been, as far as possible, combined (or perhaps better: *united*) with the primary one in a meaningful context, so that the result has become a single event whole.

Hence the elements no longer move in relation to one another. The distance between them is constant since they are the terminal points of a rigid body (a rod, etc.). There is in the cases studied here[31] no longer any dissociation into components; no separation of different systems of motion. Instead of two different two-dimensional systems, we have a stationary three-dimensional system, and a unitary complex motion within this, e.g., a screwing motion. In other words, the motion analysis may cease when the three-dimensional manner of apperception is introduced.

Velocity Analysis

In this investigation of motion, the author has found it practical to distinguish between the three following groups of motion constellations, as regards relations between rectilinear paths of motion:

(a) constellations where the paths of motion have different directions,

---

[30] It may even occur in other combinations, in conjunction with motion synthesis.

[31] Cf. note 32, page 89. See also page 100.

(b) constellations where the paths of motion are parallel,

(c) constellations with the paths of motion along the same line.

In the investigation of group formations, due to temporal relations, group (b) was considered to afford the greatest possibilities of yielding a neutral combination of elements, from a spatial point of view. Consequently, this method was employed for this series of experiments.

Since in the present chapter the role of spatial relations was to be the central point, we found it natural to commence with paths of motion that had different directions; i.e., group (a). We were thus led to study the fascinating problems of system dissociation.

In the following experiment, the third constellation possibility mentioned was utilized. This was done in order to determine whether the system dissociation was merely dependent on relations between different directions of motion.

In mathematics the simple harmonic motion of a particle can be divided into two components, both in the shape of simple harmonic motions, which act simultaneously on the particle along the same track.

Fig. 38 gives a graphic representation of this. *a* and *b* are two sine curves that illustrate two simple harmonic motions with the same frequency and amplitude, but which have a 90° phase angle in relation to each other (x-axis = time, y-axis = amplitude). The curve *ab*, which is also a sine curve, shows the resultant of the two other motions. As regards phase, it is, as shows the diagram, midway between the two components, and has thus a phase angle of 45° with

respect to both of these. Its amplitude in relation to the components is as $\sqrt{2}:1$.

On the basis of these facts it may be asked: What will be the consequence if two objects execute along the same line simple harmonic motions which are equal to the resultant and one component in Fig. 38; *ab* and, for example, *a*?

Will the motions be seen in conformity with the curves of the diagram, or will a dissociation in components occur in such a way that the component in *ab,* which is identical with *a*, will be dissociated from its remaining component *b*? That is to say, does a dissociation of velocity components along a common track take place in a manner similar to that which we found to exist in the case of direction components?

Fig. 38

This theoretical discussion has encouraged us to make the following experiment:

> *Experiment 26.* Two elements move along the same line. They have the same frequency, and their amplitude is 20 mm respectively 28.5 mm. Their respective phase difference is 45°. The medium positions of the paths of motion are made to coincide.

The experiment, which was carried out with a relatively large number of Os, gave a quite unequivocable result. The descriptions may differ from each other in manner of expression, but in principle they are in complete agreement. An object *(ab)* is seen to oscillate along the common track, with another object *(a)* as the center of motion, in the middle of the path of this motion. At the same time, this aggregate moves to and fro. It is the latter object, that which is at rest in relation to the former, which is the carrier of this motion. This object *(a)* moves continuously to and fro, while the other *(ab)* seems to follow suit, and oscillate in relation to *a*.

There is, however, another variant, which several Os mentioned. *ab* can be seen to *circulate* about *a*. It is the three-dimensional variant which we meet also here. "For me it is a little sun that moves to and fro in a miniature universe, with a planet that moves in an orbit round the sun," is the way one of the Os describes it. This simile is perhaps the one best suited to give the reader a conception of the motion combination from the point of view of a spontaneous observer, whether the motion is conceived to be two-dimensional or three-dimensional.[32]

These descriptions can only be interpreted in one way. *ab executes one motion in relation to a, and another in conjunction with a.* Two separate motions are perceived with regard to *ab*. *This is a case of motion analysis,* and characteristic for the motion combination in question is the completely coercive nature of the motion analysis. It is quite inconceivable, by force of will, to see *ab*'s motion as a single unitary motion in accordance with the stimulation.

Has the motion analysis complied with the hypothetical conditions laid down in our framing of the question? In one respect, the answer is without any hesitation in the affirmative. The two components of *ab* are incontestably simple harmonic motions. That the component which corresponds with *a*'s motion is so need not be stressed, since according to the given conditions *a* executes a motion of this description. But the motion relative to *a* can be thought of with advantage as a circular motion with *a* in the center. This is a positive proof that it is a simple harmonic motion that *ab* executes relative to *a*. The projection of a

---

[32] It ought to be pointed out that we here meet motion analysis also in connection with the three-dimensional variant.

uniform circular motion along the diameter of the path is a simple harmonic motion.

According to the mathematical conditions on which the hypothesis rests, the two components into which *ab*'s motion is to be dissociated are exactly alike, except for the phase difference. The following simple control test shows that the same applies as regards perception. When the Os had become acquainted with the motion in Experiment 26, the experimenter stopped the motion of *ab,* and let this element remain stationary at the middle point of the path of motion (this change was done in a few seconds). It was found that without exception, Os confused the objects, and maintained that the only change that had taken place was that *a* was stationary. The circular or the oscillatory motion is identical, although it is now the motion of the other object, and consequently the other component that Os see as the oscillatory motion. Thus the two motions that were perceived were, in accordance with the mathematically given motion components of the hypothesis, respectively alike.

CHAPTER V

Derivation of Laws of Motion Configurations

In the present chapter we intend to continue our study of system dissociation, and to compare the results obtained in this study with those of the experiments described in Chapter III.

On the basis of the material we have thus collected, we shall attempt to frame laws of decisive importance for the genesis of motion configurations.

We shall commence by attempting to derive the fundamental principles which determine system dissociation.

Experiment 27. Two dark points, 3 mm in diameter are visible against a bright background in a window (9 x 9 cm). One point, as depicted in Fig. 39, executes a vertical oscillating motion, while the other moves in a circular orbit. The respective positions of the paths of motion are also shown in the figure. The frequency is about 0.5 c/sec.

Os are shown:

(a) both objects simultaneously in motion,

(b) object *a* alone; or, object *b* alone.

Description of a Simple Form of Motion Analysis

As the purpose of the experiment is to establish a possible system dissociation, the following instructions were given to Os: "Describe the motions of the two points." Three trained and a number of untrained Os took part in this and the two following experiments. The more differentiated analysis which appears in some cases in this series is due also to the author's own observations.

In the experiment now under discussion essentially the same motion combination is present as was in Experiment 18, but the actual experiment represents a simplification, inasmuch as there are only two elements. Our main aim is to give a more comprehensive phenomenological description of the motion combination, as a point of departure for the continuation of the investigation.

Fig. 39

The descriptions that were obtained may be summarized as follows: During the first stage of the experiment, two points (*a* and *b*) are seen to move up and down. At the same time, *b* moves to and fro along a horizontal path. The horizontal and the vertical motions appear to be entirely separated from each other. When the element *a* is removed, *b* is seen to have a circular motion. When *b* is removed, *a* has still a vertical motion.

At the initial stage of the experiment, no instructions concerning fixation were given. During the course of the experiment, Os were requested to concentrate their gaze on *a*, and then to state whether they detected any change. Next, they were to concentrate on *b*, and subsequently make a statement. It proved, however, that in this experiment fixation of a specific object did not lead to any appreciable alteration in the motion pattern.

It is hardly necessary to point out that we are dealing here with a typical case of *motion analysis*. The physically given circular motion of *b* has been separated into two components in perception; it has, in fact, been separated into two simple harmonic motions without any respective interconnection. Thus *b* has no longer a uniform motion but two periodic ones. We can attempt to elucidate more fully the character of the perception in question by the vector diagram in Fig. 40.

The horizontal vector arrow represents the motion which is particular to *b* alone. We have thus a motion within the motion whole *ab;* a motion relative to the element *a* and without any connection with the fixed reference system, relative to which *ab*'s vertical motion is determined.

Outline of a Hypothesis

We shall take this description as our point of departure, and shall inquire why this system dissociation takes place (why do we not perceive a vertical and a circular path of motion?), and what are the laws by which it is governed.

To start with, we can conclude from the experiment in question, that the presence of element *a*, is a necessary condition for the splitting up of *b*'s circular motion into separate components. Consequently we shall term *a* the influencing element, and *b* the affected element, and then take the next step by asking: Why does this effect occur?

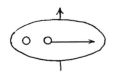

Fig. 40

It can be of importance to point out that also here, the splitting up into components is mathematically correct. The actual, physical circular motion may be described as built up of two components, corresponding to the two separate motions that the element in question takes part in. (Two simple harmonic motions with the same amplitude and frequency in the same object, which motions are at right angles to each other, and have a phase difference of 90°.)

Furthermore, in our case, we can assert that the vertical motion of the affected element is exactly equal with that of the influencing element. The two motions correspond as regards the direction of motion, its length, and the distribution of the velocity along the path of motion. They are also in phase.

In view of the fact that in Chapter III we found that identically equal motion of two objects causes them to form a perceptual unit, and that this was especially the case when a divergent motion was present in the same field, it can be expedient to point to this fact as possibly constituting the conditions for motion analysis. For some reason, according to such a hypothesis, a motion component which is equal to another motion should join with the latter and form a unit, a motion whole. The remaining component is then left as an independent motion.

With regard to such a preliminary hypothesis, let us examine whether full equality is a necessary condition for motion analysis, or, if this is not the case, which of the equality factors that have been mentioned are respectively primary or secondary. When we keep the temporal form of the event constant as an invariant experimental condition, there remain two variables: (a) phase relations, (b) relations of the length of the motions for the two unified motions and inevitably connected with this, the relations of the velocity of the motions.

Variation of the Length of Paths of the Common Motion

Our first step is to vary the length of the paths of motion, and consequently also to change the velocity relations of the motions.

Experiment 28. The experimental conditions are the same as in Experiment 27, except that *b* now describes an ellipse and not a circle. Fig. 41 illustrates the motion combinations in question.

The result of this experiment is a distinct motion analysis. Thus *b* is seen to execute a horizontal motion which is very conspicuous. At the same time, it can be seen to carry out a vertical motion together with *a;* but the latter in its turn, is perceived to move vertically, independently of the common vertical motion. The diagram in Fig. 42 depicts the motion combinations in question. We should point out that the common vertical motion is secondary to a striking extent. Several of the Os did not detect it. This signifies that only the respective interplay of

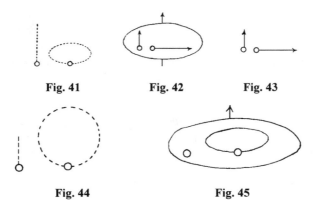

Fig. 41   Fig. 42   Fig. 43

Fig. 44   Fig. 45

motion within the whole is perceived. The common motion relative to the background (which is represented by the arrow from the inclosing ellipse) disappears, and we then have the combination as shown in Fig. 43.

As soon as *a* is removed, *b*'s elliptical path is clearly discernible.

Experiment 29. Here again we have a rectilinear vertical path (a), and a circular path (*b*). The vertical path of *a* is, however, shorter than the diameter of the circular path of *b* (see Fig. 44).

On first impression, it seems that *a* executes a short vertical motion, and that *b* describes an elliptic path. But on closer study it is seen that *b* participates in *a*'s vertical motion. Hence the motion combination in the latter case can be represented as shown in Fig. 45. It may be pointed out that the dominant feature of this experiment is the elliptic motion.

As will be gathered from this description, also here, we are dealing with a motion analysis, but only with a partial one. The elliptic motion in perception signifies that a part of the vertical component in the circular motion of the stimulus, corresponding with the length of *a*'s motion, has been detached. This will be evident by comparing the two figures 44 and 45.

Analysis of Experiments 28 and 29

If we relate these two experiments with the question that they are intended to answer, we shall see that the question in its most general meaning has received the reply that *motion analysis can take place, in spite of the inequality of the length of the paths of motion, and of the velocities of the motions.*

But at the same time, the experiments have manifested more complex relations between the influencing and the affected motions than our preliminary hypothesis had assumed to exist. Let us try to inquire further into this.

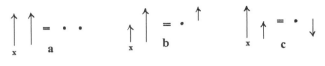

Fig. 46

An examination of the result of Experiment 28 shows that, as depicted in the diagram in Fig. 42, we have here to deal with a double motion analysis: a velocity and a direction analysis. The common motion has only the length exhibited by the vertical component of *b*; and the remaining motion pertaining to *a* persists as a vertical motion relative to *b*.

This shows that our distinction between an influencing and an affected *object* is inadequate, when it is a question of motions that are not exactly alike. It was evident that in reality, it was *the motion* in *b* that corresponded with *a*'s motion, that was the determinant, inasmuch as it constituted the frame of reference for the diverging motion both in its own object of motion and in the other.

That actually *a*'s entire motion has not determined the motion analysis of *b* can be demonstrated by the following argument, which gives some facts regarding relative motion:

Seen from a point in rectilinear motion, a point with exactly the same motion appears to be at rest (see Fig. 46a).

If on the other hand, the accompanying point is moving in the same direction as the reference point, but at a higher velocity, then the former will move in relation to the latter, in the common direction of the motion, and with a velocity that is equal to the difference between their velocities, relative to the fixed system of reference (Fig. 46b). If we finally consider the case that is illustrated by Fig. 46c, where the accompanying point has a *lower* velocity than the point of reference, the result is clearly a motion relative to the reference point, which is in the opposite direction to the common motion. Its velocity is equal to the difference in velocity in the common direction.

This last case covers the relations between the vertical motions of our two objects *a* and *b* in Experiment 28. If we start out by assuming that *a* is alone the reference base for *b*'s motion, this would signify that we have to count with a vertical motion in *b*, in the opposite direction to *a*'s motion and half the length of the latter. That is to say, *b* would continue to have an elliptic motion, for this vertical component relative to *a*, has its phase angle changed to 180°, compared with the same component relative to the fixed framework; therefore there is still a phase difference of 90° between the vertical and horizontal components of *b*. As a consequence of the phase angle being changed to 180°, *b* should, however, reverse its direction of motion and circulate in the opposite direction.

But as we know, this does not take place. The difference in velocity is instead transferred to a separate motion of a. This signifies that we are here dealing with a motion relation as shown in Fig. 46b, if by the reference point (x) we refer to the element b. *The element a moves vertically relative to b.*

In Experiment 29, it is again a's vertical motion which is the reference basis for b's motion. As shown in Figs. 44 and 45 is the vertical axis of the phenomenal path of motion of the element b equal to b's real vertical motion relative to a. *The vertical component of the circular motion has thus lost as much of its length as corresponds with the length of a's path of motion.* The *equal* displacement of both elements in relation to the background, has also here become fused and has formed the particular motion of the whole system.

These experiments make it evident that *it is the shorter, of the two otherwise equal displacements that* we *have compared, which determined the character of the actual system dissociation.* The common motion, the system's own motion, acquired just the magnitude that this shorter displacement represents. The longer of the two vertical displacements with which we are concerned has, in other words, been deprived of that part which corresponds to the other vertical displacement that in other respects is equal to it.

Motion as a Frame of Reference

The author's investigation of velocity configurations established, inter alia, that two objects in respective motion are phenomenally connected by powerful forces. These carefully quantified results led to a distinction being made between two types of motion relations: (1) motion–rest, and (2) motion–motion.

The results in question afford a good guide for the tracing of the effects of the system dissociation. It is reasonable to assume that the effect in question is dependent on this condition of superiority—subordination between, on the one hand, the forces that bind the elements to the background, and on the other hand, the stronger attraction of the respective motion between the elements.

According to such a theory, on account of the hierarchic relationship referred to, the respective displacement that takes place between the two objects should in perception be separated from the motion they have in common. The latter then merely becomes a displacement relative to the background. According to such a theory, the stronger attraction should produce the primary motion component which would then, at every moment, be directed towards the other object.

During, inter alia, the work with variations of the length of the motion paths of the equal directional components, facts were observed, however, that were particularly difficult to account for on the basis of this theory. It was found that the divergent motion was not always directed towards the other object. Experiment 28 furnishes a pregnant example, and we shall consequently return to it.

We should bear in mind that the movable frame of reference in the experiment in question was found to have the same motion as the vertical component of b's elliptical motion. In relation to this common vertical motion, a horizontal motion is observed in b, and a vertical motion in a.

A single glance at Fig. 42, shows us, however, that this distribution of motion is not in accordance with the theory just outlined. If b's divergent motion were directed towards a, it would not run along a horizontal path, but the path would be sloping at the upper part of b's vertical path (or perhaps we ought to say the path would be curved).

A thorough supervisory control with trained Os, has shown, however, that such a divergence does not occur. Disregarding the vertical motion, it is impossible to see anything else than the *element b moving horizontally.* Consequently, we can consider it as certain that b does not direct its motion towards the other object.

This appears very puzzling. The results of the investigation of velocity are firmly based on a comprehensive experimental material, with carefully quantified results. Consequently, they appear to be inevitable. And yet, it seems that after a long series of confirmations, we are faced by an exception.

Up to the present, we have accepted as self-evident the assumption that it must be material objects that form the frames of reference in an interplay of motion. Since we consider the assumption that an attraction exists between differently directed motions as incontestable, it is expedient, in our attempt to solve our dilemma, to concentrate our attention on this former still unconfirmed assumption.

We then discover that, however "natural" the assumption in question may appear, yet it is just this that is found to be inadequate. If we liberate ourselves from this conception, then the experiment under discussion shows us that it is the common *motion,* that is to say, the system of motion's own motion, which forms the basis of reference. This applies so literally that it is this *motion* and not the *object a* which disrupts the anchorage to the background and binds the divergent motion in b.

This may at first appear quite startling. One wishes to protest that the motion in question has no independent carrier. We must retort, however, that the conception of motion, with which we are dealing here, is not at all an abstract production. They are strict phenomenological descriptions that have furnished us with the motion in question. What appears startling here we have come across long before, and were compelled to accept. It consists in the fact that the same object at the same time can execute two quite separate motions. The conclusion that we are now forced to draw is when considering the matter more closely, only a consistent consequence of this fact. From this point of view the motion has two carriers. That in addition, the same object simultaneously executes other motions, is another matter.

Instead, we can now state that we have attained a very important correction of the rule that two objects in motion attract each other. *It is not the objects in themselves which give rise to attraction, but it is the very motion that they execute.*

This knowledge must influence our whole outlook on the perception of motion. In a radical way, it brings the motion itself into the foreground, the motion independent of the object which is its carrier. Many of the observations made, during our experimental work, have already pointed in the same direction. We can mention as a typical example, the way in which motions of a number of scattered points are spontaneously experienced as meaningful motions in a unitary object. This is another proof that in the perception of motion, it is primarily the *motion* and not the spatial configurations that are seen.

By placing the phenomenon in question in this connection, we also obtain a satisfactory explanation of the otherwise puzzling high frequency of images in our experiments with motion. Os frequently perceive in these experiments a well-known uniform motion, and not a configuration such as the elements in a spatial sense would give rise to.

Variation of the Phase Relation

The experiments with different length of motions or motion components that constitute the common motion have proved very instructive. They have shown clearly that it is not only the same direction of the motions in question which is decisive in motion analysis. The two conjoint motions were found to be similar both as regards direction and magnitude. The experiment in question has shown, in other words, that the common motion, from a mechanical point of view, *is composed of equal vectors*. (A vector is mathematically defined as a quantity that possesses both magnitude and direction. Two vectors that possess the same magnitude and the same direction are thus, from a mathematical point of view, equal.)

In the introductory section of this chapter, we inquired about the importance of the phase relation in the genesis of motion analysis. We shall now continue our analysis by considering this question more closely. We have found that the conjoint motion components must be equal vectors, but in this there is still no absolute determination of time. Two equal vectors need not be simultaneous. Our question concerning phase relations just touched on this point: simultaneity or an interval in time between two otherwise equal courses.

The preceding experiments suggest that simultaneity is a necessary condition for motion analysis. Especially important in this respect are the experiments with velocity analysis. But we shall leave the decision to special experiments.

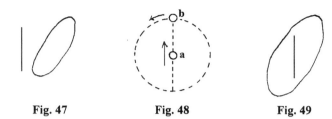

| Fig. 47 | Fig. 48 | Fig. 49 |

Experiment 30. This is a repetition of Experiment 27, but with the exception that a phase difference between the two conjoint vertical motions is now introduced. The phase angle is 90°.

Os were requested to give element *a* their principal attention, and then to describe *b*'s path of motion. They were also supplied with paper and pens so that they could make a sketch of it.

Three trained Os took part. All of them, without any hesitation, described a path in form at an inclined ellipse. Fig. 47 gives an example of the sketches that were made, and which were respectively quite alike.

The experiment was also carried out with a somewhat different constellation of elements. In this case, *a* did not move alongside of *b*'s path of motion, but along the vertical diameter of the latter (see Fig. 48). This did not give rise to any change whatsoever in *b*'s phenomenal elliptic path. The phenomenal paths of motion, sketched by an observer, are shown in Fig. 49.

Beside the two-dimensional type of perception just described, a three-dimensional variant also occurs, where the elliptic path is comprehended as the perspective of a circular motion. We shall shortly return to this variant, but we first intend to analyze the ordinary, two-dimensional type.

We find at once that the phenomenological description does not contain any mention of double motions in the element, as was the case in Experiment 27. The simple elliptic motion is alone found to be present. *In other words, motion analysis has not taken place.*

We shall instead try the same kind of mechanical description of the physical motion constellation as we applied in Experiment 21, and which was graphically represented in Fig. 34. As our point of departure we choose Fig. 48. We then obtain the diagram shown in Fig. 50. The element *a* which is to function as the reference point for *b*'s motion is situated in the middle of its path. According to the conditions prescribed, *b* is to have a phase angle of 90° in relation to *a*, and has thus, in the same moment, the position *b*. The position of each element for every 30° of a cycle has been marked along their paths of motion. We now give *b* a vertical motion in addition to its own circular motion, and let this vertical motion, during every marked time interval (30°) exactly correspond with *a*'s motion during the same interval, but with the opposite direction. Thus after 30°

we find b at ab_1 and in another 30° at ab_2, etc. In this way, during one revolution b describes the ellipse as indicated by the connecting dotted line.

In other words, our construction fully covers the description of the phenomenon, which will be readily seen by comparing Figs. 49 and 50. We observe
in both cases the same elliptic path and the same inclination of the ellipse. Also
the fact that the larger axis of the ellipse is considerably longer than the diameter
of the original circle is readily confirmed by a renewed study of the phenomenon.

What we have described is a motion synthesis, which in principle corresponds entirely with the one found in Experiment 21. *We can consequently assert that the phase difference has given rise to a motion synthesis.*

We shall now consider the three-dimensional variant. Also in this case, we
start with the grouping of elements as shown in Fig. 48.

The motion figuration can alter in different ways. The dominant form is,
however, when the element b moves in a circular path, which the Os think they
see obliquely from one side. The motion system is illustrated in Fig. 51. Most

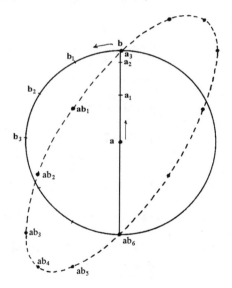

Fig. 50

Fig. 51

frequently, the whole system appears to execute a more or less pure vertical motion, while *b* circles round *a*. Thus we are here dealing with a three-dimensional motion analysis. It must be pointed out, however, that usually, this analysis is not "pure," but that *a*'s vertical motion is more striking than *b*'s. (An experience of activity on the part of *a*, and a corresponding "attendance" on *b*'s part, was also observed. The following is typical for the observations of the experimentees: "It is as if one were swinging a pair of scissors or a ruler round a pencil." This involuntarily makes one think of Michotte's causality effects.)

If *a*'s amplitude is reduced by about a third, it is found that the three-dimensional motion analysis becomes much more pronounced.

A comparison with the corresponding velocity analysis has also been carried out, both as regards the original, and the shortened amplitude of *a*. This is easily accomplished, by excluding the horizontal component of *b*'s motion. It is found that the result, from the point of view of motion analysis, is entirely analogous, even after such a change has taken place. *The three-dimensional motion analysis in Experiment 30 is thus a counterpart of the velocity analysis which the two vertical components would give rise to alone.*

We shall now proceed to study the effect of the phase relation which implies that the two motions have always opposite directions.

Experiment 31. The only difference here, as compared with Experiment 30, is that the phase angle between the vertical motions is increased to 180°. The respective positions of the paths of motion are as shown in Fig. 48.

The same Os as in Experiment 30 took part. All of them declared at once that one object described a standing ellipse, that the other moved along a vertical path inside the ellipse, and that this path is considerably shorter than the ellipse. Fig. 52 gives an example of the sketches that were made. They were all similar.

A three-dimensional variant could also occur here. This signifies that the two elements were described as terminal points on a rod. This was directed obliquely backwards behind the screen, and either tipped up and down over its middle point or rotated about it.

When we examine the *two-dimensional* variant, we find that also here, each object describes only one motion. That is to say, a motion analysis does not occur. But on the other hand, there is a pronounced motion synthesis. This will be

Fig. 52

clearly seen by looking at Fig. 53. The latter, like Fig. 50, is a graphic representation of system dissociation. The motion of the element a has been transferred
to b. The result is also here an elliptic path. The similarity between the construction shown in the diagram and the sketches made by Os is very striking.

The *three-dimensional* variant here, in contrast to the same variant in Experiment 30, shows no tendency towards motion analysis. There is only motion
in relation to a stationary center of motion. This fact appears quite consistent, if
we, in the same way as in Experiment 30, compare with the motion perception
received when the horizontal component has been excluded. In this case, we obtain (a phase angle of 180°), as pointed out previously, a pure velocity synthesis.
This synthesis is clearly seen in the phenomenal doubling of the vertical component of element b, as shown in Fig. 53.

Our results may be summarized as follows: The phase difference that we introduced has not proved to be an absolute obstacle to motion analysis. In Experiment 26 (velocity analysis) we came across a motion analysis in the presence of phase difference. We have now been able to show that an analogous
effect can occur even when the physically given motions have different directions, and the equal directional components are in different phases.

On the other hand, the experiment has clearly shown that it is not the vectors
in the motion constellation that have the same magnitude and direction that are
in themselves decisive. If a phase difference exists between these, then it is the
vector components that are included in these vectors, and that exhibit simultaneity, which are the cause of motion analysis. It is these motions that have the
same direction and magnitude *during the same time interval,* which give a frame

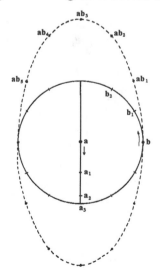

Fig. 53

of reference for divergent motions. Simultaneity is thus an indispensable condition for motion analysis. That is why a phase angle of 180° (opposite phases) cannot give rise to motion analysis, but only to motion synthesis.

We can now finally formulate the principles for motion analysis in the following manner: *Where in the motions of the stimuli there are equal and simultaneous vectors, motion analysis can occur.*

The author has conducted a large number of experiments similar to the ones now described. A deductive method has frequently been applied; that is to say, the mathematical principles, which we have previously employed in our analysis of different motion combinations, have given a hypothetical basis for the configuration that a certain motion constellation is to give rise to. These experiments have confirmed that the perception of motion always follows the principles we have described in the foregoing.

The Law of the Common Motion State

A fundamental result of our experimental series in Chapter III concerning the role of temporal relations was that simultaneity in motions that are otherwise equal gives rise to a stable whole. This was especially pronounced in constellations, where also from a temporal point of view, different motions were present. The effect of such simultaneity of motion was most frequently that the elements affected were experienced as belonging to the same spatial unit.

In the preceding section, the role of the temporal factor in the formation of configurations has been further clarified. We have succeeded in demonstrating that simultaneity is a necessary factor for the formation of primary wholes. The study of motion analysis has also taught us that, irrespective of the physically given paths of motion, such a formation of a primary whole occurs if the displacements, to some extent, imply equal motions during the same moment of time. These equal and simultaneous components of motion form a motion unit as a background for divergent motions.[33]

We are here dealing with a principle that is fundamental for motion perception; a general principle for the formation of configurations among the elements of motion. We can summarize this as follows:

When the stimulation contains two or more spatially separated motions or motion components, which are equal in magnitude and direction (that is to say, according to mechanics, they are equal vectors) and are also simultaneous, they

---

[33] It should be pointed out that by the term *primary whole* is meant the phenomenal unit which is the result of the common motion condition. On the other hand, we speak of a phenomenally *primary motion relation* between divergent motion states, on account of the attention-attracting quality of this relation.

are perceived as a single unit. These simultaneous and equal displacements are literally seen as a *single* motion.

We shall in connection to David Katz call this law *"the law of the common motion state."* [34]

Relational Hierarchy in the Perception of Motion

Duncker has, as we have already pointed out, founded the system dissociation primarily in a hierarchical rank order of spatial relations between the objects he worked with (inclusion relation). From our own experiments with, in a figurative sense, quite similar elements, we have been able to show that this restriction is not at all justified.[35] But without doubt, the factor in question is of essential significance when it is a question of facilitating or preventing a motion analysis. A more detailed investigation is required in this field.

But even if Duncker's hierarchical principle, founded on figurative relations, cannot be simply transferred from the sphere of motion induction to ordinary perception of motion, yet the hierarchical point of view in itself is of considerable value in the study of all types of interplay of motion. The demonstration of a hierarchical order between different motion systems is, without question, one of the most essential results of Duncker's investigation, which as a whole carries great weight.

In our own investigations we have constantly observed a separation between perceptually primary and secondary motions and motion relations. In this connection, the investigation of velocity is of fundamental importance; we have referred to this on several occasions. It has given rise to a radical distinction between the relation motion–motion, and the relation motion–rest, and has also established the absolute dominance of the former relation type.

In the temporal experiments in Chapter III, we came across a similar rank order between primary and secondary motion connections, where the smallest time interval produced the primary connection. The dissociation of the systems of reference in its different forms has also shown a pronounced hierarchical rank order. Thus, for example, in motion analysis, the common motion relative to the background was, from a hierarchical point of view, the most fundamental event, while the divergent motion, the change in the distance between the objects, dominated perception. In this way we have obtained a triad: rest–common motion–divergent motion.

---

[34] Cf. note 5 page 39.

[35] In experiments with numerical precedency which were conducted by the author, no such factor was observed to influence the genesis of the motion unit formed of the common motion. The presence of a single element with divergent motion was thus sufficient to give rise to a pregnant motion analysis for 15 other similar elements.

When we in this way survey the whole series of experiments, it becomes evident that every motion forms, what we may call, in analogy to Rubin's well-known terminology, *figure* against the stationary *background*. The change in distance between two elements, both of which are in motion, becomes in its turn a figure in relation to a simultaneous common displacement which thus functions as a background or as a frame of reference. From a theoretical point of view, this hierarchical system could be extended by further stages of respectively similar and divergent motions, even if we have not carried this out experimentally.

The Law of the Divergent Motion States

It is evident that we have to look for a factor of decisive importance for the hierarchical rank order, in the manner in which our visual perceptual apparatus reacts to the simultaneous presence of divergent motion states. (When we speak of a motion state in this connection, we consider, in agreement with Duncker,[36] what, from a perceptual point of view, is a static state, *rest,* also as a motion state.) In connection with the preceding section we can make the following assertion: *When a relation between divergent motion states occurs simultaneously with relations between identical motion states, the former relation is always dominant from a perceptual point of view.*

We are here dealing with a general principle governing motion perception, and shall term it *the law of divergent motion states.*

The Principle of Lowest Velocity

The law which we formulated in the preceding section only states that the relation "divergent motion states" is dominant as against "common motion state." It tells us nothing as to which of the two divergent motion states is the carrier of the displacement, and which is the frame of reference.[37]

Such a distribution is determined, however, by a general principle, a matter that we have had ample opportunity of establishing in the preceding pages. We shall now go into this matter more fully.

We choose as our point of departure a general fact, which is conspicuous both in every kind of psychological motion study and in our daily experience.

---

[36] Cf. Duncker, op. cit., p. 245, footnote 3.

[37] Here, as previously, we only take into consideration the motion relations, and leave out of account the influence of the spatial factors that Duncker (and Oppenheimer) demonstrated.

The static environment forms (when the subject is himself present in this motion state) the reference frame, and every divergent motion is the figure. The eyes, as is well known, are practically forced to direct themselves to some object in motion.

As our next step we point at a fundamental principle that we found to exist in motion analysis: It is invariably the lowest velocity of the motions participating in the analysis that is the frame of reference.[38] It is this which forms the common motion.

From these facts it follows that in ordinary motion perception, it is the subject's own motion state, whose velocity is thus zero, which is the most fundamental frame of reference. They also show that the hierarchical principle which perception follows implies that *the lower velocity becomes the frame of reference for the divergent higher velocity.*

We can conveniently term this hierarchical principle *the principle of the lowest velocity.*

Final Derivation of the Grouping Effects Established in Chapter III

In the last section of Chapter III (pp. 66ff), we left an important question in abeyance until we had ascertained the part played by the spatial relations. We shall now reconsider this question, and shall also conduct an experimental investigation.

The respective positions of the various paths of motion were chosen in the temporal experiments with a view to making the spatial relations as far as possible neutral, with regard to the spatial configurative factors. By arranging the elements along a horizontal line and making the vertical paths of motion relatively short (in relation to the distance between the elements), it was possible to prevent the distance between the different elements from being altered to any great extent.

We shall anew test some of the combinations with phase differences that we have worked with, but now with *horizontal* paths of motion, in spite of the horizontal line of elements. Thus all the elements move along the same line, and when there is a phase angle, we have a continuous change in distance between the elements affected, inasmuch as these approach and recede from one another along the common path.

Experiment 32. The respective position of the elements and the length of the paths of motion are shown in Fig. 54. The length of the

---

[38] Cf. page 96 (see also page 43).

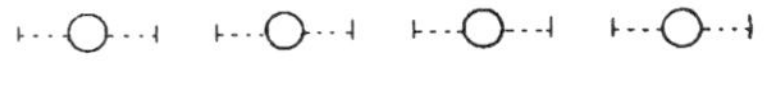

├···◯···┤ ├···◯···┤   ├···◯···┤ ├···◯···┤

Fig. 54

paths of motion is thus 8 mm, and the distance between the middle point of the paths is 12 mm. As usual, the frequency is 0.7 c/sec. *a* and *b* are in phase, and so are *c* and *d*, and the phase angle between these groups is 180°.

Two groups of elements are seen to approach and recede from one another. Each group *(ab,* respectively *cd)* constitutes a pregnant and self-evident unit.

An examination of the possible groupings remaining, *ac, bd* and *ad, bc* shows that in all cases, phase sameness gives rise to the corresponding configurations, known from Chapter III.

Experiment 33. This experiment repeats the phase relations of Experiment 13. Thus we have the following series of phase angles: 0°–45° –180°–225° (see Fig. 16). For the rest, the conditions are the same as in Experiment 32.

Also as regards the result, the experiment is a repetition of Experiment 13. Thus the two groups *ab* and *cd* are still present. The connection between the elements that form the groups is very pronounced, and the difference between the groups themselves is equally clear. Each group forms a whole; and these two wholes approach and recede from each other. In each of the two groups, the elements move respectively.

The experimental result is a case of velocity analysis. The elements execute a motion towards and away from each other within the group, and at the same time the group, as an independent unit of motion, executes a motion relative to the other group. Thus in principle, this is a motion analysis of the same type as was found in Experiment 26. There is a marked tendency within the groups only to see motion of the elements relative to each other (i.e., a motion which presupposes a phase difference of 180°), and in the same way, to perceive a motion between the groups which is diametrically opposite. In this manner, neither of the two objects in a group is in itself a carrier of the group motion, relative to the other group. It is, rather, a kind of imaginary center of motion which moves. (If sight is concentrated on either object in a group, then this moves at considerably lower velocity than the other, and at the same time becomes the point of reference for the motion of the latter, and is also the carrier of the common motion relative to the other group.)

The group formation in this experiment thus follows the principle of lowest velocity. The elements which in their motion relative to one another have the least amplitude, and consequently also the lowest velocity, form the reference basis for the higher velocity of the respective motion of these groups.

At least when the paths of motion have the respective positions as in Experiment 33 (i.e., along the same straight line) *the group formations which are determined by the temporal relations can be explained as a result of system dissociation,* in accordance with the laws of the lowest velocity and common motion state.

Can we generalize these results, so as to make them also applicable for the group formations in the temporal experiments that we previously studied? If so, then we have found an answer to the question that has been discussed.

The answer is unmistakably in the affirmative. Experiment 26 has also been repeated but with the paths of motion parallel, instead of them coinciding with one another, as they did in the original experiment. It was found that the effect of the system dissociation was identical in both variants.

An examination of the descriptions given at the temporal experiments shows, in fact, that effects of system dissociation are often present, although it is not systematically developed in this experimental series. (The relatively small movements of the objects in the series in question has proved a negative factor in this respect.) The smoothness of the motion which proved characteristic for phase differences below 180° is a feature that should be specially noticed. This signifies a common velocity component, in addition to the respective divergent motion.

It is also characteristic that 180° phase difference is often termed mechanical. No common component is present there, but the motions are relative to a common center of motion which is *at rest* (for instance the middle point of a rod). On the other hand, the more complex interaction of relative motions, which the smaller phase differences bring about, are often associated with the movements of living creatures where every joint can be a point of reference for a movement. We may also point out that it is the pregnant velocity synthesis occurring when the phase angle is 180° which makes the motion seem so energic at this phase relation.

At an earlier stage (p. 66) we discussed some experiments with rhythmic sequences and found that they indirectly supported a hypothesis that the temporal succession was the active organizing factor, e.g., in Experiment 13. As a continuation of this method, the author has tried to reproduce exactly the same temporal sequence as that which we worked with in the temporal experiments, but without any spatial change taking place. This was done by means of changes in luminosity in stationary planes. The result of these experiments was that an experience of motion did nevertheless occur; we obtained an apparent motion.

This result which is very interesting in itself will be thoroughly studied in the following chapters. Because we got also here a motion effect, the experiments in question cannot supply a decisive answer regarding the question of the direct configurative function of temporal relations.

In the meanwhile, we have the possibility also in this respect of connecting it with the result of Experiment 33. Contrary to the original experiment (13), this does not lend any support to the hypothesis of succession, or it may even be said, to make this hypothesis seem less probable. In the perception of the inter-action of motion in Experiment 33, there is nothing resembling before–after; i.e., succession of some accentuated moments of the motions, as the arrange-ment of the vertical motions in the original experiment gave rise to. In Experi-ment 33, the entire structure of the event configuration contradicts the assump-tion that an indication of succession occurs. This should be sufficient reason for dropping the succession hypothesis.

For this hypothesis we now substitute definitively the laws established at the study of system dissociation. The forming of part wholes in the experiments de-scribed in Chapter III is in all cases due to the simultaneity factor of the *law of common motion state*. This holds good also for Experiment 13, and thus there is no function of any nearness factor.

CHAPTER VI

Constellations of Light Areas with Periodical Changing Intensities

In Chapter 1 was brought forward the question whether the principle of perceptual organization due to coordinated temporal change in spatially separated elements is unique for perception of moving elements. This problem is taken up in Chapters VI and VII. The first sentence in Chapter VI says:

As the next stage in the programme outlined on page 37 we shall now test the possibility of producing event configurations in the dimension of change which we have termed change in intensity.

----

*Thus, here starts the search for answers to the question in the field of visual perception, and this search is continued in Chapter VII. The experiments described in these two chapters introduce the study of the effects of change of **brightness** in two or four stationary "windows" presented on a screen. These windows had a circular form and a diameter of 15 mm. They were lined up in a horizontal row with 50 mm of element-to-element distance and in the experiments this display was seen from a distance of about 1.25 meters. The brightness of the circular surfaces was clearly higher than on the rest of the screen and it could be brought to vary over time in a sinusoidal way. The intention was to study whether coordinated changes of brightness over elements and time would result in perceptual formation of groups similar to those in the experiments with moving elements.*

The outcome of these experiments was quite different from what the author had expected. Quotation:

The result was a very unexpected one. The four elements formed, in their way, a very pregnant event configuration—but not one that remained at rest. The constellations of elements produced a strong impression of motion even now.

Initially, a hypothetical grouping due to phase relations in changing brightness in four elements, ac, bd (similar to the grouping studied in Chapter III) was sought for. In order to study the unexpected perception of motion under simpler conditions, a set of experiments with only two such windows were carried out in

Chapter VI. Investigating perceptual grouping in a row of four windows was left to Chapter VII.

In the basic experiment, Experiment 34, the brightness of two windows varied sinusoidally with a mutual phase difference of 180° and with a frequence of .5 c/sec. Its result is described as follows.

The phenomenon is very quickly stabilized, and the two circles then no longer remain two more or less light areas; but instead of this, they become two semi-transparent windows, etc., in the otherwise opaque screen. Through these two small holes or windows is seen what is taking place behind or in the screen. *And this is always a light, a luminous body, that passes to and fro in the space between the windows.*

Thus, coordinated changes of brightness of two surfaces are perceptually interpreted as a motion of an object with a constant brightness. A certain relation to the stroboscopic motion is pointed to. Also in that case a continuous motion between stationary positions is perceived. The effect thus detected was termed "wandering phenomenon," abbreviated w-phenomenon.

In the rest of the chapter a number of experiments are described with variation of: (1) phase difference, (2) the distance between the windows, (3) changing the windows' position in three dimensions in the laboratory. The results were summarized as follows:

A New Type of Constancy Phenomenon

A phenomenon that was observed in all the foregoing experiments in which we studied the w-phenomenon is that the luminosity of the phantom does not change during the event. This event consists in *motion* and not in a change in luminosity. We have also found that the same thing holds good with regard to the color of the phantom, in all cases that are applicable. Changes in luminosity and color which can be detected in the part events, or differences between the latter in these respects, is in the perceptual act relegated to special conditions which are not connected with the primary phenomenon.

Constancy in perception, in spite of changes in the conditions of excitation, is a fact that modern perceptual psychology is well aware of. It is a description of that which the various constancy phenomena have in common: color constancy, constancy of shape, constancy of size, etc.

The phenomenon we have observed, can in other words, be described as a special kind of constancy phenomenon: *constancy during an event*.

We can distinguish two aspects of this. Firstly, we have the basic form which consists of coordinated variations of luminosity being experienced as a constant light in motion. Next, there is the phenomenon that is the outcome of the complexities that were introduced in Experiments 41 and 42.[39] In these experiments the absolute differences in luminosity and color were ascribed to the attributes of the windows (different density or color); and in this manner the phantom continued to appear as constant in these respects. In Experiment 44[39], where the interplay of changes was made still more intricate two motions occurred—while the intensity and color both of the ordinary phantom and the phantom consisting of the movable curtain remained constant.

CHAPTER VII

Transference of Temporal Event Patterns from the Investigation of Motion Configurations to Another Dimension of Event

----

In Chapter VII the same variations of phase relations between the four elements as in Chapter III were studied. The main result in this respect was summed up in the following sentence:

Experiments 48 and 49[39] gave rise to a phenomenal connection between simultaneous part elements which is in complete agreement with the theory of motion configuration referred to. The simultaneous and equal motions have formed a unit which is experienced as a figure with constant form. The apparent motions that occur here have brought about the same grouping effect as do the corresponding real motions.

---

[39] Not reproduced in this edition.

CHAPTER VIII

Parallel Investigation from the Sense of Hearing

In this chapter the study of possible w-phenomenon effects evoked by auditory stimulation was described. Its introductory first sentence formulates the problem as follows:

Is the w-phenomenon with which we became aquainted in the two previous chapters something unique for the special contrivance which we used for the production of light fluctuations, or is it a function of the changes in intensity in general?

An apparatus was constructed, functioning by analogy with the apparatus producing the visual w-phenomenon. Applying the electronics of that time, two earphones (or alternatively, two loudspeakers) were given the same sine wave tone. This tone varied sinusoidally in volume in the same way as the brightness in the experiments on vision. The frequency of this change of volume could be changed, but as in the experiments on vision, .5 c/sec was the standard.

The basic experiment and its results are described as follows.

Experiment 51. The two earphones which are a part of the apparatus described above were fastened to an ordinary telephone mounting. They were attached to the O's head in such a way that each ear was supplied with a phone. The frequence of the potentiometer, when this is set in motion, is .5 c/sec. This is also the standard frequency for the experiments that will be described later.

The instructions to Os merely request them to describe naively what they experience when the apparatus is set going.

It is found that *an experience of motion occurs as soon as the apparatus is started.* Though this appears paradoxical to an observer, it is nevertheless astonishingly distinct; in fact, it is often quite inescapable. A tone is heard which is in motion in space. For the majority of Os who took part in the experiments, it passed straight through the head, from one ear to the other, turned, went back and continued in this manner, in a kind of oscillating motion inside the skull of O, for as long as the apparatus was working.

The tone phantom, for we must speak of it as such, seems to acquire an almost substantial character for a number of the Os. Those stated that it was an uncanny reality when they experienced this sounding substance ("a kind of round sound clump") passing through their heads. The position of the phantom in the head can also be located at any given time. This is especially the case when the motion is slower (3–4 sec per cycle). Not less than 7 out of 10 Os have described the phenomenon as thus wandering through their heads.

Of the remaining three Os, two described the motion of the sound as an arch over the head stretching from ear to ear. Here it seems to follow the earphone mounting. Finally, the third declared at once that it was something like the "buzzing of an angry bee" round his head. Here we have an example of circular motion.

After a description more in detail of the subjects' reports and further confirmation from informal demonstrations, the following conclusions are drawn:

Thus we are fully entitled to summarize as the common feature of the different varieties of experience, that it is a sound phantom with constant pitch and constant intensity of sound which is heard, and that this phantom moves in the space immediately around, or within, the observer's head.

This means that also an auditory wandering phenomenon exists, a fact which subsequently will be confirmed more fully by a number of variants of this experiment.

The chapter continues with a number of variations of the experimental conditions similar to those described in the last chapter and also some conditions specific for audition. In these experiments were studied the effects of different absolute volume of the sound (condition 2); diotic stimulation (same stimulation to both ears from different sources with the sources of sound located on a table in front of the subject, condition 3); irregular course of the change of the volume (condition 4); stimulation from a single source, two experiments (condition 5); change of pitch, together with the change of volume (condition 6).

The results from these experiments indicated that all conditions except Condition 5 brought about perception of a moving sound. Condition 5 with a single source of changing sound was perceived as a stationary sound, the intensity of which was periodically changing.

Thus, these experiments made clear that coordinated changes of intensity of spatially separated sources of sound will also under most artificial conditions evoke auditory perception of a unitary moving sound. (As the reader realizes, these studies in the 1940s were earlier than the present era of enjoying stereophonic sound from earphones and loudspeakers.)

CHAPTER IX

Parallel Investigation from the Cutaneous Field

As the title of this chapter says, here is investigated the wandering phenomenon as evoked by cutaneous stimulation. Two kinds of such stimulation were studied, namely vibration and air pressure. The experimental arrangements and results will be briefly summarized as follows.

Stimulation by vibration*: A variant of the apparatus described in Chapter VII produced electromechanical vibration in two handles (200 c/sec) with a sinusoidal change of its amplitude corresponding to the sinusoidal changes of volume of the sound.*

Experiments*: Four different conditions, similar to those in the preceding chapter were investigated. The introductory one is described below.*

The Experiments and Their Results

Experiment 58. O can take the vibrators and hold one in each hand in a natural position in front of him, keeping them about 30 cm apart. The generator is set for a frequency of 200 c/sec, and the pulsating frequency is as usual .5 c/sec.

Result of this experiment (quotation):

The descriptions of the phenomenon can vary somewhat from one O to another, when it is a question of depicting the path of motion, etc. One states that the vibrations move along a curved path that dips slightly downwards between the vibrators, a second maintains that they describe a straight line, while a third considers that they emanate from the hands, etc.

But when it comes to the fact that there is a "something" that passes through the empty space between their hands or the vibrators, all are in full agreement. A movement is experienced immediately, which is apprehended by the resting hands. Consequently these function here as a kind of distant receptor analogous to eyes and ears.

It is evident that we in this experiment have produced in principle the same motion phenomenon that Katz and Thiel have demonstrated before. We will now proceed to a description of some complementary experiments carried out in accordance with our general scheme for intensity changes.

In the following three experiments, Experiments 59, 60, 61,[40] *the effects of positions in space of the hands relative to the body, the effect of variation of vibrations recorded by only one hand, and finally the outcome from jerky changes of the amplitude of vibration, were studied. Experiments 59 and 61, dealing with different positions of the hands and non-sinusoidal change of phase respectively, resulted in descriptions of events similar to those from Experiment 58. Experiment 60, however, studying the effect of stimulation with only one vibrator, brought about negative or nearly negative results.*

Stimulation by air pressure. *Apparatus: Two jets of air were generated by a reversed vacuum cleaner. The hose of this vacuum cleaner was connected to an air tank where an air pressure was produced. Two tubes attached to this tank were equipped with throttle valves. When the apparatus was running an electrical motor brought these throttles to perform a partial sinusoidal rotation in counterphase to each other. The air jets from this device were fed into two circular holes in the back side of a wooden board. The diameter of these holes was about 12 mm and the distance between them was 25 cm.*

In the experiment (Experiment 62)[40] *the subjects were told to cover the holes on the front side of the board with their hands, one hand on each hole, and report what they experienced.*

Result of the experiment: *The result was an evident perception of pressure of constant strength, wandering to and fro between the hands. It was experienced as similar to the wandering light phantom described in Chapter VI. Thus, it was established that cutaneous perception of the w-phenomenon not is limited to recording of vibration.*

---

[40] Not reproduced in this edition.

CHAPTER X

Studies of Events in the Form of Continuous Qualitative Changes in Stimuli

with Constant Intensity

Problems concerning the perceptual dimension called quality in contrast to intensity earlier was touched at only in connection with observed interactions between these entities. In the present chapter was taken up the problem about possible w-motion perception exclusively caused by coordinated changes of "quality" as such in spatially separated locations of auditory and visual such stimulation. Thus, the possible occurrence of perceptual events in form of "wandering" of pitch and color, with the intensity kept constant, was investigated. Eight experiments attacking these problems are described.

The chapter starts with a description of two experiments, characterized as being of pilot study character. These are Experiments 63, dealing with sinusoidal opposite phase variation of pitch in two spatially separated sources, and Experiment 64, studying similar continuous changes from one color to another in two windows. Prototypes of apparatus for generating adequate stimulation are described.

Results of the pilot studies. The experiments on pitch gave a very clear-cut result. Continuous change of pitch was heard, but "there was no trace of an experience of motion". Reservations about the validity of this statement due to certain deficiencies in the experimental set-up are discussed. It is concluded, however, that the type of imperfection pointed out could not explain the result. Quotation:

The absence of any tendency to motion was so categorical in the experiment that any idea of such a possibility was quite unthinkable for an observer.

This conclusion implied that further experiments on pitch were not needed.

The results from the color-wandering experiment, on the other hand, were far less informative. These results were reported as follows:

When the experiment was carried out with this apparatus, an impression of motion was observed. The impression of motion was not particularly distinct, but it was undoubtedly present according to the unanimous reports of several Os who were well trained as regards wandering phenomena.

An analysis showed that it was mainly the one color red that moved. The other (*green*) functioned as a stationary background. The analysis also showed that there was reason to believe that this effect was due to the fact that difference in brilliance did occur in spite of all precautions. Thus the wandering phenomenon observed was perhaps still due to changes in intensity taking place, or these could at least act as a contributory factor.

As a consequence of such considerations a far more complicated apparatus was built. In this apparatus additive color mixing was applied. Technically, it is very problematic to vary the color of a surface from one color to its complement without simultaneously changing the perceptual brightness. However, an apparently rather acceptable approximation was accomplished by introducing, by means of a photocell, photometrically regulated constant luminance, coordinated with change of hue. For the middle and long wavelengths of the visible spectrum the characteristics in this respect of the apparatus were approximating the reaction of the human eye.

The Basic Experiment

We shall commence the report on the experiments in question by describing the basic experiment where, mutatis mutandis, the basic form of the experiments with wandering of light was copied.

Experiment 65. The apparatus was installed in a room with electric lighting. Red and green color filters, already described, were employed. The frequency alternation was .5 c/sec. The Os were placed 75–150 cm in front of the windows of the apparatus. They could choose the distance themselves between these limits.

The instructions, as usual, requested the Os to describe, while the apparatus was working, what they saw in the windows. Only after they had given their report, were any questions put to them, if this proved necessary.

Ten subjects, inexperienced on the w-phenomenon, took part together with three experienced subjects. Their descriptions indicate that no perception of smooth motion between the windows was seen. The perceptions generally were described as an iterated, sudden change of color inside the two circles and rather constant colors in between. Thus a wandering of colors was not perceived.

CHAPTER XI

Summary of the Principal Results of the Investigation

The summing up of the results of the project is given under two headings. The first one of these sections will be reprinted word-forword:

Configurations in Event Perception

With reference to the introductory framing of the questions, the most essential results of our experimental study of the problems of event perception can be summarized under the following points (the experiences gained in connection with the investigation of velocity which have been referred to in this paper are inserted here without this being alluded to in every particular case) :

1. All the event combinations tested have given rise to configurations of various kinds. This holds good of all three event dimensions, and of all the sensory fields that were examined.

2. Temporal relations were found to exert a decisive influence on the character and structure of the configurations. Nevertheless it must be considered an established fact that in the motion configurations (as long as no conflict arises between temporal and spatial factors) it is *not* the perception of temporal sequence which is the active factor. What here is decisive is instead *simultaneity.* The simultaneous vectors which are equal form phenomenally a single motion, a motion unit.

3. Experiments with analogous event constellations in the same event dimension (changes in intensity) and with the same temporal event pattern have been carried out in various sensory fields (sight, hearing, vibration, pressure). These experiments have resulted in quite analogous configurations being observed in the different sensory fields.

4. Our experiments, with a repetition of the same event pattern in different event dimensions, have shown that *the experience of motion occupies a special position.* Changes, which objectively belong to one of the other two event dimensions, are preferably assigned to the motion dimension. We were thus able to establish:

(a) Changes in the stimulus *intensity* in sight and hearing and in the cutaneous senses in one objectively stationary stimulus may be experienced both as a change in intensity and as motion. The latter manner of perception is often found preferable, and at times is even difficult to avoid.

(b) Temporal coordination between two or more such events which are spatially separated most usually gives rise to a compelling experience of motion.

(c) Temporal coordination between two events in form of changes in the *quality* of stimuli gives rise, in the sense of sight, often to an experience of motion and not to an experience of changes in quality.

5. A certain degree of parallelism exists between event configurations in the form of changes in intensity and in form of changes in quality, inasmuch as both may give rise to a perception of motion; the differences, however, remain very marked.

6. In accordance with points 3, 4, and 5, we can observe that a transposition from one sensory field to another, with reference to the matter now under discussion, implies less change than does the transposition from one event dimension to another. The experimental material is, however, much too limited to allow for a definitive conclusion being drawn.

7. We have observed interesting constancy phenomena in connection with this perceptual transposition of event constellations from the event dimension, which the stimulation implies, to motion. Even in "adequate" experience of motion, i.e., motion experience caused by spatial changes, we have observed constancy phenomena, which are conditioned by the event. We have termed all these phenomena *constancy phenomena in event perception.*

The second section of the summary deals with the general appearance of perception of some kind of phenomenal constancy found in the studied aspects of event perception. (The constancy phenomena attracted great interest at that time.) It is stated that event perception of the types studied implies perception of moving carriers with some kind of constant characteristics.

Rigidity, Stability, and Motion in Perceptual Space[†]

A discussion of some mathematical principles operative in the perception of relative motion and of their possible function as determinants of a static perceptual space.

Gunnar Johansson

Uppsala University

Changing excitation as a condition for perception.

Thomas Hobbes, the father of English empiricism, once said that to perceive one and the same thing is tantamount to perceiving nothing.

Some recent experiments on vision have clearly demonstrated the truth of this statement, reformulated in the following way: To get the same excitation is equivalent to perceiving nothing. Change of excitation has been shown to be a *necessary* condition for visual perception.

Some years ago, Hochberg showed, in his ingenious variant of Metzger's famous *Ganzfeld* experiments, that a constant color stimulation results in a fading out of color perception.

The recent technique, elaborated especially by Ditchburn, Riggs, and Ratliff, which employs a mirror attached to a contact lens for absolute fixation of an image on the retina, indicates that this is true, in a still higher degree, also of form perception. The perception of a hair line, with good brightness contrast, fades out completely within one or two seconds, provided the image of the hair line falls constantly on the same place of the retina.

In this way the modern physiological view implies that continuous change is characteristic of all retinal excitation, and that this is a necessary condition for perception. In most theories of space perception we seek in vain, however, for an explicit discussion of these essential facts and their relevance to perceptual space. Osgood's more general application of Marshall's and Talbot's statistical theory of visual acuity may be mentioned as an exception. The theoretical discussion on visual space perception has primarily been concerned with static

[†] From *Acta Psychologica*, 1958, *14*, 359–370. Paper read before the XVth International Congress of Psychology, Brussels 1957. Reprinted by permission of Elsevier Science Publishers B.V.

stimulus patterns, and has also tacitly assumed a static retinal excitation as a correlate for visual space perception.

For me, the problem was first stated in a more advanced way by Marshall's and Talbot's discussion on physiological nystagmus and visual acuity, and as regards the purely psychological aspect, by Koffka's account of distal and proximal stimulus, and by Gibson's discussion of ordinal stimulation and his definition of proximal stimulus, in contrast to eye scanning.

For my present purpose, I shall use the term proximal stimulus mainly in the way it is employed in Gibson's discussion. It will refer to the geometric (not ordinal) distribution of radiant energy, reflected or emitted from the environment into the eye. In one respect, however, I shall deviate slightly from Gibson by defining it as a spheric picture rather than as corresponding to a picture *plane*.

I would also mention that for the sake of simplicity, my discussion in this paper will deal exclusively with the condition where the observer is at rest.

Some mathematical principles in percepts from combinations of real motions.

I shall now take the principle of *change* as the main theme of my comments on space perception.

Change in space is the same as motion, and I shall start by discussing some fundamental principles affecting the perception of relative motion.

I hope that I may succeed in making clear how, in this respect, our vision functions in accordance with strict mathematical principles. I shall then show that these principles are probably valid also for some more general problems of space perception.

As you are well aware, the field of "real motion" has been very largely neglected. So much so, that it is quite easy to mention the scientists who have made essential contributions to our knowledge of this domain. In the first place, Karl Duncker, Edgar Rubin, Wolfgang Metzger, J. F. Brown, Hans Wallach, and Albert Michotte. In recent years, James Gibson and his co-workers at Cornell have also carried out some excellent studies.

I am also especially interested in the perception of change, and I have tried to contribute towards a somewhat better understanding of the mechanisms operative in the perception of relative motion. In this work I have drawn heavily on the investigators just mentioned.

Of course, every motion is relative. It is displacement relative to some frame of reference. But in perceptual psychology, the static background is often taken as a frame of reference for description and analysis of a displacement, and we usually speak of relative motion only when the motion is related to another displacement, relative to the static space.

In our everyday life we always describe motion in terms of paths, relative to the static space. However, this principle holds true for *perception* only in special, simple cases. The static space is definitely not a general frame of reference for motion perception. Perceptual motion is mathematically *related* to the tracks, represented in proximal stimulus, but often it is not perceived as proceeding along these tracks.

Edgar Rubin (1927) mentions the example where you see a person waving to you from a moving train. Relative to the static space his hand describes a sinusoidal track, but, in fact, you see his hand moving vertically up and down and at the same time following the translatory motion of the train. If perhaps you argue against Rubin, that you have no possibility of seeing the hand as related to the static background, I will give you another example. Imagine instead, that a person riding a bicycle is waving to you. In this case, you see his hand against the static background, but you still see it moving up and down, and not in a sinusoidal track. In quite an analogous way you see the wheels of the train or bicycle rotating around their axles together with a translatory motion of the axles. It is not possible for you to detect the cycloid component in the motion tracks, which every part of the wheels (except the very center) describes relatively to the static background. Follow, for instance, the valve of a bicycle wheel with your gaze. Perceptually it rotates around the axle of the wheel, and this means that you see a circular motion relative to a translatory motion, which is translatory relative to the street, and not the "real" cycloids relative to the street.

Of course we regard all these things as absolutely self-evident. However, we do so only till we have tried to discuss them in terms of perceptual theory—or to associate them with the common conception of our eyes functioning like a camera. Systematic experiments with motion constellations demonstrate clearly the inadequacy of taking the static space as the single frame of reference for analysis of motion percepts. Experimental results indicate that our visual apparatus does not function like a cinematographic camera, registering motion tracks, but rather in close analogy with a computer capable of calculating and summing differentials and integrals of motion vectors inherent in the "real" motion tracks of the proximal stimulus.

In fact, the percepts correspond to the results of such a vector analysis along a common time axis; we find that all vectors, which are equal at a given moment, and thus have the same size and direction, combine perceptually into units of motion. We find what may be termed (according to Duncker) a perceptual dissociation of motion systems.

As an illustration, I shall give a very brief account of the results of certain experiments with some motion constellations, which I described in a monograph some years ago (Johansson, 1950).

1. Two circular dots oscillate on a homogeneous screen in simple harmonic motions (pendulum motions) along rectilinear tracks as diagrammed in Fig. 1. The experiments were arranged in such a way that the proximal stimulus could be described in terms of motions on the screen. The oscillations of both dots have the same frequency (0.5–2 periods/sec) and they are in phase (turn at the ends of their tracks at the same moment).

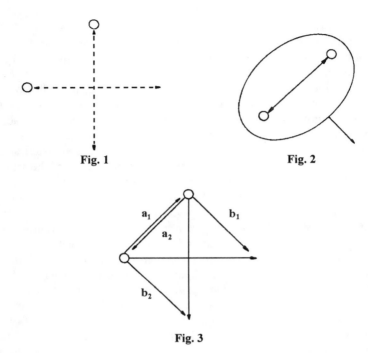

Fig. 1   Fig. 2

Fig. 3

The perceptual outcome of this stimulus pattern is that we see two dots moving towards and away from each other along a sloping path, which, simultaneously, is seen to be moving along the opposite diagonal. The dots seem to cross in the middle of the common path. Fig. 2 is a diagram of the *perception*.

Fig. 3 represents a vector diagram from a mathematical point of view of the motions in the proximal stimulus as presented on the screen. Each stimulus motion is here split up into two component vectors. The motion components along the perceptually given path (a_1, a_2) are abstracted, and the residual equal vectors (equal as to size, direction, and time) b_1, b_2 are drawn.

Thus our vector diagram is a perfect representation of the perceptually given motion combination: two dots moving diagonally, relatively to each other, and together moving in a common unitary motion. This common motion, which functions as the real frame of reference for the mutually diverging motions will be termed in the following discussion: the *common motion state*.

2. Another example: We use the same arrangement as the one described and diagrammed in Fig. 1, except for phase relations. Instead of phase equality (or 180° phase difference) a phase difference of 90° is introduced.

This gives radically changed perceptual patterns. The pattern perceived with resting gaze is diagrammed in Fig. 4.

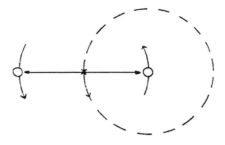

Fig. 4

Thus, we have here a common rotation around a common center, and the latter also describes a circular path around the interception of the stimulus paths. The reader will find that also this is a mathematically correct description of the stimulus motion constellation. (Because simple harmonic motions in 90° spatial angle and 90° phase angle acting on the same particle give rise to circular motions.)

The same stimulus pattern may produce two other perceptual variants, which result from fixating either of the two dots and following it with the gaze. These variants must be described as the integration in perception of the two motions in proximal stimulus, and in both cases a circular motion is seen in the element not fixated.

These and other experiments are treated in greater detail in Hochberg's report on the Cornell Symposium on perception (Hochberg, 1957).

The Minimum Principle.

The perceptual principle of combining equal vectors to form units, which I have tried briefly to demonstrate, may also be described, though perhaps in a somewhat metaphysical sense, as a "resistance" to change, or as a principle of "least amount of change" in a perceptual field.

Most of the members of the Cornell Symposium, which was held in 1954, accepted the following formulation of a "Minimum Principle": "other things equal, that perceptual response to a stimulus will be obtained which requires the least amount of information to specify" (Hochberg, 1957, p. 83). The perceptual vector analysis, which we are now discussing, was then regarded as supporting this Minimum Principle.

Change in change.

Before we leave motion perception, let me point out another characteristic feature of percepts from single harmonic motions, which may be looked upon as also furnishing a good demonstration of the minimum principle, since this feature represents an effort to allow for only the least possible amount of change in perception.

The type of simple harmonic motion which I have demonstrated may be described mathematically as a two-dimensional motion with a velocity which continually changes in accordance with the sine curve. It is equally correct, however, to describe it as the plane projection of a rotary motion in depth, and with constant velocity. In the latter case, it represents a spatial change whose second derivative, throughout the whole cycle, is zero.

If the second description is adopted, there is no change in the change: no acceleration or retardation of the motion. Thus, if the least degree of change is a value; this is the simplest description possible.

In experiments with simple harmonic motions as stimuli, we very frequently meet with such three-dimensional percepts and constant velocity, and we find that they, once seen, are highly preferred. Among other investigators, Metzger and Wallach have studied such effects, and I have done so myself.

Such experimental situations demonstrate not only a minimum principle but also a stimulus ambiguity which may evoke different percepts, all of which are mathematically correct when related to proximal stimulus.

Proximal stimulus–Excitation–Percept.

I started my discussion by pointing out the theoretical problems inherent in the relations between proximal stimulus and retinal excitation, which have practically never been investigated.

In the triad stimulus–excitation–percept, I have so far discussed only relationships between the two extreme members of the triad: between stimulus and percept. Probably you have already caught me committing the very fault to which I have directed your attention. In the last three paragraphs I have discussed the relationships between proximal stimulation and percept, as if there were no problems connected with the retinal correlate to proximal stimulus.

However, I shall now try to take the next step and attempt to bridge this gap, or still better, to connect all the three members of the triad. The main purpose of the foregoing discussion was to make this step possible. To start with, I shall consider the relations between a percept of a static rigid space and the continuously changing retinal excitation.

We are, of course, fully justified in making the assumption that the proximal stimulus, in the form of a geometric pattern of reflected radiant energy, is unchanging when reflected from a static outer world. This stimulus pattern strikes a retina which is continually moving on account of both physiological nystagmus and more or less voluntary scanning movements.

From this it follows that the diagram of change in excitation on the retina may be described in mathematical terms as comprising equal vectors of change, with the retinal surface taken as the frame of reference.

If, on a given point on the time axis, all equal vectors of change, corresponding to the eye movement, are subtracted from the pattern of excitation change, we obtain the static pattern of the proximal stimulus as a residual.

This is equivalent to saying that all changes, due to the eye movements, form a common motion state, and that the spatial relations within this common motion state correspond to the proximal stimulus.

We may add head movements, for instance, as a further source of complication in the changing pattern of excitation. However, this change is also represented by equal vectors, which may be subtracted, and the remainder is still the common motion state corresponding to the proximal stimulus.

Consequently, we find that the retinal excitation may very appropriately be treated in exactly the same way as was the proximal stimulus in our motion experiments. When applying the principle of minimum perceptual change, we may split up retinal excitation into groups of simultaneously equal vectors.

When the description is based on a changing proximal stimulus pattern, we know that our visual apparatus is able to carry out what must be termed a vector analysis of this character. We also know that our visual apparatus seems to function spontaneously in this way, in accordance with a principle of minimum of change.

Then, and *this is my central point*, instead of proximal stimulus, why not now introduce into the discussion on motion the really fundamental variable: *retinal excitation?* If we do so, we shall find that we are able to state exact mathematical relationships between changes in excitation and the percept (either percept of motion or of resting space). Moreover we are also able to adduce cogent arguments, based on experimental results, for the actual existence of a corresponding perceptual mathematization: the principle of common motion state.

If we extend the principles of motion perception to include not only visual reactions related to stimulus motions, but preferably also all visual reactions to retinal excitation, and speak of a general principle in the treatment of excitation changes, we are able to indicate the way in which our visual apparatus abstracts, from changing excitation, information about the external world. The percept of a rigid world is a direct correlate to a unified gradient of change in excitation: the common motion state relatively to which spatial motions are seen.

When we do this, we take as a starting point for our approach the basic principle of the organism for gaining information from stimuli. We have started by accepting change, and need to speak only of relative changes and relative invariances. The static space in perception is no longer regarded as a result of static excitation but of a common component in a more or less complex pattern of excitation changes.

Rigidity of space and stability.

My theoretical application of the principles of motion perception with regard to static space perception is intended to explain how space can be experienced as rigid and unchanging in spite of continuous changes in excitation. It has not—and this must be explicitly stated—a definitive relevance to the *stability* of perceptual space. Every common motion state can move relatively to a frame of reference. This is the fundamental principle.

Such a frame of reference for visual space may consist of proprioception from different sources: eye movements, head movements, vestibular stimulation, etc. When such stimuli are in conflict with the retinal pattern, we may expect to perceive a rigid but moving space. Artificial eye movements afford a simple but good demonstration of this. Such movements result in the perception of a rigid but moving space. (Press lightly on your eyeball and you will see that your space moves but remains rigid.)

Induced distortions of excitation patterns.

If we accept my application of the principles for perception of relative motion, and thus regard them as general visual principles, we shall be in a position to take further steps: We may, systematically, make the pattern of excitation more complex, and then *predict the perceptual outcome.*

In our discussion, we have already briefly touched on one way of doing this, namely the possibility of building up series, hierarchies, of common and diverging motion states. Several other examples may readily be given from the field of interacting visual events.

However, I prefer to mention here another very important field. I wish to point out the very extensive ability of our visual apparatus to compensate for experimentally induced distortions; an ability which has been experimentally demonstrated.

The best examples of this ability are afforded by a fascinating series of experiments with long-time adaption to distortions of the retinal image, which are going on especially at Innsbruck (Kohler) and in Cape Town (Taylor).

In one of the Innsbruck experiments (Kohler, 1951), a horizontal displacement of the upper part of the visual field, as related to the lower, was induced by means of special spectacles. This resulted in all vertical lines appearing to have been cut off and somewhat displaced in a horizontal direction. See Fig. 5. The common line of intersection moved vertically with head and eye movements.

Distortions of the kind mentioned complicate the retinal pattern of excitation to a very high degree. However, the complications in the pattern of change are intimately connected with head and eye movements; they are systematic, and consequently they may be described mathematically. This means that the systematic changes in retinal excitation, due to the distorting glasses, may be described as a component in the changing pattern of excitation which, principally in the same way as changes in eye movements themselves, can be subtracted from the total pattern.

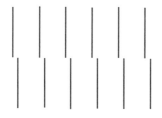

Fig. 5

Thus, when we subtract from this pattern both changes due to eye movements and those caused by the glasses, we again obtain, as a residual, an excitation pattern which is a correlate to the proximal stimulus *outside* of the glasses.

What Ivo Kohler's experiment shows is that this residual in our analysis of the excitation gets, after some weeks of perceptual learning, an exact correlate in perception. The distortion is no longer seen.

The following is an appropriate expression of this fact: The visual apparatus has proved its ability to abstract from the highly complex excitation pattern three groups of invariances with continuous changes relative to each other: static space, changes caused by glasses, and thirdly, eye movements.

Experiments with complex motion constellations sometimes result in what must be termed incomplete or defective analysis of the stimulus pattern. This seems to apply also in respect of preliminary incomplete perceptual correction of distortions.

Objectivistic and subjectivistic theories compared.

I feel rather confident that many readers will consider that part of my discussion may be regarded as an attempt to apply, in the field of event perception, Gibson's program for perceptual psychophysics. What are my motion vectors other than higher-order variables in Gibson's meaning of the term? Therefore, I wish to state that this is my own opinion.

I had begun to work along these lines before Gibson gave us his famous "Visual World"; but in several respects, my work in this field follows his program, and his psychophysics has greatly influenced my own theoretical position. I find that especially his programmatic search for higher-order variables as correlates for perception is of the greatest value and is able to give us new and fruitful aspects of the discussion on space perception.

In the current discussion on perceptual theory, two lines may be readily distinguished: the objectivistic, stimulus bound, and the subjectivistic, which deals also with what may be regarded as more subjective factors.

If we take Gibson as a representative of the former line, we may mention M. Vernon as representing the latter. She has stated in a recent paper that "it is possible to hold the view that percepts are constructed from sensory data though not wholly a function of them" (Vernon, 1955).

There is, of course, a theoretical difference between the two positions; this should not be denied. In my opinion, however, this difference has sometimes been exaggerated by both sides. My own point of view is that there should not be any radical cleavage between a whole-hearted acceptance of the fundamental principles of the gradient theory and a somewhat "subjectivistic" standpoint. On the contrary, if we regard a percept as an outcome from an economical combining of equal vectors in excitation, rather than, for instance, as a correlate of external space, we may find it natural to accept, not only one description, but a variety of different descriptions arising from the same excitation pattern. Different perceptual habits or differences in previous learning sometimes seem to lead to a preference for what I should like to term different "gradient systems."

As a matter of fact there often seems to be a possibility of choosing between two or more percepts, different, but all representing correct mathematical descriptions of the stimulus constellation; this is so, at least, when it is a question of event perception of the type I have been discussing here.

As an example, I shall mention the possibility of seeing a simple harmonic motion as either a two-dimensional pendulum motion or a uniform rotation in depth. I have already pointed out these alternatives. Expectancies of past experiences may, in such cases, determine the "choice" between several possible gradient systems.

If, in accordance with Gibson's theory and my own arguments in this paper, we regard perception as mathematical, gradient bound, and not factual, bound to an image, we must accept whole-heartedly also the plasticity of mathematical descriptions. This plasticity in the choice of gradient systems (often only termed "stimulus ambiguity") may perhaps be discussed in terms of schemata. If so, then for me, this implies that sometimes the choice of gradient system for an actual percept is determined not by the most elegant mathematical description (considered from the standpoint of economy), but by the subject's past experience and actual expectancy.

Sometimes the "subjectivity" which is found to exist may, perhaps in part, depend on the psychologist's inability to find adequate higher-order variables.

Hence, the character of a perceptual response may be regarded as being more or less *economical* rather than more or less subjectivistic, in the sense that it is not a consequence of excitation.

Summary

In the past, the relation between perceptual static space and the stimulus has been one of the problems with which most of the theorizing about visual space perception bas been concerned. A basic assumption, with regard to this problem, has been that a static pattern of excitation corresponds to perceptual space. In accordance with this assumption, perceived motion has been regarded as a special case which ought to be explained by the general principles for static space, or possibly even by principles conflicting with those for static space (e.g., "Kurzschluss").

The purpose of the present paper is to demonstrate how the concept of relative change is probably a more adequate starting point, from a theoretical point of view, than the classical approach.

It is shown that mathematical relationships in the continuously changing energy distribution on the retina may be substituted for the classical, static retinal picture, as the source of information from the external world. This substitution is regarded as an application of Gibson's gradient theory.

The possibility of choosing between various mathematical descriptions, which has been demonstrated, is taken as an indication that much of the conflict between subjectivism and objectivism has no real foundation. The problem with which this conflict is concerned is a result of the old "static" theories. From the present writer's point of view, it is mainly a problem for differential perceptual psychology. It has no evident bearing on the general problem of the relationship between stimulus and response.

References

Hochberg, J. (1957). Effects of the Gestalt revolution: The Cornell symposium on perception. *Psychological Review, 64,* 73–84.

Johansson, G. (1950). *Configurations in event perception.* Uppsala: Almqvist & Wiksell. [Chapter 2, this volume.]

Kohler, I. (1951). *Über Aufbau und Wandlungen der Wahrnehmungswelt.* Wien: Sitzungsber. Oesterr. Akad. Wiss. 227.

Rubin, E. (1927) Visuell wahrgenommene wirkliche Bewegungen (Visually perceived real motions). *Zeitschrift für Psychologie, 103,* 384–392.

Vernon, M. (1955). The functions of schemata in perceiving. *Psychological Review, 62,* 180–192.

Perception of Motion and Changing Form[†]

A study of visual perception from continuous transformations of a solid angle of light at the eye

Gunnar Johansson

Uppsala University

Abstract: It is shown how geometrically changing projections of objects which move and/or change their shape carry no specific information about form and three-dimensional motion. How, then, does the visual apparatus produce specific percepts from such non-specific changing stimuli? By applying an analogue computer technique, changing projections of artificial objects are generated on a CRT screen. These projections are fed into the eye by means of an optical device where they form a continuously changing solid angle of homogeneous light. The main conclusion is that it is a principle of perceptual three-dimensionality which gives specificity to the percepts. Preliminary statements of principles for prediction of perceived motion in depth from a given change in proximal stimulus are presented.

A basic group of problems in visual perception is concerned with how an organism gets information about the three-dimensional physical environment from light impinging on its retinal surfaces. The investigation to be presented here has bearing on a part of this group of problems, for the solving of which there are still rather few experimental data. As a first approximation, our problem may be stated in the following form: Motions of objects and changes of form of objects in the visual field of a human being (or motion of the organism) are accompanied by transformations of the spatial pattern of light entering the eye. Does this transformation of the array of light provide any specific information for the organism if it is isolated from other possible sources of information in visual stimulation? If it does, which are the relevant stimulus parameters?

[†] From *Scandinavian Journal of Psychology*, 1964, *5*, 181–208. Reprinted with permission from the journal.

Discussion of the Problem

The problem of the third dimension applied to changing proximal stimuli

Before specifying the problem further we ought to state explicitly that the eye is a sense organ, which reacts primarily to differences and changes in the array of light energy focused on its retina. The actual distribution of this energy may be described in terms of angular measures at the eye. It is also conveniently described in terms of image projection on a "picture plane" (or on a picture sphere) which is oriented at right angles to the direction of gaze (Gibson, 1950). In accordance with Gibson, we will refer to this distribution of light as the proximal stimulus.

We will also repeat a statement which is classic in the psychology of depth perception and given in many ways: The construction of the visual apparatus and the geometry of optics allow a description of light as stimulus only in terms of a two-dimensional distribution as measurements of a cross-section of the array of light entering the eye or as angular measurements of this array at the eye. This fact is the very source of the old depth-perception problem. However, most discussions and experiments concerning this problem have dealt primarily with the perception of static space, while our present problem is a problem of event perception. Since Helmholtz, there has been agreement that motion parallax is a forceful secondary cue for perceiving the third dimension, but few experiments have yet been performed to substantiate this. Classically, cues to depth have been divided into monocular and binocular. Our problem here exclusively concerns monocular vision.

In the environment of man there are both rigid motions of objects and form changes of objects. Perhaps rigid motions are more frequent, but there are also plenty of instances of form changes. Thus, the bending movements of, for example, branches and grass in the wind, can be described as continuous variations in form. Other examples are the ever-changing flames of a fire, cloud formations, and the complex wave patterns on a water surface. Many types of animal (and human) movements and some aggregations of small animals (e.g., swarming of mosquitoes) also belong to this category. Therefore, in our discussion, we must take into account both types of space-time events.

Most of the above examples involve simultaneous form changes and motions.

A geometric and conceptual reference frame

In accordance with our problem setting, we will choose the following conditions as a starting point and reference frame for our further discussions:

(1) Monocular vision.

(2) A reversible system, in accordance with principles of projective geometry, consisting of: (*a*) a station point in the locus of the eye; (*b*) a three-dimensional space (described in X-, Y-, and Z-coordinates, here termed the *projective*

space); and (*c*) a two-dimensional *projection plane* (the picture plane, with X- and Y-coordinates). This system with the station point on the Z-axis and its projection plane in the X-Y-plane, we will term the *projection system* (see Fig. 1).

(3) A continuously changing pattern of light on the picture plane. Because the system is thought of as reversible, this pattern may alternatively be regarded in one of the following two ways. (*a*) It may be a *projection of an object* in the projection space which changes its shape or moves (rotation and/or translation) in space or changes its shape and moves simultaneously; or (*b*) the pattern may be regarded as projected into the projection space in the form of a specific three-dimensional representation, moving and/or changing its shape.

Thus, we will discuss both projection *from projection space to the picture plane* and projection *from the picture plane into the projection space.*

Projections and specificity of information

The relationships between the three-dimensional and the two-dimensional representations of the same optical events in the projection system pose the problem of how information is translated from one representation in the system to the other. Under specified conditions of projection, the moving and/or changing object in three-dimensional space generates a unique transformation of the pattern on the picture plane. Thus, we are always able to determine from a given change in space what two-dimensional change will occur on the picture plane and thus also on the surface of the retina. (Some complex changes in space, however, may have the effect of no change on the picture plane.)

Next, we will try to describe the events in the three-dimensional projection space, starting from the information given in the picture plane with the conditions indicated above. When doing so, we immediately find that there is in fact *no specific information* for this purpose in the changing pattern on the picture plane, and thus in the changes in the optical array. A two-dimensional changing pattern cannot specify both form-size changes of an object and at the same time its instantaneous localisation in three-dimensional space. This has been stated explicitly also by Hochberg and Smith (1955). For example, every change of size and shape of this pattern may represent change of size of the object, motion in the Z-dimension, change of orientation relative to the X-Y-plane, as well as combinations of these changes. Thus, we will find that every continuous change of size, shape, or location of the two-dimensional image representing the retinal light distribution may specify an infinite number of combinations of continuous motions and changes of form of an object in three-dimensional space. We might add that under the conditions given, even an image on the picture plane which does not change or move also represents an infinite number of possible combinations of motion and change of shape in the projection space.

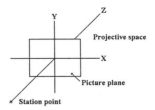

Fig. 1. The projective system.

Elaboration of the problem

So far, our discussion would seem to indicate that continuous transformations of the proximal stimulus, when isolated from other kinds of information to the eye, cannot supply any specific information about events in a three-dimensional space. Thus, the first part of the problem raised, viz the question "Does the continuous transformation of a retinal pattern carry any specific information to the organism?" is very far from being rhetorical. There is no possibility of mathematically specifying any such stimulus variables (of any order) which carry veridical information about three-dimensional space. This conclusion follows as soon as we accept the possibility of both rigid motions and elastic motions of perceived objects in the three-dimensional perceptual space.

However, experimental data demonstrate just the opposite conclusion. Investigations on the perception of depth from motions and transformations of shadow patterns which are generated by objects moving behind a screen (Metzger, 1934-35; Wallach & O'Connell, 1953; Gibson & Gibson, 1957), indicate that such patterns often give rise to veridical perceptual representations of the object motions behind the screen. These results are obtained under good experimental control and ought to be regarded as reliable.

The present writer is of the opinion, for reasons given above, that for solution of our problem we must seek principles inherent in the perceptual process which bring about specificity. As we have stated, the proximal stimulus pattern is by geometrical necessity unspecific with reference to form-depth, and the percept is specific. Inherent in these facts are questions of the following type: (1) Which treatments of the stimulus data would allow a possibility for specific percepts? (Percepts = the information products of perceptual processes.) (2) Which treatments would make the percept specific, but also in correspondence with the distal change causing the optical transformation at the eye (thus veridical)? (3) Which of these restrictions are applied by the eye? The first two questions are formulations for theoretical speculation about our problem (or for geometrical analysis). The last question is an experimental one, and if an answer is possible, it will be an empirical one.

Before we proceed to describe our attempt to give an experimental answer, let us become acquainted with some attempts to give answers to the first two questions.

Some Earlier Viewpoints on Our Problem

Berkeley's and Helmholtz' answer

The classic way of dealing with problems of visual space perception is well known. The solution along this line is primarily concerned with the problem of perception of a static space. However, it is often expanded to include perception of changes and ought to be mentioned here as the most common way of thinking about our problem. In fact it has been so common that it has sometimes been looked upon not as a speculative answer but as a factual one. This theoretical solution was characterised by the most radical restriction when it came to hypothesising ways for getting information about three-dimensional space from the two-dimensional stimulation. According to this approach there is no primary information available in the optic array other than information about two-dimensionality. In the same way a changing pattern gives perfectly specific visual information which, however, very seldom is veridical. According to this theory, veridical percepts are built up by adding different kinds of depth cues and by hypothesised psychological processes.

Perhaps the best demonstration of the common theoretical acceptance of this hypothesis is that "kinetic depth effects," "stereokinetic effects," etc., have often been looked upon as strange phenomena, deviating from the normal way of perceiving.

Poincaré's outline to a solution

The famous French mathematician Poincaré (1913, pp. 250ff.), clearly formulated our problem in an interesting discussion, which has since been taken up in a paper by von Fieandt & Gibson (1959). Poincaré clarifies what we have stated above—the impossibility of distinguishing between change of position of an object and change of form ("state") of this object, starting from changes in the optical array. He also accepts the obvious fact that the organism seems to be able to make such a distinction in visual event perception, and gives an interesting and fresh hypothesis for explaining this fact. By an active movement of his body, the observer (or animal) is theoretically able to compensate for the transformation caused by rigid motions of objects, but not to interfere with transformations caused by form changes. From this point of view, therefore, these two types of changes belong to two different groups of changes.

Most interesting of all in Poincaré's attempt to solve our problem is the allusion to an active exploration of the array by changing it in a systematic way. If we elaborate Poincaré's outlines the process may be thought of in the following way: (1) initially, the organism cannot specify the information given in the stimulus; (2) attempts at compensatory bodily movements immediately reveal whether the changing optical pattern is due to rigid motion in the distal object or not; (3) specific perceptual information from the optical transformation at the eye is gained by applying one of the two "rules" given by the characteristics of the two groups of responses to the compensatory motions. (For compensatory changes in proximal stimulus, the percept is rigid motion in space; for non-compensable changes, the percept is elastic changes and no displacements in depth.)

However, an analysis will reveal that Poincaré's attempt to solve the problem is at best a partial solution. We can mention at least two conditions which give percepts not covered by Poincaré's principle for "rule"-detection:

(1) The principle implies no possibility of getting a specified percept from optical transformation caused by an object which changes its shape and moves spatially at the same time. But such changes are, as we have mentioned above, rather common in the environments of both man and animals.

(2) It follows from the principle that a motionless observer cannot differentiate between the two groups of changes. However, recent experiments using shadow-casting technique and a stationary eye with an eyepiece (von Fieandt & Gibson, 1959) seem to validate an opposite conclusion.

Poincaré's discussion did not solve our problem, but his attempt, so astonishingly fresh and "modern" from our point of view, and his clear statement of the problem is worth mentioning.

von Fieandt's and Gibson's approach

In the paper already referred to, von Fieandt and Gibson (1959) discuss Poincaré's problem and his proposed solution. They accepted the problem as a very fundamental one for space perception but proposed another method for its solution. "It would be that an eye, for reasons to be investigated is sensitive to a change of form, and, moreover, to the *type* of a change of form. In this respect, an eye is to be contrasted with a camera. The eyes of animals and men are very good at detecting motions; perhaps they are just as good at discriminating *types* of motions. It might be that the one group of continuous transformations, the perspectives of rigid objects, constitutes one kind of stimulus for vision and that the other group, the 'rubbery' transformations, constitutes another kind of stimulus for vision."

This discussion is an application of Gibson's gradient theory in a special context. It is evident that, when this hypothesis was set forth, Gibson and von Fieandt accepted the perceptual dichotomy *rigidity and motion* vs. *elasticity and non-motion* as the exclusive possibilities. In this respect, their problem discussion is very closely related to Poincaré's problem setting. Consequently, their proposed problem solution has the same weakness as Poincaré's: It does not take into account the perception of combined motion and form changes. Because von Fieandt and Gibson essentially built their theoretical approach on a distinction between perspective and non-perspective transformations, it is hard to see how to handle any case of the above-mentioned combinations in the distal stimulus with their theory.

Their experiments demonstrate quite convincingly that the subjects were able to distinguish between the rigid and non-rigid transformations given. The

authors also seem to draw a valid conclusion when they point out that their experiments did not give direct support to the hypothesis set forth but that it demonstrated the existence of a discriminatory ability in the subjects which is the
prerequisite for this hypothesis.

Previous viewpoints from the writer

In previous theoretical discussions about motion and space perception, the
present writer has followed lines rather parallel to those of Poincaré, and von
Fieandt and Gibson. He has thought about invariances in proximal stimulus
changes as deciding principles. In fact, these speculations have included both
invariances giving constant shape, as is the case with the authors mentioned
above, as well as, e.g., constant velocity (Johansson, 1958).

Principles Behind Our Experimental Approach

Light-not objects as stimuli

It is changes in the distribution of light entering the eye which bring the eye
visual information about spatial changes and motions in physical space. For the
eye it makes no difference whether this array of light is generated by light reflected from touchable objects moving or changing their shape, or whether it is
generated in any other way. If the arrays of light, generated in different ways,
are exactly equal, the percepts must be equal under the conditions when no other
perceptual information about the "source" of stimulation is available.

This fact—so self-evident that it hardly requires mentioning—forms a basis
for our experimental approach to the problem stated. It provides us with a possibility of generating perceptual "objects" by an appropriate manipulation of
light and also of introducing form changes and motions in these "objects," otherwise hard to get in physical objects reflecting light. Such a generation of artificial perceptual objects is a necessary condition for the experiments, which
statement will be clarified later. In this way it is also possible to avoid interactions of different cues which are characteristic in perception of "real" objects in
motion.

Percepts as functions of changes in proximal stimulus

One of the classic questions in perceptual theory research concerns stimuli
for "veridical" perception. This means that special attention is paid to the relationships between distal stimulus and percept. Those percepts whose description
deviates from accepted descriptions of the distal stimulus are said to be illusions.
The research on perceptual constancies, culminating in Brunswik's distal-
stimulus oriented theoretical approach is the best example.

The present approach will form a contrast to this. In order to solve our
problem, we will restrict ourselves to a study of lawful relationships between

percept and *proximal* stimulus. We will have no distal stimulus reflecting light and therefore no question of veridicality. The proximal stimulus in the form of a changing array of light is the only kind of physical event causing perception. There are no real objects to use for a determination of degree of veridicality. This means that we will pass over the problem of veridicality, because our experiments will be experiments in object perception without real objects.

However, behind our forthcoming discussions is the assumption that there are lawful relationships between proximal stimulus and percept from a mathematical point of view as an explicit hypothesis. This hypothesis, of course, includes the assumption that perception is a function of stimulation (Gibson, 1959) and it has as its strongest support the high level of veridicality found in everyday perception. Therefore every response which is in accordance with the geometric principles for projection from the picture plane in our system and into the projection space is in our experiments a correlate to a veridical response.

Spatial changes in proximal stimulus as the independent variable

The above discussion means that we will choose changes in the proximal stimulus programmatically as our independent variable. We will introduce a systematic variation of changes in proximal stimulus and ask for percepts (i.e., perceived distal objects). The stimulus will ideally consist of a solid angle of light at the eye, which has a homogeneous light intensity in its cross section (i.e., the picture plane). In this solid angle of light will be introduced continuous and mutually independent changes of angular size in the X and Y dimensions.

In this way we get spatial transformations of our stimulus patterns. These transformations have no relationship to perspectivity and most of them are not possible as geometric transformations from rigid objects in motion.

In one way our experiments are appropriately classified as a continuation of the experiments on kinetic depth effects and slant perception already referred to (Wallach & O'Connell, 1953; Gibson & Gibson, 1957; see also Braunstein, 1960). From the methodological point of view, however, there is a radical difference. It is evident that the above-mentioned experiments have one characteristic in common: manipulation of real distal objects induces the proximal changes, and these are therefore always projections of rigid objects. Also the search for relationships between this distal object and the percept is common for these experiments. The Cornell studies on slant are especially characterised by a consequent endeavour to get perfect projections in accordance with the principles for polar projection. In this way it is the distal stimulus or its projection which has been the independent variable in most of the previous experiments alluded to (this holds true also for Green's, 1961, and Braunstein's, 1962, experiments), while we will programmatically introduce the proximal stimulus as independent variable.

Technical principles for generating proximal stimulus

The proximal stimulus was generated electronically. Electronics provide convenient means for generating and combining different kinds of voltage changes as functions of time and to transform them into optical changes. Basically, our apparatus consisted of a set of function generators, a cathode ray tube (CRT) and an optical device. Appropriate combinations of functions in this set-up resulted in exactly controlled, continuously changing patterns of light from the CRT into the eye of our subjects. In most of the experiments to be reported in this paper, the image on the CRT face was a homogeneous area of light in the shape of a rectangle, square, or parallelogram. This area changed continuously in size along the X- and Y-dimensions. The X- and Y-changes could proceed quite independently of each other. In addition, a continuous change of angles in the parallelogram could be introduced.

The problem of conflicting projections

A picture representing three-dimensional space, and printed or traced on a sheet of paper or projected on a screen, brings about a complication in the stimulus conditions for space perception. The paper and the screen form a surface in a perceived space, and this space is represented in the eye of the observer in accordance with the principles of projective geometry. However, this surface also introduces to the eye a projection of a kind of "secondary" space, the picture, under very different conditions of projection. Thus, the picture is seen as a surface in space which is carrying a more or less vivid representation of a secondary space.

These facts have important bearing on space perception experiments, when, as is the case here, one of the main problems is a choice between two-dimensional and three-dimensional perceptual correlates of the proximal stimulus. In order to allow valid conclusions to be drawn from the experiments, our proximal stimulus pattern should represent only one projection system. This means that our experimental conditions have to exclude every possible visual cue to a surface as a carrier of the pattern of light brought to the eye, and of course also exclude other possible inferential visual cues from the environment.

Such conditions in our experiments were brought about by means of an optical telescope system giving the eye the pattern of light on the CRT in the form of a magnified virtual image against a totally dark background covering the whole visual field.

Type of spatial change chosen

It is a well-known fact that Lissajous patterns on an oscilloscope screen, generated from sinusoidal voltage changes, often are perceived as a rotation of rigid three-dimensional figures. The same effect from two-dimensional sinusoidal motion on a frontal screen is known from experiments on visual motion perception. The present writer has earlier set forth the hypothesis that this effect of sinusoidal motion (which may be described as a projection of a rotary motion with constant angular velocity) is due to a tendency in the functioning of the visual apparatus to prefer perceived motion with constant velocity in a stimulus situation allowing choice between perceived constant velocity (= three-dimensional motion) and acceleration (= two-dimensional motion).

Of course, we will avoid depth effects due to the character of motion. Therefore, in the forthcoming experiments, only non-sinusoidal changes were introduced (with one exception where such effects were intended). The triangular waveform, giving constant speed and periodically changing direction, was found to be an adequate standard type of change for the experiments.

Description of the Apparatus

The electronic part of the apparatus

The main part of the apparatus was an oscilloscope for X-Y plotting, Tectronix 502. The CRT of this scope had a P 11 screen, which is characterised by a very short afterglow.

A bright rectangular area of homogeneous brightness was generated on the CRT by connecting two alternating voltages of rather high, mutually different, audio frequency (10–100 kc/sec) and triangular waveform to the X-Y inputs of the oscilloscope respectively.

These two high frequencies had the function of carriers for two very low modulating frequencies (0.2–1 c/sec). The modulation was obtained in specially built modulators and was of the amplitude modulation type.

The effect of modulating the amplitude of the high frequency along, e.g., the X-axis is, of course, a shrinking-growing of the rectangle in that dimension. The frequency of this shrinking-growing is the frequency of the modulating alternating voltage (ca. 0.5 c/sec), its amplitude is proportional to the modulating amplitude and its spatio-temporal pattern during one cycle is equal to the wave form of the modulation frequency.

In this way the modulating low frequencies bring about and control a continuous transformation of the rectangle on the screen. It always has rectangular shape, but shrinks and grows continuously in both X- and Y-directions.

The course of change can readily be controlled and adjusted by plotting the two modulated carrier frequencies against a common time axis on a double beam oscilloscope having a conventional CRT-screen afterglow.

Fig. 2 gives a simplified block diagram of the apparatus.

A component of the carrier voltage in the Y-dimension (the higher frequency) could be introduced into the horizontal channel and mixed with the carrier in this dimension. In this way a change of angles is obtained. The figure is still a parallelogram, but the vertical sides are sloping.

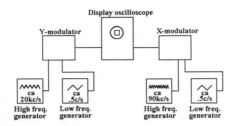

Fig. 2. Block diagram of the stimulus generator.

If this carrier component is modulated a continuous change of angles in the parallelogram will be the result. Thus, the figure on the screen can be made to shrink and grow in the X- and Y-dimensions and change its angles at the same time, and these changes can be tied together or made independent of each other.

Here are described mainly the methods of generating some standard patterns which were used in the present investigations. By using special types of function generators and modulators other patterns can readily be obtained (e.g., trapezoidal figures, ellipses, etc.).

The optical device

As mentioned above the subjects are not allowed to look directly at the CRT-screen and see the tube face. They see the pattern when looking through the eyepiece of a kind of telescope. The first lens of this device is fixed at a distance of its double focal length from the CRT, thus yielding an inverted real image in magnification 1:1 on the opposite side of the lens. The eyepiece consists of a magnifying lens (8:1) and this gives (in the same way as the eyepiece of an ordinary telescope) a magnified virtual image at the eye. This optical device is diagrammed in Fig. 3.

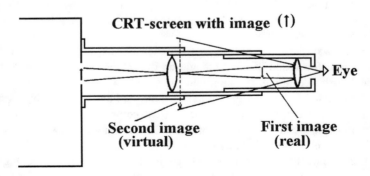

Fig. 3. Diagram of the optical device.

The oscilloscope and the other parts of the apparatus are masked by a large screen through which the telescope tube is protruding. Therefore the subjects get the impression of looking into a tube and seeing something happen in space on the other side of the screen.

The stimulus

When the brightness of the CRT is correctly adjusted and the subjects are not allowed to become dark adapted, their impression when looking through the eye-piece is that of seeing a light plane surface in a dark space. The darkness covers the total field of view except for the figure, which covers a visual angle of about 5°–10° in the centre of the field.

The brightness of the image changes of course with its size, because it is the constant intensity of the beam distributed over the area of the image which controls the brightness. In planning the technical equipment the writer believed it necessary to keep the brightness of the image constant by a compensating modulation of the brightness of the beam. However, it was found that the change of brightness mentioned was perceptually insignificant and did not interfere with the perceived spatial changes (motions and form changes). Therefore in the series of experiments to be reported below the brightness was allowed to change with image size.

Stimulus via film projector

At a later stage of the experiments the patterns on the CRT were filmed. This film was projected from behind onto a small translucent screen attached in the place of the CRT face in the optical device and in this way the patterns were brought into the eye of the subject without direct use of the electronic equipment during the experiment.

Experimental Technique and Subjects

The experiments to be reported were carried out on three groups of subjects. In the primary experiments 20 graduate students acted as subjects. They received a typed instruction requesting them to classify perceived change or motion in a given set of categories and also to rate the relative strength of each impression on a 5-point scale. Some of the experiments were carried out with 24 school children 10–11 years old. However, here no formal instructions were used. The "instruction" was just the following: "Look into this tube and describe what you see."

Most of the children used hand movements for illustrating observed motion, and in general their reports were simple and clear, yielding data which were well possible to categorise in the above scheme. However, in some cases complementary questions were found necessary. Of course, care was taken not to make leading questions in any respect.

The third group consisted of 23 students. This group got the same instruction as the children and in some of these cases the complementary questions were also found necessary in order to get complete descriptions.

For this latter group the conditions were somewhat different from a technical point of view. The method using the film projector instead of the oscilloscope described above was introduced. The projector sound was masked. The visual angle of the patterns was the same as in the original experiments. The main reason for duplicating the experiments on different agegroups of subjects was to investigate the possibility of generalising the results. The same holds true for the change of instruction. The reason for introducing the film technique was to test the possibility of using a more convenient apparatus than the complicated set-up of function generators and oscilloscopes in future research.

The order of the different patterns was random, changing from subject to subject in the first two groups.

In the experiments using film technique, the order was the same for all subjects. In the following the group of 20 graduate students will be referred to as group A, the group of 23 undergraduate students as group B, and the group of 24 children as group C.

Experiments Part I

The stimuli in the experiments to be reported in this section form a set of 4 different continuous and periodic transformations of a solid angle of light at the eye of the subject. The cross section of this solid angle has initially the shape of a square. In the following detailed descriptions, the stimuli will be described as projections on a picture plane. It follows from the description of the apparatus that this is equivalent to a description of the pattern of change on the CRT screen. For these periodically changing stimuli we will use the term *transformation pattern* or the abbreviated term *pattern*.

Only the A-group of subjects received all the eight transformation patterns as stimuli.

Transformation pattern 1

Description: A graphic description of the transformation over time of the stimulus pattern is presented in Fig. 4. As this diagram demonstrates, the horizontal dimension of the pattern remains constant, while it shrinks and grows continuously with a linear velocity in the vertical direction.

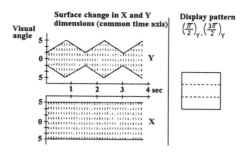

Fig. 4. Transformation pattern 1.

Results: The reports from the total number of 67 subjects fall into two distinct categories. These are: (1) change of shape of a frontally oriented, bright surface, and (2) motion of a surface with constant area. Category (2) includes several variants of the description, e.g., rotation of a rigid plane surface about a central horizontal axis or a symmetric bending in depth about a horizontally oriented symmetry axis (a "book-folding"). Many subjects reported seeing both main alternatives, usually starting with the two-dimensional form change (1).

Table 1 gives the frequencies of the two types of responses in our three groups of subjects. Because many subjects reported both alternatives, the sum of responses is higher than the number of subjects.

Discussion: The results demonstrate that under our experimental conditions (no static visual reference frame, triangular wave form, untrained subjects), the indefinite information contained in the proximal stimulus has evoked percepts which are characterised by some degree of ambiguity. This means that the percepts are to a very limited extent unspecific, and this holds true both within and between subjects. In this way our tentative conclusion from the transformation pattern is that this type of nonperspective transformation with change in only one dimension of the two-dimensional proximal pattern gives ambiguity between two-dimensional and three-dimensional percepts, but never results in percepts which are combinations of these categories.

Table 1. Frequencies of responses in groups A, B, and C.

Subjects		Description of percept	
Group	n	2-dimensional form change	Bending or rotary motion
A	20	13	10
B	23	21	8
C	24	19	8
Sum	67	53	26

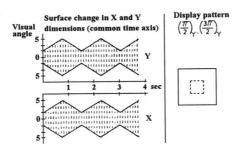

Fig. 5. Transformation pattern 2.

Transformation pattern 2

Description: Fig. 5 gives the diagrams for this pattern. Here identical changes are introduced in X and Y dimensions. In this way the pattern forms a continuously growing-shrinking square.

Results: The result may be summarised as follows: 66 subjects out of 67 reported perceiving an object moving in depth, toward and away from the observer. Many subjects spontaneously demonstrated the perceived motion by hand movements which made clear that this motion was a translatory motion along the optical axis of the apparatus.

The *A group* of subjects had received the special instruction to try to perceive the pattern also as an expanding-contracting surface if they found this possible. Among the 19 subjects reporting strong and dominant motion in depth, 4 subjects reported the two-dimensional percept as a possible alternative but gave it the lowest value in the rating scale (as contrasted to the highest value for the motion-in-depth percept).

In the *B group* experiment, 11 subjects reported the possibility of seeing the pattern as a two-dimensional expansion-contraction, but all of them described the motion in depth of an object of constant size as the spontaneous percept.

The descriptions from the *C group* were unequivocal with regard to the motion in depth. The children very often illustrated the perceived motion by hand movements. No one in this group described the percept as a two-dimensional event. However, after a question from the experimenter about constant or changing size of the object, most children (17 subjects) described it as expanding-contracting during its motion in depth. This means that the descriptions from the children deviate from the description given by the two groups of adult subjects in one important respect. However, this difference may possibly be due to inadequate description from the children or simply an effect of questioning. The material available is not sufficient for answering the important question whether there is a real difference in this respect between children and adults. Therefore, in the following discussion about relationships between two-dimensional and three-dimensional percepts we will restrict our discussion to the either-or responses given by the two groups of adult subjects. However, when applying this restriction we know that we have opened a very basic question for future research about ontogenetic development of perception of motion and form changes.

Discussion: It seems adequate to generalise the hypothesis from this experiment that under our experimental conditions a continuous angular change in both dimensions of a proximal stimulus pattern will evoke, in most observers, a strong and in many cases unequivocal percept of motion in depth in a three-dimensional perceptual space. It might be added that evidently, the perceptual three-dimensionality is generated by the change introduced in the proximal pattern.

Transformation pattern 3

Is invariant form of the proximal image a prerequisite for the transformation of combined X- and Y-changes in this image to a perceptual Z-motion? This question, in fact critical to the "motion-of-a-constant-shape-" hypothesis, is the main problem behind transformation patterns 3 and 4.

Description: Pattern 3 is the same as Pattern 2 with but one exception. The amplitude of the horizontal motion is diminished to give the relationship 2:3 between the horizontal and the vertical motion amplitudes. Thus, during each transformation cycle, the proximal image changes from a square shape to a horizontally oriented rectangle and back again to a square. The diagrams are given in Fig. 6. This pattern was presented only to the A and B group. However, for group B it was the vertical (Y) motion instead of the horizontal motion (X) which was shortened.

Results: All subjects in both groups reported seeing an object moving backwards and forwards in space as the spontaneous and strongly dominant percept. Among the 43 subjects, 30 reported form change of the surface during motion

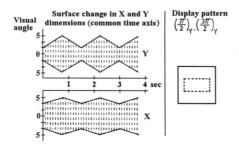

Fig. 6. Transformation pattern 3.

and there were 16 reports indicating rotation or "book-folding" of the object. The length of the perceived Z-motion was in some cases reported as shorter than the same Z-motion in Pattern 2.

Transformation pattern 4

Description: The only difference between Pattern 3 and 4 is that in Pattern 4 the relation between the horizontal and the vertical motion is 2:3. This experiment was carried out only with the subjects in group A.

Results: The descriptions recieved from this pattern were analogous to the descriptions from Pattern 3. The depth variant was quite dominating and there were 11 reports about rotation, etc.

The main interest behind introducing Pattern 4 was the perceptual effect of shortening the horizontal motion. Also in this respect the result was clear. All subjects who were given the opportunity of systematically comparing Patterns 2, 3, and 4 reported that the lengths of the percieved motions in depth formed a series in which Pattern 2 gave the longest and Pattern 4 the shortest motion track. When we compare the dominant percepts from Pattern 1 and 2 with the dominant percepts from Pattern 3 and 4 we find an interesting fact. The two first are both closely related to the two latter, which in fact are to be regarded as combinations of Patterns 1 and 2. The component of form change (or of rotation, etc.) in the percept from Patterns 3 and 4 has a direct counterpart in the outcome from Pattern 1. In the same way the translatory motion in depth characteristic for Pattern 2 forms the residual component of change in Patterns 3 and 4.

Analysis and Outline of a Model

Geometric description

The set of experiments reported above gives material for a more systematic analysis of the relationships between transformations of proximal stimuli and percepts.

We start this analysis with the supposition that there are strict mathematical relationships between the percept and the proximal stimulus pattern in this field of perception (cf. Johansson, 1950, 1958). From this follows that these stimulus-percept relationships may be given in terms of projective geometry and trigonometry and also that we are justified in representing the percepts diagrammatically in accordance with geometrical principles.

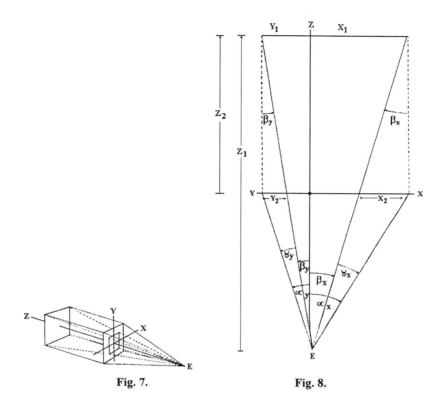

Fig. 7.   **Fig. 8.**

Fig. 7. The projection system.

Fig. 8. Projection of simultaneous and linear X-Y-changes to motion along the Z-axis of a lane perpendicular to this axis.

Fig. 7 illustrates a simple three-dimensional projection system given with Cartesian coordinates. E is the locus of the eye and the station point in the system. The Z-axis coincides with the optical axis of our apparatus. The proximal stimulus pattern is represented on the X-Y-plane in two opposite phases, and the changing size of this pattern has been transformed into a change of localisation of a rigid surface along the Z-axis and at right angles to this axis. This will be our basic figure. In order to present a more detailed diagram, Fig. 8 was devised. This figure is nothing more than a "folding out" of the positive parts of the X-Z-plane and the Y-Z-plane about the Z-axis. It allows convenient comparisons of effects of simultaneous X- and Y-changes projected in the Z-direction.

Transformation pattern 2 had the form of a square. This is a special and simple case where equal and simultaneous changes in the X- and Y-directions give changing size but invariable form. For our discussion we want a more general case. Therefore Figs. 7 and 8 illustrate the case of a rectangle. It is easily seen from Fig. 8 that the general condition for a projection of the change in the pattern to a rigid translatory motion in the Z-direction (the typical percept from Pattern 2) is that the changes in X and Y over the same time interval cover the same proportions of the initial angles at the eye in the X-Z- and Y-Z-planes. In Fig. 8,

$$\tan\beta_x = \frac{X_1}{Z_1} = \frac{X_2}{Z_2} \quad \text{and} \quad \tan\beta_y = \frac{Y_1}{Z_1} = \frac{Y_2}{Z_2}$$

Thus, $$\frac{Z_2}{Z_1} = \frac{X_2}{X_1} = \frac{Y_2}{Y_1}$$

For the angular size of the patterns used in our experiments ($< 10°$), the following relationships also hold true within very small error limits:

$$\frac{X_2}{X_1} = \frac{\gamma_x}{\alpha_x}; \quad \frac{Y_2}{Y_1} = \frac{\gamma_y}{\alpha_y}$$

The stated proportionality between X and Y displacements of any point on the X-Y-plane as a condition for a translatory motion of a rigid surface along the Z-axis in our projection system may also be conveniently pictured in the two-dimensional coordinate system represented by the picture plane. This is shown in Fig. 9. From any point (a) on the contour of the rectangle (e.g., one of the corners) a line is drawn through the origin of the coordinate system. A vector drawn from (a) along this line is the two-dimensional representation of Z motion parallel to the Z-axis of the point (a) on the contour. Thus, if this vector is split up in two components with X- and Y-directions, these vectors represent the Z motion in terms of X and Y changes on the picture plane. This fact gives the following rule for combining X and Y changes in our diagram in order to get a correct representation of a translatory Z motion of a surface with unchanging shape and size: When the magnitude of the displacement vector in, e.g., the X-direction is known, the Y-vector must be given a magnitude which, if the X- and Y-vectors are added, gives the resultant a direction towards the origin.

Because our X-Y diagram in Fig. 9 is a picture of the proximal stimulus as generated on the oscilloscope screen, and as projected onto the retina, we will use diagrams of this type in the following discussions. They are very simple, and the starting point for the present investigation is proximal stimulation with X- and Y-changes without any reference to distal objects. However, as already pointed out, our X- and Y-measures may also be used as radian measures of the respective angles at the eye (α_x, γ_x; α_y, γ_y) in accordance with Fig. 8. Therefore, our forthcoming discussions in connection with X- and Y-vectors in the proxi-

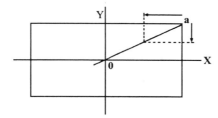

Fig. 9. Displacement vectors for X and Y displacements on the picture plane.

mal stimulus (Fig. 9) may easily be converted into terms of angular measures in the projection system formed by the eye and its proximal stimulus.

Analysis of the results from Pattern 3 and Pattern 4

We will now try to analyse the stimulus-percept relationships in the percepts from Pattern 3 and Pattern 4. In doing so, we will attempt to describe the proximal pattern of change in terms of motion vectors in a way which corresponds to the description of the percepts, but which is also a correct mathematical description of this pattern of change.

Common to all reports from Patterns 3 and 4 was the percept of a Z-motion. Patterns 2, 3, and 4 given to group A form a systematic series of different X-amplitudes. The reports from the subjects indicate that the amplitude of the perceived Z-motion varied with this amplitude. The same holds true for Y-amplitudes in Patterns 2 and 3 given to group B. This may be taken as a preliminary indication that the Z-amplitude is a function of the relatively smaller motion amplitude in the proximal stimulus. No formal quantification of the relationship between the relatively shorter amplitude in the proximal stimulus and the perceived Z-motion has yet been made, but will be included in a forthcoming investigation. Until then, the very probable assumption of linear relationships will be accepted.

In accordance with our discussion in the foregoing section, the geometric condition for a translatory motion, parallel to the Z-axis in the visual projection system, of a point in the proximal pattern on the picture plane is X- and Y-vectors of the same relative magnitude for this point. In order for this condition to be fulfilled in Patterns 3 and 4, we must regard the larger amplitude (Y) as a sum of two vectors of the same direction, one of which is proportionally equal to the X-vector. Applying such a description of the proximal pattern results in a very satisfactory correspondence between stimulus and percept. The *residual* vector in Y in our stimulus description has a direct correspondence in the change of shape of the perceived object which some subjects reported, or in the rotary motion about a horizontal central axis as reported by other subjects. In the latter case, the translatory Z-motion is the motion of the axis of rotation. The

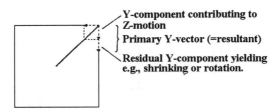

Fig. 10. Diagram of vector analysis representing Z-motion of the centre point plus shrinking or rotation of the object in the projection system.

diagram of the vector system of the proximal stimulus corresponding in this way to the reported percepts is given in Fig. 10.

We will summarise and also tentatively generalise in the following way: For every changing proximal pattern, irrespective of shape but with simultaneous X- and Y-changes of the same direction relative to the origin, the percept will, under our experimental conditions, be in accordance with the following description:

(1) The proportionally smaller of the two vectors representing motions of the contours in the X- and Y-direction (more exactly, motions of the points on the contours) determines the length of a perceived translatory Z-motion of an object in a three-dimensional perceptual space.

(2) The proportionally larger of these vectors will be treated as a sum of two independent vectors simultaneously acting in the same direction. One of these components is made proportionally equal to the vector simultaneously acting along the other axis. These two proportionally equal vectors together specify with geometric correctness the translatory Z-motion of a perceived frontal object (or the translatory Z-motion of the axis of rotation of a perceived object).

(3) The residual vector under (2) is perceptually described (*a*) as a form change of the frontal surface or (*b*) as a rigid rotary motion of a surface (or some other related change) or (*c*) as a combination of a rotation and form change.

A strict application of this model for relations between proximal stimulus and percept makes it necessary to explicitly distinguish between the Euclidean geometry of stimulus and the geometry of percept. Those two descriptions of space must not necessarily be linearly related to each another (see also page 165).

Experiments Part II

The percepts from Patterns 3 and 4 clearly demonstrate that constant shape of an expanding-contracting proximal pattern is not a prerequisite for the per-

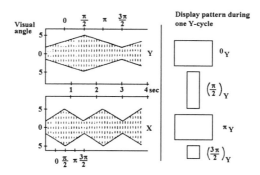

Fig. 11. Transformation pattern 5.

ception of specific motions in depth under our experimental conditions. These patterns also indicate that the existence of proportionally equal simultaneous vectors in stimulus adding to a resultant directed towards the origin of the coordinate system is a sufficient condition for perception of motion in depth. The following patterns were designed in an attempt to determine whether this is also a necessary condition.

Transformation patterns 5 and 6

Description of Pattern 5. In this pattern, the frequency of the changes in X- and Y-direction were unequal and of the relationship 1:2. Thus, for every two cycles in the horizontal direction, there was one cycle in the vertical direction (see Fig. 11). This pattern was presented only to group A.

Description of Pattern 6. In this pattern, the two frequencies were also different. The only difference between Patterns 5 and 6 is that in Pattern 6 there is no simple relationship between the two frequencies. The X-frequency was about 0.7 cps and the Y-frequency about 0.3 cps. This means that while there is one repetition of the pattern every other second in Pattern 5, the repetition cycle extends over more than 20 seconds in Pattern 6 and thus in fact gives percepts without any noticeable cyclical character. This pattern was given to both group A and group B. However, for group B the frequency relationships between X and Y were inverted.

Results: These patterns also gave as a perceptual outcome a clearly dominant motion in depth of exactly the same character as Patterns 2, 3, and 4. The frequency of the perceived Z-motion was controlled by asking the subjects to reproduce the forward-backward motion which they described. This was done by simple counting or reproducing the motion by movements of one hand. In this way, it was found that the Z-motion was always determined by the frequency and amplitude of the change in the direction having the lower frequency. Thus, the Z-motion continued even during the time intervals when the X- and Y-vectors in our diagram had opposite directions.

Discussion: We will summarise the experimental results from Pattern 5 and Pattern 6 by the following three points:

(1) Different frequencies in the X- and Y-directions of the stimulus pattern give perceptions involving motion in the Z-direction.

(2) The lowest frequency determines the Z-motion.

(3) There is always a change of shape or a rotatory motion of the perceived object, in addition to the depth motion.

We will now apply the method given on page 149 ff. describing these stimulus patterns in terms of vectors corresponding to perceived motions or changes. The phases of change in the proximal stimulus where X and Y have the same direction relative to the origin of the coordinate system are, of course, analogous to the changes in Patterns 3 and 4, and need no further discussion. A description of a phase where the X- and Y-changes have opposite directions relative to the origin is given in Fig. 12.

In this diagram, a component vector is introduced, which has no physical counterpart but which is perceptually (and mathematically) represented in the Z-motion reported. It is, of course, in our diagram, made proportionally equal to the motion along the other axis. In order to get a mathematically correct result we have to subtract this component 1 from the resultant. The vector remaining after this subtraction is component 2 in the diagram. It will be found that this residual vector has the same direction as the primary motion in the pattern but a magnitude which is the algebraic sum of the primary motion track (resultant) and component 1. This vector has a direct representation in the percepts in the form of the reported expansion-contraction or rotation in the X-direction.

We will expect to find vector component 2 represented adequately in perception not only for direction but also for magnitude. As mentioned before, no direct quantification has been attempted in the present study. However, the frequency relationship in Pattern 5 was devised primarily in order to test the above

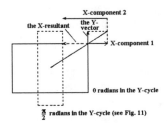

Fig. 12. Vector analysis of the transformation in Pattern 5 (0 radians to $\pi/2$ radians in the Y-cycle) when described as a translatory motion in Z direction.

prediction in a semi-quantitative way. If the prediction is correct, the perceived object ought to behave in accordance with the description given in Fig. 12. In fact, the reports from the subjects confirmed the prediction very convincingly.

Transformation pattern 7

Description. The experiments with Patterns 3–6 have demonstrated an un-predicted and astonishingly strong perceptual tendency to transform simultaneous X- and Y-change in the proximal stimulus to Z-motion, in spite of both amplitude and frequency differences in the stimulus pattern. Pattern 7 represents an attempt to break the perceptual interaction between X- and Y-changes.

In this pattern the X-change is an exact projection of a rotary motion and thus, in accordance with known fact, will evoke a very strong tendency to be seen as a rotation in the third dimension. This effect is well known from Lissajous figures created on oscilloscope screens or in other ways (Metzger, 1934–35; Fisichelli, 1946; Johansson, 1950). Thus, the X-change was taken to form a perceptual time-space configuration where perceived velocity and perceived motion track are determined fairly definitely and probably hard to break. To this horizontal event configuration was added our ordinary triangular Y-change. The frequency relationships were: X = 0.9 cps; Y = 0.3 cps. Fig. 13 shows some phases of a Y-cycle.

In Patterns 3–6, it has always been possible to describe geometrically the residual change as a rotation or form change of the perceived object. It is evident that if the horizontal change in Pattern 7 is described as a projection of a rotation about one vertical edge, then there is no possibility of splitting up this change into two vectors in accordance with the above given principles. Therefore, the vertical motion ought to introduce nothing more than a change of form during the revolutions of the object. The pattern has the form of a square in one phase of the Y-change, and a rectangle in the opposite phase.

Results: In the primary experiments 8 subjects from group A and the 24 children in group C took part. The perceptual outcome is very definite. All observers reported a rotating or oscillating object, the axis of which was moving back and forth in depth with the frequency of the vertical component. The object is either seen as continuously rotating about one of the vertical edges or as describing a pendulum motion to and fro about this axis with a swing of 180 degrees or less. (Most of the subjects saw it as rotating.) The surface, of course, changed its form from a square to a rectangle (proportions 2:3) during the Y-cycle. However, astonishingly enough, only a few subjects reported this change spontaneously. The complete descriptions of the percepts may be summarised as follows: A rectangular surface rotates about one of its vertical edges. The axis of rotation moves continuously toward and away from the observer. During this motion and synchronous with it, the surface shrinks and grows in the horizontal

Fig. 13. Change over time of shape and X-localisation of Pattern 7. Time along axis.

dimension. When it is far away it has the shape of a horizontally oriented rectangle and when it is at the closest turning point it has the form of a square.

Discussion: This outcome from the stimulus pattern does not correspond to the expectation behind its construction. On the contrary, it seems to demonstrate that any combination of changes in X- and Y-direction has a strong tendency to generate a perception of motion in depth (if the velocities chosen allow it).

The result is of special interest from a theoretical viewpoint. It demonstrates in a very convincing way the difficulties in applying principles of "least action" for prediction of percepts from stimulus patterns. The perceptual description given necessarily contains three rather independent events: (1) rotary motion, (2) translatory motion in Z-direction, and (3) shrinking-growing of the rotating surface in the X-direction. A percept in the form of (1) rotary motion of an object, and (2) simultaneous shrinking-growing in the vertical direction would be in equally good geometric correspondence with the stimulus pattern. It also would be much simpler, considering that it contains only two independent events of exactly the same kind as we have found in the reported percepts. It seems hard to find a more convincing demonstration of the strength of the perceptual tendency to transform changes in two stimulus dimensions to a motion in the third dimension.

In accordance with the principles given above for relating stimulus and percept in an adequate way, the stimulus pattern ought to be described as follows: The sinusoidal change in the X-direction represents a rotation with constant speed and consequently there is no component left which can be transformed into a linear Z-motion. The perceived Z-motion therefore means that we have to add an X-component proportionally equal to the Y-change. This vector is then counter-balanced by a vector of the same magnitude but in the opposite direction acting along the same contour (see Fig. 14).

The mathematical vector sum of these two vectors along the X-axis corresponding to the perceived Z-motion and form change in the X-direction is zero.

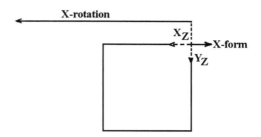

Fig. 14. Vector description of Pattern 7 in accordance with reported percepts.

The percept contains representations of both and is therefore in principle mathematically correct.

Thus, the existence of a stimulus change in X, which has a definitive perceptual representation is demonstrated to be a sufficient condition or cause for perceptually introducing a counterpart in the X-direction to the Y-change (plus a simultaneous opposite change giving a mathematically correct stimulus-percept relationship as a result). If we compare this result with the perceptual outcome from Pattern 1, we find that when there was no change in one dimension of proximal stimulus there was never a perceptual translatory Z-motion.

In this connection, it is perhaps of interest to remember that most of the subjects did not spontaneously report the form change from Pattern 7. This change was seemingly rather unimportant from a perceptual point of view.

Transformation pattern 8

A surface which perpetually changes its shape while its area or circumference remains constant seems to provide a type example of an elastic motion in perception. Our last attempt to get a definite two-dimensional percept from our proximal patterns consisted of generating such an elastic surface on our oscilloscope screen, thus matching perceived two-dimensional elasticity against perceived depth. The elasticity principle means that in our diagram there will always be different directions of the X- and Y-vectors relative to the origin. There is, then, at no instant of time, a common component corresponding to Z-motion.

Pattern 8 is a repetition of Pattern 2 with one exception: There is a phase difference of 180 degrees introduced between the X- and Y-changes. Thus when there is an expanding motion along one axis, there is always a contraction along the other axis.

This motion combination means, of course, that the length of the circumference of the figure is not changing during the cycle of form change ($X + Y = K$). Also the area remains approximately constant during the form change because the relation between maximum and minimum length of a side is 2:1. The maximal deviation from constant size of area is, under these conditions, not more than 10 percent of the initial size. The exact function for constant area: $Y =$

k(1/X) was also generated, but the difference between the two functions was found to be hardly perceptible, and both gave the same outcome in pre-experiments. Therefore, the formal experiment was restricted to Pattern 8, which was presented to all three groups of subjects.

Result: In the two groups of adult subjects 22 reported seeing a surface moving in depth and changing its form or rotating during this motion, while 21 reported seeing a two-dimensional static surface, which changed its shape in an elastic way. Among the 24 children only 3 reported motion in depth. The rest of the C group described a frontal surface which just changed its shape.

Discussion: The results indicate that this pattern also is often perceived as an object moving in depth by adult observers. In spite of the ideal conditions for elasticity, this way of perceiving the pattern was no more than one alternative from a rather ambiguous stimulus condition.

The percept implying Z-motion is diagrammed in Fig. 15.

This percept is in principle equivalent to the percept from certain phases of Patterns 5 and 6. An important difference between the patterns is, however, that in Pattern 8 the two motions on the screen never combine (at any instant of time) to a resultant giving a Z-motion in the projection system. Fig. 16 (a and b) illustrates three phases of the surface change in the proximal pattern as a projection of a combination of rotatory and translatory Z-motion.

These figures should help the reader to visualise the perceived event during one cycle of change. Ideally, the subject sees a frontal rectangle (phase 1). This rectangle rotates about its central vertical axis and also moves toward the observer at the same time. When it is nearest the observer (phase 3), it has made a swing around its axis covering an angle of about 75 degrees (which is the angle required of a rectangle with the proportions 1:2 between the sides for giving the proportions of phase 3 as a projection).

The perceptual outcome from Pattern 8 and Pattern 7 compared with the result from Pattern 1 makes it clear that the existence of simultaneous changes in the X- and Y-dimensions of a proximal stimulus pattern (irrespective of direction) is a sufficient but also necessary condition for perceiving a translatory motion in depth.

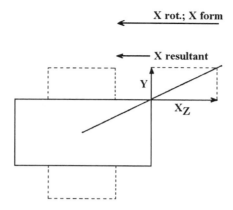

Fig. 15. Vector description of Pattern 8 in accordance with reported percepts.

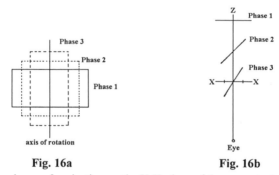

| **Fig. 16a** | **Fig. 16b** |

Fig. 16a. Three phases of projection on the X-Y-plane of the perceptual object.
Fig. 16b. Three phases of motion of the perceptual object (when rotating) over the X-Z-plane.

Summary and Conclusions from the Experiments

Two-dimensional versus three-dimensional percepts

When the proximal stimulus was characterised by change in only one dimension, the percept was ambiguous with regard to dimensionality. This holds true for both variation between subjects and within subjects. A change in one dimension is seen as a change in form of a frontal surface or as a rotation or bending of a more or less rigid surface.

Simultaneous changes in both the X- and Y-dimensions of the proximal stimulus brought about a different result. In six out of seven cases, characterised by a systematic search for two-dimensional percepts from such patterns, the result was perceived translatory motion in the third dimension. In almost all reports, there has been no real ambiguity between two- and three-dimensionality. The exceptional case was found when an elasticity of the stimulus surface, with constant area, was generated. This pattern resulted in ambiguity between perceived elasticity of a frontal surface and motion in depth of an object.

Perception of motion in depth from a proximal pattern changing in two dimensions has, under our stimulus conditions, proved to be rather inevitable, and thus a spontaneous consequence of stimulation in most cases. Even the sophisticated observers found it impossible to avoid this percept. It may also be mentioned, as a good indication of the same fact, that some of the students of psychology who acted as subjects raised questions after their experimental session about the technique for producing the stimulus and giving it motion, which revealed that they took for granted the fact that they had seen 'real' motion in depth.

Referring to the perceived motion in depth, we may sum up our results as follows: (1) It has not been possible under the conditions of speed of change chosen to design a proximal stimulus pattern of change of a rectangle which does *not* give depth perception; (2) in all but a very special case, depth perception is reported by practically all subjects; (3) this depth perception reported by the subjects allows practically *no alternative* spontaneous percept.

These three facts taken together allow only one interpretation: Projection of the proximal pattern into the third dimension is a general and basic perceptual principle under our experimental conditions. We are therefore able to state that the principle of primary three-dimensionality given above is something of a basis for perceptual "interpretation" of changing stimulus patterns at least under stimulus conditions analogous with those characteristic of our experimental situation (homogeneous dark background).

The principle of the lowest rate of change

The perceived motion in depth in the experiments has always been determined by the component of change in proximal stimulus (i.e., the X- or Y-component) which was characterised by the lowest velocity relative to the origin in the projection system. This velocity was determined by (1) the proportionally smaller amplitude of motion of the contours, or (2) the lower frequency. If both relative amplitude and frequency were equal, but the motions were in opposite phases (Pattern 8), it seems to be the vertical component which is usually spontaneously seen as the carrier of the depth motion. (Cf. the vertical-horizontal illusion.)

A special study will be carried out in order to investigate the generality of this principle of lowest rate of change relative to the origin as a determinant of the perceived depth motion. Because we have found no exception to it in the present series of experiments, we will accept it as a valid formulation in our actual discussion. If it should prove to need a reformulation (i.e., that it is not the velocity mentioned but, for example, the time factor involved in frequency which is also a deciding factor) this will not interfere with our conclusions in this discussion.

Perceptual vector analysis

Good evidence is advanced (in an as yet non-quantitative way) that the depth motion in perception from our stimulus inputs is due to a process analogous to a mathematical vector subtraction in the proximal pattern of change. This process is tentatively thought of in the following way: (1) The proportionally slowest rate of change, which in accordance with our earlier statement seems to determine the depth motion, "absorbs" a proportionally equal component of change in the other dimension, and in this way the geometric conditions for a translatory motion in depth are satisfied. The remaining component of change is perceived as a more or less independent motion or form change in the perceptual object. This perceptual "splitting up" of the physical change relative to a static reference system is in no way a unique characteristic for the depth perception now studied. On the contrary, it has been found to form something of a general principle for motion perception (cf. Duncker, 1929; Johansson, 1950; Wallach, 1959). It is highly satisfying, from a theoretical point of view, to meet this principle again in pure form in the perception of depth through motion.

Three-dimensionality as a primary condition for perceptual vector analysis

In the percepts from Patterns 5, 6, 7, 8, but especially in Patterns 7 and 8, we find a very embarrassing fact: Even when there is no common component in X- and Y-changes of the pattern which is granting depth motion in perception in accordance with the principles broadly set forth above, depth motion is perceived in accordance with the principle of proportionally least change. The compelling depth motion from Pattern 7 and the tendency to see Pattern 8 in this way, could not be predicted from the principle of common vectors of change in X- and Y-dimensions. It seems as if we have to accept these experimental results as being indicative of the existence of an unknown principle for the action of the visual system under conditions analogous with our experimental conditions. (This principle was unknown and also unexpected, at least for the present writer.) It has already been stated above but may now be expressed as follows: When there are simultaneous form changes in two dimensions of a structure in the proximal stimulus, there will be found with but few exceptions perceptual motion in the third dimension. Thus, three-dimensionality seems to be a very basic perceptual response to proximal patterns changing in two dimensions—a change which also involves, in almost every case, variation in size of the proximal pattern. Change in two dimensions seems to be a necessary condition, but once this condition is fulfilled, the percept is basically determined as an event happening in a three-dimensional space.

Perspective and non-perspective transformations

These three principles for stimulus-percept relationships (the principles of three-dimensionality, of vector subtraction and of "least change") specify, in combination, all geometric projections from moving rigid bodies. It is easily seen but ought perhaps to be stated explicitly that given a changing projection generated by a rigid body in complex motion in space, these principles will specify just one description; the "veridical" motion of the body.

In this way these principles will predict, e.g., the percepts received from the changing shadow patterns at Cornell and elsewhere. However, they are more general than the perspectivity principle hypothesised by Gibson (1959) because they also cover projective transformations caused by objects which change their shape during motion. Most of our stimulus patterns of change are to be described as non-perspective transformations. The experimental results indicate that such non-perspective transformations provide a good perceptual distinction between motion of an object and the simultaneous form change of this object. In this sense, we also have full specificity in spite of the fact that the change of the object under our impoverished stimulus conditions may be seen in more than one way.

This last point is of considerable interest, and worth an extra note. When a subject has described the residual change as a "shrinking-growing" of the object, this is a correct description from a mathematical point of view. This is not perfectly true, however, when the subject describes a partial rotation of the object. If the residual change is described as a rotation, we will still have, geometrically, another residual change remaining. This is based on the fact that all our patterns are parallelograms at every instant, while rotations would imply change to trapezoidal shape. Because the patterns cover visual angles larger than 5 degrees on an average and the relation between the smallest and largest angle during a cycle of change is of the ratio 1:2, the deviation from true shape constancy during rotation ought to be easily perceptible. Thus, if the relative expanding-contracting of the pattern in one dimension is described as a rotation 60 degrees about a central axis of the perceived object, the relative size of the two opposite, unequal sides will be approximately in the ratio 9:10.

It is an interesting fact that this hypothetical residual form change due to perceived rotation in accordance with principles of geometry also seems to have a definite representation in perception, at least in trained observers. When observed, the percept is described as a rectangle or square which, during its rotation, changes elastically to a trapezoid (the contour which is farthest away seems to expand). A systematic study of this effect, however, was beyond the purpose of the present investigation.

The results applied to the theoretical problem of the investigation

The problem set forth in the first part of this investigation was the following: Does a continuous transformation of the proximal stimulus provide specific information for the organism? If it does, which are the relevant stimulus parameters?

Our experiments have quite decisively given an affirmative answer to the first question. On the basis of our experimental results, we can state explicitly the answer also to the second question: The results quite clearly invalidate the hypothesis of primary perceptual two-dimensionality as a solution. Instead, they prove exactly the contrary. The fundamental principle for gaining specific information from proximally changing stimuli is *perceptual three-dimensionality.*

The hypothesis that the decisive factor is perceptual discrimination of perspective or non-perspective transformations has also been proved too specialised and therefore inadequate. This hypothesis concurs with the data only in the special case where the transformation is a perspective one. Our experiments show that also a transformation of the proximal stimulus implying motion of a changing form, thus a non-rigid transformation, gives information about this motion which is often perfectly specific.

Our experiments have proved, as stated above, *that projection into the third dimension* of every complex change in the two dimensional proximal stimulus is the basic rule for obtaining specific information. Given this basic rule, the principles of *vector analysis* and *least change*, revealed in our present (as well as earlier) research on motion perception, render in principle full specificity to every percept caused by a proximal stimulus in the form of a changing two-dimensional energy flux.

Thus, we know that these three principles give an adequate formulation of the relationship between stimulus and percept under our experimental conditions. They allow us to specify what characteristics of physical change have an approximately linear relationship to perception in our experiments.

The expression "approximately linear relationship" may be interpreted to indicate the assumption that, under our experimental conditions, perception of distance in depth is related to the three-dimensional description of stimulus change in accordance with the psychophysical equation $R = S^n$, where $n \approx 1$. Until experiments allowing better quantification have been carried out, this relationship represents the best hypothesis. Of course a possible curvilinear relationship indicated by a value of the exponent clearly deviating from 1.0 would not invalidate our discussion about the principles of vector analysis and least change. Strictly speaking those principles are related to *perceptual* space. If this space would deviate from the Euclidean space, all that we have to do is to transform our data in an adequate way.

Are we also willing to generalise from these experiments to other situations with changing proximal stimuli—perhaps the most common type of visual stimulation? In one way the answer is easy. If we want to build a theory for monocular perception of motion in three dimensions, we have to generalise from the experimental data available. The principles given have been shown to cover all data in the present investigation and also the data from earlier research in the same field. Thus, the best alternative at this level of knowledge is to explicitly generalise our three principles as valid formulations for stimulus-percept relationships in visual space perception, and accept this generalisation as a hypothesis to be tested in further research.

However, some restrictions must be added if we want to use our data as the basis for a theory. It is the opinion of the writer that these data contain some very important pointers toward a theory, but also that they are as yet in some respects too unstructured to be used as good cornerstones.

I should like to specify in the following way:

(1) In one important respect, our results form a firm basis for a theory of visual space perception from changing stimulus patterns. This basis is given by our principle of primary three-dimensionality. Everything in our experiments worked against this principle. It holds true, for example, for the extremely impoverished stimulus conditions in combination with the non-perspective transformation in stimulus change. Every added structure of the stimulus pattern ought to increase information on depth. Therefore, when the principle of primary three-dimensionality is a general principle underlying our experimental conditions, it ought to be regarded as a basic principle behind every visual perception from proximal patterns of light changing continuously over time, within the rate of angular change applied in our experiments.

(2) The principles of vector analysis and of least change are in our discussion given in strict quantitative terms. The outcome of the experiments, however, gives from this point of view just a simple categorisation. Thus, the present investigation ought to be followed up by experiments able to give true quantitative data before these principles are fully accepted.

(3) The stimulus conditions in our experiments have been varied only with regard to combination of changes. Further research on, for instance, the effects of different types of changes, the complexity of the patterns, the frequency or speed span giving three-dimensionality, etc., have to be carried out.

(4) The three principles given are probably not the most general or not the most elegant formulation of the stimulus-percept relationships (it would be strange if they should prove to be so). We know that they are valid under our experimental conditions and also cover earlier known facts. Therefore, they can be used as preliminary formulations of these relationships. The present writer, however, should like to find some still simpler formula for the same relationships.

The main contents of this report may be summarised as follows:

(1) The starting point for this investigation was a question about principles inherent in the visual perceptual processes for getting specific information from changing patterns of proximal stimulation. The problem was broadly given in the following form: "Does a transformation of the array of light provide specific information for the organism? If it does, which are the relevant stimulus parameters?"

(2) Two theoretical attempts at a solution were discussed. (a) The classic solution assuming that a primary two-dimensional percept gives a good perceptual specificity to every stimulus flow. (b) Possible perceptual differentiating between transformations due to motions of rigid objects and transformations due to form changes (Poincaré, 1913; von Fieandt & Gibson, 1959).

(3) Experiments were carried out in which the eye was given a proximal stimulus pattern which consisted exclusively of a solid angle of approximately homogeneous light. The cross section of this solid angle always had the shape of a rectangle or square and changed continuously in different well-controlled ways.

(4) The main result of the experiments (67 subjects) may be summarised as follows: When there is change in only one dimension in the stimulus, there is ambiguity between two-dimensional form change and changing slant (depth). All our stimulus patterns which simultaneously changed in two dimensions gave rise to descriptions of percepts in terms of motion in depth of objects which were rigid or changed shape during motion. Seven such proximal stimuli (Patterns 2-8) were investigated, and all but one gave practically 100 per cent responses indicating motion in depth as the dominant percept. One pattern (Pattern 8) gave ambiguity between two-dimensional elastic form change and depth motion.

(5) The deciding principle in perceptual filtering of information inherent in our stimulus patterns with changes in two dimensions seems to be very simple. It is definitely not two-dimensional form change, but neither is the result in conformity with the shape constancy (rigidity) principle discussed. Instead, it simply seems to be a principle of primary perceptual *three-dimensionality* which gives specificity to the percepts from changing stimulation.

Most of the experiments in the series were designed in order to find stimulus conditions which give unequivocal two-dimensional percepts. Therefore, the principle stated ought to be hypothesised as a general principle underlying perception from patterns changing simultaneously in two dimensions.

(6) Preliminary statements of principles for prediction of the exact character of perceived motion in depth from a given stimulus change are given.

Note

This investigation was carried out at Cornell University. I am sincerely indebted to Dr. J. J. Gibson for initiating my visit to his laboratory, and for placing its facilities at my disposal.

The investigation was made possible by grants from the National Science Foundation, U.S.A., and the Swedish Council for Social Science Research which also fully covered the costs of publication.

References

Braunstein, M. L. (1960). *Rotation of dot patterns as stimuli for the perception of motion in three dimensions: The effects of numerosity and perspective.* Ph.D.-thesis, University of Michigan. Mimeo. Cornell Aeronautical Laborarory.

Braunstein, M. L. (1962). Depth perception in rotating dot patterns: Effects of numerosity and perspective. *Journal of Experimental Psychology, 64,* 415–420.

Duncker, K. (1929). Über induzierte Bewegung (On induced motion). *Psychologische Forschung, 12,* 180–259.

Fieandt, K. von & Gibson, J. J. (1959). The sensitivity of the eye to two kinds of continuous transformation of a shadow-pattern. *Journal of Experimental Psychology, 57,* 344–347.

Fisichelli, V. R. (1946). Effect of rotational axis and dimensional variations on the reversals of apparent movement in Lissajous figures. *American Journal of Psychology, 59,* 669–675.

Gibson, J. J. (1950). *The perception of the visual world.* Boston: Houghton Mifflin.

Gibson, J. J. (1959). Perception as a function of stimulation. In S. Koch (Ed.), *Psychology: A study of a science* (Vol. 1, pp. 456–501). New York: McGraw-Hill.

Gibson, J. J. & Gibson, E. J. (1957). Continuous perspective transformations and the perception of rigid motion. *Journal of Experimental Psychology, 54,* 129–138.

Green, B. F. (1961). Figure coherence in the kinetic depth effect. *Journal of Experimental Psychology, 62,* 272–282.

Hochberg, J. & Smith, O. (1955). Landing strip markings and the Expansion Pattern. *Perceptual and Motor Skills, 2,* 81–92.

Johansson, G. (1950). *Configurations in event perception.* Uppsala: Almqvist & Wiksell. [Chpter 2, this volume.]

Johansson, G. (1958). Rigidity, stability, and motion in perceptual space. *Acta Psychologica, 13,* 359–370. [Chapter 3, this volume.]

Metzger, W. (1934-35). Tiefenerscheinungen in optischen Bewegungsfeldern (Depth perception in optical motion patterns). *Psychologische Forschung, 20,* 195–260.

Poincaré, H. (1913). *The value of science.* New York: Science Press.

Wallach, H. (1959). The perception of motion. *Scientific American, 201* (1), 56–60.

Wallach, H. & O'Connell, D. N. (1953). The kinetic depth effect. *Journal of Experimental Psychology, 45,* 207–217.

On Theories for Visual Space Perception[†]

A letter to Gibson

Gunnar Johansson

Uppsala University

Dear Friend,

For many years we have both been engaged in experimental research and theoretical work aiming at a better understanding of visual space and object perception. A main theme has been the important role played by changing stimulus patterns, thus, event perception, as contrasted to static perception. During these years we have exchanged many personal communications which, for me, have been highly stimulating.

The purpose of the present paper is to continue the discussion about some parts of your recent book: *The Senses Considered as Perceptual Systems*, in which we were involved during your visit to Uppsala some months ago. Both I, personally, and other members of the Uppsala group had some principal objections to your application for the "ecological optics" in your book. I promised to analyze this conception a little further and to communicate the result in a discussion paper. Here you have our points of view. I hope that a discussion of some essential divergences may be fruitful for both of us.

I will analyze your construct "ecological optics" in two ways; first, from a systematical point of view, and then I intend to scrutinize the validity of your application of its basic rules in your theory for space perception.

What is "Ecological Optics?"

From several declarations in your book it seems clear that you regard ecological optics as a special but very little studied field of general optics. I hope that I have understood your book right when I say that the main function of "ecological optics" is to *develop a model for how reflected light carries visually decodable information about an organism's environment* (see, e.g., op. cit. p. 186).

[†] From *Scandinavian Journal of Psychology*, 1970, *11*, 67–74. Reprinted with permission from the journal.

In terms of distal-proximal stimuli this means that you start with the distal environment and ask what information about it is available proximally at the eye. Such detailed knowledge is, to be sure, a highly important condition for a theory of visual space perception, and I regard your consequent endeavor in this respect as a highly important contribution.

In your discussion the central question is an analysis of the information available in the optical convergence points in space and given by the network of rays from reflected light. [The reader is reminded that the optical convergence point (the station point) is a point where rays reflected from the environment cross. Light rays cross in every point in a room reflecting light and such a crossing is a necessary condition for the functioning of an eye or a camera. Fig. 1 gives a diagrammatic illustration taken from Gibson's book.]

Formulated in this way the problem is primarily a geometrical one. It has direct relevance for a study of the eye as an optical instrument, but also for other optical instruments, for instance the camera. However, it has the same relevance for the perspective drawer. In this way ecological optics in accordance with your treatment has a near relationship to the most classical part of optics, namely geometrical optics on the one hand and the geometry of perspective on the other. I will in the following briefly touch upon both these fields.

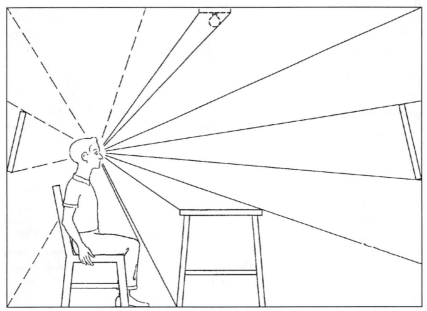

Fig. 1. The effective array at a stationary convergence point (Stage 5). The solid lines represent the sample of the total optic array that is admitted to a human eye in a given posture. The dashed lines represent the remainder of the array, which is available for stimulation but not effective at this moment.

In your treatment you stress the very special character of ecological optics. You speak about the "quite unfamiliar laws of ecological optics" and that known laws of physical optics need to be supplemented with these laws (p. 188). You also say that "this protodiscipline cannot be expected to have the mathematical elegance of classical optics but it is closer to life" (p. 187). I want to stress another position. I agree wholeheartedly in your endeavor to develop an optics specially adapted to our common theoretical problems, but I think that in the two above-mentioned branches of geometry and optics we have rather adequate basic principles and rules ready for borrowing.

Ecological optics as a part of geometrical optics

Currently, optics is divided into three parts: geometrical optics (where the "ray" conception has fundamental relevance), physical optics (primarily wave theory), and quantum optics (= interaction between light and matter).

Geometrical optics introduces the concept of "ray" and studies, among other things, how light is reflected from more or less opaque surfaces, how it is refracted, etc. In this way it gives the well-known principles for image generation from reflected rays crossing in a point in space. In fact, the insight that rays from a surrounding hemisphere are crossing in every point in space is the basis for optical image generation—even if this fact is not often explicitly pointed out. From this point of view, ecological optics may be regarded as a special application of geometrical optics. Optical image generation is macroscopic in character in the same way as you have stressed for ecological optics and it is submitted to the well-developed mathematics of geometrical optics. The "image" may be regarded as a convenient way of describing some of the information available in the convergence point. Used in this way it is a geometrical concept rather than a visual one.

Ecological optics and perspective geometry

In your book *Perception of the Visual World* (1950) you made much use of the laws of perspectivity. The perspectivity gradients played a central role in your theory structure.

In the present book you seem to be rather disappointed with the results of experimental work along these lines. The concept of gradients has vanished. [Parenthetically I wish to say that this is a reaction which perhaps will prove to be a little premature.] However, I know that you are aware of the near relationship between the perspective geometry and your ecological optics. But even here you have a well-developed science. Perspective geometry was the origin of projective geometry. Thus, you have here again the powerful mathematical tools of a highly developed and sophisticated science.

Information contained in the optical convergence point, or the station point, may be described in many different but theoretically equivalent ways. Now, you want to leave the traditional picture plane method and use a construct with hemispheres. This, I think, depends on your ambition to discuss in terms of wide-angle perspective. From a geometrical point of view this is adequate. The question is not, however, a very important one, it is just a question of choice between spherical and linear representation of the same information contained in the convergence point. What is of key importance is the knowledge that all the visually useful information in reflected light is available in the optical crossing point loosely represented by the pupil of the eye.

About multiple reflection and information about illumination

What I have so far touched upon concerns primarily the stimulus counterpart for contour vision and perception of forms. In traditional terms this is the stimulus background for *shape constancy*. There is, however, a third part of the system you have named ecological optics, and in my opinion the most "ecological" part of it. This concerns the consequences of multiple light reflection between surfaces in terms of reduction of energy and change of spectral characteristics. Both number of reflections and type of reflecting surfaces have specific effects and give the ray a "history." These ecological characteristics of light are highly important for perception of illumination. They are the stimulus

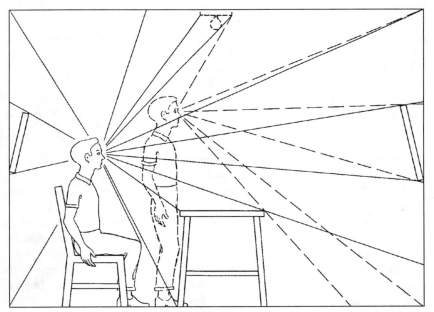

Fig. 2. The transformation of the optic array obtained by a locomotor movement (Stage 6). The solid lines represent the optic array before the observer stands up the dashed lines after he has moved. The path of locomotion of the head is forward and upward. The whole array is transformed, including the invisible portion behind the head, but the latter is not represented in the drawing.

counterpart for *brightness constancies and color constancies.*

I am a little astonished to find that you have not explicitly treated this section of the ecology of light. [You have mentioned it at p. 12.] These aspects of the information contained in the convergence point (and surely used by the visual apparatus) seem to give special problems for proximal stimulus analysis. Here, perhaps, your declaration about the lack of adequate methods for stimulus analysis is more justified than ever.

Information About the Third Dimension in the Convergence Point

After these comments on your treatment of the optical-geometrical relation between environment and convergence point (distal stimulus–proximal stimulus) we can take the next step. This concerns the essential question of the information about space available in the station point. If we regard the light reflection to a convergence point as a geometrical projection (in accordance with projective geometry) we can speak about the visual "reconstruction" of physical space from proximal light distribution as a reversal of this process, thus a *reverse projection.*

The general problem is well known from Bishop Berkeley. We can express it in the following questions: How is specific 3D perception possible from the information available in the convergence point. How is the third dimension given in vision? We know that the classical cue theory for static perception is unsatisfactory. It does not cover the ordinary type of visual perception: perception of changes and of motion. However, there is an important difference between your theoretical positions in this field and my own, and my main purpose with the present paper is to sort out this controversy.

I will start with an effort to summarize from your text (Gibson, 1966) your present position in the following two statements. I hope that you will find my digest of your text correct.

1. It is not possible for the eye to get specific and veridical information about space from a single static convergence point (pp. 198–199). [You argue with data from the Ames distorted room.]

2. A set of convergence points in space can, taken as a unit, bring about specific and veridical information about this space (p. 191–192, stage 3). Locomotion (motion) of the eye through a series of convergence points represents a successive combination of information in the same way and therefore gives specific 3D information (p. 199) about a rigid environment.

I borrow Fig. 2 from your book as a very clear but static illustration of the effect of locomotion.

These statements seem to me to form the basis for your main theorem: The visual system receives optically no specific information about the environment when it is in a static state but a moving organism obtains such information due to its motion. You assume that it is gained from combining information available in a set of static points along the motion track. There we have our main point of controversy.

Let me comment on your position.

1. You state that there is no specific 3D information available in one single static convergence point. Here I agree and will add that we have at our disposal also decisive geometrical arguments for this position; arguments of ecological optics-type taken from projective geometry (equivalent figurations). These arguments are given in, e.g., Johansson (1964) and Johansson and Jansson (1968), but also in the theoretical discussions behind Ames's demonstrations.

2. The second paragraph concerns motion and changing patterns of proximal stimulus information. Your position would have been correct there also if you had included a highly important restriction. But it is lacking. Without a priori assuming the existence of 3D rigidity there is no specific information about space available in visual stimulus even in connection with locomotion. The visual apparatus has to introduce a set of decoding principles for data treatment with the signification that the expanding and changing proximal patterns represent motion in a rigid 3D world. Taken *per se* the changing information pattern due to locomotion does not contain specific information about a 3D space.

I know that you dislike any attempt to introduce what may be regarded as subjective moments in visual perception (like "assumptions," "schemata," etc.) Your main thesis has been that there is available in proximal stimulus all the information needed and that the problem is to find an adequate stimulus description in terms of higher order variables. Now, you have changed your position when it is a question of static perception, but seem to believe in the possibility of keeping the position when it is a question of the categories of changing stimulation where the changes are due to locomotion.

As you know, I am of the same opinion as you regarding the need of reformulation of traditional stimulus description. We have also the same position regarding the decisive importance of motion and changing visual stimulation for an understanding of visual perception. For that same reason I feel that it is necessary to make it clear what is valid in your approach and what is an erroneous consequence of an incomplete analysis.

When you restrict your discussion about information in visual change to such changes caused by locomotion it seems to me that you stop halfway. You stop at locomotion instead of analyzing the more pure case concerning a stationary eye and its changing stimulation due to motions and form changes of objects. Locomotion in 3D space surely introduces also non-optical components of sensory information. So far, as I understand, however, there is no place for such added information in your ecological optics.

You may answer that a main theme of your book is to demonstrate how different sense channels interact and form unitary perceptual systems and that perhaps we have here the most important example of such interaction. I agree wholeheartedly. I am convinced that space perception in a freely moving animal or man is the result of a highly complex interaction between vision and a number of different receptor systems for mechanical forces.

Our discussion here, however, concerns the isolated visual component. Our problem is to find out how far pure optical information in a convergence point can contribute to the organism's orientation in its environment. Therefore, in the interest of theoretical clearness I want to stress the distinction between possible optical information and possible mechanical information.

From this follows the question: Is space perception from visual perception necessarily due to interaction with non-visual sense channels (outside the eye)? This is, I think, a crucial question for theoretical development.

In order to get an answer to this question, the appropriate step is, of course, to study visual effects of changing optical structures in an approximately static convergence point. Suppose that we are able to demonstrate experimentally that this condition can also give specific (and perhaps veridical) space perception. The consequence would be that we had shown that bodily motion is not a necessary condition for specific 3D perception from optical motion. And we would also know that isolated optical stimulation of this type is enough for obtaining space perception.

We have, as you well know, many such affirmative results. You have given excellent affirmative answers yourself. Your "looming" experiments with various species have convincingly demonstrated how expanding patterns on resting retinas yield perception of motions in depth. I could also mention the kinetic depth effects (Wallach & O'Connell, 1953) or my own studies about motion perception already referred to.

Strangely enough you have just in your arguments for what I will call the locomotor theory (p. 199) pointed to the looming effects as an experimental support. I hope that you will agree when I stress that these effects are, on the contrary, an argument for the proposition that an eye resting in space is able to get specific 3D perception from changing stimulation. If so, let us make it clear that it is continuous optical change in the convergence point that is the decisive condition. Whether such changes are due to locomotion or to moving objects is rather equivalent from the point of view of 3D information.

We have to accept that (1) there is geometrically no specific information about space available in the pattern of change in the station point, and (2) that the visual system presents specific information from such stimulus patterns. This poses a problem which you have not solved.

There is also another important reason for me to say that your theory for motion perception is not sufficiently developed. You have not taken into consideration a highly important characteristic of the perceptual pick-up of optical information.

I am aiming at the property of the visual decoding for which I once have used the term *motion analysis* (Johansson, 1950; see also 1958, 1964). The term refers to the automatic and unavoidable splitting up into unitary components of the complex pattern of change in the optical convergence point. This analysis follows simple laws of mechanics. Its consequence is that a complex pattern of optical change in the station point is perceptually split up and grouped into mutually equal and divergent components. This function of the visual system seems to be a necessary condition for the visual ability to perceive a rigid world and rigid objects from the complex optical information flow at the eye.

I have discussed (Johansson, 1958) how this characteristic of the visual treatment of stimulus data not only makes it possible to get adequate information about locomotion or about object motion, but also to perceive both types of event at the same time. Locomotion gives one component of change in the whole pattern and the object motion another and these components are perceptually perfectly separated. A hunting animal, for instance, seems to perceive in a perfect way its motion over a field and simultaneously also the motion of the prey. The same analyzing principle is in work when we are able to walk along a crowded sidewalk or to drive our car in ordinary city traffic. We control visually our own motion and the motion of several distinct objects at the same time. It seems appropriate to point to the fact that the ear demonstrates an analogous analyzing capacity. From the complex wave pattern of the eardrum we are able to distinguish a chosen voice in party chatter or one of the instruments in an orchestra.

But, let us now return to our main point of controversy: the role of the organism. Above I have characterized your position in this respect as the result of an incomplete analysis. Thus, I mean that a more thorough analysis brings about a deviating position. Therefore, in order to give you an object for your criticism, let me sketch out the structure of my own theory structure. It has been developed on the basis of experiments, which I have tried to make as critical as possible for the problem.

I will stress that the visual system itself in a decisive way contributes to the perceptual outcome from the proximal stimulus flow also to an eye of approximative rest. The efficiency of the system is given by a set of rules for stimulus data treatment (the programming of the visual computer, if you accept this metaphor), rules which work in an automatic way, but which result in veridicality when the proximal stimuli are projections from moving rigid objects and/or a rigid environment in motion relative to the eye. The principle of motion analysis mentioned above may be regarded as a general summarizing formulation of these decoding principles.

Such rules have been shown experimentally to work in a blind, mechanical way and leave basically nothing for subjective choice. Therefore, I prefer to regard them as indicating a primary neurological "wiring." Their basic effect seems to be to filter out rigidity in space.

Together with my co-workers, I have tried to give some special and preliminary formulations of these stimulus decoding principles (Johansson, 1964; Johansson & Jansson, 1967).

Further analyses are found in Marmolin and Ulfberg (1968), Jansson and Runeson (1969), and Jansson and Börjesson (1969). Much more experimental and theoretical work remains, but I think that we begin to discern the main lines. This means that I (and I think all members of the Uppsala group) hope to be able to arrive at generally valid and specific formulations of perceptual rules for visual stimulus data treatment.

It is our opinion that our research program will help us to avoid a not uncommon appeal to subjectivity in the basic functions of the visual apparatus, but at the same time to avoid following the pendulum swing to the other extreme: an unstructured belief in stimulus information.

It was, of course, appropriate to characterize the theory type now outlined as a pure nativistic one. Your own theory, then, would be described as belonging to the empiristic type. I regard, however, these two old polar categories as rather unsatisfactory for the purpose of characterizing both our theory types. The structure I have outlined here concerns the primary biological programming of the visual system and has thus been concentrated on the nativistic component. But for a more complete theory we must include also the ability to adapt to induced distortions of various kinds. We are dealing with both basic and rather rigid decoding principles (apparently common for all types of visual systems of retinal type) as one category and, as another, a more or less advanced ability to adapt the outcome from this primary decoding scheme when needed. This may perhaps be regarded as some kind of analogy to a basic programming together with a possibility of changing some instructions and constants within the program of a computer. What is your own opinion in this respect?

References

Gibson, J, J. (1950). *The perception of the visual world.* Boston: Houghton Mifflin.

Gibson, J. J. (1966). *The senses considered as perceptual systems.* Boston: Houghton Mifflin.

Jansson, G. & Börjesson, E. (1969). Perceived direction of rotary motion. *Perception & Psychophysics, 6*, 19–26.

Jansson, G. & Runeson, S. (1969). Measurement of perceived oscillation. *Perception & Psychophysics, 6*, 27–32.

Johansson, G. (1950). *Configurations in event perception.* Uppsala: Almqvist & Wiksell. [Chapter 2, this volume.]

Johansson, G. (1958). Rigidity, stability, and motion in perceptual space. *Acta psychologica, 13*, 359–370. [Chapter 3, this volume.]

Johansson, G. (1964). Perception of motion and changing form. *Scandinavian Journal of Psychology*, *5*, 181–208. [Chapter 4, this volume.]

Johansson, G. & Jansson, G. (1968). Perceived rotary motion from changes in a straight line. *Perception & Psychophysics*, *4*, 165–170.

Marmolin, H. & Ulfberg, S. (1967). Rörelseperception och formförändring (Perception of motion and change of form). Unpublished report. Uppsala University, Department of Psychology.

Wallach, H. & O'Connell, D. N. (1953). The kinetic depth effect. *Journal of Experimental Psychology*, *45*, 205–217.

On Theories for Visual Space Perception[†]

A reply to Johansson

James J. Gibson

Cornell University

Dear Friend,

It is 19 years since you published *Configurations in Event Perception* and I published *The Perception of the Visual World*. During all these years we have been in fundamental agreement about the perception of events and the perception of space. That is why our disagreements are worth discussing. Each of us always knows what the other is talking about, at the very least, and this is a very satisfying situation. I understand your criticisms and I will try to meet them, or at least some of them.

Ecological Optics

First, about ecological optics. You say that I seem to regard it as a special branch of the existing science of optics, but a neglected branch. You imply that ecological optics could be derived from physical and geometrical optics without introducing any radically new postulates. Well, when I think about it, I disagree. It seems to me that ecological optics is a discipline of *higher order* than physical optics, and that the new definitions and postulates give us a truly different level at which to study light. The *seeing of light* is a problem in sensory physiology. But *the seeing of things by means of light* is so different a problem that the very meaning of the term 'light' is altered. The light that radiates from a source and the light that illuminates the surfaces of a room are different because new laws emerge for the latter. What I am saying, in a sense, is that there are Gestalt laws not only for physical objects and not only for the brain, but also for light.

You say that the aim of ecological optics is to explain "how reflected light carries visually decodable information about an organism's environment." That is approximately right but I have two reservations about it. First, the light which reverberates in the air instead of being propagated through empty space reaches a steady state. It is not just reflected light, but *multiply* reflected light. It "fills"

[†] From *Scandinavian Journal of Psychology*, 1970, *11*, 75–79. Reprinted with permission from the journal.

the air. It does not therefore so much *carry* information as *contain* information. The information exists in the set of all the ambient arrays at each of the station points. The air, in other words, is filled with geometrical projections, not just with waves or particles. Second, the information in an ambient array, consisting of geometrical projections, is not the kind that can be coded and decoded as messages and signals can. It is information in a quite different meaning of the term.

I do not believe that the existing disciplines of physical and geometrical optics can explain how light carries or contains information about the environment so long as light is conceived merely as radiant energy or rays. Rays can carry information about the *atoms* of a surface that radiates light, or is excited to emit it, but not about the gross layout, structure, and composition of the surface.

If, as you seem to suggest, we simply borrow the rules of physical and geometrical optics we must assume that an observer has to *construct* a perception of his environment out of light rays; that is, he must build up a picture of the world from elementary point sensations. You and I both know the theoretical difficulties to which this leads. My solution of this theoretical problem is to assume that there are genuine units in the array of ambient light, units that are not reducible to a distribution of points of light, or to a matrix of independent stimuli.

I think you are assuming that the information in the array of light coming to a convergence point *has* to be analyzed in terms of the direction, the amplitude, and the wavelength of each ray at that point. I agree that this analysis is possible but I do not think it is appropriate for the study of perception. The information can be analyzed in terms of relations, contrasts, discontinuities, and invariants. Your kind of information could be transmitted along a fiber of the optic nerve as a signal; my kind of information could not be transmitted in this way—in fact it could not be transmitted at all. But then I do not believe that the visual system is a channel for transmitting signals from the retina to the brain. I believe it is a system for *sampling* the ambient array.

I do not deny, of course, that visual sensations from the retina can be noticed—afterimages for example—but I assert that they are irrelevant for perception. Optical information as I conceive it is not conveyed over a channel; it is picked up by an active observer. And that means that the observer's brain cannot be compared to a computer, or to a processor of information delivered to it. It means that the environment does not send messages to a little perceiver in the head of an animal. And it means that the concept of information used by the mathematical theory of communication, however suggestive, is not applicable to vision considered as a perceptual system.

Information for the Perception of a Rigid Spatial Environment

Next we come to a deeply puzzling problem that has concerned us both for many years. We agree that optical *change* in some sense of that term contains information for the perception of space. You speak of "changing form" where I speak of "transformation." You still like to talk about the third dimension of "space" where I like to talk about the "layout" of surfaces. But despite our use of different terms we both understand the importance of a changing array as distinguished from a frozen array in time. There is less ambiguity in a changing array than there is in a frozen array, and we seem to agree about this. The difficulty between us arises, I think, from the assumptions I have made about the ecological *causes* of optical change. Let me try to make them explicit.

I assume there are four different kinds of material events that give rise to four distinct kinds of optical change. They are, first, rigid motions of objects relative to a stationary earth with a stationary observer, second, elastic motions of certain substances when the remaining environment and the observer are stationary, third, locomotions of the observer in a stationary environment and, fourth, elastic movements of the observer's extremities, such as his hands. I assume that the fundamental layout of the environment is rigid, since it is mostly matter in the solid state, not viscous or liquid. Hence a motionless observer is surrounded by an optic array which is for the most part frozen in time. He thus detects his immobility relative to the environment and this information is much more trustworthy than what might be provided by the joints, muscles, and vestibular organs, since he may have to work in order to stay in the same place, like a bird in a wind. When he moves (actively or passively) this ambient array undergoes "motion perspective" (as I call it) and he thus detects his locomotion relative to the environment (Gibson, Olum, & Rosenblatt, 1955).

I then assume that the optical change resulting from either the motion of a rigid object or the locomotion of an observer is of a special mathematical kind, whereas the optical change resulting from the *elastic* motion of an external surface or that of one's own skin is of a *different* mathematical kind. Being different, they are capable of being distinguished. The rigidity and non-rigidity of things can thus be detected. The difference has to be noticed of course; it has to be picked up by the visual apparatus, but that does not mean that the brain has to know a priori that space is rigid. I don't think that there are any built-in assumptions in the brain, but it is a great distinguisher of differences (Gibson, 1969).

I think it is a fact, a geological fact, that the surface of the earth tends to be rigid and tends to be composed of evenly distributed units. This is the basis of the assumption that the laws of perspective projection hold for terrestrial space.

You say that I overstate the importance of the locomotion of the observer in space perception and neglect the importance of the motion of objects. But surely the locomotion of the observer is necessary for large-scale space perception, for the awareness of the whole environment. Do you not agree that the *ground*, the *earth*, is the fundamental frame of reference for both locomotions and the motions of objects? Motion perspective for the surface of the earth is therefore the first case to analyze. The same laws no doubt will apply to both kinds of motion but the detecting of locomotion by vision is required for the *control* of locomotion (Gibson, 1958). However I have never doubted or denied that depth perception can arise from the motion of objects relative to the earth with no motion of the observer relative to the earth.

My guess is that the optical change over time in the optic array is what specifies both the locomotion of the observer and the motion of an object whereas the non-change over time in the changing array is what specifies the spatial arrangement of the environment and of the object in the environment. If I am right about this, then we shall have to understand the mathematical *invariants* under optical transformation instead of the old-fashioned "cues for depth" if we hope ever to understand space perception.

This last point may well be a crucial one for understanding the difference between our positions. The truly *specifying* information for the layout of the faces of an object or of the surfaces of the environment may be something that only emerges over time. It takes time since an invariant can only be detected if something does not vary along with something else that does. Such an invariant, you must agree, could not be transmitted over a nerve in the way a signal can be transmitted. It would have to be detected, registered, or "picked up" by an active perceptual system that works in a radically different way than the channels of sensory input work.

My notion of invariant properties during the course of change in the optic array is an alternative to your notion of applying vector analysis to the change in the optic array. You try to reduce the highly complex changes of the array to the simplest component motions (is that right?) whereas I try to separate the parameters of change in the array from the properties that do not change. Your motion analysis follows the laws of mechanics, as you say, and appeals to analytic geometry whereas my theory says that optical changes occur at a different level of abstraction than do mechanical motions and appeals to what has some times been called synthetic geometry.

Perhaps your analytic approach and my synthetic approach can be reconciled in the end, but for the present I cannot do so. Your idea that the information for ego-motion and that for object-motion are different *components* of change in the optic array is a good one. As I would put it, the first is "propriospecific" information and the second is "exterospecific." But I do not understand how you can say that this idea of component changes is derived from mechanics and vector analysis. The components are properties of the optic array, not the velocities of bodies in space.

I suggested a year ago (Gibson, 1968) that the changes in an optic array should not be called "motions" at all. They are changes that can *specify* environmental motions or locomotions without having to be *like* the motions that are specified. Hence what gives rise to the *perception* of motion is not itself motion. This is a radical conclusion, I must admit, and it is disconcerting. But I predict you will be forced to it, as I was, by the evidence. The hypothesis that a displacement of the retinal image over the retina is necessary for any kind of perception of motion is simply incorrect as I tried to show. And yet you seem to accept that hypothesis when you advocate the analysis of complex motions into simple components.

My reasons for believing that the rigidity of the terrestrial world in general and the elasticity of certain parts of it are distinguishable have been set forth recently in another publication (Gibson, 1969) and need not be repeated here. It is a deeply puzzling problem, as I said at the beginning, but it goes to the heart of many other problems and we must try to solve it.

The Contribution of the Perceiver to His Perception

You argue that the visual system itself *contributes* to the perceptual outcome resulting from stimulation. You have a theory of how this contribution is made in terms of rules for treating the stimulus data. You say that my theory of stimulus information goes to an extreme and does not recognize the contribution of the organism to perception. This is your final and most general criticism.

My answer is that it is false to put into opposition the contribution of the perceiver and the contribution of the external stimulation. It is impossible to weigh the subjectivity of perception against the objectivity of perception. They are not commensurable. If perception is essentially an act of attention, as I maintain, and is not to be confused with imagination, hallucination, or dreaming, then the perceiver does not *contribute* anything to the act of perception, he simply *performs* the act.

When you postulate rules for treating the stimulus data or principles for decoding the data you are taking it for granted that the data themselves are insufficient for perception. You imply that they are meaningless. Both nativist and empiricist theories of perception begin with this assumption. The nativist assumes innate ideas (or the basic "programming" of the nervous system in computer terms) whereas the empiricist assumes acquired memories (or new connections in the nervous system). But both theories are alike in supposing that perception is a process of contributing to the data of sense. My theory of available stimulus information outside the eyes of an observer and explored by him avoids *both* nativism and empiricism.

For me, perception is an awareness of the world. An awareness of the self *accompanies* it but does not *contribute* to it. Proprioception, as I put it, goes along with perception but is not the same thing. There is a subjective aspect and an objective aspect to every phenomenal experience but this does not mean that there is some degree of subjective *determination* of objective perception. The old idea that a perception is determined partly from the outside and partly from the inside is nothing but a muddle of thought. So when you argue that we should avoid the two extremes of perceptual theorizing, the "appeal to subjectivity" on the one hand and the "belief in stimulus information" on the other, I do not agree, for I think the issue is false. It is just as false as the issue between nativism and empiricism.

My theory of perception is not going to be clear unless you understand that it goes hand in hand with a theory of *proprioception*. One cannot be aware of the world without also being more or less aware of existing in the world, sometimes staying in the same place and sometimes moving about or being moved. If this had been clear to you, you would not have said that I had a "locomotor theory" of space perception. Locomotion is one biological function and space perception is another; the former does not explain the latter. I think you still believe that the third dimension must be added to depthless sensations by motion. But I do not any longer believe in the "cues for depth." I think a perceiver picks up information about the layout of the environment directly, and does so more readily when the object moves or when he himself moves.

References

Gibson, J. J. (1968). What gives rise to the perception of motion? *Psychological Review, 75*, 335–346.

Gibson, J. J. (1969). Further thoughts on the perception of rigid motion. In *Contemporary research in honorem Kai von Fieandt sexagenarii* (pp. 57–61). Helsinki: Porvoo.

Gibson, J. J. (1958). Visually controlled locomotion and visual orientation in animals. *British Journal of Psychology, 49*, 182–194.

Gibson, J. J., Olum, P. & Rosenblatt, F. (1955). Parallax and perspective during aircraft landing. *American Journal of Psychology, 68*, 372–385.

Visual Perception of Biological Motion and a Model for its Analysis[†]

Gunnar Johansson

Uppsala University

Abstract: This paper reports the first phase of a research program on visual perception of motion patterns characteristic of living organisms in locomotion. Such motion patterns in animals and men are termed here as biological motion. They are characterized by a far higher degree of complexity than the patterns of simple mechanical motions usually studied in our laboratories. In everyday perceptions, the visual information from biological motion and from the corresponding figurative contour patterns (the shape of the body) are intermingled. A method for studying information from the motion pattern per se without interference with the form aspect was devised. In short, the motion of the living body was represented by a few bright spots describing the motions of the main joints. It is found that 10–12 such elements in adequate motion combinations in proximal stimulus evoke a compelling impression of human walking, running, dancing, etc. The kinetic-geometric model for visual vector analysis originally developed in the study of perception of motion combinations of the mechanical type was applied to these biological motion patterns. The validity of this model in the present context was experimentally tested and the results turned out to be highly positive.

With very few exceptions, research on visual motion perception has dealt with simple patterns of mechanical motions. As a rule, rigid objects in rotary or translatory motion have been chosen as the distal stimuli, and the proximal stimulus patterns investigated have been projections of such objects in motion.

Stimulus patterns representing living animals in motion have rarely been studied. Michotte's (1963) study of perception of larva motion may be pointed to as an important exception. This relative lack of studies concerning visual per-

[†] From *Perception & Psychophysics*, 1973, *14*, 201–211. Reprinted by permission of Psychonomic Society, Inc. This research was supported by a grant from the Swedish Council for Social Science Research. Experimental assistance was provided by Ragnar Johansson.

ception of animal and human motion patterns has no relation to the biological importance of this type of visual perception. It seems evident that, throughout animal evolution, valid information about other animals' motion has achieved a very high survival value.

Our everyday experience also tells us that human vision not only detects motion directions in man and animals, but also distinguishes different standard types of limb motion patterns. We immediately see whether a person is walking, running, or dancing, and also if he is moving forward with identical speed in these three cases. It is also a common experience that our visual apparatus is very sensitive to small deviations from such standard patterns. We immediately recognize, for instance, a slight limp in walking, we distinguish between a tired and an elastic gait, etc. Furthermore, we think we sometimes can recognize a person exclusively from his style of walking, his gestures, etc.

The geometric structures of body motion patterns in man and higher animals (e.g., the patterns of walking) are determined by the construction of their skeletons. Human walking, for instance, as well as the same types of motion in most domestic animals can readily be described as combinations of several pendulum-like motions of the extremities relative to a joint. These motions are often combined with an elastic bending of the spinal column. The time relations in the series of iterated pendulum motions as a rule are highly regular. This interaction brings about a body displacement with a rather constant speed. Different types of human displacement, i.e., walking, running, dancing, skating, etc., are all built up from such combinations of pendulum-like motions, which are highly specific for the different types of motions. The typical character of the pendulum motions about the hip and the knee joints during walking of a young man and their phase relations are shown in Fig. 1.

The present study is the first in a planned series of investigations on perception of such rather complex patterns of live motion and their outcome in body displacement. It will provide an empirical and theoretical basis for forthcoming studies in this field. The aim here will be to study the visual information from

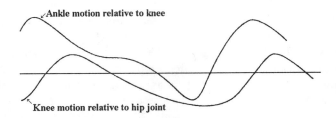

Fig. 1. The relative pendulum motion components of knee and ankle of a walking person. The two motions are plotted against their common time axis, and therefore the diagram also illustrates typical phase relations between the two motions.

some typical motion patterns of the human body when the pictorial form aspect for these patterns has been abstracted. For this purpose, it was important to develop methods for giving the Ss an adequate motion stimulation without any interference from figural perception.

Methods

A Method for Isolating Information in Motion Patterns from Information in Form Patterns

When analyzing motion in physics, it has, as is well known, been found necessary to introduce the concept of *particle*, i.e., abstract mathematical points as carriers of the motion. In an analogous way, it has, in the experimental (and/or theoretical) study of motion perception, sometimes been found advantageous to work with artificially isolated stimulus elements. Bright or dark spots moving against a homogeneous, contrasting background are typical as elements in such experiments.

Allowing such elements to represent the motion structure to be studied experimentally makes it possible to load the structure with well-controlled motion information. A classical example is found in Wertheimer's (1923) demonstration of the "law of common fate." Wertheimer demonstrated that when in a static "Gestalt" built up of a pattern of dots, some dots begin to move in a unitary way, the static form is broken up, and the moving dots form a new unit. Johansson (1950) has applied the same method to the analysis of motion perception in a rather programmatic way. Another example is Green's excellent study of coherence in motion patterns (Green, 1961).

This method of using bright spots as carriers of element motions in complex motion patterns has been applied also in the present study. It will allow us to analyze human motion patterns without interference from the pictorial information inherent in perception of the moving pattern.

It goes without saying that the method described has nothing to do with the old sensation-perception controversy recently reactivated by Gibson (1966). The point motions will not be thought of as some kind of motion sensations. The model here is chosen for methodological reasons and has no theoretical implications. In fact, all experiments applying this method in a highly convincing way demonstrate how a theory of sensation type is extremely inadequate for motion perception.

Methods for Producing the Proximal Patterns of Stimulus Motion

Two bright spots seen in motion against a structureless background are perceived as end points on a moving, invisible, rigid line or rod. In the same way,
four points representing the corners of a square bring about visual information
about motion of a rigid square (Johansson, 1950, 1964; Johansson & Jansson,
1968; Börjesson & von Hofsten 1972, 1973).

From a mechanical point of view, the joints of the human body are end
points of bones with constant length, and at the same time the points of connection between such motion units. Consequently, the motion tracks of the main
joints were chosen as representative motion elements.

So far two similar methods for generating the proximal pattern of spot motion have been developed. The original one makes use of a film technique and,
in a later alternative, a video recording technique is applied. Both of these methods are constructed for producing proximal stimuli representing perfect projections of the live motions under study. In a forthcoming study systematic variations of such patterns will be treated, in which a computer technique will be
applied.

Method 1

This is the originally developed method. Flashlight bulbs (6 V, .5 A) were
fitted into small dull black funnel-shaped holders and attached to the main joints
of an assistant dressed in tight-fitting dark clothes (see Fig. 2). The lamps were
powered by a variable transformer. When the assistant walked over the studio
floor along a rectilinear track, the motion tracks of these joints were recorded by
a 16-mm film camera. There was no lighting in the studio except the faint light
from the flashlight bulbs.

This method gives a very good recording of the motion tracks of the different joints without revealing any traces of the background or the body contours.
However, it has also some limitations and drawbacks. The arrangement with
lamps on the body and their wire connections to a transformer is rather incon-
venient and clumsy, and the problems were serious when other than rectilinear
motion directions were introduced. Therefore, Method 2 was devised.

Method 2

Here a video technique is applied. It has many advantages when compared
with the film technique. The principle, with bright spots representing the joints,
is the same, but these spots are generated in another way with this technique.
The possibilities of manipulating the signal relations in a TV record are taken
advantage of. In this way light-reflecting spots rather than light-emitting spots
can be used.

Small patches of tape (15 mm ∅), which have a surface of glass-bead retroreflective material ("reflex patches"), were attached over the joints of the as-

sistant actor. In one variant, instead of using reflex patches, ribbons of this material were attached around the joints. (This is to be preferred in some studies where the actor is moving in curvilinear tracks.)

The actor is now flooded by the light from one or two searchlights (1,000-4,000W) mounted very close to the lens of a TV camera. In this way, practically all the light hitting the reflex patches is reflected back into the camera. The result is an extremely high brightness contrast between the reflex patches and the background (and consequently a large difference in signal amplitude).

The movements of the actor are recorded by a videotape recorder. In the experiment, this record is displayed on the screen of a TV monitor, adjusted in a special way. Its contrast control is turned to its maximum setting thus yielding a "supercontrast," which amplifies the brightness difference between the reflex patches and the actor's skin. The brightness control is set near its minimum. These control settings result in a blocking of all signals except the high-intensity signals from the reflex patches. These stand out as bright spots with sharp contours against a totally dark screen.

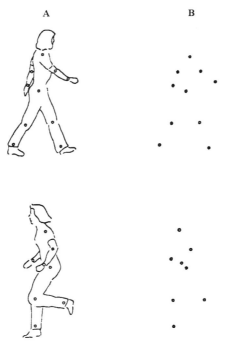

Fig. 2. Outline contours of a walking and a running subject (A) and the corresponding dot configurations (B).

Perception of Walking and Other Related Human Motion Patterns

Demonstration 1

Stimulus Material

The stimulus material will be described here as produced by Method 2.

Reflex patches were fastened to each side of the main limb joints of the "actor," as shown in Fig. 2A. The actor walked in a normal style over the scene from the left to the right and back, in a direction fronto-parallel to the camera lens. About eight steps in each direction were within the angle covered by the camera lens chosen. The start and turning were outside the angle of recording, and therefore the actor was walking into and out of the field of view. Fig. 2B shows the isolated dot pattern in the same moment of motion, and Fig. 3 is an example of motion tracks of the elements during walking.

This motion pattern is displayed on a TV monitor and shown to the Ss. The visual angle subtended by the screen in the experiments was about 15 deg. Thus, the height of the swarm of bright spots representing the walker was about 3 deg. of visual angle. (Ordinarily, in motion-and-space research, it is not recommended that the proximal stimulus be displayed on a visible screen. For discussion, see Johansson (1964). In the present demonstrations, however, it was found to be acceptable.)

The Perception from Demonstration 1

The combination of spot motion in Demonstration 1 when looked at on a TV screen (or, in the film version, on a movie screen) always gives an O the most vivid impression of a person walking in fronto-parallel direction.

This motion pattern has been shown in many class demonstrations as well as under more strict experimental conditions. It always evokes the same spontane-

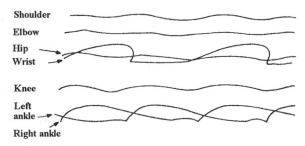

Fig. 3. Typical motion paths of seven elements representing the motions of the right side joints plus the ankle joint of the left leg of a walking person.

ous response after the first one or two steps: This is a walking human being! This perceptual effect has been observed without exception. Perceiving a walking person in the motions of these 10 spots seems to be equally as self-evident and natural as seeing a real man walking in a motion picture. The O has the freedom neither to combine the moving points in other groupings by an act of concentration nor to see these elements just as a series of unrelated points in motion. It might be added that when the motion is stopped, the set of elements is never interpreted as representing a human body (cf. Fig. 2B).

The moving dot pattern from Demonstration 1, together with a number of similar ones representing various types of human bodily activities, is included in a film in progress. This film illustrates some main results from the Uppsala research on visual motion perception.[1]

Because of the manifest character of the perceptual response to this pattern of element motions, it is reported here as a demonstration rather than in terms of an experiment on identification. Before starting an analysis concerning the rationale for the perhaps somewhat unexpected outcome of this stimulus configuration, some important generalizations will be reported.

Demonstration 2

In Demonstration 1, the distal motion path of the actor had a fronto-parallel direction. In this case, the analysis of the proximal pattern is especially simple, because just in this projection the constant lengths of the skeletal bones result in constant distances between their proximally projected end points.

Far more complex geometrically is the general case where the distal track can represent any angle between 0 and 90 deg. to an O's fronto-parallel plane. Under these conditions of projection, the distally constant distances between couples of joints will be represented in the proximal stimulus by continuously changing distances between the elements representing these joints.

From the point of view of theory, this general case is of course more interesting than the fronto-parallel case, but also far more complex. Demonstration 2 shows that, obviously, there do not exist any extra problems for the visual apparatus in its spontaneous "treatment" of such patterns.

Stimulus Material

Either one of the two methods described above can be used for producing the stimulus material. The flashbulbs or the patches of reflex tape are now attached to the frontal side of the actor's main joints. It may be regarded as prefer-

---

[1] Produced by James B. Maas, Cornell University, and distributed by Houghton Mifflin Co., Boston, Massachusetts. It is also possible to receive, from the present writer, at cost, a film copy of some demonstrations described here.

able in this case to attach stimulus patches (or flashbulbs) to the shoulder joints and two hip joints (12 elements instead of 10). However, this is not essential for the result.

The actor is instructed to walk toward the camera in directions between 80 and 45 deg. to the fronto-parallel plane. The scenes are recorded on videotape or film. A lens with rather short focal distance is preferred because of the more drastic change in pattern size during an approach which is obtained in this way.

Results

This pattern has also been shown to a large number of Os both under well-controlled experimental conditions and on motion picture screens in class demonstration. The outcome is wholly analogous to the results from Demonstration 1. All Os immediately reported seeing a person walking toward them. Furthermore, the perceived direction of motion track roughly corresponds to the recorded one.

These results were found without any exception. Every O immediately reported the correct motion pattern. Also, in this case, the degree of perceptual vividness appears to be very high for all Os.

Demonstration 3

Human walking is also readily recognized when the number of recorded elements in the stimulus pattern is reduced. Five elements representing the hip-and-legs part of the pattern in Demonstrations 1 and 2 were used in Demonstration 3.

This element combination has been found to give correct responses irrespective of motion direction. Os always report seeing a walking human being. In most cases the Ss describe this pattern as two walking legs. A few Ss, however, have described the upper point (points) as shoulders of a walking man.

Demonstrations of Other Types of Human Motion Patterns

The walking pattern was chosen as some kind of standard pattern in our studies of human motion. However, a number of other demonstration patterns have also been produced and studied. These patterns include running in different directions and also in a circular track, cycling, climbing, dancing in couples, various types of gymnastic motion, etc. In all these cases, spontaneous and correct identification of the types of activity has been made without exception.

Two Main Lines of Analysis

How can 10 points moving simultaneously on a screen in a rather irregular way give such a vivid and definite impression of human walking? This question forms the main theoretical problem of this paper. We will now take the first steps toward its solution.

The first spontaneous answer to the above question perhaps would be a reference to previous experience. We would guess that there exists a heavy overlearning in seeing human walking, which makes it natural for us to see this motion pattern of the joints' motion as representing a walking man.

Surely, experience plays a certain role, perhaps also a rather important role. We can, for instance, state that the identification of the perceived motion constellations as representing human walking must be an effect of previous experience. But saying that the perceptual grouping of elements is made meaningful by previous visual experience of walking is not the same as saying that the grouping is *determined* by experience. Furthermore, in our case, it was most probably the first time in their lives that our Ss had seen a walking pattern built up from moving spots. Why did these spots evoke the same impression of motion as the outlines of a walking man usually does?

Let us make the problem a little more explicit by raising the following question: Is the perceptual grouping to a human Gestalt determined by a recognition of the walking pattern, or is this recognition dependent on a spontaneous grouping in consequence of some general principles for grouping in visual motion perception?

I think that the best a priori guess would be to suppose that the definite grouping is determined by general perceptual principles, but that the vividness of the percept is a consequence of prior learning. If the grouping were mainly due to learning, we would expect that it might be possible to see, at will, the points as moving independently of each other or to see other structures.

As a matter of fact, my study of biological motion started from the theoretical position that the principles found in studies of perception of mechanical motions should also be revealed in the perceptual outcome from the complicated systems of biological motion. The vividness and strength of the visual motion configurations from biological motion patterns, however, were even more definite than expected. Perhaps the perceptual learning factor is responsible for this effect. In experimental studies to be reported here, as well as in some forthcoming studies, I will try to throw some light on this problem complex. In the next section, I will give an outline of the theoretical framework for a model able to include both mechanical and biological motion patterns.

The geometrical frame finally chosen for this analysis is not the traditional one, based on the parallel axiom, but the geometry of central perspective where convergent lines are also treated as parallel.

Visual Vector Analysis

For many years, the present writer has been engaged, together with a number of co-workers, in research on visual motion perception. Data from this research have successively been condensed to a model for motion and space perception, i.e., the vector analysis model. The presently chosen geometrical frame for this analysis however, is not the ordinary Euclidean one represented by the Cartesian coordinate system. Instead, it is the geometry of central projection from 3-space to 2-space (or 1-space) which has given the reference frame (cf. Johansson, 1971).

This model is not yet fully structured, but its main outline is established. It consists of a set of simple rules for a mathematical vector analysis of the proximal visual experience of walking is not the same as saying motion patterns, within the geometrical framework mentioned, the results of which form a near analogue to the corresponding percept.

Among the studies that yield the basic material for this model of perceptual vector analysis, or that are concerned with its theoretical structure, the following may be mentioned: Rubin (1927), Duncker (1929), Johansson (1950, 1958, 1964, 1966, 1971), Hochberg (1957), Marmolin and Ulfberg (1967), Johansson and Jansson (1968), Börjesson and von Hofsten (1972, 1973). The most complete review to date is found in Johansson (1971).

This model, which initially was worked out from studies of simple mechanical motion perception, has so far been found also to make theoretically understandable the perceptual outcome of biological motion patterns. Therefore, it will be tentatively applied here. Before proceeding to such an analysis, it is advantageous to repeat the main characteristics of this model. This will be done by (1) giving short explicit formulation of the basic principles, and (2) describing a few empirically found examples which have a special bearing for our present analysis of biological motion patterns.

Basic Principles of Visual Vector Analysis

Principle 1

Elements (= inhomogeneities, in the projected light distribution, see p. 188) in motion on the picture plane of the eye are always perceptually related to each other. This principle was investigated in a systematic way in Johansson (1950) (cf. Wertheimer, 1923; Cohen, 1964; Johansson, 1971). As a matter of fact, it can be deduced from most experimental studies of motion perception.

Principle 2

Equal and simultaneous motions in a series of proximal elements automatically connect these elements to rigid perceptual units.

This is, strictly speaking, hardly more than a consequence of Principle 1 above. Far from trivial, however, is the following third principle, which in itself encompasses Principle 2 as a simple special case.

Principle 3

When, in the motions of a set of proximal elements, equal simultaneous motion vectors can be mathematically abstracted (according to some simple rules), these components are perceptually isolated and perceived as one unitary motion. More or less complex hierarchies of equally diverging perceptual motions often turn out to be the consequence of this visual stimulus analysis.

This third principle is, of course, the essential principle of perceptual vector analysis.

The term "equal" introduced in Principles 2 and 3 above has a very special definition. It is, as mentioned above, defined in the framework of central perspective. Equal motion directions and velocities for translatory motion are therefore not only Euclidean parallel motions with the same velocity. (This latter description is valid only for projections from fronto-parallel motion.) The term "equal" also includes all motions (1) that follow tracks that converge to a common point (a point at infinity) on the picture plane, and (2) whose velocities are mutually proportional relative to this point. This will be further developed in connection with the examples. See also, especially, Johansson (1971).

The perceptual motion analysis forms the basic mechanism in visual motion and space perception. It has the consequence that the ever-changing stimulus pattern on the retina is analyzed to maximal rigidity in coherent structures. The finding that it follows in a mechanical way the rules of central perspective means that we automatically obtain perceived size constancy as well as form constancy from projections of rigid objects in motion. However, what is critical for perceiving rigidity is not rigidity in distal objects, but rather, the occurrence of equal motion components in the proximal stimulus. This has been demonstrated in experiments using artificially generated changing light distributions. These experiments have also made clear how this process is fully automatic and independent of cognitive control (see Johansson, 1964, 1971).

Clearly, the vector model for motion perception represents a proximal approach to the stimulus-percept problem and is in this way contrasted with the traditional distally anchored object constancy model.

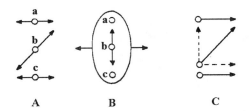

Fig. 4. Examples of the main principle in visual vector analysis. (A) proximal pattern; (B) diagram of the percept from this stimulus combination; (C) vector analysis of the motion of the middle point corresponding to the percept. For further description see text.

Experimental Examples on Visual Vector Analysis

Example 1

This example, illustrated in Fig. 4., shows how a translatory motion in one element in the proximal pattern is perceptually split up into two translatory components in accordance with the principles of perceptual vector analysis. The stimulus pattern consisting of three elements in translatory motion is shown in Fig. 4A. Two elements, a and c, follow horizontal tracks, and the third, b, moves in a diagonal direction. All the three elements move to and from in accordance with a triangular function. They have the same frequency and are in phase. Optimal frequency is .5–1.5 Hz.

An O perceives this pattern as follows: Three dots, forming a vertical line, move horizontally to and fro. During this motion, Point B moves vertically up and down along the line. This percept is given in diagram form in Fig. 4B.

In Fig. 4C, a vector analysis of the motion of element b is given in accordance with the percept description. The diagram demonstrates the correctness of the analysis from the mathematical point of view (cf. Johansson, 1950, 1958; Hochberg, 1957).

Example 2

Fig. 5 presents some proximal combinations of motions of four dots arranged as a square. The motions diagrammed are all examples of Principle 2, above. It is easily understood that Fig. 5A gives the impression of a fronto-parallel motion of a rigid square. The four dots are seen as connected by some invisible rigid structure. Figs. 5B and 5C show proportionally equal motions of the elements relative to Point 1. These patterns always result in perception of motions in depth of a rigid square. For a systematic analysis, see Johansson (1964).

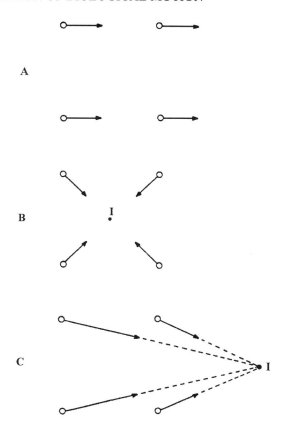

Fig. 5. Three examples of element motion which are equal in the geometry of the model. Element motions or components in element motion of this character are seen as a unit motion. The dots with common motion are seen as forming a rigid unit.

Example 3

Fig. 6 shows a more complex motion pattern. Geometrically, there exists no common element motion here. We can abstract from the element motion, however, a common component of convergence toward Point 1 (point at infinity). Experiments with such patterns have also made it clear that all Ss perceive a motion in depth corresponding to this equal component. The residual components are seen as a form change or sometimes as a rotation in depth (see Johansson, 1964).

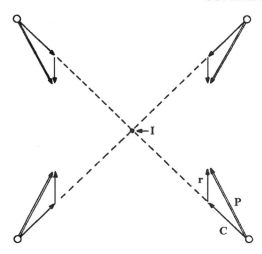

Fig. 6. Motion analysis in a nonperspective shrinking configuration represented by four elements. A common concurrent component (C) in the motion pattern is perceived as a translatory motion in depth. The residual (r) is seen as a shrinking or sometimes as a rotation in depth; p is the physical motion of the element.

Example 4

In Example 3, a rotary motion is sometimes seen. This percept is not stable, and it is, to a certain degree, inadequate from the geometrical point of view. (We have here some kind of ambiguity between polar and parallel projection.) Example 4 illustrates a case of vector analysis with an enforcing and mathematically correct perception of rotation.

Let the two points, C and P, in Fig. 7a represent the axle point and the periphery point on a wheel rolling along a straight line in a fronto-parallel direction relative to an O.

From geometry, we know that the center point in such a configuration will describe a translatory motion and that the peripheral point will describe so-called cycloids, as indicated in the figure. A cycloid (which is a special type of trochoid) can be described mathematically as composed of a circular-motion component and translatory-motion component equal to the motion of the center point of the circle.

If only Point P is visible to the O, he will always describe (or draw) it as moving in a curve, as in Fig. 7b. Adding Point C, however, immediately changes the perceived motion of P. The following description is typical: "I see one of the points rotating around the other one. Both move forward together. It is like a rolling wheel." This percept is diagrammed in Fig. 7c.

It is evident that this percept description represents a correct mathematical vector analysis. The motion of P is split up in one component common with the

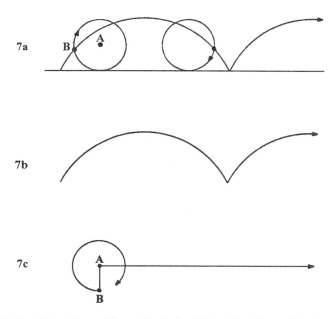

Fig. 7. (a) A point on the periphery of a circle which rolls without slip along a line is generating a cycloidal curve. The center point, A, generates a straight line. All points between A and B describe prolate cycloids. (b) The percept from exposure of Point B alone; the point is seen as moving in a cycloidal track. (c) Percept from exposure of both center point and periphery point; Point A is seen to rotate about Point B while B is moving in a linear track. The two points are seen as rigidly connected and, therefore, AB is perceived motion of (a) represents a correct analysis of its motion in a circular and a translatory component.

motion of the center point, C, and a residual rotary component. This perceptual vector analysis gives no option. Perception of combinations of trochoidal motions has been the subject of a recent study (Johansson, 1973).

Example 5

Our last example concerns perception of pendulum motions and therefore has a direct bearing on perception of human motion patterns. Fig. 8 shows three combinations of motions in two elements, perceptually representing the end points of a rod in pendulum motion (cf. Principle 1 above). Experiments have shown that change of angle, but at a constant distance between the elements, results in perception of a fronto-parallel pendulum motion (Fig. 8A), and that change of both angle and distance produce perception of a pendulum motion in depth (Fig. 8B).

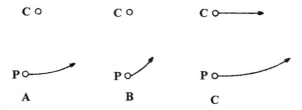

Fig. 8. Three pendulum motion combinations of two stimuli. (A) This combination is perceived as a fronto-parallel pendulum motion of Point P about C (constant distance between the elements, but change of angle). (B) This is always reported as a pendulum motion in plane in a certain angle (30–60 deg.) to the fronto-parallel plane (change of distance and angle). (C) is finally seen as the same pendulum motion as in (B), but the axis is now moving during the cycle.

In Fig. 8C, we finally meet again a case of perceptual vector analysis. This motion pattern is built up from the pattern in Fig. 8B plus an equal component of translation added to both elements. This common component is effectively separated perceptually and seen as a reference frame for the pendulum motion.

Analysis of the Walking Pattern

The experimental examples, 1–5, given above have one characteristic in common: In the proximal pattern, a component can be mathematically subtracted that is common for all elements in the configuration. We have also stated that such a perceptual separation of common motion components from the rest of the motion pattern has always been found in experiments critical in this respect. This perceptual separation of a common component is a typical example of perceptual vector analysis.

When the common component was subtracted in the examples given, the residual motion formed a translatory motion, a rotary motion, or a pendulum motion. These motions were also perceived in accordance with the mathematical analysis. The main conclusion exemplified with these examples is that the common motion is just a reference frame for the deviating component. Changes in this component do not change the perceived primary motion: the rotation, pendulum motion, etc. (In this sense, also, the static background forms a common motion state: the null motion.)

The motion patterns of the element combination forming the demonstrations of biological motion as described above can be analyzed in the same way by subtracting common motion components. In this analysis, the semitranslatory motion of the hip and shoulder elements (= the trunk) will be found in the motions of all elements. The motions of the knees and the elbows are rigid pendulum motions relative to this moving reference frame. Thus, the motions of these elements ought to be perceived in exactly the same way as the corresponding elements in Examples 4 and 5 above (cf. Figs. 7 and 8).

The principle, however, can also be applied to the ankle and wrist elements. We are in this case concerned with the next step in a hierarchy of reference frames. The ankle describes a pendulum motion relative to the knee motion, which, in its turn, is a pendulum motion relative to the hip, while the hip describes a translatory motion relative to the ground. This is diagrammed in Fig. 9.

The motion of the hip (and shoulder) forms a common component in this analysis, inherent in all the other element motions relative to the ground. This fact affords the possibility of testing the validity of the motion analysis model when it is a question of biological motion. Let us raise the question: Is the recognition of walking from the motion of our 10 points independent of the course of the common component?

It is evident that when accepting the motion analysis model as hypothetically valid for live motion perception also, we have to give an affirmative answer to this question. This fact was used for a partial test of the general applicability of the motion analysis model. Accepting the model enforces us to the following prediction: The semitranslatory component in walking (cf. Fig. 3), which is inherent in the motion of all our 10 elements, will play no decisive role for the identification of this pattern. Therefore, introducing drastic experimental changes in the common translatory component can be used as a test of the validity of the model.

It is also evident that accepting a hypothesis that identification of the walking patterns were due primarily to extended experience and overlearning would result in another prediction about the outcome from the experiment proposed. From this starting point, we have to assume that drastic changes of the most important component in walking will more or less destroy the identification. In this way, the experiment under discussion to a certain extent is critical also for the choice between a theory based on the experience factor and a model of the information analysis type.

The hypothesis testing discussed was carried out in the following three experiments.

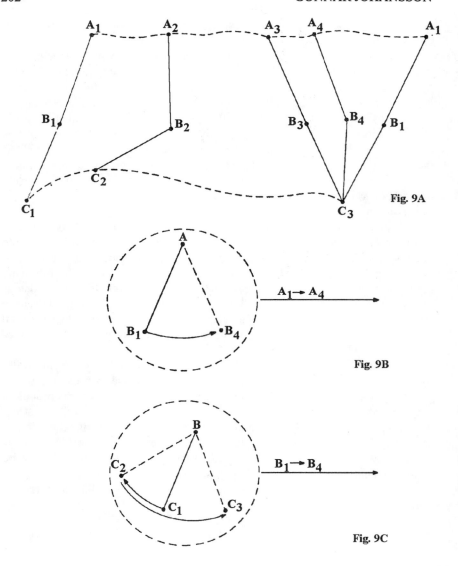

Fig. 9. Graphical analysis of leg motion during walking in accordance with the model of perceptual motion analysis. (A) The motions relative to the static background of the hip (A), the knee (B), and the ankle (C) during one step. (B) The common semi-translatory component in A and B and the residual pendulum motion of B relative to the common component. (C) The common component in B and C and the residual pendulum motion in C.

Experiment 1

This experiment was designed to study the effect of subtracting a common component from the element motions in the walking pattern.

A typical diagram of the elements' motion tracks in walking patterns and their time relations is given in Fig. 3. The slightly wavy motion track of the hip (and the shoulder) in this diagram represents the maximum of equal motion in this combination of element motions.

This wavy motion can be looked upon as composed of two components: a major, horizontally directed one and a minor, vertical component.

In the experiment, we will subtract only this horizontal translatory component, leaving the up-and-down motion as a small common motion residual. (The reasons for this are technical.)

Method

The video technique described above was applied. About 10 steps of fronto-parallel walking over the scene were recorded. With one exception, the recording arrangements were exactly the same as in the recording of Demonstration 1, described above. The exception was that by careful panoraming, the actor's image during the recording was "locked" in a hair cross marking on the monitor screen. In this way, the horizontal translatory motion of the dot pattern was subtracted from the record.

The stimulus pattern was presented to the Ss against a background of total darkness. This was accomplished in the following way: The TV monitor was placed in a dark tunnel, 5 m in length. In the front gable of this tunnel was a window measuring 15 x 8 cm. The tunnel was placed in a normally lit room. Therefore a visual-contrast black was seen through the window. The Ss were told to look binocularly into the tunnel.

Owing to this arrangement, the Ss could see the room and the outside of the tunnel but not any traces of the inside of the tunnel through the window or the TV screen. The pattern of bright spots was seen against a homogeneous black background. (A consequence of this was that some Ss reported seeing the walking pattern as a real, little manikin walking in the back part of the tunnel. The strange miniature size of the walker was, of course, due to the conditions with perceived tunnel size, the angular size of the pattern, and the total darkness in the tunnel.)

Procedure and subjects. Ten students from another faculty took part as Ss and were tested for spontaneous recognition of the pattern. None had seen our biological motion pattern before or knew that they would be shown such a pattern. They were given a neutral instruction to describe what they saw through the tunnel window. After seeing a full scene (about 10 steps), they had to describe what they had perceived.

In addition to these naive Ss, a number of Ss who had seen human walking patterns before were tested.

Result

All Ss immediately reported seeing a walking person. The perceived miniature size was sometimes commented on. Some of the Ss also spontaneously described the event as a walking on some kind of a moving belt. The (invisible) ground then was experienced as moving backward.

Experiment 2

The 100% correct recognition responses in Experiment 1 made it necessary to manipulate the amount of information given to the Ss. The consecutive steps in the sequence mentioned mean a tenfold iteration of the step cycle and thus a considerable redundancy. Therefore, in Experiment 2, a tachistoscopic presentation was introduced.

Procedure and Subjects

A presentation time of 1.0 sec was chosen. This means that the S was shown a little less than half a step cycle (one "step"). This interval was chosen randomly during the walking period. Technically, the exposure time was controlled by an electronic timer switching the electron beam of the picture tube on and off. In other respects, the stimulus material and the arrangements were identical with those described under Experiment 1. The same holds true for the choice of Ss. Ten naive Ss took part.

Result

After the first exposure, all Ss, without any hesitation, reported seeing a walking human being.

Experiment 3

In Experiments 1 and 2, a common motion component was subtracted. From the point of view of vector analysis, this can be regarded as representing a simplification of the original stimulus pattern. In Experiment 3, the opposite principle was applied. Here, instead, an extra component was added to the primary motion of each element. This extra motion was a circular motion with a diameter of the circle covering about one-third of the distance between the foot and the shoulder elements.

This extra component was produced by an arrangement with a slowly rotating mirror in front of the camera lens, oriented at a 45-deg. angle to the optical axis of the lens. The mirror was mounted on its axle at an angle which deviated somewhat from 90 deg. Therefore, when the mirror rotated, the image was not stable but described a circular motion. The mirror reflected into the TV camera the scene to be recorded, and in this way the extra component was generated.

The scene recorded in this way was the same as in Demonstration 1 and in Experiment 1.

This stimulus pattern contains a rather complex common motion. It is the result of an addition to the ordinary semitranslatory common component in the walking pattern of a superposed rotary motion. Mathematically, it is an approximation to a special form of trochoid (a curtate cycloid). See also Example 4 above, where the element on the periphery of the rolling wheel describes pure cycloids.

Procedure and Subjects

A stimulus sequence of three to four steps was shown to 10 Ss under the same experimental conditions as in Experiment 1. Furthermore, the same sequence was shown a little more informally to a group of Os, who had seen Demonstration 1.

Results

All Ss immediately reported seeing a walking man. The walking pattern seems to be spontaneously seen in the same way as in Demonstration 1 and in Experiment 1. All Ss also said that the walker moved in a highly strange, "wavy" way.

Conclusions from Experiments 1–3

The experiments were designed for limited hypothesis testing. The results are highly conclusive. The general result is that subtracting or adding common components to the element motions do not have a disturbing effect on the identification of the walking pattern.

This result means that, in the essential respects covered by the hypothesis underlying the experiments, the vector analysis type of model has also proved valid for perception of complex motion patterns representing biological motion.

Discussion

The demonstrations described have in a conclusive way made clear that 5–10 elements in adequate combinations of proximal motion give the visual system highly efficient information about human motion. Five points are enough for identification of human legs in motion.

From the theoretical reasons given above, a more or less positive outcome was expected from the experimentation with such point patterns. The overwhelmingly positive result reported here, however, was a surprise. In short, the results mean that the proximal motion patterns presented have been found to carry all the essential information needed for immediate visual identification of such human motions.

In the formulation of the problem, the question was raised about the role of experience in the identification of biological motion patterns. It seems to me that the experimental answer is rather decisive. We can, with a high degree of confidence, conclude that it was not previous learning of motion patterns which determined the perception of walking in our Experiments 1–3. Instead, we have found that it seems to be a highly mechanical, automatic type of visual data treatment that is most important. Mathematically lawful spatio-temporal relations in the proximal stimulus pattern (complex or impoverished) determine the perceptual response. Strongly in favor of such a position is also the unexpected result from Experiment 2, namely the finding that an unfamiliar dot pattern becomes perceptually organized in less than 1 sec.

At the same time, we ought to remember that what the experiments have shown is the validity of some main principles determining the *possibility* of recognizing a biologically meaningful motion type in spite of more or less drastic changes in the original proximal pattern. It seems very probable that the vividness in the perception and the 100% correct responses which have been so typical for identifying the patterns as human motions can be derived from prior perceptual learning.

The model for stimulus-percept analysis which has been applied here is in a programmatic way anchored in a geometric-kinetic analysis of proximal stimulus. This anchorage in the proximal stimulus is a consequence of the insight that all the information available is given in the continuously changing light distribution entering the pupil.

Biological motion represents motion combinations which are far more complex than the mechanical motions from the studies of which the model originally was developed. So far, however, this model of proximal motion analysis has proved valid for biological motion, too.

The model describes visual motion perception as being built up from structuring the changing proximal pattern in hierarchies of equal and deviating motion components. Our experimental tests of the validity of the model for biological motion have studied only the effects of manipulation of equal components of the first degree, that is, motion components common for all motion elements. Thus, the tests, while perfectly positive for the applicability of the model, must be regarded as more or less partial. At the same time, however, these experiments may be regarded as a highly informative first step in a more conclusive series of experimental checks aiming at verification/falsification (or modification) of the model. The rationale for this is easy to give. When the model has been found to predict adequately the basic effects of motion analysis we have good reasons for expecting it to also cover (perhaps after some modification) some remaining, more limited aspects of visual information from the proximal stimulus.

References

Börjesson, E., & von Hofsten. C. (1972). Spatial determinants of depth perception in two-dot motion patterns. *Perception & Psychophysics, 11*, 263–268.

Börjesson, E., & von Hofsten, C. (1973). Visual perception of motion in depth: Application of a vector model to three-dot motion patterns. *Perception & Psychophysics, 13*, 169–179.

Cohen, R. (1964). *Problems in motion perception.* Uppsala: Almqvist & Wiksell.

Duncker, K. (1929). Über induzierte Bewegung (On induced motion). *Psychologische Forschung, 12*, 180–259.

Gibson, J. J. (1966). *The senses considered as perceptual systems.* New York: Houghton & Mifflin.

Green, B. F. (1961). Figure coherence in the kinetic depth effect. *Journal of Experimental Psychology, 62*, 272–282.

Hochberg, J. E. (1957). Effects of the gestalt revolution: The Cornell Symposium on Perception. *Psychological Review, 64*, 73–84.

Johansson, G. (1950). *Configurations in event perception.* Uppsala: Almqvist & Wiksell. [Chapter2, this volume.]

Johansson, G. (1958). Rigidity, stability, and motion in perceptual space. *Acta Psychologica, 14*, 359–370. [Chapter 3, this volume.]

Johansson, G. (1964). Perception of motion and changing form. *Scandinavian Journal of Psychology, 5*, 181–208. [Chapter 4, this volume.]

Johansson, G. (1966). Geschehenswahrnehmung (Event perception). In W. Metzger (Ed.), *Handbuch der Psychologie, Band 1, Wahrnehmung und Bewusstsein* (pp. 745–775). Berlin: Springer.

Johansson, G. (1973). *Motion perception. A model for visual motion and space perception from changing proximal stimulation* (Report No. 98). Uppsala University, Department of Psychology.

Johansson, G., & Jansson, G. (1968). Perceived rotary motion from changes in a straight line. *Perception & Psychophysics, 4*, 165–170.

Marmolin, H., & Ulfberg, S. (1967). *Motion perception and form change.* Unpublished report. Uppsala University, Department of Psychology.

Michotte, A. (1963). *The perception of causality* (T. R. Miles & E. Miles, Trans.). London: Methuen. (Original work published 1946.)

Rubin, E. (1927). Visuell wahrgenommene wirklische Bewegungen (Visually perceived real motions). *Zeitschrift für Psychologie, 103*, 384–392.

Wertheimer, M. (1923). Untersuchungen zur Lehre von der Gestalt (Studies on the theory of the Gestalt). *Psychologische Forschung, 4*, 301–350.

Spatio-Temporal Differentiation and Integration in Visual Motion Perception[†]

An Experimental and Theoretical Analysis of Calculus-Like Functions in Visual Data Processing

Gunnar Johansson

Uppsala University

Abstract: Perceptual organization during short tachistoscopic presentation of stimulus patterns formed by 10 moving bright spots, representing a human body in walking, running, etc., was investigated. Exposure times were .1 sec to .5 sec.

The results reveal that in all Ss the dot pattern is perceptually organized to a "gestalt," a walking, running, etc., person at an exposure time of .2 sec. 40% of Ss perceived a human body in such motion at presentation times as short as 0.1 sec. Under the experimental conditions used the track length of the bright spots at the threshold of integration to a moving unit was of the size order 10' visual angle.

This result is regarded as indicating that a complex vector analysis of the proximal motion pattern is accomplished at the initial stage of physiological signal recording and that it is a consequence of receptive field organization. It is discussed in terms of vector calculus.

Introduction

In a recent paper (Johansson, 1973a) the present writer reported that a few bright spots (5–12) in adequate simultaneous motions evoke a vivid impression of a walking, running, etc., human being. The technical principle applied is to represent each of the main joints under study (hip, knee, ankle, shoulder, elbow,

---

[†] From *Psychological Research*, 1976, *38*, 379–393. Received September 1, 1975.

wrist) by a bright spot tracing the motion of the joint.[1] It was further shown that the visual processing of the proximal stimulus pattern could be described in terms of a vector analysis of the element motions in common and relative components.

During the experimental studies of such biological motion patterns formed by a number of moving spots it was also found that the percept of the motion of, for instance, a walking man could be structured in a fraction of a second. This finding, which was hardly expected, has an evident theoretical interest. It highlights an aspect of perceptual processing of changing stimulation which to my knowledge has not been studied in a direct way. Described in mathematical terms this visual process under perceptually liminal time conditions implies an analogue to a differentiation of motion vectors together with an integration to common and relative motions.

A detailed study and theoretical analysis of these temporal aspects of motion perception was regarded as a task of its own and left to a separate investigation. In the present paper such a study will be reported. It deals with the type of motion pattern described: the motions relative to a static background of the joints of a walking man. Some later preexperiments using nonsense combinations of similar mechanical motions have indicated that these also will be perceptually organized to complex units in the same short time interval. Therefore, the effects mentioned most probably are indicators of a basic way of sensory data treatment.

Experiment 1

Problem

What is the liminal time interval for perceptual integration to meaningful unit of a number of element motions representing human limb-body movements?

Method

Ten bright spots representing the motions of the ten visible main joints of a man walking in fronto-parallel direction relative to the observer were displayed on a TV-monitor screen (see Fig. 1). The screen was seen through a window in the front end of a dark tunnel, 4 m in length. The monitor was set up in the rear end of the tunnel. The visual angle between the shoulder and ankle elements in the swarm of dots was about 3° and the pattern was presented to the Ss in binocular vision.

---

[1] A demonstration of this effect is given in full length in two educational films from Houghton C. Mifflin produced by James B. Maas: Motion perception I, Motion perception II.

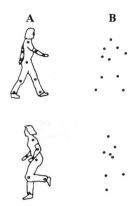

Fig. 1. Outline contours of a walking and a running subject (A) and the corresponding dot configurations (B)

The motion pattern was produced in accordance with the video technique described in Johansson (1973a). It was recorded on videotape and played back on the monitor. The electron beam of the monitor was blacked electronically, except for small time intervals. An electronic timer controlled these time intervals. No fixation point was given, but Ss were instructed to fixate the center of the visual field when a signal was given.

The following series of exposure times was chosen: .1 sec, .2 sec, .3 sec, .5 sec. A pilot study had indicated that .5 sec always gives a clear percept of a walking man. The lower limit (.1 sec) was set primarily for technical reasons, namely the scanning frequency of the video system.

E observed a second monitor out of S's sight and manually released the stimulus pattern to the S's monitor when the image of the walker passed the center of the screen. The exposures were sampled randomly from a continuous record, and therefore the phase of the step cycle varied randomly from exposure to exposure. Thus, there was a random variation of the proximal pattern both at intra-subject and inter-subject level. The fixation signal was given 1–2 sec before exposure. The series of exposures was given in increasing order, starting with the shortest exposure time. Each exposure time was given only once. The verbal reports from Ss were recorded by a tape recorder.

Instructions

The Ss were told that they would be shown "something" moving in the rear end of the tunnel during a very short period of time. They were instructed to describe verbally immediately after each exposure what they had perceived. The instruction also required Ss to fixate the center of the field when signaled to do so.

Table 1. Proportion of Ss who perceived a walking man. Four exposures, .1–.5 sec length, given in serial order. N = 10.

Duration sec	Proportion correct responses
.1	4/10
.2	10/10
.3	10/10
.5	10/10

Subjects

Ten students from a gymnasium (senior high school), age 16–18, took part in the experiment as paid Ss. They were totally ignorant about the problem and about the type of pattern to be shown. Communication between "used" and "unused" Ss was prevented.

Results

The reports fell into two categories: descriptions in terms of (1) a walking human being and (2) a number of bright spots in unorganized motion. Table 1 shows for each time interval the number of reports belonging to category (1).

The table shows that for all Ss an exposure time of .2 sec was enough for perceptual organization of the pattern to a meaningful unit. Four Ss out of ten perceived a walking human being already during the shortest time interval. Thus, .1 sec seems to be something like a mean threshold for this type of pattern.

Discussion

The variation in detection at the .1 sec interval was probably to some extent a consequence of the variation over subjects of amount of useful information resulting from the random phase sampling over the step cycle.

In the experiment only the exposure time factor is varied, not the speed of motion. Of course the exposure threshold, Δt, must be thought of as dependent on the corresponding displacement, Δs, measured in visual angle. From the stimulus description given above, we can find that the angular displacement of the hip and shoulder elements during a tenth of a second amounts to about 12 minutes of arc. This ought to be compared with the traditional acuity measure (1') for static vision. A motion over about 10 static threshold steps has here proved to be enough for complex organization of the type studied.

Experiment II

Problem

In Experiment I the problem was the minimum time necessary for perceptual interpretation to an organized unit of the swarm of moving dots. The next step concerns liminal time for identification of specific types of motion patterns in such a unit and this formed the problem for Experiment II. In this experiment S's task was to identify the type of motion pattern presented during a short time interval. Thus the perceptual task was now to differentiate under liminal time conditions between the motion patterns of the joints in, e.g., a walking and a running person. The Ss had to choose between 9 different patterns of this type.

Method

The same method for stimulus generation and presentation as in Experiment I was used. However, nine different patterns were presented. Six of these were recorded from real human motion and three from devices of the type used on puppet shows, crudely simulating human limb motions. The series consisted of the following: (1) walking to the right, (2) walking to the left, (3) walking backwards right, (4) walking backwards left, (5) slowly running (jogging) to the right and (6) to the left, (7) puppet "walking" right, (8) puppet "walking" left, (9) frontal "jumping jack" motion.

The translatory component in the human motions was subtracted from the records by carefully "panning" the moving object during video recording, in order to avoid this type of directional information. Also the puppets were recorded as stationary. Thus, the shoulder and hip spots were approximately stationary in all patterns and only the limbs described their characteristic combinations of pendulum motions. The nine patterns were presented in random order in five time intervals between .1 and .5 sec. As in Experiment I the phase of motion was chosen at random for each exposure, thus making impossible the mechanical recognition of the patterns.

Instructions

The session started by showing Ss all patterns in the series and asking them to describe each pattern in the terms given above. Ss never had any difficulty in identifying the patterns. Then S was told that he/she would be shown these patterns during very short time intervals and had to try to identify them. If necessary a blank answer could be given.

Subjects

Ten students from a gymnasium took part as paid Ss. They had not had any previous contact with this type of experiments.

Table 2. Percepts from nine different motion patterns and five exposure durations. (1) walking right (WR), (2) walking left (WL), (3) walking backward right (WBR), (4) walking backward left (WBL), (5) running right (RR), (6) running left (RL), (7) puppet "walking" right (PR), (8) puppet "walking" left (PL), (9) frontal jumping jack (PF). Exposure duration- .1, .2, .3, .4, .5 sec. N = 10.

Table 2a. Stimulus duration .1 sec.

STIMULUS								
PERCEPT	WR	WL	WBR	WBL	RR	RL	PR	PL	PF
WR	8			5	1		1	1	
WL		5	5	1		1	5		2
WBR			1				1		
WBL				2	2			1	
RR	1			1	4			4	1
RL	1	2	3			5	1	1	1
PR					2		2		
PL						1		3	
PF		1							5
	10	8	9	9	9	7	10	10	9

Table 2b. Stimulus duration .2 sec.

STIMULUS								
PERCEPT	WR	WL	WBR	WBL	RR	RL	PR	PL	PF
WR	9		1	2			1		
WL		9	2	2				4	
WBR			4	1					
WBL			1	5			2		
RR	1		1		7		1	1	
RL		1				9			
PR					3		4		
PL			1				1	3	1
PF						1		1	9
	10	10	10	10	10	10	9	9	10

Table 2c. Stimulus duration .3 sec.

PERCEPT	WR	WL	WBR	WBL	RR	RL	PR	PL	PF
				STIMULUS					
WR	10			1					
WL		9	1	1				3	
WBR			8						
WBL				8				1	
RR					9			1	
RL		1				10	1		
PR					1		8		
PL			1				1	5	
PF									10
	10	10	10	10	10	10	10	10	10

Table 2d. Stimulus duration .4, .5 sec.

PERCEPT	WR	WL	WBR	WBL	RR	RL	PR	PL	PF
				STIMULUS					
WR	10								
WL		10							
WBR			10						
WBL				10					
RR					10				
RL						10			
PR							10		
PL								10	
PF									10
	10	10	10	10	10	10	10	10	10

Results

The results are summarized in Table 2. At intervals as short as .1 sec four out of nine patterns were correctly recognized by more than 50% of Ss. With an exposure time of .4 sec all Ss had given a correct response. With minimum detection time as a criterion the difficulty varied between the patterns. As seen in Table 2 the "artificial" patterns with profile puppets were hardest to recognize. This may be an effect of familiarity with real human movement patterns. However, the frontal puppet with symmetric jumping jack movements apparently was special enough to be rapidly identified.

Comments

The common translatory component in the stimulus pattern was excluded in this experiment. Left as source of information about coherence were only the various pendulum motions of the limbs. In the thigh bones these motions usually covered an arc peak-to-peak of about 35°–40° while the arc traced by the shin-bones is of the same order of size or somewhat larger. Converted to measures in terms of visual angle traced by the knee element during .1 sec we get a maximum length of about 18' and a minimum length of about 1'. The actual length of course was determined by the randomly chosen phase interval. Table 2 shows that "real" forward walking was correctly identified by more than 50% of the Ss at the .1 sec interval. At the .2 sec interval the same holds true for the whole spectrum of motion patterns.

Discussion

Visual motion perception implies recording, in a functionally effective way, spatial change as a function of time, $s = f(t)$. Our experiments have demonstrated that also within a perceptually liminal time interval an analysis of the proximal motion pattern has been accomplished which, when described in mathematical terms, must be rather advanced. The relations between the proximal pattern of element motion and its perceptual correlate indicate that it might be adequate to describe the basic process of sensory data treatment in terms of vector calculus. Consequently, we will apply such a model to our results. The perceptual process will be described in terms of (1) a continuous perceptual vector differentiation and (2) a simultaneously ongoing integration of the vector differentials thus abstracted.[2]

Perceptual Vector Differentiation

The basis for our analysis was given in Johansson (1973a). In this paper a model for perceptual vector analysis of the motion patterns of the human limb joints was elaborated. It was shown how the perceptual "treatment" of the proximal flow of energy corresponds to an analysis of the proximal motion of the joints in vector components, common for all elements and in components of element-relative motions. In the present paper Experiment I gives a typical example. The shoulder and hip elements form a perceptual unit, moving horizontally in the frontal plane. Relative to this unit the elbow and knee elements are seen as describing pendulum motions. In an analogous way the wrist and ankle elements perceptually are performing pendulum motions relative to the elbow and knee, respectively. Because of the similarity between the motion patterns of

---

[2] Cf. the discussion about perceptual space/time derivatives in Johansson, 1966, 1974c.

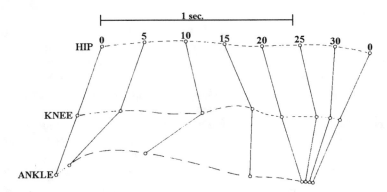

Fig. 2. Typical paths of the hip, knee, and ankle elements over one step cycle, plotted from a film record. The paths are recorded relative to the static background and the time scale is given in units of five film frames with equal time intervals.

the arm and leg systems we will in the following limit our analysis to the hip-knee-ankle system. In Experiment II the translatory hip motion component was canceled out. In our analysis, however, we will treat the general case exemplified by the stimulus pattern in Experiment I.

In accordance with the percept description given we will analyze the proximal pattern as motions relative to a set of reference systems, one fixed and anchored to the perceptually static space and two moving relative to the fixed one. Typical paths of the three elements relative to the static background are shown in Fig. 2.

The stimulus represents a fronto-parallel motion and thus the simplest case from the point of view of projection. This makes the following analysis relatively simple because distally constant distances between the elements are projected as constant distances. For a discussion about perspective projections and visual perception see Johansson (1974a, 1974c).

In Fig. 3 let A represent the hip element of a walking man, let B represent the knee, and C the ankle point of the same leg. The motions of these three stimulus elements in accordance with Fig. 2 and over an interval of time, Δt, will be described in terms of vector calculus in a way corresponding to the percept description. As our primary reference frame we choose a static two-dimensional Cartesian coordinate system (O, x, y), forming a scalar field with the unit vectors i and j in the x and y dimensions, respectively.

At time (t) the element A is at position (x_A, y_A). Thus, at this moment its position vector (denoted $\overline{OA}$) is

$$\overline{OA}(t) = \bar{i} x_A + \bar{j} y_A \tag{1}$$

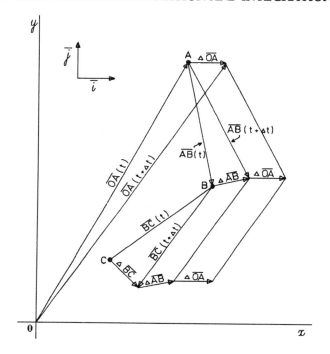

Fig. 3. Perceptual change of position vectors over an interval of time (Δt) in one fixed and two moving systems. See text.

At time ($t + \Delta t$) its position vector is

$$\overline{OA}(t+\Delta t) = \overline{OA} + \Delta\overline{OA} = \bar{i}(x_A + \Delta x_A) + \bar{j}(y_A + \Delta y_A) \tag{2}$$

as shown in Fig. 3.

Accordingly the velocity vector of A, (v_A) can be determined by differentiation as

$$\overline{v}_A = \frac{d\overline{OA}}{dt} = \frac{d\overline{OA}}{ds} \qquad \frac{ds}{dt} = \bar{i}\frac{dx_A}{dt} + \bar{j}\frac{dy_A}{dt} \tag{3}$$

with s measured along the path of the element. However, because we are dealing with element motions along curvilinear paths, it is more convenient to speak in terms of tangential ($\overline{T}$) and normal ($\overline{N}$) unit vectors:

$$\overline{T} = \bar{i}\cos\phi + \bar{j}\sin\phi \tag{4}$$

where ϕ is the angle between the x-axis and the tangent to the motion path. $\overline{N}$ is obtained by rotating $\overline{T}$ 90° counter clockwise. Then, because

$$\overline{T}_A = \frac{d\overline{OA}}{ds} \tag{5}$$

and with reference to Equation (3) the velocity vector $\overline{v}_A$ can be written

$$\overline{v}_A = \overline{T}_A \frac{ds}{dt} \tag{6}$$

Instantaneous sensory information about radius of curvature of the motion path and about the two components of acceleration in the relation between elements has been found to play an important role in visual motion perception. In order to formalize also these aspects of visual analysis of proximal patterns of motion we differentiate Equation (6) with respect to time. This gives the acceleration vector (a) with its two components, the tangential and the normal ones:

$$\overline{a} = \frac{d\overline{v}}{dt} = \overline{T} \frac{d^2 s}{dt^2} + \overline{N} \frac{v^2}{|\rho|} \tag{7}$$

where ρ is the radius of curvature at the point under study. For perceptually rectilinear paths the normal component of course is zero.

So far we have performed a traditional differentiation of the proximal motion of the element A. More interesting is our next step which deals with the perceptual motion of element B, the knee element. As pointed to above this element will not be described as moving in the same reference system as A (the coordinate system O, x, y). It is perceived as moving relative to A. Therefore in order to bring the mathematical description in correspondence with the percept we have to introduce a secondary reference system, a parallel coordinate system moving relative to the primary system. This moving system has the same unit vectors as the fixed system. We denote it O*, x*, y* and give it the motion of the element A in the fixed system. In this starred coordinate system the equation for the velocity vector of element B is analogous to the equation for element A in the static system (Equation 3), thus

$$\overline{v}_B* = \overline{i} \frac{dx_B*}{dt} + \overline{j} \frac{dy_B*}{dt} = \overline{T}_B \frac{ds*}{dt} \tag{8}$$

Because of the relation between the two coordinate systems we get:

$$\overline{v}_B = \overline{v}_A + \overline{v}_B* \tag{9}$$

which indicates that the proximal velocity of B is treated as the sum of two independent components.

The thigh-bone describes pendulum motions about the hip joint and there-fore the knee element traces an arc of a circle in our coordinate system O^*, x^*, y^*. This means that in the starred system the distance between A and B is kept constant and that a normal component of acceleration of B at every moment is directed toward A. It has previously been found that a characteristic in a proxi-mal pattern allowing such an interpretation generally is determining for the per-ceptual structuring (Johansson & Jansson, 1968; Börjesson & von Hofsten, 1972, 1973; Johansson, 1974a, 1974b). This holds true not only for the simple case of fronto-parallel projection studied here, but is a general rule. The theo-retical importance of the present results and what the mathematical model will indicate is the demonstration that the sensory relation A - B is formed instanta-neously.

The perceptual analysis of the motion of the foot element (C) forms a close parallel to that of the knee element and need not be carried out in detail. It re-sults in a geometrically correct percept of C as describing a circular path with the moving element B as the center. Consequently we introduce in our model a second moving coordinate system, denote it O^{**}, x^{**}, y^{**} and give it the mo-tion of B relative to the basic reference system. The proximal velocity vector motion of C as specified in this double-starred system (v_c^{**}) covers the percept and we get the following relation:

$$\overline{v}_C = \overline{v}_A + \overline{v}_B{}^* + \overline{v}_C{}^{**} \tag{10}$$

indicating that the proximal motion of C is broken up into three separate mo-tions.

About Principles Determining Visual Vector Differentiation

We have found that the chosen set of coordinate systems in relative motion gives a simple model for the stimulus-percept relations under study. However, so far the model may look like an ad hoc construction which perhaps is valid only for the stimulus pattern studied. A critical reader probably already has asked for an anchorage of the analysis in principles covering perceptual interpretations also of other types of proximal motion patterns. This question is justified and in fact it touches on a research problem which I regard as basic but still far from solved. At present only some main lines toward formulation of generally valid principles can be discerned, but in fact it is these approximations that have formed a background for the above analysis. I would like to make the relevant part of this background explicit in the following tentative form.

1) Spontaneous isolation of sets of spatially invariant relations in the stimul-us flow (search for perceptual form and size constancy) is a generic principle in the visual analysis.

2) In the relation between moving perceptual units, as specified above, the perceptually lower speed generally forms a reference frame for the higher one.

The geographic environment is perceived as static and, thus, its motion state acts as a basis.

3) The eye fixation can play an important role for perceived structure. What is fixated on tends to act as a primary reference for other motion components. Therefore principle (2) above is fully valid only under fixation on the background. (As is well known, also under full cue conditions the static background seems to move backwards during pursuit eye movement.)

These empirically based principles for perceptual data treatment form a theoretical basis for the model. Applying them on our short-exposure walking pattern has the following consequences:

1) Disregard fixation attitude. The critical exposure intervals are too short for evoking pursuit eye movements and thus we are dealing with a "balanced" stimulation in this respect. (To some extent Experiment 2 simulates the effect of pursuit eye movement with fixation on the hip element.)

2) The line AB represents the projection of a rigid structure and thus must be treated as a unit. The same holds true for the line BC. Because B is a connecting point for the two lines we might expect the pattern ABC to form a unit of higher order.

3) The hip-shoulder unit has the lowest mean speed relative to the background and it connects the four pendulum subsystems to a unified system of higher order. Therefore the hip element was taken as a starting point in our stimulus-percept analysis.

It must be said, however, that our analysis has been only partially adequate from a perceptual point of view because of the restriction of the display to a presentation of the three leg elements used (or motion of an isolated "real" leg). This is because the foot of a walker has contact with the ground during about half a cycle and thus has the lowest relative speed during this half cycle. As a consequence of the rule proposed, an analysis covering this period would start from element C, describe CA as a unit in pendulum motion about C and BA as the next unit performing a pendulum motion about B. Thus, the choice of starting point for the analysis had been depending on the phase of cycle displayed. Displaying the motion pattern of a single leg over several step cycles shows that such a cyclical change of percept anchorage really occurs.

Perceptual Integration in Motion Perception

It may seem almost trivial to remind the reader of the necessity to presuppose some kind of memory function in connection with motion perception. Motion is spatial change over time and therefore supposing the existence of motion perception without some process of tying together or integration would imply a logical contradiction. In a broader context, U. Neisser has in his already classic book *Cognitive Psychology* (Neisser, 1967) analyzed visual short-term memory functions in a highly instructive and important way. Although dealing with percept of static type, he also stresses the central role of such memory functions in motion perception. His analyses are mainly anchored in results from static tachistoscopic studies but also studies of stroboscopic motion perception are included. In these analyses the actual aspects of the short-term visual memory are described as visual integration over time of the sensory message. As a consequence of the character of the stimulus material analyzed, Neisser discusses visual short-term memory in terms of some kind of temporal integration of static "snapshots" rather than integration of continuous functions. In his treatment of stroboscopic motion he says for instance: "The example of apparent motion gives us good reason to believe that perception involves genuine integration of successive patterns" (Neisser, 1967, p. 145).

The present study of real motion perception and the visual vector analysis highlights another short-term memory effect, which it is fully possible and consequent to describe as a standard mathematical integration of a continuous spatial function of time. Given the vector differentials abstracted above, it is consistent to proceed along Neisser's line and hypothesize a visual memory function which is an analogue to a regular mathematical integration of a continuous space/time differential function. We can specify velocity and acceleration as derived from our experimental results. Their integrals over the experimental time intervals of .1 sec to .5 sec would then be immediately given in the actual percepts.

Integrating the various component differentials, sensorially abstracted from the stimulus flow, gives the motion tracks in the hierarchies of moving reference systems. In our examples with biological motion we get the system of pendulum motion and the displacement of the body unit relative to the basic reference frame formed by stimulation from the stationary ground. This means that we now as a model accept an instantaneous visual analysis of the proximal stimulus flow in a number of vector differentials together with simultaneous and continuously ongoing processes of integration of this material.

Final Remarks

The most significant finding from the experiments reported is the clear indication that the perceptual organization of the stimulus patterns is an initial act, fully accomplished at the perceptual spatial/temporal threshold level. Our results also indicate that the sensitivity of the analyzing system is very high. The slightest coordinated displacement in the optical flow is enough to accomplish an immediate organization in coherent perceptual structures.

There are strong reasons for assuming that the perceptual motion analysis is a primary and direct effect of integrated receptive field processes.

As a consequence of its mathematical structure the model for perceptual motion analysis elaborated in the present paper has been given in rigidly quantitative terms. In this respect also the present model represents a considerable simplification and does not cover more than a basic scheme of the perceptual process. The visual system works in a far too flexible way to be fully covered by a rigid formula. Instead it seems as if a basic goal for the visual process is to find functionally useful approximations at each instant rather than producing mathematically perfect solutions, and that incessant corrections and shifts occur as a consequence of instantaneous information received.

References

Börjesson, E., & von Hofsten, C. (1972). Spatial determinants in depth perception in two-dot motion patterns. *Perception and Psychophysics, 11*, 263–268.

Börjesson, E., & von Hofsten, C. (1973). Visual perception of motion in depth. Applications of a vector model to three-dot motion patterns. *Perception and Psychophysics, 13*, 169–179.

Johansson, G. (1962). Perceptual overestimation of small motion tracks. *Psychologische Beiträge, 6*, 570–580.

Johansson, G. (1966). Geschehenswahrnehmung (Event perception). In W. Metzger (Ed.), *Handbuch der Psychologie, Band 1, Wahrnehmung und Bewusstsein* (pp. 745–775). Berlin: Springer.

Johansson, G. (1973a). Visual perception of biological motion and a model for its analysis. *Perception and Psychophysics, 14*, 201–211. [Chapter 7, this volume.]

Johansson, G. (1973b). Monocular movement parallax and near-space perception. *Perception, 2*, 135–146.

Johansson, G. (1974a). Projective transformations as determining visual space perception. In R. B. MacLeod & H. L. Pick (Eds.), *Perception: Essays in honor of J. J. Gibson* (pp. 117–138), Ithaca, NY: Cornell University Press.

Johansson, G. (1974b). Vector analysis in visual perception of rolling motion. *Psychologische Forschung, 36*, 311–319.

Johansson, G. (1974). Visual perception of rotary motion as transformations of conic sections. *Psychologia, 17*, 226–237.

Johansson, G., & Jansson, G. (1968). Perceived rotary motion from changes in a straight line. *Perception and Psychophysics, 4*, 165–170.

Neisser, U. (1967). *Cognitive Psychology*, New York: Wiley.

Studies on Visual Perception of Locomotion[†]

Gunnar Johansson

Uppsala University

Abstract. The problem about visual discrimination between seeing objects in motion and perception of motion of the perceiver (locomotion) was taken up. A flow of vertical motion was presented to limited areas of the far periphery (45°–90°) of the retina simultaneously with optical information about a stationary room over the rest of the retina. The result was that most subjects perceived themselves as sitting in an elevator continuously moving upward or downward. Thus, peripheral motion stimulation over a few percent of the retinal area determines locomotion perception in apparent competition with information about a static state over the rest of the retina. The same type of stimulus presented to the central part of the retina always brought about perception of object motion and a static perceiver.

Effects of size and localization of the area stimulated with the motion flow was studied. Theoretical consequences and problems for further experimental analyses are discussed.

1 Introduction

Ordinarily the sensory information about locomotion stems from a number of interacting sensory subsystems. Traditionally we distinguish between information from the skeletal and muscular systems, the cutaneous senses, the vestibular apparatus, and vision. All these channels usually interact in the perception of *active* locomotion, that is, displacements due to muscular effort like walking, running, etc. That vision plays a dominant role in this complex system has recently been demonstrated by Lee and his co-workers (Lishman & Lee, 1973; Lee & Aronson, 1974; Lee & Lishman, 1975).

Starting from specific neurophysiological problems about interaction between the visual and vestibular channels, Dichgans and a number of his co-

[†] From *Perception*, 1977, *6*, 365–376. Received March 11, 1977. Reprinted with permission from Pion Limited, London.

workers have also during recent years given highly significant contributions in this field (Dichgans et al., 1972, 1973, 1974; Brandt et al., 1973, 1975; Held et al., 1975).

Transport of the perceiver by vehicles like boats, trains, cars, elevators, moving pavements, or escalators, etc., is termed *passive* locomotion. [Strictly speaking, the term locomotion denotes "motion of an organism from place to place by means of its own organic mechanism" (Warren, 1933). However, in common usage of today the term "locomotion perception" includes also perception of transport of a passive perceiver. Therefore, we will explicitly distinguish between active and passive locomotion.] Under rectilinear and smooth transport with constant speed, the only sensory information available about locomotion stems from vision. When a passenger under these conditions shuts his/her eyes, a stationary state is perceived. Therefore, with the interest centered about *visual* perception of locomotion, experiments with the passive aspect afford a good starting point.

Transport of a perceiver (man or animal) generates a geometrically specific optic flow pattern in his eyes. Such flow patterns generated by motions relative to a rigid and static environment form continuous perspective transformations (Gibson et al., 1955; Gordon & Michaels, 1963; Gordon, 1965; Lee, 1974) and are supposed to bring about locomotion information. However, objects in motion relative to a perceptually stationary perceiver also can generate flow patterns in the eye, which have similar or even identical characteristics but which regularly elicit perception of object motion. Thus, it seems as if the visual system can separate object motion from locomotion by utilizing some other sources of information than the geometric structure of the optical flow pattern.

Such considerations form the background for the research project from which the present paper is the first report. The general problem can be expressed thus: *How does the visual system discriminate between passive locomotion and object motion?*

In a first attempt to answer this question it is relevant to point to the fact that locomotion most often generates a continuous flow over the whole retina, while object motion most often brings about local flows, often overlaid on a total flow representing the stationary environment. However, it is easy to find that the distribution of stimulus pattern over the whole retina is hardly a deciding condition for perceiving locomotion. From our daily life we can find many examples that the visual system in certain situations often reacts, with locomotion perception, to stimulus patterns of motion covering rather limited retinal areas. For instance, when we are sitting in a closed vehicle, say a train compartment or a bus which is moving linearly and with a constant speed, the nonvisual information about transport is rather faint and unspecific. In this situation most of the area of the retinas gets a projection from the closed compartment, which is approximately stationary relative to the perceiver, and often the projections from the side windows are the only motion stimulation available. In spite of this we perceive the terrain seen through the windows as stationary and the vehicle as moving. This "window" situation was taken as a model for the experiments to be presented below.

2 Experiment 1

2.1 Problem

Does stimulation of limited parts of the retina with a uniform motion flow evoke locomotion perception in a stationary subject when the rest of the retina receives stimulation from the stationary environment? This was the problem for experiment l. Because the investigation will deal with problems of perimetric type, the specification of stimulated area will be given in terms of angular measures relative to the fovea.

Binocular vision was used and effects of motion stimulation in an area 45°–90° from the fovea on the nasal side of both retinas were investigated. See Fig. 2 for further details. As a complement, effects from corresponding stimulation of central sectors of various size were also studied.

The interest for the dichotomy of central versus peripheral areas has several sources. (i) Brandt et al. (1973) have shown that the periphery of the retina (more than 30° from the fovea) plays a totally dominant role for perception of locomotor rotation in a subject sitting inside a rotating striped drum. (ii) The speed of a retinal flow pattern stemming from locomotion over a plane surface usually is near zero in central vision but relatively high in the far periphery. This holds true in the general case when the visual axis roughly coincides with the direction of motion. (iii) A great number of our own pilot studies have given positive results only when peripheral parts of the retina were stimulated.

2.2 Technical arrangements

The apparatus is diagrammed in Fig. 1. It essentially consists of an endless moving belt with a random dot pattern, a video camera, and two video monitors (visible surfaces 42 cm × 42 cm). The camera was facing the moving belt and it filled the screens of the monitors with a vertically moving random pattern of black dots. The size of the dots was about 2° of visual angle; the mean density of dots was such that the black-to-white ratio was about 1:4. The brightness and the contrast were on normal video level. Within certain limits the speed of motion was not critical for the effect studied. It could vary from perceptually low to "moderate" speed; in the experiment it was $10 \times 5° \text{ s}^{-1}$.

The subject sat at a table with his head on a chinrest and with one monitor on each side of his head. The centers of the monitor screens were on his eye level and each video screen covered a horizontal visual angle 45°–90° from the optic axis of the eyes with the gaze directed straight forward. Vertically the video screen covered an angle of about 40°–53° as shown in Fig. 2. The appa-

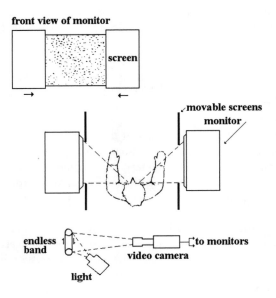

Fig. 1. The experimental arrangements; see text.

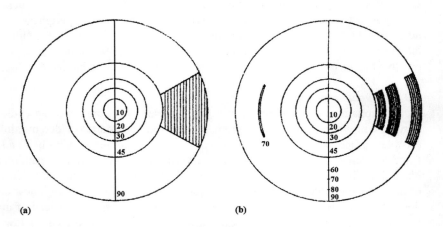

Fig. 2. Perimetric charts of the retina. Part (a) shows the retinal area (hatched) exposed to motion stimulation in experiment 1. In (b) the right side shows the three areas, each 10° in width stimulated with a motion pattern in experiment 2. To the left in (b) is indicated the 1° line which was the liminal condition in experiment 2. All the stimulated areas were located on the nasal side of both retinas.

ratus was set up in a laboratory room with plenty of furniture and equipment. The ceiling light was switched on during the experimental sessions. The distance from the subject's seat to the front wall was about 4 m. In order not to weaken the contrast on the monitor screens these were shaded from direct ceiling light.

2.3 Procedure

The instructions were as follows: Please sit down with your chin on this chinrest and look freely toward this area of the front wall. Do not look at the TV sets at your sides. The pattern on these sets will begin to move in a moment. Just sit relaxed, and if you eventually should get a clear impression of sitting in a moving elevator, tell me this immediately. Tell me also whether the elevator is going up or down.

In the case when the subject reported perception of going by elevator, he was instructed to report every change in perceived motion: if it stopped, changed speed, changed direction, etc. After 45 s from report of perceptual locomotion the moving belt was stopped and after a delay of about 3 s it was started again in opposite direction. Six such presentations were given to the subjects with positive responses to the first presentation. The subjects lacking locomotion perception after 3 min of motion stimulation were classified as negative. The initial direction of motion alternated between odd and even numbered subjects. Only subjects reporting a realistic and compelling perception of sitting in a moving lift were classified as positive. A few subjects reported some weak or diffuse impression of elevator motion and consequently these subjects were regarded as negative cases. The reason for choosing this strong criterion for acceptance was that the pilot studies had indicated that the locomotion perception from stimuli of the type chosen most often was literally spoken, of all-or-none character. There was typically a sudden shift from static perceiver in a static room and moving video patterns to a moving perceiver and room (and a static pattern behind the "windows"). Typically, the percept is not "as if" sitting in a moving elevator; it is perception of *real* elevator motion.

2.3.1 Subjects. Twenty subjects took part in the experiment; most of them were students from a first-year course in psychology and the rest were laboratory personnel. Three subjects in the latter category had been subjects in a pilot experiment with a similar apparatus.

2.4 Results

Table 1 gives the individual data from experiment 1. As shown in the table two-thirds (13/20) of the subjects after a longer or shorter delay perceived vertical locomotion in accordance with the criteria chosen. The rest of the subjects instead perceived a pattern moving over the screens during the whole 3 min session or did not perceive any manifest or consistent locomotion.

Table 1. Latency times (s) over six iterations for 13 subjects (out of 20 tested) reacting with locomotion perception.

Subject	Iteration					
	1	2	3	4	5	6
1	-					
2	3	2	4	0	1	0
3	15	8	6	4	4	2
4	15	2	0	1	0	0
5	10	0	0	0	0	0
6	20	0	0	0	0	0
7	2	0	0	0	0	0
8	24	44	26	37	14	12
9	15	7	5	0	0	0
10	-					
11	30	22	16	20	12	6
12	-					
13	-					
14	58	30	38	15	12	0
15	37	13	16	15	10	14
16	42	24	41	5	10	28
17	40	2	3	0	0	0
18	-					
19	-					
20	-					
Approximate mean	24	12	12	7.5	5	5

As indicated in the table, the delay in locomotion perception in the "locomotion" group at the first presentation varied between 2 s and about 1 min.

Table 1 also shows that iteration of the stimulus as described above brought about practically immediate locomotion perception in about one-half of the "positive" group and a decreasing latency in the other half. The change of the mean of the whole group over iterations is shown in Fig. 3.

2.4.1 Effect of motion stimulation of a central area. It was mentioned in the description of the problem for experiment 1 that also a condition was studied where the central and the peripheral areas had changed roles: a stationary pattern in the periphery and motion stimulation in the central area. This was also carried through in several variants with the motion pattern covering central areas from 30° to 10°.

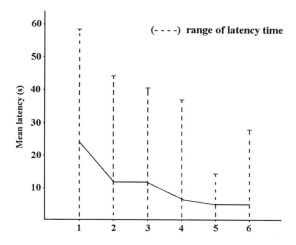

Fig. 3. Mean latency time as a function of iteration, n = 13 (experiment 1).

In this experiment the two monitors in experiment 1 were removed and one of them placed at different distances in front of the subject. In no case was locomotion perceived but always a motion over the monitor screen. This corresponds to the result in Brandt et al. (1973).

2.5 Discussion of experiment 1

Initially all the subjects perceived the dot pattern as moving and the room as stationary. For most subjects, however, the visual response changed after some seconds of passive viewing and they suddenly found that the whole laboratory with the monitors was moving vertically like a very large elevator cage. From the onset of locomotion perception an observer paying attention also to the moving patterns perceived these as a stationary environment in form of vertical walls. (This perception of static "walls" of course was paradoxical. The surfaces visually acting as the walls of an elevator shaft were seen as much closer to the head than were the laboratory walls.)

Iteration of motion stimulation after stop and change of direction typically brought about a shortening of the latency time to onset of locomotion perception; for some subjects the locomotion started without any delay.

These were the main results of experiment 1. From the point of view of theory it certainly is noteworthy that localized peripheral stimulation under full cue perception of the stationary room brings about a compelling locomotion perception. However, the fact that not all subjects reacted in this way also is significant. This latter result suggests that there was involved in the experimental situation some sort of sensory conflict which resulted in different results in different perceivers. One reason for assuming such a conflict is that, at least at the onset of locomotion perception, there must exist a sensory conflict between visual indication of locomotion start and a lack of the vestibular signals usually paired with such visual information. Dichgans et al. (1973) have demonstrated that in the rabbit also a visual stimulus can elicit activity from vestibular nuclei. Therefore, our results probably could be interpreted as indications about intersubject differences in the relative dominance of the two sensory channels, differences that result in different percepts.

However, there are good reasons to assume that our experimental situation has introduced a conflict within the visual system itself. There seems to be considerable evidence that the visual system is built up of the two rather independent subsystems, what Trevarthen has called the focal and the ambient systems (Trevarthen, 1968; Ingle, 1967; Schneider, 1967). (The finding that the central part of the retina did not elicit locomotion perception in our and in Brandt et al.'s experiments gives support to Trevarthen's theory. For further discussion see section 3.5.)

Our experimental arrangement produced sharp borders between motion stimulation in the far periphery of the retinas and the information about a stationary state over the rest of the retinal surface (thus a peripheral window). In our daily environment, however, locomotion usually brings about a continuous perspective flow over the whole retina. We might guess that interindividual differences in balance between the two hypothetical visual subsystems could explain the difference between our subjects in their response to isolated peripheral motion. As a partial check on the probability of this guess, a new experiment with some of the "locomotion negative" subjects was carried out. In this was used a classical device, a vertical drum, striped inside and slowly rotating about the subject sitting in its center. In this device the total visual field is covered by moving stimuli and thus the hypothetical system rivalry was excluded. It was found that under this condition all subjects after a short delay perceived a stationary drum and rotary motion of their own bodies. Brandt et al. (1973) also used this type of device and got 100% locomotion perception.

The next interesting outcome was the existence of latency times and their change with iteration. A delayed onset of locomotion perception seems to be a rather general characteristic for experiments like this (Brandt et al., 1973; Held et al., 1975). This latency seems to vary very much between the subjects and also between conditions. In experiment 1 the first mean latency time was relatively long (25 s) when compared with the drum condition, where it averaged around 10 s. Also Brandt et al. found mean latency times on the order of 10 s. It is of interest to compare this with the experiment of Lee and Aronson (1974), in which the "swinging room" (constructed by Lee) was used. There the response to a very small motion of the room (with an infant standing on a stationary floor) was immediate and drastic. The children regularly lost their balance in attempts to compensate for the perceived locomotion, and the same held true for adult subjects standing on a beam in this room (Lee & Lishman, 1975). Thus, we probably can regard the latency time as another hint about system rivalry under our conditions.

3 Experiment 2

3.1 Problem

In experiment 1 a considerable part of the far periphery of the nasal side of both retinas was exposed to motion locomotion. The result from this experiment made it natural to ask about the liminal area within this sector still yielding locomotor response when stimulated with a motion flow, and also to ask about possible differences in sensitivity in this respect at different angles from the fovea. In experiment 2 these two questions were taken up. To some degree this experiment had the character of a pilot study. The basic purpose was to get some insight into the main characteristics rather than to perform a detailed mapping. In the experimental design was included also a study of a possible effect of perceptual size of the environment presented in the central part of the visual field. The risk of systematic changes in response because of adaptation made it necessary to keep the number of presentations low and to stop the motion only a few seconds after onset of locomotion perception at each presentation.

3.2 Technical arrangements

The apparatus described under experiment 1 was used after a minor modification. Immediately in front of each of the two monitors were set up two movable screens as shown in Fig. 1. These screens made it possible to screen the moving pattern with the exception of the area under study. The largest possible display was the 45°–90° area studied in experiment 1, and the smallest possible, still under good control, was a band, measuring 1° of visual angle. The dot pattern from experiment 1 was used.

3.3 Procedure

The experiment was run in two steps. First the same retinal area as in experiment 1 was exposed to the motion stimulation and then this area was reduced to form a vertical band, 10° in width, and located on different parts of the retina. In a second phase a more elaborate search for the threshold size of the stimulus area that still evoked locomotion perception was carried through.

The experiment was carried out under two different conditions of the visual environment in the central 90° area of the visual field. In the first (condition A) the subject saw the laboratory room from a distance of about 4 m to the front wall. The next condition (B) restricted the frontal visual field by means of a screen 12–15 cm from the subject's face. The screen simply consisted of the subject's own hands kept side by side in front of the face. Thus, under this condition the subject saw only the monitors with their screening in the far periphery, and his/her own hands in the central sector. The two conditions were rotated ABAB during the experiment. The reason for adding condition B was the finding during some methodological work that limiting the visual space to a near space in central vision probably had a highly facilitating effect for eliciting locomotion perception from peripheral stimulation.

In the first phase of the experiment the following areas were displayed: 45° –90°, 45°–55°, 80°–90°, and 60°–70° in this order. See Fig. 2. Between the presentations the motion was stopped, the localization of the stimulus band changed and the direction of motion shifted. The time interval between the presentations was about 20 s.

Each condition was presented just once. The instruction was the same as in experiment 1. If locomotion perception was not reported during a presentation, the presentation was ended after 2 min, and the next condition was presented. Thus, all subjects were presented all conditions.

The second phase started with presenting again the stimulus band 60°–70°. For all subjects reacting with locomotion perception in the first randomly presented condition (A or B) the area was gradually diminished in steps of 1°, until the subject reported that the locomotion had stopped or until the 1° width was reached. This procedure was repeated for the next condition. Thus, in this phase the liminal width of the stimulus band still retaining ongoing locomotion perception was sought.

3.3.1 Subjects. Fifteen subjects took part in the experiment, most of them students in an elementary course in psychology and the rest other volunteers without previous experience in experiments on locomotion.

3.4 Results

The quantitative results of experiment 2 are given in Table 2 and Table 3 and are summarized in diagram form in Fig. 4. Table 2 makes clear that there hardly is any difference in the mean latencies between different 10° peripheral areas in the reaction to motion stimulation. Next, it again indicates that there is a pronounced interindividual variability in the tendency to react to peripheral motion stimulation with locomotion perception. Third, it demonstrates that our condition B, thus the condition with central nearspace, is much better for evoking locomotion perception than is the open-laboratory condition. From a total of 60 stimulus presentations on various retinal areas under each of the two conditions A and B, condition B brought about 55 locomotion responses (thus in about 92% of all presentations) while condition A resulted in 34 such percepts (about 57%). It is also only condition B which shows some lengthening of the latency time with stimulus displacement toward the extreme periphery.

Table 3 and Fig. 4 report the result from the second phase of the experiment, the search for the limiting size of the area stimulated with motion, which still

Table 2. Latency times (s) to onset of locomotion perception after stimulation of four different retinal sectors and under two different viewing conditions: A is far space, B is near space.

Subject	Retinal sector (measured from fovea)							
	45°–90°		45°–55°		60°–70°		80°–90°	
	A	B	A	B	A	B	A	B
1	30	0	-	0	-	1	-	1
2	35	0	28	0	15	0	30	0
3	30	0	22	0	-	1	-	2
4	4	0	7	0	-	0	-	0
5	-	7	-	10	-	20	-	-
6	55	20	50	22	35	14	-	-
7	5	1	10	0	0	0	5	0
8	-	10	48	42	27	30	-	38
9	52	16	36	14	20	5	70	26
10	-	10	-	28	-	8	-	5
11	-	-	56	14	-	95	-	-
12	6	4	7	3	12	9	18	11
13	15	2	5	1	1	1	20	1
14	-	-	-	15	-	17	-	70
15	25	10	24	2	100	6	-	12
Approximate mean for "positive" responses	26	6	27	10	30	14	29	14
Number of "negative" responses	5	2	4	0	7	0	10	3

evokes locomotion perception. These data in a still higher degree reveal the relative superiority of condition B in eliciting locomotion perception. It also demonstrates an exclusive proneness of the peripheral retina to react in this way.

Most subjects perceived locomotion also when the sector measured only 1° in width. This means that under some conditions a few dark spots moving vertically in a row are enough for retaining locomotion perception and that the threshold size of the area was not reached in this experiment.

Table 3. Liminal size of stimulus area retaining locomotion perception in subjects initially perceiving locomotion in a 10° area.

Subject	Threshold area (°)	
	A	B
1	-(45)	<1
2	<1	<1
3	-(30)	<1
4	-(30)	<1
5	-	10
6	3	<1
7	3	<1
8	-(10)	<1
9	8	<1
10	-	3
11	-	<1
12	3	<1
13	4	<1
14	-	5
15	8	<1

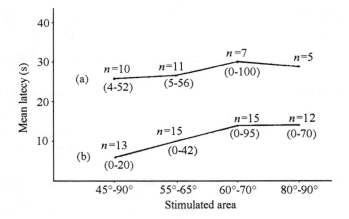

Fig. 4. Mean latency time (s) in experiment 2 as a function of stimulated retinal area: (a) the basic condition with the laboratory space exposed; (b) reduced frontal view (see text). Numbers in parentheses indicate range of latency times (s) in the group of subjects reporting locomotion perception, n denotes the size of these groups for each condition.

3.5 Discussion of experiment 2

The first stimulus presented was identical with the stimulus in experiment 1. This of course was done in order to make possible a direct comparison between the two groups of subjects. The results, both when it was a question of number of "positive" subjects and when it was a question of length of latency time, came out to be very similar.

The main outcome from experiment 2 is the documentation that a continuous optical flow in very narrow bands in the far periphery of the visual field (some thousandths of the retinal area) regularly is interpreted as locomotion. This holds true for most subjects also when the total visual stimulation, except this narrow band, informs about a well-structured stationary environment.

In connection with the result from experiment 1 this result strongly indicates that the retinal periphery is especially tuned for transferring information about locomotion rather than about object motion when there is otherwise unequivocal information about a static state. This holds true at least when it is a question of a continuously ongoing and coherent stimulus flow.

This interpretation of the result seemingly is at variance with the well-established observation that the periphery of the retina is very sensitive to object motion and that such motion in the periphery effectively triggers fixation behavior. Therefore, the following tentative explanation may be called upon. Hypothetically, peripheral parts of the retina have two major functions. (i) When the optical flow is continuously ongoing (and is bisymmetric relative to the optical axis of the eyes) the system responds with locomotion perception. (ii) When a unilateral motion stimulation in the periphery suddenly occurs, the system reflexively reacts with object motion perception and a reflexive change of fixation and attention.

This assumption about qualitatively different reactions to *onset* of motion stimulation and *ongoing* motion stimulation also would make understandable the latency time phenomenon typical in artificially evoked visual locomotion perception (cf. Brandt et al., 1973, 1975; Held et al., 1975). From this standpoint the delayed onset of locomotion perception could be regarded as belonging to a prevalent paradigm in visual data treatment.

As mentioned above, Trevarthen (1968) has strongly suggested that from the point of view of neurophysiology there are two parallel processes in vision, one controlled from the central part of the retina and another from the peripheral parts. Trevarthen says:

> "Experiments with split-brain monkeys led me to consider that vision of space and vision of object identity may be subserved by anatomically distinct brain mechanisms. In this paper I examine the visual mechanisms of the brain to test the idea that vision involves two parallel processes; one *ambient*, determining space at large around the body, the other *focal* which examines detail in small areas of space. In vertebrates there is a

projection from eye to midbrain of a detailed topography of body-centered behavioral space. This visual map is integrated with the bisymmetric motor system to obtain correspondence between visual loci and the goals for movements. The midbrain visual system governs basic vertebrate locomotor behavior. The phylogenetically more recent forebrain visual system looks almost exclusively at central behavioral space, and cortical motor control is likewise concerned with the formulation of highly specific acts in the same central territory."

Evidently these conclusions about dissociation of the visual system into two parallel subsystems have a direct relevance for the interpretations of our results. This was touched on in the discussion of the results from experiment 1, and in a still clearer way the outcome of experiment 2 demonstrates a very strong functional constraint in the perceptual interpretation of motion stimulation in the periphery of the visual field. In a planned investigation the problem about two parallel systems will be taken up in a further study.

4 Concluding Remarks

As stated above, our experiments have given strong support to the hypothesis that one of the main functions of the retinal periphery is to control the organism's motor behavior relative to its environment. We found that, when stimulated with a continuous motion flow, liminally small areas in peripheral retina can elicit locomotion perception and that this regularly happens also when the rest of the retina in an obviously competing way gets information about a stationary position of the perceiver in his environment. Perceptually this apparent dilemma is solved by a percept where the perceiver's own body and his visual environment get a common motion. In this way we get the "elevator illusion." That this percept has a sensory basis is evident. In some pilot studies the subject was facing the window of the laboratory (with the blind drawn up) rather than a laboratory wall. This had no influence on the perception of locomotion. The whole outdoor environment seen through the window: the streets, houses and trees, and the old castle on its hill in the background were seen as a rigid unit continuously moving vertically in a direction opposite the stimulus motion. Thus, a very limited and unstructured motion stimulation in the retinal periphery was enough to supersede cognition and experience.

Of course this is just a laboratory parallel to a known illusion. This illusion can occur for some persons when standing before streaming water; they perceive themselves as moving in a direction opposite to the stream (cf. Fröbes, 1923, p. 397). A personal experience of this type may be mentioned as a good example. Near to my parents' house there was a shallow lake. As a child I early found that sometimes when standing in a moored boat looking into the rippled water I suddenly felt myself and the boat moving over the water in a most realistic way. During such occasions, combining perception and imagination. I often undertook many fantastic voyages!

Locomotion perceived while looking out through the window also verifies an interesting preliminary observation about perceived speed. The perceived speed of locomotion seems to be a function (probably not linear) of perceptual distance to the centrally fixated point, in a way reminiscent of Emmert's law. Thus, fixation of the distant castle gave a perceptual speed of the vertical motion of many meters per second, while fixating the laboratory wall reduced the perceptual speed to some decimeters per second, and finally introducing a screen at a short distance from the eye resulted in a perceptual speed of a few centimeters per second.

The motion stimulation pattern used in our experiments was the simplest possible from a mechanical point of view. It represented a continuous flow with constant speed over the whole stimulated surface seen on a vertical screen. The vertical direction of stimulus motion was chosen mostly for technical reasons. Pilot studies had made clear that every direction of stimulus motion was followed by perceptual locomotion in the opposite direction.

Thus, the present study has actualized a number of questions and problems concerning peripheral motion stimulation and locomotion, which ought to be studied experimentally before we are in a position to establish a more elaborate answer to the general problem raised in the introduction. From the above, the following problems are brought to the fore:

(i) the double role of peripheral retina as an organ for locomotion perception, but also for signaling peripheral object motion;

(ii) the functional difference found between our conditions A and B;

(iii) the relation between focally perceived distance and perceived locomotion speed from a standard stimulus speed (Emmert's law analogue);

(iv) perceptual effects of more complex motion patterns, including perspective transformations.

References

Brandt, Th., Dichgans, J., & Koenig, E. (1973). Differential effects of central versus peripheral vision on egocentric and exocentric motion perception. *Experimental Brain Research, 16*, 476–491.

Brandt, Th., Wist, E. R., & Dichgans, J. (1975). Foreground and background in dynamic spatial orientation. *Perception & Psychophysics, 17*, 497–503.

Dichgans, J., Diener, H. C., & Brandt, Th. (1974). Optokinetic-graviceptive interaction in different head positions. *Acta Oto-Laryngologica, 78*, 391–398.

Dichgans, J., Held, R., Young, L. R., & Brandt, Th. (1972). Moving visual scenes influence the apparent direction of gravity. *Science, 178*, 1217–1219.

Dichgans, J., Schmidt, C. L., & Graf, W. (1973). Visual input improves the speedometer function of the vestibular nuclei in the goldfish. *Experimental Brain Research, 18*, 319–322.

Fröbes, J. (1923). *Lehrbuch der experimentellen Psychologie* (Textbook in experimental psychology), Band I. Freiburg im Breisgau: Herder.

Gibson, J. J., Olum, P., & Rosenblatt, F. (1955). Parallax and perspective during aircraft landings. *American Journal of Psychology, 68*, 372–385.

Gordon, D. A. (1965). Static and dynamic visual fields in human space perception. *Journal of the Optical Society of America, 55*, 1296–1303.

Gordon, D. A., & Michaels, R. M. (1963). Static and dynamic visual fields in vehicular guidance. *Highway Research Record, 84*, 1-15.

Held, R., Dichgans, J., & Bauer, J. (1975). Characteristics of moving visual scenes influencing spatial orientation. *Vision Research, 15*, 357–365.

Ingle, D. (1967) Two visual mechanisms underlying the behavior of fish. *Psychologische Forschung, 31*, 44–51.

Lee, D. N. (1974). Visual information during locomotion. In R. B. MacLeod & H. L. Pick, Jr. (Eds.), *Perception: Essays in honor of J. J. Gibson* (pp. 250–267). Ithaca, NY: Cornell University Press.

Lee, D. N., & Aronson, E. (1974). Visual proprioceptive control of standing in human infants. *Perception and Psychophysics, 15*, 529–532.

Lee, D. N., & Lishman, J. R. (1975). Visual proprioceptive control of stance. *Journal of Human Movement Studies, 1*, 87–95.

Lishman, J. R., & Lee, D. N. (1973). The autonomy of visual kinaesthesis. *Perception, 2*, 287–294.

Schneider, G. E. (1967). Contrasting visuomotor functions of tectum and cortex in the golden hamster. *Psychologische Forschung, 31*, 52–62.

Trevarthen, C. B. (1968). Two mechanisms of vision in primates. *Psychologische Forschung, 31*, 299–337.

Warren, H. C. (1933). *Dictionary of Psychology*. London: George Allen and Unwin.

Toward a New Theory of Vision
Studies in Wide-Angle Space Perception[†]

Gunnar Johansson and Erik Börjesson

Uppsala University

Abstract: This is the first article from a project aimed at developing a new type of theory for visual space perception. The article is limited to the first basic part of this theory: the wide-angle recording of slants of plane surfaces under self-motion. This article is composed of two parts. The first part presents the theory for wide-angle slant perception. Its approach must be characterized as unique in the sense that it utilizes the hemispheric form of the retina. It ends up with an analogue to visual slant perception in the form of a three-dimensional metrical specification of slant information in the optic flow. The second part of the article describes three experiments supporting the theory.

Experimental research on visual space perception in humans implies, with very few exceptions, studies of perceptual effects from more or less isolated stimulation of the macular region. Psychologists (ourselves included) have been accustomed to extrapolate, most often implicitly, from isolated small-angle experiments to the wide-angle space perception of our daily life.[1] There exist, however, experimental results indicating that the retinal periphery in fact plays an important, probably even independent role in space perception. These are experiments carried out in a real wide-angle environment. J. J. Gibson (1950, pp. 183-187) described some pioneering, illustrative experiments. His famous book, *The Perception of the Visual World*, can be read in its entirety as a consistent argument for the necessity of accepting wide-angle perception as the basis for the theory of space perception. The Edinburgh experiments with the "swinging room" (Lee & Lishman, 1975; Lishman & Lee, 1973; Stoffregen, 1985, 1986) are also relevant.

Experiments such as these tell us that a perspective wide-angle optic flow yields information about the observers' physical position in their environment and their motion relative to it. We also mention the studies on the difference be-

---

[†] From *Ecological Psychology,* 1989, *1,* 301–331.

[1] In the following, we use the term *small angle* for angles less than 10° and the term *wide angle* for angles greater than 10°.

tween wide-angle effects of vection (Dichgans & Brandt, 1978, on circular vection; Berthoz, Payard, & Young, 1975, and Johansson, 1977a, 1977b on linear
vection) and such effects of visual angles less than, say, 20°. A most direct indication of active peripheral contribution to everyday space perception is well
known also from ophthalmology. *Tunnel vision*, which is the retinal disease that
spoils peripheral vision while leaving the foveal area intact, is known to gravely
disrupt the patient's orientation in space.

In an early search for the principles determining the hierarchical order of
relative motion components in visual motion perception, one of us (Johansson)
found that the component in the optic flow stemming from self-motion in the
environment generally acts as the ultimate common motion component,
underlying all perceived relative motions. This component is extended over the
whole retina and it has the character of a continuous, perspectively invariant
transformation (Johansson, 1986). Furthermore, from a geometrical point of
view, its content of spatiotemporal information is increasing from the fovea to
the periphery.

Such thoughts about the role of peripheral stimulation inspired my
(Johansson) first experimental studies in this field. The two first (Johansson,
1977a, 1977b) were limited to the question about possible visually relevant information in highly reduced stimulation of the retinal periphery. These results
indicated an advanced control of self-motion perception also when the stimulus
pattern was a few bright spots (or just one) moving 70° or more peripherally on
each side of the head.

Another critical question was whether or not the retinal periphery with its
low degree of optical resolution really can abstract projective invariances in perspective transformations. This question resulted in a tentative pilot study
(Johansson, 1982) going straight to the point: Will continuous perspective transformation in wide-angle optic flow, simulating aspects of stimulation under everyday conditions, bring about veridical three-dimensional perception? The term
wide-angle perception implies that under such conditions central and peripheral
parts of the retina are simultaneously stimulated by the component in the optic
flow stemming from self-motion. Therefore, these experiments (and also those
presented herein) concern central as well as peripheral parts of the retinal hemisphere. The results of these studies were so positive and promising that we pursued this research further.

This article describes the basic outcomes of our project to date, in two parts:
(a) a description of a theory as worked out in detail with special regard to slant
perception and (b) our experimental support for this aspect of the theory. Although the theory was constructed after the experiments were done, our work is
best understood if the theory is presented first.

A New Type of Theory

A consequence of the traditional concentration on small-angle perception is that in these connections the proximal stimulus could be, and always has been, described as a projection on a flat surface. The curvature of the parafoveal surface covering only a few degrees of visual angle could be regarded as negligible. This is the hardly ever questioned Berkeley-Helmholtzian small-angle pictorial approach.

When studying the effects of geometrically coherent optic flow patterns extended over larger parts of the retina, this flat-surface model must be given up. The proximal stimulus under everyday conditions is light refracted by the lens of the eye and focused onto a hemisphere. Thus, the optical and geometrical conditions correspond to central projection from the lens onto a spherical surface. This means that in the eye all distal straight lines will be projected onto the retinal surface as curves, namely, approximations of arcs of great circles. For instance, an image of a triangle projected in this way will not be a straightsided triangle but a triangle with curved sides, a spherical triangle with an angle sum exceeding 180°.

Therefore, in connection with our experimental work, we have developed the basic structure of a new theory of vision, a theory based on the hemispheric projection. According to this approach, the proximal stimulus is defined as angles read at the nodal point of the lens of the eye rather than as images on the retina.

The Model

Our theory takes into account the anatomical structure of the eye with its lens and its hemispherical retina. It is founded on a model for recording the optic flow as projected on a spherical surface. This model is composed of two parts: (a) a set of assumptions about the neurophysiological processing and control, and (b) a geometrical framework for three-dimensional specification of the information available in the optic flow under wide-angle conditions. This geometrical part is a three-dimensional variant of projective geometry, namely, the geometry of central projection of a plane on a sphere from the center of the sphere (gnomonic projection, Coxeter, 1969, pp. 92–95).[2] We call the geometrical part of the model the *optic sphere* and the neurophysiological part the *processor*. We start by describing the processor.

The processor. The specification of the processor consists of three assumptions. The first one says that the visual system "knows" about the anatomical measures in the eyeball such as the position of the lens relative to the retina, the

---

[2] This projection is famous in mathematics because it is the model for the elliptic non-Euclidean geometry (Hilbert & Cohn-Vossen, 1952, pp. 235–242).

spatial relations between stimulated retinal spots in terms of distance nodal point-to-retina (radian measures), and so on. This assumption is in no way original. For instance, measurement of distances on the retina is a prerequisite of the retinal image concept, and Helmholtz (Warren & Warren, 1968), for example, explicitly accepted spatial ordering on the retina as innate. In fact, our assumption is just an example of the general sensory capacity for recording positions of stimulated points on and in the body and for localizing body parts in space without visual support. In the model, this assumption makes possible metrical recording of stimulated positions in a spherical coordinate system.

The second assumption concerns the relation of the model to the physical world. We presuppose that the well-documented neural interaction between the vestibular and the visual systems (Dichgans & Brandt, 1972, 1978) introduces the sensorially recorded direction of the gravitational force as the polar axis in the optic sphere. This will, figuratively speaking, lock the model to the physical world with its up and down directions, thereby also specifying the perception of the horizontal plane.

Measurement in the horizontal dimension is in the theory anchored in the perceiver's motion, namely in the direction and change of direction of the perceiver's eye sockets relative to the environment. The sagittal direction is set as the zero point on the horizontal scale and thus, in the model, the angles as read on this scale will continuously change when the perceiver moves in a curve or just turns his or her head.

Finally, our model utilizes a basic characteristic of all sensory systems, their adaptability. The exact form of the vertebrate chambered eye varies over species. Most probably no such eye satisfies the intrinsic demands of our geometrical model concerning shape of the retina and position of the nodal point. The human eye is far from perfect in these respects. Therefore, we take into account the purposive adaptation to its environment that is fundamental for the visual system. In our model, this adaptation concerns the self-motion-generated optic flow. As examples from vision we refer to the much studied long-term adaptation to stimulation that has been distorted by lenses, prisms, mirrors, and so forth (e.g., Gibson, 1933; Held, 1965; Kohler, 1964; Stratton, 1897). These experiments reveal a flexible visual calibrating and recalibrating capacity in connection with self-motion. We assume that in the visual system such calibrating adjustments have corrected the incoming optical information to accomplish optimal projective invariance in the self-motion-generated component in the optic flow.

The optic sphere. The optic sphere is thought of as being independent of the retina (cf. Gibson, 1961). It is a physical sphere of light, read by the scanning retina. In accordance with Gibson (1961, 1966), it is the potential array of light reflected from the environment to the momentary position of the nodal point of the eye. As a pencil of rays of light it is purely physical. Therefore, we regard the optic sphere as belonging to the distal world. Fig. 1 shows the optic sphere with a unit radius and two angular coordinates θ and φ.

The gnomonic projection mentioned earlier has some special characteristics of great interest for an understanding of wide-angle space perception. For instance, it allows a three-dimensional recording of the optic flow and it makes possible a metrical recording of this flow in terms of spherical coordinates.

The optic sphere is shown in Fig. 1 as a sphere standing on a plane, its foot plane. Because we are dealing with a variant of projective geometry, this plane is regarded as the projective plane. It is called the *distal plane* (D-plane). The point O is the center of the sphere.[3] The optic sphere has the following essential characteristics.

1. As illustrated in Fig. 1, each end point of a distal line, the *distal point* (D-point), is at the moment of stimulation represented by a directed line, a *projected line* (P-line), through the sphere (a ray of light) intersecting the sphere on two points. In this way the D-point is mapped on the sphere in a one-to-two way (it is mapped on two antipodal points on the sphere), but in accordance with a common convention the mapping is mathematically regarded as singular. Therefore, *projected point* (P-point) denotes the point of stimulation read by the ret-

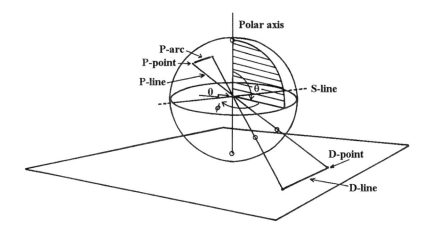

Fig. 1. The optic sphere with a unit radius and two angular dimensions θ and φ. A distal line (D-line) is projected from the center of the sphere onto the sphere. The projection has the form of an arc of a great circle. Together with the center of the sphere this arc specifies a plane.

---

[3] Because the optic sphere represents the eye bulb, its depicted size should be only a small fraction of its height above the ground. We have chosen the eyeeight as the unit for its radius only for making the figure readable.

ina. The direction of the P-lines in three-dimensional space is specified in the coordinate system of the sphere as the direction from point 0 to the P-point.

2. A straight line, a *distal-line* (D-line) on the D-plane is projected as an arc of a great circle, a *projected arc* (P-arc), on the sphere. See Fig. 1. The angular size of this arc is determined by the angle at point 0 between its limiting P-points. Together with the center of the sphere (0), this arc specifies a *projected plane* (P-plane). Geometrically this abstract plane has a distinct direction in three-dimensional space, and thus it specifies the full great projected circle on the sphere. We assume that this great circle is recorded automatically in the sensory analogue to the spherical coordinate system of the model.

3. From the preceding, it follows that a closed figure on the D-plane (e.g., a triangle, a square, or any other polygon) generates a volume in the model: a directed space angle at the center of the sphere.

Summing up, in the optic sphere, a D-point is represented as a directed line, a D-line is represented by a directed plane, and a closed figure on a D-plane is represented by a directed volume.

On Applications of the Model

There is a great difference between the specifications of the model's two components. The optic sphere, as being strictly geometric, could be conclusively referred to (in the opening paragraph on our model) by a single sentence supported by a reference. In contrast to this, the specification of the processor, which consists of a set of assumptions concerning neurophysiological "processing," must be limited to the demands set by the actual problem. In this article, the processor part could be restricted to three assumptions. When studying other aspects of space perception (e.g., perception of shape), the optic sphere would be applied in its present form while further assumptions must be added to the processor.

Relations to J. J. Gibson's Ecological Optics

Gibson, Olum, and Rosenblatt (1955) introduced an innovative description of the optic flow at the eye of, for example, a flying bird or an airplane pilot. Gibson went on to develop his ecological optics (Gibson, 1961, 1966, 1979; see also my discussion with Gibson in Johansson, 1970, and Gibson, 1970).

The geometrical part of our model is built on the foundation laid by Gibson in his ecological optics. Thus in accordance with Gibson, we have anchored the description of available optical information in a 360° array of reflected light potentially passing the nodal point of the eye of a moving perceiver. Like Gibson, we treat this array—our optic sphere—as belonging to the physical environment rather than to the retina. The retina is supposed to scan and read that part of the optic sphere that, by eye and head movements, is potentially available for the scanning hemispheric retina.

From Model to Theory

The spherical model offers radically new ways to an understanding of the functioning of the visual system. As was mentioned in the introduction, the approach from which this model was born implies that it concerns simultaneous central and peripheral recording of optic information. In the following we abstract from the optic flow—to our knowledge, for the first time—a three-dimensional metrical specification of the optical information of the slant of a distal surface. Advantages inherent in this approach should stand out clearly when it is contrasted with traditional theories with their lost third dimension and consequences such as the shape-slant problem.

The perception of slant was chosen as the starting point partly because it offers an excellent opportunity for an objective, quantitative recording of wide-angle perception. Still more essential, however, was that light reflected from the ground is the source of the fundamental common component in the optic flow. It acts as the frame of reference relative to which all object motion is seen (Johansson, 1982, 1986). Therefore, the part of the theory described in this article is a cornerstone in our forthcoming development of the theory to comprise form and distance perception.

In our analysis we set the line as the fundamental element and dot patterns are regarded as a network of rigidly interconnected virtual lines. The justification for the latter statement is the well-established experimental fact that central projection of two moving distal dots with constant distance is perceptually equivalent to a rigid line. The most advanced examples of the exclusive strength of this perceptual effect are found in the research on biological motion (Johansson, von Hofsten, & Jansson, 1980). The application of this effect makes our theory highly efficient as an analogue to everyday space perception because all perceptible stationary spots on a surface are in the processor treated as a network of lines.

We now introduce motion of the optic sphere relative to the D-plane in a way schematically corresponding to a person's walking straight forward on level ground. The optic sphere as presented in Fig. 1 is in Fig. 2 shown in a translatory motion relative to a D-line on the D-plane, here drawn as horizontal. The figure shows in side and top projections two snapshots along the motion track.

As described earlier, the D-line is projected as a P-arc on the sphere. Together with the center of the sphere this arc specifies a P-plane in three-dimensional space.

Due to the height of the center of the sphere above the D-plane (the eye-height), the P-plane has a certain vertical angle to the D-plane. Generally, this angle changes continuously during the motion of the optic sphere (see Fig. 2, the side view). Consequently, under the perceiver's self-motion the P-plane rotates vertically with the D-line as its axis of rotation. However, the D-line is projected onto the optic sphere from the center of the sphere. Therefore as seen in the figure, the P-plane simultaneously rotates on a line on the center of the sphere. Two constraining axes of rotation on the same plane imply that the axes are parallel. Thus, according to the geometry of the optic sphere, there exists on the center of the sphere a distinct diameter on which the P-plane rotates, and this diameter is parallel to the D-line. We call this second axis of rotation the *slant line* (S-line), and its intersections of the optic sphere are called *slant points* (S-points). The geometrical fact that there exists in the model a three-dimensionally directed line parallel to a corresponding distal line is, of course, decisively important for the theory. Before commenting more about this, however, let us take the next step.

We assume that on the distal plane there are a great number of lines, real or virtual with random directions and lengths. As already shown, each one of these

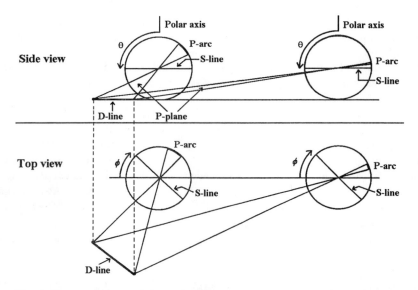

Fig. 2. Two snapshots of the optic sphere moving linearly one eyeheight above a horizontal plane with a distal line (D-line) to the left of the motion path. A side and a top view are shown. The figure shows the rotation of the projected arc of a great circle (P-arc) and the stationary slant-specifying S-line parallel to the D-line. The direction of the S-line is specified by the θ and the φ angles.

Fig. 3. This is a photo of a real three-dimensional model of the optic sphere. In the photo, a distal-line is projected from the center of the sphere as an arc of a great circle. This great circle with a sector specifying a plane (the P-plane) and the center point of the sphere is shown. Furthermore, the corresponding slant-informing S-line is seen as lying on the S-circle which is parallel to the distal plane. (See text.)

D-lines has a parallel S-line on the center point of the optic sphere.[4] Because all the D-lines are lying stationary on the same slanted plane the corresponding S-lines together specify a *slant plane* (S-plane) constantly parallel to the distal plane. Thus, the S-points lying on a common great circle, the *slant-circle* (S-circle), specify in terms of spherical coordinates the slant of the distal plane. For easier visualizing of the P-plane with the corresponding S-line, see Figure 3.

Generalizing to Everyday Perception

Although the P-arc and the P-circle are continuously changing during linear motion, the θ-angles and φ-angles of the S-points remain stationary. This is demonstrated in Fig. 2. Let us now see what happens when the perceiver's eye

---

[4] This implies that each S-line has its own specific direction in the optic sphere except those from parallel D-lines. Parallel D-lines of course get common S-lines.

sockets are moving in curved paths. The zero point of the ϕ-scale is bound to the momentary sagittal direction of this motion. This means that when the perceiver moves along a curved path, the ϕ-scale rotates on the S-circle in the opposite direction. The θ-coordinate of each S-point, however, as indicating its angle to the polar axis, does not change. Consequently, the S-circle stays constant relative to the environment under any kind of motion of the perceiver. It stays parallel to the distal plane also under such diverse perceiver motions as bending, jumping, sitting down, and lying in bed.

About the Recording of Slant Information

Finally, we address a potential objection to using the S-plane, S-circle, S-line, and S-point as valid information about distal slant. They are only secondary geometrical constructs without direct representation in the stimulation. The only stimulation underlying the specification of these constructs is the motion of arcs of great circles projected on the optic sphere and read by the retina. Can the processor identify the S-points as constituting the S-circle? The answer is yes. Under the self-motion-induced rotation in the sphere of any P-plane, all records specifying the corresponding P-circle are, as clarified in the last section, continuously changing, except the θ-angles for its S-points. This implies that on each P-circle, there exist two diametric points that are characterized by zero change over time in the vertical direction. According to the assumed capacity of the processor, the visual system automatically expands the P-arcs to full great circles (see the first assumption in specifying the processor and the essential characteristics of the optic sphere). Therefore, in the framework of the theory the S-points are identifiable by locating on the P-circle the points that do not change in the vertical direction. These points are the S-points.

Because all structural spots on the D-plane visually act as end points of connecting virtual lines, there exist under real-life conditions myriads of slant-informing S-lines in the optic sphere. The visual recording of this information is thought of as being achieved by an automatic parallel processing in the neural network.

About the "Smart Mechanism" Character of the Model

The way of specifying the stimulus for perceived slant as direction in three-dimensional space of an intraocular plane, as we have done, has evident advantages. It helps in visualizing and making tangible relevant angular information in the three-dimensional optic flow. It also illustrates that with its hemispheric retina, the eye is a very smart anatomical construction (Runeson, 1977). A complicated transformation of the impinging array of light can be thought of as accomplished by a simple location of nonchanging θ-coordinates on the optic sphere.

A possible disadvantage is that from this type of mechanism it is probably not easy to understand its underlying mathematical principle. Therefore, we remind the reader of what we said earlier about the geometric model. Basically, the optic sphere is an application of gnomonic geometry, the subject of which is central projection on the sphere from its center. According to this geometry, the following holds true: When the sphere stands on its foot plane, the great circle on the sphere parallel to the foot plane—thus the equator of the sphere—is the projection of the line at infinity of the foot plane (regarded as the projective plane).

Transferring this to our abstracting of information in the optic sphere in terms of distal, projected, and slant variables implies that according to gnomonic geometry the S-circle is the projective line at infinity for the D-plane and as such parallel to the D-plane (or more correct, is on the D-plane). Furthermore, the S-points are the points at infinity of the respective D-lines.

In fact, our model was constructed for the purpose of transforming three-dimensional projective invariances to a Euclidean metric, an operation possible in gnomonic geometry.

Applying this metric model, we could demonstrate that the hemispheric form of the retina makes possible a valid specification of three-dimensional space without reference to the abstract mathematical structure of the geometry of three-dimensional central projection but in direct accordance with its theorems.

Conclusions

1. Accepting that there exist neurophysiological capacities analogous to the assumptions constituting the processor part of our model, we have shown that our theory is capable of explaining real-life slant perception.

2. The processor's three assumptions do not go beyond what is known from experiments and experience. They only make explicit what most often has been implicitly accepted.

3. The demands on the visual system for processing capacity corresponding to a mathematical computation are in our theory very elementary. This holds true in absolute terms and still more when compared with current theory proposals applying two-dimensional models. In our theory the pickup of optic information is limited to a retinal recording of positions together with the recording of angles between such positions at the nodal point of the lens. A recording capacity of this kind might be regarded as just an example of the general sensory function resulting in localization of stimulation and recording of relative directions, a capacity necessary for survival of all species.

The Experiments

The problem for the experiments was how well the slant of a plane could be discriminated perceptually under wide-angle conditions and different conditions of structural information in the optic flow.

On Application of a Pictorial Wide-Angle Effect

In our experiments, we have taken advantage of a limitation in the application of wide-angle perspective. An old rule in teaching architects and draftsmen in perspective drawing says that the constructed visual angle of the object must be less than 28°. With a larger visual angle the drawing will appear distorted (also for untrained eyes). Parallel lines will appear diverging; length of lines, slants of surfaces, and so on will appear distorted; and all these distortions will change with change of the perceiver's position relative to the picture (McCartney, 1963). Artists, when aiming at perfect realism, apply far more restrictive principles.

Geometrically these distorting effects are due to the fact that in the viewing of drawn, or in other ways artificial perspectives, the eye (in the same way as in the perception of real objects) acts as the pole, the station point, of the perspective. Therefore, from a strict geometric point of view, a "veridical" perception of the picture is possible only when the eye is on the station point of the perspective and thus the pictorial and the perceived perspective coincide. This difference between produced and perceived projection, however, is small for angles less than 10° but accelerates rapidly.

From these considerations, it follows that when viewing an extremely wide-angle display (drawn or computed, static or dynamic) observers should be very sensitive to the discrepancy between the station point and their own point of view if their (active) eye is not on the geometrical station point, and they therefore should see the depicted object as something other than the corresponding real object. This is especially true for the extreme wide angles employed in our experiments ($\approx 70°$) and is the effect we utilize to manipulate perceived slant.

The effects of wide-angle picturing are demonstrated in Fig. 4. This figure also demonstrates the way we have made use of wide-angle distortion of slant in the experiments. The figure is a wide-angle perspective of a square with four parallel lines. The station point of the perspective is located at a distance from the page of 4/10 of the length of the bottom line of the figure and at right angles to the vanishing point (point VP). The effects of changing the spatial relation eye-to-station point can be easily demonstrated in the following way. Make the figure page flat, if necessary by means of a piece of cardboard or the like (or better, make a copy enlarged 4:1). Then keep this flat "display" close to your right temple as shown in Figure 4B and at the distance and angles of the eye relative to the VP prescribed earlier. Apply monocular vision and look freely at

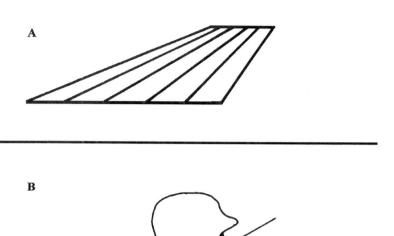

Fig. 4. An extreme wide-angle perspective of a square striped by four parallel lines. See text for instructions about viewing.

the figure. (Directing your gaze inside the figure and not far from its far bottom corner might be advantageous.)

You are likely to find that the figure is sticking out from the page. It becomes perceptually three-dimensional. You will also find that its shape and direction in space change considerably under small displacements of your head relative to the display. Try to make the figure an approximation to a square and then move your head slightly up and down relative to the figure. This way of changing the perceived slant had been found to be sensitive and metrically correct; therefore, it was employed for simulation of slant in two of the experiments. A second observable geometric effect, the elongation of the figure in depth, does not influence the simulated slant (for a geometric specification of the direction of perceived slant as a result of displacing the eye from the computed station point, see Fig. 9).

Experiment 1

This experiment had three objectives: (a) to check the method chosen for the subject's reproduction of perceived slant; (b) to study typical human perceptual capacity in recording a surface's slant as seen under full-cue, wide-angle conditions and as measured with this method; and (c) to make possible an evaluation of the efficiency of slant perception from such full-cue conditions as compared with slant perception from simulated planes to be used in subsequent experiments.

Method

Stimulus. A rectangular board as shown in Fig. 5 was used as the stimulus with the longer sides AB and CD 118 cm and the shorter sides BC and AD 110 cm. The board was covered by black cloth onto which seven strings painted with self-luminous color were attached. The strings were separated 17 cm and parallel to the shorter sides of the board. The board could be rotated round the AB side as shown in Fig. 5 and positioned in any slant. A pole was placed close to the corner B of the board. It was displaced 30 cm from the imaginary extension of the AB side, and 3 cm from the extension of the BC side. On the top of the pole a chin support was mounted 79 cm above the level of the AB side. In the experiment, nine different slants were presented, namely, the horizontal and ± 8°,± 16°, ± 24°, and ± 32° deviation from the horizontal. A response device was made of a rectangular metal board 20 × 13 cm. At the middle of one of its longer sides, the response board was attached to a horizontal axis of rotation parallel to its shorter sides. The board could be rotated by hand to match perceived orientation of the stimulus board. A potentiometer attached to the axis of rotation recorded the orientation, which was read on a digital voltmeter.

Subjects. The subjects were 11 undergraduate psychology students. They received course credit for their participation.

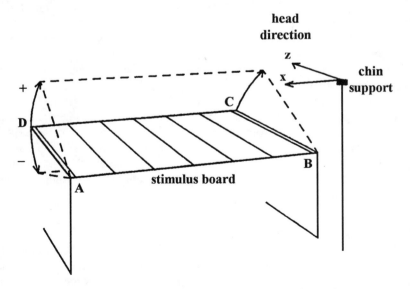

Fig. 5. The stimulus board used in Experiment 1.

Viewing conditions and procedure. The viewing conditions were varied with respect to spatial information available and to head orientation. In the full-cue condition, the laboratory was well lighted and binocular vision was applied. The only perceptual restriction from normal perception was that the subjects were not allowed to move their heads from the chin support while looking at the board. In the impoverished condition, the room was totally dark and only the self-luminous strings attached to the board were visible. Furthermore, the subjects watched the set of parallel lines monocularly. In both conditions, the subjects were allowed to move their eyes. Two head orientations were used. In one orientation, the sagittal axis of the head (x-direction in Fig. 5) was parallel with the AB side of the stimulus board and, in the other orientation, the sagittal axis (z-direction) was parallel to the BC side. In the impoverished condition the subjects used their right eyes with their heads in the x-direction and their left eyes with their heads in the z-direction.

Nine orientations of the stimulus board, two levels of visibility, and two head directions made 36 different conditions that were presented once in randomized order. Before each trial, the subjects put their heads on the chin support in the proper direction and closed their eyes. The slant of the stimulus board was set and, in the impoverished condition, the light turned off. Then the subjects looked at the stimulus board for the time needed. When ready, the subjects closed their eyes, turned around, and, with their backs to the stimulus board, produced a slant, seeing the response device binocularly in full light.

Results

One subject gave extremely odd results and it was obvious that her measures suffered from some fault. Consequently, her data were discarded from the data analysis. For each viewing condition and stimulus board orientation the mean has been calculated, summarizing over subjects. In Fig. 6, these means are plotted against objective slant for each of the four viewing conditions. The straight lines indicate the correct slope. A positive angle indicates that the board is slanted upwards (i.e., the farther CD side is higher than the closer axis of rotation), and a negative angle indicates that the board is slanted downwards. As can be seen, the reproduced slants agree very well with objective slants; this is also apparent from the intercepts and the slopes of the regression equations.

Although small, there were significant effects of experimental conditions. Thus, there was a significant difference between the full-cue condition (M= -2.91°) and the impoverished-cue condition (M = 0.07°), $F(1, 9) = 20.29$, $p <$ .01. Similarly, there was a small but reliable difference between the x-direction (M = 2.75°) and z-direction (M = - 0.09°), $F(1, 9) = 10.29$, $p < .05$. When comparing the four different viewing condition groups with the Newman-Keuls test for pairwise comparisons, it was found that the impoverished condition with z-direction differed significantly, $p < .01$, from the other three conditions between which there was no significant difference. These facts are illustrated in Fig. 6

where reproduced slants in the impoverished condition with z-direction lie above the straight line. This means that upward positive slants were perceptually overestimated and downward negative slants were underestimated. The other three conditions showed opposite tendencies. These effects cannot be explained at present. The effects were small, however, and the main results from Experiment 1 are that matched slants agree very well with objective slants. This indicates that the experimental setup with the response device as a tool for reporting perceived slant works in a fully satisfactory way. The data also provide a basis for comparisons with the following experiments.

Experiment 2

The aim of Experiment 2 was to study how well and in what way the visual system utilizes perspective information in wide-angle stimulation in the percep-

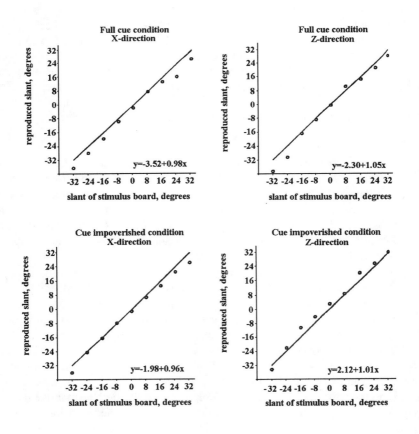

Fig. 6. Reproduced slants in Experiment 1.

tion of slanted planes. In connection with this objective, the effectiveness of different sources of perspective information for veridical perception was studied.

Method

Stimulus patterns. A viewing situation was simulated such that an observer sat close to the side of a window and without moving his head, looked monocularly at a moving plane, for instance, a sidewalk. The background outside this plane was empty. The direction and speed of motion simulated the motion of a walker strolling along such a sidewalk. This situation can equivalently be thought of as representing two different conditions: either a stationary observer seeing a moving plane outside the window or an observer sitting in a slowly moving vehicle looking at a stationary plane outside its window. Fig. 7 shows this simulated scene from above (A) and from the rear (B). As shown in the figure, the plane is simulated as being at level with the lower border of the window. The terms *distal plane, distal element*, and so forth as used in the following, for the sake of brevity, stand for the *simulated* distal plane, *simulated* distal element, and so forth.

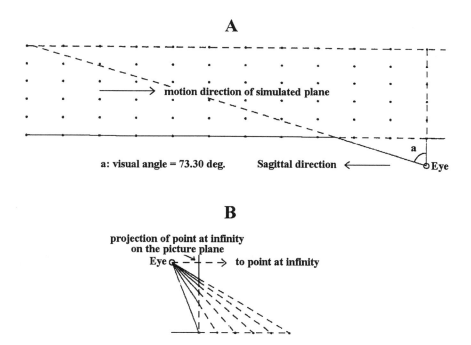

Fig. 7. The viewing situation with a simulated plane in Experiments 2 and 3 as seen from above (A) and from behind (B).

A perspective projection on a picture plane with the eye as the nodal point was computed by an IBM AT PC (accepting its regrettably bad resolution because we had not found any deteriorating influence on the perception of slant due to this technical weakness). A set of 200 "frames," representing a stepwise perspective transformation in accordance with the data for the simulated motion, was then displayed on the monitor screen (ECD) and filmed frame by frame with a 16-mm camera. This film was glued end to end, thus forming an endless loop. During the experiment, such film loops were continuously run in a specially adapted 16-mm projector.

Twelve different films served as stimuli. Three different types of distal elements, constituting the distal plane, were used: (a) points as displayed on the screen of the computer (here called dots), (b) short lines, and (c) small filled squares. The perspective projection of such an element in itself was assumed to carry different amounts of spatial information about the distal plane, ranging from no such information in the dot to distinct length in the lines to linear perspective in the square.

About 50 elements of one of these types constituted a display. They were distributed on the D-plane either ordered in rows and columns or randomly. The randomly distributed lines and squares, however, were linearly oriented as shown in Fig. 8. As can be seen in the figure, the distribution of elements in rows and columns provides clear indications of a linear perspective in a stationary display irrespective of element type. This, however, is not the case when the elements are randomly distributed. Each such pattern was shown as continuously moving along the screen or as stationary.

Crossing three types of elements, two kinds of structures, and two motion states makes 12 conditions. Each plane was presented in nine different slants. Thus, we used a factorial design comprising 108 different conditions.

Viewing conditions. The subject's head was firmly positioned by a combined chin and forehead support (called the *headrest*). Because eye position was crucial in this experiment, an aiming device was used. It consisted of a self-illuminated ring (5 mm) and a light-emitting diode. The ring and the diode were placed 400 mm and 900 mm, respectively, in the sagittal direction from the geometrically correct position of the pupil of the subject's right eye. The ring, the diode, and the eye were all 174 mm from the projection screen. Using this aiming device the subjects had to adjust the headrest till they saw the diode surrounded by the ring and to control the position of the head when needed. The combination of headrest and aiming device ensured that the subject's eye was as exactly as pos-sible in the correct position relative to the station point of the perspective on the screen. This position is shown in Fig. 7 where the visual angles of the displayed patterns are also given. The patterns on the screen measured 570 mm horizontally and 350 mm vertically. Due to stray light from the screen, the screen itself and its surroundings were visible.

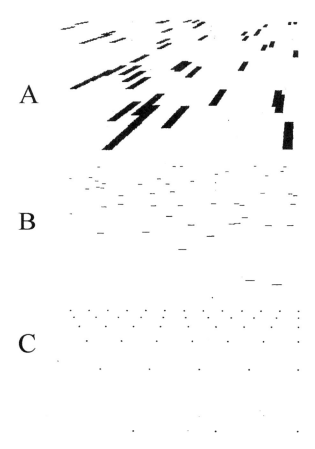

Fig. 8. Three of the stimulus patterns used in Experiment 2: randomly distributed squares (A), randomly distributed lines (B), and regularly distributed dots (C).

In accordance with the pictorial wide-angle effect described in an earlier section, the perceived slant was expected to vary with the vertical displacement of the eye relative to the display and vice versa. In the experiments, the eye was kept stationary and the change of displayed slant angle was accomplished by varying the position of the display vertically. (See Fig. 9 for the computation of exact position of the eye relative to the display for desired slant angles.) Nine different angles were presented in random order, namely, horizontal, ±8°, ±16°, ±24°, and ±32° slant from the horizontal direction.

The same response device as the one used in Experiment 1 was placed in front and to the left of the subjects within comfortable operating distance. To

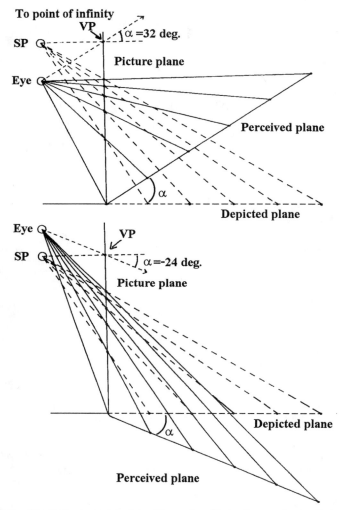

Fig. 9. In the section on pictorial wide-angle effects, it was shown that perceived slant varies with deviations of the perceiver's eye from the position of the station point of a wide-angle perspective. The figure shows in a vertical section how the change of perceived slant can be determined geometrically. The method utilizes the basic consequence of perspective drawing that a line from the station point to the position on the picture plane.

Therefore in our experiments, the perceived slant was expected to vary with changes of the angle α as shown in the figure. In the figure, *picture plane* stands for the display, SP denotes the station point in the constructed perspective, and the point EYE is the position of the subject's eye relative to the display. Thus, when in the experiments the display was raised or lowered a small predetermined distance yielding the angle α, the geometric information to the visual system about slant of the perceived plane was expected to vary accordingly.

see the response device, the subjects had to turn their heads a little and it was not possible to see the stimulus patterns and the response device simultaneously.

Subjects. Sixteen students participated in Experiment 2. They received course credit for their participation.

Design and procedure. Twelve stimulus films in nine different positions made a total of 108 different conditions. To reduce possible effects of learning and boredom, each subject either saw the films with the elements ordered in rows and columns or the films with randomly distributed elements in the nine positions. Consequently, randomized groups with 8 subjects in each group were used with respect to the distributions of elements. Repeated measurements on each subject were used with respect to type of surface element, motion or not, and display position. Each subject saw the 54 conditions once in randomized order. Two dependent measures were taken. First, the subject had to rate how distinctly they could perceive a plane with a specific slant, on a 7-point scale ranging from *no plane at all* (1) to *a distinct plane with a specific slant* (7). Next, the subjects had to match the perceived slant with the response device. This task was demanded only when the first rating exceeded 2.

Each session started with headrest adjustment to get the subject's right eye in the correct position. Then the tasks were described and the rating scale explained, including the fact that a rating of 1 and 2 indicated that no specific slant was perceived and no matching was called for in these cases. Two test trials were run before the real experiment started. The subject looked monocularly in darkness at the presented pattern and was allowed to look freely at the pattern. When ready the subject gave ratings and, when these exceeded 2, matched the slant of the response board with perceived slant. The subject was allowed to look back and forth to match as exactly as possible. Half the 54 presentations for each subject were completed in about an hour. Thereafter a pause was introduced. Some subjects continued after a rest of approximately 15 min. The other subjects continued with the remaining presentations the next day.

Results and Conclusions

The ratings of distinctiveness of a slanted plane are shown in Fig. 10. There is a significant effect of element type, $F(2, 28) = 92.38$, $p < .01$. As expected, the square was the most effective type of element. There was also a significant motion effect, $F(1, 14) = 26.26$, $p < .01$, the motion patterns of course yielding higher ratings than patterns with no motion. Type of element interacted significantly with motion, $F(2, 28) = 10.09$, $p < .01$. Thus, the square elements apparently contained so much information that the motion did not substantially affect the ratings. Compared to the squares, the lines and dots contain less information and the addition of motion to patterns with the latter surface elements contributed greatly to the perception of a plane with a specific slant. Further, there was a significant effect of distribution of elements, $F(1, 14) = 4.65$, p < .05, with higher ratings for the regularly distributed elements where linear perspective is present regardless of type of surface element. Finally, there was a significant interaction between distribution of elements and motion, $F(1, 14) = 7.05$, p < .05. When there was no perspective information, neither from the distribution of the dots nor from motion, the ratings decreased, as can be seen in Fig. 10.

The matches of slant are presented in Fig. 11 and Table 1. In the table, the intercepts and slopes are given for the different conditions together with the number of reproduced slants (the maximum being 9 simulated slants x 8 subjects = 72). Because no slant match was requested when the ratings of distinctiveness were less than 3, the number of matches varies for the different conditions, being of course less when the amount of information is decreased. In particular, the motionless dot pattern with random distribution of elements has an extremely low number of slant matches; therefore its regression equation is very uncertain.

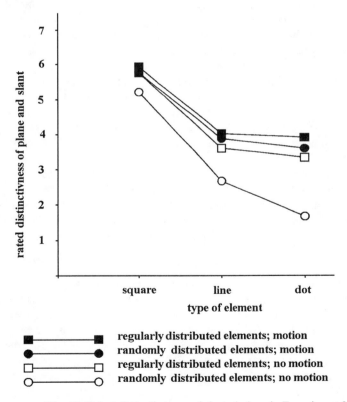

Fig. 10. Rated distinctiveness of slanted plane in Experiment 2.

Table 1

Intercepts and Slopes of Regression Equations of Reproduced Slant on
Simulated Slant for Different Conditions in Experiment 2

Condition		Square	Line	Dot
Motion				
Regular	*a*	0.20	0.09	3.22
distribution	*b*	0.714	0.647	0.707
	n	72	67	65
Random	*a*	1.47	-1.39	3.57
distribution	*b*	0.667	0.558	0.648
	n	72	57	58
No motion				
Regular	*a*	2.33	6.56	8.39
distribution	*b*	0.619	0.580	0.593
	n	71	54	53
Random	*a*	2.61	16.97	30.09
distribution	*b*	0.686	0.196	0.729
	n	70	27	7

Note. a = intercept of regression equation; b = slope of regression equation; n =
total number of slant matches out of 72.

It is evident from Fig. 11 and Table 1 that the simulated slant has affected
perceived slant. With square elements, the reproduced slants are reliable and
close to the simulated slants and it is clear that the visual system is able to utilize
perspective information to determine absolute slant in a wide-angle stimulus
situation. There is, however, a small but consistent underestimation of simulated
deviation from the horizontal plane and this underestimation becomes greater
when the deviation from the horizontal plane increases.

When perspective information is reduced, as in the static line and dot patterns with randomly distributed elements, the slant matches change in two respects.

First, the intercept increases. This means that a more positive slant upward is
perceived. A positive slant is an adjustment toward the projection screen which
has a slant of 90°. This change can be given the tentative interpretation that a
loss of perspective information increases the influence from the slant of the
projection screen. The perceived slant will be a compromise between traces of
useful information about the simulated slant and that of the projection screen.
Second, the regression coefficients decrease and the random variation in the reproduced slant increases. Thus a natural consequence of the missing information

is that variation of simulated slant determines perceived slant less. This result also agrees with the presented ratings of distinctiveness of a slanted surface.

Experiment 3

In Experiment 3, the study of sources of perspective information continued by investigating the effect of number of surface elements on slant perception.

Method

Stimulus patterns. The simulated viewing situation and the principles and techniques for film production were the same as in Experiment 2.

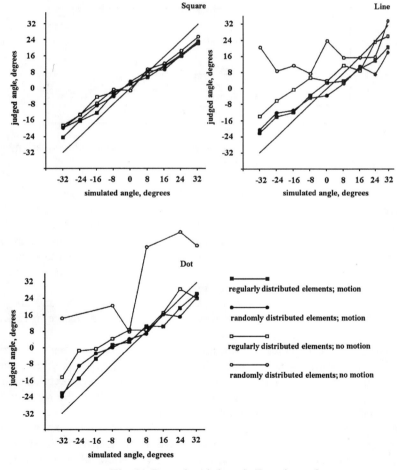

Fig. 11. Reproduced slants in Experiment 2.

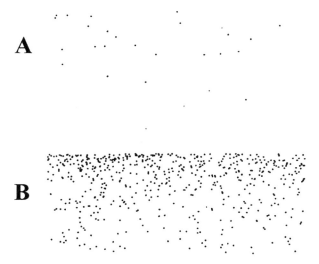

Fig. 12. Two of the stimulus patterns used in Experiment 3: 25 dots (A) and 600 dots (B).

Five films served as stimuli. They were simulated planes composed of randomly distributed dots moving beyond the imaginary window. The films differed only in the number of dots being displayed, about 25, 50, 100, 300, and 600 dots, respectively. The film with 50 dots was the same film as the one used in Experiment 2. The films with the minimum and maximum number of dots, 25 and 600, are shown in Fig. 12.

Subjects. Eight subjects participated in Experiment 3. They received course credit for their participation.

Viewing conditions and procedure. The viewing conditions and the procedure were identical with those of Experiment 2 with one exception. Just seven different slants were simulated, namely, horizontal and deviations upwards and downwards from the horizontal of 10°, 20°, and 30°. Five films and seven slants make a total of 35 different conditions which were shown once in randomized order for each subject.

Results

Mean ratings of distinctiveness of plane and slant are shown in Table 2. It is evident that distinctiveness increased significantly when the number of dots increased, $F(4, 28) = 8.99$, $p < .01$.

Table 2

Judged Distinctiveness of Slanted Plane and Intercepts and Slopes of Regression
Equations of Reproduced Slant on Simulated Slant in Experiment 3.

Measure	Number of Dots				
	25	50	100	300	600
Mean of rated distinctiveness	3.4	4.0	4.3	5.1	5.2
a	2.81	1.84	1.81	1.00	1.94
b	0.578	0.690	0.681	0.793	0.973
n	39	47	50	52	52

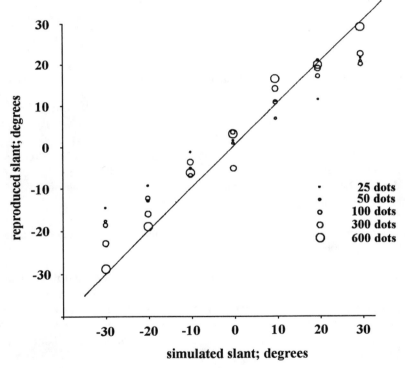

Fig. 13. Reproduced slants in Experiment 3.

In Table 2 and Fig. 13, the reproduced slants are shown. As in Experiment 2, these depend on simulated slant. This strongly supports the notion that the visual system utilizes perspective information in this impoverished situation.

The number of dots intercept does not change in a consistent way. The pattern with 600 dots was almost correctly perceived yielding an intercept of 1.94

and a slope of .973. When the number of dots decreases, the slope decreases, whereas the intercept does not change in a consistent way. This means that, with few dots, simulated deviations from the horizontal orientation are not so well detected and that the tendency to underestimate these deviations becomes greater when the deviations from the horizontal are great. A similar tendency appeared in Experiment 2 when the amount of perspective information was reduced. However, even as few as 25 dots randomly distributed over a great visual angle convey perspective information that is surprisingly well utilized. Finally, it should be noted that the 50-dot pattern appeared in both Experiments 2 and 3. The distinctiveness ratings and reproduced slants remained relatively constant from one experiment to the other in spite of different subjects and different contexts of the other patterns (distinctiveness ratings = 3.6 and 4.0, intercepts = 3.57 and 1.84, and slopes = .648 and .690, for Experiments 2 and 3, respectively).

General Discussion of the Experiments

In Experiment 2, three ways of varying spatial information in the elements were employed: (a) static - kinetic presentation, (b) ordered - random distribution of the structured elements, and (c) three levels of perspective information in the elements themselves. These three levels represented the three geometrical classes, point, line, and surface. Except for the perspectivity in the pattern, there was no information available about an object behind the screen.

Beforehand it was hypothesized that squares would be the most efficient element type with lines as next best. The projection of a single square carries two-dimensional information whereas line information is one-dimensional. The dots, regarded as lacking dimensionality, are naturally devoid of any perspective information of their own.

The results from Experiment 2 indicate that the squares had conveyed a geometric component of visually important information about slant, lacking in the two other types of elements. Generalizing over the conditions in Experiment 2, the results indicate that under static conditions, only perspective indications of parallel lines in two dimensions on the distal plane will evoke efficient wide-angle slant perception from artificial two-dimensional perspectives (this effect is closely related to the classical linear perspective cue). Further, any type of randomly distributed elements on a plane, seen under continuous wide-angle perspective transformation, will bring about perception of a distinct slant of the plane. Therefore, relative motion between the distal plane and the eye seems to be the condition that generally brings about veridical perception. Considering the evolution of the vertebrate eye, it is interesting to observe in this connection that linear perspective must be regarded as being exceptional in projections of environments not touched by humans. Practically all strict linear perspectives originate from human activity: houses, furniture, streets, plow furrows, to name a few.

The finding from Experiment 3 about effects of density of dots is of great interest from a methodological as well as a theoretical point of view. When the number of dots was increased to 600, the reproduced slants became practically equal to those from the full-cue condition in Experiment 1. The methodological significance of this result is that our method was proven adequate for wide-angle research. This result also makes clear that the deviations from geometrically correct slant under all other conditions apparently were real perceptual effects. The systematic variation of the slope of the regression lines as a function of number of dots on the display (Table 2) also indicates this.

The result from the other extreme in the series, the 25-dot display, is rather astonishing. When the number of dots seen simultaneously in the "window" was reduced to 25 and thus the angular distances between the dots in most cases were great, the data still showed a strict linear slant function and a y-intercept close to zero. This is of a great theoretical interest and will be further studied.

In the dynamic condition, our subjects in Experiment 2 and Experiment 3 recorded the horizontal orientation with remarkable precision. The y-intercepts in Tables 1 and 2 show that with a moving pattern, the largest deviation from 0° was less than 4°. This should be compared with the corresponding result from Experiment 1. In this experiment, the full-cue condition (binocular vision of a real stationary plane seen in full lighting) resulted in a y-intercept of -3.52°. The conclusion must be that, for perceiving a horizontal plane, all needed information is available already in our most impoverished stimulus patterns, if motion is present.

Under our experimental conditions, however, perspective transformations do not yield fully veridical slant percepts when the distal plane deviates from the horizontal orientation. Our data from the two experiments with simulated distal stimuli reveal a clear tendency to a regression toward the horizontal. This tendency seems to vary with amount of appropriate information.

As already described, the slant variations in our experimental setup were produced solely by changing the vertical level of the display relative to the subject's eye and consequently also the angles between the elements on the screen at the nodal point of the eye. This method was chosen in accordance with findings in the pilot studies. Our general result—that perceived slant varied linearly with these displacements of the stimulus pattern—validated in a rather exclusive way our method. We are able to state that the directional projection onto the retina acted in our experiments as the primary geometrical information about slant.

Final Remarks

As pointed out in the introduction, experimental research on wide-angle space perception is a severely neglected field. To our knowledge, the theory we have proposed is the first one worked out with a special regard to effects of wide-angle stimulation. Consequently, when it was a question of experimental methodology, we had to start from scratch; as for the theory, we know of just one forerunner, J. J. Gibson. This means that the type of displays used in our experiments has resulted from a process of successive construction and study of a very great number of displays. In these studies we have mainly worked in the Helmholtzian way, drawing conclusions from our own observations. As discussed earlier, the work on a new type of theory started soon after the publishing of Johansson's (1982) article. Its present form, however, was first worked out after finishing the formal experiments described herein. Therefore, we do not refer to these experiments in the traditional way as post hoc support for the theory. Instead we limit ourselves to the following statements:

1. The experimental findings indicate that the visual system is highly sensitive to wide-angle optic flow carrying information about slant of plane surfaces. This holds true also under extremely impoverished conditions.
2. The theory is in full concordance with these experimental findings.

Acknowledgments

We are indebted to Peter Juslin for running the experiments.

This research was made possible by grants to Professor Gunnar Johansson from the Swedish Council for Research in the Humanities and Social Sciences.

References

Berthoz, A., Payard, B., & Young, L. R. (1975). Perception of linear horizontal self-motion induced by peripheral vision (linear vection): Basic characteristics and visual-vestibular interactions. *Experimental Brain Research, 23*, 471–489.

Coxeter, H. S. M. (1969). *Introduction to geometry.* New York: Wiley.

Dichgans, J., & Brandt, T. (1972). Visual vestibular interactions and motion perception. In J. Dichgans & E. Bizzi (Eds.), *Cerebral control of eye movements and motion perception* (pp. 327–338). Basel, Switzerland: Karger.

Dichgans, J., & Brandt, T. (1978). Visual-vestibular interaction: Effects on self motion perception and posture control. In R. Held, H. Leibowitz, & H.-L. Teuber (Eds.), *Handbook of sensory physiology* (Vol. 8, pp. 755–804). New York: Springer-Verlag.

Gibson, J. J. (1933). Adaptation, after-effect and contrast in the perception of curved lines. *Journal of Experimental Psychology, 16,* 1–31.

Gibson, J. J. (1950). *The perception of the visual world.* Boston: Houghton Mifflin.

Gibson, J. J. (1961). Ecological optics. *Vision Research, 1,* 253–262.

Gibson, J. J. (1966). *The senses considered as perceptual systems.* Boston: Houghton Mifflin.

Gibson, J. J. (1970). On theories for visual perception. A reply to Johansson. *Scandinavian Journal of Psychology, 11,* 75–79. [Chapter 6, this volume.]

Gibson, J. J. (1979). *An ecological approach to visual perception.* Boston: Houghton Mifflin.

Gibson, J. J., Olum, P., & Rosenblatt, F. (1955). Parallax and perspective during aircraft landings. *American Journal of Psychology, 68,* 372–385.

Held, R. (1965). Plasticity in sensory-motor systems. *Scientific American, 213,* 84–94.

Hilbert, D., & Cohn-Vossen, I. (1952). *Geometry and the imagination.* New York: Chelsea.

Johansson, G. (1970). On theories for visual space perception. A letter to Gibson. *Scandinavian Journal of Psychology, 11,* 67–74. [Chapter 5, this volume.]

Johansson, G. (1977a). Studies on visual perception of locomotion. *Perception, 6,* 365–376. [Chapter 9, this volume.]

Johansson, G. (1977b). *Visual perception of locomotion elicited and controlled by a bright spot moving in the periphery of the visual field* (Psychological Reports No. 210). Uppsala, Sweden: Uppsala University, Department of Psychology.

Johansson, G. (1982). Visual space through motion. In A. H. Wertheim, W. A. Wagenaar, & H. W. Leibowitz (Eds.), *Tutorials on motion perception* (pp. 19–39). New York: Plenum.

Johansson, G. (1986). Relational invariance and visual space perception: On perceptual vector analysis of the optic flow. *Acta Psychologica, 63,* 89–101.

Johansson, G., von Hofsten, C., & Jansson, G. (1980). Event perception. *Annual Review of Psychology, 31,* 27–63.

Kohler, I. (1964). *The formation and transformation of the perceptual world.* New York: International Universities Press.

Lee, D. N., & Lishman, J. R. (1975). Visual proprioceptive control of stance. *Journal of Human Movement Studies, 1,* 87–95.

Lishman J. R., & Lee, D. N. (1973). The autonomy of visual kinesthesis. *Perception, 2,* 287–294.

McCartney, T. O. (1963). *Precision perspective drawing.* New York: McGraw-Hill.

Runeson, S. (1977). On the possibility of "smart" perceptual mechanisms. *Scandinavian Journal of Psychology, 18,* 172–179.

Stoffregen, T. A. (1985). Flow structure versus retinal location in the optical control of stance. *Journal of Experimental Psychology: Human Perception and Performance, 11,* 554-565.

Stoffregen, T. A. (1986). The role of optical velocity in the control of stance. *Perception & Psychophysics, 39,* 355–360.

Stratton, G. (1897). Vision without inversion of the retinal image. *Psychological Review, 4*, 341–360.

Warren, R. M., & Warren, R. P. (1968). *Helmholtz on perception: Its physiology and development*. New York: Wiley.

Visual Vector Analysis and the Optic Sphere Theory

Gunnar Johansson

Introduction

My initial study of the perceptual separation of common and relative components of motion in the optic flow, called "perceptual vector analysis," was published in 1950. It was the result of my research on event perception, especially real motion perception, in the last part of the 1940s and was submitted for a Swedish doctor degree that year (Johansson, 1950).

The theory of visual vector analysis, which was the main result of this project, differed fundamentally from the theories on visual perception prevalent at that time. These theories applied *pictorial* analyses of the optical stimulation and mainly were dealing with analyses of static "retinal images." This holds true for the traditional Berkeley-Helmholtzian approach as well as for the Gestalt psychology.

Unlike these theories, perceptual vector analysis programmatically concerned perception of *events*, thus spatial change over time, and a mathematical model borrowed from mechanics was applied. At that time a description of the optical stimulation in such technical terms probably differed in a too radical way from the traditional analyses of information in retinal images. Therefore, demonstrations of perceptual vector analysis effects most often were treated as indications of an interesting group of illusions rather than as applications of a basically different type of theory.

Since the 1970s, however, the interest in the perceptual vector analysis type of approach to visual event perception has been rapidly growing. In my opinion, there were two closely related causes for this change of attitude. The first one was the introduction of the "biological motion" effect and its explanation in terms of perceptual vector analysis (Johansson, 1973, 1976). These papers, together with an educational film about the Uppsala research on event perception, illustrating a number of effects of visual vector analysis, and among them the biological motion phenomenon, started a rich, still ongoing research on this latter type of perceptual vector analysis under real-life conditions. The second cause was the at that time rapidly growing interest among psychologists in computational specifications of visual event perception combined with an evident AI engagement in the biological motion problem. Mathematical specifications of stimulation for visual space perception became in vogue and this started something like a creative paradigm shift.

From visual vector analysis to the optic sphere theory.

My work of many years on the theory of visual vector analysis entailed a, for me, successively growing, disturbing implication. A great number of early experiments, and especially the biological motion research, had demonstrated that the vector model was a reliable model for stimulus-to-percept relations in motion perception. The results of my studies of perception of motion and changing form, evoked by non-perspective transformations (Johansson, 1964), however, had brought in their train a theoretical problem. These results indicated a visual preference for three-dimensionality and rigid motion (a finding that has played an important role in recent computational theories on visual event perception). This observation seemed to imply that, when the ambition is to include principles of this character in the paradigm, special processing rules must be added to the vectorial theory. Such rules, however, probably imply a demand on the visual system about a capacity for processing, similar to more or less complicated mathematical computations.

From a biological point of view such a demand hardly is possible to combine with what is known about the evolution of the chambered eye and about vision in primitive animals. It is known that most animals with very primitive brains have efficient visual systems. This fact indicates that a capacity for a mathematical processing of visual stimulation hardly can be supposed to be built-in in the neural part of the visual system of such animals. Consequently, in my opinion the vector analysis theory as applied in Johansson (1964) asked for specifications of additional automatic mechanisms separating rigid and non-rigid motion.

Tentatively, I interpreted these observations as revealing some kind of limiting restraints in the technical specification of the stimulation rather than in the relational approach as such. This interpretation resulted in a search for a theoretical framework, more generally applicable than the initial vector theory.

With the construction of the optic sphere theory (Johansson & Börjesson, 1989) my guess about a limitation in the technical structure of the vector theory was confirmed. In the present paper I will make clear that in the optic sphere theory the processing of the optic flow in terms of common and relative motion, also when it is a question of stimulation of the type studied in Johansson (1964), stands out as belonging to the *technical-mechanical* basis of the visual system. According to this theory, recording of optical stimulation is performed mechanically and without any demands for a neural computation. This has been accomplished by incorporating in the theory continuous, spatial information, especially from the vestibular and kinesthetic senses. Also in primitive animals the control of movements of the components of the own body relative to the environment generally is very much to its purpose. Therefore, in the new theory,

visual space and motion perception is treated as an outcome of interaction between different sense channels in a way closely related to Gibson's "sensory
systems" (Gibson, 1966).

On the structure of the optic sphere theory.

For the reader's convenience, I will interfoliate a brief description on the basic geometrical structure of the optic sphere theory as presented in Johansson
and Börjesson (1989) and also add a relevant information from Johansson and
Börjesson (1990). Beside this material, some not yet published outcomes from
my work on the new theory will be taken advantage of. (In the following I will
often speak about the optic sphere theory as *the new theory* or just *the theory*
and about the theory of visual vector analysis as *the vector theory*.)

The theory is composed of two parts: (1) a set of experimentally established
and commonly accepted statements about sensory processing of stimulation, and
(2) an optical-geometrical model. The geometrical part takes advantage of the
fact that the retinal surface is hemispherical. Therefore, the optic flow is specified as projected on a spherical surface and a special form of central projection,
the geometry of gnomonic projection, can be applied. Gnomonic projection is
central projection of a plane on the sphere from the center of the sphere. In this
geometry a point on the plane is represented in the sphere by a distinct line, and
a line on the plane is represented by a distinct plane in the sphere ("gnomonic"
means something like "indicating directions").

When applied in the theory, this geometry says that any light-reflecting distal spot is represented in the optic sphere by a distinct ray on the center of the
sphere, ending on a distinct point of stimulation *on the sphere* (not on the retina
as such). The visual system interprets two distal points in relative motion as end
points of a distinct straight line segment. (This perceptual effect is in a definite
way established in, for instance, the great number of experimental studies of
perceptual vector analysis.) In the geometry of the theory the projection of two
distal dots represent, together with the center of the sphere, a distinct plane in 3-
space.

The geometrical construction called "optic sphere" consists of a specification
of the wide-angle pencil of rays entering the lens of the eye and impinging on
the hemispherical retina. For simplifying the geometry, the nodal point of the
lens is treated as lying on the origo point of the sphere. Thus the rays can be
treated as radii in the sphere and their directions can, without any transformations, be specified in spherical coordinates. The polar axis of the spherical coordinate system is locked to the vestibular and kinesthetic recording of the direction of gravity. Thus, also in this respect the optic sphere has its anchorage in
the physical world. The directions of the rays of light passing the center of the
sphere are in the theory supposed to be automatically recorded by the scanning
retina and by head and body movements (cf. Gibson on "ecological optics,"
1966, 1979). For detailed description see Johansson and Börjesson (1989).

Consequently, what is stated as being recorded is *not* the stimulation as located on the retina as such. Instead it is the momentary angular position of each ray in the hemisphere of rays, read by the moving retina, that determines the percept.

Presently the theory is only worked out for monocular perception while the experiments on visual vector analysis usually have been run binocularly. This, however, will not limit the conclusions from the analyses. The experiments to be analyzed with respect to the optic sphere theory concern projections of dots on a frontal screen and thus during the experiments the two eyes have received the same stimulation.

On optic-sphere recording of rotary motion.

Recording of rotary motion of a line was not treated in Johansson and Börjesson (1989). Therefore the geometrical background for the above statements about optic sphere specifications of this category of motion will here be briefly sketched. The description concerns object motion relative to a static environment.

A rotary motion of a distal line about one of its end points (like the second hand of a clock) will, when projected into the optic sphere, bring about rotation in the sphere of the plane specified by the line. The plane will rotate about the ray projected from the distal center of rotation to the projection in the sphere of the axis of rotation of the distal line.

In an active perceiver's eye there continuously exists an optic flow due to motion of the eye socket relative to the environment. This holds also for the rotating line and its center of rotation. Therefore, added to the rotary motion of the great circle in the sphere, caused by the object rotation on the distal plane, there simultaneously exists an ongoing change of direction relative to the eye of the ray acting as the axis of rotation of the great circle. Thus we get a rotation about an axis which continuously changes its direction in the sphere.

Pendulum motion.

Pendulum motion differs from rotation mainly in the respect that the pendulum oscillates to and fro over a certain angle. This implies that the arc plane in this case rotates in pace with the pendulum. It rotates about the ray on O from the axis of the pendulum, and over the same angle as the pendulum motion.

Visual Mechanics

As mentioned above, a basic principle of the optic sphere theory is the transforming of the optic flow in the eye bulb to mechanical events, recorded in spherical coordinates. This base of the theory was presented in Johansson and Börjesson (1989). The application of the mechanical model as described in this paper, however, only concerned the perception of slant of planar surfaces. In the present paper we will be dealing also with perception of directions of single lines and planes in a way not treated in the earlier papers referred to. This will call for some further information. Such information is added in the formal specification of the mechanical model given below, to the extent and in the form to be used in the present paper. The model will here be described in two respects, namely: (1) a specification of the basic material for its construction, available in the optic sphere theory, and (2) a description of the principles for its function.

Material to be used.
1. Moving distal points. Will be called *spots* or *dots*.
2. Distal line segments in motion. Will be called *lines* or, when specification is needed, *line segments* or distal lines.
3. Lines emanating from spots, passing the center of the sphere (Origo) and ending on the sphere. Will be called *rays*.
4. End points of rays on the sphere. Will be called *points*.
5. Geodesics on the sphere. Will be called *arcs*.
6. Projections of distal line segments. Will be called *arc planes*.
7. Great circles on arc planes. Will be called *great circles*.

Principles for application.
   (These principles are abstracted from the geometry of gnomonic projection and the specifications of the processor.)
1. Any distal spot specifies a directed ray on Origo and its end point on the sphere. This point is in the theory specified in terms of the spherical coordinate system with the polar axis directed along the sensorially recorded gravitational force.
2. Two or more spots on a distal line is in the processor treated as a line segment.
3. A distal line segment specifies in the sphere a plane on Origo with a specific arc and great circle on this plane.
4. Arcs can move on their great circle.
5. Points on an arc can move on their arc.
6. During orbit motion, great circles rotate on the sphere about the diameter which is parallel to the corresponding distal line.
7. Translatory motion (a translatory component of motion) of a distal line segment on its line brings about a corresponding motion of its arc on its great circle.
8. Translatory motion of a distal line segment (or of a component of translatory motion of the line segment), not on its line, brings about a rotary motion of the corresponding great circle. The great circle will rotate about the specific diameter parallel to the moving distal line.

9. In the special case when the distal plane of a translatory motion and the arc plane are coincident, the rotation of the great circle during translation is zero.

10. Rotary motion of a distal line segment about a spot on the segment brings about a parallel rotation in the sphere of the arc and great circle about the ray from the distal axis of rotation.

11. Rotation on Origo of the axis of rotation of a great circle and the rotation of the great circle about this axis can occur simultaneously.

On My Research on Perceptual Vector Theory

Starting from my dissertation of 1950, I will describe the basic trend in my contributions to an understanding of the perceptual separation of common and relative components. My account will be anchored in presentations of the results of a few, for my present purpose especially relevant experiments, together with comments on their theoretical implications. In the last part of the paper these results will be interpreted in terms of the new theory.

The start.

The initial work on the perceptual vector analysis was planned as a study of perception of two-dimensional motion. An unexpected complication met with, however, was that a number of my stimulus patterns designed for the study of perception of such motion sometimes also evoked specific perception of rigid motion in depth. This brought about a widening of the study by including also such effects. This widening later proved to be of a great importance for the further development of the theory. Therefore, as material for my present study, I have chosen two experiments from this early study which are especially instructive concerning both two-dimensional and three-dimensional vector analysis.

Johansson 1950, Experiment 19.

As my first example I will use the constellation shown in Fig. 1 (op. cit., Experiment 19, p. 89 f[1]). This constellation of two dots is commonly used as the type example of vector analysis, and referred to in many connections. In the experiment the two dots were moving periodically according to the same sine function along tracks forming a right angle. They moved in phase and with a cycle time of about 1.4 sec. Thus, they met once a period. These motions are illustrated in Fig. 1A.

According to the at that time traditional retinal-image specification of the optical stimulation, the two dots should be seen as moving along a vertical and a horizontal path respectively. This does not happen, however. The dots are in a rather unavoidable way seen as moving on the screen toward and away from

---

[1] p. 73, this volume.

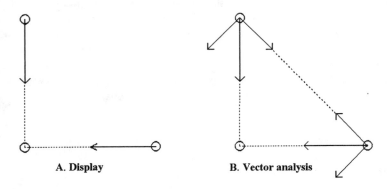

A. Display   B. Vector analysis

Fig. 1

each other along a common diagonal track. Simultaneously this track can be seen as moving as a unit at right angles to the common track of the to and fro motion between the dots. In Fig. 1B it is shown that the two simultaneously perceived motions correspond to a vectorial separating of the two physical motions on the screen in one common and two relative components of motion.

The implication of this demonstration is that the optic flow, generated by the dot motions on the screen, has been sensorially treated, not in a pictorial way but in a way analogous to a mathematical separation of relative and common components.

This was the initial percept, reported by all subjects. However, some subjects after a while spontaneously told about seeing the event in another way. This shift was in the monograph commented on in the following way. I quote:

> "Our description, however, is not complete yet. For a number of Os (mostly the best observers) the experience of motion can suddenly change its character. Instead of a two-dimensional motion along a common path of motion of two separate elements a three-dimensional motion of a rigid object is then seen. 'It becomes a rod with a knob at each end which twists around an inclined axle. It moves a quarter of a revolution forwards and then a quarter of a revolution backwards; and at the same time, it rises and falls,' one O stated. 'It screws up and down a steeply inclined thread.' " (op. cit. p. 90[2]).

At that time I found the possibility of perceiving the two dots as a rigid object performing a three-dimensional motion highly interesting—but also puzzling. The perceived screwing motion was a unitary motion in 3-space. Geometrical indications about motion in depth, however, were lacking or extremely

---

[2] p. 74, this volume.

poor. When geometrically interpreted as a rotation in depth the display namely represented a parallel projection of rotary motion on a sagittal plane. A question that at that time suggested itself was whether the vector analysis phenomenon under study really could be studied as limited to two-dimensional events. Was that percept an indication about a preference for seeing also such projections as events in 3-space?

Johansson, 1950, Experiment 26.

This experiment—an experiment which I am still happy about—gave me a rather convincing answer to this question. In order to make clear the theoretical background for this experiment, I will before describing the experiment quote a part of its introductory problem setting:

> "In mathematics the simple harmonic motion of a particle can be divided into two components, both in the shape of simple harmonic motions, which act simultaneously on the same particle along the same track. Fig. 38[3] gives a graphic representation of this. a and b are two sine curves, that illustrate two simple harmonic motions with the same frequency and amplitude; but which have 90° phase angle in relation to each other (x-axis = time, y-axis = amplitude). The curve ab, which is also a sine curve, shows the resultant of the two other motions. As regards phase, it is, as shows the diagram, midway between the two components, and has thus a phase angle of 45° with respect to both of these. Its amplitude in relation to the two components is as $\sqrt{2}:1$.

> On the basis of these facts it may be asked: What will be the consequence if two objects execute along the same line simple harmonic motions which are equal to the resultant and one of the components in Fig 38[3]; ab and for example, a?" (Op. cit., p. 114[4].)

Next I quote about the experiment:

> "Two elements move along the same line. They have the same frequency, and their amplitude is 20 mm respectively 28.3 mm. Their respective phase difference is 45°. The medium positions of the paths of motion are made to coincide.

> The experiment, which was carried out with a relatively great number of Os, gave a quite unequivocal result. The descriptions may differ from each other in manner of expression; but in principle they are in complete agreement. An object (*ab*) is seen to oscillate along the common track, with another object (*a*) as the center of motion, in the middle of the path of this motion. At the

---

[3] Fig. 2 below.

[4] p. 88, this volume.

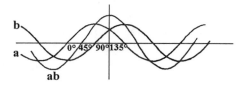

Fig. 2

same time, this aggregate moves to and fro. It is the latter object, that which is at rest in relation to the former which is the carrier of this motion. This object (*a*) moves to and fro, while the other (*ab*) seems to follow suit, and oscillate in relation to *a*.

There is, however, another variant, which several Os mentioned. *ab* can be seen to circulate about *a*. It is the three-dimensional variant which we meet also here. 'For me it is a little sun that moves to and fro in a miniature universe, with a planet that moves in an orbit round the sun' is the way one of the Os describes it. This simile is perhaps the one best suited to give the reader a conception of the motion combination from the point of view of a spontaneous observer, whether the motion is conceived to be two-dimensional or three-dimensional." (Op. cit., p. 112[5])

To this quotation I will just add that it also was shown experimentally that either element could play the role of being the "sun," that is, act as the carrier of the common motion component. It was found that it always was the fixated element that got this dominant role. Thus pursuit eye movements will in this respect determine the percept.

This experiment added a lot to my growing understanding of event perception and perceptual vector analysis. It not only convinced me about the occurrence of three-dimensional vector analysis, it also in a simple but still convincing way demonstrated the possibility of a strict mathematical lawfulness in the visual processing of proximal stimulus. An effect which had tentatively been predicted from pure geometrical considerations had turned out to be experimentally verified in a totally convincing way. The finding that visual perception could be specified and predicted mathematically was at that time commonly regarded as rather unbelievable.

I will sum up the level of development of the vector analysis model in this book in the following three points.

1. The initial problem and therefore also the experimental set-up concerned the study of fronto-parallel, translatory motions. Perceptual fronto-parallel vector analysis was the primary result.

---

[5] p. 89, this volume.

2. In most experiments, but in these experiments only by some subjects, perception of rigid motion in depth in a single object or a constellation of rigid motions suddenly could substitute the fronto-parallel vector analysis. This alternative, once appeared, was preferred by the subjects.

3. A one-dimensional projection could bring about both a perceptual fronto-parallel vector analysis and a vector analysis on a sagittal plane.

Vector Analysis in Three-Dimensional Visual Space

In the 1960s an invitation to me from J. J. Gibson to stay for a period at his laboratory gave me a good chance to take a crucial step toward generalizing the vector analysis approach. At the Cornell laboratory I tried to gain a general understanding of vector analysis processing, resulting in perception of motion in depth and change of form. As said above, I had observed these problems and had, for a special aspect, been able to assimilate them in the initial paradigm of perceptual vector analysis. The general problem in this respect about three-dimensional visual perception, however, was unsolved.

The finding in these initial studies that even extremely impoverished indications about central perspective sometimes evoked perception of motion in depth, had astonished me. I found it hard to avoid the conclusion that these observations indicated a visual tuning for perception in accordance with central projection. Therefore, I decided to test this supposition as critically as possible. My objective was to find out whether geometrical possibilities for perspective in the flow was a necessary condition for three-dimensional vector analysis or if it was not.

By applying an analogue computer technique I created a number of artificial two-dimensional objects on an oscilloscope screen. These "objects" changed their form and size in a non-perspective way. Also the simulated characteristics of the motion and the change of form of the simulated objects intentionally were made highly unnatural and artificial from a mechanical point of view. It namely was produced by a triangular function yielding sudden start and stop moments at the turning points and a constant speed in between. The maximal visual angle of these objects was between 5 and 10 degrees and the cycle time was 1.4 seconds.

In these experiments the subjects were looking at the oscilloscope screen through a specially built telescope. The telescope was mounted on a board, screening the oscilloscope and other apparatus. This resulted in seeing the changing figures as freely hanging in a dark, empty space. In this way visual effects of the environment and a visible screen as a frame of reference were avoided.

From the summingup of the experimental results I will quote the following paragraph.

"The main result of the experiments (67 subjects) may be summarized as follows: When there is change in only one dimension in the stimulus, there is ambiguity between two-dimensional form change and changing slant (depth). All our stimulus patterns which simultaneously changed in two dimensions gave rise to descriptions of percepts in terms of motion in depth of objects which were rigid or changed shape during motion. Seven such proximal stimuli (patterns 2–8) were investigated, and all but one gave practically 100 per cent responses indicating motion in depth as the dominant percept. One pattern (Pattern 8) gave ambiguity between two-dimensional elastic form change and depth motion." (Johansson, 1964, p. 207[6])

As examples of vector analysis effects in this investigation I have chosen two displays which together are especially informative in this respect. Because of their clear demonstration of the visual capacity for separating components representing rigid motion combined by changes of form, I have also earlier in theoretical connections (Johansson, 1975, 1978) made use of these displays. These two displays are:

Display 1. The description of this display was in the original paper (Johansson, 1964) given by a reference to a figure, reproduced below as Display 1 in Figure 3. The figure represents a square (A) symmetrically shrinking to one

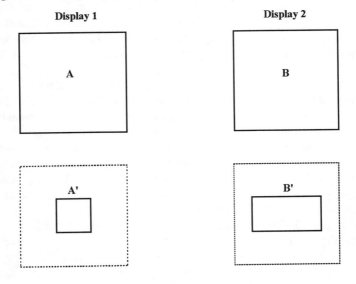

Fig. 3

third of its linear size, then growing to its initial size, etc. The cycle time was 1.4 sec. The subjects reactions to this pattern were reported in the following way:

"The result may be summarized as follows: 66 subjects out of 67 reported perceiving an object moving in depth, toward and away from the observer. Many subjects spontaneously demonstrated the perceived motion by hand movements which made clear that this motion was a translatory motion along the optical axis of the apparatus." (Op. cit., p. 192[7])

Display 2. The only difference between this condition and the one described above was that the extent of shrinking in the X-direction has changed from 1:3 to 2:3, resulting in a cyclical transformation from the square form to a horizontally extended rectangle and back again to a square, and so on. See Display 2 in Fig. 3. The result was summarized in the paper as follows:

"All subjects in both groups reported seeing an object moving backwards and forwards in space as the spontaneous and strongly dominant percept. Among the 43 subjects, 30 reported form change of the surface during motion and there were 16 reports indicating rotation or 'bookfolding' of the object. The Z-motion was in some cases spontaneously reported as shorter than the same Z-motion in Pattern 3[8]." (Op. cit., p. 193[9])

Biological Motion

I regard introducing research on the "biological motion" area of research on vector analysis (Johansson, 1973, 1976) as my probably most effective experimental contribution to the development of the initial vector theory. In my own work it brought about an important generalization of the theory and it has revealed a precision in the perceptual reaction to a maximally thinned out optic flow information, never before thought about as possible to study experimentally. Especially the studies by Cutting and his colleagues (Cutting & Kozlowski, 1977; Cutting, Proffitt, & Kozlowski, 1978) and by Runeson and Frykholm (1981, 1983) have documented this.

The distal stimulus patterns in this type of experiments and demonstrations consist of a number of moving dots (usually 12) forming complicated "trees" of common and relative motions. Each new branch of these trees is indicated only by one added dot. For instance the joint at one of the hips is seen as moving relative to the moving backbone-pelvis system but simultaneously also as being transported by this center of motion of the body. In the next branching the knee

---

[7] p. 148, this volume.

[8] Here Display 2 in Fig. 3.

[9] p. 149, this volume.

joint of the corresponding leg moves in common with the hip but simultaneously it also performs a pendulum motion relative to this joint. Such branchings can proceed in a theoretically predictable sequence down to the most peripheral joints of the toes and the fingers. Such displays always evoke perception of constant distance between the respective joints, irrespective of direction in the third dimension of the connecting imaginary line.

As is well known nowadays, such biological motion patterns regularly result in a highly detailed perception of the specific activity of a human being. Still more, this percept immediately stands out in three dimensions with rigid connections between the respective joints. There never is an initial phase of seeing a two-dimensional pattern of moving dots. In Johansson (1976) it was found that school children, who never before had seen such biological motion patterns, reported seeing a human being from exposure of the moving dots during one to two tenths of a second. This is another impressive indication about visual space as three-dimensional but also about vector analysis as a "primitive" and in this meaning fundamental visual function.

Vector Analysis in the Optic Sphere Theory

Optic sphere theory and small angle stimulation.

In Johansson and Börjesson (1990), it was shown that the optic sphere theory is applicable also for studies of isolated stimulation on the foveal and parafoveal regions of the retina during pursuit eye movements. This finding is important as a warrant for the validity of the analyses to be presented below. To my knowledge, all studies of visual vector analysis have concerned foveal and parafoveal stimulation.

In the investigation referred to, however, it was also found that the metrical precision in perceptual recording was somewhat lower under small angle conditions. This finding will be of evident interest in a following theoretical analysis.

On mechanical recording of moving objects.

The studies of visual vector analysis generally have concerned perception of moving *objects*. The conditions for specifying the perception of objects moving relative to the static environment, however, was not taken up in Johansson and Börjesson (1989). Therefore, when it is a question of analyzing the relations in this respect between the optic sphere theory and the vector analysis effects, a comment on the basis of the optic sphere recording of object motion might be useful.

I will start by reminding that in the new theory it is the directions of rays in the optic sphere (the eye bulb), as recorded by its neural analogue to the spherical coordinate system, that determine the percept. This is a new variant of Lotze's theory about local signs (Lotze, 1886). Thus, according to the new theory, when the eye performs saccadical jumps, the information in the optic flow as such, reflected from a static environment through the stationary lens, does not change. Saccades without orbit motion cause a change of fixation point in the visual field but the records of ray directions in the eye bulb do not change.

When a moving object is fixated and followed by pursuit eye movements, the situation will be somewhat more complicated. The basic outcome is that the object motion is recorded kinesthetically in a most precise way. In real-life situations the fixated object is experienced moving relative to the static environment. When especially observed, however, there exists in fact a certain tendency of instead perceiving the background as simultaneously moving in the opposite direction. This tendency, the so-called Filehne illusion, is easily observed under experimental conditions.

In the optic sphere theory *kinesthetic* information of pursuit eye movements, like such information about orbit motion, is taken into account. Thus, these movements inform about the fixated object's motion *relative to the own body*.

According to my experience, the subject's spontaneous reaction in experiments on vector analysis generally is anchoring the gaze on the component of *common* motion in the pattern (thus performing pursuit eye movements, controlled by this component), while primarily observing the relative-motion components. This spontaneous attitude is, as I later will show, related to a specific optic sphere mechanism for separation of the common motion and relative motion systems.

After these comments on some relations of the optic sphere geometry and the perception of object motions I will now, by applying this theory, explain the vector analysis effects appearing in the two experiments from Johansson (1950) described above.

Experiment 19 in Johansson 1950 interpreted by the optic sphere theory.

In this experiment, the display consists of two dots specifying a moving and shrinking-growing line, as described above and illustrated in Figure 1. Basically this display affords an example of a perceptual two-dimensional, fronto-parallel vector analysis. This optic "line" with its two visible end points is seen as moving to and fro at right angles to its direction.

According to the optic sphere theory, the projection into the eye of the two spots specifies, together with the origo point, a great circle and a distinct arc on that great circle. The projected arc is attached to the great circle as a "passenger" but it can freely move on the great circle and also change its length. Therefore, when the two spots on the distal pattern move relative to each other, the end points of the arc behave in the same way.

The translatory motion of the distal line at right angle to its direction brings about in the sphere a rotation of the great circle. It will rotate about the diameter in the sphere that is parallel to the distal line. Due to the symmetrical motions of the distal spots to and from each other, the arc is periodically shrinking-growing.

Thus, in optic sphere specifications, the motions of the two distal spots are represented by a shrinking-growing arc on a great circle in pendulum motion. The pendulum motion of the great circle about its axis brings about the common component in the vector analysis. Therefore, in terms of mechanics, the rotating great circle acts as a moving frame of reference, while the motions of the points on the great circle specify the motions of the distal dots relative to each other in this moving reference system.

In this way the two-dimensional variant of this first example of vector analysis has been explained as being in full geometric accordance with the mechanical function in the visual system when described in optic sphere terms. It is also evident that the great circle-and-arc mechanism *automatically* performs a vector analysis of the optic flow.

On the three-dimensional "screwing motion" variant.

As was called attention to in the introductory part above, the display under study is ambiguous in the meaning that it sometimes will be described in a way resembling a parallel projection of a rotary motion in depth on a plane sagittal to the eye. This variant illustrates a projection in depth under the most impoverished conditions but still it has been rather regularly met with in experiments of the type described here. In the following I will in more general terms discuss the problems connected with this alternative. Here I will restrict myself to concluding that perception under impoverished stimulus conditions, like those presently under study, experimentally has been found to be more or less ambiguous and that this implies that the information in the optic flow studied in this type of experiments evidently permits two perceptual variants.

Geometrically, projection on a sagittal plane is equivalent to projection on a line. Therefore, the above analysis of the dominating fronto-parallel alternative of vector analysis also encloses a geometrical possibility of reacting with the three-dimensional variant. The difference is perceptual rather than geometrical. Consequently, the perceptual ambiguity means that in both perceptual variants the visual system reacts in accordance with the geometrical analysis applied in the optic sphere theory.

Summing up, I conclude that in the optic sphere theory there is no need for assuming a processing of computational character as an explanation of the vector analysis met with in the results from this experiment. Both the two-dimensional and the three-dimensional vector analysis effects are results of the mechanical function of the visual system, when described in terms of the optic sphere theory.

Discussion of Experiment 26 in Johansson 1950.

This experiment is of great significance for the understanding of visual perception of moving objects as analyzed in terms of the optic sphere theory. It exemplifies a most severe reduction of spatial information in the optic flow; just two elements seen as moving on an invisible stationary line or alternatively on a plane sagittal to the nodal point of the eye. Still, it provides an example of a pictorially one-dimensional event, representing a most impressive vector analysis.

In this display the two dots are in a complicated way moving relative to each other along the line. That the line is stationary implies that there exists no rotary motion of the great circle carrying the projected arc. Thus, the information about the common motion component available in Experiment 19, analyzed above, now is lacking.

Still, all subjects described the event in a way clearly indicating vector analysis. The explanation is as follows: The typical visual reaction when looking at such a display is, as pointed out above, to keep one of the dots fixated during pursuit eye movements (fixating a stationary point under the conditions of Experiment 26 more or less destroys the vector analysis). In this way the kinesthetic recording of the pursuit eye movement provides the common motion component in the optic flow. The visually recorded motion of the not fixated spot relative to the fixated one determines the component of relative motion. Therefore it always was the fixated dot, the dot controlling the pursuit eye movements, that acted as the carrier of the common motion (the "sun"). This holds true for the two-dimensional as well as for the three-dimensional way of perceiving the event which was found to appear also in this experiment. In a similar way as in Experiment 19 the line indicated by the motions of the two dots perceptually could represent a sagittal plane. Thus, also in this one-dimensional case there existed an ambiguity between fronto-parallel motion and motion in depth in accordance with the geometry of the optic sphere theory. The experiment also nicely makes clear the role of kinesthetically controlled and recorded eye movements in the perception of moving objects.

Vector analysis of changing surfaces in the optic sphere theory.

The experiments in Johansson (1964), described above, concern perception of moving and changing homogeneous flat surfaces.

Principles for optic sphere specification of perception of moving objects in general have not yet been worked out in a definite way. The basic principles sufficient for analyses of the now actual two-dimensional, rectangular stimulus patterns, however, are known. Contours of such objects consist of straight lines forming closed units. Therefore each such line will in the present context, in the same way as applied above, be specified in terms of a moving great circle and invariant or changing arcs on this great circle. Since such a contour is a closed line, its replication in the sphere will consist of a series of arcs linked together to an endless chain. Mechanically, the type of linking is rather special; the arcs are

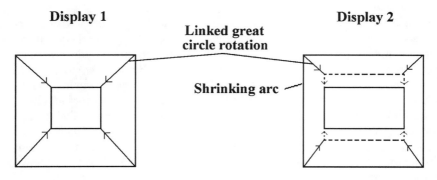

Fig. 4

united in the meaning that at each joint two arcs have their end point in common. This point can act like a ball-and-joint socket, connecting the arcs but also
allowing them to change direction relative to each other. Thus, we get a quadri-
lateral, flexible in three dimensions.

Rigid motion in depth.

Fig. 4 is derived from Fig. 6 in Johansson (1964) to which has been added
some detailed specifications of the ongoing shrinking and change of form of the
figures. These specifications will be used below when describing such changes
in the conceptual framework of the optic sphere theory.

Display 1 in the figure depicts the elementary case of shrinking-expanding
of a fronto-parallel square. The square continuously changes its size without
changing its form. Geometrically, such a pattern also can represent a central
projection of a square of constant size moving sagittally in depth.

I will now describe this event in terms of the optic sphere mechanics. As said
above, in this system the projection of each one of the four distal contour lines
specifies in the sphere a distinct arc and its great circle. The distal contour lines
are pairwise parallel and consequently the corresponding great circles in the optic sphere have on Origo a common axis of rotation which is parallel to the respective couple of contour lines. During a cycle of shrinking-growing of the distal pattern the angle between each pair of the great circles varies correspondingly. Simultaneously, the arcs on the great circles, representing the lengths of
the distal contours, vary perspectively with the shrinking-growing of the contour
lines. Thus, the two-dimensional event on the screen is in the optic sphere represented by a perspectively correct motion in depth. Because the plane of each
great circle is the plane on the distal line and on Origo, the continuous angular
change between the great circles geometrically corresponds to the shrinking-
growing of the distal square.

My own experience of this pattern was that in the experimental situation (seeing the display through a telescope) it in fact is impossible to really *perceive* it as a stationary shrinking-growing surface. Without exceptions this was found to be the reaction also of a number of colleagues watching this display.

These observations are of evident interest in connection with the optic sphere theory. As said above, geometrically the stationary square with a changing size is equivalent with a central projection of a sagittally moving square with a constant size. The mechanical event in the optic sphere, as described here, however, seems to allow only the latter interpretation.

Motion in depth and change of forms.

In Fig. 4, Display 2, a component of non-perspective form change was added. The figure is shrinking-growing and at the same time changing its form. The two horizontal sides have larger amplitude of their motion towards and from each other as compared with the vertical ones. Their relative change of length, however, is less than the corresponding change of the vertical sides.

The specification of this event as projected on the optic sphere is as follows: Each one of the four contour lines are represented by a specific arc of a great circle. The vertical motion of the two horizontal lines brings about a rotation of their great circles towards and from each other about their common horizontal axis on Origo. (Parallel distal lines have in the optic sphere a common axis of rotation of the corresponding great circles, but different slopes relative to the polar axis.) This common axis of rotation is parallel to the distal lines. In the same way, the horizontal motions of the two vertical parts of the contours introduce rotations of their great circles about a common vertical axis.

Because the end points of the arcs act as joints between the vertical and the horizontal arcs, these move together over the same angle. The common motion of the corners is in Fig. 4 indicated by the diagonal arrows at the corner points. The dotted horizontal lines connecting the arrow-heads show the maximal extent of common shrinking. The extent of this shrinking is determined by the horizontal sides because these points indicate the maximal amplitude of vertical motion also for the vertical ones. Thus, this motion is common for the four corners. The change of length of the vertical sides, in excess of those of the horizontal ones, is represented in the spherical projection by a shrinking-growing of the vertical arcs, as shown in the figure.

Thus, also here we find that the perceptual component of common motion is in the mechanical model represented by motions of great circles, while changes in their arcs inform about changing form. It also makes clear that in the optic sphere there exists specification of a distinct motion in the third dimension of an object simultaneously changing its form.

In this way also the vector analysis of simultaneous, three-dimensional motion, and change of form of a planar surface is explained as a result of the regular function of the visual system, when analyzed in terms of the optic sphere theory.

The rotating-square alternative.

This alternative is another example on the variant with seeing motion in depth in accordance with transformation of parallel perspective projection. Here it may appear still more mystifying because we now are dealing with rotary motion in depth of a planar surface. In order to clarify the character of the problem, I will before proceeding say a couple of words about a difference between a parallel projection and a gnomonic projection.

Parallel projection (a case of affine geometry) means that all rays projected from one plane to another have the same direction and thus are parallel. Therefore, under such transformation projected lines can change direction and length while the angular relations in the figure still will stay invariant. From this follows that, as an alternative to the frontal change of form during sagittal motion in depth, the display in the actual experiment can in an ambiguous way represent a parallel projection of a square rotating about a horizontal axis on its center.

If the display instead is described as a central projection of a planar surface rotating in depth, the constant right-angled shape of the figure will in the projection represent a continuous change of form of the rotating surface. The changing distances polar-point-to-horizontal contours during half a cycle of rotation in our example will in the projected figure introduce a change from a moment of right-angular shape to a changing trapezoidal form. Thus, in the geometry of the optic sphere, the rectangular projection should evoke seeing the figure as a rotating and continuously changing trapezoid (because its corner points not are moving in a way indicating rigid motion) and not as the rotating square reported by the subjects.

This seeming contradiction between theory and percept, however, turned out to have a simple explanation. Under the conditions of the experiment the maximal visual angle of the figure was between 5 and 10 degrees and the vertical shrinking was as 1:3. When the figure was seen as rotating about a horizontal axis in the middle of the figure, the corresponding perspective transformation would represent a successive, angular change of direction of each vertical contour of about 20 minutes of arc during each half a cycle of rotation (10 minutes at each corner). Evidently, under the conditions given the total angular change was below or slightly above the neighborhood of the subjects' threshold for effective visual information and therefore not observed by the subjects. The change of form could not or would not be apparent.

Informal observations after increasing the visual angle of the figure to considerably more than 10 degrees resulted in an unambiguous perception of the predicted change during rotation, from a square to a trapezoidal form and back to a square, etc. This indicates that perception also in this case corresponds to the geometry of the optic sphere. The percepts indicating parallelity was the effect of a too much reduced optical information.

In this way perception of transformation of hypothetical parallel projections can (at least in this case) be set aside as a pseudo-problem. However, this is not the only important outcome of the analysis. The basic problem in Johansson (1964) concerned sensory recording of the experimentally documented perceptual separation of a component of rotary motion in depth from a component of change of form of the surface. We have found that in the optic sphere theory this problem is solved by its automatic great circle-and-arc mechanism.

Optic Sphere Specification of Biological Motion

Biological motion patterns are the outcome of combinations of translatory motions and pendulum motions in a group of dots moving on a flat screen. These dots represent projections of the main joints of the human body when performing some kind of movements. Such a pattern of moving dots evokes an immediate and compelling perception of a moving person. This depends on the fact that, generally, two neighboring dots are perceived as rigidly connected and in this way representing the bone between two joints. I will now explain the sensory processing of this perceptual effect by describing it in terms of the optic sphere theory.

Figure 5 illustrates a snapshot of the projection of a person's moving arm into the optic sphere of a perceiver's eye. We will suppose that, like in the stud-

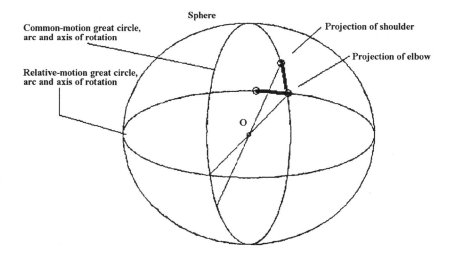

Fig. 5.

ies of biological motion, only the joints of the person are visible and are seen as bright spots.

Let the arc on the vertical great circle be the projection of the swinging upper arm of the person when he/she is stretching for a tool, a cake, or the like, lying on a table in front of the person. Let us also for a moment accept that the shoulder joint of the person stays stationary.

Under these conditions the motion of the upper arm introduces in the sphere a rotary motion of the great circle, representing the upper arm. This great circle will rotate about the diameter on the projection of the shoulder point of the arc. For reaching the object, the person also must stretch his/her arm, thus simultaneously rotate the forearm. Because the forearm is jointed to the upper arm by the elbow joint, the rotation of the forearm must be about the diameter on the elbow point, common for the two arcs.

From this follows that the axis of rotation of the arc-and-great-circle unit, representing the forearm, must rotate in the sphere together with the great circle, specified by the motion of the upper arm. Simultaneously the forearm is rotating about its own axis. Thus, the motion of this great circle represents rotation in a moving coordinate system. In this way this is an example of perceptual vector analysis described in terms of the mechanics of the optic sphere when specifying a complex, rigid rotary motion.

So far we have in an artificial way treated the joint of the shoulder as being stationary in space. Such a situation never will occur in the actual course of events. In our example the shoulder, for plain anatomical reasons, will take part in the activity. This motion was temporarily excluded only for getting a simpler start. In a real person the shoulder (and body) certainly will take part in the stretching. The shoulder point is in this case moving relative to the center of gravity of the body and this center is moving relative to the visible static environment. In the optic sphere this environment is represented by a projectively coherent, optic flow produced by the motion of the orbit of the eye. Thus, this global flow acts as the framework relative to which the shoulder point is moving on the sphere. This point, together with the elbow and wrist points, will be seen as a mechanical system, moving forward in three-dimensional space and stretching towards the cake.

Theoretically, an arbitrary number of new links can be added to such a chain of pendulums moving relative to one another. The anatomy of vertebrates offer striking examples on their existence under real space perception. We can just think of the six-pendulum shoulder-to-fingertips system in man. (Own not published experiments on biological motion of the human arm and hand have in a most convincing way demonstrated the perceptual efficiency of such patterns.)

In fact, also perception of continuous bending would be possible to explain in this theoretical framework. The principles for such biological motion linkages belong to the perception of vertebrate movements but they are of course general for perception of all kinds of (most often far simpler) mechanical linkages.

The above transcription of vector analysis of biological motion to optic sphere processing shows that in this framework biological motion patterns on a screen result in iterations of an elementary type of process, namely with arcs representing distal lines of a constant length. Due to the neural parallel processing in the sensory system, the manifold of pendulum motions of straight lines will not imply any complications.

An essential outcome from this analysis is that the cause for the vivid perception of three-dimensionality, typical for the biological motion patterns, has been found inherent in the mechanics of the optic sphere. It was shown that, due to the great circle-and-arc mechanism, projection of a distal, rigid rod with constant length and in pendulum motion automatically will be recorded with a constant length and moving in the same direction as the corresponding distal rod. This explains the immediate and compelling perception of motions in depth found in the biological motion patterns.

It is also of interest to observe that perceptually a static biological motion pattern has no resemblance with a human body. What will be perceived is just a stationary group of randomly spread dots. This is what must be predicted from the optic sphere theory. When there is no relative motion between the dots their projections will, due to the self-motion of the head of the perceiver relative to the environment, represent a group of stationary dots on a stationary vertical plane in the static environment.

Final Comments

In the present paper I have tried to elucidate the relations between two theoretical approaches to visual event perception which superficially might appear rather different. Still, as the reader has found, in my theoretical work they are closely associated. In fact, both derive from some fundamental experimental findings during my initial research on visual event perception, published in Johansson (1950). The result of my analyses here indicate that the principles for application of the perceptual vector analysis also belong to the basic structure of the optic sphere theory. In this latter theory they are shown to be the consequence of the anatomy and adaptability of the visual system, when the sensory interaction between this system and other senses, especially the kinesthetic one, is taken into account.

The relations between these two types of theory have been analyzed with material from three publications of mine, namely Johansson (1950, 1964, 1973), representing three steps of advancements of the theory of visual vector analysis. The result was that the "great circle-and-arc" mechanism in the optic sphere theory, in all the cases analyzed, has made understandable the sensory separation of common and relative components of motion in the optic flow. Thus, the initial *postulate* in the vector theory about automatic visual separation of common and relative components in the optic flow has in the optic sphere theory been replaced by an *explanation*.

Common for both approaches is the specification of optical stimulation in terms of mechanics and geometry. Purposive mechanical reaction to light is one of the most fundamental biological reactions known. It is a basic function already in the vegetable kingdom and we meet it in unicellular animals. This implies that we must assume that also in vertebrates there exists an inherited, but also in an advanced way expanded capacity for purposive mechanical reaction to changing directions of pencils of light.

In current approaches to visual event perception various types of algebraic models for sensory processing, called "computational theories," have been proposed. My own theoretical position is anchored in the biology of the sensory systems. Seen from such a position these models seems to have a serious limitation. Also when mathematically they can specify and predict visual perception of motion and change of form, they cannot make understandable the sensory processing of the optic flow, resulting in functionally valid space perception. The visual system of man is inherited from very primitive ancestors with their evident collaboration between the visual and kinesthetic senses and there has in this respect not been found any sudden jumps in the evolution of the visual system of vertebrates. Therefore, also if qualified brain processing in man, in accordance with such mathematical models, could be accepted as possible, it seems totally impossible to imagine that primitive animals like, for instance, snails and other mollusks, or amphibians like the frog should have such a capacity for such neural computations. Still, with regard to the anatomy, they all have the same type of chambered eyes as that of man. We also know that, when it is a question of visual control of the organism's behavior relative to its environment, most of these animals have a visual capacity on at least the same level of efficiency as the human visual system. Thus, while the computational type of theories can afford mathematical analogues to event perception, these theories cannot solve the old problem about the visual processing of reflected light, instigated by Kepler and Berkeley. Therefore, from my theoretical standpoint, such descriptions cannot in this respect be accepted as valid explanatory models. As I have tried to show in the present paper, the mechanical type of model representative for the optic sphere approach is far more promising in this respect. In such a theory there is no need for any cognitive-like sensory functions and therefore it is applicable even on the most primitive species with chambered eyes. Furthermore, the mechanical model also seems to be applicable on the ommatidie eyes of the insects.

The base for the perceptual vector analysis is strictly quantitative and so is the optic sphere theory. Therefore, these approaches of course can be formulated algebraically and in this meaning classified as computational theories. Consequently, what I have criticized here does not concern the mathematical form of these theories as such. It is the lack of biologically relevant components, necessary for the understanding of the sensory processing resulting in visual space perception in man and animals, to which I will draw attention.

I will end up with a personal declaration concerning my work on the optic sphere theory. I regard this theory in its present rather uncompleted form as the final step in my work on the establishing, at least for myself, the mechanical aspect of the visual processing of optical stimulation. My intention has been to demonstrate that optic stimulation in connection with sensory recording of movements of the organism affords relevant information about the environment. This model for sensory processing is applicable not only in man but also in at least the whole part of the animal kingdom equipped with chambered eyes. It must be regarded as successively developed during the evolution. At first when we can understand vision in animals with rudimentary brains we will be able to explain in a relevant way visual space perception in man.

References

Cutting, J. E., & Kozlowski, L. T. (1977). Recognizing friends by their walk. Gait perception without familarity cies. *Bulletin of the Psychonomic Society, 7*, 353–356.

Cutting, J. E., Proffitt, D. R., & Kozlowski, L. T. (1978). A biomechanical invariant for gait perception. *Journal of Experimental Psychology. Human Perception and Performance, 4*, 357–372.

Gibson, J. J. (1966). *The senses considered as perceptual systems.* Boston: Houghton Mifflin.

Gibson, J. J. (1979). *The ecological approach to visual perception.* Boston: Houghton Mifflin.

Johansson, G. (1950). *Configurations in event perception.* Uppsala: Almqvist & Wiksell. [Chapter 2, this volume.]

Johansson, G. (1964). Perception of motion and changing form. *Scandinavian Journal of Psychology, 5*, 181–208. [Chapter 4, this volume.]

Johansson, G. (1973). Visual perception of biological motion and a model for its analysis. *Perception and Psychophysics, 14*, 201–211. [Chapter 7, this volume.]

Johansson, G. (1975). Visual motion perception. *Scientific American, 232* (6), 76–88.

Johansson, G. (1976). Spatio-temporal differentiation and integration in visual motion perception. *Psychological Research, 38*, 379–393. [Chapter 8, this volume.]

Johansson, G. (1978). Visual event perception. In R. Held, H. W. Leibowitz, & H.-L. Teuber (Eds.), *Handbook of sensory physiology, Vol. VIII. Perception* (pp. 675–711). Berlin: Springer.

Johansson, G., & Börjesson, E. (1989). Toward a new theory of vision. Studies in wide-angle space perception. *Ecological Psychology, 1*, 301–331. [Chapter 10, this volume.]

Johansson, G., & Börjesson, E. (1990). *Experiments on the optic sphere theory. Slant perception from central stimulation* (Uppsala Psychological Reports, No. 424). Uppsala University, Department of Psychology.

Lotze, H. (1886). *Outlines of psychology.* Translated and edited from the 3rd German edition. Ginn and Company

Runeson, S., & Frykholm, G. (1981). Visual perception of lifted weight. *Journal of Experimental Psychology: Human Perception and Performance, 7,* 733–740.

Runeson, S., & Frykholm, G. (1983). Kinematic specification of dynamics as an informational basis for person and action perception: Expectations, gender recognition, and deceptive intention. *Journal of Experimental Psychology: General, 112,* 585–615.

Tracing Gunnar Johansson's Theoretical Development

Looking at Perceptual Theory Through a Johansson Lens

William Epstein

University of Wisconsin-Madison

Abstract. This essay traces the development of Gunnar Johansson's theoretical commitments from his earliest studies of configurations in event perception to his ongoing work on optic sphere theory. Throughout Johansson's theoretical premises are considered in the context of other theoretical approaches which have contributed to the development of his ideas.

The aim of this essay is modest: I propose to offer a number of observations concerning the Johansson enterprise from the earliest studies of configurations in event perception to the current proposal of optic sphere theory. The first of these observations conditions all the rest. In his writings Gunnar has been theoretically reticent. He has been disinclined to provide explicit renderings of the metatheoretical foundations that support his empirical work. As a consequence, I have had to read meanings into the Johansson canon that are not explicit. In view of the inherent subjectivity of this interpretive enterprise, at times during this talk, Gunnar may feel himself to be a stranger at his own birthday celebration.

My observations are embedded in a nonlinear history of Gunnar's long trek (like another, better known trek, this one also lasted 40 years), from the land of Gestalt theory to the land of direct perception. I will start by tracing a shift of emphasis in Gunnar's work from a concern with organization of perception to a concern with the meaning of stimulation. Next I will comment on a number of fundamental aspects of perceptual theory: the way in which the problem of perception is formulated, the nature of information, the character of the perceptual process. I will conclude with a brief critical exposition of optic sphere theory. Throughout I will refer often to the work of other theorists to provide a broader framework for consideration of Gunnar's ideas.

Two Aspects of the Problem of Perception

Two broad aspects of the analysis of perception are commonly distinguished. One aspect is reflected in Koffka's (1935) famous formulation "Why do things look as they do?" The other aspect may be denoted in an expanded version of Koffka's question: Why do the way things look agree with the way things are? The first question is concerned with the syntax of perception, that is, the laws governing the organization of perception. The second question has a semantic focus; it is concerned with the meaning of stimulation.

Gestalt theory (Koffka, 1935; Köhler, 1947) adopted the syntactic focus. For Gestalt theory the principal task of psychology was to secure an understanding of the organization of experience. Gibson (1966, 1979), on the other hand, adopted the semantic focus. What impressed Gibson was the fact that the perceiver typically is "in contact" with the environment. For Gibson the principal task was to secure an understanding of the grounding of this salient fact. Adopting the syntactic focus encourages an investigative strategy that aims to uncover the processes that underlie perception. Adopting the semantic focus encourages an investigative strategy that aims to identify the information contained in stimulation.

As an aside, notice that when the aim is to elucidate the laws of perceptual organization, no restrictions on the design of experimental displays arise from consideration of the relationship between stimulation and environment and no guidelines for the assessment of the perceptual report arise from consideration of the relationship between the perceptual report and the environment. Instead, in the early stages of investigation the design of displays is guided by intuitions concerning the optical inputs that will challenge the visual system and that will, in consequence, reveal organizational processes. In the later stages, when intuition is supplanted by data-based theory, it is the process model that directs display design. These tendencies are evident in Gunnar's early writings on event perception (Johansson, 1950) and on perception of motion and changing form (Johansson, 1964).

In contrast to the syntactic focus, adoption of the semantic focus brings with it explicit demands on the design of experimental displays. The optical input provided by the display must stand in a principled relationship to a designated distal arrangement. In presimulation times, this commitment required presentation of an actual environmental configuration. With the introduction of simulation capabilities, exact reproduction of distally correlated optical structures replaced the actual distal configuration. But for both procedures, design of the display begins with consideration of the environment.

The earliest of Gunnar's major published works, *Configurations in Event Perception*, takes the syntactic focus. Gunnar set out to do for motion configurations what the Gestalt psychologists intended to do for perception of static forms. In reviewing Gunnar's more recent work from the investigations of biomechanical motion (Johansson, 1973) to the optic sphere theory (Johansson & Börjesson, 1989) I have the impression of a shift from the syntactic focus to the semantic focus. I construe the fundamental objective of the optic sphere theory to be establishment of a direct mapping between spatial layout and virtual structures in the optic sphere and between these latter structures and properties of retinal flow that will allow retinal flow to specify spatial layout directly. The concern with the nature of perceptual processing that is prominent in Gunnar's early work is de-emphasized in the optic sphere theory. Although there is talk about a processor this turns out to be not so much talk about processing as about attributes assigned to the visual system that allow it to make use of the properties of the optic sphere, e.g., that the visual system "knows ... the spatial relations between stimulated retinal spots in terms of distance nodal point-to-retina (radian measured)" (Johansson & Börjesson, 1989, p. 304[1]).

The optic sphere theory is essentially a semantic enterprise: The task it is designed to accomplish is not merely to provide an account of perception but to supply an account of veridical perception.[2] To this end the displays in the later studies are designed from the environment in, that is, they originate in a description of the environment. Of course, this tendency is also evident in the displays designed for the study of biological motion. But the tendency is more pronounced in the recent work, e.g., the studies of slant perception from central stimulation.

What accounts for the shift in focus or at least for the adoption of a dual focus? One factor may be the influence of ecological realism. Another factor may be that inclusion of the semantic focus provides the challenge that perceptual theory needs to keep it honest.

The Problem of Perception

Gunnar is to be counted among the few originals in the field of perception in the past half century. It is all the more striking, therefore, to note that in his framing of the fundamental problem of perception Gunnar has remained faithful to the traditional formulation: *Given a particular distal arrangement the optical input is uniquely determined, but given an optical input, static or dynamic, no distal arrangement is picked out. These coupled assertions are mathematical truths. If in the face of these unimpeachable assertions perception is specific and predictable how is this fact to be understood?* In this formulation, Gunnar has many cosponsors: The Gestalt theorists, the neo-Helmholtzians such as Rock

---

[1] pp. 241f., this volume.

[2] One example: "Will continuous perspective transformations in wide-angle optical flow, simulating aspects of stimulation under everyday condition, bring about veridical three-dimensional perception?" (Johansson & Börjesson, 1989, p. 302; p. 240, this volume).

(1983), and the contemporary computational constructivists such as Marr (1982) all agree that optical input presents the visual system with an ill-posed problem.

By hewing to the established formulation Gunnar has distanced himself from Gibson. At first glance the cause of this separation appears to be a difference between Gunnar and Gibson concerning the possibility of information in stimulation. Gibson affirms that optical structures contain information sufficient to pick out a unique distal state of affairs. Gunnar denies the possibility. I think that the difference between Gibson and Gunnar regarding the prospect of information is indeed real, but it is more nuanced.

Concerning the availability of information, Gibson often wrote as if he believed that a level of description of optical structures can be found that will allow optical structure and the environment to exhibit one to one mapping *unconditionalized on a description of the environment*. It is the latter clause that causes Gunnar to dissent.[3] However, if this clause is relaxed to allow that when specific constraints are satisfied then optical structure *can* specify the distal state Gunnar is likely to agree. Consequently, Gunnar and Gibson do not differ in respect to the availability of information. Their difference concerns the conditions that must be satisfied in order to underwrite claims for information.

Another, more important difference respecting information separates Gibson and Gunnar. The difference rests on the distinction between availability of information and extraction of information. Gibson accorded to the extraction of information only cursory attention in the form of unelaborated adumbrations to information "pick up." In contrast, early on, Gunnar saw a need to postulate decoding principles that operate on optical input. The vector analysis set out in the treatment of mechanical and biological motion (Johansson, 1973, 1976) is the primary example.

In his concern with processing rules, Gunnar exhibits the influence of preexisting Gestalt theory as well as an anticipation of contemporary computational theory. In common with Gestalt theory there is the emphasis on processes that operate on proximal stimulation, although in sharp contrast with Gestalt theory Gunnar considers that the optic array is structured while the Gestalt theorists denied that structure is a property of the optical input.

Gunnar's stance regarding information is similar to the general view promoted by the computationalists. The canonical statement of the computational

---

3 "Your position would have been correct there also if you had included a highly important restriction. But it is lacking. Without *a priori* assuming the existence of 3D rigidity there is no specific information about space available in visual stimulus even in connection with locomotion. [The visual apparatus has to introduce a set of decoding principles for data treatment with the signification that the expanding and changing proximal patterns represent motion in a rigid 3D world.] Taken *per se* the changing information pattern due to locomotion does not contain specific information about a 3D space" (Johansson, 1970, p. 71; p. 174, this volume.).

approach is Marr's (1982) *Vision*. Marr criticized Gibson for failing to give constraints their due and for failing to recognize the need to postulate processes that would make explicit the information that is implicit in optical input. Marr's assertions might seem to echo Gunnar's insistence on this point, but Marr did not observe that his concerns were anticipated by Gunnar at least a dozen years earlier.

The Nature of Johansson's Decoding Principles

In surveying the variety of theoretical approaches at least three types of processes may be distinguished.

1. *Intrinsic process:* One form is intrinsic to the nature of the system that instantiates the process. The process is a characteristic of the system; it is a "design feature" having no reality independent of the system. The clearest example is provided by Gestalt theory. The organizational principles are intrinsic to the physical system, the brain, which instantiates the principles. The principles *per se* are not represented in the system. It is just that the brain has evolved to operate the way it does. The only medium in which organizational principles are represented is the mind of the scientist who describes the system.

2. *Computational algorithms:* The algorithms deployed in computational style theory comprise the second type. These algorithms are designed to get the job done and they are independent of the machine that implements them. In devising the algorithm the theorist may look to the biological hardware for clues but the chief directive influence flows from consideration of the task. The algorithms discussed in Marr's *Vision* are familiar examples.

3. *Perceptual rules:* A third form is exemplified by the processing rules that are at the heart of cognitive constructivism. Rock's (1983) neo-Helmholtzian theory proposes that perception is the product of constructive operations that are rule-following. The rules are represented in the language of perception and it is the semantic content of the rules that is causally active in the perceptual process. These are the features that mark the approach as cognitive.

Where do Gunnar's decoding principles fit in this scheme? The decoding principles certainly are not rules in the sense I have attributed to cognitive constructivism. Nor do they have the character of intrinsic processes; for example, nowhere in Gunnar's writings is it implied that vector analysis is an inherent property of the visual system. I think that the decoding principles are most aptly described as computational algorithms. Indeed, occasionally, Gunnar has explicitly deployed the computer program as a metaphor in characterizing the nature of the decoding principles.

About Constraints

The processes generate unique solutions to the inverse projection problem. Earlier I observed that talk about information in stimulation entails talk about constraints. A similar entailment may be observed in relationship to the processes. It is only when the constraints are posited that the process can work its way. The nature of the constraints that are posited vary, particularly respecting the locus of attribution. Constraints may be attributed to the environment, to the process, or to the perceptual world.

Consider first *environmental constraints*. These are requirements that the environment must satisfy in order that a unique solution become a possibility. Absent postulation of environmental constraints there will be a persistent residual ambiguity and an algorithm capable of picking out a unique solution cannot be devised. If the posited constraints are too special the algorithm will lack generality. (Witness the fate of toy world algorithms.) If the constraints are not satisfied the algorithm will generate a misleading solution. Heavy reliance on environmental constraints is explicit in computational algorithms. Examples are rigidity in Ullman's (1984) structure from motion algorithm and the continuity constraint in Marr and Poggio's (1979) stereopsis algorithm. It should be emphasized that environmental constraints need not be represented in the visual system; they are properties of the environment, not properties of the process.

Next consider *process constraints*. The classic example is Prägnanz or the minimum principle. (For an analysis of the diverse implementations of the minimum principle see Hatfield & Epstein, 1985.) The Gestalt psychologists asserted that the brain is a highly interactive self-organizing system that settles or relaxes into the simplest distribution of activity. Minimization is a property of the process. In addition to the classical deployment in Gestalt theory, minimization theorems are favored by a number of contemporary computational theories that propose massively parallel self-organizing processes.

Parenthetically, notice that in the sense intended by Gestalt theory, the minimum principle operates quite differently than the economy principle developed by Leeuwenberg (1971; Leeuwenberg & Buffart,[4] 1983) or the maximum rigidity constraint proposed by Ullman (1984) in the revision of the original SFM algorithm. In both of these latter cases the perceptual system is presumed to select among candidate perceptual representations in an iterative procedure that is guided by maximum economy (minimal code, minimal change). In the Gestalt-oriented deployment, there is no choosing and there are no intermediate approximate perceptual representations.

Finally, there are constraints that are localized in the web of perceptual interrelations. This type of constraint is prominent in rule-based cognitive construc-

---

[4] Restle's (1979) application of Leeuwenberg's coding theory to Gunnar's motion configurations is germane.

tivism. The contention is that perceptual representations are knit together in perceptual structures and that a particular perceptual representation must comply with the constraints set by the perceptual structure. One illustration will suffice. Given a moving observer, represented relative angular velocity associated with points on the surface of a 3D object, perceived absolute distance and perceived exocentric depth are presumed to be linked in an invariant perceptual structure. Accordingly, when represented relative angular velocity and perceived absolute distance are specified, perceived exocentric depth is determined. Exocentric depth is constrained by the requirements of the perceptual structure. It is as if percepts are required to conform to an internalized natural geometry.[5]

A version of the minimum principle has figured prominently in many of Gunnar's early analyses. The minimum principle has appeared in various forms; least change and maximum rigidity are most frequent. Gunnar's construal of the minimum principle bears a family resemblance to Ullman's (1984) maximum rigidity principle and to the economy principle in Leeuwenberg's coding theory. In all three cases what is minimized is change of the perceptual representation; for Gunnar the perceptual system settles on a representation which exhibits least change; for Ullman the perceptual system maintains an internal model of the viewed object and modifies it at each instant by the minimal nonrigid change that is sufficient to account for the occurrent optical transformation; for Leeuwenberg the perceptual system favors the description that can be instantiated in minimal code. Restle's (1979) application of Leeuwenberg's coding theory to the analysis of the perceptual reports elicited by Gunnar's original motion configurations is the best realization of this latter approach.

This commonality notwithstanding, it seems to me that there is an important difference between Gunnar and the others. For Ullman and for Leeuwenberg (Restle) the minimum principle directs a process of successive approximations and comparisons. For example, in Ullman's maximizing rigidity scheme, over time, as the simulation of the proximal input undergoes cumulative cycles of transformation, the structure-from-motion algorithm makes step by step modifications of the mental model, each modification observing the maximum rigidity constraint, until no further change is needed to accommodate the optical input. The final solution is preceded by many tentative preliminary approximations. Ullman reports an implementation of this scheme in the form of the output of a computer program on a Lisp machine. The error of the internal model is shown to diminish step by step over 10 revolutions (Ullman, 1984, Fig. 5). And in Restle's application of coding theory, a picture is presented of a process that

---

[5] The notion of natural geometry may seem farfetched but it has had considerable appeal. For an older version, see Descartes' advocacy of natural geometry and Berkeley's (1709) critique. For a contemporary version see Shepard's (1984) treatment of putative internalized constraints revealed in apparent motion.

evaluates the information load of various candidate descriptions, comparing the outcomes, and choosing the description that is expressed in minimal code.

Like his Gestalt predecessors, neither the language nor the machinery of choice appears in Gunnar's deployment of the minimum principle. I think that Gunnar has in mind that the perceptual algorithms go directly to the minimal solution without assessing alternatives.[6] Somewhat like the "mathematical" procedure, in contrast to the "experimental" procedure for solving mathematical problems, if the procedure is executed correctly, only the correct solution will be computed; it is not necessary to compute imperfect or incorrect solutions along the way.

Optic Sphere Theory

This brings me to the optic sphere theory.[7] Optic sphere theory represents a significant change of theoretical course, one which cast a new light on the road Gunnar has traveled since 1950. Throughout the four decades leading up to optic sphere theory, Gunnar's writings have been marked by a certain diffidence or reticence in matters of theory. In another individual one might have remarked a tolerance for eclecticism. But the correct reading is quite different. I think that these equivocations were manifestations of a tension in Gunnar's thinking; a tension emanating from an approach-avoidance conflict that Gunnar experienced in the presence of Gibson's theory. From early days Gunnar has been attracted by the prospects of a theory of direct perception but put off by Gibson's version because he could not accept that it was sufficient to the task. The conflict and the resultant tension have now been resolved and dissolved by the development of optic sphere theory. The optic sphere theory is nothing less than a Johanssonian theory of direct perception.

As a program the optic sphere theory bears an obvious Gibsonian stamp. But owing to its special Johanssonian character it allows a theory of direct perception to go through, at least in principle. (I hasten to add here that while Gibson intended to offer a theory of the direct perception of almost everything, Gunnar aims to account for the more traditional contents of perception, e.g., spatial layout, motion.)

Two incontrovertible assertions, one concerning anatomy, the other geometry, are the starting points for optic sphere theory. The first is that the retina is

---

[6] As Gunnar observes in a recent formulation, respecting biological motion displays: "this percept immediately stands out in three dimensions with rigid connections between the respective joints. There never is an initial phase of seeing a two-dimensional pattern of moving dots" (p. 282 in this volume).

[7] Optic sphere theory is in an early stage of evolution. The commentary that follows will certainly need significant revision as the theory assumes more mature form.

hemispherical and the second is that any shaped surface can serve as a projection surface for light reflected from the environment. The next step is to adopt a sphere as a projection surface. This geometric construction is designated the optic sphere. The notion of the optic sphere activates in me mental images of Gibson's optic array. Despite their proximity in my representational space, the two constructs are quite different. First, the optic sphere *is* a projection surface. Gunnar has always insisted that projective geometry is the appropriate tool for the analysis of optical structure. In contrast, the optic array explicitly avoids a projection surface. Instead, optical structures are described in terms of a complex array of nested, solid visual angles. Secondly, the optic sphere allows for the construction of virtual structures that mimic the 3D structure of the environment. The "lost" third dimension is alive and well and present in the optic sphere.

But this much is only geometry. And we are not equipped with sensory transducers for treating geometric abstractions or virtual surfaces and structures. I am reminded of Bishop Berkeley's complaint lodged against the "natural geometry" proffered by his predecessors (Descartes, Kepler) in accounting for perception of spatial layout: "But these *lines* and *angles*, by means whereof *mathematicians* pretend to explain perception of distance, are themselves not at all perceived ... (moreover) those lines and angles have no real existence in nature, being only an hypothesis framed by mathematicians ... that they might treat of that science (optics) in a *geometrical* way" (Berkeley, 1709, Sec. XII–XIV). It is here that the anatomical fact comes into play. Owing to the hemispheric shape of the retina, and granting a number of processor assumptions, it becomes possible to delineate properties of retinal flow that are specific to the virtual structures. And so there has been demonstrated a 1:1 mapping from environment to optic sphere and from optic sphere to properties of retinal flow and by extension a 1:1 mapping between perception and the environment.

What does the optic sphere contribute that is different from the optic array? The answer is that the optic sphere makes available copies or iconic models of the distal world whereas the optic array is supposed to present only optical correlates. This is a decidedly odd attribution to make to Gunnar, but it seems unavoidable on a straightforward reading of the initial published version of the theory (Johansson & Börjesson, 1989). And in his most recent tentative elaboration of the theory Gunnar himself comments, "... optic sphere theory introduces a renewal of the classical retinal image theory. Again the visual system has got a kind of picture to 'look' at ..." (Johansson, 1991).

But what is the cash value of pictures or copies? Perhaps Gunnar will explain. All that is needed in order to sustain the principal function of the visual system, supporting successful action, is information and it would seem to make no difference what form this information assumes. I have the impression that what has troubled Gunnar respecting Gibson's information theory of perception is that the spatiotemporal optical structures that inform the visual system resemble neither their source nor their product. In optic sphere theory, distal, optical, and perceptual states are isomorphic. And this relationship of resemblance seems to ease the way for Gunnar to advocate an information-based theory of direct perception.

Gunnar is fully aware that postulation of a new conception of the optical environment, even one with the mimetic powers of the optic sphere is only one component, however important it may be, in a theory of perception. Two additional components are needed: a description of mechanisms that can access the optic sphere and a program of psychophysical experimentation that evaluates the utilization of the putative information.

Gunnar approaches the first of these objectives in his description of processor assumptions. The importance of these assumptions cannot be overestimated. Without them, the optic sphere remains only an ingenious application of projective geometry. Consequently, it is important to assess their plausibility. We can make one a priori test by applying the following rule: Inasmuch as these are assumptions about an *actual* biological vision system, not merely a conceptual visual system, no attributions should be made for which we cannot offer a candidate real detector or transducer at some level in the visual system. Consider, for example, assumptions concerning registration of retinal coordinates. Neuronal detectors can only detect actual physical energy, so one can accept without qualms that the retinal location that is activated by the light originating in a distal point may be registered. In fact, that a complete map of local signs may be available. Indeed, this has been assumed explicitly or implicitly at least since Helmholtz. But how does the following assumption stand up to the test: "the visual system 'knows' ... the spatial relations between stimulated retinal spots in terms of distal nodal point-to-retina (radian measures) ..." (Johansson & Börjesson, 1989, p. 304[8]). What sort of neuronal unit could possibly be sensitive to relations that involve the nodal point as a term?

Finally, turning to the psychophysical component, what sort of experimentation would strengthen the case for the optic sphere theory of perception? Initially, it would be a mistake to ask too much. At the outset, a non-Popperian verification strategy is sensible. This verification strategy eschews the logic of exclusion. Instead, a program of experimentation is executed with the aim of determining whether data in the domain covered by the theory will be compatible with the theory. This is the strategy that Gunnar has adopted in these early days of optic sphere theory. But at some stage the theory must be subjected to a sterner test, one that will pick out optic sphere theory from among its rivals.

I have offered a retrospective overview of Gunnar's travels from his starting point in Gestalt theory to his current location in optic sphere theory. Retrospecting can be 20:20; prospecting is usually fuzzy. But this much is clear: The radical character of optic sphere theory has the potential to inspire a revolution in

---

[8] pp. 241f., this volume.

the formulation of the problems of perception and a redirection of experimental research. For this prospect, we are once more, as we have been in the past, indebted to Gunnar Johansson.

Acknowledgment

This essay originated in a talk given on August 21, 1991 at a symposium that was convened in Uppsala to celebrate Gunnar Johansson's 80th birthday. I wish to express my appreciation to Sheena Rogers for her help in preparing the talk and this article.

References

Berkeley, G. (1709). *An essay toward a new theory of vision.* Dublin: Yeremy Pepyat.

Gibson, J. J. (1966). *The senses considered as perceptual systems.* Boston: Houghton Mifflin.

Gibson, J. J. (1979). *The ecological approach to visual perception.* Boston: Houghton Mifflin.

Hatfield, G., & Epstein, W. (1985). The status of the minimum principle in the theoretical analysis of visual perception. *Psychological Bulletin, 97,* 155–186.

Johansson, G. (1950). *Configurations in event perception.* Uppsala: Almquist & Wiksell. [Chapter 2, this volume.]

Johansson, G. (1964). Perception of motion and changing form. *Scandinavian Journal of Psychology, 5,* 181–208. [Chapter 4, this volume.]

Johansson, G. (1970). On theories for visual space perception: A letter to Gibson. *Scandinavian Journal of Psychology, 11,* 67–74. [Chapter 5, this volume.]

Johansson, G. (1973). Visual perception of biological motion and a model for its analysis. *Perception and Psychophysics, 14,* 201–211. [Chapter 7, this volume.]

Johansson, G. (1976). Spatiotemporal differentiation and integration in visual motion perception. *Psychological Research, 38,* 379–393. [Chapter 8, this volume.]

Johansson, G. (1991). *Elaborating the optic sphere theory.* Unpublished manuscript.

Johansson, G., & Börjesson, E. (1989). Towards a new theory of vision: Studies in wide-angle space perception. *Ecological Psychology, 1,* 301–331. [Chapter 10, this volume.]

Koffka, K. (1935). *Principles of Gestalt psychology.* New York: Harcourt, Brace.

Köhler, W. (1947). *Gestalt psychology: An introduction to new concepts in modern psychology* (Rev. ed.). New York: Liveright.

Leeuwenberg, E. (1971). A perceptual coding language for visual and auditory patterns. *American Journal of Psychology, 84,* 307–349.

308   WILLIAM EPSTEIN

Leeuwenberg, E., & Buffart, H. (1983). An outline of coding theory: A summary of related experiments. In H. G. Geissler, H. Buffart, E. Leeuwenberg, & V. Sarris (Eds.), *Modern issues in perception*. Amsterdam: North-Holland.

Marr, D. (1982). *Vision*. New York: W. H. Freeman.

Marr, D., & Poggio, T. (1979). A computational theory of human stereo vision. *Proceedings Royal Society London B, 204*, 301–328.

Restle, F. (1979). Coding theory of the perception of motion configurations. *Psychological Review, 86*, 1–24.

Rock, I. (1983). *The logic of perception*. Cambridge, MA: MIT Press.

Sheperd, R. (1984). Ecological constraints on internal representation: Resonant kinematics of perceiving, imagining, thinking and dreaming. *Psychological Review, 91*, 417–447.

Ullman, S. (1984). Maximizing rigidity: The incremental recovery of 3-D structure from rigid and nonrigid motion. *Perception, 13*, 255–274.

Comments on Epstein: Looking at Perceptual Theory Through a Johansson Lens

Gunnar Johansson

Uppsala University

The editors have asked me to convey some personal reactions to Bill's paper. I will do so by commenting on the text under some of the main headings in his paper. Before starting this, however, I will express my admiration for Bill's account of how my theoretical stance has evolved and finally come to some degree of relative maturity. In my attempts to achieve an objective retrospective view I find that—after disregarding a number of too positive ingredients—I clearly recognize my own profile in Bill's description.

Bill starts by saying that his task not was an easy one. I quote: "In his writings Gunnar has been theoretically reticent. He has been disinclined to provide explicit renderings of the metatheoretical foundations that support his empirical work" (p. 297). I understand Bill's difficulties in this respect. This in fact has been a deliberate attitude and it is the consequence of my lack of a real anchorage in any one of the current theoretical trends. (It seems to me as if in his preceding analysis Bill himself has made this observation.)

Two Aspects of the Problem of Perception

Bill's distinction of syntactic and semantic focusing is interesting. I never before have met this categorization of perceptual theories formulated in such a distinct way. Of course I agree in Bill's statement that my *Configurations in Event Perception* (1950) is a clear example of a syntactic approach. I also find that his analyses of my successive theoretical progression mainly are correct. The influences from my close contact with Gibson, with his clear emphasis of the semantic aspect, is evident. Possibly I myself would emphasize that in my opinion a firm syntactic basis must be regarded as a prerequisite for a fruitful work along the semantic line, but also that both components are necessary for an understanding of the language of visual perception.

The Problem of Perception

Bill is right in saying that I have been faithful to the traditional fundamental problem of perception, which he has given the following formulation: "Given a particular distal arrangement the optical input is uniquely determined, but given an optical input, static or dynamic, no distal arrangement is picked out. These coupled assertions are mathematical truths. If in the face of these unimpeachable assertions perception is specific and predictable how is this fact to be understood?" (p. 299). My present research still concerns this fascinating problem. However, to the traditional formulation I would add an important demarcation of epistemological character. Thus I prefer to read Bill's text as follows (with my addenda italicized): "Given a particular distal arrangement the optical input is uniquely determined *in immediate visual recording*, but given an optical input, static or dynamic, no distal arrangement is picked out *from recording only the optic input*. This coupled assertions are mathematical truths...." I regard these addenda as necessary because I accept the possibility of a more complicated geometrical specification of visual information in the optic flow. Such a possibility was touched on in Johansson (1964) and it was made substantial in Johansson & Börjesson (1989). If I am not mistaken, Bill will agree with me when I assert that my 1964 paper with its experimental studies of distinct rigid motion and simultaneous distinct change of form of an object and with its introduction of assumptions of functional constraints in the neural processing, pointed to a possible new way toward a solution of this problem. I myself reacted in that way. Börjesson's and my present work on the optic sphere theory should be looked at as a continued advancing in this direction.

The Nature of Johansson's Decoding Principles

Bill distinguishes three different theoretical types of approach to visual space perception. These are (1) accepting intrinsic processing, (2) specification in terms of computational algorithms, and (3) introducing perceptual rules like those of cognitive constructivism (p. 301). He finds that my decoding principles are not related to the perceptual rules in cognitive constructivism. Neither do they seem to him to have the character of intrinsic processes. He concludes that they are "most aptly described as computational algorithms" (p. 301).

I must declare that to me this classification does not hit the point. I would feel more at home in the intrinsic category—after widening that domain considerably. For me the term "intrinsic" in connection with sensory psychology means inborn *in the neural system*. My decoding principles (principles for decoding the information in the optic flow) are thought of as inherent, that is "programmed" neurophysiologically, in the interconnections and functional interactions in the network of neurons constituting the visual system from the receptor cells through the mid-brain and spread in the cortex. In this meaning they are "intrinsic"—but as such the specialized outcome of a phylogenetic programming.

With this standpoint of mine the logic underlying Bill's conclusion is understandable. To a certain extent I regard the visual system as being analogous to a neural computer, albeit a computer slowly programmed during the successive evolutionary trial-and-error-and-progress construction of the hardware.

It is correct that occasionally I have in a metaphorical way referred to computer programming. I now find, however, that, in order to avoid misunderstandings, I should also have said that essentially the "programs" called decoding principles are *builtin* into the specific visual systems of the species.

Given a digital computer, the desired output can be generated by a number of differently constructed algorithms. This does not apply to visual perception as I understand it. In the visual system a flexible software does not exist. It lacks capacity for basic restructuring or plasticity. This distinguishes my view from the pure computational approach. I will also underline, however, that while in my view the visual system is a system constructed for an automatic processing of optic information, it also is "preprogrammed" for automatic recalibration and for refining the outcome by perceptual learning. Furthermore, these automatized functions do not prevent occasional appearance of ambiguity or indistinctness. However, as is well known, under such everyday situations the organism spontaneously will try to gain distinct information by displacing the head.

These viewpoints concern the automatic operations of the system. However, I also will declare that my thinking about the functioning of the visual system broadly conceived also includes attentional factors and intentionality as essential components. Already during my studies of the effects of intentional fixation in my 1950 book I learned a lot about the sometimes crucial role played by such functions. My current work on the optic sphere theory has again brought to the fore this aspect of a forthcoming *general* theory of visual perception. This aspect hardly can be characterized as belonging to the traditional cognitive camp. However it includes a kind of "higher order" functions in the organism and in this meaning it seems to have clear relations to this type of theory. Therefore, if intentional fixation can be regarded as a cognitive process I will not exclude a certain relation also to traditional "cognitive" components from my present theoretical profile. Let me also add that from my point of view the current theoretical cleavage between perception and thinking is irrelevant and unhappy. Active perception is a search for knowledge while thinking and forming of concepts basically means organizing of memorized such knowledge.

To sum up: When I try to characterize my position with regard to the three common types of theoretical approaches discussed, I find that my position in fact seems to be possible to characterize as a conglomeration of components related to all of them. (What a theorist!)

About Constraints

Under this heading I find nothing to add to Bill's application of the constraint concept and no changes to propose. As already mentioned, I introduced this concept in Johansson (1964) using the term "restriction." In my theorizing it solely concerns the category here called process constraints. It is highly satisfying to find that Bill has noticed this and also has observed and underlined that for me a constraint implies spontaneous and immediate application.

Optic Sphere Theory

Reading Bill's analysis of the present state of the optic sphere approach and his comments to this venture has been highly stimulating. First I will mention my deep satisfaction when finding that I here meet a colleague who has thoroughly penetrated the material available so far—and genuinely has understood my intentions. Second, I highly appreciate his very useful restrictive and critical comments. Third, given his solid background, Bill's declaration of his general appreciation of the approach of course for me is very gratifying.

Bill starts by pointing out that the classical problem about the "natural geometry" vanishes in the geometrical framework of the optic sphere. I agree. For instance this remark tells me how thoroughly he has penetrated the consequences of this new approach.

Next he compares the optic sphere with Gibson's optic array and makes a theoretically important observation, an observation that puzzles him. While the optic array "is supposed to present only optical correlates," the optic sphere "makes available copies of or iconic models of the distal world" (p. 305). This makes Bill profoundly embarrassed—he does not recognize the notorious pursuer of the retinal image concept and finally he asks, "But what is the cash value of pictures or copies? Perhaps Gunnar will explain" (p. 305). I will try to do so by the following comments.

Regrettably I must start by criticizing myself for a careless and erroneous use of the term "picture" in the sentence quoted by Bill, but I will also thank him for directing my attention to that error. In the study of visual perception "image" and "picture" are concepts belonging to sensory reactions to optical stimulation. However, both only allude to some kind of *optical copies*, not to real *physical things*. Talking about the visual reaction when looking at a physical object, say a chair, we say: "I see a chair." It would be erroneous and misleading to say "I see a picture of a chair." However, what I now must accuse myself for is just that I, in the quoted sentence, have committed that mistake.

In the vocabulary of the science of vision the theorist until rather recently has made use of the term "image" also for characterizing the sensory (or cognitive) process in question. Gibson's change from retinal image to optic array, my own event perception approach with its study of sensory interaction of pictorial elements, and the recent computational approach successively have made irrelevant the specification of the visual process in terms of image. However, instead the theorists found themselves compelled to think about visual representation of seen objects in terms of a cerebral processing.

For me personally also this new type of approach came to an end with my construction of the optic sphere theory. A for me most fascinating consequence of this new approach is that now I am no longer enforced to work with the mentioned type of abstract representations. In the manuscript quoted by Bill I have sketched how in this new theoretical framework a preprogrammed function automatically locates the neural reaction of each stimulating ray hitting the retina onto the distal point in space from which it was reflected. Thus, according to the theory the perceiver in my example above really sees the fixated object as such in its physical position, with its physical three-dimensional form and size, and in his/her physical environment. He/she will *see* it as painted by the neurochemical reactions to light in the stimulated retinal receptors.

A "painted" object still is an object, and not a picture. My forgetting of this caused my error in the manuscript—and probably Bill's problem.

When scrutinizing the processor part of the theory Bill applies the following rule: *"Inasmuch as these are assumptions about an actual biological vision system, not merely a conceptual visual system, no attributions should be made for which we cannot offer a candidate real detector or transducer at some level of the visual system"* (p. 306, my italics). I agree.

An essential component in the optic sphere theory concerns determining the directions in three dimensions of the incoming rays. This was attained by the processor specifications of the positions of two special points in the eye: the retinal point stimulated by a given ray and the location of the nodal point of the lens. Referring to his rule Bill accepts the application of our variant of Lotze's old local sign theory when it is a question of the localization of the relevant retinal point. However, he calls in question the assumption that sensory information about the position of the lens really exists.

This assumption is of a deciding significance for the directness and geometrical simplicity of the theory. Therefore, Bill's strong question mark must be taken seriously and I am very anxious to clarify the arguments for my accepting of this assumption.

I wholeheartedly agree with Bill that his rule is essential. In fact, my insight about the importance of the principle now set forth by Bill was the basic reason for constructing the processor (with its *explicit* specifications of the essential assumptions) as a separate part of the theory. This principle also was determining in Börjesson's and my discussions about the components of the processor. I will proceed with explaining why the actual assumption, also when examined in this way, was added to the processor.

When anew reading the actual text in Johansson and Börjesson (1989) I have found an imperfection in the text that might at least partially explain Bill's reaction. The nodal point of the lens is a geometric entity lacking a corresponding visual receptor. Therefore the rule as formulated by Bill in a literal sense could mean that this assumption should not be accepted. In the paper our argument for its relevance is only very briefly hinted at by saying in passing that the assumption "is an example of the sensory capacity for .... and for localizing body parts in space without visual support" (Johansson & Börjesson, 1989, p. 304; p. 242 in this volume). This statement was not supported by a reference to earlier known data. This is a deficiency. Therefore I will here to full length present my underlying theoretical and empirical reasons for accepting the assumption about known position of the lens of the eye and its nodal point.

A fundamental component in the optic sphere theory as developed by Johansson and Börjesson (1989) is accepting that there exists an intimate interaction and "overhearing" between the visual and the kinesthetic senses. The assumption that the visual system knows the functional position of the lens basically is founded on this principle. In this special case it is supported by an empirically well-established rule about kinesthetic control of spatial distances and relations in the own body. This latter rule will be formulated thus: *The spatial relations between components of the body which are activated by the motor system are continuously recorded in the central nervous system.* The doctor's traditional tests for undisturbed brain function in these respects are outcomes of this classical finding. The patient is for instance instructed with closed eyes to hit his/her nose with an index finger or, in a somewhat more advanced test, to try under the same condition to bring the index fingers of the two hands to meet tip-to-tip in front of him/her. Manifest lack of this ability is taken as an indication of disturbances in the kinesthetic/motor control of the body.

The described capacity in man (and animals) presupposes an exact information in the respective brains about the specific dimensions of the own skeleton together with an equally efficient, continuously renewed information about the spatial effects of the ongoing intentional muscular activity. Such information is a necessary condition for all types of intentional locomotion.

Should this sensory capacity be regarded as relevant also in the case of recording the position of the common point of convergence of rays passing the lens? With regard to the construction of the theory with assumed overhearing between vision and kinesthesis the answer must be yes. The question concerns a spatial location in the eye bulb and socket. These positions are controlled by two uniquely sensitive muscular systems: (1) the system for accommodation by the ciliary muscle connected to the lens and controlling its refractive power, and (2) the intricate oculomotor system for controlling movements and directions of the optic axis fovea-to-nodal-point relative to the socket of the eye.

It is also easy to find examples of implicit applications of our assumption in current, geometrically less well-specified theories on space perception. Moreover, a special application of this perceptual effect exists in the theories on information from binocular disparity. There the positions in the skull of the eye sockets and the distance between them (without relevant optical stimulation) are taken into account. This presupposes an implicit assumption about sensory "knowledge" of a distance in the skull and about the actual angles of convergence of the optic axes. Thus, assumptions similar to the one discussed here.

Finally Bill touches the question about relevant conditions for experimentation in the framework of the optic sphere theory. Experiments with *simulation* of an optic flow representing a specific environment must satisfy a highly restrictive condition generally ignored in earlier research. This is the demand for control of a chosen distance eye-to-projection surface together with regulation of the simulated motion of the specific optic element. This is due to the three-dimensional metric in the new theory.

These demands only concern research with a *simulated* environment. It is easily seen that in experiments with perception of real objects or spatial elements (in motion relative to the nodal point of the eye) no such restrictions will exist. In this case the changing real distance and direction of each ray with its automatic corresponding variation of the angular motion at the nodal point will do the job in optic sphere terms.

Börjesson and myself still are in the initial stage of experimentally testing the validity and efficiency of the theory. Our principle so far has been to investigate selected problems, considered as especially interesting, while applying a standardized technical principle and set-up. Probably we will proceed some further steps along this line. Owing to this present lack of technical variation, I find it premature to give more distinct comments on the possibilities of future experiments with different problems and techniques. However, with reference to our experiments so far, I am decidedly optimistic.

References

Johansson, G. (1950). *Configurations in event perception.* Uppsala: Almqvist & Wiksell. [Chapter 2, this volume.]

Johansson, G. (1964). Perception of motion and changing form. *Scandinavian Journal of Psychology, 5*, 181–208. [Chapter 4, this volume.]

Johansson, G., & Börjesson, E. (1989). Toward a new theory of vision. Studies in wide-angle space perception. *Ecological Psychology, 1*, 301–331. [Chapter 10, this volume.]

Applied Research

Human Factors in Road Traffic

An applied part of Gunnar Johansson's research work

Kåre Rumar

Swedish Road and Traffic Research Institute, Linköping

Abstract. Gunnar Johansson was a Swedish pioneer in human factors research. His interest in this area was primarily concerned with the interaction between the driver and the vehicle lighting, the road sign system and the braking of a car in surprise situations. His main methods and findings in these areas are presented and commented upon. Now, 25 years after his active research in road traffic, it is evident that his work constitutes an enduring achievement. Johansson's findings continue to contribute to road traffic planning around the world.

Introduction

The science of human factors, human engineering, became prominent during the Second World War. By then the growing complexity of modern weapon systems made it clear to most responsible decision makers that selection and training were no longer enough to adapt man and technology to each other. This fact became especially evident within air and submarine warfare.

However some unusually clearsighted scientists had long before that understood that the science of psychology could make important contributions by analyzing and specifying human characteristics and human limitations so that the technological surroundings (instruments, controls, signs, signals, systems, rules, etc.) could be designed for and adapted to man in advance of training. It is probably not a coincidence that J. J. Gibson was one of the pioneers in this field (Gibson & Crooks, 1938).

Gunnar Johansson was the human factors pioneer in Sweden. When he became a professor at the University of Uppsala in 1957 psychology was a "soft" science closely related to philosophy. However he immediately realized that his expertise and knowledge in perception and research methodology in experimental psychology could be used to study and specify how various types of equipment should be designed in order to maximize human performance and minimize human effort and errors. He was consulted by industry, military and air force representatives to improve, for instance, inspection procedures and equipment and instrument designs.

His decision to move into the area of human factors was probably also influenced by the fact that work in this area presented one of the few possibilities to obtain and build the kind of equipment that Gunnar needed to carry out his more basic studies in space and motion perception—for instance oscilloscopes and other electronic apparatus. Only a few years after he became the leader of the Department of Psychology it had more external contracts and money than the rest of the faculty of social sciences combined.

The initiative to start human factors studies in the area of road traffic was taken by Gunnar himself. To that point nobody in the road traffic society had understood the need for basic perceptual research as a basis for decisions to improve road safety. His initiative was met by considerable skepticism both from government administrators and from industry. It was not until many years later when the results were confirmed (often in studies carried out abroad) that his pioneering work was really appreciated. We, who have followed in his footsteps, however, have enjoyed the advantages of his ice-breaking activities.

During about 10 years of active studies of road traffic problems, Gunnar covered many areas. Below an effort is made to give an idea of his research within three of these areas:

- Driver visual performance in night traffic conditions
- Driver information acquisition from road signs
- Driver reaction times in real traffic

For each area one of his early publications is described to illustrate his style of analysis. It should be noted here that many of the studies in road safety were published in Swedish. The publications used in this article however are based on the international publications. These often appeared 3 to 5 years after the Swedish publication.

Vision in Night Traffic

In the late 1950s it was well known from road accident statistics that the risk of having an accident during night was more than two times that during daylight. It was also known that human visual performance during lower levels of illumination is comparatively poor. Other reasons for the high accident rate were considered to be fatigue, alcohol, proportionally more young drivers, and cars in bad condition at night. In the United States, United Kingdom, and the Netherlands, studies were carried out to establish how vehicle lighting characteristics influenced the distance of clear perception and the identification of objects on the road. Typically these studies were carried out by the automobile lighting industry and were not very well controlled or reported. The clear motive was to improve headlight performance.

Gunnar managed to receive a grant from the Swedish Road Safety Council to study driver visibility distances in night traffic on roads without stationary lighting. He set out very systematically by starting to investigate the methodology that could be used to measure visibility distance. Previous studies had simply registered detection distance to obstacles when approaching them. Could that subjective methodology have enough reliability?

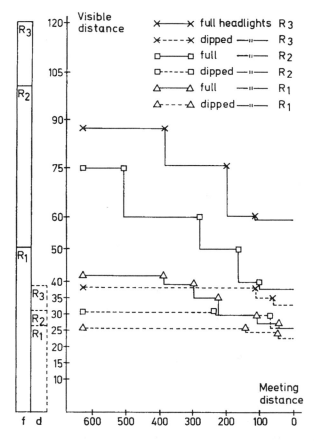

Fig. 1. Mean values of visible distance (meters) for full (f) and dipped (d) symmetrical headlights, for three different signal reflectances, plotted against meeting distance. The height of the columns on the left-hand side of the graph show visible distances where there is no approach light, for the three different signal reflectances (from Johansson et al., 1963).

In order to study this problem he used a versatile eye movement recorder he had constructed for other purposes (Johansson & Backlund, 1960). The subjects were seated in a stationary car fixating an object facing the subjects placed on a rotating carousel at some distance in front of the vehicle. Oncoming cars were approaching with their headlights on and when the glare became too severe the subjects could no longer follow the swinging object with their eyes. This was immediately recorded by the eye movement recorder and an objective distance was received at which the subject lost sight of the object. It was shown that the objective and the subjective methodology gave the same results. Consequently the more simple subjective methodology was used in the following series of studies.

The next methodological problem to be studied was whether a simple detection measurement and a method based on the psychophysical method of limits (falling scale) could yield similar results. The subjects were again seated in a stationary car with a number of stationary objects placed in front of the car on different distances. They were to report the farthest away object they could see. Initially the subjects could see most of the obstacles but as the approaching car created increasing glare the subjects gradually lost sight of the obstacles. This method worked fine and was much more effective from a data collection point of view. However it gave somewhat longer visibility distances than the detection method (Johansson et al., 1963).

The results obtained in these earlier studies were striking: The visibility distances that normal drivers had to dark obstacles on the road when encountering an oncoming vehicle was no greater than 25 meters! Considering the speeds that were normal on dark roads all over the world this meant that drivers had no possibility to brake before a dark obstacle if it happened to be in front of the vehicle in the most critical part of an encounter. The automobile and the automobile lighting industry did not want to believe the results. The authorities doubted it seriously and did not want to take action. However, the results were confirmed in later studies by Johansson and his collaborators (e.g. Johansson & Rumar, 1968) and by international studies. It was not until about 10 years later that these results were accepted by everybody and forceful action was taken to counteract the night visibility problem.

Already in the early studies Gunnar showed that one simple countermeasure to bad visibility is extensive use of retroreflective material (Johansson et al., 1963). A retroreflective pedestrian tag can change the detection distance of a dark obstacle in low beam from 25 meters to 125 meters. In later studies Gunnar and his co-workers also investigated other countermeasure possibilities such as asymmetric low beams, silhouettes, halogen light sources, and polarized headlights (Johansson & Rumar, 1970, 1971a; Rumar, 1974).

Night Driving with Full or Dipped Headlights

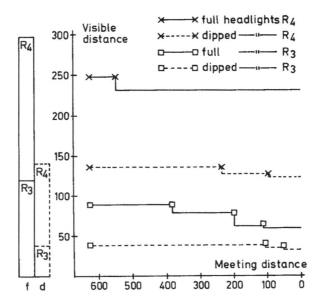

Fig. 2. Mean values of visible distances (meters) for full (f) and dipped (d) symmetrical headlights, for two reflectances, R_3 = 25% and R_4 = reflector tape, plotted against meeting distance. The columns on the left-hand side have the same significance as those in Fig. 1 (from Johansson et al., 1963).

The pioneering work carried out by Gunnar in the area of night driving visibility during the 1950s and 1960s is still found as reference papers in most traffic engineering and road safety handbooks. His pupils keep up his reputation and Sweden is still a well-recognized country from a night visibility research point of view. The methodologies he developed are still used.

His main idea that human visual performance and human visual characteristics should be the basis for design of stationary and mobile lighting systems is now generally accepted. His own work is one of the main reasons for this development.

Information from Road Signs

All around the world authorities put up road signs to inform drivers about possible dangers, prohibitions, interesting points, direction, and distance to various destinations, etc. It is more or less taken for granted that drivers read and use this information. A large number of studies have investigated the way road sign design influences the legibility of a sign. Other studies have tried to establish how symbols should be designed in order to be understood by as many drivers as possible.

Gunnar, however, had his doubts from a basic psychological point of view. It is not natural for human beings to continue to use information cues that are normally of no interest or incorrect. Such cues must eventually lose their signal value and become more of a background noise. Furthermore, human attention is known never to be continuous. Lapses of attention are commonplace. These were the main thoughts behind some pioneering investigations into the effectiveness of common road signs as carriers of road and traffic information to road users, primarily drivers.

The first series of studies was carried out in the early 1960s but not published in English until 1966 (Johansson & Rumar, 1966). It contained two experiments. In the first one the problem was to find the maximum level of performance in recording (seeing and understanding) road signs. To our surprise it became evident that the authorities did not know exactly which road signs were placed along a specific road. Therefore the first task was to establish the true number of road signs (what characterized a road sign in this context was carefully defined). This had to be done by subjects. Two cars were sent out along the 170 km road, each with two passengers whose only task was to record the road signs passed. It was concluded that the true number of signs was "at least" 424. This figure however contains some uncertainty.

In the experiment five subjects were driven in an estate car instructed to press a silent switch every time they passed a sign. The results showed that the proportion of correctly reported signs for the five subjects varied from 87 to 96 percent. The mean correct percentage was 91. It was concluded that the maximum performance level of drivers to register road signs is in the order of 90 percent.

The second experiment was more important and of a completely new character. For the first time the effectiveness of road signs was studied in realistic situations outside the laboratory. Five road signs were set up temporarily at a specific site along the road between Stockholm and Uppsala. Drivers were stopped and asked a number of questions—mainly "What was the last road sign you passed?"

The results (see Fig. 3) show that on the average drivers only registered about 50 percent of the road signs. However, more interesting was that clear differences can be shown between different signs of similar perceptual characteristics. Those signs that were of primary importance to the passing drivers also were registered to a much higher degree. Drivers tend to register mainly signs they consider to be of importance to themselves. Society should know that signs only function as far as they are of importance and interest to the passing driver. You cannot put up signs to warn for every eventual danger without risk of the "cry wolf" situation. These results stirred a lot of interest and initiated a number of similar experiments around the world. Most of them confirmed Johansson´s original and striking results.

Later Johansson and Backlund (1970), using a corresponding methodology, tried to analyze in greater detail which factors govern the probability of registering a road sign. The results from this study are worth a lot more interest than they have received. It can be concluded from their results that the first thing that drivers tend to leave out when the situation becomes difficult and complicated is artificial signals such as road signs. On the other hand the last thing they stop registering is the road itself. This seems to be the most important information to the driver. Other road users and traffic in general seems to fall in between the previous two categories. In conclusion, most road signs are of secondary or lower interest to the drivers. Johansson raised a considerable interest with these new results.

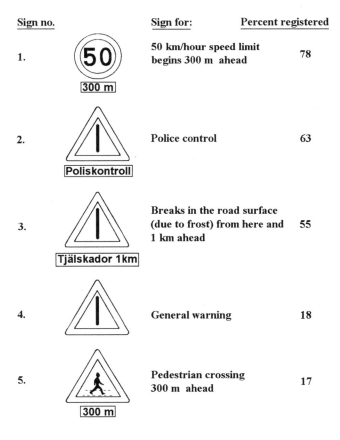

Fig. 3. Percent registered road signs in the Johansson and Rumar (1966) study.

Drivers' Brake Reaction Times

It is generally agreed that a quick and adequate brake reaction time is a crucial variable in driver road safety. Many studies have been carried out to establish how various conditions influence the brake reaction time of drivers. However, most of these studies have been carried out in laboratory and/or stationary conditions. They rely to a large extent to the basic studies of simple reaction times that were so common in earlier psychological research. Unfortunately, these studies have comparatively limited relevance for real traffic conditions. The reason is that when you are prepared the reaction time is both short and accurate. The problem appears when you are surprised, when a situation suddenly evolves and you have to react quickly.

Gunnar (Johansson & Rumar, 1971b) realized this and started out with the ambition to investigate drivers' brake reaction times in unexpected, sudden situations. The second purpose was to study the variation of brake reaction times that could be expected among a sample of drivers in real traffic conditions. To solve these problems he set out with two methods:

- To measure the brake reaction times of a large number of drivers in an anticipated situation.

- To measure the brake reaction times of a small number of drivers in a completely unexpected situation.

The relation between these two measurements offers a kind of a correction factor that can be applied on the large sample to get both the unexpected brake reaction times and the distribution of brake reaction times.

The anticipated situation was set up in such a way that every driver passing the test road was stopped and instructed that somewhere within the next 10 km he would hear a strong klaxon horn at the side of his car. When he heard the horn, he was to make a short but immediate braking response. His brake lights were registered by a trained observer whose reaction time was continuously checked. Figure 4 gives the results obtained at this experiment. The median for the 321 drivers tested was .66 sec, the 75th percentile was .90 sec and the range varied between .30 and 2.0 sec.

In order to get the correction factor, each car of five subjects was equipped with an apparatus that triggered a strong buzzer in the car with preset random intervals at two levels. In the first part the buzzer was released within about 10 km (cf. Experiment 1). In the second part the buzzer was released with very long intervals. It could sometimes be as long as a week between signals. For each subject the ratio between the 10 measurements in the unexpected situation and the 10 measurements in the anticipated situation was then used as a correction factor to calculate the unexpected brake reaction times for the large sample of drivers.

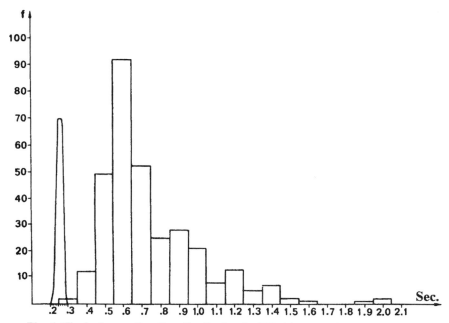

Fig. 4. The brake-reaction-time distribution for 321 drivers on the road and the reaction-time distribution of the experimental assistant responsible for the measurements (from Johansson & Rumar, 1971b).

As it turned out the correction factor was found to be 1.35. That is to say, each point in the distribution of anticipated brake reaction times (Figure 4) should be multiplied by 1.35 to obtain the calculated brake reaction times in unexpected situations. Doing so the median moved from .66 to .90, the 75th percentile from .90 sec to 1.2 sec and the 90th percentile from 1.1 to 1.5 sec.

This study was for many years the only brake reaction study which gave information on which brake reaction times could be expected in a sample of drivers in unexpected, surprise situations. It is therefore found as a basic reference in many road traffic handbooks.

Final Words

Human factors research in the area of road traffic was only a secondary interest to Gunnar Johansson in his research work. He worked actively in the area for only about 10 years. He had nobody to follow but had to break new ground. In spite of all these complications he has left behind him a number of new problem analyses, some innovative methodologies and not least a number of results that are still valid and frequently used in the road traffic society. Also as an experimental road traffic psychologist, Gunnar Johansson is certainly more recognized abroad than in Sweden.

References

Gibson, J. J. & Crooks, L. E. (1938). A theoretical field-analysis of automobile driving. *American Journal of Psychology, 51*, 453–471.

Johansson, G., Bergström, S. S., Jansson, G., Ottander, C., Rumar, K., & Örnberg, G. (1963). Visible distances in simulated night driving conditions with full and dipped headlights. *Ergonomics, 6*, 171–179.

Johansson, G., & Backlund, F. (1960). A versatile eye-movement recorder. *Scandinavian Journal of Psychology, 1*, 181–186.

Johansson, G., & Backlund, F. (1970). Drivers and road signs. *Ergonomics, 13*, 749–759.

Johansson, G., & Rumar, K. (1966). Drivers and road signs: A preliminary investigation of the capacity of car drivers to get information from road signs. *Ergonomics, 9*, 57–62.

Johansson, G., & Rumar, K. (1968). Visible distances and safe approach speeds for night driving. *Ergonomics, 11*, 275–282.

Johansson, G., & Rumar, K. (1970). A new polarized headlight system. *Lighting Research & Technology, 2*, 28–32.

Johansson, G., & Rumar, K. (1971a). Silhouette effects in night driving. *Scandinavian Journal of Psychology, 12*, 80–89

Johansson, G., & Rumar, K. (1971b). Drivers' brake reaction times. *Human Factors, 13*, 23–27.

Rumar, K. (1974). Visibility distances with halogen and conventional headlights. *Scandinavian Journal of Psychology, 15*, 21–25.

A Note on the Synergy Between Basic and Applied Research

Herschel Leibowitz

Pennsylvania State University

Abstract. Suggestions are offered to account for the remarkably creative career of Gunnar Johansson. Some of his direct contributions to the transportation safety literature are described as well as an important implication of his research on biological motion for the enhancement of night-time pedestrian visibility.

This symposium has provided a welcome opportunity for some of Gunnar's many admirers to both express their appreciation for his many contributions and to evaluate the impact of his creative career. This is also an appropriate time to attempt to analyze why he has been so productive. Of course, there are many variables which enter into this equation: intelligence, motivation, personality, etc. However, I feel that it is not insignificant that his academic career started relatively late in life. He did not enter the University until the age of 29. The PhD was awarded in 1950 at the age of 39. In retrospect, this may have been an advantage because his "non-academic" years not only provided interaction with the real world, but possibly served to free him from the encumbrance of previous approaches and theories. As we all know, psychology is a "faddish" science and we inadvertently direct the thinking of our students in directions which happen to be popular at the moment. It is interesting to speculate whether Gunnar's lack of exposure to historical theories and concepts during a formative period of his life played a role in his remarkable originality.

The presentations in this symposium have concentrated on Gunnar's perceptual and theoretical contributions. It should be pointed out that he has also contributed significantly to the human factors literature. A prime example is the classical study on reaction time of drivers in traffic (Johansson & Rumar, 1971). For many years this was accepted as the standard and references to it appear frequently in textbooks, manuals, articles, and accident reports. He has also made significant contributions to the literature on illumination problems in driving (Johansson et al., 1963; Johansson & Rumar, 1968). It is no mean achievement to contribute substantially to any literature be it basic or applied. It is extraordinary to be recognized by both communities.

Gunnar always recognized the artificiality of the distinction between basic and applied research. The initial step in solving an applied problem is often to first elucidate the underlying fundamental mechanisms. This is nicely illustrated by the phenomenon of biological motion, a field of investigation which Gunnar pioneered and in which he is credited with outstanding discoveries.[1] Gunnar has shown that the recognition of biological motion is rapid, taking place within a fraction of a second (Johansson, 1976). Recently, researchers from Franklin and Marshall College, USA, have utilized this phenomenon to improve pedestrian visibility at night. Pedestrian visibility is a serious public health problem. In the United States alone, there are annually about 5,000 pedestrian deaths on the highways. From the point of view of human factors engineering, the problem is primarily one of visibility. The average recognition distance of a pedestrian wearing dark clothing at night when illuminated by low headlight beams is 80–100 feet (Olson & Sivak, 1981). If an automobile traveling at a speed greater than 21 miles/hour unexpectedly encounters a dark-clothed pedestrian, it is un-likely that the driver will have time to take evasive action. One effective solu-tion is to increase visibility by wearing light clothing or retroreflective materials. However, the Franklin and Marshall group has demonstrated that by attaching the retroreflective materials to the appropriate parts of the body so that the pat-tern of lights invokes biological motion, recognition time is decreased signifi-cantly (Francis, Owens, & Antonoff, 1992). Thus, one of Gunnar's fundamental contributions has led to an important application which has the potential for saving lives. The object lesson here is that one never knows how or when crea-tive research will be useful in relation to societal problems. It is particularly re-warding that Gunnar, who has devoted his career to both fundamental percep-tual studies and traffic safety problems, was the inspiration for a development which incorporates both aspects.

---

[1] For his many contributions to experimental psychology, Gunnar was awarded the cov-eted distinguished contribution award of the American Psychological Association in 1987. The citation on this occasion was the following: "For his penetrating theoretical insights into human visual perception, combined with ingenious and creative experi-mental research. His analysis of how environmental regularities are exploited by per-ceptual decoding principles anticipated current thinking about constraints and inferen-tial processors. His experimental studies have provided much of the foundation for our understanding of motion and depth perception. Together with his students, he devel-oped a substantial body of innovative research on perceptual vector analysis and on the perception of minimal events, biological motion, nonrigid motion, self-motion, and natural motions. His advanced thinking provides continuing leadership and inspiration for current researchers in visual perception."

References

Frances, E. L., Owens, D. A., & Antonoff, R. A. (1992). Biological motion and pedestrian safety in night traffic. *Investigative Ophthalmology and Visual Science, 33,* 1415.

Johansson, G., (1976) Spatio-temporal differentiation and integration in visual motion perception. *Psychological Research, 38,* 379–393. [Chapter 8, this volume.]

Johansson, G., Bergström, S. S., Jansson, G., Ottander, C., Rumar, K., & Örnberg, G. (1963). Visibility distances in simulated night driving conditions with full and dipped headlights. *Ergonomics, 6,* 171–179.

Johansson, G., & Rumar, K. (1968). Visibility distances and safe approach speeds for night driving. *Ergonomics, 11,* 275–282.

Johansson, G., & Rumar, K. (1971). Driver's brake reaction times. *Human Factors, 13,* 23–27.

Olson, P., & Sivak, M. (1981). Headlamps and visibility limitations in night-time traffic. *Journal of Traffic Safety Education, 28,* 20–22.

Commentaries on Selected Aspects of Gunnar Johansson's Contributions

Vector Analysis

Vector Analysis

Jan J. Koenderink

State University Utrecht

Abstract: The human perceiver is not very adept at the estimation of absolute directions, but very good at relative judgments. This means—among other things—that it is unlikely that global coordinate systems have much relevance for the description of human spatial judgments in small field situations. It is more likely that the simultaneous-successive mutual order between visual directions will have to play a key role. "Vector analysis" is one method to implement such relative structural descriptions. I show in this paper how an elementary vector analysis method greatly simplifies the solution of the "Shape from Motion from Two Views Problem" as compared to standard methods based upon global coordinates. It is one example of the power and simplicity of such methods.

Why Vector Analysis?

"Vector analysis" proper is a branch of mathematics that is required for freshmen in the natural sciences and engineering. I mean something different here: The term is also used in visual psychophysics to indicate a manner of analysis of "optic flow" or "dynamic perspective" that emphasizes the analysis of changes in *relative location* in the optical input. Moreover, it has been used to refer to the phenomena in human visual perception that are most naturally described in such terms. I refer, of course, to the classical contribution to the field by Gunnar Johansson (1950, 1973). However, in this short paper I always intend the term in the sense of an optic flow analysis mode, although the result will have implications for the psychology of perception.

In the setting of "optic flow" one conceives of a "point observer" and a bundle of "visual rays" tied to this "vantage point." The rays are labeled with identifiable points in the physical environment. It is as if a bundle of taut elastic strings was attached to the vantage point and to any number of pointlike features on environmental objects. If the observer moves and/or the world changes, then

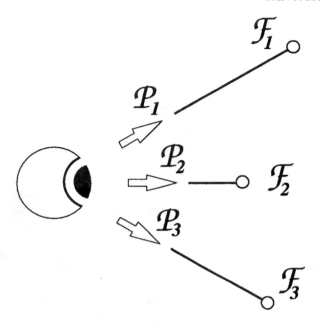

Fig. 1. Euclid's model of vision. The "visual rays" $\{\mathbf{P}_1, \mathbf{P}_2, \mathbf{P}_3\}$ point to recognizable feature points $\{\mathbf{F}_1, \mathbf{F}_2, \mathbf{F}_3\}$ in the environment (no propagation of a quid intended). These directions $\{\mathbf{P}_1, \mathbf{P}_2, \mathbf{P}_3\}$ (think of unit vectors: the lengths of these vectors is abstracted away from) are elements of the "optic array," or "visual field." The rays end on the feature points $\{\mathbf{F}_1, \mathbf{F}_2, \mathbf{F}_3\}$ which are elements of three-dimensional environmental space. The eye itself is a singularity: Its direction is undefined.

the mutual angular order of the strings in the bundle changes over time. The strings can be followed because they retain their individuality, as inherited from the external objects. One calls the space of all possible string directions (which has the topology of the sphere) the "optic array," and the flux of angular order the "optic flow." This may well be the simplest reasonable model of human vision. (See Fig. 1.) It has been thoroughly investigated around 300 B.C. by Euclid (cf., the translation by Ver Ecke, 1959), but the subject cannot be considered closed even today.

A visual ray may be labeled in a different manner, through the use of "coordinates." This presupposes that a suitable "coordinate system" has been agreed on. The human condition is such that the vertical direction and the horizontal plane are important, and that in the horizontal plane the straight ahead and left—right directions are singled out. Thus it makes good sense to use latitude and elevation angles as convenient egocentric coordinates. (See Fig. 2.) Once a coordinate system has been established, the motion of a *single* visual

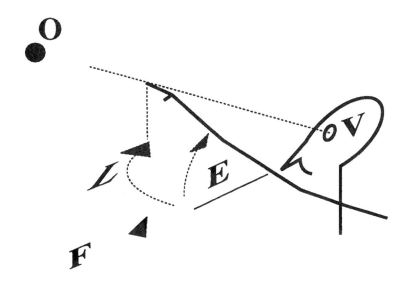

Fig. 2. Typical coordinate system. **O** denotes the object and **V** the vantage point. **F:** frontal direction, **E:** the elevation, **L:** the latitude.

ray can be described as a temporal change of its coordinates. For instance, the instantaneous rates define the angular velocity of a ray. Theories of optic flow are typically formulated in such terms. Notice that an invariant label is required to track a ray over time: The coordinate values themselves are of no use here!

One rather obvious problem with the use of coordinates is that they require a pre-established coordinate system. This requirement presents no problems in machine vision applications, but it is very problematic in the case of biological systems. Human observers are bad estimators of absolute direction (ray coordinates), but very good at the estimation of *mutual relations* in a configuration of rays. A theory of optic flow fit for human vision shouldn't relate the direction of a ray to any fixed global coordinate system, but to its relation to other rays in its neighborhood. Even better, the *temporal change* in the simultaneous order of rays should be described relative to the *current order* (which could be quite arbitrary). Then the optical structure *itself* acts as the reference system.

The case of binocular vision is quite similar. Instead of a *moving* vantage point one considers a *split* one. Formally, the geometry of bicentric perspective is identical to the geometry of dynamic perspective. Again, one should preferentially frame descriptions in relative terms. (In this case: disparity and its gradients and rates.)

Although all this is almost too obvious to mention, it remains the case that almost all existing theory is firmly tied to absolute coordinate systems. This is not at all necessary, and has to be considered bad practice: In modern geometry the emphasis is on "coordinate free" methods, and for excellent reasons, too. In this paper I indicate possible ways to do away with coordinate systems altogether.

Local Theory of Relative Position

Although it is possible to handle the general case I consider only the case of narrow angle vision in this paper. This will allow me to stick to the simplest possible formalism. Thus the theory will apply quite well to foveal vision under fixation and pursuit, that is, mainly to the visual estimation of three-dimensional shape and attitude in space, less to visually guided behavior such as orientation and navigation. Narrow angle vision means that the angles between relevant visual rays will be small, thus all rays are nearly parallel. Notice that "narrow" is not the same as *zero*: Thus apparent size (I mean angular extent) *does* depend on distance in narrow angle vision (as different from the more familiar case of "orthographic projection"). The approximation of narrow angle vision allows one to consider the "visual field" (which really has the topology of a sphere) as *flat*. This simplifies the discussion considerably whenever vectors at different location have to be compared with each other. For the point I want to make in this paper the narrow angle approximation suffices.

Since the visual field is two-dimensional, the simplest configuration of points that "spans it" consists of three not collinear points, "in general position" is the common phrase. (The convex hull of three points is two-dimensional, whereas that of fewer points is not, and more points will never raise the dimension above two.) Let's take such a triple of points $\{P_0, P_1, P_2\}$ (say). Then one can use simple vector scaling and addition operations to specify the position of an arbitrary fourth point Q (say) relative to this fiducial triple. How one does this is illustrated in Fig. 3.

Construct the bilocal objects ("displacement vectors") $\overrightarrow{P_0P_1}$, $\overrightarrow{P_0P_2}$, and $\overrightarrow{P_0Q}$. Then you can find (unique) coefficients (α_1, α_2) such that

$$\overrightarrow{P_0Q} = \alpha_1\overrightarrow{P_0P_1} + \alpha_2\overrightarrow{P_0P_2}.$$

This merely involves the solution of two simultaneous, linear equations. Instead of proceeding numerically, one may alternatively use the classical "parallelogram of forces" method to combine or decompose vectors. The coefficients then arise as ratios of collinear stretches. The pair of coefficients (α_1, α_2) serves as a convenient description of the position of the point Q relative to the triple of fiducial points.

When one repeats the construction for other points one can describe arbitrary point configurations in terms of the fiducial triple. One may pick any triple *ad*

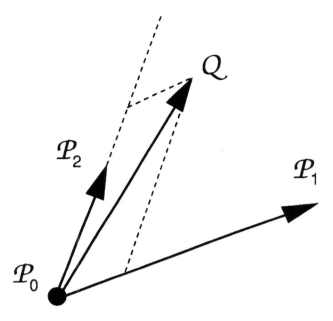

Fig. 3. Simple example of vector analysis. The point **Q** is the point P_0 shifted 0.25 times the vector $\overrightarrow{P_0P_1}$ plus 1.5 times the vector $\overrightarrow{P_0P_2}$. The "parallelogram of forces" method is used for the decomposition.

libitem, as long as the triple spans the plane ("is in general position"). If one switches from one fiducial triple to another all coefficient pairs change numerically. However, the mutual relations between points shouldn't depend on the description, and certain relations between the coefficient pairs should reflect that. Indeed, if three points $\{Q_0, Q_1, Q_2\}$ with coordinate pairs $[(\alpha_{01}, \alpha_{02}), (\alpha_{11}, \alpha_{12}), (\alpha_{21}, \alpha_{22})]$ are in the relation $(\alpha_{01}, \alpha_{02}) = \xi_1(\alpha_{11}, \alpha_{12}) + \xi_2(\alpha_{21}, \alpha_{22})$, then this relation is conserved when one fiducial triple is swapped for another. That is to say, although the numerical values of the coefficient pairs depend on the particular choice of the fiducial triple, the values of the coefficients (ξ_1, ξ_2) do not change. Mathematically this is a rather trivial consequence of the linearity of the constructions. Figure 4 shows two equivalent point configurations. Both could have arisen as a particular view of a single planar configuration of four points. They constitute the same simultaneous ray order.

Thus two observers who happen to use different fiducial triples can simply compare notes on the shapes of point configurations without any prior agreement on any fiducial triple.

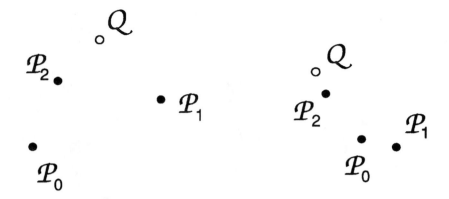

Fig. 4. These point configurations are equivalent. Both result in the same vector decomposition as illustrated in the previous figure.

This convenient system is bought at a price: There exist deformations of point configurations that go undetected if one considers just the coefficient pairs. These are the *affine transformations*: arbitrary concatenations of translations, rotations, similarities, and shears. This can be considered an asset rather than a drawback though: One automatically gains position, orientation, and size invariance. The insensitivity with respect to shears may seem a problem. One can always get rid of that by pointing out some special fiducial triple though, for instance, an equilateral triple.

Vector Analysis and Optic Flow

Suppose one has N points ($N \geq 4$) in the visual field. One may pick any three of them (in "general position") and find the coefficient pairs of the $N - 3$ remaining points in the usual manner. Suppose the point configuration changes over time, that is, one monitors an optic flow. I assume that the flow is generated by a general movement of the observer relative to a rigid three-dimensional configuration (the usual setting for optic flow problems, actually more constrained than is really necessary here). Then the only way it might happen (except for singular cases like no movement at all) that the coefficient pairs don't change, is that all points happen to be *coplanar*. The reason is simply that movement relative to a plane in narrow angle perspective generates affine transformations in the visual field. If the coefficient pairs change (as they typically will of course), then one may conclude that the configuration is not coplanar, that is, one has gained information that concerns the third dimension!

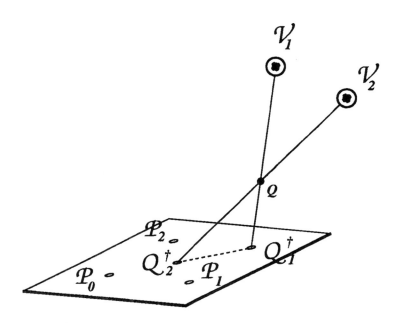

Fig. 5. Two views, from the vantage points V_1 and V_2, of a non-coplanar configuration of four points $\{P_0, P_1, P_2, Q\}$. The point Q is "real," the points $Q_1^\dagger$ and $Q_2^\dagger$ are "fictional." The affine order in the optic array changes when one moves the vantage point. The distance $Q_1^\dagger - Q_2^\dagger$ is proportional with the distance from the real point Q to the fiducial plane $P_0P_1P_2$.

Label the points $\{P_0, P_1, P_2, Q_1,...,Q_{N-3}\}$ after having picked the fiducial triple at pleasure. *Conceptually* one may consider a *planar* configuration

$$\{P_0, P_1, P_2, Q_1^\dagger,...,Q_{N-3}^\dagger\}$$

in which the fiducial triple is the same, but the other $Q_i^\dagger$ points are in the same visual directions as the Q_i, but shifted in depth such that they are in the plane defined by the fiducial triple. This is pure fiction, but it enables one to get a firm grasp on the optic flow problem. Notice that the notation doesn't distinguish between points in the visual field (visual rays, directions) and points in three-

dimensional space. It is essential to keep in mind that the points Q_i and $Q_i^\dagger$ are really *the same* point in the visual field: They are only interpreted as the projections of *different* points in the three-dimensional space. In cases where confusion is likely to arise I will indicate the meaning in parentheses. (Fig. 5 illustrates the geometry.)

Of course one doesn't know the "fiducial plane" at all (since one has no way of knowing the distances toward the fiducial points), but one may rest assured that it *exists*, because three points always specify a unique plane in space. If one moves, then one need only follow the fiducial triple in order to know all points

$Q_i^\dagger$. (In the visual field that is.) One can predict the positions of these points in the visual field because the affine coefficients cannot change, whatever one's movement. Of course one will not be surprised to find the actual projection of the Q_i at some *different* place than predicted (because the configuration is unlikely to be really planar to begin with, for the planarity assumption was purely

fictional). At this point one conjectures that the distances $\left\| Q_i Q_i^\dagger \right\|$ are finite. The

line segments $Q_i^\dagger Q_i$ (in threedimensional space!) that were first seen "end on" and thus projected into *points* now are revealed as *arcs* in the projection.

Notice that all line segments $Q_i^\dagger Q_i$ are *parallel* in three-dimensional space, because they all point in the visual direction of the first view. The result is that the coefficient pairs $(\alpha_{1i}, \alpha_{2i})$ will change in such a way that they differ from the initial values by variously scaled versions (scale factors μ_i say) of a single "affine optic flow direction" (ω_1, ω_2) (say). The scale factors μ_i are proportional

with the lengths $\left\| \overrightarrow{Q_i^\dagger Q_i} \right\|$, *i.e.*, with the distances of the object points from the fiducial plane $P_0 P_1 P_2$ in three-dimensional space. This means that I have actually reconstructed the three-dimensional point configuration *modulo* an arbitrary affine transformation in three-dimensional space (Fig. 6). The result is not a trivial one if the number of points exceeds $N = 4$.

For four points one can at most ascertain that the point Q is not coplanar with the fiducial triple. This is because one may only derive *ratios of distances* from the fiducial plane, but not the absolute distances themselves.

Notice that I have described an algorithm that solves both the "Shape from Motion" as well as "Motion from Motion" problem (and that from two views) in the most obvious manner. Indeed, I have hardly performed anything more than elementary vector analysis. Notice how this method compares very favorably with respect to complexity when confronted with any currently standard method.

Conclusions

Vector analysis (Johansson, 1950, 1973) is a convenient means to refer spatial structure to parts of itself. It thus obviates the need for pre-established coor-

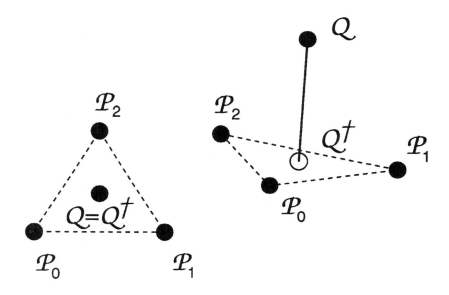

Fig. 6. Two views of the same point configuration in three-dimensional space. In the first view I conceptually split the point **Q** into two distinct points in three-dimensional space, namely **Q** (the "real" point) and **Q**† in the fiducial plane. In the second view one can predict **Q**† by vector analysis. The difference with the projection of the real point is a measure of the deviation from the fiducial plane.

dinate systems. I have shown how the method applies to the "Shape from Motion Problem," and in fact thoroughly trivializes the solution.

Of course this solution is only a *partial* solution (although it is a true three-dimensional solution). Part of the ambiguity is easily resolved in a single view itself, by the use of a metric ("eye measure") that immediately lifts the affine ambiguity in the visual field. What remains are depth ambiguities (see Fig. 7).

In many cases a partial solution may well be all that is really needed. In other cases additional information may have to be sought. Such problems are relatively easy to resolve. For instance, in many cases the depth scale can be calibrated by taking a single side view.

The present example is only that—an example. The principle of vector analysis has far wider applicability.

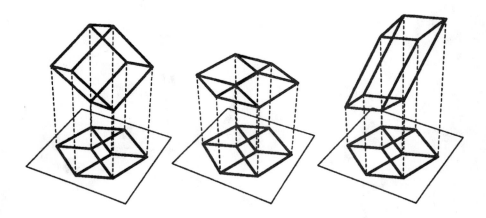

Fig. 7. An example of the depth ambiguities for the shape from motion algorithm based upon vector analysis for two views.

References

Euclid (1959). Optics. In P. Ver Ecke (Trans.), *Euclide, l'optique et la catoptrique* (Euclid: Optics and catoptics). Paris: Albert Blanchard.

Johansson, G. (1950). *Configurations in event perception.* Uppsala: Almqvist & Wiksell. [Chapter 2, this volume.]

Johansson, G. (1973). Visual perception of biological motion and a model for its analysis, *Perception & Psychophysics, 14,* 201–211. [Chapter 7, this volume.]

Can the Johansson Vector Analysis Be Applied to the Perception of Illumination, Color and Depth?

Sten Sture Bergström

Umeå University

Abstract: An earlier published attempt to apply Johansson's vector analysis to the perception of illumination, color, and 3D form is discussed. It is assumed that light reflected from illuminated objects is automatically analyzed into common and relative components. The common component corresponds to perceived illumination and the relative components to reflectances (colors). A minimum principle is assumed as to the number of perceived sources of light. The empirical evidence for the commonality assumption about illumination seems to be overwhelming, and so is the sculpturing effect of spatial modulation of illumination. Some new evidence concerning spatio-temporal modulation of the illumination and induced object motion in depth is presented, which resembles Johansson's (1950) wandering phenomenon. It is discussed as evidence for the assumed minimum principle as to the number (and constancy) of perceived sources of light. So far a critical experiment showing the analysis to be a vector analysis is still missing, however.

Background

In the 1970s I visited Edwin Land's laboratory and saw his Mondrian demonstrations of color constancy. In one of his demonstrations Land varied the illumination of a Mondrian display until a red field reflected the same white light as a white field in white light. Still the red field looked red and the white looked white. Back in Uppsala I decided to replicate some of them in my own laboratory and I was very successful. The color constancy seemed to be very robust under the Mondrian conditions. According to the Retinex theory (Land & McCann, 1971) the complexity of the display is essential in order to get constancy. I decided to find out what degree of complexity would be sufficient. To my surprise I got a high degree of color constancy as long as the Mondrian consisted of at least two colors. One single color did not suffice, however, which is quite in line with Katz' (1911) findings that color constancy is zero when using a reduction screen. A reduction screen is a peep-hole making only the target visible but not its surrounding. A Mondrian consisting of two fields of different color was enough, however, to give a color constancy of the type Land had demonstrated, that is, our subjects reported the same color name under very different illuminations. As two is the lowest number to have something in common, this observation gave me the idea that an analogy to Johansson's (1950) analysis of object motion into common and relative components could be applied to color constancy. And the common component in this case is, of course, illumination. Figure 1 sketches the analogy between seeing a red and green object in yellow illumination and seeing a Johansson motion configuration.

Figure 2 illustrates the analysis of a luminance profile across an achromatic Mondrian illuminated from one side. The vector approach to color constancy was first published in Bergström (1977).

The Model Summarized

The main postulate of our model is that the visual system performs a *perceptual analysis of light reflected from illuminated objects into common and relative components.*

The *common component* is assumed to correspond to the illumination. Just as the visual system immediately extracts a common motion component even from a very complex pattern of moving objects, so it extracts a common component of illumination from a complex pattern of reflected light. So far the common component is not supposed to be a certain level and it is not uniform, it is a complex spatial modulation depending on (and informing about) the 3D layout of the environment including the position of (or the direction towards) the source of light. The modulation of illumination always depends on the 3D layout of the environment including the position of the source of light (and nothing else). It might well be fruitful, however, to assume a further analysis of this complex common component.

The *relative components* correspond to the variation of the materials illuminated, their variation in space and/or time as to degree of reflectance, selectivity of reflectance, and so on. (A further analysis of the illumination might result in an extension of the relative components to include shape and shading leaving us with a simpler illumination vector.)

A *minimum principle* is applied in the theoretical model in the assumption that a minimum but geometrically sufficient number of light sources is percei-

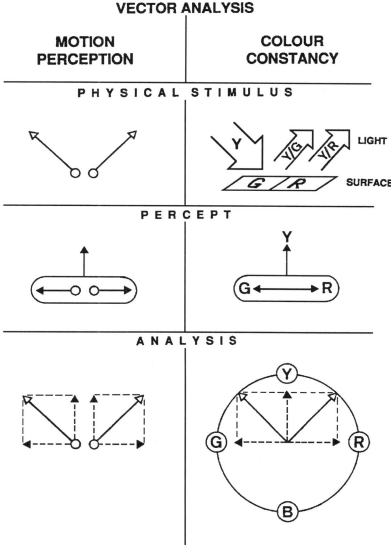

Fig. 1. The analogy between a Johansson vector analysis of a two-dot motion and an analysis of light reflected from a red/green surface illuminated by yellow light.

ved. The minimum principle is here a theoretical construct to explain the tendency to perceive the smallest number of light sources that could give the actualproximal stimulation. For a further discussion of the status of the minimum principle in theories of visual perception see Hatfield and Epstein (1985).

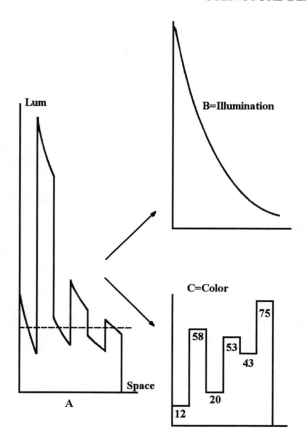

Fig. 2. A sketch of the luminance gradient across an achromatic Mondrian (A) and the analysis into a common illumination (B) and relative lightness components (color, C). The figures denote reflectances from black (12%) to white (75%). (From Bergström, 1977).

In the original paper (Bergström, 1977) *a functional difference between edges and gradients* was assumed. This assumption is not a central one in the model, but it was made to explain the Craik-O'Brien-Cornsweet phenomena. These phenomena are typically illustrated by a concentric disc-ring display, where the border between the disc and the outer ring consists of a combination of a luminance step and a gradient (see, e.g., Cornsweet, 1970, pp. 270 ff.). The gradient "restores" the luminance of the disc to the same level as that of the ring. Still the disc and the ring perceptually are different in lightness (brightness?). (These phenomena have usually been demonstrated using a rotating disc which makes its surface color characteristics questionable). According to our assumption the luminance step is supposed normally to correspond to a reflectance edge and its effect can not be canceled or compensated for by a gradient, which corresponds to a variation of illumination (e.g., a shadow). The central disc should appear convex or concave in depth rather than having the same degree of whiteness as the ring.

Empirical Evidence

In a recent paper (Bergström, in press) I have tried to put together the empirical evidence that supports our model both from the literature and from experimental studies carried out in my own laboratory.

The model, that is the commonality assumption plus a minimum principle as to the number of perceived light sources, has been applied to a number of color (lightness) constancy studies (both constancy and non-constancy results), to Land's Mondrian demonstrations, to Gilchrist's (1980) two classes of experiments, one class giving a radical shift of perceived lightness and the other giving lightness constancy, and to Metelli's (1983) demonstration of a hole in a screen appearing like a surface color.

Most of our own experiments have been within an experimental paradigm that could be labeled "shape from shading." This means that a cast shadow (mostly a square-wave grating) has been projected on different Mondrian displays and as they have simulated attached shadows they have also made the Mondrian appear pleated in depth. Figure 3 shows a Mondrian display with the superimposed modulation, in this case a defocused square-wave grating, which gives a compelling 3D appearance. (A sharp grating gives a pleated appearance, but can be ambiguous.)

One conclusion to be drawn from our experiments is that a spatially modulated illumination has a very strong "sculpturing" capacity. A number of experiments (e.g., Bergström, Gustafsson, & Putaansuu, 1984) show that structured displays are perceived as more distinctly pleated under the square-wave illumination than are homogeneous ones. According to traditional theories of depth perception the geometrical structure of the Mondrian (i.e., the edges of the squares and rectangles of the Mondrian) should inform about its flatness thus making the structured displays more resistant to the sculpturing effect of the modulated illumination. But our results are consistently in the opposite direction: The structured Mondrians appear more distinctly pleated than the homogeneous ones.

In one experiment (Bergström, Gustafsson, & Jakobsson, 1993) the number of reflectance edges within a square Mondrian was varied between zero and three. The edges were either crossed by or parallel to the projected grating. A paired comparisons method was used and the subject's task was to choose the display in each pair which appeared most distinctly three-dimensional (i.e.,

Fig. 3A

Fig. 3. A black and white photo of a Mondrian without (A) and with (B) a superimposed grating. When the grating is sharp, the display appears pleated in depth, but when it is out of focus as in (B), the display appears as consisting of cylinders (pipes).

pleated). The results show clearly that the distinctness of the three-dimensional impression increases with number of reflectance edges. This holds true whether the reflectance edges are crossed by the grating or parallel to it. We got the lowest degree of distinctness (i.e., the lowest proportion of preferences in the paired comparisons) for the homogeneous display, and then in order of increasing distinctness of depth came: one edge parallel, three edges parallel, one edge crossed, and finally three edges crossed by the illumination grating. So, crossings between illumination edges and reflectance edges seem to reveal the common component characteristics of the illumination. But three crossings are better than one. And even reflectance edges parallel to the grating seem to do the work. And three of them do it better than one. The conclusion is that the reflectance edges, which should inform about the flatness of the display since they

Fig. 3B

remain straight and parallel, reveal the illumination edges and make the darker phases of the grating appear like attached shadows. It takes variation to reveal invariances, and more variation does it better than less. In the case of parallelism the variation is not along the same illumination edge but across the whole grating, which is not as compelling but still better than no variation at all. We interpret these results as support for the assumption that illumination is a common component, the spatial variation of which informs about three-dimensional form.

Using "O'Brien modulated" illumination we have also demonstrated that the inner disc of the disc-ring display in the O'Brien phenomenon really appears convex or concave in depth and that this three-dimensional form is more distinct when the circular display is divided into sectors by reflectance edges which are crossed by the O'Brien contour (Bergström, Gustafsson, & Jakobsson, 1993). Again, it takes variation to reveal invariances.

In still another type of experiments (Putaansuu & Bergström, 1992) two square displays are used, one of which can be (a) moving back and forth in depth in a pendulum motion, and/or (b) illuminated by a temporally modulated illumination either in phase with or in counterphase to the physical motion. The reference display is always stationary and evenly illuminated. In one of the pilot studies nine subjects marked the front (i.e., close) and back turning points of the moving display on a piece of paper in a 1:1 scale. The position of the static (reference) display was marked on the paper. This was done for monocular and binocular vision under four conditions: *baseline* (real motion 5 cm, 1/3 Hz, even illumination); *induced* (static, illumination modulated temporally, 1/3 Hz); *phase* (illumination modulated in phase with real motion, i.e., highest when the object is closest); *counterphase* (illumination modulated in counterphase with real motion).

Object motion in depth was perceived under all conditions. The length of the perceived object motion was calculated as the distance between the front and back turning points as marked by the subjects. Monocularly the induced object motion in depth was of the same length as the real motion of the baseline condition. The modulation of the illumination in the phase condition seems to lengthen the perceived motion in depth but the counterphase modulation does not foreshorten it. The subjects reported problems with the counterphase condition, however. They had a feeling that the object when judged to be at the front turning point suddenly "jumped" to the back turning point. This means that there might be an ambiguity here, sometimes the real motion and sometimes the modulation of the illumination (i.e., the hypothesized superimposed induced motion) determines the perceived position of the object. A later experiment, where the subjects had to press a switch every time the object was at the close turning point seems to give some support to the ambiguity hypothesis. For technical reasons control experiments have to be run, however.

The fact that a temporally modulated illumination of an object induces a perceived object motion in depth can be interpreted to mean that the temporal modulation of the illumination is not perceived. Instead a spatial modulation is perceived and the object appears to move in and out of the illuminated area. This phenomenon resembles Johansson's (1950, pp. 141ff.; pp. 110ff. in this volume) *wandering phenomenon.* Johansson presented two circular bright areas on an opaque screen and varied their luminance sinusoidally and in counterphase. His subjects described the event like a constant source of light moving behind the screen between two semi-transparent windows in the screen. In our case, however, it is the illuminated object and not the light that is moving. The type of constancy is the same, however, that is *constancy during an event* to use Johansson's terminology. He states that *periodic changes of the luminosity of a surface at rest tend to give a perception of motion* (p. 152; not reprinted in this volume).

Conclusions

The empirical evidence for our commonality assumption seems almost overwhelming. And so is the evidence for the sculpturing in depth by modulated illumination. And Johansson's (1950) wandering phenomenon can be interpreted as one evidence supporting our minimum principle as to the perceived number of sources of light. Not only is their number at a minimum, they also seem to be constant over time at least during short events. What is still missing, however, is a good support for the assumption that our perceptual analysis of reflected light is a vector analysis. Maybe the induced object motion will give us the opportunity to test the vector hypothesis. So far we do not have an algorithm for our model. The closest thing to an algorithm for our type of perceptual phenomena is probably Adelson and Pentland's (1990) workshop metaphor.

References.

Adelson, E. H., & Pentland, A. P. (1990). The perception of shading and reflectance. *Vision and Modeling Technical Report* (No. 140). Cambridge, MA: MIT Media Laboratory.

Bergström, S. S. (1977). Common and relative components of reflected light as information about the illumination, color, and three-dimensional form of objects. *Scandinavian Journal of Psychology, 18*, 180–186.

Bergström, S. S. (in press). Color constancy. Towards a vector model for the perception of illumination, color, and depth. In A. Gilchrist (Ed.), *Lightness, brightness and transparency*. Hillsdale, NJ: Erlbaum.

Bergström, S. S., Gustafsson, K.-A., & Putaansuu, J. (1984). Information about three-dimensional shape and direction of illumination in a square-wave grating. *Perception, 13*, 129–140.

Bergström, S. S., Gustafsson, K.-A., & Jakobsson, T. (1993). Distinctness of perceived three-dimensional form induced by modulated illumination: Effects of certain displays and modulation conditions. *Perception & Psychophysics, 53*, 648–657.

Cornsweet, T. N. (1970). *Visual perception*. New York: Academic Press.

Gilchrist, A. L. (1980). When does perceived lightness depend on perceived spatial arrangements? *Perception & Psychophysics, 28*, 527–538.

Hatfield, G., & Epstein, W. (1985). The status of the minimum principle in the theoretical analysis of visual perception. *Psychological Bulletin, 97*, 155–186.

Johansson, G. (1950). *Configurations in event perception*. Uppsala: Almqvist & Wiksell. [Chapter 2, this volume.]

Katz, D. (1911). Die Erscheinungsweisen der Farben und ihre Beeinflussung durch die individuelle Erfahrung. *Zeitschrift für Psychologie, Ergänzungsband 7*.

Land, E. H., & McCann, J. J. (1971). The retinex theory of color vision. *Proceedings of the Royal Institution of Great Britain, 47*, 23–58.

Metelli, F. (1983). *Three perceptual illusions: Their meaning for perceptual theory.* Paper read at the Sixth European Conference on Visual Perception, Lucca, Italy, August 28–31,1983. *Perception, 12*, A1–A40.

Putaansuu, J., & Bergström, S. S. (1992). *Perceived object motion induced by temporal modulation of the illumination.* Unpublished manuscript.

Seeing Structure in Space-Time[†]

Joseph S. Lappin

Vanderbilt University

Abstract: A fundamental distinction between Gunnar Johansson's research and much other contemporary research on vision involves the representation of the optical information for vision. In Gunnar's research, the structure of visual stimulation is regarded as based on spatio-temporal relationships intrinsic to the optical patterns themselves. Gunnar's experiments elegantly illustrate how space, motion, and shape should be regarded as interrelated aspects of visual stimulation.

One hypothesis suggested by Gunnar's research on visual vector analysis and perception of biological motion is that information about the global structure and motion of motion configurations is provided by local optical properties. Indirect support for this hypothesis is provided by several recent experiments on the discriminability of globally coherent and incoherent motion, but efforts to identify specific local optical properties that carry such global information have not yet succeeded.

The general hypothesis that perceived spatial structure is governed by intrinsic properties of moving patterns is examined in (a) recent theoretical and experimental research on the perception of surface structure from motion, and (b) research on the "optic sphere theory." Currently available evidence indicates that vision is very sensitive to information about surface shape provided by the local differential structure of moving images. Gunnar's hypothesis that visual information for locating environmental objects and the observer within a 3D environmental framework is given by the structure of the "optic sphere" deserves continued experimental attention.

[†] Support for preparation of this manuscript and for research reported herein was provided by NIH grants EY005926 and P30EY08126. This paper has also benefited substantially from important contributions of Changnian Sun, Warren Craft, Farley Norman, and Lyn Mowafy in collecting and analyzing data reported in this paper and from discussions of the theoretical issues with these persons and with David Gilden, Steven Tschantz, and James Todd.

Introduction: Representing Optical Information

Gunnar Johansson's research on motion perception is familiar to nearly all students of visual perception. But familiarity sometimes breeds neglect; contemporary research and thinking about visual perception have not yet fully accommodated the implications of this research. Gunnar's research still offers timely insights about the visual perception of motion configurations and spatial patterns.

A principal theme elegantly illustrated in Gunnar's experiments is that perceived *space, motion,* and *shape* are interdependent aspects of the structure of optical patterns: Perceived space conforms to the shapes and motions it contains; perceived shapes and motions are scaled by the space in which they are framed. The purpose of the present paper is to review some theoretical issues and experimental evidence associated with the concepts of space, motion, and shape in vision.

A common misunderstanding about vision is that the elementary visual representation of the spatial structure of optical patterns is specified by reference to the spatial structure of the retina—an extrinsic coordinate system, independent of the patterns imposed on it. Similarly, the temporal structure of optical stimulation is also assumed to be represented by reference to some extrinsic coordinate system that is independent of both the temporal and spatial characteristics of the specific stimulus patterns. This form of representation of optical data patterns is a fundamental assumption guiding the computational theories of Ullman (1979), Marr (1982), and many others. Despite its intuitive plausibility, this representation of the optical input is neither theoretically useful nor empirically valid for understanding the perception of form and motion.

As Marr (1982) pointed out, vision and computation may both be regarded as transformations of input into output. Representing the input and output of such a system is equivalent to representing the computational problem that it must solve; the design of a computational process that can accomplish this transformation is shaped by the representation of input and output. Representing optical patterns by reference to an extrinsic coordinate system imposes difficult computational problems on vision because this representation is incommensurate with the output perception of environmental objects and motions. The retinal coordinates are generally assumed to have an inherent metric structure that specifies the retinal distance between each pair of points, but these spatial relations in the retinal images do not correspond to those on the environmental surfaces or in the spaces between objects. The mapping of these environmental distances into their retinal images changes with relative translations and rotations between the observer and the objects. Thus, the mapping from this representation of the retinal images into the shapes, distances, and motions of environmental objects is many-to-many and ill-defined. Solution of these computational problems is commonly believed to require perceptual or computational processes involving logical inference.

These computational problems may be greatly simplified, however, by representing optical input information by the *intrinsic* spatial and temporal structure of the optical patterns. As Gibson (e.g., 1966, pp. 54, 165) emphasized, information about the structure of the environment is "in" the ordered structure of the light; the anatomical arrangement of the photoreceptors is of secondary importance.

Gunnar Johansson's research is distinguished from much other contemporary vision research in part by the fundamental idea that the structure of optical stimulation is visually represented by spatial and temporal relations intrinsic to the optical patterns themselves.

Visual Vector Analysis

Evidence that optical stimulation is visually represented by reference to the intrinsic structure of the optical patterns is provided by most of Gunnar Johansson's experiments. In the wonderful set of experiments in Gunnar's doctoral thesis (Johansson, 1950), the direction and velocity of a given moving point were shown to be perceived in relation to other neighboring points rather than by positions on the retina or display screen. For example, a point of light moving with equal velocities in the horizontal and vertical axes appears to have a diagonal trajectory when it is the only visible light, but is seen as moving up and down within a horizontally translating frame when additional horizontally moving lights are visible at both ends of the apparent vertical path. Other experiments in this study demonstrated that similar phenomena occur with rotating as well as translational motions, that rotations in the picture plane can be perceptually organized as translations, and that translations in the picture plane can be perceived as rotating relative to other points when the directions and phase relations are suitably chosen. The effect of such added context usually is visually irresistible; one can barely imagine, let alone see, the paths of individual points relative to the display screen or retina. Gunnar's vector analysis showed that the trajectory of a given moving point can be efficiently described as an additive composition of multiple vectors—global common motion plus local motions relative to the global framework. Restle (1979) also showed that the perceived organizations of these motion configurations were predictable from the relative simplicity of their representations as common and relative motions. Thus, these perceptual organizations of space and motion should not be regarded as cognitive reinterpretations but as valid descriptions of the optical patterns themselves.

Related phenomena were also illustrated by Gunnar's later experiments on biological motion (Johansson, 1973, 1976). These experiments demonstrated that perceptual organizations of common and relative motions apply to several hierarchical levels of groups and subgroups: The pendular motion of a pair of points on the forearm of a human walker (one at the wrist and another at the elbow) is perceived as a subgroup moving relative to the pendular motion of the whole arm (specified by three points, at the wrist, elbow, and shoulder), which in turn is perceived as a subgroup moving within the larger group of points associated with the trunk and two arms, which is also perceived as a subgroup of the whole body consisting of the legs as well as upper body. Evidently, this organization of groups and subgroups of common and relative motions is seen as a whole coordinated structure—as indicated by the fact that naive observers can quickly identify individual friends in briefly presented patterns by subtle characteristics of bodily movement and gait.

Even human infants as young as 4 months can discriminate point-light patterns produced by human walkers from patterns of independently moving points or from 180° rotations of the same patterns (Fox & McDaniel, 1982), and can discriminate computer simulations of human walkers from incoherent patterns of the same local motions (Bertenthal, Proffitt, & Cutting, 1984; Bertenthal, Proffitt, & Kramer, 1987). Blake (1993) recently found that cats can discriminate a computer-simulated point-light pattern of a walking cat from a temporally asynchronized pattern of the same local motions. Of course there is uncertainty in these experiments about precisely what spatio-temporal relationships the infants and cats are perceiving and discriminating. Nevertheless, these findings reinforce Gunnar's hypothesis that visual analysis of common and relative motions is "accomplished at the initial stage of physiological signal recording ... a consequence of receptive field organization" (Johansson, 1976, p. 379; this volume, p.208).

A Local Mechanism for Perceiving Globally Coherent Motion?

How might such a visual vector analysis be accomplished? How is information about global structure and motion obtained from the local motions of individual points? Could such global information be associated with local properties, as Johansson (1976) suggested? Such questions about the mechanisms underlying motion perception constitute a basic but poorly understood problem. When the individual moving points are assumed to stimulate spatially separate motion-sensitive mechanisms, and when these local neural mechanisms are regarded as the initial carriers of information about the individual motions, then global organization of the whole pattern is implicitly assumed to require integration and reconstruction by higher-order neural mechanisms. Precisely how such global organization might be accomplished, however, is seldom discussed.

Indications that simple local properties may carry information about global structure are given by recent experiments on the discriminability of coherent vs. incoherent motion. These experiments have used a method described in other papers (Lappin, Norman, & Mowafy, 1991; Mowafy, Blake, & Lappin, 1990)—where the spatial positions of several dots or other features are rapidly and randomly "jittered," and observers must discriminate patterns of coherent vs. incoherent motion, where the displacements of all the dots are correlated or where one or more dots move independently.

When the components of these randomly moving patterns have high luminous contrast with the background, then the coherent and incoherent motions are very easily discriminated. Indeed, the discriminability of correlated vs. uncorrelated motion is nearly equal to the detectability of any motion at all—as if little information is lost after the initial motion detection. The coherent structure and motion of these patterns is easily detectable under many conditions—over wide spatial separations between dots (Lappin, Wason, & Akutsu, 1987), for patterns of both fine- and course-grained contours (Mowafy et al., 1990), over a range of temporal rates of motion (Mowafy, Lappin, Anderson, & Mauk, 1993), and for patterns undergoing rotations, expansions, or deformations as well as translations (Lappin et al., 1991).

The spatial structure of these jittering patterns seems to be perceived as a whole—with a single independently moving dot constituting a local discontinuity in a globally coherent spatial field, detected independently of the number of dots in the pattern. Some recently collected data that demonstrate this effect are shown in Fig. 1. The patterns contained either 7, 19, or 37 points in hexagonal arrangements. As may be seen, the detectability of a single incoherently moving dot decreased with lower contrasts and larger retinal areas, but the number or density of dots had no noticeable effect on detectability. This lack of effect of the number of dots indicates that the incoherently moving dot is seen as a local discontinuity in an otherwise smoothly connected field. If the component motions were detected in parallel by statistically independent local processes, then a larger number of dots would necessarily produce a lower probability of detecting any given discrepant motion. Evidently, the spatially distributed motion signals do not arise from independent local processes.

What type of mechanism might yield such efficient performance in carrying information about global structure and motion? Could *local* mechanisms provide such global information, or is information about global structure detected by second-stage *multi-local* mechanisms sensitive to correlations within an earlier stage of local motion signals? The performance characteristics described above—little loss of information beyond initial motion detection, sensitivity to a variety of geometric transformations, and nonindependence of neighboring concurrent directional signals—all suggest the operation of local mechanisms or local interactions that carry information about global structure.

Additional relevant evidence has been obtained in recent experiments conducted with Changnian Sun and David Gilden which have found large effects of certain optical image properties—contrast, spatial frequency, spatial separation, and displacement distance—on the visibility of coherent motion. The large in-

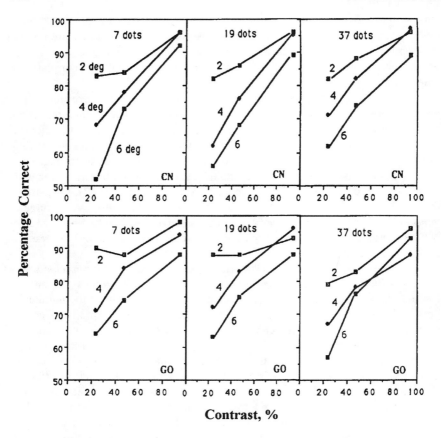

Fig. 1. The accuracy in detecting a single independently moving dot within hexagonal patterns of 7, 19, or 37 dots undergoing otherwise random translational motions. The two sets of graphs in the upper and lower parts of the figure are for two different observers. The parameters for the three curves in each graph refer to the diameter of the patterns. Most data are based on 100 trials; a few points at the higher levels of accuracy are based on 50 trials.

fluence of these variables indicates that visually detected information about coherent structure and motion is closely related to these characteristics of the optical images.

In comparison with the robust visibility of coherent motion of high-contrast dots, we were surprised by the poor discriminability of coherent motion of balanced dots separated by only 2 deg or so. The principal characteristic of balanced dots is that they reduce the low spatial-frequency components of both the individual dots and of the pattern as a whole, and the visibility of this low spa-

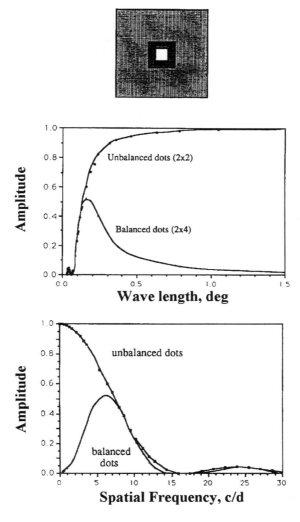

Fig. 2. Schematic description of a balanced dot. The upper figure illustrates a balanced dot. Balanced dots in this experiment were composed of a 2 x 2 pixel (2 min arc per pixel) inner white area and a 1 pixel wide dark border. When displayed on a properly calibrated gray-scale monitor the contrast of the spatially integrated luminance from the central white area plus the surrounding dark border relative to the surrounding gray border is zero, but this illustration is not so calibrated. The lower two graphs illustrate the one-dimensional amplitude spectra for a horizontal or vertical cross-section through the balanced and unbalanced (only the central white 2 x 2 pixels) dots. The same amplitude values are plotted in both figures, as a function of wavelength in the middle figure and as a function of spatial frequency in the lower figure.

tial-frequency structure seems to be related to the visibility of coherent motion. Balanced dots consist of a light central area surrounded by a dark border and displayed on an intermediate gray background, with luminances adjusted so that the total light energy from the balanced dot equals that of the background, yielding zero net contrast. A schematic illustration of such a balanced dot is shown in Fig. 2 along the amplitude spectra of balanced and unbalanced dots. (Detailed descriptions of balanced dots are given by Carlson, Moeller, & Anderson, 1984, and Gilden, Bertenthal, & Othman, 1990.) Unlike balanced dots, ordinary unbalanced dots add to the total luminance of the visual field, have a large "DC" component at zero c/deg spatial frequency, and usually do not become invisible with decreasing visual resolution. Accordingly, ordinary dots will stimulate visual neurons with large receptive fields centered on the retina at some distance from the center of the dot; but balanced dots will stimulate neurons only in a much smaller neighborhood, neurons whose receptive fields are differentially stimulated by the center and border of the balanced dots.

Balanced and unbalanced dots produce different local motion signals. Increases in displacement distance have opposite effects on coherence discriminations of balanced and unbalanced dots: Accuracy declines with displacement distance for balanced dots, but improves with larger displacements of unbalanced dots. This result is consistent with other experiments on the effect of the spatial-frequency spectrum on the detectability of motion over varying distances (e.g., Chang & Julesz, 1983; Nakayama & Silverman, 1985; Baker, Friend, & Boulton, 1991), and also consistent with theoretical proposals that motion-sensitive mechanisms are composed of paired receptive fields in "quadrature phase," making them maximally sensitive to displacements of about 1/4 of the dominant wavelength (e.g., Adelson & Bergen, 1985; Watson, 1990).

The difference in spatial frequency compositions of the balanced and unbalanced dots produces other important effects on the visibility of coherent motion. The joint effects of spatial separation, contrast, and displacement distance for both balanced and unbalanced dot patterns are illustrated in Fig. 3. These data were obtained for patterns of seven dots in a hexagonal arrangement, with one dot in the center and six dots at equal radial distances. On half the trials the motion pattern was coherent, with all seven dots moving rigidly, changing positions randomly every 54 msec, and on the other trials one of the six outside dots moved independently. The observer's task was to discriminate between these two patterns, coherent vs. incoherent. The three values of contrast (between center and border) for the 4 min. arc motions of balanced dots were initially set to cover a relatively broad range, and then the contrasts for the remaining conditions were adjusted independently so that the accuracy at 1 deg separation would be approximately equal to that for the corresponding contrast (high, medium, or low) for the 4 min. arc motions of balanced dots.

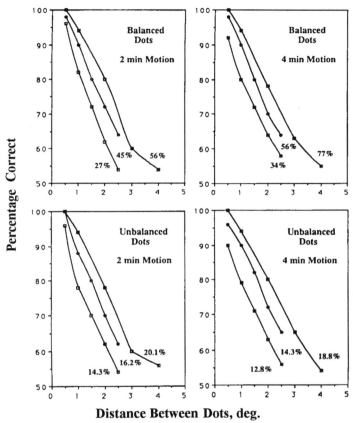

Distance Between Dots, deg.

Fig. 3. Accuracy in detecting the presence of a single independently moving dot in a hexagonal pattern of 7 balanced dots as a function of the spatial separation between the dots, contrast, and displacement distance, for both balanced and unbalanced dots. The contrast values were free parameters, selected to produce similar accuracy levels at 1 deg separations for the balanced and unbalanced dots at both of the two displacement distances. Most data points represent 100 trials for a single well-practiced observer; a few data points at the highest accuracy levels are based on 50 trials.

Three principal effects are illustrated in Fig. 3: (1) Coherent motion was detectable at much lower contrasts for unbalanced than for balanced dots. Moreover, performance for unbalanced dots was more sensitive to changes in contrast than was that for balanced dots. (2) Given suitable adjustments of contrast, increases in spatial separation produced essentially the same decline in performance for each of the four sets of conditions, with varying spatial-frequency content (balanced vs. unbalanced dots) and displacement distance (2 vs. 4 min. arc). (3) Increased displacement distance had opposite effects on the visibility of coherent motion of balanced and unbalanced dots, since the compensating contrast adjustments were opposite for these two cases. In general, the discriminability of coherent and incoherent motion depends mainly on contrast in the low spatial frequencies.

Why should low spatial frequencies be especially important for the visibility of coherent motion? One hypothesis about a possible local mechanism is that local information about global coherence might be provided by phase shifts at spatial wavelengths equal to the separation between dots. When one of the dots moves independently, then the global phase spectrum of the pattern undergoes greater relative changes at long wavelengths (low spatial frequencies) corresponding to the separation between the dots; when the whole pattern moves coherently, then these relative phase shifts do not occur. Such phase shifts should be detectable by local mechanisms with large receptive fields responsive to luminance variations at the appropriate low spatial frequencies. Since the balanced dot patterns have little energy at these long wavelengths, coherent and incoherent motion would be much more difficult to discriminate, approaching chance as the separation increases to 2 deg and more. In other words, the hypothesis is that discriminability of coherence is governed by the energy at long wavelengths corresponding to the separation between dots. Two testable predictions are the following: (1) Balanced and unbalanced dots should yield equal performance at contrasts that produce equal energy at a wavelength matching the separation between dots. (2) Declining performance with larger inter-dot separations should be correlated with decreasing energy at these longer wavelengths.

Neither of these predictions is supported by the results in Fig. 3 together with analyses of the spatial-frequency spectra of the patterns: First, unbalanced dot patterns have much greater energy at these long wavelengths than do the equal-performance balanced dots. Second, the small amount of energy in the balanced dot patterns at these wavelengths changes only negligibly with changes in contrast between the center and border of the balanced dots.

Could another form of local information account for these results? Analyses of the Fourier power spectra have found indications that balanced and unbalanced dot patterns yield similar performance when their energies are similar at spatial frequencies of about 3–4 c/deg, though this comparison is not consistent across all conditions. Even so, it is not yet clear how luminance variations at this spatial frequency would provide information about the global coherence.

Thus, we cannot yet identify the specific optical properties that provide visually detected information about the coherent structure of motion configurations like those in our experiments or in Johansson's experiments. Several lines of evidence offer indirect support for Gunnar's hypothesis that information about such global structure and motion is carried by local properties of the initial optical and physiological input to the visual system, but the form of this information has not yet been discovered. Perhaps the underlying mechanism is multi-local, involving sensitivity to correlations among the motion signals arising from separate retinal locations.

Perceiving Surface Structure from Retinal Image Motion

The preceding discussion has concerned only the perceived connectedness and coherence of motion configurations. Another basic aspect of Johansson's ideas about visual vector analysis involves the perceived spatial relations among the component points and their motions—spatial relations that he suggests are determined by intrinsic properties of the moving pattern. One important form of this spatial information is associated with the structure of surfaces and their images.

A fundamental fact about the geometry of vision is that the differential structure of visible regions of environmental surfaces and the differential structure of their retinal images are isomorphic [Note 1] (cf. Koenderink & van Doorn, 1975, 1976a, 1976b, 1976c; Lappin, 1990, 1991; Lappin & Love, 1992). This isomorphism holds for images defined by rotation in depth, stereoscopic disparity, and texture. (Isomorphism does not hold for shaded images defined by variations in luminance, but a correspondence does exist between certain properties of the two differential structures [Koenderink & van Doorn, 1980].) Both the surface and its image are 2D manifolds, so the projective mapping of a surface onto its image involves no loss of dimensions. Moreover, this mapping from the surface onto its image is locally described simply by a linear coordinate transformation; and the inverse transformation from the image onto the surface is also well-defined. The parameters of this transformation vary smoothly with changes in the relative orientation of the surface, except at isolated local discontinuities (sharp corners and peaks, occluding contours, and boundary contours). The critical points of the surface—minima and maxima, ridges and troughs, parabolic lines (inflections, separating convexities and concavities), saddlepoints, and discontinuities—are duplicated in the retinal image. Thus, the differential structure of the image constitutes information about the structure of environmental surfaces.

Given this simple relationship between the differential structure of surfaces and their images, one would expect vision to be sensitive to this information. Experimental evidence on this issue is not extensive, but available evidence supports the hypothesis that surface structure is a fundamental aspect of the optical information that vision detects. Surface structure has been regarded by many vision researchers (not Johansson nor Gibson) as a derived property, requiring inferences from perceived differences in depth. Presently available evidence, however, indicates that surface structure is probably fundamental rather than derived, associated with intrinsic properties of the optical pattern rather than inferred from local retinal cues. Experimental evidence on perceiving struc-

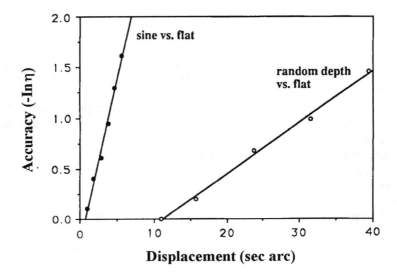

Fig. 4. Accuracy in detecting relative depth and motion as a function of the distance of relative motion. The left curve gives the accuracy in discriminating a sinusoidal surface (0.75 c/deg.) from a flat pattern; the right curve is for discriminating between a flat pattern and a volumetric pattern thickened in the depth axis in which dots with differing depths were randomly distributed in the image. The control variable on the horizontal axis refers to the maximum displacement of a single dot in the depth pattern relative to that for the flat pattern. For the sine-wave patterns, this relative displacement corresponds to the peak-to-trough amplitude of the modulation in depth, with near dots moving in one direction and far dots moving in the opposite direction. For the sine waves, the distance between dots with the maximal relative difference in displacement was 40 min. arc. The measure of discrimination accuracy is the choice theory measure, approximately the log odds of a correct response (cf. Luce, 1963). The data are for a single observer, with 60 trials per data point.

ture from motion and on stereopsis indicates that vision is more sensitive to variations in surface structure than to depth differences per se among disconnected points. Vision also seems to be more sensitive to qualitative variations in curvature (second spatial derivatives and/or Gaussian curvature) than to depth gradients (first derivatives, such as texture density gradients) of planar surface patches. Qualitative variations in surface structure are isomorphic with easily detected spatial variations in image motions.

Evidence about the visual primacy of surface structure has been obtained in experiments on structure from motion, where depth differences in random-dot patterns were more easily detected when depths varied smoothly as if on a slightly curved surface rather than being randomly distributed within a volume.

Relevant data were collected in an unpublished experiment in my laboratory by Changnian Sun. Random-dot patterns were displayed on a computer-controlled cathode ray tube and oscillated horizontally as if rigidly rotating in depth around a central vertical axis, 5° in each direction from the frontal-parallel plane [Note 2]. On half the trials the dots moved as if on a flat plane, and on the remaining trials they moved as if their relative depths varied over some fixed range; the observer's task was to discriminate between these two alternative patterns—that is, to detect differences in relative depths [Note 3]. Two sets of conditions differed by whether the depths varied smoothly, as on a sinusoidally corrugated surface (with horizontal peaks and troughs), or were randomly distributed over the same image area.

Depth variations were much more easily detected when the moving images resembled those of a smooth surface rather than a random volume of points. Fig. 4 shows psychometric functions for discriminating each type of pattern from a flat plane. As may be seen, relative motions of very small amplitude were accurately detected when they corresponded to depth rotations of a smooth surface. When the configuration was a random volume of dots, however, the detectability of relative motion and depth was greatly reduced. The threshold displacement (at an accuracy of -log η = 1.0, equal to 73.1% correct) for the smooth sine waves was only about 3 sec arc, but was greater than 30 sec arc for the random patterns. Interestingly, this result is quantitatively similar to a corresponding difference found by Stevenson, Cormack, and Schor (1989) for detecting depth in random-dot stereograms.

The smooth and random motion configurations in this experiment yielded subjectively different perceived patterns: The smoothly varying image motions were usually seen as rigid rotations in depth, whereas the random patterns, when their motions were visible at all, were seen as disconnected motions in the image plane. The flat patterns were also seen as moving only in the image plane, with slight contractions in the horizontal axis being barely visible. We have also found in other experiments that such planar patterns are usually not seen as rigidly rotating in depth (Norman & Lappin, 1992). Thus, smooth variations in image motion may be necessary for perceiving rigid rotation in depth.

The remarkable sensitivity to depth differences described in this experiment—with image motion thresholds much smaller than the spacing between cones in the central fovea—suggests that the visibility of motion in depth is probably limited only by the visibility of any motion at all.

As indicated by the difference in performance between the smooth and random patterns in this experiment, the detection of relative motion and depth depends on the spatial configuration of the motion. As the spatial frequency of the motion and depth variations increased from 1 to 6 c/deg, the detection thresholds rose approximately linearly from less than 5 to about 30 sec arc. This finding is similar to earlier results by Nakayama and Tyler (1981) and Rogers and Graham (1982).

Vision is sensitive not merely to the presence of depth variations in smooth surfaces; the shapes of these surface variations are also quite visible. Local image information about the qualitative curvature [Note 4] and shape of a surface is provided by the second spatial derivatives of its image—that is, with changes in the gradients of the motion, disparity, and texture fields of the image. However, since two views of a surface via binocular disparity or the KDE are ambiguous with respect to scale in depth (Koenderink & van Doorn, 1991; Todd & Bressan, 1990; Todd & Norman, 1991), the *metric* curvature and shape are also ambiguous in these images. Moreover, Todd and Bressan (1990) and Todd and Norman (1991) have found that human observers seem unable to integrate spatial information over temporal sequences of more than two successive frames. Even though metric information is theoretically available in sequences of three or more frames (Ullman, 1979), human observers have not yet been shown to be sensitive to such information except in the restricted case of planar motion (Lappin & Love, 1992). Rather than metric curvature or shape, vision seems to obtain information about the affine structure of the surface—ambiguous with respect to scale of the depth axis. Despite this ambiguity, the second spatial derivatives of the image constitute rich information about surface shape: The sign of the Gaussian curvature at a point on a surface is the same as that of its image, invariant under perspective and affine transformations. Thus, the relative signs of two orthogonal second spatial derivatives of the image are sufficient to determine whether the surface is locally planar, parabolic (cylindrical), elliptic (ellipsoidal), or hyperbolic (saddle-shaped) and whether it contains a local discontinuity. The local shape of any smooth surface is one of these four types.

Very little psychophysical research has studied the perception of surface curvature from motion. A recent PhD thesis by Farley Norman (Norman, 1990; Norman & Lappin, 1992) is one of the few such investigations. Norman evaluated the detection and discrimination of surface curvature from motion in random-dot KDE patterns. Among his main findings were the following: (1) Observers could accurately discriminate between two ellipsoids that had very similar relative depths but qualitatively different curvature profiles. (One ellipsoid was slightly extended and the other slightly compressed in depth relative to a sphere.) The threshold difference in the length of this axis for 75% correct discrimination between the two ellipsoids was about 5% (±2.5% deviation from a sphere) [Note 5]. (2) Discriminations were less accurate for noncurved dihedral edges with the same depth range and same average slant as the ellipsoids. (3) Discriminations were invariant under large changes in the size of the displayed patterns, indicating that discriminations were based on shape rather than on the local values of image velocities, depths, or curvatures per se. (4) Discriminations were also invariant under large changes in the perspectivity of the projected patterns, although this too had a large effect on the image velocities, indicating that visual information about the shape of the object was obtained from the intrinsic structural constancy of the object rather than from an extrinsic coordinate space. (5) *Detections* of curvature (discrimination between curved and planar surfaces) had a threshold of only about 15 sec arc for the maximum difference in image displacements for the two surfaces. (6) Curvature was more easily detected perpendicular to the direction of rotation than in the direction of rotation, inconsistent with the common idea that surfaces are derived from depth maps of individual points. (7) Planar surfaces usually did not appear to rotate rigidly in depth, suggesting that depth variations may be necessary for perceiving rigid structure from motion [Note 6].

Thus, Norman's study indicates that rotation in depth provides sufficient information for accurately discriminating the shapes of surfaces in 3D space. Even though the scale of the depth axis may be ambiguous, the qualitative local shape of the surface is potentially visible from the local structure of the image motions. When the rotation carries the shape through a sufficiently large angle, then ambiguity about scale in depth is effectively resolved, and the metric shape is perceivable.

A schematic illustration of the relationship between the local structure of the image motions and the structure of the environmental surface is given in Fig. 5. These four alternative patterns of relative motions are associated, respectively, with local surface patches that are planar, parabolic, elliptic, or hyperbolic [Note 7]. The local structure of any smooth surface is one of these four types. As may be seen, each of these types produces a unique pattern of differential image motion when the surface rotates rigidly in depth. The central point in these illustrations is shown as stationary, corresponding to removal of the common motion of the points; the remaining relative or differential motions of the four outside points determine the surface structure. The relative image motions of three approximately collinear points provide a measure of the second spatial derivative of the image motion, associated with the curvature of the surface in that direction. Thus, measures of these second derivatives of the relative image motion in two orthogonal directions provide information about the relative surface curvatures in those two directions [Note 8].

How efficient are real human observers in identifying these alternative surface shapes? Natural image motions produced by objects moving in 3D space include additional vector components: Theoretically, image motions produced by any rigid motion in 3D space may be described by combinations of translation, rotation, expansion, and deformation of the image; only the deformations carry information about surface shape (cf. Koenderink, 1986). Can human observers perceive surface shapes by visually analyzing such complex motion configurations?

An experimental study of this issue was conducted by Lappin, Craft, and Tschantz (1991). Patterns of 19 dots in a hexagonal arrangement (with collinear subsets of five dots) were displayed on a computer-controlled CRT and subjected to random jittering movements corresponding to rotations of surfaces in depth, independently around both horizontal and vertical axes [Note 9]. These

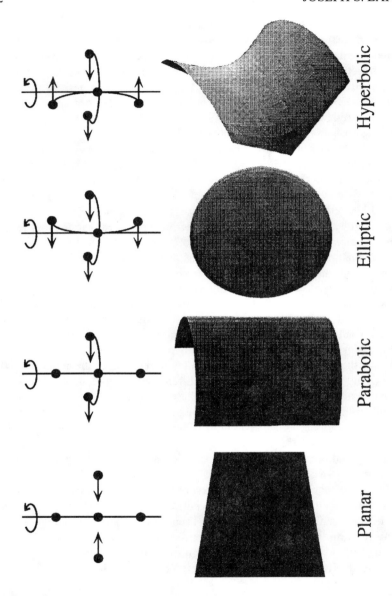

Fig. 5. Schematic illustration of the relative motion patterns associated with each of the four possible categories of local shape of a smooth surface: planar, parabolic (cylindrical), elliptic (ellipsoidal), and hyperbolic (saddle-shaped). These relative motions specify the second spatial derivatives of the image motion in the local neighborhood of the central point.

rotations produced slightly different patterns of image motion depending on the shape of the underlying surface. Without motion, the patterns were identical; the surface shapes were revealed only by the rotations in depth. The hexagonal arrays of dots were projected onto one of four alternative surfaces—plane, cylinder, sphere, and saddle, as illustrated in Fig. 5. The surface patches were 3 cm in diameter (1.5° arc) on surfaces with a 12 cm radius of curvature. (These small surface curvatures produced only slightly different patterns of motion; the maximum rotation of 40°, from one extreme position to the other, yielded less than 1.5 min. arc differential displacement of dots on opposite outside edges of the pattern. Surfaces with increased curvatures were more easily discriminated.) The visibility of coherent structure and motion of these patterns was further challenged by adding other independent image motions: horizontal and vertical translations, expansions and contractions (corresponding to translations in depth), and 2D rotations in the image plane. The magnitudes of image displacements associated with these transformations were essentially the same as those associated with the 3D rotations—a maximum value of about 3.9 min. arc in both horizontal and vertical directions. The displacement of each point was the vector sum of these transformations. Five different types of image motions were presented in separate blocks of trials: (a) 3D rotations alone; (b) 3D rotations plus translations; (c) 3D rotations plus expansions; (d) 3D rotations plus 2D rotations; and (e) 3D rotations plus translations, expansions, and 2D rotations. The observer's task in all conditions was to identify which one of the four alternative surface shapes was presented on each trial.

The average accuracies of four observers in identifying the four surface shapes from these various patterns of image motion are shown in Fig. 6. The accuracy was usually highest for identifying the sphere and saddle and lowest for the cylinder. The greatest numbers of confusions were between the plane and cylinder; the least confusions were between the sphere and saddle. The plane was often identified by its lack of apparent rigid motion in depth. Thus, it is clear that these surface shapes could be identified by these randomly moving patterns in which the shape information was provided only by image deformations between successive pairs of frames. It is also evident that the most easily perceived surfaces were those curved in two directions.

The principal issue addressed by these data concerns the effects of the combined image transformations on the accuracy of shape discrimination. Although accuracy generally declined with additional image transformations, the detrimental effect was not large when a single image transformation was added to the 3D rotations. In particular, accuracy in identifying the sphere and saddle shapes was affected very little by addition of either expansions or translations, remaining about 80% correct with or without these transformations, but declining to 60–70% correct with addition of the 2D rotations. Although accuracy declined sharply when all four groups of image transformations were combined,

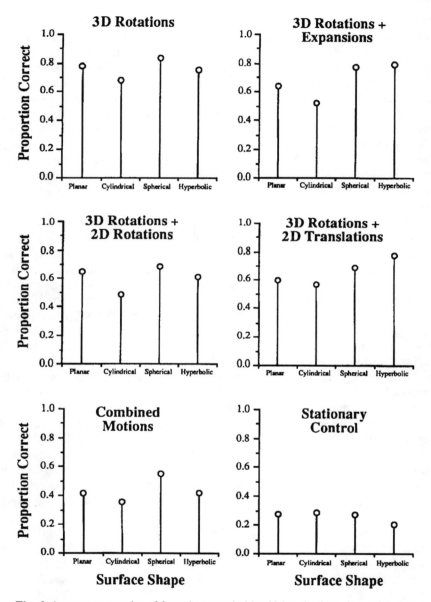

Fig. 6. Average accuracies of four observers in identifying the four alternative shapes in each of the image motion conditions. In the stationary control condition, the shapes were presented in a single stationary position rotated to one of the extreme rotational positions; this condition was used to check on the discriminability of the surface shapes without the image motions. These data points are based on 240 trials, 60 for each of the four observers.

the task could still be performed and led to the same qualitative pattern of pair-wise con-fusions among the shapes (shown by other analyses). The decline in accuracy with increasing image transformations is not surprising, since in-creased transformations produced increased magnitudes of image displacement, and this tended to decrease the detectability of coherent motion. Despite this decline in accuracy, the observers' success in detecting the coherent structure of these complex motion patterns suggests that the visual system can indeed per-form a type of vector analysis to identify the relative motions associated with curved surfaces amid the superimposed effects of translation, expansion, and 2D rotation. This vector analysis seems to be based on the second spatial derivatives of the global image motion of the whole surface patch: The local motion of any given dot was essentially the same for all of these image transformations; and the expansions produced the same displacements of pairs of points on opposite sides of the pattern as did the 3D rotations; but these locally similar motions in-terfered little with perceptions of 3D rotation and surface shape.

The experiments in this section illustrate the continuing relevance of Gunnar Johansson's ideas about the visual interdependence of space, motion, and shape. Visual information about the shapes of objects moving in 3D space is defined by the local differential structure of the image motions. Other cues or assumptions about the structure of an abstract 3D space are unnecessary.

Perceiving 3D Spaces

The spatial relations relevant to experiments in the preceding section involve only the structure of smoothly connected surfaces. The three-dimensionality of the surrounding space derives from the objects and motions it contains. But this space is defined only in the neighborhood of a smoothly connected surface.

What are the sources of information about the space between disconnected objects, and about the relative locations of objects and the observer within an environmental framework? Is vision sensitive to such information? Everyday achievements of moving observers in coordinating bodily movements with po-sitions and motions of environmental objects—for instance, in athletic games such as baseball, tennis, and basketball—clearly indicate that vision is an im-pressively effective detector of such information.

Optical information about the geometric structure of the environment has two complementary aspects: One part, discussed above, is *local* and involves information about surface structure. The other part is *global* and involves the perspective embedding of the images into 3D Euclidean space (E^3). This per-spective embedding locates both objects and the observer within a 3D environ-mental framework. Johansson's recent research on wide-angle vision and the "optic sphere theory" (Johansson, 1977; Johansson & Börjesson, 1989, 1990,

1991) provides valuable evidence about this fundamental aspect of vision that has been much too neglected in vision research.

Optical information about perspective may be described in terms of the "optic array"—the collection of light rays passing through a focal point. This optic array is specific to the location of the focal point within the surrounding environment. Expanding the optic array from a point yields a spherical image, the "optic sphere." The retinal image is a sample of this optic sphere. Thus, physiological information about the position of the retina within the optic sphere provides optical information about the observer's direction and orientation within the environment. The studies of Johansson and Börjesson demonstrate that vision is quite sensitive to this information when the images stimulate the far periphery of the retina.

Perspective projection from E^3 onto the optic sphere maps lines parallel in E^3 onto lines that converge toward a common vanishing point in the image, and all lines parallel to a plane in E^3 converge toward a great circle in the optic sphere. All lines parallel to the ground plane converge toward a great circle called the horizon line. A concrete horizon line does not occur in most images, and its abstract optical specification is equally ambiguous as the orientation of the ground plane, but it partitions the image into regions above and below the eye. Similarly, images of lines in E^3 parallel to the observer's median sagittal plane converge toward a great circle partitioning the visual field into objects on the right and left sides of the viewing direction. This linear perspective associated with the images of lines and planes that are parallel in E^3 provides information about the metric structure of the environment: Since parallel lines are equidistant from one another in E^3, their images provide a scale for associating certain spatial relations in the image with distances in E^3. When the global perspective parameters are correctly inferred, then a uniform geometric scale is conferred on the image such that apparent sizes and shapes of objects are invariant under motion. Conversely, optical information about perspective is provided by (a) motions of the observer, (b) motions of environmental objects, and/or (c) repeated images of a given shape in multiple locations in a stationary scene. Linear perspective and texture density gradients are special cases of the latter form of spatial information involving only implicit but not real motion. All these forms of metric spatial information involve the same basic principle, *congruence under motion*: If the same object occupies two different spaces, then these two spaces are congruent. The geometry of vision seems to be based at least in part on this principle for defining space (cf. Lappin & Love, 1992).

Movements of the observer offer an especially rich source of perspective structure: "Optic flow" patterns of the image trajectories of environmental points correspond to lines that are parallel and equal in length in Euclidean space-time. When the observer translates in the direction of gaze, these image trajectories radiate in the image from a "focus of outflow" corresponding to the observer's heading direction.

The *retinal* flow patterns, however, described with respect to retinal coordinates rather than with respect to the intrinsic structure of the optic sphere, may in general be significantly more complicated summations of multiple vector components. When the observer fixates an environmental point not in the direction of heading, or when the eyes are moved during locomotion, or when the observer's path is not a linear translation, then the retinal flow patterns have added rotational components. If the visible information consists of these retinal flow patterns, then the radial structure of these patterns must be obtained by analytic decomposition of the complex retinal flow patterns. The processes by which such an analysis might be accomplished are an important subject of current research and controversy.

If Johansson is correct, however, that the visual input is the intrinsic structure of the optic sphere, then such decomposition may not be necessary at all. This issue concerning the proper representation of optical information about the perspective embedding of moving retinal images into E^3 is fundamental for understanding how we see the spatial locations and motions of ourselves and objects within a stable environmental framework. This issue has not yet been resolved, but it deserves energetic and creative experimental attention.

In this case as in several other basic issues in vision, Gunnar Johansson's research on the optical information for vision and on the visual interdependence of space, motion, and shape remains central to contemporary understanding of vision. May the energy and creative efforts of other researchers resemble the standard set by Gunnar Johansson.

Notes

[1] Actually, natural surfaces are probably usually not smooth but fractal—nondifferentiable everywhere and at every scale (cf. Mandelbrot, 1983). Even though the physical structure of many contours and surfaces may not be smooth (differentiable), the organized structure seems to be visually described by a smooth approximation, with unsystematic roughness seen as an added noisy component (Gilden, Schmuckler, & Clayton, 1993).

The retinal images of motion patterns used in laboratory experiments, including those of Johansson, are often composed of discrete components, such as dots, that are certainly not spatially continuous. But the spatial organization of even these discrete patterns appears to be visually approximated by a smooth contour or surface. The neurophysiological representation of retinal images, involving synaptic interactions sensitive to spatial and temporal gradients in neurophysiological responses, might well approximate smooth patterns. In any case, because the organized spatial structure of optical patterns is typically perceived by a smooth approximation, we will adopt the assumption that both environmental surfaces and their images are smooth.

[2]   These patterns were composed of 600 dots randomly positioned in a 2 deg^2 area on a computer-controlled point-plot CRT. The patterns oscillated at 1 Hz, rotating through an angle of 10° around a central vertical axis, 5° in each direction from the frontal-parallel plane. Each cycle was constructed from a sequence of 12 frames portraying 6 different equally spaced orientations in depth. Each frame was displayed for about 83 msec with no interframe interval. Each pattern was displayed for a total of 3 sec. The spatial frequency of the sine-wave patterns in this experiment was 0.75 c/deg, with the depth values modulated in the vertical direction of the display, producing horizontally oriented peaks and troughs. In another set of patterns, the same set of depth values as in these sine-wave patterns was distributed within a volume of space by randomly changing the vertical positions of dots in the sine-wave patterns, leaving positions in the horizontal and depth axes unchanged.

[3]   This discrimination task does not directly evaluate the perception of depth and 3D structure. Discriminations between the flat plane and either the sine-wave surface or random volume required only the detection of relative motion. Subjectively, however, the sine-wave patterns generally did appear as rigid surfaces rotating in depth when the differential motion was visible.

[4]   The curvature in a given direction at a given point on a surface refers to the derivative of the direction of a surface normal with respect to the arc length over the surface in that direction. The standard measure of curvature for a plane curve is the reciprocal of the radius of the best-fitting circle, $k = 1/r$. The curvature at a given point on a surface can be characterized by the curvatures in two perpendicular directions, and it is customary to use the "principal" directions for which k is a maximum and a minimum. These measures of curvature are *extrinsic* in that they are defined only by reference to an external coordinate system for the space in which the surface is embedded. An *intrinsic* measure of surface curvature, however, is given by the Gaussian curvature, $K = k_{max} k_{min}$. K can be defined by intrinsic relations confined to the surface itself regardless of its embedding in any other coordinate space. These measures of curvature also depend on size; Koenderink (1990, pp. 319-324) presents other useful formulae in k_{max} and k_{min} that provide separate measures of size and "curvedness," and suggests specific indices of shape related to curvature.

[5]   These discriminations were based on the presentation of one of the two alternative ellipsoids on each trial, with one alternative slightly extended and the other slightly compressed in depth relative to a sphere. This axis of extension was parallel to the depth axis before the ellipsoid was rotated in depth. The ellipsoids were rotated through an angle of 70° around a central vertical axis, displayed in 15 different positions with 5° between successive positions and each frame displayed for 28 msec. There were three cycles of this oscillating horizontal motion on each trial, lasting for a total of 2.5 sec.

Before rotating in depth, these two shapes were equivalent under a scalar transformation of the depth axis, but this affine equivalence did not hold after the shapes rotated away from the central position so that the axis in which they differed was no longer parallel to the depth axis. When the patterns were displayed in just two positions in which the central axis was on either side of the depth axis, they were virtually indiscriminable; but if the central axes of the ellipsoids were rotated 35° from the depth axis, then two views were sufficient to produce discrimination similar to that obtained with 15 views distributed over 70° rotation. Thus, seeing these shapes in positions in which they were not equivalent under a scalar change of the depth axis was critically important for the accurate shape discriminations obtained when the shapes were rotated through 70°.

[6]   The inadequacy of planar surfaces for producing perceived rigid rotation in depth seems to be limited to the case in which both the plane and the axis of rotation are in the frontal-parallel. If the plane is tilted around the horizontal axis and this tilted plane then rotates around the vertical axis, so that the image contains a spatial gradient of velocities perpendicular to the axis of rotation, then rigid rotation in depth is perceived.

[7]   The isomorphism between these four alternative patterns of differential image motion and the four alternative types of smooth surface structure was pointed out by Steven T. Tschantz, a faculty member in Mathematics at Vanderbilt.

[8]   In practice, the image measurement problem is more complex than shown in these illustrations: Relative motions must be measured in more than just these two orthogonal directions in the image since the principal curvatures of the surface may not be aligned with these two directions. Moreover, the relative motions of just three approximately collinear points may be insufficient to provide reliable visual measures of curvature. We have found in laboratory experiments that these simple five-point patterns are subjectively ambiguous for most observers; increasing the number of points in each collinear set from three to five produces a great improvement in discriminating the 3D structure, and still greater dot densities often yield more compelling percepts.

[9]   The patterns were displayed on a computer-controlled CRT using the same equipment as in the previously described studies by Changnian Sun and by Farley Norman on perceiving structure from motion. The positions of the dots were displaced every 50 msec in random directions and distances corresponding to independent rotations around both the horizontal and vertical axes, with the angle of rotation uniformly distributed in the range ±20°. Each pattern was presented in a random sequence of 40 different positions, displayed for a total of 2 sec on each trial.

References

Adelson, E. H., & Bergen, J. R. (1985). Spatiotemporal energy models for the perception of motion. *Journal of the Optical Society of America, A, 2*, 284–299.

Baker, C. L., Friend, S. M., & Boulton, J. C. (1991). Optimal spatial displacement for direction selectivity in cat visual cortex neurons. *Vision Research, 31*, 1659–1668.

Bertenthal, B. I., Proffitt, D. R., & Cutting, J. E. (1984). Infant sensitivity to figural coherence in biomechanical motions. *Journal of Experimental Child Psychology, 37,* 213–230.

Bertenthal, B. I., Proffitt, D. R., & Kramer, S. J. (1987). The perception of biomechanical motions: Implementation of various processing constraints. *Journal of Experimental Psychology: Human Perception and Performance, 13,* 577–585.

Blake, R. (1993). Cats perceive biological motion. *Psychological Science, 4,* 54-57.

Carlson, C. R., Moeller, J. R., & Anderson, C. H. (1984). Visual illusions without low spatial frequencies. *Vision Research, 24,* 1417–1413.

Chang, J. J., & Julesz, B. (1983). Displacement limits for spatial frequency filtered random-dot cinematograms in apparent motion. *Vision Research, 23,* 1379–1385.

Fox, R., & McDaniel, C. (1982). The perception of biological motion by human infants. *Science, 218,* 486–487.

Gibson, J. J. (1966). *The senses considered as perceptual systems.* Boston: Houghton Mifflin.

Gilden, D. L., Bertenthal, B. I., & Othman, S. (1990). Image statistics and the perception of apparent motion. *Journal of Experimental Psychology: Human Perception and Performance, 16,* 693–705.

Gilden, D. L., Schmuckler, M. A., & Clayton, K. N. (1993). The perception of natural contour. *Psychological Review, 100,* 460-478.

Johansson, G. (1950). *Configurations in event perception.* Uppsala: Almqvist & Wiksell. [Chapter 2, this volume.]

Johansson, G. (1973). Visual perception of biological motion and a model for its analysis. *Perception & Psychophysics, 14,* 201–211. [Chapter 7, this volume.]

Johansson, G. (1976). Spatio-temporal differentiation and integration in visual motion perception. *Psychological Research, 38,* 379–393. [Chapter 8, this volume.]

Johansson, G. (1977). Studies on visual perception of locomotion. *Perception, 6,* 365–376. [Chapter 9, this volume.]

Johansson, G., & Börjesson, E. (1989). Toward a new theory of vision: Studies on wide-angle space perception. *Ecological Psychology, 1,* 301–331. [Chapter 10, this volume.]

Johansson, G., & Börjesson, E. (1990). *Experiments on the optic sphere theory: Slant perception from central stimulation* (Uppsala Psychological Reports, No. 424). Uppsala University, Department of Psychology.

Johansson, G., & Börjesson, E. (1991). *Studies on perception of waves: A contribution to the optic sphere theory.* Preliminary manuscript. Uppsala University, Department of Psychology.

Koenderink, J. J. (1986). Optic flow. *Vision Research, 26,* 161–179.

Koenderink, J. J. (1990). *Solid shape.* Cambridge, MA: MIT Press.

Koenderink, J. J., & van Doorn, A. J. (1975). Invariant properties of the motion parallax field due to the movement of rigid bodies relative to the observer. *Optica Acta, 22,* 773–791.

Koenderink, J. J., & van Doorn, A. J. (1976a). Local structure of movement parallax of the plane. *Journal of the Optical Society of America, 66,* 717–723.

Koenderink, J. J., & van Doorn, A. J. (1976b). Geometry of binocular vision and a model for stereopsis. *Biological Cybernetics, 24,* 51–59.

Koenderink, J. J., & van Doorn, A. J. (1976c). The singularities of the visual mapping. *Biological Cybernetics, 24,* 51–59.

Koenderink, J. J., & van Doorn, A. J. (1980). Photometric invariants related to solid shape. *Optica Acta, 27,* 981–996.

Koenderink, J. J., & van Doorn, A. J. (1991). Affine structure from motion. *Journal of the Optical Society of America, A, 8,* 377–385.

Lappin, J. S. (1990). Perceiving the metric structure of environmental objects from motion, self-motion, and stereopsis. In R. Warren & A. H. Wertheim (Eds.), *Perception and control of self-motion* (pp. 541–547). Hillsdale, NJ: Erlbaum.

Lappin, J. S. (1991). Perceiving environmental structure from optical motion. In W. W. Johnson & M. K. Kaiser (Eds.), *Visually guided control of movement* (pp. 39–61). Moffett Field, CA: NASA Conference Publications.

Lappin, J. S., Craft, W. D., & Tschantz, S. T. (1991). Perceiving shape from motion. *Investigative Ophthalmology and Visual Science, 32,* (Suppl., ARVO Abstracts), 1277.

Lappin, J. S., & Love, S. R. (1992). Planar motion permits perception of metric structure in stereopsis. *Perception & Psychophysics, 51,* 86–102.

Lappin, J. S., Norman, J. F., & Mowafy, L. (1991). The detectability of geometric structure in rapidly changing optical patterns. *Perception, 20,* 513–528.

Lappin, J. S., Wason, T. D., & Akutsu, H. (1987). Visual detection of common motion of spatially separate points. *Bulletin of the Psychonomic Society, 25,* 343.

Luce, R. D. (1963). Detection and recognition. In R. D. Luce, R. R. Bush, & E. Galanter (Eds.), *Handbook of mathematical psychology, Vol. 1* (pp. 103–189). New York: Wiley.

Mandelbrot, B. B. (1983). *The fractal geometry of nature.* New York: Freeman.

Marr, D. (1982). *Vision.* San Francisco: Freeman.

Mowafy, L., Blake, R., & Lappin, J. S. (1990). Detection and discrimination of coherent motion. *Perception & Psychophysics, 48,* 583–592.

Mowafy, L., Lappin, J. S., Anderson, B. L., & Mauk, D. L. (1993). Temporal factors in the discrimination of coherent motion. *Perception & Psychophysics, 52,* 508–518.

Nakayama, K., & Silverman, G. H. (1985). Detection and discrimination of sinusoidal grating displacements. *Journal of the Optical Society of America, A, 2,* 267–274.

Nakayama, K., & Tyler, C. W. (1981). Psychophysical isolation of movement sensitivity by removal of familiar position cues. *Vision Research, 21,* 427–433.

Norman, J. F. (1990) *The perception of curved surfaces defined by optical motion.* Ph. D. dissertation, Vanderbilt University.

Norman, J. F., & Lappin, J. S. (1992). The detection of surface curvatures defined by optical motion. *Perception & Psychophysics, 51,* 386–396.

Restle, F. (1979). Coding theory of the perception of motion configurations. *Psychological Review, 86,* 1–24.

Rogers, B., & Graham, M. (1982). Similarities between motion parallax and stereopsis in human depth perception. *Vision Research, 22,* 261–270.

Stevenson, S. B., Cormack, L. K., & Schor, C. M. (1989). Hyperacuity, superresolution and gap resolution in human stereopsis. *Vision Research, 29,* 1597–1605.

Todd, J. T., & Bressan, P. (1990). The perception of 3-dimensional affine structure from minimal apparent motion sequences. *Perception & Psychophysics, 48,* 419–430.

Todd, J. T., & Norman, J. F. (1991). The perception of smoothly curved surfaces from minimal apparent motion sequences. *Perception & Psychophysics, 50,* 509–523.

Ullman, S. (1979). *The interpretation of visual motion.* Cambridge, MA: MIT Press.

Watson, A. B. (1990). Optimal displacement in apparent motion and quadrature models of motion sensing. *Vision Research, 30,* 1389–1393.

Perception of Biological Motion:
The KSD-Principle and the Implications of a
Distal Versus Proximal Approach[†]

Sverker Runeson

Uppsala University

Abstract: Underlying the perceptual efficiency of Gunnar Johansson's point-light displays is the fact that natural kinematic patterns contain unique information about dynamic properties; they provide *kinematic specification of dynamics (KSD)*. Because Johansson used recordings of natural events–a *distal approach*–the KSD-information was preserved. Thus, although reduced to a handful of moving points, the displays could still support unmitigated perception of the characteristic dynamics of human action. Other researchers have instead taken a *proximal approach,* using synthetic human-like displays assembled from elemental motions. In such displays there is no underlying dynamics. What gets specified, inadvertently, to a KSD-oriented perceptual system, is bound to have an inanimate and pseudodynamic character. Results obtained in this way have no obvious relevance for the understanding of the perception of biological motion. The argument is applied in a critical examination of some well-known studies based on computer animated displays, including the role of the so called center-of-moment in gender recognition and the role of occlusion in point-light displays. The related problem of *symbolistic degeneration* of perception experiments is also discussed.

[†] Work on this chapter was made possible by grants from The Swedish Council for Research in the Humanities and Social Sciences (HSFR) and The Bank of Sweden Tercentenary Foundation (RJ). Thanks are due to Diane Berry and Dankert Vedeler for valuable comments. Parts of the exposition are based on a paper presented at the ICEPA4 conference in Trieste, Italy (Runeson, 1987).

The Distal vs. Proximal Approach Distinction

Gunnar Johansson's studies of biological motion (1973, 1975, 1976) differ in an important respect from his previous research. Until then, his experiments had concerned *synthetic* events presented to the observers. In contrast, the studies of biological motion employed events that were basically *natural*. The difference can also be described as a swing from a *proximal* to a *distal* approach in the study of perception (Runeson, 1977/1983).

In producing the famous point-light displays, Gunnar Johansson filmed the normal movements of persons in action and subjected them only to *subtractive* manipulations. Certain global aspects were, one may say, filtered out. Small lights were attached to the main joints of the person and the exposure was adjusted so that all except the lights was made invisible on the film. Thus the acoustic and olfactory media were removed. Normally visible features such as shapes, colors, clothing, and facial expressions got extricated as well. Essentially, only the gross kinematic aspect was retained. The point is that despite the manipulations, the displays remained natural in an important respect: The configuration and motion of the ensemble of visible points were still faithfully rendered. The experimenter was not directly in control of the proximal events (the patterns of motion on the screen)–only of the choice of the distal events (i.e., the persons and their actions) and the subtractive manipulation. This procedure is characteristic of a *distal approach* because the occurrences on the display screen are constrained by a real or hypothetical event occurring, as it were, beyond the screen (Runeson, 1977/1983). Thus, what was made available to the observers in the experiments were samples of the richness and complexity of real-life human kinematics–even though its nature was largely unknown.

This is in contradistinction to the *proximal approach* characteristic of Johansson's previous research contributions (e.g., 1950, 1964). In these, the patterns presented to observers were produced by synthesis and manipulation of events on a screen. This direct control of the proximal pattern extends, in effect, to a control of the optic array at the experimental subjects' eyes. Unlike the production of the patch-light displays, there were no distal events that determined what was put on the screen. At most the experimenter was guided by informal or intuitive notions about distal occurrences and how they might constrain proximal patterns. Moreover, the procedure was *additive:* The resulting proximal patterns contained only those features that the experimenter deliberately put in there.[1]

---

[1] In addition, the displays may have included some inadvertent properties, arising, for instance, from the limitations of the CRT technique. Although not controlled by the experimenter, they were still not due to properties of any distal event that the experimenter may have tried to simulate.

It might seem that this difference is not of great significance since, either way, sets of moving points, lines, or geometrical forms are presented on a screen and subjects are asked to report on how they are perceived. To wit, in several later studies human-like patch-light displays have been produced by computer animation (see the reference list for works by Bertenthal, Cutting, Proffitt, and Todd) and used in much the same way as Johansson's natural recordings. Although these displays could be called simulations of human motion, they were produced by direct manipulation of the movements as such, as they occurred on the screen, and therefore instantiate the proximal approach.

However, the use of proximal and distal displays can pass as equivalent only as long as perception research is confined to the study of arbitrary subjective impressions. In a more circumspect approach, the *adaptive utility* of perception, thus the perceptual *achievements* people are capable of in real life, become foremost concerns. In that case, the proximal and the distal type of research strategies differ quite radically in their implications. To see how, a principled understanding of the *informational* relation between proximal patterns of motion and distal events is essential.

Kinematic Specification of Dynamics

Gunnar Johansson's works on biological motion brought into evidence a highly significant and intriguing category of perceptual achievement. Such a discovery should lead directly to a concern for the nature of the available information that makes the perceptual achievement possible. Hence, for the case of point-light biological motion, the important question is what the movements, that is, the *kinematic pattern*, of a person in action may specify concerning the person and the event. Towards an answer, it was important to note that in watching the recordings made by Johansson and his colleagues, the perceptual outcome is in fact much richer than the mere discernment of the fact that the recordings are of persons engaged in walking or other activities.[2] Despite that only about a dozen moving points appear on the screen, the impression one gets has a vividness that comes close to that obtained from recordings of people in normal illumination.[3] In particular, one can perceive how effortful the push-ups

---

[2] See Bingham (1991) for a discussion of the distinction between identification and scaling in perceptual functioning.

[3] As a historical note, this observation was corroborated in our work on two educational films (Maas et al., 1971a, 1971b). According to the original script, each point-light film sequence was to be followed by the same sequence shot in full illumination so that the audience could verify their first impressions. However, the idea had to be dropped since the repetition turned out to be very boring, seemingly adding nothing of interest beyond what the audience had already seen in the point-light sequence.

are and that the person who climbs up on a ladder does not actually start painting a wall–only pretends to do so. Indeed, one can see that the bicycle ride is not real. Instead it is a fake pan-shot of a ride on a stationary exercise bike set to minimal friction, leaving the moment of inertia of the flywheel as the only resistance the rider is confronted with. Hence, it appears that information about a number of inner or causal properties of the person and the event are also conveyed by the point-light displays, and perceptually apprehended.

Observations such as these suggest that the point-light displays provide *kinematic specification of dynamics*. This notion, the *KSD-principle*, was first developed for the case of collisions between inanimate objects (Runeson, 1977/1983; Runeson & Vedeler, 1993), where it entails that the resulting kinematic pattern uniquely specifies the mass ratio and the efficient damping characteristics of colliding objects. Bringing it to bear on Johansson's results on biological motion perception and some later works (Cutting & Kozlowski, 1977; Kozlowski & Cutting, 1977; Runeson & Frykholm, 1981), the KSD-principle was generalized and its applicability was shown to extend also to animate events (Runeson & Frykholm, 1983). In this context, the KSD-principle entails that properties pertaining to a person that have a *dynamic* ("causal") role in the generation of his or her movements are specified by the resulting kinematic patterns. Hence, information is available to make perception of such dynamic properties potentially possible. In particular, there is information to specify the difference between true and faked (mimed) properties or acts.

The necessary complement to the study of *available information* is of course the testing of its usefulness or *perceptual efficiency*. Thus, in a series of experiments, all employing the patch-light technique, it was shown that this kind of information is indeed often used by ordinary perceivers, sometimes with remarkable acuteness (Bingham, 1993; Runeson & Frykholm, 1981, 1983; see also Berry, 1991; Cutting & Kozlowski, 1977; Frykholm, 1983; Henderson, Bush, & Stoffregen, 1993; Kaiser & Proffitt, 1984; Kozlowski & Cutting, 1977; Stoffregen & Flynn, 1993; Sumi, 1993). These experiments extend Johansson's findings. They show that patch-light displays provide eminently usable information not only concerning the presence of a person in action and the category of action engaged in, as Johansson had shown. They also confirm that there is efficient information concerning a number of finer properties of the person and the event: the mass of an object handled by a person, the expectations or deceptive intentions he or she may have concerning its mass, the gender or identity of the person, etc.

Importantly, many of these properties would be labeled dispositional or "hidden" in traditional theorizing, with the implication that they could only be inferred from, or attributed on the basis of, a person's "behavior," perhaps only over an extended time. Taken together, the results of the patch-light studies and the KSD-principle demonstrate the inadequacy of the timeworn distinction between visible and hidden properties. The fact is that we can *see* the weight of an object handled by a person. The fundamental reason we are able to do so is exactly the same as for seeing the size and shape of the person's nose or the color of his shirt in normal illumination, namely that *information* about all these properties is available in the optic array. The kinematic-optic properties that specify box-weight may be analytically very complex. However, as exemplified in other contributions to this volume, the complexity of the optical information for three-dimensional size and shape and for surface color is far from trivial either. Although a dimension-analytic difference exists (see the concluding discussion), it would be unwise to assume that the latter types of information are fundamentally simpler or more accessible than that for lifted weight.

The KSD-principle expresses the exceedingly large specification power of naturally complex kinematic patterns. Thus it provides a theoretical basis for understanding the overall success with Johansson's original studies of biological motion. It holds for most organisms that other organisms, their properties, expectations, intentions, etc., have high biological adaptive relevance, hence *incentives* for perceiving them have always existed. The KSD-principle adds to this the insight that a category of excellent *opportunities* for such perceiving is available in the form of *firmly based* and *directly relevant* kinematic information. Thus it is plausible to expect that the evolution of the visual system has made it suitable for exploiting these opportunities. Furthermore, one can expect that individual organisms indulge in perceptual learning, that is, acquisition of perceptual skills that extend and refine this category of perceptual performances.

To appreciate the relevance of the above, it is important to note that an organism's use of analytically complex informative properties need not require complicated information processing. This insight is implicit in Johansson's reliance on vector-analytic stimulus descriptions and in Gibson's introduction of higher-order invariants as the basis for perception. As discussed by Runeson (1977, in press) under the label *smart mechanisms*, it is a mistake to think that real instruments or sensing devices respond in a pure way to elemental physical variables. Instead their response can, in principle, be described by an invariant function of elemental variables. The adequacy of a physical measuring device depends on the extent to which the target variable, whether elemental or complex, has been made to quantitatively dominate the response invariant. By the same logic, we can expect that the response characteristics of natural perceptual mechanisms have become dominated by the sort of complex invariants that have high biological informative relevance. Thus it is both physically and biologically more plausible that the way the KSD-type of information is exploited is through direct pickup in the Gibsonian sense rather than through inferencing from meaningless elemental sensations.

In summary, we can say that patch-light displays recorded from real events may *superficially* be very impoverished, however, they do in fact preserve much of the very powerful information contained in animate kinematic patterns. They therefore tap right into one of the strongest functional aspects of visual perception, with remarkable immediacy and refinement in the ensuing perceptual achievements.[4]

Searching for the Efficient Information

The KSD-principle, in itself, is a statement as to the general *existence* of a certain category of information, hence, in addition, it sets the stage for attempts at discovering actual instances of it. This has been successfully done for inanimate collisions (Runeson, 1977/1983). In contrast, the complexity of the dynamics of animate action, and the relative lack of knowledge about it, has proved a monumental obstacle to the explicit description of informative properties in human kinematic patterns. The analysis provided in Runeson and Frykholm (1983) essentially took the form of a demonstration of *non-substitutability among dynamic factors* in human action: It is not possible to substitute a change in one dynamic factor (e.g., an actual increase in the mass of a lifted box) with changes in other factors (e.g., an intention to move as if lifting the heavier box) and yet obtain the same kinematic pattern. Hence the kinematic pattern could not be ambiguous concerning the dynamic structure of the event, which is to say that information in the specificational sense is necessarily present.

Although derivation of informative properties directly from knowledge about how action is generated has not been possible, a number of investigators have set out to identify relevant information from the empirical end instead. This work entails measurement of various anatomical and kinematic properties in search for those that may covary with a particular dynamic factor, or with the way the factor is perceived.

Lifted weight

In search for the information that may be responsible for the judgments of lifted weight in patch-light displays, Bingham (1987) has taken an interesting approach. In the original works of Runeson and Frykholm (1981, 1983) the discussion of potentially relevant informative properties concerned several whole-body kinematic characteristics such as backward lean, movements due to the travel of reactive impulses through the body, and compensatory movements that maintain or restore balance and integrity. However, to circumvent the forbidding complexity of these multiple degrees-of-freedom properties, Bingham chose to start from the opposite end by investigating one-arm curl lifting with elbow and shoulders immobilized. Although this procedure no doubt freezes out many of the more powerful instances of KSD-type information, the purpose was

---

[4] Another of the strongest aspects, presumably, is the fundamental ability to perceive the three-dimensional layout of the environment, under static or moving conditions, and ones own location in it (cf. Lee, 1977).

to study the information that might be engendered by the lowest-level constraints involved: the energetic characteristics of the muscles.[5]

The single-joint movements were found to exhibit a characteristic kinematic form, which confirms that information-relevant constraints occur already at the level of muscle energetics. However, the kinematic form did not change appreciably between weights in the low and middle range. Only in the upper range, as the lifter's strength began to be taxed, did the kinematic forms distinguish the weights. These findings corresponded well with the judgments obtained from observers; weights were properly scaled in the upper weight range but the curves flattened out in the midrange and below. As expected, the judgments were also linked to the strength of the lifter, hence relative effort, rather than weight, appeared to be the perceived property.

Bingham's (1987) study not only identified relevant kinematic information for the single joint case but also clarified its basis in muscle-energetic constraints and the extent of its perceptual utility. Since the original lifted-weight results demonstrated perceptual discrimination over a larger range, we can now be sure that further searching for efficient information will have to consider the specific constraints inherent in multiple degrees-of-freedom actions as well. In addition to backward lean and the consequences of reactive impulses, Bingham calls attention to the subsidiary movements in adjacent joints that occur because differences in lifted weight require the use of different muscle groups which, in turn, differ in the number of joints they span.

In this context, a more recent finding is of importance. Several authors, in reviewing Runeson and Frykholm's (1981, 1983) original results, have presupposed that the conformance of the judgments with the absolute weight of the lifted box was due to the presentation of a standard weight, separately for each lifter. These presentations might have informed the observers about the individual lifter's strength and thus, it is implied, the property actually perceived could only have been the lifter's relative force or exertion (e.g., Gilden 1991; Todd, 1983). However, a recent study by Bingham (1993) proves otherwise. His main experiment was a better controlled replication of that of Runeson and Frykholm (1981). In addition, lifters varying more extensively in size and strength were used and no standards were presented. Despite this, the judgments conformed quite well with the *absolute* weight of the lifted box. It appears therefore that the kinematic pattern can contain useful information about the lifter's size and strength as well. More precisely, we can conclude that the effective information about lifted weight, provided by the kinematic pattern, exhibits at least a rudimentary *invariance* under variations in lifter characteristics. Thus the sophistication inherent in KSD-type information and in the perceptual use of it, hence

---

[5] For a discussion of the necessary role of constraints, that is, real-world laws and regularities, as grantors of information, see Barwise and Perry (1983) and Runeson (1988, 1989).

the challenge to perception research, proves to be even greater than it appeared before.

Gender recognition and the Center-of-Moment hypothesis

In a continuation of a series of studies of gender recognition in point-light walker displays (Kozlowski & Cutting, 1977, 1978), Cutting, Proffitt, and Kozlowski (1978) put forth a biomechanical property of the observed person which, they argued, has a decisive role in determining the impressions of maleness-femaleness obtained by observers. The property they suggested was the location of the so-called center of moment (C_m). This point was defined as the intersection of the lines that diagonally connect the shoulder joints with the hip joints and sits somewhat higher in the torso of women than it does in men. The C_m is not visible as such, however, it was argued that its location is revealed through the movements of the limbs, for which it provides an abstract center mediated by torsions that occur in the torso. Although no kinematic invariants that might specify the C_m were given, the analogy with the way that cycloids specify the center of a rolling wheel was suggested and the Gestalt law of common fate was referred to (however, for an elaboration, see Cutting, 1981).

Empirically, significant correlations between the C_m measure and the proportions of male/female judgments were found. It is important to note, however, that there are innumerable other intercorrelated anatomical and biomechanical measures on which men and women differ (see Bernstein, 1967, for examples). One possible way that the C_m could prove to have a special role would be if its correlation with the judgments was substantially higher than those of the other properties. No such comparisons were made, however. Alternatively, a case for the C_m could be made if the judgments exhibited a strict functional relation to the C_m.[6] The relatively modest correlations obtained (up to $r = .86$) provide little hope for this though. The conclusion must therefore be that Cutting et al.'s (1978) hypothesis, that the C_m is of crucial importance in enabling patch-light gender recognition, has not received sufficient support from these results. (A test of the C_m hypothesis by means of computer animated displays will be discussed below.)

The KSD-principle provides an alternative perspective on this issue. The fact to note is that all or most of the gender differences that occur in various measures are ultimately due to, that is, dynamically constrained by, the genetic difference that defines gender. It is this difference that constitutes the most relevant "underlying property" (cf. Schwarz, 1979) and which engenders the gender-specific differences in people's movements. The C_m property thus occupies an

---

[6] Since the judgments are binary, a qualitative-response model (Amemiya, 1981) would have to be applied. In such methods, the dependent variable is related to the independent by way of a psychometric threshold function such as the normal ogive. See Runeson and Vedeler (1993) for a related application.

unclear intermediate position between the kinematic "surface" and the definitive dynamic "deep structure" (quoted terms used by Cutting et al., 1978). It should be granted, though, that in the search for the perceptually efficient gender-specific properties of human kinematics–no doubt a tough and long-standing challenge–it may turn out to be tactically fruitful to identify intermediate dynamical entities. The C_m could in principle become useful in that context.

Gender differences in ankle motion

A further example of empirical search for efficient information is provided by Kruse, Stadler, and Vogt (1992; Kruse & Stadler, 1991). They have identified a characteristic gender difference in the kinematic pattern exhibited by the foot (ankle) in normal walking. To ascertain the perceptual efficiency of this property they presented recordings of moving ankle points and found that untrained observers were about 61% correct in judging gender (77% if trained). This figure is of course quite low in comparison with the 85% recognition level found by Runeson and Frykholm (1983) with extended whole-body patch-light scenes. However, given that only a single moving point was shown, Kruse et al.'s results come remarkably close to the figure obtained with full patch-light walker displays by Kozlowski and Cutting (1977). Given the difficulties pertaining to Cutting et al.'s (1978) work on the C_m, it might be that the ankle motion difference identified by Kruse et al. is the only clear example we have so far of a kinematic property that can be effective in gender recognition.

The status of empirically determined informative properties

To conclude the discussion of the search for efficient kinematic information we should note that informative properties identified on purely empirical grounds have a much weaker status than what would be the case if they were derived from explicit knowledge of the biomechanics of human action – the way it has been done for inanimate collisions. Even if a strong covariation between a proximal property and a distal source property is found, one does not know to what extent the relation will hold up under more variable conditions, that is, whether the proximal property will qualify as a specificational invariant. The covariation between specifier and the property specified may be contingent on one or more constraints that do not prevail throughout the relevant range of conditions (Runeson, 1989). For example, the gender-specific foot-placement property found by Kruse et al. (1992) obviously pertains only to walking. Kinematic information about gender is basically a consequence of the gross anatomical differences between men and women. We can therefore expect that there exist more general gender-specific kinematic properties, of which the foot-placement property is only a special case.

For the following discussion wee need to make clear that, despite a few limited but positive exceptions, *we are in no position to say which parts or properties of a natural patch-light display are of perceptual importance*, and which are not. Hence, to qualify as a true patch-light display, with undisputable relevance for illuminating and extending Johansson's original findings, we must require that even its finer details are intact. Real patch-light displays entail no control of the informative kinematic properties but provide a way of ensuring that the information is there. This predicament brings us back to the issue of a distal versus proximal approach in perception research. A distal approach appears to be indispensable. Hence, it will be necessary to examine the relevance, or lack thereof, of computer-generated (animated) displays of human motion.[7]

Computer Animated Displays

If we had full knowledge about how human action is generated, and complete biomechanical dynamic equations were available, it would have been possible to create simulated point-light displays that were kinematically identical to natural recordings. Thus they would be equally valid for perception research. Likewise, if full knowledge were available concerning the informative invariants of human kinematics then it would be possible to explicitly control and manipulate the informational content of the simulations. The proximal pattern would be derived, through a strict procedure, from a full-fledged *distal model* of a person in action. The use of displays simulated in such a way would be consistent with a distal approach, and would conform to the notion of laboratory studies of perception advocated by J. J. Gibson. However, as he put it, "the controlled displaying of *information* is vastly more difficult than the controlled applying of stimulation" (Gibson, 1979, p. 3, emphasis added). When it comes to biological motion, this difficulty is probably larger than within any other domain of visual perception research. As of today, the possibilities of fully valid dynamical simulation just do not exist (but see Bruderlin & Calvert, 1991, for a "hybrid" attempt).

Nevertheless, several recent studies that purport to address issues with a bearing on Johansson's biological motion work have used computer-animated patch-light-*style* displays instead of recordings of real events. Typically, the limb segments of an imaginary stick figure have been rotated in sinusoidal pendular fashion to produce, in most cases, the pattern of a walking person. The relative sizes of the limb segments have been "fitted by eye" and the amplitudes and phase relations of their movements, along with some other parameters, have been "chosen simply because they yielded the most natural-looking movements" (both quotes from Cutting, 1978a, pp. 396–397). Hence, the animations are purely geometric/kinematic with no involvement of dynamic factors such as mass, elasticity, energetic processes, or neural mechanisms, nor are any of the

---

[7] Similarly, the relevance of acted (mimed) events should be critically evaluated in the light of the KSD-principle (not discussed here, but see Runeson & Frykholm, 1983).

laws of motion taken into account. The motions are injected as such and do not arise as ad hoc results of simulation of the dynamic interplay among the limbs and with the environment.[8] Animations of this kind instantiate the proximal approach because the underlying model is very primitive as concerns the anatomical makeup and, especially, the way the movements come about. The approach is proximal also because motion parameters are adjusted ad hoc, that is, they are chosen on the basis of the programmer's preferences in viewing the result rather than derived through a strict procedure from a competent dynamic model.[9] The majority of these studies have used or been based on one and the same walker animation program developed by Cutting (1978a, 1978b; for an exception, see Todd, 1983).

Animation Test of the Center-of-Moment Hypothesis

To further investigate the center-of-moment hypothesis for gender recognition, Cutting (1978a) presented animated walker displays in which the C_m location was varied while all other parameters were kept constant. The above-mentioned animation of a patch-light walker figure was developed for this purpose (Cutting, 1978a, 1978b). Positive experimental results were reported and the conclusion drawn in this part of the study was that the C_m hypothesis had received further support.

As Cutting admits, the outcome of this procedure could only demonstrate perceptual sufficiency of the C_m. Other properties could still be equally potent in producing male or female appearance, hence the C_m variation might not be necessary. However, a more important problem with the study is that the variation in C_m location was greatly exaggerated in the animated displays: the range was made *ten times larger* than what occurred in the group of natural walkers measured by Cutting et al. (1978). Since the range was covered by only five stimuli, all except the middle one, designed to be gender neutral, were a long way outside the largest or smallest values that occur naturally among men and women. Moreover, the results show, by interpolation, that the C_m had to be exaggerated about 5.7 times in order to yield the same modest level of gender recognition performance that occurred with the natural patch-light walker displays.

---

[8] The terminology adopted here restricts the use of "simulation" to cases in which, at least rudimentarily, the motions are obtained by letting them *unfold* from a distal model subject to dynamic laws. Otherwise, when motions are synthesized as such, "animation" is the preferred term.

[9] Specialists in computer animation have found this distinction important too. Thus Bruderlin and Calvert (1991) use the terms *dynamic* and *kinematic approaches* and acknowledge the principled advantages of the former.

The author of the study points out that the C_m variation may not have captured all gender differences in walking and makes reservations concerning unnaturalness of the animations used. Moreover, the "hypernormality" of the C_m variation is discussed, however these several caveats are typically not retained when the study is reviewed by other authors (e.g. Bruce & Green, 1985, pp. 293–294). Hence the impression is conveyed that these results provide an extension to, even an explanation of, the results obtained with naturally recorded point-light material. For the reasons discussed above, the more proper conclusion is that the results pertain only to the specific type of animations used. Because of the absence of male-female discrimination in the animated displays at normal levels of C_m variation, the study has not really provided any evidence in support of the role of the C_m in animated displays either. One can glean that the overall quality or naturalness of the animations has been quite low, a suspicion that was confirmed in a later study that used the same animation program (Proffitt, Bertenthal, & Roberts, 1984). After viewing the walker display for 1.5 minutes, only a third of the observers said they saw a walker. Thus the animation study, too, has failed to provide support for the role of the C_m in gender recognition.

Symbolistic degeneration of perception experiments

Generally, how can one know that an experiment taps into *perception proper* and has not degenerated into a demonstration of *symbolistic perception*? The latter will very probably be the case if the experimental setup and the manipulated variable do not provide proper (natural) information for the entity studied. Rather than giving null and void answers, ambitious observers are then likely to base their judgments on whatever property of the display appears to vary saliently from trial to trial, irrespective of what they were instructed to judge and what percepts are actually engendered. An anomalous variation in an experimental variable may aggravate the problem since the exaggeration itself could make the varied property more salient. Hence the results may spuriously appear to confirm the experimenter's hypothesis.

The results reviewed above suggest that Cutting's (1978a) animation-based study of gender recognition is an instance of symbolistic degeneration. Confirming evidence can be found in a later study, designed to compare the accuracy of C_m-based gender recognition under conditions of normal versus off-joint placement of the point-lights. Despite that only the two extreme, hence most salient, C_m values were used, Cutting (1981) reports that without training several observers consistently based their gender judgments on the gender-irrelevant light-placement variable instead. Obviously, the center-of-moment variable does not have an intrinsic perceptual relation to gender. Thus the evidence suggests that the (relative) consistency of the results obtained in the initial experiments is in good part due to the single-variable nature of the display material used, leaving the C_m as an uncontested symbol for gender. Its adventitiousness is revealed by its susceptibility to displacement when another, irrelevant, variable is present.

The symbolistic interpretation stands in contrast to Cutting's (1978a) suggestion that the extreme C_m values function as hypernormal gender information. A hypernormal display should be one that qualitatively retains the informative specificity of the normal case and adds to that an augmented saliency. Facilitation and stability of gender recognition should follow. This expectation is not confirmed by the evidence reviewed above and the symbolistic interpretation is favored instead. It remains, hypothetically, that the imperfections of the walker animation have interfered and that the C_m variation might be functional, both normally and hypernormally, in a more adequate simulation. As yet, there is no evidence to suggest so though.

The Role of Occlusion in Patch-Light Walker Recognition

The walker animation provided by Cutting (1978a, 1978b) was used again in a study by Proffitt, Bertenthal, and Roberts (1984; see also Bertenthal, Proffitt, Spetner, & Thomas, 1985). They were concerned that the animations exhibit "multistability," that is, viewers experience Necker-cube type reversals of the near and far side of the walker. Such reversals do not occur in viewing Johansson's recordings (e.g., Maas et al., 1971a, 1971b) and are at least very rare in other natural point-light displays. Proffitt et al. experimented with occlusion of the points that are not visible during parts of the step cycle in the natural case. The purpose was to test whether the absence of such occlusion in Cutting's original animation was responsible for the instability of the perceptual impression. Hence, occlusion was introduced in the animation by switching some of the points on and off at appropriate points in the cycle. The results confirmed the expectation: Reversals were less frequent and recognition of the display as a walker rose from 33% to 83%. It was concluded that occlusion is an important factor in stabilizing the depth relation in point-light displays.

The obvious objection is that the observed effects of presence vs. absence of occlusion in the animated displays do not allow conclusions as to its role in natural displays. It might very well be the case that occlusion has a contributory effect only when the animations are poor, hence sparse or contradictory in what information they provide. The poorness of the animation was evidenced by the figure given above: Even after 90 seconds of viewing the enhanced version, only 83% of the observers reported they saw it as a walker. This contrasts sharply with the immediacy of recognition that occurs in watching Johansson's natural point-light recordings and, specifically, with his demonstration that observers can distinguish humans in action from agitated puppets in fractions of a second (Johansson, 1976). A more proper test would instead remove the occlusion that occurs in natural recordings. Such a manipulation may turn out to have no effect on the perceiving of a walking person, its orientation, etc., and may just make the walking human figure look transparent. If so, the truth about occlusion in point-light walker perception would be the exact opposite of what it seemed to be when studied with the proximal animation method: It has no important role in perceiving the basic stable walking-person event; it only pertains to the perceiving of a certain secondary feature, the opaqueness or transparency of the figure.

Occlusion in natural recordings

A recent study by Pardo (1992) satisfies the requirements just described. Natural patch-light recordings were digitized frame by frame and the locations of the patches were identified and stored in computer files so that the scenes could be recreated and displayed on the computer screen in real time. To achieve the non-occluded condition, alternative files were prepared in which a copy of the near-side points was phase-lagged by half a step cycle and then added in again so as to visibly represent the far side.

The natural and the disoccluded natural sequences were then compared by means of an experimental design similar to that of Proffitt et al. (1984). The results confirm the above expectations very well. First, the number of observers who reported seeing a walker in the displays was 100% in both conditions. Second, although perspective reversals did occur to some extent, the manipulation of occlusion did not affect their frequency. Also, ratings of naturalness differed slightly albeit in the opposite direction, that is, they were higher without occlusion (not statistically significant though). In summary, Pardo (1992) notes that the results "indicate no overall effect of the manipulations of occlusion in the perception of a natural point-light walker" (p. 19). In many contexts, occlusion no doubt contributes perceptually useful information. However, the weight of the evidence now runs contrary to Proffitt et al.'s conclusion and suggests that the role of occlusion is instead very small in comparison with the information entailed in the interrelated motion functions that make up *natural* patch-light walker displays. Although Proffitt et al. admitted that their displays may not have captured all the information that occurs in Johansson's point-light displays, they suggested that constructors of processing models should abandon their exclusive preoccupation with motion functions and give occlusion information a more prominent role. It now appears that one might be better advised to let occlusion wait and to probe for the more sophisticated informational aspects of kinematic patterns instead, at least for the case of biological motion. Generally, the occurrence of occlusion effects in the study by Proffitt et al. (1984), and their absence in that of Pardo (1992), confirms that those informative properties that make natural displays so compelling are lacking in the walker animation originated by Cutting (1978a, 1978b), with or without occlusion.

The Validity of Animation Studies

The authors of animation-based studies often comment on the validity of their results. Thus Todd (1983), in a study of the kinematic information that may underlie perception of running vs. walking gaits, made it clear that "the method of simulation ... was never intended to model the physical processes involved in human gait" and that "the specific parameters ... were determined by trial and error solely on the basis of perceptual criteria" (Todd, 1983, p. 33). However, the animations were taken to be quite accurate on the grounds that observers described them as compelling and because the motions generated were similar to those recorded on real subjects.

Whereas the studies based on Cutting's (1978a, 1978b) walker animation obviously have a low validity, one gets the impression that the quality of the animation, thus also the validity, of Todd's gait perception study may have been a good deal better. This is a likely possibility because the underlying model may have incorporated a few more biomechanical constraints, and because the upper half of the walking figure was not included and the experimenter could concentrate on making the movements of the legs and feet look good. Nonetheless, it is hard to find conclusive evidence for the validity of Todd's study. For instance, the naturalness ratings that were obtained covaried in a meaningful way with experimental manipulations, however, they can say nothing about the absolute level of naturalness (the same holds for Cutting's, 1978a, study). Likewise, when observers remarked that the displays were "extremely compelling" (Todd, 1983, p. 33) they may have had the current computer animation technique, rather than natural gait, as the implicit reference. Although reported as high, the similarity with published recordings of real gait motion functions was not perfect, and the differences can not be dismissed as informationally or perceptually irrelevant.

It is also important to note that even though we can trust the researchers that they have done their best in adjusting their animations until the most natural-looking displays were obtained, the results may have been far off the mark nevertheless. The reasons are twofold. First, each animation only has a finite (small) number of variables, hence a natural-looking result may not occur anywhere in the parameter space available to the programmer. Second, even if it does, the optimization procedure can only proceed on one dimension at a time and the chances of finding the optimal combination of parameter values are therefore small, in particular since nonlinear interactions between the variables are likely to occur.[10]

A general discussion of the validity of computer animated displays in perception research is provided by Proffitt and Kaiser (1986). Thus they mention that, ideally, simulations should be validated against natural events. However,

---

[10] For a discussion of the difficulties inherent in multi-variable optimization, as they appear in the context of action skill acquisition, see Fowler and Turvey (1978).

they summarize current practices very well by saying that "we *tend to assume* that the differences are irrelevant to the questions under study and that findings with computer-generated stimuli will generalize to natural events" (p. 491, emphasis added). As we have seen above, this belief is ill founded and has lead researchers to present misleading results and to draw some unwarranted conclusions on issues relating to Johansson's patch-light studies. An alternate statement in Proffitt and Kaiser's article should therefore be brought forth and emphasized: "We recommend caution in making unqualified generalizations about human sensitivities to natural events from studies on perceiving computer-animated displays" (p. 491). The situation is well captured by Pardo (1992): "The limitations of computer-generated displays are unknown due to the uncertain status of the model used to generate the kinetics. Overall, edited natural displays offer the better mix of control and generalizability" (p. 21).

Concluding Points

Our exposition has shown that, when it comes to perception of biological motion, radical differences exist between proximally and distally oriented research. The two approaches can lead to severely divergent results and conclusions. When that happens, the distally based results have the advantage of an undisputable relevance towards the scientific understanding of natural perception, while the value of results obtained with proximally generated displays becomes correspondingly marginal. Unfortunately, it does not help matters to dedicate proximal results to a process-modeling context since the uncertainty of their relevance will then only be extended to the modeling enterprise as well.

Moreover, the fact that proximal results have been proven wrong or irrelevant by a subsequent distal study–and that there is a theoretical backing, the KSD-principle, that helps explain the discrepancy–puts the searchlight on other proximal studies as well, even though there may not be any corresponding distal results to compare them with as yet. Clearly, the general lack of evidence for validity that pertains to animation studies is not just an in-principle difficulty that could be taken lightly in practice.

The two approaches may be further apart from each other in biological motion than in other areas of perception research. Valuable results have no doubt been obtained through proximally oriented experiments in research on the perception of three-dimensional structure, with Johansson's (1964) work on motion in depth as a good example. This may have been possible because some informative distal-to-proximal relations in this area are quite accessible and not so difficult to analyze. Hence, through several rounds of research, intuitions and relatively simple projection-geometric analyses may have been sufficient to funnel proximal experimentation in the direction of displays that incarnate relevant information.

Basically, visual perception of static or changing spatial layout is a matter of geometry, kinematics, and projective relations (not completely though; see Runeson, 1988). To the contrary, in the perception of events, as opposed to mere motion, dynamics comes to the fore (Runeson, 1977/1983). The proximal properties that specify dynamic distal properties are less amenable to common sense because the informative relations occur between properties that differ more deeply in the dimension-analytic sense. Spatial layout properties are kinematic (sometimes only geometric), which means they are composed of length and time dimensions, and the proximal optical properties that specify them are composed similarly. As we turn to dynamic events, the information remains kinematic whereas the dynamic properties specified include the dimension of mass (or force) as well. Thus the dimensional isomorphism that pertains to proximal-distal relations in spatial layout perception (except for the number of length dimensions) does not hold for perceptually salient aspects of biological events.

The intriguing question is, what is it about real biological motion that is so important perceptually and so often missing in the animations? While applying the KSD-principle we first compare, for example, a leg of a walking person and a geometrically similar free-swinging mechanical device. Kinematic differences that potentially specify the dynamical difference between them should be fairly easy to find. However, since the overall motions of both systems are relatively smooth and pendular, the kinematic difference could not be captured in terms of elemental motions such as sinusoidal versus linear (triangular-wave) motion. Thus, although the example is crude, we can say that the information must reside in the specifics of the motion functions of the parts of the system and the phase relations between them. For short we will refer to this as *kinematic details*.

We can assume that the more subtle the differences on the dynamic side, the smaller will be the kinematic details required to specify them. To gauge the relevant scale of these details we should note that perceptual ability goes far beyond mere distinguishing between animate and inanimate events. As reviewed above, perceivers are capable of many fine qualitative and quantitative discriminations within each category. It follows that *the scale of the perceptually efficient informative proximal properties that specify distal dynamic properties extends into very fine-grained kinematic details*. The details should be understood as relational properties of high analytic complexity and subtlety, usually defined over the whole pattern and over time.

As a consequence, whenever a recorded natural kinematic pattern is manipulated it is very likely that informative details get altered. If so, it will have noticeable effects on the perceived dynamic properties of the event. If large alterations are made, or the details altered are of crucial importance, the impression of animacy may be lost entirely.

Turning instead to proximal animation, the important restriction is that one has to work off from elemental, not natural, motions. This may give satisfactory results for portraying, say, simple pendulums or other oscillators because such systems are limiting cases in which elemental motion concepts fit the real dynamics quite well (directly or through simple equations). Unfortunately, this match breaks down as soon as the intended system gets more complex (e.g., a complex pendulum). The motions are then describable only through differential equations that usually do not have explicit solutions. For very complex events, animate ones in particular, even setting up the equations may be beyond reach.

Proximal animation thus necessarily starts out with a pattern that is far off the mark and is then subjected to piecemeal alterations aimed at approaching the natural. Given the special nature of the target patterns, and the tightness of the perceptually relevant tolerances, it is not realistic to expect that passable approximations can be achieved in this way. We can therefore conclude that, for purposes of perception and perception research, proximal animations do *not* specify the intended type of complex events, whether animate or inanimate, nor any other reasonably normal events either.

The lesson for proximal animation is that sinusoidal or other elemental motion does not provide the right kind of approximation to animate motion, as it may do for simple inanimate oscillation. Composing a walker figure from sinusoidal motion does not result in a default or generic walker which could then be given special character by various alterations to the basic sinusoidal pattern.

In principle, it could be the case that when no reasonable dynamics are specified the visual system abandoned its quest for KSD-type information and just registered the kinematic pattern—we'd only be seeing the motions as such. A more plausible possibility follows from Runeson's (1977/1983) suggestion that perception is *fundamentally* geared to underlying dynamic properties. Thus it can be expected to function the same way even when nothing reasonable is specified. In other words, the visual system proceeds as if distal dynamics could be meaningfully retrieved also from proximally created displays.

There is a kind of "unreasonable" dynamics that perception could fall back on in such cases. This would be systems in which all or several of its parts are being individually moved by invisible actuators through prescribed ("programmed") trajectories. The actuators would have to be anchored externally and strong enough to override all reactive forces that arise because of the masses and other dynamic aspects of the parts of the system. Such systems could be called *a*-dynamic or *pseudo*-dynamic. It follows that by being composed basically of sinusoidal motion functions, manipulated proximally, and presented to a perceptual system geared to KSD-type information, *proximal computer animations do in effect specify inanimate pseudodynamic devices* rather than humans in action.

Perceivers are obviously very sensitive to this distinction in the information provided. As Bruderlin and Calvert (1991) report, "figures often look as if they were pulled by strings" (p. 309), thus illustrating both the shortcomings of computer animation and the steadfast KSD-gearing of visual perception.[11] In fairness, therefore, the observers in the study by Proffitt et al. (1984) who did not report a walker were actually perceiving correctly. It should be noted though that, in a sense, even for these displays a walking person figures in the underlying causal structure. The difference from natural recordings is that the walker occurs at a far greater causal remove from the resulting kinematic pattern: as a mental notion, held by the programmer, which by way of his intuition constrains the composition of the proximal motions. Thus the observers who did report a walker may have been correct too–but only in the sense that they had managed to discern the programmer's *intention to depict* a walker.

Naturally, experiments with full-blown natural patch-light displays cannot provide all the evidence needed for a full understanding of the perception of biological motion. We need to find an adequate parsing of natural kinematic patterns into potentially efficient informative properties. Then we need to control and manipulate each of those properties experimentally in order to study how they get used by the visual system. Only when that becomes possible could the distinction between a distal and a proximal approach be said to vanish.

Given the advanced nature of the informative properties in animate kinematic patterns it is not likely that this goal can ever be reached from the proximal end. The more promising approach will be to continue from the distal end and go further along the subtractive line inaugurated by Johansson's point-light work. It appears that the procedure can be meaningfully subtractive in two ways. First, it can follow the lead of Pardo (1992), who subtracted and controlled a candidate informative property, occlusion, from the full patch-light pattern. With modern digitization technique the opportunities to pursue this line have improved considerably. Second, meaningful subtraction is possible concerning the complexity, that is, the number of degrees-of-freedom, of the distal event. Such a procedure was exemplified by Bingham's (1987) study of single-joint weight lifting. At this level, it should be possible to experimentally manipulate recorded kinematic patterns in interesting ways. Of course, the next step would have to be to add back degrees-of-freedom one by one by removing the various supports and restraints. However, it might also be possible to start with the full patch-light pattern and freeze out selected degrees-of-freedom. In the pursuit of such approaches there will be a need for criteria and methods for evaluating the absolute level of naturalness–methods that bypass the "under the circumstances" reference. Straight naturalness ratings will not do, as explained above, but alternatives are not easy to suggest. Possibly, observers could compare the naturalness of experimental displays with that of corresponding natural patch-light displays. However, there might be some advantages in doing such

---

[11] The cited phrase aptly describes the appearance of the Cutting (1978a) type of walker animations as well (personal observation of the Proffitt et al., 1984, displays).

comparisons indirectly by studying discrimination performance concerning some property of the observed event, such as the weight of a lifted object. A deterioration in performance for the manipulated displays would then indicate that the manipulation has hit upon and tampered with the efficient information for the target property.

The primary value of Gunnar Johansson's work on biological motion perception is that it has opened an area of research directed at a strong and important side of human perceptual functioning. More than that, however, it has implications at the metatheoretical and methodological levels that present tough challenges to perception research. The identification of relevant information has become a more acute issue, which in turn puts the researcher in great need for qualified knowledge about that which is perceived. In biological motion perception the distal object is animate action, the study of which is an active and demanding field of research itself. The consequences we must face are that the study of perception can no longer be conducted in the relative isolation from work in other branches of natural science that much of experimental psychology has enjoyed before.

References

Amemiya, T. (1981). Qualitative response models: A survey. *Journal of Economic Literature, 19*, 1483–1536.

Barwise, J., & Perry, J. (1983). *Situations and attitudes.* Cambridge, MA: MIT Press.

Bernstein, N. (1974). *The co-ordination and regulation of movements.* Oxford, England: Pergamon Press.

Berry, D. S. (1991). Child and adult sensitivity to gender information in patterns of facial motion. *Ecological Psychology, 3*, 349–366.

Bertenthal, B. I., Proffitt, D. R., & Cutting, J. E. (1984). Infant sensitivity to figural coherence in biomechanical motions. *Journal of Experimental Child Psychology, 37*, 213–230.

Bertenthal, B. I., Proffitt, D. R., & Kramer, S. J. (1987). Perception of biomechanical motions by infants: Implementation of various processing constraints. *Journal of Experimental Psychology: Human Perception and Performance, 13*, 577–585.

Bertenthal, B. I., Proffitt, D. R., Spetner, N. B., & Thomas, M. A. (1985). The development of infant sensitivity to biomechanical motions. *Child Development, 56*, 531–543.

Bingham, G. P. (1987). Kinematic form and scaling: Further investigations on the visual perception of lifted weight. *Journal of Experimental Psychology: Human Perception and Performance, 13*, 155–177.

Bingham, G. P. (1991). *The identification problem in visual event perception. Part I: Rate structures in optic flow and the degrees of freedom problem.* Indiana University Cognitive Science Research Report (Report No. 52).

Bingham, G. P. (1993). Scaling judgments of lifted weight: Lifter size and the role of the standard. *Ecological Psychology, 5,* 31–64.

Bruce, V., & Green, P. (1985). *Visual perception: Physiology, psychology and ecology.* Hillsdale, NJ: Erlbaum.

Bruderlin, A., & Calvert, T. W. (1991). Animation of human gait. In A. E. Patla (Ed.), *Adaptability of human gait* (pp. 305–330). Amsterdam, The Netherlands: North-Holland, Elsevier.

Cutting, J. E. (1978a). Generation of synthetic male and female walkers through manipulation of a biomechanical invariant. *Perception, 7,* 393–405.

Cutting, J. E. (1978b). A program to generate synthetic walkers as dynamic point-light displays. *Behavioral Research Methods and Instrumentation, 10,* 91–94.

Cutting, J. E. (1981). Coding theory adapted to gait perception. *Journal of Experimental Psychology: Human Perception and Performance, 7,* 71–87.

Cutting, J. E., & Kozlowski, L. T. (1977). Recognizing friends by their walk: Gait perception without familiarity cues. *Bulletin of the Psychonomic Society, 9,* 353–356.

Cutting, J. E., Proffitt, D. R., & Kozlowski, L. T. (1978). A biomechanical invariant for gait perception. *Journal of Experimental Psychology: Human Perception and Performance, 4,* 357–372.

Frykholm, G. (1983). Action, intention, gender, and identity, perceived from body movement. *Acta Universitatis Upsaliensis: Abstracts of Uppsala Dissertations from the Faculty of Social Sciences,* Serial No. 31.

Fowler, C. A., & Turvey, M. T. (1978). Skill acquisition: An event approach with special reference to searching for the optimum of a function of several variables. In G. Stelmach (Ed.), *Information processing in motor control and learning* (pp. 1–40). New York: Academic Press.

Gibson, J. J. (1979). *The ecological approach to visual perception.* Boston, MA: Houghton Mifflin.

Gilden, D. L. (1991). On the origin of dynamical awareness. *Psychological Review, 98,* 554–568.

Henderson, C. W., Bush, J., & Stoffregen, T. A. (1993). Visual perception of caught weight. In S. S. Valenti & J. B. Pittenger (Eds.), *Studies in perception and action II: Posters presented at the VIIth International Conference on Event Perception and Action* (pp. 40–43). Hillsdale, NJ: Erlbaum.

Johansson, G. (1950). *Configurations in event perception.* Uppsala: Almqvist & Wiksell. [Chapter 2, this volume.]

Johansson, G. (1964). Perception of motion and changing form. *Scandinavian Journal of Psychology, 5,* 181–208. [Chapter 4, this volume.]

Johansson, G. (1973). Visual perception of biological motion and a model for its analysis. *Perception and Psychophysics, 14,* 201–211. [Chapter 7, this volume.]

Johansson, G. (1975). Visual motion perception. *Scientific American, 232,* (6), 76–89.

Johansson, G. (1976). Spatio-temporal differentiation and integration in visual motion perception. *Psychological Research, 38,* 379–393. [Chapter 8, this volume.]

Kaiser, M. K., & Proffitt, D. R. (1984). The development of sensitivity to causally relevant dynamic information. *Child Development, 55*, 1614–1624.

Kozlowski, L. T., & Cutting, J. E. (1977). Recognizing the sex of a walker from a dynamic point-light display. *Perception and Psychophysics, 21*, 575–580.

Kozlowski, L. T., & Cutting, J. E. (1978). Recognizing the gender of walkers from point-lights mounted on ankles: Some second thoughts. *Perception and Psychophysics, 23*, 459.

Kruse, P., & Stadler, M. (1991). Kinematic cues in gait perception: Gender-specific movement gestalts. In P. J. Beek, R. J. Bootsma, & P. C. W. van Wieringen (Eds.), *Studies in perception and action: Posters presented at the VIth International Conference on Event Perception and Action* (pp. 154–160). Amsterdam, The Netherlands: Rodopi.

Kruse, P., Stadler, M., & Vogt, S. (1992). *Kinematic cues in gait perception: Improved recognition through reduced information.* Unpublished manuscript, University of Bremen, Department of Psychology.

Lee, D. N. (1977). The functions of vision. In H. L. Pick & E. Saltzman (Eds.), *Modes of perceiving and processing information* (pp. 159–170). Hillsdale, NJ: Erlbaum.

Maas, J. B., Johansson, G., Jansson, G., & Runeson, S. (1971a). *Motion perception I: 2-dimensional motion* (Film). Boston, MA: Houghton Mifflin.

Maas, J. B., Johansson, G., Jansson, G., & Runeson, S. (1971b). *Motion perception II: 3-dimensional motion* (Film). Boston, MA: Houghton Mifflin.

Pardo, J. (1992, January). *Perceptual sensitivity to information in complex motion.* Unpublished manuscript. New York, NY: Barnard College, Department of Psychology.

Proffitt, D. R., Bertenthal, B. I., & Roberts, R. J. (1984). The role of occlusion in reducing multistability in moving point-light displays. *Perception and Psychophysics, 36*, 315–323.

Proffitt, D. R., & Kaiser, M. K. (1986). The use of computer graphics animation in motion perception research. *Behavior Research Methods, Instruments, & Computers, 18*, 487–492.

Runeson, S. (1977). On the possibility of 'smart' perceptual mechanisms. *Scandinavian Journal of Psychology, 18*, 172–179.

Runeson, S. (1983). On visual perception of dynamic events. *Acta Universitatis Upsaliensis: Studia Psychologica Upsaliensia*, Ser. number 9. (Originally published, 1977)

Runeson, S. (1987, August). *Perception of human action: Comparing the merits of natural, acted and simulated kinematic displays in empirical studies.* Paper presented at the Fourth International Conference on Event Perception and Action, Trieste, Italy.

Runeson, S. (1988). The distorted room illusion, equivalent configurations, and the specificity of static optic arrays. *Journal of Experimental Psychology: Human Perception and Performance, 14*, 295–304.

Runeson, S. (1989). A note on the utility of ecologically incomplete invariants. *International Society for Ecological Psychology Newsletter, 4:1*, 6–9.

Runeson, S. (in press). Psychophysics: The failure of an elementaristic dream. *Behavioral and Brain Sciences.*

Runeson, S., & Frykholm, G. (1981). Visual perception of lifted weight. *Journal of Experimental Psychology: Human Perception and Performance, 7,* 733–740.

Runeson, S., & Frykholm, G. (1983). Kinematic specification of dynamics as an informational basis for person and action perception: Expectation, gender recognition, and deceptive intention. *Journal of Experimental Psychology: General, 112,* 585–615.

Runeson, S., & Vedeler, D. (1993). The indispensability of precollision kinematics in the visual perception of relative mass. *Perception and Psychophysics, 53,* 617–632.

Schwartz, S. P. (1979). Natural kind terms. *Cognition, 7,* 301–315.

Stoffregen, T. A., & Flynn, S. B. (1993). Identification versus discrimination in the perception of dynamics. In S. S. Valenti & J. B. Pittenger (Eds.), *Studies in perception and action II: Posters presented at the VIIth International Conference on Event Perception and Action* (pp. 36–39). Hillsdale, NJ: Erlbaum.

Sumi, S. (1993). Biological motion perception of the moving point-lights generated by human hand movements. In S. S. Valenti & J. B. Pittenger (Eds.), *Studies in perception and action II: Posters presented at the VIIth International Conference on Event Perception and Action* (pp. 52–56). Hillsdale, NJ: Erlbaum.

Todd, J. T. (1983). Perception of gait. *Journal of Experimental Psychology: Human Perception and Performance, 9,* 31–42.

Perceptual Processing

Perceived Bending Motion, the Principle of Minimum Object Change, and the Optic Sphere Theory

Gunnar Jansson

University of Uppsala

Abstract. This paper (1) presents some main points of certain investigations of perceived bending motions of quadrangular figures), (2) discusses a principle of minimum object change applied to these motions, and (3) looks at bending motions in the light of the optic sphere theory.

Application of the minimum principle to visual perception introduces complex and controversial issues (see, e.g., Hatfield & Epstein, 1985; Hochberg, chapter 21 in this volume). Gunnar Johansson has often deployed this concept. One of the contexts where he has done so is in studies of visual perception of bending motion. The aim of this paper is to present some studies on this kind of motion and relate them to a special version of the minimum principle, as well as to the optic sphere theory.

The Bending Motion Studies

Bending motion may be subsumed under the general rubric of non-rigid motion, that is motion of an object that does not have a constant form during its motion. Non-rigid motion may be divided into mechanical and biological motion, the former comprising motions of inanimate objects and the latter motions of living creatures. Bending motions appear in both contexts. The examples given here are mechanical variants, but the principles instantiated in these mechanical variants are applicable to biological motions as well. In the programmatically proximal approach chosen by Gunnar Johansson in several of his studies (see especially Johansson, 1964), the stimuli are, in many cases, strictly not possible as transformations of rigid objects in motion. (Cf. Note 1.)

The starting point for the investigations of bending motion to be discussed was a stimulus pattern used by Johansson (1964); see Fig. 1. In this stimulus pattern all the corners were moving towards the center of the figure, the perceptual result being a translatory motion in depth. The main "decoding principle"

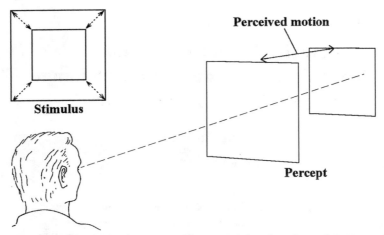

Perceived motion

Stimulus

Percept

Fig. 1. Proximal stimulus pattern of a square changing size and corresponding percept, originally studied in Johansson (1964). [From G. Johansson, Visual motion perception. Copyright © 1975 by Scientific American, Inc. All rights reserved.]

found for this stimulus and others in the same series was a principle of primary three-dimensionality, meaning that 2D proximal patterns of this kind strongly tended to give rise to a perceived motion in 3D space of an object as rigid as the proximal pattern allowed.

In order to test this principle, Gunnar Johansson tried to find proximal stimulus patterns falsifying it, that is finding stimuli with 2D motions that did not elicit percepts of events in 3D space. Examples of such stimuli are patterns with different amplitude and frequency in the horizontal and vertical changes, respectively, of a quadrangular figure. But these patterns also produced percepts of dominantly 3D motion (Johansson, 1964). Another case was a pattern consisting of two stimulus points moving in a rectangular path with 180° phase difference (Johansson, 1974). This 2D pattern continuously changed the distance between the proximal points, but, in spite of this, the percept was a 3D motion of a rigid (invisible) "rod" the two points forming its endpoints (Fig. 2). An amusing case, in the context of biological motion studies, was the introduction of an extra circular motion of the point light of the knee of a walking person where the knee was perceived to perform a strange back and forth movement in 3D space (Johansson, unpublished). Thus, in none of these cases the principle of primary three-dimensionality was falsified.

The bending motion studies were started in this context (Jansson & Johansson, 1973). What would be perceived if only one or two corners of an original square were moving? The perception of a rigid plane surface is geometrically impossible in several of these cases. Would 3D motion be perceived all the same or would the principle of primary three-dimensionality be falsified?

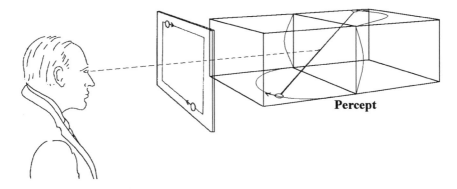

Fig. 2. Proximal stimulus with two points moving in a rectangular path with a 180° phase difference, as well as corresponding percept of a rigid (invisible) "rod" moving in 3D space. [From G. Johansson, Visual motion perception. Copyright © 1975 by Scientific American, Inc. All rights reserved.]

The most interesting cases were motions of two opposite corners or of only one corner (Fig. 3). The experiments demonstrated very clearly that these stimuli were perceived three-dimensionally in nearly all cases. Rotary motion was the dominating percept of the stimulus with two corners moving, and bending motion in the case with only one corner moving (Fig. 4).

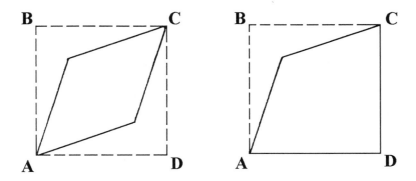

Fig. 3. The "turning forms" of two of the proximal stimuli in the bending motion experiments, the left one being perceived as 3D rotation of a flat object and the right one as 3D bending. [From Jansson & Johansson, (1973), *Perception, 2,* 321–326, Fig. 1. Reprinted with permission from Pion Limited, London.]

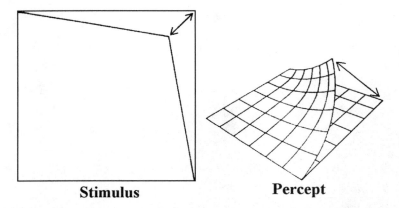

Stimulus   **Percept**

Fig. 4. Proximal stimulus for bending and corresponding percept as studied by Jansson & Johansson (1973). [From G. Johansson, Visual motion perception. Copyright © 1975 by Scientific American, Inc. All rights reserved.]

The Principle of Minimum Object Change

In explaining the results, Jansson and Johansson (1973) offered a principle of minimum object change. This principle is related to the minimum principle in the Gestalt tradition (cf. Hochberg, 1957), but also to the principle of primary three-dimensionality mentioned above. It means that motion in 3D space of an object of constant form is perceptually preferred in comparison with a 2D form change. It should be emphasized that both 3D motion and constancy of the object are stressed, not only the rigidity of the moving object. When Johansson (1964) summarized the results of the experiments reported in this paper, he even rejected a rigidity principle and suggested instead the principle of primary perceptual three-dimensionality (p. 207; p. 167 in this volume).

The following main aspects of the principle of minimum object change are especially relevant in the context of bending motion.

(1) The world contains many non-rigid motions.

The fact that non-rigid motions are abundantly occurring in natural environments means that we can expect that animals have adequate perceptual mechanisms to perceive these variations. Gunnar Johansson has several times alluded to the existence of non-rigid motions. Already in his first main work, on the first page of the first chapter (Johansson, 1950), he chose as an example of an object changing its form: a tree, with its leaves and branches, moving in the wind. In his paper on the perception of motion and changing form (Johansson, 1964) he never avoided stimuli where the object was involved in form changes. Rather form change is an often-appearing aspect of the percept of the experimental stimuli. In one of his most recent reports (Johansson, Börjesson, & Vedeler, 1993) the topic is the perceived surface of the most important liquid, water waves. Thus, non-rigid motions are common in the natural environment and experimental simulations have shown that observers are sensitive to them. In fact, non-rigid motions are so common that it is reasonable to consider them as the general case, rigid motion being a special case when there is no form change.

(2) Universal application of the principle is not expected.

The principle states that predictions, with a very high probability of being verified, can be made that if a proximal pattern contains a geometrically possible alternative in reverse projection of a rigid object moving in 3D space, this event is perceived. However, even if the principle of minimum object change is a forceful principle with a wide application, it can be overridden by other principles, for instance concerning projective information as in the Ames window case. This seems to be in agreement with a "soft" interpretation of the rigidity principle suggested by Braunstein and Anderson (1986). This kind of interpretation is gradually gaining adherents; even Ullman (1986) has turned away from a "strong" version of the rigidity principle.

It may also be noted that perceived constant distances between points are not a necessary condition for adequate slant judgments. When comparing the perceived slants of bending and stretching lines, Jansson (1977) found the two kinds of motion equally adequate. Perceived distances between the points *changing over time but internally equal* seemed to function as well as distances *constant over time.* There seems to be a hierarchy of perceptual preferences, constant distances over time being a first alternative, and distances internally equal but with the common length changing over time being a second option.

A related result was obtained by Todd (1984) when he found that accurate structure may very well be obtained in the case of non-rigid motion.

(3) The principle suggests a hierarchy of perceptual preferences.

A special feature of this version of the minimum principle is that it states a hierarchy of preferences. The interest in many contexts has been focused on only the distinction between rigid and non-rigid motion (e.g., von Fieandt & Gibson, 1959; Todd, 1982). However, there are many different kinds of non-rigid motions, and it would be useful to be more specific.

In the bending case there is a hierarchy of perceptual preferences: (1) *Rotation* of a flat object (complete rigidity); (2) *Bending* of an object where the intrinsic surface properties, such as contour and angles, are constant but the way the surface is embedded in space is changed (partial rigidity; for a mathematical definition of bending, see Hilbert & Cohn-Vossen, 1952; cf. also Note 2); (3) *Stretching*, that is 2D form change (non-rigidity, but with retention of the flat form). In (1) and (2) a prerequisite is that the options given are geometrically possible. (For other perceptual categories, see Note 3.)

Bending Motion and The Optic Sphere Theory

In their first paper on the optic sphere theory, Johansson and Börjesson (1989) announced that new assumptions of the processor part of the model are needed when aspects of space perception such as shape are studied (p. 306; p. 244 in this volume). When the model is applied to the perception of waves, Johansson, Börjesson, and Vedeler (1993) started with "the experimentally well-documented fact that two distal spots moving in space as if rigidly connected will be perceived as end points of a recorded but invisible line segment." This seems to be an application of the principle of minimum object change, but on a more local level. The recording of corresponding geometrical entities "is presupposed to occur automatically in the sensory analogue in the spherical coordinate system." (Cf. Note 4.)

The principle of minimum object change seems to survive in the optic sphere theory but as a theory for local analysis. As stated so far, it has the character of a universal rule built into the sensory system.

Notes

[1]   There are also efforts of studying proximal stimuli of mechanical non-rigid events produced with distal stimuli in mind. von Fieandt and Gibson's (1959) investigation was clearly of this kind, and the introduction of changing texture gradients in stimuli for bending motions (Jansson, 1977) was a move in the same direction, as was Johansson's (unpublished) study of a line of (quite few) points performing bending and folding motions in 3D space. In the biological motion studies (Johansson, 1973) the stimuli were strictly constructed as proximal transformations of distal events (cf. Runeson, chapter 19, this volume).

[2]   Partial rigidity may mean several things. It means here that some (global) aspect(s) of the object is/are constant, while others are not. It may also mean that the total pattern is divided into several different but internally rigid parts (Ullman, 1986).

[3]   Another example of further specification of non-rigid motion is the difference between bending proper and folding, that is flexion of the whole surface versus folding of two plane triangular surfaces connected via a hinge (see Fig. 5; Jansson & Runeson, 1977). In this study, where phase differences between the motions of two opposite corners were introduced, a clear tendency to perceive bending proper best at small phase differences was found, but with decreasing frequency when the phase difference increased. Instead, the frequency of folding increased with difference in phase.

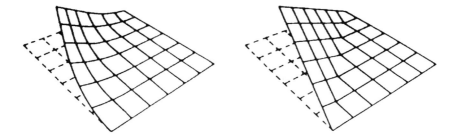

Fig. 5. The meaning of bending proper (left) and folding (right). [From Jansson & Runeson (1977), *Perception, 6*, 595–600, Fig. 3. Reprinted with permission from Pion Limited, London.]

The ambiguity in this case is probably related to the lack of surface information in the original bending motion patterns which consisted of either homogenous surfaces or outline figures. It disappeared when texture gradients, corresponding to bending proper, were introduced (Jansson, 1977). These stimuli were never perceived to fold.

[4] It may be noted that Ullman (1986, p. 646) suggested that two points in motion are not sufficient for the rigidity to be applied while this number is the basis for Johansson's theory. Ullman's result may be related to the condition that Ullman's theory dealt with successive images; Johansson analyzed continuous motions.

References

Braunstein, M. L., & Andersen, G. J. (1986). Testing the rigidity assumption: A reply to Ullman. *Perception, 15*, 641–646.

Fieandt, K. von, & Gibson, J. J. (1959). The sensitivity of the eye to two kinds of continuous transformation of a shadow pattern. *Journal of Experimental Psychology, 57*, 344–347.

Hatfield, G., & Epstein, W. (1985). The status of the minimum principle in the theoretical analysis of visual perception. *Psychological Bulletin, 97*, 155–186.

Hilbert, D., & Cohn-Vossen, S. (1952). *Geometry and the imagination*. New York: Chelsea.

Hochberg, J. E. (1957). Effects of the Gestalt revolution: the Cornell symposium on perception. *Psychological Review, 64*, 73-84.

Jansson, G. (1977). Perceived bending and stretching motions from a line of points. *Scandinavian Journal of Psychology, 18*, 209–215.

Jansson, G., & Johansson, G. (1973). Visual perception of bending motion. *Perception, 2*, 321–326.

Jansson, G., & Runeson, S. (1977). Perceived bending motions from a quadrangle changing form. *Perception, 6*, 595–600.

Johansson, G. (1950). *Configurations in event perception.* Uppsala: Almqvist & Wiksell. [Chapter 2, this volume.]

Johansson, G. (1964). Perception of motion and changing form. *Scandinavian Journal of Psychology, 5,* 181–208. [Chapter 4, this volume.]

Johansson, G. (1973). Visual perception of biological motion and a model for its analysis. *Perception & Psychophysics, 14,* 201–211. [Chapter 7, this volume.]

Johansson, G (1974). Visual perception of rotary motion as transformations of conic sections—A contribution to the theory of visual space perception. *Psychologia - An International Journal of Psychology in the Orient, 17,* 226–237.

Johansson, G. (1975). Visual motion perception. *Scientific American, 232* (6), 76–88.

Johansson, G., & Börjesson, E. (1989). Toward a new theory of vision. Studies in wide angle perception. *Ecological Psychology, 1,* 301–331. [Chapter 10, this volume.]

Johansson, G., Börjesson, E., & Vedeler, D. (1993). *On perception of waves. A study of monocular wide angle space perception.* Manuscript. Uppsala University, Department of Psychology.

Todd, J. T. (1982). Visual information about rigid and nonrigid motion: A geometrical analysis. *Journal of Experimental Psychology: Human Perception and Performance, 8,* 238–252.

Todd, J. T. (1984). The perception of three-dimensional structure from rigid and nonrigid motion. *Perception & Psychophysics, 36,* 97–103.

Ullman, S. (1986). Competence, performance, and the rigidity assumption. *Perception, 15,* 644–646.

Vector Analysis, Perceptual Intention, and the Hidden Rules of Visual Perception (or Mental Structure)

Julian Hochberg

Columbia University

Abstract: Close examination of three among the many surprising and theoretically important phenomena discovered by Johansson and his colleagues suggests that those phenomena reveal (and open for study) major hidden rules of cognitive processing (mental structure), and are not merely due to reverse projection constrained by a rigidity or minimum principle.

In his work *Configurations in Event Perception*, Gunnar Johansson (1950) described a class of phenomena that he had discovered, often called perceptual vector analysis, which offers an immediately meaningful starting point for the study of event perception (and demonstrates that our perceptions are not transparent to the motion detectors studied in early vision). The new optic sphere model (Johansson, 1993; Johansson & Börjesson, 1989, 1990) offers an immediately meaningful, distortion-free way to deal with wide-angle slant perception (and also seems able to predict the traditional vector-analysis phenomena as well as any approach can now do). Both the phenomena and the theories seem challenging and exciting. But I have serious questions about the larger theoretical context in which the facts and theory must be set.

Most broadly, I don't believe that such robust phenomena and generalizations as Johansson has repeatedly given can be explained "directly" by the stimulation in the optic array. Instead, they reflect hidden rules of mental processing and therefore will help to discover what those hidden rules really are.

My specific argument addresses three of the topics with which the 1991 Uppsala conference dealt, the first of which is whether with only geometrical constraints on reverse projection (see Johansson, 1964) or on organization, we can predict the events and objects that are perceived.

(1) Against the Rigidity Constraint (and the Minimum Principle, as Well)

The rigidity (or invariance) constraint simply cannot serve as a strong principle which supersedes the traditional depth cues, which is what Gunnar Johansson (e.g., 1982) and Gunnar Jansson (e.g., 1977), along with Jimmy Gibson, have on occasion argued, and that Gunnar Jansson (Chapter 20, this volume) has talked about during this conference. Admittedly, with relative motion between viewer and a rigid 3D layout, a rigidity constraint is *sufficient* to specify the 3D *stimulus* structure, without recourse to depth cues, inference, organizing principles, etc., which is why it keeps being assumed. But because the rigidity constraint is not logically *necessary* to the recovery of 3D structure, however, *the occurrence of such perceptions can in no way prove that the rigidity constraint is operating.* Indeed, we have known for about 70 years that simple, rigid 3D objects can appear in reverse perspective even when they (or the viewer) are moving, though they then appear to be rubbery and grossly nonrigid. We are still trying to pinpoint why this occurs in the most familiar case, a rotating wire cube (Fig. 1A; Note la), but in many other cases the static depth cues of the situation *seem* to offer a sufficient account (e.g., that we construe the thicker wires in Fig. 1B as nearer even when they are further).

That is, it does not seem true that the static depth cues—at least those of relative size (or perspective convergence), and of interposition—work only in impoverished vision or are powerless in the face of relative motion (I describe viewer-produced motion specifically because that is often apparently believed to possess magical properties): In Fig. 3C, a static Ames window, with the large end further from the viewer, appears to counter-rotate in illusory concomitant motion (Gogel & Tietz, 1992; Hochberg & Beer, 1991). Note that this is *against* a rigidity constraint: Remember, the veridical static trapezoid is the *only* rigid solution to the transforming optic array received by the self-moving viewer.

It is important that in all cases referred to by Figs. 1–3 in this paper (including replications of the experiments of Figs. 1A, 1B), displays are viewed under at least two different conditions of instruction, using the *opposed set* procedure (Hochberg & Peterson, 1987; Peterson & Hochberg, 1983). In this, two or more possible construals are described, and subjects are asked to try to see one of them for as long as possible. (Given that we know that attention seriously affects the processing of size-at-a-distance and of shape-at-a-slant (Epstein & Broota, 1986; Epstein & Lovitts, 1985; Rock & Nijhawan, 1989), something like the opposed-set procedure seems essential.) Spontaneous alternations occur; we take the relative durations as a quantitative measure of each alternative's strength. Note also that in order to avoid having subjects merely saying they see whatever they have been asked to see, we do *not* in most cases ask them to report on that *instructed* or *intended attribute*. Instead, they are to report some perceptually coupled concomitant (Note 1b). Thus, in Fig. 3C, if instructed to

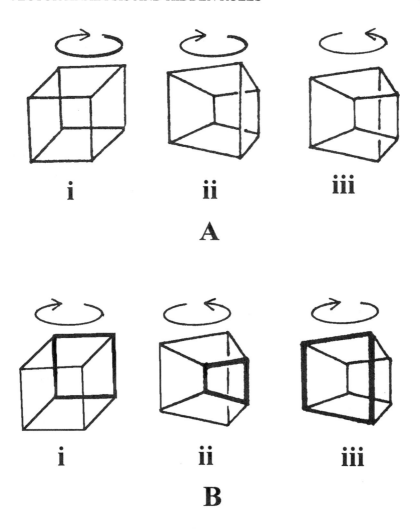

Fig. 1. (A) Rotating wire cube: (i) True rotation direction; (ii, iii) Alternating perspectives and their apparent rotation directions (von Hornbostel, 1922).

(B) Rotating wire cube with four thicker wires: (i) True rotation direction; (ii) Apparent rotation direction when thick wires are to rear (as they are in (i)); (iii) Apparent rotation when thick wires are in front (from Schwartz & Sperling, 1983).

see the left side nearer and to report perceived motion, subjects predominantly see motion m' far more than they do when they are asked to try to see it further (as it really is: Hochberg & Beer, 1991; Note 1c).

This cannot show that there is absolutely no perceptual preference for rigidity: A local rigidity constraint (more properly, a continuity constraint, or a coherency preference) might work in tandem with other cues (see Note 1d), but in any case, as Braunstein and Anderson (1984, 1986) and I (Hochberg 1984, 1987) have repeatedly pointed out, we cannot now put any substantial theoretical burden on a rigidity constraint without a lot of reservations. And that in turn means that we cannot simply discard "cues" when we introduce "invariants."

Johansson (1964) and Jansson (1977, 1993) have already shown us objects that, while moving in depth, change forms non-rigidly, but these could not satisfy a rigidity constraint in any case. The point that I want to stress is that objects which are in fact rigid can, quite robustly, be perceived as non-rigid. To the extent that a rigidity or constant-shape constraint (e.g., see Johansson, chapter 11, this volume) is actually needed in the optic sphere model (and in the biological motion formulations), therefore, it cannot be merely as the working of some general principle. Indeed, it must come with limits—some rules for when it will and will not apply.

When dealing with the striking ways in which moving dots and lines are perceptually transformed into quite different and simpler organizations, it is very tempting to invoke some "simplicity principle," as Gunnar Jansson has done at this meeting and in the past (Jansson, 1977; Jansson & Johansson, 1973). I, myself (Hochberg & MacAlister, 1953; see Hochberg, 1988), and many since, have tried to so phrase this intuition as to allow quantitative analysis and comparison of the alternative construals. No one has yet succeeded, because it is easy to generate exceptions by pitting local features that act as depth cues (which are hard to phrase in simplicity terms, and hard to bound spatially) against overall object-wide simplicity (which can readily be assessed and bounded). In its static form (Fig. 3B), the partially covered wire cube is strongly fixed in its apparent orientation and form when fixated (or attended?) at point (1), whereas it alternates freely (perhaps only locally, but that is hard to tell) at point (2) (Hochberg, 1982). In its dynamic form, relative motion (including viewer motion) and the opposed-set procedure (described above, p. 418) provide much more periodic illusory concomitant motion when attended at point (2) than at point (1) (Note 1e; Hochberg & Peterson, 1987; Peterson & Hochberg, 1983). Although some are unconvinced by this point (cf. Hatfield & Epstein, 1985; Boselie & Leeuwenberg, 1986), I do not believe that a minimum principle can be taken seriously unless this class of local-vs.-global problem is confronted and solved. A similar problem arises, as next we see, in connection with the Johansson event-configuration phenomenon.

(2) Unexpected Robustness and Unexpectedly Contingent Nature of the Johansson Effect

First, the *Johansson effect* (I use this term in place of "vector analysis," for reasons I soon describe) is far more robust than it should be, according to existing explanations: It occurs in the presence of stationary surrounds and fixation points, giving it an even greater theoretical and practical importance.

In an example of one of Johansson's most powerful discoveries the distal and retinal displacements in Fig. 2A are seen instead as in Fig. 2B. No input from any hypothetical early motion detector sensitive to the diagonal in 2A is discernible in 2B. According to any strict reading of Johansson's original interpretation of his discovery, a stationary framework of any kind should destroy the phenomenon in Fig. 2A & 2B (although the literature has recently seen some confusion about this point: See Note 2a). In fact, however, as we have known since 1976, the introduction of additional stationary dots, indicated by the crossed dots in Figs. 2C–F, does not necessarily destroy the effect (Note 2b). Indeed, Fig. 2B is what everyone perceives most of the time, and some viewers perceive all of the time, *even on a television screen in a normally lighted room*. As some of you saw at the New Orleans Psychonomics meeting recently, the stationary framework provided by room, TV screen, etc., are not enough to ensure that everyone sees the diagonal motion at all. This fact argues that we need some say to parse the optic array as to what will and will not be included in our motion analysis. Using the opposed set procedure (described above, p. 418) we can now say that such viewing conditions (as compared to total darkness and no framework at all) only decreases somewhat the relative duration with which the Johansson effect is reported. (The new effects sketched in Fig. 2 are from Hochberg & Beer, 1990.)

Second, the Johansson effect is more contingent than it should be (as Johansson has himself noted at several points): It can be shown to depend on the configuration of moving (and stationary) elements, not only on their vectors; it depends on where one looks (or attends); and—most suggestive of all—when these events are viewed in a framework or lighted surround, spontaneous alternations or reconstruals occur between different perceived motion organizations. Moreover, the relative durations of these competitive reconstruals are in part a function of what the viewer has been asked to try to see and of where the viewer has been asked to fixate.

Thus, the event in Fig. 2C looks essentially like Fig. 2B, even when fixation is held on the stationary point. (This, incidentally, rules out uncompensated pursuit eye movements as an explanation for the Johansson phenomenon, which Stoper (1973) proposed; see Note 2b). It is not that we somehow simply ignore stationary elements: In Fig. 2D, in which the stationary element is in line with the diagonal (*and the rate of change in separation along that line which joins the middle and stationary points is proportionally greatest*) subjects perceive the

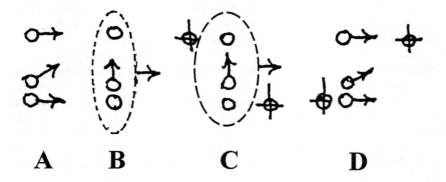

⊕ **same as other dots,
but stationary**

Fig. 2. (A) Three dots moving on a video screen. Arrows show objective velocity vectors (linear, nonsinusoidal) for 1/2 cycle.

(B) The Johansson effect: How the 3 dots at A are perceived.

(C, D) With the two stationary dots as at C, D, respectively, and the objective motion of A, the appearances indicated by the vectors predomiate.

(E, F) With the objective pattern of movement as at E, and with fixation on the right stationary dot, the appearance indicated at F predominates. With the same movement pattern and with fixation on the leftmost stationary dot, with prior instruction in what the actual movements are, and with effort to see that arrangement, the pattern of E predominates (Hochberg & Beer, 1990).

diagonal motion much of the time even when they are trying to see the vertical, and see the diagonal motion virtually all of the time on trials when they try to do so (Hochberg & Beer, 1990).

We have considered various reformulations phrased in terms of stimulus properties. Here is a case that ruled out several of them: In Fig. 2E, viewers mostly perceive the diagonal motions *only* when they fixate the *left* stationary dot, *although even then those diagonals may first have to be described and pointed out to them,* whereas they see the cruciform motion (sketched in Fig. 2F) almost exclusively when fixating the right stationary dot in the identical stimulus pattern. As with "impossible" figures (including the one that the perfectly consistent cube of Fig. 3B turns into when it reverses), and of complex patterns in general, I am not sure that I can attend all of the individual component motions simultaneously. There seem to be explicit detailed motions embedded in some global generally consistent motion flows. Having some specific motion-schemes to test also seems to make a difference. (And this is why I would like to know about the reconstruabilities of coherence (Note 1d) and whether biological motions can be reconstrued when the viewer is made familiar with one of the nonveridical alternatives.)

Where one fixates affects which alternative one sees, as Gunnar Johansson himself noted (1979, p. 390), but we see in these examples that even though a stationary point is fixated in all cases, the effect depends on the configuration—perhaps, on what lines of motion have been made most salient. Moreover, even with fixation constant, there are attentional effects that should surely affect our understanding of what is going on.

Different, alternative motion organizations are perceived in response to a single stimulus pattern. As in static patterns that are relatively easy to reconstrue (see Note 2c), the perceived motions alternate spontaneously during a single viewing session when the viewer knows what to look for and when some stationary reference is present, and then only one alternative is perceived at a time (or so it seems). I add to this that the viewer's knowledge of what can be perceived, and the opposed-set instructions of what he or she should try to perceive, had clear effects on relative report durations. Because we did not use a concomitant response as our measure here (we have not yet figured out how to do so in the Johansson effect) viewers *might* have been merely reporting whatever they were asked to perceive, without actually perceiving it. But I don't think so, partly because the behaviors are so similar to cases in which concomitant coupled responses are in fact used (see above), and also because the stimulus manipulations had strong and significant effects: For example, there were very few responses of the diagonal, even when asked to see it, in Fig. 2A, 2C, and in 2E with the right-hand fixation and many fewer cases of the vertical in Fig. 2D, even when asked to see that.

These facts may yet place all of these phenomena at a higher processing level—one that involves what I think should be called "perceptual intentions" and "mental representations," as these terms are used (without any necessarily introspective connotations) throughout contemporary cognitive psychology.

(3) On Daring to Say "Mental Structure" in Uppsala

I raise this issue most specifically in reference to Bergström (1982; chapter 17, this volume), but I think it applies as well to the intimations of "directness" that hovered at the edges of the conference discussions.

It would be unparsimonious to invent the notion of mental structures merely to explain some otherwise-unexplained aspects of the Johansson effect, considered by itself, but the issue is a quite general one in the study of visual cognition, arising in the difference between proximal and distal properties. The distal properties of objects in our surroundings can be viewed as coupled pairs (and higher conjunctions), each with an environmental member and an object-property, in which the proximal stimulus provided by the object varies lawfully with the conditions of seeing as determined by the environmental member. Thus, an object's reflectance is specified by its luminance in conjunction with illumination it receives; for a given projection, an object's shape varies with the object's slant to the line of sight; the object-motion is specified by a displacement in the field of view only when any change in viewpoint (eye or head movement) is taken into account, etc. We can identify *perceptual couplings*, or percept-percept couplings corresponding to these physical couplings: Whenever changes are induced in the environmental member of a perceptually-coupled pair of attributes, the other attribute appears to change appropriately, more or less in accord with the coupling.

This is, of course, the paradigm for which "unconscious inference" offered a general principle, providing a first pass at an explanation for all perceptual couplings (and for much more besides). Most of the more specific attempts to develop this too general principle have been pursued in connection with some version of what came to be called the size-distance invariance hypothesis (see Epstein, 1961b; Epstein, Park, & Casey, 1961): that with a given image size or visual angle, perceived distance varies with perceived size, and vice versa. Note that such explanations grant causal status to a perceptual variable which, by its nature, cannot be publicly observed or directly measured. We would now call that variable a *mental representation*. And the causal relationship between the two mental representations (e.g., that perceived size is proportional to perceived distance) would itself be publicly unobservable, i.e., a *mental structure*. (Presumably, such mentalism must last only until we know enough about the underlying neurophysiology.)

But such mentalistic explanation at first seems unnecessary: There are aspects of the proximal stimulus pattern other than retinal extent that will normally vary with both the object's size and distance, so that we are perfectly free to assert that an object's perceived size and perceived distance covary only because of the covariation in the higher order dimensions of stimulation by which these perceptions are each directly specified, and to which they are each direct responses (Gibson, 1950). This answer replaces the messy problem of trying to be more specific about how one mental state (perceived distance) might "cause" another (perceived size), with the clean and mathematically inviting task of describing the stimulus information in ways that correspond to distal attributes and to the discriminations and judgments that visually guided organisms seem able to make. (This was the agenda that Gibson first laid out, one to which many at this conference have made admirable contributions. But not, I think, the line pursued at Uppsala: Each of the major discoveries that has come from the latter was found through the use of what Gibson should have dismissed as highly impoverished stimulation; most have been strong illusions. Johansson writes of encoding, of memory, of the effects of gaze-direction, which simply do not exist in the Gibsonian optic array.)

Although the direct approach is clearly the simpler, that advantage shrinks rapidly when we add alternative channels of depth information. For example three quite different such channels, or depth cues (e.g., binocularity, perspective, and motion parallax) can all feed interchangeably into the same mental representation of depth, D', and equivalently affect apparent size, or anything else that makes use of D'. In direct terms on the other hand, each channel that specifies depth information (DI_{1-3}) specifies a size, as well, *but in what sense (other than distal measure) are those perceived sizes equal or equivalent?* An answer might be devised (e.g., in terms of new convergent potential affordances), but the apparent parsimony vanishes.

As to evidence: Whereas I can think of no evidence that *any* perceptual coupling comprises responses that are "direct" in any well-defined sense of that word, I know of many cases in which they *cannot* be: Cases in which there is no stimulus information present that will, without attributing causal status to mental structure, account for the dependent response. The different relative sizes in the optic array that are projected by two objects of the same distal size offer specifiable distance information, but a retinal image of the same size would offer different information to viewers who are and who are not familiar with the distal size of the object. Such assumed or *familiar size* does indeed affect distance judgments (Epstein, 1963, 1965; Eriksson & Zetterberg, 1975; Ittelson, 1951; Ono, 1969) and reaching behavior in babies aged 7 (but not 5) months (Granrud, Hake, & Yonas, 1985; Yonas et al., 1982). Such findings seem to move perceived depth to a later stage. I originally argued that familiar size works at a later stage than relative size, and is therefore not "truly perceptual" (Hochberg & Hochberg, 1952), a view shared by Gogel (1969, 1981; Gogel, Hartman, & Harker, 1957) and by Predebon (1992), but in any case the work with infants, and the present absence of clear criteria for what is truly perceptual, makes this question moot for now.

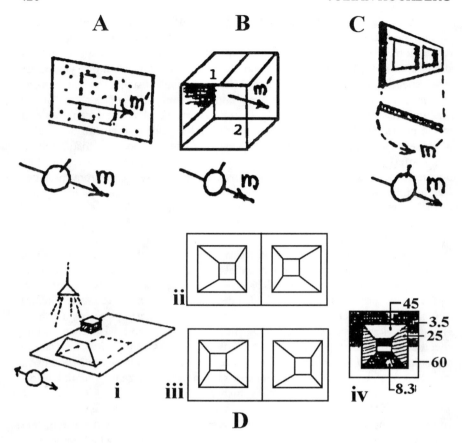

Fig. 3. (A) With a viewer moving laterally (m) before an ambiguous stereogram, the direction of concomitent motion m' depends on which depth organization the viewer is instructed to try to see (Peterson, 1986).

(B) With a partly covered cube, fixed by interposition at junction (1), reversals of orientation are perceived at junction (2) and illusory concomitant motion m' then accompanies lateral viewer motion, m (Hochberg & Peterson, 1987).

(C) Illusory concomitant motion in the stationary Ames window: See text.

(D) (i) Effect of changes in apparent spatial arrangement to illumination: real layout (see text; Hochberg & Beck, 1954).

(ii, iii) Effect of changes in apparent spatial arrangement to illumination: Computer-presented stereogram and its reverse (see text).

(iv) Luminances for 3D (ii, iii) in foot-Lamberts (Hochberg & Beer, in preparation).

Among other examples, the illusory concomitant motion that Gogel and Tietz (1974) have demonstrated with misperceived stereoscopic distance can be demonstrated using the opposed-set procedure and no change at all in the stimulus display: When a viewer moves laterally (m) while viewing an ambiguous stereogram, the central region moves in an illusory concomitant motion (m'), as In Fig. 3A, with a direction that (although reversals occur) largely depends on whether the viewer is instructed to hold the central region of dots as nearer or as further than the surround (Peterson, 1986).

Or, closer to the original Helmholtzian example and to the issue that Bergström has raised in print (1982) and at this symposium (chapter 17, this volume): Layouts of surfaces that differ from each other in their luminances (within a normal range of variation, i.e., less than 30:1), but whose luminances remain fixed, nevertheless change in their apparent relative reflectance or surface color when their apparent orientation to the source of illumination is changed. For instance, the trapezoid in Fig. 3Di, cut and viewed so that it appeared (monocularly) to be a square lying flat on a table, was made by four different means (binocular viewing, lateral viewer motion, waving a black stick behind it and waving a white stick behind it) to change from that perceived orientation and to appear closer to its true upright position. When illumination clearly came from above the layout, the target was judged to be lighter whenever any of those very different but spatially equivalent stimulus manipulations (i.e., depth cues) were provided; with illumination from in front, it appeared darker with depth cues present; and with illumination from the side, it appeared unchanged (Hochberg & Beck, 1954). The original experiment has been repeated several times, with only binocularity as a depth cue, sometimes replicating and sometimes failing to do so (Note 3a).

Because real objects may provide microhighlights that offer different criteria for lightness depending on how depth is construed, and because the replications used only one cue, binocularity (which could conceivably be directly linked to lightness in some way; Note 3b), we have currently revised the procedure substantially (Hochberg & Beer, in preparation).

First: displays are in VGA monochrome (640x350), either moving or static, viewed normally or stereoscopically (with crossed or uncrossed disparity), eliminating any possible microtextural bases for reflectance judgments. (With real objects, the latter could be differently used with different apparent illumination angles; Note 3c.)

Second: To sidestep the lightness/brightness thicket, viewers are not asked to report target lightness. Instead, we explained and illustrated surface color (reflectance) and took discrete or categorical ratings by several methods, mostly using keypresses for alternative responses. (Troost & deWeert, 1991, have used an even better procedure, naming object hues, which we want to try next.) This let us use the opposed-set procedure (see p. 418), viewers being asked to try to perceive one of two possible 3D layouts while reporting (by keypresses) which reflectance difference they are perceiving at any time.

For example, when shown versions of Fig. 3Dii and 3Diii, viewed with no disparity, with normal disparity (Fig. 3Dii), and with crossed disparity (Fig. 3Diii), and either asked to try to see a truncated pyramid or a hollow square tunnel, viewers' reports of high-reflectance differences predominate in Fig. 3Diii, and low difference predominates with Fig. 3Dii. Moreover, confirming the seminal observation made by Mach about a century ago (Mach, 1895/1959) in the no-disparity conditions, the low reflectance difference predominates when subjects are asked to perceive the truncated pyramid, and the high difference predominates when they are asked to perceive the square tunnel—*even though the stimulus array remains unchanged between the two conditions*. Reflectance and 3D structure-under-illumination are clearly a perceptual coupling. What does it mean?

This does *not* prove that *perceived depth* "causes" *perceived illumination* (or reflectance): I have suggested (Hochberg, 1974) that there are alternatives to unconscious inference-like processes which would generate the same outcome. That is why I have used the more neutral term *percept-percept coupling*, rather than unconscious inference (see also Epstein, 1982). Here is one such alternative (Hochberg, 1974): Perhaps a stimulus pattern—say, an object at some specific distance and visual angle—mobilizes a set of alternative coupled perceptual responses, or construals, each already structured so that, say, size and distance differ but their product is constant. This requires nothing like a reasoning process, but does imply a mental representation which is constrained by an internal structure (what Gogel, 1990, has aptly called a *phenomenal geometry*).

During this meeting, the issue of perceptual couplings is raised most explicitly by Sten Sture Bergström in his discussion of the reflectance/illumination relationship and of "the assumption that the analysis of the proximal stimulus is a vector analysis." Such a vector analysis would represent the kind of hidden rules that I think we must seek, but only if we recognize that it does not rest only on the information in stimulation.

More generally, I am suggesting that the formulae that Johansson and his colleagues use to explain and explore the robust and surprising perceptual phenomena that they have given to psychology are not concerned with the information about the distal stimulus that is to be found in the optic array, but rather to describe in each case an operation performed, at some hidden level, upon the proximal stimulus pattern. These offer immediately applicable distortion-free ways of summarizing or accounting for the specific class of phenomena being introduced. Thus, the optic sphere theory is not merely an alternative to the Gibsonian flow patterns, as some at the symposium seemed to assume. Of course, the information in the one must necessarily also be found in the other but, as Johansson said during the discussion, "enough pictures." I take this to mean that if we start with the optic flow, the information in the array, like that in a display of pictorial depth cues, must be transformed, extracted, operated upon, in order to get to the attributes of the perceived world. The elements of the new theory more directly disclose those attributes and their relationships, particularly so in the striking and important wide-angle egomotion phenomenon that he showed us during the meeting.

Couched though they may be in terms of optical anatomy and physics, these theories nevertheless comprise what I have called hidden rules, or mental structures: These are not just stimulus-information analyses, but models enriched by mechanisms (especially, the optic sphere) not found in the optic array. But as I have been arguing, they need amendment (although I do not yet know whether the optic sphere phenomenon will also show the same evidence of central attentional participation when appropriately "weakened.") In any case, the optic sphere theory needs further development (e.g., as emerged in discussion of David Lee's tau) and needs comparison with other far less ambitious efforts that deal with similar phenomena (e.g., Matin & Li, 1992; Warren & Kurtz, 1992).

(4) How Not to Deal with Mental Structure

Some of us feel the need for notions like mental structure and mental representation, and some do not. I used to be among the latter, now I incline reluctantly toward the former, along with most cognitive psychologists (and now, cognitive neurophysiologists). But without principles to describe and predict the operation of such constructs, the issue is not very fruitful (see Cooper & Hochberg, 1994).

Virtually any rule will fit some cases; the challenge is to find a rule that can be applied with some predictive confidence (i.e., that has only principled exceptions). One such traditional rule is that representations reflect distal physics (i.e., the "likelihood principle"); although sometimes classed among its supporters, I don't think it viable without an enormous amount of as-yet unprincipled hedging. Another such rule derives from the Gestaltist's *minimum principle*; although I helped start the still-current coding version some 39 years ago, it is just 30 years since I decided that it can't work either, since we can at will generate exceptions, and since what one perceives can depend so much on where one attends and on what one intends (see Hochberg, 1988, or Peterson & Hochberg, 1989, for reviews).

But since the simple "big principles" can't really be used, I think that the kinds of robust and striking surprises that have been so regularly discovered here in Uppsala are more diagnostic of underlying processes than mere mirrors of distal attributes can be. And because these processes are so clearly lawful, any exceptions we can find are theoretically important.

Notes

[1a] Hochberg and Cooper (in progress); Lynn Cooper has observed that with increased familiarity the reversed perspective becomes predominant, an observation seconded by Ian Howard and James Cutting. For early observations, see von Hornbostel (1922); for use as specific challenge to rigidity theories, see Schwartz and Sperling (1983), Amira, Peterson, and Hochberg (1983), Hochberg, Amira, and Peterson (1984), Braunstein & Andersen (1984, 1986), Hochberg (1987). For a recent review of this issue, see Hochberg (1988).

[1b] The use of percept-percept coupling to achieve convergent definition of perceptual experience was discussed in Hochberg (1956); illusory concomitant motion as a possible measure of misperceived distance was measured by Gogel and Tietz (1974), and used to measure perceived object structure by Peterson (1986), Peterson and Hochberg (1983, 1989), Hochberg and Peterson (1987) and Hochberg & Beer (1991).

[1c] Hochberg and Beer (1991): Viewing distance, instructed intentions, and the presence or absence of a uniform texture which could provide additional information as to true slant, all affected (but did not reduce to zero) the duration of illusory concomitant motion.

[1d] Ullman, 1984: Something like a minimum principle reemerges here, but the extents, distance functions, and relative strengths are not only left open, but it is not clear that it can be brought to testability and applicability. A coherency principle (cf. the remarkable findings of Lappin, Norman, & Mowafy, 1991; Mowafy, Blake, & Lappin, 1990) seems more plausible and potentially powerful, but may still face problems. See Gillam (1972) and Gillam and Broughton (1991).

[1e] Intention, binocularity vs. monocularity, information at the intersection, and viewing distance all affected (but did not reduce to zero) the duration of illusory concomitant motion.

[2a] See Wallach (1990), Wallach, Becklen, and Nitzberg (1985) and the reply by Johansson (1985); for brief discussion, see Hochberg and Beer (1990).

[2b] Hochberg and Fallon (1976); Hochberg, Fallon, and Brooks (1977); For example of extreme effect of stationary point, see Wallach, Becklen, & Nitzberg, in Note 2a, and examples like Fig. 2D in this paper, taken from Hochberg and Beer (1990). The TV in a lighted room is from Hochberg and Beer (1990) and many classroom demonstrations.

[2c] Girgus, Rock, and Egatz (1977) have shown that unless viewers know of the alternative construals, displays that characteristically fluctuate readily do so far less.

[3a] The set of experiments described in connection with Fig. 3Di are from Hochberg and Beck (1954). Luminance range was well within 30:1, and effects were small. Several attempts were made at partial replication (none included similar efforts to test the effects of more than one "depth cue" and of orthogonal illumination directions, so that in each case there is the danger that the stimulus change itself, with no intervening coupling, would be sufficient to account for whatever differences were found).

The attempts at replication have met with some success (Beck, 1965; Gilchrist, 1977) and some failure (Epstein, 1961a; Flock & Freedberg, 1970).

[3b] Also, by drastically increasing the luminance ratio, Gilchrist (1977) greatly increased the effect size, so that the replication of the Hochberg and Beck (1954) finding might seem secure, but as Bergström (in press) argues, this ratio-increase may have changed the issue. The research described here, with computer displays in a range of about 21:1, and a perceptually depth-coupled relative lightness response, should serve as an unequivocal replication.

[3c] See Hochberg (1972, pp. 421–422); for the nearest relevant evidence, see Flock, Wilson, and Poizner (1966); for a more stimulus-constrained and less intention-dependent proposal, see Bergström (1977, 1982, in press).

References

Amira, L., Peterson, M., & Hochberg, J. (1983). Apparent tridimensionality differences in computer-generated sequences of skeletal objects. *Proceedings and Abstracts of the 54th Annual Meeting of the Eastern Psychological Association, 62* (Abstract.).

Beck, J. (1965). Apparent spatial position and the perception of lightness. *Journal of Experimental Psychology, 69,* 170–179.

Bergström, S. S. (1977). Common and relative components of reflected light as information about illumination, color, and three-dimensional form of objects. *Scandinavian Journal of Psychology, 18,* 180–186.

Bergström, S. S. (1982). Color and three-dimensional form. In J. Beck (Ed.), *Organization and representation in perception* (pp. 365–378). Hillsdale, NJ: Erlbaum.

Bergström, S. S. (in press). Color constancy: Toward a vector model for the perception of illumination, color, and depth. In A. Gilchrist (Ed.), *Lightness, brightness, and transparency.* Hillsdale, NJ: Erlbaum.

Boselie, F., & Leuwenberg, E. (1986). A test of the minimum principles requires a perceptual coding system. *Perception, 15,* 331–354.

Braunstein, M. L., & Andersen, G. J. (1984). A counterexample to the rigidity assumption in the visual perception of structure through motion. *Perception, 13,* 213–217.

Braunstein, M. L., & Andersen, G. J. (1986). Testing the rigidity assumption: A reply to Ullman. *Perception, 15,* 641–644.

Cooper, L. A., & Hochberg, J. (1994). Objects of the mind: Mental representation in visual perception and cognition. In S. Ballesteros (Ed.), *Cognitive approaches to human perception* (pp. 223–239). Hillsdale, NJ: Erlbaum.

Epstein, W. (1961a). Phenomenal orientation and perceived achromatic color. *Journal of Psychology, 52,* 51–53.

Epstein, W. (1961b). The known size-apparent distance hypothesis. *American Journal of Psychology, 74,* 333–346.

Epstein, W. (1963). The influence of assumed size on apparent distance. *American Journal of Psychology, 72,* 257–265

Epstein, W. (1965). Nonrelational judgment of size and distance. *American Journal of Psychology, 78*, 120–123.

Epstein, W. (1982). Percept-percept couplings. *Perception, 11*, 75–88.

Epstein, W., & Brouta, K. D. (1986). Automatic and attentional components in perception of size-at-a-distance. *Perception & Psychophysics, 40*, 256–262.

Epstein, W., & Lovitts, B. E. (1985). Automatic and attentional components in perception of shape-at-a-slant. *Journal of Experimental Psychology: Human Perception and Performance, 11*, 355–366.

Epstein, W., Park, J., & Casey, A. (1961). The current status of the size-distance hypothesis. *Psychological Bulletin, 58*, 491–514.

Eriksson, S., & Zetterberg, P. (1975). *Experience and veridical space perception* (Report No. 169). Uppsala University, Department of Psychology.

Flock, H., & Freedberg, E. (1970). Perceived angle of incidence and achromatic surface color. *Perception & Psychophysics, 8*, 251–256.

Flock, H., Wilson, A., & Poizner, S. (1966). Lightness and matching for different routes through a compound scene. *Perception & Psychophysics, 1*, 382–384.

Gibson, J. J. (1950). *The perception of the visual world.* Boston: Houghton Mifflin.

Gilchrist, A. (1977). Perceived lightness depends on perceived spatial arrangement. *Science, 195*, 185–187.

Gillam, B. (1972). Perceived common rotary motion of ambiguous stimuli as a criterion of perceptual grouping. *Perception & Psychophysics, 11*, 99–101.

Gillam, B., & Broughton, R. (1991). Motion capture by a frame: Global or local processing? *Perception & Psychophysics, 49*, 547–550.

Girgus, J. J., Rock, I., & Egatz, R. (1977). The effect of knowledge of reversibility on the reversibility of ambiguous figures. *Perception & Psychophysics, 22*, 550–556.

Gogel, W. C. (1969). The effect of object familiarity on the perception of size and distance. *Quarterly Journal of Experimental Psychology, 21*, 239–247.

Gogel, W. C. (1981). Perceived depth is a necessary factor in apparent motion concomitant with head movement: A reply to Shebilske and Proffitt. *Perception & Psychophysics, 29*, 173–177.

Gogel, W. C. (1990). A theory of phenomenal geometry and its applications. *Perception & Psychophysics, 48*, 105–123.

Gogel, W. C., Hartman, B. O., & Harker, G. S. (1957). The retinal size of a familiar object as a determiner of apparent distance. *Psychological Monographs, 71* (No. 442), 1–16.

Gogel, W. C., & Tietz, J. D. (1992). Absence of compensation and reasoning-like processes in the perception of orientation and depth. *Perception & Psychophysics, 51*, 309–318.

Gogel, W. C., & Tietz, J. D. (1974). The effect of perceived distance on perceived movement. *Perception & Psychophysics, 16*, 70–78.

Granrud, C. E., Haake, R. J., & Yonas, A. (1985). Infants' sensitivity to familiar size: The effect of memory on spatial perception. *Perception & Psychophysics, 37*, 459–466.

Hatfield, G., & Epstein, W. (1985). The status of the minimum principle in the theoretical analysis of visual perception. *Psychological Bulletin, 97,* 155–186.

Hochberg, C. B., & Hochberg, J. E. (1952). Familiar size and the perception of depth. *Journal of Psychology, 34,* 107–114.

Hochberg, J. (1956). Perception: Toward the recovery of a definition. *Psychological Review, 63,* 400–405.

Hochberg, J. (1972). Perception: Color and shape. In L. A. Riggs & J. A. Kling (Eds.), *Woodworth & Schlosberg's experimental psychology* (pp. 395–550). New York: Holt, Rinehart & Winston.

Hochberg, J. (1974). Higher-order stimuli and inter-response coupling in the perception of the visual world. In R. B. MacLeod & H. Pick (Eds.), *Perception: Essays in honor of James J. Gibson* (pp. 17–39). Ithaca, NY: Cornell University Press.

Hochberg, J. (1982). How big is a stimulus? In J. Beck (Ed.), *Organization and representation in perception* (pp. 191–218). Hillsdale, NJ: Erlbaum.

Hochberg, J. (1984). *Visual worlds in collision: invariances and premises, theories vs. facts.* Presidental Address, Division of Experimental Psychology of the American Psychological Association, Toronto, Canada.

Hochberg, J. (1987). Machines should not see as people do, but must know how people see. *Computer Vision, Graphics, & Image Processing, 37,* 221–237.

Hochberg, J. (1988). Visual perception. In R. Atkinson, R. Herrnstein, G. Lindzey, & D. Luce (Eds.), *Stevens' handbook of experimental psychology, Vol. I, Perception and motivation* (pp. 295–375). New York: Wiley.

Hochberg, J., Amira, L., & Peterson, M. A. (1984). Extensions of the Schwartz/Sperling phenomenon: Invariance under transformation fails in the perception of objects' moving pictures. *Proceedings of the Eastern Psychological Association, 55,* 44 (Abstract).

Hochberg, J., & Beck, J. (1954). Apparent spatial arrangement and perceived brightness. *Journal of Experimental Psychology, 47,* 263–266.

Hochberg, J., & Beer, J. (1990). Alternative movement organizations: Findings and premises for modeling. *Proceedings of the 31st Annual Meeting, p. 25* (Abstract). (Copy of presentation available; talk currently being expanded to submit for publication.)

Hochberg, J., & Beer, J. (1991). Illusory rotations from self-produced motion: The Ames window effect in static objects. *Annual Meetings of the Eastern Psychological Association, p. 34.* (Copy of presentation available; talk currently being expanded to submit for publication.)

Hochberg, J., & Beer, J. (in preparation). *The virtual lightness of virtual objects* (tentative title).

Hochberg, J., & Cooper, L. A. (in preparation). *As the cube turns: When and why mental objects are made of rubber.*

Hochberg, J., & Fallon, P. (1976). Perceptual analysis of moving patterns. *Science, 194,* 1081–1083.

Hochberg, J., Fallon, P., & Brooks, V. (1977). Motion organization in "stop-action" sequences. *Scandinavian Journal of Psychology, 18*, 187–191.

Hochberg, J., & MacAlister, E. (1953). A quantitative approach to figural "goodness." *Journal of Experimental Psychology, 46*, 361–364.

Hochberg, J., & Peterson, M. A. (1987). Piecemeal organization and cognitive components in object perception: Perceptually coupled responses to moving objects. *Journal of Experimental Psychology: General, 116*, 370–380.

Hornbostel, E. M. von (1922). Über optische inversion. *Psychologische Forschung, 1*, 130–156.

Ittelson, W. H. (1951). Size as a cue to distance: Static localization. *American Journal of Psychology, 64*, 54–67.

Jansson, G. (1977). Perceived bending and stretching motions from a line of points. *Scandinavian Journal of Psychology, 18*, 209–215.

Jansson, G., & Johansson, G. (1973). Visual perception of bending motion. *Perception, 2*, 321–326.

Johansson, G. (1950). *Configurations in event perception.* Uppsala: Almqvist & Wiksell. [Chapter 2, this volume.]

Johansson, G. (1964). Perception of motion and changing form. *Scandinavian Journal of Psychology, 5*, 181–208. [Chapter 4, this volume.]

Johansson, G. (1979). Memory functions in visual event perception. In L.-G. Nilsson (Ed.), *Perspective in memory research* (pp. 93–103). Hillsdale, NJ: Erlbaum.

Johansson, G. (1982). Visual space perception through motion. In A. H. Wertheim, W. A. Wagenaar, & H. W. Leibowitz (Eds.), *Tutorials on motion perception* (pp. 19–39). New York: Plenum.

Johansson, G. (1985). Vector analysis and process combinations in motion perception: A reply to Wallach, Becklen, & Nitzberg (1985). *Journal of Experimental Psychology: Human Perception and Performance, 11*, 367–371.

Johansson, G., & Börjesson, E. (1989). Toward a new theory of vision. Studies in wide-angle perception. *Ecological Psychology, 1*, 301–331. [Chapter 10, this volume.]

Johansson, G., & Börjesson, E. (1990). Experiments on the optic sphere theory, slant perception from central stimulation. (Uppsala Psychological Reports, No. 214). Uppsala University, Department of Psychology.

Lappin, J. S., Norman, J. F., & Mowafy, L. (1991). The detectability of geometric structure in rapidly changing optical patterns. *Perception, 20*, 513–528.

Mach, E. (1959). *The analysis of sensations.* (Revised 5th ed., C. M. Williams, Trans.). New York: Dover (Original work published 1895.)

Matin, L., & Li, W. (1992). Visually perceived eye level: Changes induced by a pitched-from-vertical 2-line visual field. *Perception & Psychophysics, 18*, 257–289.

Mowafy, L., Blake, R., & Lappin, J. S. (1990). Detection and discrimination of coherent motion. *Perception & Psychophysics, 48*, 583–592.

Ono, H. (1969). Apparent distance as a function of familiar size. *Journal of Experimental Psychology, 79*, 109–115.

Peterson, M. A. (1986). Illusory concomitent motion in ambiguous stimuli: Evidence for non-stimulus contribution to perceptual organization. *Journal of Experimental Psychology: Human Perception & Performance, 12,* 50–60.

Peterson, M. A., & Hochberg, J. (1983). The opposed-set measurement procedure: The role of local cues and intention in form perception. *Journal of Experimental Psychology: Human Perception & Performance, 9,* 183–193.

Peterson, M. A., & Hochberg, J. (1989). Necessary considerations for theory of form perception: A theoretical and empirical reply to Boselie and Leeuwenberg. *Perception, 18,* 105–110.

Predebon, J. (1992). The role of instructions and familiar size in absolute judgments of size and distance. *Perception & Psychophysics, 51,* 344–354.

Rock, I., & Nijhawan, R. (1989). Regression to egocentrically determined description of form under conditions of inattention. *Journal of Experimental Psychology: Human Perception & Performance, 15,* 259–272.

Schwartz, B. J., & Sperling, G. (1983). Non-rigid 3D percepts from 2D representations of rigid objects. Investigative ophthalmology and visual science. *ARVO supplement, 24,* 239 (Abstract).

Stoper, A. E. (1973). Apparent motion of stimuli presented stroboscopically during pursuit movement of the eye. *Perception & Psychophysics, 13,* 201–211.

Troost, J. M., & deWeert, C. M. M. (1991). Naming versus matching in color constancy. *Perception & Psychophysics, 50,* 591–602.

Ullman, S. (1984). Maximizing rigidity: The incremental recovery of 3-D structure from rigid and nonrigid motion. *Perception, 13,* 255–274.

Wallach, H. (1990). The role of eye movements in the perception of motion and shape. In E. Kowler (Ed.), *Eye movements and their role in visual and cognitive processes* (pp. 289–305). Amsterdam: Elsevier.

Wallach, H., Becklen, R., & Nitzberg, D. (1985). Vector analysis and process combination in motion perception. *Journal of Experimental Psychology: Human Perception and Performance, 11,* 93–102.

Warren, W. H., & Kurtz, K. J. (1992). The role of central and peripheral vision in perceiving the direction of self-motion. *Perception & Psychophysics, 51,* 443–454.

Decoding Principles, Heuristics and Inference in Visual Perception[†]

Myron L. Braunstein

University of California

Abstract: In 1970 Johansson outlined a theory of perception in which perceptual processes were characterized as decoding principles. This approach provided an alternative to both constructionist theory and direct perception. This chapter discusses the relationship between decoding principles, perceptual heuristics, inductive inference, and a formal theory of perception introduced recently by Bennett, Hoffman, and Prakash (1991).

The articles and commentaries in this book review a number of theoretical concepts introduced by Gunnar Johansson. One concept that is especially important in clarifying the nature of perceptual processing is the decoding principle (Johansson, 1970). Although the phrase "decoding principle" is not widely used in the perception literature, the concept of a decoding principle is central to a complete understanding of perception. Decoding principles present an answer to perhaps the most ancient question in perception: How do physical objects in the external world give rise to perceptions that are internal to the perceiver? To be more specific, and slightly less ancient, we can rephrase the question in a way that assumes that we have some knowledge of the physics of light: How does light reflected (or emitted) from objects in the external world lead to the perception of surfaces, objects, and events? There have been many interesting attempts to answer this question over the centuries, some of which are described in a fascinating book by Pastore (1971). Modern theory is characterized by two somewhat opposite poles—constructionist theory and direct perception. These approaches encompass very different views of how much of the information in perception is in the stimulus and how much must be provided by the observer. Johansson's decoding principles provide a third approach—one which has directly or indirectly influenced other current approaches to understanding perception. Most of the remaining discussion will be about recovery of 3D structure from 2D images. This is an especially clear-cut problem for illustrating different

[†] Preparation of this paper was supported by NSF Grant BNS 88-19565 and DBS 92-09773. I am grateful to George J. Andersen and Donald D. Hoffman for comments on an earlier draft.

concepts of how much information is in the stimulus. The discussion applies, however, to perception in general.

Perhaps the most extreme version of the constructionist approach is Ames' transactionalist theory (Ittelson & Kilpatrick, 1952). This theory presents perception as a "transaction" between the observer and the physical world. It is a transaction between an ambiguous stimulus and the observer's beliefs about what is really present in the external world. This is a form—albeit an extreme form—of Helmholtz's (1962) unconscious inference (also see Uttal, 1981). Unconscious inference usually refers to an activity, very much like conscious reasoning, about what is likely to be present in the environment—but an activity that takes place without conscious awareness. This in a way is an unfortunate choice of terminology because it gives inference, as used in perception, a connotation of a process of deliberate reasoning. The meaning of inference (e.g., in logic) is much broader than that. With a definition of inference divested of cognitive connotations it becomes clear that inference can describe *smart mechanisms* (Runeson, 1977) and indeed all of perceptual processing (Bennett, Hoffman, & Prakash, 1991).

Overall, perception according to the constructionist approach uses considerable internal knowledge of what is likely in the environment in determining what is perceived when a certain pattern of light is presented to the eye. As an illustration, again using transactionalism as an extreme case of a constructionist theory, consider the Ames trapezoidal window illusion (Ittelson & Kilpatrick, 1952). The Ames explanation of the illusion is essentially that the object looks like a window and since most windows with which we interact are rectangular, it looks rectangular. Once it is interpreted as rectangular, the larger projected side should always appear closer, hence the illusion of oscillation.

Direct perception is intended as an alternative to constructionist theory. The emphasis is on the information present in the stimulus. Whereas this information may appear inadequate for perception of complex properties of the environment without cognitive reconstruction when only elementary stimulus dimensions are considered, higher order properties of the stimulus can provide sufficient information for perception. These higher order variables, which are based on combinations or higher derivatives of the elementary variables, provide invariants which, according to this approach, can form the basis for direct perception. An example of an invariant is the horizon ratio: The proportion of an object on a level ground plane with the observer that projects above the horizon is invariant over viewing distance (Gibson, 1979).

Overall, direct perception holds that the required information is in the stimulus. A process of unconscious inference is not required. But if the information is in the stimulus, how can we have illusions—especially dynamic illusions like the rotating trapezoid—when dynamic stimuli are in most cases especially informative? One explanation is that illusions occur when the natural active perception of the human (or animal) observer is artificially impeded. If the observer moves very close to the trapezoid or views a trapezoid rotating about a vertical axis from above, the true direction of rotation of the trapezoid will be perceived. One might therefore argue that active perception can eliminate the illusion. However, the illusion persists over a considerable range of active exploration, including viewing positions that provide sufficient information to determine the rotation direction of other forms, such as rectangles. Although the observer can determine the true direction of rotation of a trapezoid by moving closer or viewing it from above, this exploration does not eliminate the illusory perception that occurs at more distant viewpoints. (See Gehringer & Engel, 1986, for a similar analysis of the Ames distorted room illusions.)

Decoding Principles

Johansson has shown that there is an alternative to the constructionist and direct perception approaches. It is not, on the one hand, necessary to postulate a reasoning-like unconscious inference process between the light projected onto the retina and visual perception, or between stimulation and perception in general (although unconscious inference, with the unfortunate cognitive connotations removed, may not be an inappropriate description of perception as we shall see later). On the other hand, it is not necessary to reject the concept that processes internal to the organism determine the relationship between the stimulus and perception. Indeed, it is not possible to account for perception without this concept. Johansson argues that there are processes that determine the relationship between stimulus and perception, but these are not the cognitive-like cues of the constructionists. Instead, these are decoding principles—rules that are automatically applied and may be part of the "hard-wiring" of the visual system.

How is this different from the constructionist approach? Although Johansson has not applied decoding principles to the rotating trapezoid illusion, I will illustrate how a decoding principle—probably one of several involved in this illusion—might be applied. Consider the following hypothetical decoding principle: A contour enclosed by angles that are becoming increasingly acute in the projected image is approaching in 3D. (This would probably be encompassed by a more general principle involving features adjacent to converging textures, but presenting it in a more specific form makes it easier to relate it to the trapezoid illusion.) When a rectangle is rotated, the side enclosed by angles that are decreasing in magnitude is always approaching. (In a parallel projection the angles do not change.) On the other hand, when a rotating trapezoidal shape is viewed from a sufficient distance, or shown in parallel projection, the angles enclosing the larger side decrease at times even when that side is receding (see Fig. 1). The illusion of oscillation can be predicted from these periods when the decoding principle described above would give the wrong direction of rotation (Braunstein, 1972). Note that in this explanation of the trapezoidal illusion, a

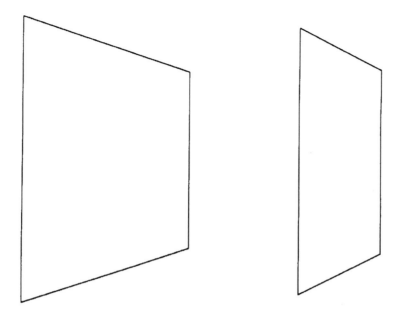

Fig. 1. The figure on the left is a frontal view of a trapezoid (but it is also consistent with a rotated view of a rectangle). The figure on the right is a rotated view of the trapezoid on the left. Note that the side enclosed by acute angles has become smaller in the projection. This is a perspective effect and indicates that the distance to this side has actually increased.

decoding principle is automatically applied to the image data. This is different from the transactionalist explanation, in that it does not require the observer, even unconsciously, to use prior knowledge about windows or even about rectangles. It does not require that the observer apply specific knowledge about the nature of objects in the environment except in the following sense: The decoding principle exists because of the nature of objects in the environment and because of the principles of projective geometry. But once it exists it is automatically applied; knowing that the object is trapezoidal in shape does not eliminate the illusion. The illusion is also not due to a lack of information caused by restrictions on active exploration. In a parallel projection, it is true that the information is insufficient for a veridical judgment of direction of rotation. However, the illusion occurs in polar projections even when the observer could correctly judge the direction of rotation if the acute and obtuse angles were eliminated (Börjesson, 1971; Braunstein, 1971).

The concept of a decoding principle is not really at variance with the tenets of ecological optics in any fundamental way. The difference seems to arise from a reluctance in the direct perception approach to be explicit about such princ-

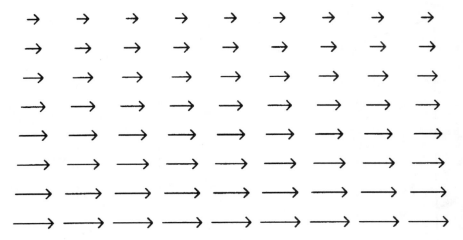

Fig. 2. A velocity gradient based on a perspective projection of points on a slanted plane moving to the right. Geometrically, the gradient is also consistent with points that are all at the same distance but happen to be moving at velocities that are a linear function of their height in the image (a very unlikely interpretation).

iples, even though they may be implicitly assumed to be part of the structure of the organism and the result of the organism's "ecological niche" (Gibson, 1979). This can be illustrated with the following example. Consider a gradient of velocities—rows of dots moving horizontally with the velocity of each dot in a row inversely proportional to its height in the image (see Fig. 2). This is likely to have the appearance of a rigidly moving planar surface slanted away at the top. A direct perception approach might argue that the slant is directly extracted from this gradient—that the gradient unambiguously conveys 3D slant information. But couldn't the dots all be at the same distance and moving independently at velocities that are just by coincidence related to their heights in the image? The answer is yes and no: Yes, it is a theoretical possibility, and no, it never happens (has a probability of occurrence of zero) in a natural environment, excluding perception labs from the category of natural environments. Still, slant can be recovered directly from a velocity gradient if we use a smart mechanism (Runeson, 1977) as part of this direct perception process. This mechanism would have to be smart enough to take into account the zero probability that the dots would move as they do if they were independently moving elements. But taking into account is not meant in a cognitive sense. The environmental knowledge is part of the structure of the mechanism, which can then operate in a fully automatic and mechanical way. This smart mechanism would be a decoding principle having, as part of its structure, a rigidity constraint (Johansson, 1970). The mechanism directly recovers 3D slant from a gradient of 2D velocities. It exists because of a rigidity constraint and principles of projective geometry. It does not have to reference this constraint or these principles as it operates—they are part of its structure. Closely related concepts have emerged in computational vision (e.g., Marr, 1982; Ullman, 1979) and more recently in observer theory (Bennett et al., 1991).

It is not difficult to find examples of smart mechanisms in the technology available today. Consider the computer modem that indicates that it is connected when it receives a carrier tone. We would certainly not regard this as a cognitive decision or even as unconscious inference. But the modem operates this way because it is designed to operate in an environment in which a certain tone implies a connection with another modem. If it somehow picked up a tone of the frequency to which it was designed to respond, and this tone had no relationship to data communications, the modem would produce an erroneous connect message (an illusion?). I use this example only to demonstrate, as did Runeson (1977), that processes that are logically equivalent to decoding principles in perception can exist in mechanisms and do not imply cognitive processing.

In computational vision it is often thought to be a requirement that a perceptual process, or a decoding principle in Johansson's terminology, must provide a guarantee against false targets. Consider Ullman's three views of four points proof. The probability is zero that three views of four points that have a rigid solution were not the result of rigid motion in 3D (a false target). This does not mean that a false target will never occur—but a solution based on rigidity can be relied on with complete confidence, unless someone (like a psychologist) is deliberately trying to create an illusion of 3D rigid motion. This process thus guarantees a correct solution if it provides any solution at all.

Heuristic Processes

Processes with zero probability of false targets, however, may not be typical of perceptual processes or decoding principles. Another possibility is that perceptual processes are heuristic processes (Braunstein, 1972, 1976, 1983). In heuristic processes the requirement of eliminating false targets is balanced against requirements for efficiency and flexibility. The concept of heuristic processes in perception is derived from the concept of heuristic search procedures in problem solving. Consider for example the problem of finding a proof for a theorem in symbolic logic. There is a procedure, known as the British Museum Algorithm, that guarantees that a proof will eventually be found if the theorem can be proven from the axioms. (It simply checks all permutations of all axioms until it finds a proof.) Newell and Simon (1972) have shown that one can reach a solution (i.e., find a proof) more quickly by using certain rules of thumb or heuristics. Heuristics in general have the characteristic of narrowing the search space by using information about characteristics of the problem space. This has the positive aspect, already mentioned, of increasing efficiency in solving the problem. But it has the negative aspect of introducing the possibility that the problem solver will sometimes miss the solution completely. Thus the problem is usually solved much more rapidly, but occasionally is not solved at all. Obviously one would want to choose heuristics that maximize efficiency while making missed solutions extremely rare.

The concept of heuristic processes in perception is similar although not exactly the same. In some ways it is closer to the heuristics proposed in decision making (Kahneman & Tversky, 1972, 1973; Payne & Braunstein, 1971). A heuristic process in perception does not fail to reach an interpretation, but may reach an interpretation that is nonveridical, that is, an interpretation that is inconsistent with the state of the physical world. One reason heuristic perceptual processes might be used even though they have a higher probability of error than other theoretically possible processes is very similar to the reason for heuristics in problem solving—to gain efficiency. A faster but less precise interpretation of a visual image may often be more valuable to the perceiver than a slower, more precise interpretation. But in vision it may be flexibility rather than speed that is most important. Processes that can provide approximate solutions for a wide range of stimulus conditions may be more useful than processes that can provide more precise solutions but operate only in a restricted range of stimulus conditions. For example, the failure to find improvement in structure-from-motion judgments as the number of views increases beyond two (Todd & Bressan, 1990) may occur because the same heuristic processes are used for multiple view displays and for two view displays (Liter, Braunstein, & Hoffman, in press). These processes provide approximations that do not take advantage of the information that is theoretically available as the number of views increases beyond two. An example of a heuristic proposed for recovering depth from motion is that perceived depth is based (in part) on the relative image motions of the projections of features on an object (Caudek & Proffitt, 1993).

Ramachandran (1985) has introduced the phrase "bag of tricks" to describe a variety of perceptual processes. These "tricks" have something of the characteristic of heuristic processes in that they are applied automatically even when they lead to a physically incorrect interpretation in the presence of sufficient information in the stimulus for a "rational" perceiver, using appropriate constraints, to reach a correct solution. The main problem with the "bag of tricks" description is that it has the connotation, whether intended or not, of an almost random, unrelated set of perceptual processes that would be difficult to rationalize as a system for perceiving the external environment. The concept of heuristic processes, on the other hand, refers to decoding principles that, while they may use approximations, taken together may well optimize some combination of accuracy, speed, and flexibility.

Observer Theory

Recently, a formal approach to the study of perception has been introduced in which the central concept is the "observer" (Bennett et al., 1991). An observer is not, in general, synonymous with a perceiving organism (although it could be), but is consistent with the concept of a decoding principle. In very general terms, the relevant image data available to the observer consists of a set S of premises from the space of all possible premises, Y. This set of premises is associated with a set of interpretations, E, by means of a map from X to Y. For example, X could be the set of 3D interpretations, Y the set of 2D projections, and the map could be a polar projection. A kernel η associates a probability for each specific interpretation to a specific configuration of image data. An observer is formally defined as "a six-tuple (X, Y, E, S, π, η) where

1. X and Y are measurable spaces; E is an event of X; S is an event of Y.

2. π is a measurable map from X onto Y such that $\pi(E) = S$.

3. η is a Markovian kernel that associates to each point s of S a probability measure on E giving non-zero weight only to points of E in $\pi^{-1}(S)$ (Bennett et al., 1991)".

To apply this approach to the velocity gradient example, consider the following decoding principle: If the 2D motions of a group of points is compatible with a polar projection of a group of points in 3D space undergoing a rigid translation, then the perceived depths and motion of these points will be depths and motions in 3D that would produce the observed 2D motions through polar projection. This is a reverse perspective geometry principle, using a rigidity assumption, as discussed by Johansson (1964, 1977). For this decoding principle to be applied, there would first have to be image data compatible with a rigid translation. Obviously any random 2D motions are unlikely to be compatible. To describe this decoding principle as an observer, we would say that the 2D motions compatible with a rigid 3D interpretation form a set S from the space of 2D point motions, Y. The 2D image data are premises in this system, and those compatible with the rigid translation are "distinguished" premises. The premises in Y are related to a space of interpretations, X, by a map, for example, projective geometry. By reverse perspective geometry (Johansson, 1977), an interpretation or a set of interpretations is associated with the premises—that is, with the image data. These interpretations are labeled "distinguished" interpretations in observer theory. If there are multiple distinguished interpretations (as, for example, in parallel projections which are reversible in depth), a probability is associated with each interpretation. A discussion of the importance of this formalism as a unifying theory of perception would be beyond the scope of this commentary, and the reader is referred to Bennett et al. (1991). The points that are of importance here are first that the observer concept is fully compatible with that of a decoding principle, and second, that observer theory clearly shows that perception can be formally described as a process of inductive inference, without the cognitive connotations of Helmholtz's unconscious inference theory. The observer is presented with premises, the image data, and reaches an interpretation by a process that may be completely mechanical (or may not be) but is nevertheless in a formal sense a process of inductive inference. It is inference because it begins with premises and ends with a conclusion that is not stated in the premises. The premises may be a series of 2D images; the conclusion may be a 3D perception. It is inductive because in all cases the conclusion is not logically required by the premises and the conclusion is thus not deductively valid (Hoffman, 1983). There is nothing in projective geometry to prevent points moving independently at different velocities from projecting velocities compatible with a rigidly moving structure. Empirically, the probability may be zero that this will happen, but the inference that it did not happen must be inductive. It is worth repeating that a cognitive reasoning process is not required. An observer may exist that produces a perception of rigid motion of points at varying distance when presented with compatible image motion because all other interpretations are improbable and such an observer is thus useful and usually veridical in its conclusions. But once the observer exists, it can operate in the blind, mechanical fashion proposed by Johansson for decoding principles. An observer does not "think" about what is probable in the environment each time it is applied. What is probable determines its structure and its structure determines what perceptual conclusion it reaches from the image data that is presented.

But an observer can reach a physically incorrect conclusion, which means that an illusory perception will occur. Consider the rotating trapezoid example, again making the observer unrealistically specific to simplify the discussion. Let us say that the distinguished premises for the observer consist of changes in the angles enclosing a vertical edge in the image that are compatible with a polar projection of a rotating vertical edge enclosed by right angles. The set of distinguished interpretations are the 3D rotations of the edge enclosed by right angles that would project the angle changes present in the image. Angles that became increasingly acute would thus have interpretations as right angles enclosing an approaching edge and angles that became increasingly obtuse would have interpretations as right angles enclosing a receding edge. But suppose that the figure is a trapezoid rather than a rectangle. Why is this observer (decoding principle) applied when its distinguished premises are based on the projected motions of rectangles (and thus it is not applicable to trapezoids)? Is it because the perceiver has decided first that the object is a rectangle? No, this sort of cognitive decision is not required. Is it because rectangular shapes (or more generally, even textures) are more common in the environment than trapezoidal shapes (or more generally, textures that diverge in one direction)? Not exactly. That may be the reason the observer exists, but not why it is applied in this particular instance. It is applied because the stimulus fits its distinguished premises. That's what an observer does. It provides an interpretation from its kernel of interpretations whenever its distinguished premises are matched by the image data. It is not stopped by cognitive knowledge about the shape of the object. Indeed, the empirical evidence indicates that cognitive knowledge that the object is a trapezoid does not prevent the illusion. When the observer is applied to a stimulus which is compatible with its distinguished premises, but which is not from the set of distinguished interpretations that map onto these premises, it has responded to a false target. Of course, an observer that frequently responded to false targets would not be useful.

Conclusions

In conclusion, Johansson's decoding principles form a basis for perceptual processes that are neither cognitive on the one hand or so direct as to exclude any processing by the perceiver on the other hand. Two variations on this theme have been discussed: (1) the proposal that decoding principles are heuristic, and (2) the formal theory of an observer that can be thought of as a formal theory of a decoding principle. Overall, a decoding principle can be a mechanism that in a formal sense instantiates inductive inference. Interpreting perception as inductive inference, with the stipulation that such inference can be instantiated by decoding principles that operate in a blind mechanical way, does not bring an unwanted cognitive component into perceptual theory.

References

Bennett, B. M., Hoffman, D. D., & Prakash, C. (1991). Unity of perception. *Cognition, 38*, 295–334.

Börjesson, E. (1971). Properties of changing patterns evoking visually perceived oscillation. *Perception & Psychophysics, 9*, 303–308.

Braunstein, M. L. (1971). Perception of rotation in figures with rectangular and trapezoidal features. *Journal of Experimental Psychology, 91*, 25–29.

Braunstein, M. L. (1972). Perception of rotation in depth: A process model. *Psychological Review, 79*, 510–524.

Braunstein, M. L. (1976). *Depth perception through motion.* New York: Academic Press.

Braunstein, M. L. (1983). Contrasts between human and machine vision: Should technology recapitulate phylogeny? In J. Beck, B. Hope, & A. Rosenfeld (Eds.), *Human and machine vision* (pp. 85–96). New York: Academic Press.

Caudek, C., & Proffitt, D. R. (1993). Depth perception in motion parallax and stereokinesis. *Journal of Experimental Psychology: Human Perception and Performance, 19*, 32–47.

Gehringer, W. L., & Engel, E. (1986). Effect of ecological viewing conditions on the Ames' distorted room illusion. *Journal of Experimental Psychology: Human Perception and Performance, 12*, 181–185.

Gibson, J. J. (1979). *An ecological approach to perception.* Boston: Houghton Mifflin.

Helmholtz, H. (1962). *Physiological optics* (Vol. 3) (J. P. Southall, Ed. and trans.). New York: Dover. (Originally published, Optical Society of America, 1925.)

Hoffman, D. D. (1983). The interpretation of visual illusions. *Scientific American, 249* (6), 154–162.

Ittelson, W. H., & Kilpatrick, F. P. (1952). Experiments in perception. *Scientific American, 185 (8),* 50–55.

Johansson, G. (1964). Perception of motion and changing form. *Scandinavian Journal of Psychology, 5,* 171–208. [Chapter 4, this volume.]

Johansson, G. (1970). On theories for visual space perception: A letter to Gibson. *Scandinavian Journal of Psychology, 11,* 67–74. [Chapter 5, this volume.]

Johansson, G. (1977). Spatial constancy and motion in visual perception. In W. Epstein (Ed.), *Stability and constancy in visual perception: Mechanisms and processes* (pp. 375–419). New York: Wiley.

Kahneman, D., & Tversky, A. (1972). Subjective probability: A judgment of representativeness. *Cognitive Psychology, 3,* 430–454.

Kahneman, D., & Tversky, A. (1973). On the psychology of prediction. *Psychological Review, 80,* 237–251.

Liter, J. C., Braunstein, M. L., Hoffman, D. D., Bennett, B. M. (in press). Inferring structure from motion in two-view and multi-view displays. *Perception.*

Marr, D. (1982). *Vision.* San Francisco: Freeman.

Newell, A., & Simon, H. A. (1972). *Human problem solving.* Englewood Cliffs, NJ: Prentice-Hall.

Pastore, N. (1971). *Selective history of theories of visual perception.* New York: Oxford University Press.

Payne, J. W., & Braunstein, M. L. (1971). Preferences among gambles with equal underlying distributions. *Journal of Experimental Psychology, 87,* 13–18.

Ramachandran, V. S. (1985). The neurobiology of perception. *Perception, 14,* 97–103.

Runeson, S. (1977). On the possibility of smart perceptual mechanisms. *Scandinavian Journal of Psychology, 18,* 172–179.

Todd, J. T., & Bressan, P. (1990). The perception of 3-dimensional affine structure from minimal apparent motion sequences. *Perception & Psychophysics, 48,* 419–430.

Ullman, S. (1979). *The interpretation of visual motion.* Cambridge, MA: MIT Press.

Uttal, W. R. (1981). *A taxonomy of visual processes.* Hillsdale, NJ: Erlbaum.

Vection and Locomotion

The Significance of Vection:
Thoughts Provoked by Gunnar Johansson's Studies on Visual Perception of Locomotion

Richard Held

Massachusetts Institute of Technology

Herschel Leibowitz

Pennsylvania State University

Abstract: Gunnar Johansson's surprising finding that a very sparse set of moving points in the visual periphery can induce motion of the self is an important clue to the nature of vection. Some of the implications of this finding are discussed in the following. When the stimulus situation is ambiguous as to the source of movement—environmental or bodily—even very impoverished stimuli can produce the illusion of self-motion which may alternate with motion attributed to the surrounding environment. This reciprocity in the attribution of motion illustrates the ubiquitous presence of the self as a platform for the distance senses. The perceived spatial relationship between this self and other objects is derived in turn, we believe, from prior actions in the object world. These considerations bear on issues of telepresence and the production of virtual worlds posed by modern technology.

We owe it to the genius of Gunnar Johansson that he was able not only to conceive and carry out seminal experiments, but also to identify the fundamentals of many perceptual phenomena. This rare ability is nicely illustrated in his studies of visual locomotion and, in particular, his investigation of the phenomenon of visually induced self-movement or "vection" (a subject reviewed in Dichgans & Brandt, 1978). In his paper on visual locomotion, Johansson (1977) reports a striking finding. The motion of only a few bright points moving vertically in the peripheral visual field of a stationary observer, situated in an otherwise normally illuminated laboratory, is sufficient to generate a compelling sense of observer-motion in the opposite direction. After a latency period, during which the points appear to be moving, they become the stationary reference coordinates while the rest of the scene, which is objectively stationary, appears to move with the observer (O). The result of this experiment demonstrates the surprising susceptibility to what is called illusory motion of O when moving stimuli of such minimal size and amplitude of displacement can become interpreted as the reference surround. The same visual sensitivity is available to provide feedback during O-produced movements of the body that entail displacements of the eye in space. But in the latter case the motion is always attributed to O moving with reference to the surround with essentially zero latency. Judging by the evidence, both types of motion—O-produced and vision-induced (vection)—can be generalized to each of the six dimensions of movement, three of rotation and three of translation (Howard, 1982).

Johansson's data are remarkable because they demonstrate saturated vection produced by very sparse stimuli. In saturated vection the objectively moving stimuli appear stationary while the observer and the objectively stationary stimuli appear to move in the opposite direction. The authors are not aware of any other study in which such minimal moving stimuli in the periphery can elicit saturated vection when the majority of the visual field is objectively stationary. None of the studies utilizing other dimensions of vection, for instance, circular and roll vection, have reported such a marked effect with minimal peripheral stimulation. The difference in the vection-inducing salience of Johansson's configuration may be related to the fact that he investigated linear vection while the other studies were concerned with alternative vection dimensions. The most common mode of body movement outside the laboratory, in the absence of concomitant vestibular stimulation (constant velocity), is linear. It may be that sensitivity to linear vection is enhanced because of its high incidence and, consequently, may be the basis for the Johansson results.

As Johansson suggests, this interpretation may also serve to explain the familiar phenomenon in which a passenger in a stationary vehicle falsely perceives self-motion when an adjacent vehicle moves. The phenomenon has been an enigma to researchers in this field because such a small area of the visual field (a few windows) is able to induce vection in spite of the simultaneous presence of stationary contours. While other factors may enter into this effect, such as expectation and the greater salience of background as opposed to foreground stimuli (Dichgans & Brandt, 1978), it may also be the case that linear vection is more easily elicited.

Johansson speculates whether the periphery is specialized for motion. Certainly in the case of linear vection, his results clearly demonstrate a heightened sensitivity of the periphery. A point which is frequently misinterpreted is that object motion perception is superior in the peripheral field. This is not the case as the thresholds for object motion increase with eccentricity (Leibowitz, Johnson, & Isabelle, 1972). However, the rate of the decrement of motion sensitivity with increasing eccentricity is slower than for resolution so that it appears as if motion is improving. This condition might provide an alternative explanation to the suggestion by Johansson that the periphery is specialized for self-motion.

The argument would be that in the periphery the conspicuity of moving stimuli is greater than the static stimuli which signal stationarity. However, in the central field, the relative strength of the two is changed so that the predominant response is reversed. Whether the periphery is specialized for motion depends on whether one is concerned with object or self-motion. It would appear that for object motion the answer is negative but that for self-motion, at least in the case of linear vection, there is evidence for specialization based on Johansson's results.

The Ambiguity of Vection

Not infrequently after a period of vection the attribution of motion may be transposed. An objectively stationary O, who, after continued surround motion feels moved in the opposite direction, may abruptly feel stationary while perceiving the surround as moving. With continued exposure the reversals will further cycle (Dichgans & Brandt, 1978). This two state alternation process has been analogized with the more familiar depth-reversible figures such as the Necker cube (Finke & Held, 1978). Such a reversible figure is ambiguous because the two-dimensional representation of the three-dimensional object is insufficient to determine a unique order of parts in depth. Similarly, the attribution of motion to O as opposed to surround is ambiguous when a stationary observer views constant velocity motion because other sensory and motor information, normally present during actual movement, is insufficient to disambiguate the two alternatives.

The Complementarity of Self and Surround Motion

One may ask the further question, why do the two states constitute the polar alternatives? After all the direction of self-motion could conceivably go off in any direction other than the reverse of the field motion. We believe that the answer derives from an internal model in the brain (conceptual) relating movements of the eye in space and image changes. As Johansson has repeatedly emphasized, such movements cause continuous and orderly perspectival transformations in the retinal image. This order derives, in turn, from the geometry and kinematics of movement in relation to visible objects. We should like to add that this is true if and only if the real movements of objects in the world, relative to the viewer, allow the orderly relationship described above. In an environment in which object movement was extensive and random in direction, the orderly relation would not occur.

To make this discussion more concrete consider rotations of the head. Discounting movements of the eyes, a displacement of N degrees will be accompanied by a displacement of the visual images of the surround of equal magnitude but reversed direction. Over time many such displacements will occur in varied directions including repetitions. We assume that these concomitances will be stored in memory. Translatory movements of the head create flows of the image which are unique to the initial orientation of the head and the direction of movement. We assume that chronic exposure to these concomitances of posture, movement, and visual change are also stored in memory. This data store can then be used to anticipate future concomitances in the following manner. Motion of the visible surround, unaccompanied by movement of the head, gives rise, after a latent period, to the "illusory" head movement in the anticipated opposite direction which, in the past, has been the habitual concomitant of such motion of the surround. The latency of this effect is presumed to result from the abrupt onset of visual motion unaccompanied by the change in vestibular stimulation with head rotation anticipated by the model. Rapid change in visual stimulation is attributed to the motion of external objects unless it is accompanied by movements of the head (again discounting movements of the eyes). However, when the steady state of motion seen at constant velocity is achieved, attributions of motion to either surround or head are equally likely to be anticipated and the consequence is vection and the alternation of states described above. In accord with the internal model, both the illusion of vection and the perception of surround motion arise as a consequence of the habitual accompaniment of surround motion and observer movement at the same velocity but in the opposite direction.

This kind of reasoning can be found at least as early as Helmholtz (1910, English translation of 1925):

"Such objects (and their motions) are always imagined as being present in the field of vision as would have to be there in order to produce the same impression on the nervous mechanism, the eyes being used under *ordinary normal* conditions" (Authors' italic and words in parenthesis).

Since the data of the internal model derive from a history of exposure, they may be altered by systematic changes in this history. The adaptation found in rearrangement experiments can be interpreted as arguing that the orderly relationship between movement and its sensory accompaniments actually determines the entries in the internal model (Held, 1961; Welch, 1978). Adaptation then reflects new entries in the internal model of the relationship which, in turn, can determine altered conditions for vection.

The Ubiquitous Self

Vection, and especially the reciprocity of motion between self and surround, calls attention to the presence of the observer as a platform for the distance senses. It does so because we are impelled to regard vection as illusory motion of the self. But the self in this sense must always be present in spatial perception whether or not motion is involved. After all we, the perceivers, are always localizing objects in space with respect to ourselves. That activity entails its reciprocal of localizing ourselves with respect to the objects. This process has been recognized in the long history of thinking about the externalization of objects in the world. British empiricist philosophers proposed a psychological basis for attributing sensed objects to an external world. J. S. Mill (1865) ascribed belief in an external world to the "permanent possibilities of sensation." In a related vein, at least since the time of Weber's (1848) paper entitled "Über die Umstände, durch welche man geleitet wird, Empfindungen auf äussere Objecte zu beziehen," the condition under which objects are perceived to be external relative to the observer has been attributed to the fact that surround and O motion are reciprocally coupled in the above sense. Moreover, if one considers the functional dependence between these movements in one or more dimensions, a metric for spatial position can be derived. A simple case is the one in which parallax is used to derive distance between observer and object. Since normally the body and its parts are never at rest, the distance-sensing organs are continually in motion and the object-observer reciprocity obtains.

Telepresence, Presence, and Virtual Worlds

In recent years, the improvements in display and movement-monitoring devices have greatly improved the technology for human control of remote operations: teleoperation for short. Such remote control is highly desirable in inaccessible and dangerous environments. The operator's movements are transduced and made to control, let us say, a remote robot with humanlike appendages. The robot's sensors, in turn, report back to the operator the visual, auditory, and other sensory consequences of the robot's movements in its environment. Under these conditions, the phenomenon called telepresence has sometimes been reported (Held & Durlach, 1992). The operator perceives himself/herself at the site of the robot. By substituting a powerful computer with a large memory it is possible to replace the robot and external environment. The operator's movements are then transduced and fed into the computer which is programmed to generate sensory consequences, contingent upon the operator's movements, which are fed back to the operator. When carefully done, a virtual world can be created with the observer acting and feeling present in it. A certain amount of mysticism has accrued to the notion of presence. After all, can one really be transported, even if it is only "as if" to a remote location? We suggest that the phenomenon is really not mysterious, that it can be comprehended on the basis of what we already know about the perception of the observer's motion and sense of location discussed above. In this manner we can see the influence of Gunnar Johansson even in the most up-to-date issues posed by new technology.

References

Dichgans, J., & Brandt, T. (1978). Visual-vestibular interaction: Effects on self-motion perception and postural control. In R. Held, H. Leibowitz, & L. Teuber (Eds.), *Handbook of sensory physiology* (Vol. VIII, pp. 755–804). New York: Springer.

Finke, R., & Held, R. (1978). State reversals of optically induced tilt and torsional eye movements. *Perception & Psychophysics, 23*, 337–340.

Held, R. (1961). Exposure-history as a factor in maintaining stability of perception and coordination. *Journal of Nervous Mental Diseases, 132*, 26–32.

Held, R., & Durlach, N. (1992). Telepresence. *Presence, 1*, 109–112.

Helmholtz, H. v. (1910). *Handbuch der physiologischen Optik*. Vol. 3. (p. 2 in English Translation by J. P. C. Southall; reprinted by Dover Press, 1962).

Howard, I. (1982). *Human visual orientation*. New York: Wiley.

Johansson, G. (1977). Studies on visual perception of locomotion. *Perception, 6*, 365–376. [Chapter 9, this volume.]

Leibowitz, H., Johnson, C., & Isabelle, E. (1972). Peripheral motion detection and refractive error. *Science, 177*, 1207–1208.

Mill, J. S. (1865). Examination of Sir William Hamilton's Philosophy.

Weber, E. H. (1848). Über die Umstande, duch welche man geleitet wird, Empfindungen auf äussere Objecte zu beziehen. *Berichte über die Verhandlungen der Königlich Sachsischen Gesellshaft der Wissenshaften zu Leipzig* (Zweiter Band, pp. 226–257).

Welch, R. B. (1978). *Perceptual modification, adaptation to altered sensory environments*. New York: Academic Press.

Measuring with the Optic Sphere

Claes von Hofsten
Umeå University

David N. Lee
University of Edinburgh

Abstract: A surreptitious recording of a conversation between two of the symposium discussants sitting drinking beer on the rocks near Gunnar Johansson's summer house on an island in the Baltic. They came to talk about the problem of perceiving specific distance and how this could be accomplished. The conclusion was that although perceived distance is always relative, it may be anchored to physical space through a number of different scaling factors. The prime function of such scaling is to establish a link between perception and action.

Claes (C). In the optic sphere theory, Gunnar (Johansson, 1991) stresses the problem of perceiving specific distance. Perceiving the specific scale of space is crucial for at least two kinds of tasks—in the guidance of actions and in the judgment of specific spatial properties. In the guidance of action, information about specific distances and sizes are essential as all movements have to be scaled relative to action space. Specific size judgments are needed, for instance, in identifying objects that come in different sizes, like humans, and in comparing objects to one's own size. In perceiving an orange, specific space perception is thus needed not only for being able to grasp the orange, but also for deciding its value—for example, whether it is big enough to satisfy one's thirst or not.

David (D). By "specific distance" I take it Gunnar means "specific to, or relative to the person or, in general, the animal." As you say, perceiving distance in this sense is critical for guiding actions. For what an animal has to do is to fit its actions to the environment. The fit, of course, has to be both spatial and temporal. In reaching out to grasp your orange, you close your fingers in synchrony with the movement of your hand toward the orange. The need to achieve a spatio-temporal fit is even more evident if the orange is thrown to you and you have to catch it.

C. Yes, and this is only possible if your perceptual system and your movement system are scaled to each other.

D. So, to get at the problem of specific distance perception that Gunnar has raised, why don't we consider a particular movement skill as an illustration? How about the problem of steering that sailboat over there tightly around a buoy? That would be something close to Gunnar's heart—particularly as he built the boat—and it would also fit in nicely with those beautiful experiments he showed us on perception of waves (Johansson & Börjesson, 1991).

C. That sounds good. The problem of sailing tightly around a buoy is in many ways similar to catching a ball, so why don't we consider both examples. Where should we start?

D. Well, one thing the sailor has to do is perceive when they will be level with the buoy so they can start turning at the right time. The information in the optic flow field about time-to-nearest-approach to the buoy is the same as for a ball (Lee, 1976).

C. Yes, in order to catch a ball, a person must be able to judge the time at which contact can be made and the location of this place of contact in space. However, unless the ball is coming straight toward the eye, the optic expansion pattern of the ball does not specify how far away from the eye the ball is going to pass. A large ball moving fast and passing far from the eye or a small ball moving slowly and passing close to the eye can produce similar optic expansion patterns. The absolute distance to the ball needs to be known to determine the right combination of values. Otherwise the person will not be able to place the hands in the appropriate area to intercept the ball. The problem is the same when turning around a buoy. Since the boat will not be heading straight for the buoy, the optic expansion pattern of the buoy does not specify how far away from it the boat is going to pass. But the passing distance of the buoy has to be perceived and regulated to get the turn right. If the expansion pattern of the ball or the buoy on the optic sphere does not supply the necessary distance information, how is the information obtained?

D. One way might be in terms of the overall flow field on the optic sphere—in particular the linear component of the flow field that is due to the linear motion of the observer relative to the environment.

C. It might also be explained in terms of the flow fields on two optic spheres, one centered on each eye.

D. I agree, but let's consider monocular vision first.

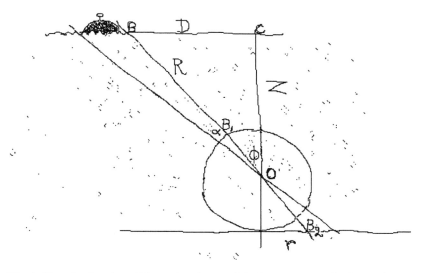

Fig. 1. How the drawing of the optic sphere and the buoy came out in the sand.

C. OK. So we have the linear component of the flow field. That is, in fact, the component Gunnar was talking about. But to be precise one needs to recognize that the flow field will normally also have a rotary component due to rotation of the optic sphere, as when the head turns. However, Warren's and Hannon's (1990) experiments show that the linear component can be perceptually separated out so I think we can agree it is reasonable to talk about the sailor picking up information from the linear optic flow.

So, let's consider an arbitrary patch B on the buoy. I think that I need to draw it up—here on this sandy patch (Fig. 1).

The cone of light from B to the point of observation O intersects the optic sphere in two points B_1 and B_2. As O moves in a straight line, B_1 and B_2 move on a great circle on the sphere. C is the point where the boat gets level with the buoy. Since the great circle, the points O and B, and the locomotor path all lie in one plane, we can just consider that plane. Since O is moving, the distances Z and R are decreasing over time while angle ϕ is increasing. D remains constant. Thus we have

$$Z/D = \cot \phi$$

and differentiating

$$\dot{Z}/D = d(\cot \phi)/dt$$

hence

$$Z/\dot{Z} = \cot \phi / (d(\cot \phi)/dt) \qquad (1)$$

$Z/\dot{Z}$ is what you've called the tau margin, in this case the time to get level with the buoy when traveling at a constant velocity.

D. Yes. This optical specification of the tau margin is particularly applicable to situations where the surface being approached has no fine-grain texture, so there are no thin optic cones reflecting from it to the point of observation; or where the surface contains an aperture through which the perceiver, in this case the sailor, is aiming to pass. All that is required for this specification to operate is the presence of "points" associated with surfaces, for instance, corners or other aspects of edges. Actually, I now think it is better, for a more general theory, to talk about the *tau function* rather than just the tau margin. The tau function (τ) of any variable X is simply X divided by its rate of change $\dot{X}$, that is

$$\tau(X) = X/\dot{X} \qquad (2)$$

Thus your equation can be written

$$\tau(Z) = \tau(\cot \phi) \qquad (3)$$

where $\tau(Z)$ is the tau function of Z, which we'd previously called the tau margin. This equation is equivalent to

$$\tau(Z) = \tau(r) \qquad (4)$$

where r is the projection of BC on a flat projection surface orthogonal to OC and unit distance behind O. This description of the optic flow field we've used before (Lee, 1980). When we consider projection onto a plane like this then $\tau(Z)$ is also equal to the tau function of the width of the optical patch of B on the plane.

C. The same doesn't quite apply to projection on the optic sphere though, does it? The basic equations there are

$$\dot{R} = \dot{Z} \cos \phi$$

$$Z = R \cos \phi$$

hence

$$Z/\dot{Z} = R/\dot{R} \cos^2 \phi \qquad (5)$$

D. The only other step needed is to consider the optic cone from the surface patch B to O. If α is the (small) angle subtended at O by B in the direction perpendicular to the plane of movement BOC, then α is inversely proportional to R and so

$$\tau(R) = R/\dot{R} = -\alpha/\dot{\alpha} = -\tau(\alpha) \qquad (6)$$

hence from (5) and (6)

$$\tau(Z) = -\tau(\alpha)\cos^2\phi \qquad (7)$$

C. That's fine as far as it goes, but we've been talking only about temporal information. What about spatial and kinematic information? For example, Johansson (1973) tested the ability of subjects to utilize motion parallax for the perception of specific distance in near space. When the subject moved his or her head, room lights were switched off and only four monocularly viewed reference lights were seen. When the head stopped moving, the reference lights were switched off, the room lights were switched on, and the subject was asked to estimate the distance to the remembered position of the reference lights by adjusting the distance to a binocularly seen pointer. Performance was almost as good as if the reference lights had been seen binocularly, which shows that motion parallax is related to an internally consistent spatial system which may be mapped onto the binocular system. However, it does not demonstrate that monocular motion parallax gives specific distance in itself. On the contrary, in order to get specific distance from motion parallax it has to be related to an external stable referent.

D. I don't think it has to be necessarily an *external* referent.

C. You mean if the movement of the person is self-produced, a possibility would be to calibrate specific visual space by sensing kinesthetically how much one is moving. This is what Johansson proposes in his optic sphere model (Johansson, 1991). The problem with such a reference system, however, is that it requires kinesthesis to supply specific spatial values, but how this is done is by no means obvious. Thus the basic problem is not solved, it is just transferred to another modality.

D. But that is inevitable, surely. It is not meaningful to talk about *absolute* distance perception. Distance perception has to be relative and this is true for all modalities!

C. The question is: relative to what? Going back to this drawing in the sand and the equations, we basically have

$$\tau(Z) = Z/\dot{Z} \qquad\qquad\qquad (8)$$

$$Z = D \cot \phi \qquad\qquad\qquad (9)$$

Therefore $\tau(Z)$ is optically specified and so is ϕ. But what about Z, $\dot{Z}$, and D? We have those three unknowns and only two equations.

D. But if we can specify one of the unknowns in terms of a quantity X say, then the equations would be solvable in terms of X. We would be measuring the unknowns relative to the quantity X. In other words X would be a scaling factor of perceived space. Under such conditions, the passing distance to the buoy would be specified in terms of X and the same would be true for the passing distance to the ball. However, X does not necessarily need be the same quantity in the sailing and the ball-catching situations. Let's see what scaling factors might be effective in these two situations.

C. Probably the best known scaling factor of perceived space is interocular distance. It could be effective in both situations. Already, Bishop Berkeley (1709) showed that if the convergence angle is known, then the distance to the point of convergence is also potentially known. More recently, however, there was much controversy about the status of convergence as information about distance, because geometrical values and perceived distance did not seem to relate in a simple way (see e.g., Woodworth & Schlosberg, 1954). However, an experiment I did a few years ago showed that convergence does have potential for scaling binocular space (Hofsten, 1976). Individual subjects' distance estimations could be precisely accounted for by the hypothesis that different subjects have different but relatively stable rest convergence and that it is the difference between the convergence to an object and the rest convergence that determines perceived distance. If the distance corresponding to rest convergence is known, then binocular space can be veridically calibrated.

A good study that supports the position that binocular information can play a role in interceptive action is one by Judge and Bradford (1988). They had subjects catch balls which they viewed with their interocular distance artificially increased by means of a telestereoscope. Though looking through the instrument had very little effect on catching accuracy during monocular viewing, the initial effect during binocular viewing was great. However, after only a short training period with the device, performance was back almost to normal. When the device was removed, subjects again missed the ball but the errors were in the opposite direction. This shows two things. First, convergence is an important factor in scaling reaching space. Second, the system can easily recalibrate (see also Hofsten, 1979).

D. Another good study on the role of binocular information in controlling interceptive action is by McLeod, McLaughlin, and Nimmo-Smith (1985), who measured subjects' performance when attempting to hit a falling ball with a bat. They found that binocular vision did *not* improve timing accuracy. Monocular information, which could have been given by tau, was quite adequate to achieve the 5 ms timing accuracy that they found. However, binocular vision did improve *spatial* accuracy. This does not necessarily mean that the improvement was due to the binocular system exploiting the *differences* between the two eyes' views, which is what binocular convergence and stereopsis are based on. Spatial perception could equally well have been more accurate because there is *concordant* information available binocularly, and having two eyes working on picking up the information can be better than having just one eye on the job (Jones & Lee, 1981).

C. That two eyes see better than one is an often forgotten aspect of binocular vision. But it is undeniable that binocular vision also exploits the *differences* between the two eyes' views to access spatial information. Both Judge and Bradford (1988) and Hofsten (1976) demonstrate that. Additional evidence has been provided by Hofsten, Rosengren, Pick, and Neely (1992). We had subjects catch balls during binocular and monocular viewing in normal room lighting and in complete darkness with a luminous ball. Catching performance was superior with binocular vision, especially under normal room lighting. However, ball catching was not exclusively dependent on binocular information. A substantial proportion of the balls in the monocular conditions were either caught or contacted with the hand by the subjects. This was also true for the dark condition. Binocular vision added precision but was apparently not necessary for catching the ball. This raises the question as to what kind of information about specific distance could be utilized by the visual system in the monocular situation.

I don't know of any experiment testing the relative importance of monocular and binocular vision in steering a sailing boat tightly around a buoy, but I can easily imagine how to set it up. That would be something to think about for the next grant proposal. First of all, we need a sailing boat to conduct the experiments.

D. What a good idea! Then we could investigate a possible monocular scaling factor—eye height—in a rather interesting situation. If a person is sailing, walking, or driving across a more or less level surface, the D coordinate (here in the drawing) of every point ahead on the ground beneath the path of movement of the eye is equal to the eye height. Thus, if we apply Equations (8) and (9) to any such element we get a solution for $\dot{Z}$, the speed of movement, in terms of eye height. And since $\dot{Z}$ is the same for all environmental surface elements, the spatial coordinates of each is, therefore, specified in terms of eye height.

This would mean that if a person were using this information and eye height were lowered unbeknownst to the person, then speed, distance, and size should all appear larger. The movie "The Incredible Shrinking Man" (1957) used this principle by placing the camera close to the floor in a doll's house. This made the house look the size of a normal house and so a cat peering in the window appeared enormous. Mark (1987) studied the effect in a very nice experiment. He had subjects stand and look through an aperture in a screen at some steps. The screen prevented them from seeing that the floor on which the steps stood was actually higher than the one on which they stood. Consequently they perceived the steps to be higher than they actually were.

C. Also, when they first introduced the Boeing 747 Jumbo jet, there were several incidents where pilots were taxiing too fast. They were, of course, all used to smaller airplanes where the cockpit was closer to the ground.

But to get back to the grant. What if we had the boat sinking as it approached the buoy? From what you have said, the person should overestimate the distance to the buoy more and more as they sank lower and lower.

D. That's right. And just as they are submerging and their eye height was shrinking to zero they would appear to be moving an infinite distance away from everything! However, I'm not sure we would get ethical approval for that experiment.

C. Yes, maybe we had better stick to catching balls. Using eye height as a scaling factor would seem to require a moving perceiver and be mostly applicable to perceiving distance to points on the ground. It appears to be less adequate for scaling the distance to an approaching ball coming out of a blue sky. Therefore, we need to find another scaling factor for the catching task, because catching is also fairly good under monocular conditions.

Might known size of an object be used? This is one of the traditional cues to distance and is founded on the fact that if the size of an object is known, the distance to it is also potentially known. Both adults (Ittelson, 1951) and infants (Yonas, Pettersen, & Granrud, 1982) have been found to be influenced by familiar size in perceiving the distance to a target. There are, however, certain shortcomings with familiar size. First, knowledge of the size of each specific target needs to be stored. Second, if objects of a specific form exist in several different sizes, there is no way of knowing which target is seen at a specific time. For instance, if known size is an important determiner of perceived specific distance, subjects should perform poorly under monocular viewing when presented with approaching balls of different sizes. Another possible source of information about specific distance to an object is gravity. Todd (1981) showed that this parameter could be utilized to determine whether a ball in flight would land in front of or behind the observer. But gravity might be more informative than that.

Watson, Banks, Hofsten, and Royden (1992) showed that if the effect of gravity is known, then the absolute distance to a falling object can be derived from the vertical acceleration of its optic projection on a plane. Going back to our drawing, the formula is simply

$$Z/g = 1/\ddot{r} \qquad (10)$$

where g is the gravitational acceleration. Since g is the same irrespective of size or any other target property, it would be of great advantage if subjects could use this source of information compared to familiar size. There is only one gravity constant to be remembered compared to numerous familiar sizes.

D. As you'll remember, Johansson and Jansson (1967) found that observers are sensitive to gravity as information about specific size or distance. When subjects viewed their films of divers diving into a pool or high jumpers descending and had to set the film speed so that the event looked natural, their settings were rather accurate. This suggests that they were, in effect, sensitive to the information in your Equation (10).

C. Yes, there is other indirect, but persuasive evidence that human observers use g as information about specific distance. Cinematographers have long been aware of the problem of making miniature objects appear full sized when filmed. If filmed at projection speed, a miniature car falling off a cliff or a miniature skyscraper collapsing look, when projected, like a miniature car and a miniature skyscraper, no matter how realistic the surroundings appear. However, if the miniature event is filmed faster than projection speed, then when the film is projected the objects appear larger and further away. If g is utilized for perceiving specific distance, the spatial scale should vary with the square of the time scale. This follows straight from Equation (10). For instance, if the miniature event were filmed at four times projection speed, then the filmed object should appear 16 times larger. When we examined the cinematography literature on special effects we found that this is exactly the rule-of-thumb that is used (e.g., Spottiswoode, 1969).

D. g might also be used as a scaling factor when it is the person that is falling rather than an object. When running, for example, the body is in short free fall once every step. Therefore, during each step the distances to environmental surface elements are specified in terms of g as per your Equation (10). Alternatively, expressing the relation on the optic sphere, the equation is

$$Z/g = 1/ (d^2 \tan \phi /dt^2) \qquad (11)$$

C. Could there be more information revealed by the subject's own activity which could act as a scaling factor of perceived space?

D. Most natural locomotor activity is cyclical, whether on the ground, in the air, or in water. The frequency of strides, wingbeats, or undulations of the body tends to be regular—though it can be changed, of course, to fit the demands of the environment. When sailing, too, the waves tend to have a regular rhythm. Suppose then that an animal is moving linearly at a constant speed with a constant locomotor rhythm. If the tau margin for an arbitrary surface element is $\tau_n(Z)$ at the start of the nth locomotor cycle, then

$$\tau_n(Z) - \tau_{n-1}(Z) = T \qquad\qquad (12)$$

where T is the period of the locomotor cycle. Therefore

$$\tau_n(Z) / (\tau_n(Z) - \tau_{n-1}(Z)) = \tau_n(Z) / T = \text{number of cycles to point of near-}$$
est approach to the element   (13)

Thus the Z and D coordinates of an element, and the time to nearest approach, can all be scaled in terms of locomotor cycles. Visual regulation of gait to hit the take-off board in long jumping (Lee et al., 1982) and when running over irregularly spaced stepping stones (Warren et al., 1986) probably involve scaling in terms of locomotor cycles. In both cases, the runner adjusts cycle time by regulating the vertical impulse applied to the ground in order to control where the foot strikes the ground.

C. I can see a problem here. You said that this method of scaling assumes that you travel with constant speed and with a constant locomotor rhythm. What happens if you speed up or slow down, and what happens when you run over rough terrain? Then the locomotor cycles might be different for every step you take.

D. In principle that should not matter. Perceived action space could be scaled afresh at each locomotor cycle. Suppose, for example, you were decreasing your cycle time as you approached, at constant speed, a stepping stone from which you wanted to spring. Then all you would need to perceive would be how long the last step cycle had to be in terms of the length of the penultimate step cycle. This you could effectively do using Equation (13). The procedure could work adequately well even if you were changing your overground speed. Providing your acceleration or deceleration was not too high, the error in effectively assuming constant speed would not be great.

C. So what you are saying is that, by performing an action, perceived space can be scaled in terms of that action.

D. Yes. And I don't think the action used for scaling needs to be of the same form as the action to be controlled. For example, animals such as cats frequently bob their heads when they are stationary and preparing to leap to something. In this case, the velocity, $\dot{Z}$, of the environmental surface elements relative to the point of observation will be determined solely by the head movement. $\dot{Z}$ is thus specified in terms of the head action. Hence, from Equations (8) and (9), the spatial coordinates Z and D of each surface element are also specified in terms of the head action and the optically specified quantities $(-\tau(Z))$ and ϕ. It is reasonable to suppose that head action could be intrinsically related to leaping action, and so distance would be specified in terms of leaping action.

C. That is an interesting idea. So, you probe perceptual space by performing a defined action. You then use the perceptual effect of the probing action to scale perceptual space and calibrate other actions to fit the space.

D. We seem to agree, then, that what is common with all the different ways of calibrating the visual system is the use of scaling factors through which perceived space can be related to physical space, whether the scaling factor is some known body dimension like eye height or interocular distance, or some known external property such as the size of an object or the acceleration due to gravity, or some defined movement.

C. Yes, and by far the most important application of specific distance perception is in controlling movement. Movements are performed in the physical world and need to be programmed in terms of specific physical values. The scaling factors used to anchor perceived space in physical space are thus also essential for mapping perceived space onto movement space. This is what is of basic importance, establishing a relationship between perception and action.

D. Scaling factors are, of course, merely intermediate variables. They comprise possible ways of connecting, say, perceptual space and movement space, but do not themselves feature in either space. They are physical properties that can be exploited to establish a link, rather like properties of electronic components in a telephone system which make it possible for two people to relate when miles apart.

C. The intermediate variables are in effect "dummy." They are only necessary for connecting perception and action. By moving around and perceiving the consequences of our movements, we can continue to keep a tight fit between perceived space and movement space. It is only if a scaling factor suddenly changes its value that the fit is upset, like when Judge and Bradford (1988) artificially increased the effective interocular separation by having subjects view the world through a telestereoscope. Thus, the role of the scaling factor, like interocular distance in this example, is to allow the connection between perceived space and movement space in the same way as a catalyst enters into a chemical reaction.

This has important implications for development. When the body grows, the values of the scaling factors increase slowly, but through active perceiving and moving around the fit between perception and action can easily be maintained. The process of recalibration is constantly going on. Every time we move and perceive the consequences of our movements, the fit is probed.

D. Talking of which, someone seems to be probing around in the dark behind us. Oh! Hi Gunnar! We were just talking about measuring with the optic sphere. This has been a tremendous party, many thanks.

References

Berkeley, G. (1709). *An essay towards a new theory of vision.* Dublin: Yeremy Pepyat.

Hofsten, C. von (1976). The role of convergence in visual space perception. *Vision Research, 16,* 193–198.

Hofsten, C. von (1979). Recalibration of the convergence system. *Perception, 8,* 37–42.

Hofsten, C. von, Rosengren, K., Pick, H. L., & Neely, G. (1992). The role of binocular vision in ball catching. *Journal of Motor Behavior, 24,* 329–338.

The incredible shrinking man. (1957). Jack Arnold (dir.) USA: Universal International. (Film)

Ittelson, W. H. (1951). Size as a cue to distance; static localizations. *American Journal of Psychology, 64,* 54–67.

Johansson, G. (1973). Monocular motion parallax and near space perception. *Perception, 2,* 135–146.

Johansson, G. (1991). *Elaborating the optic sphere model.* Unpublished manuscript. Uppsala University, Department of Psychology.

Johansson, G., & Börjesson, E. (1991). *Studies of perception of waves.* Unpublished manuscript. Uppsala University, Department of Psychology.

Johansson, G., & Jansson, G. (1967). *The perception of free fall.* Seminar paper. Uppsala University, Department of Psychology.

Jones, R. K., & Lee, D. N. (1981). Why two eyes are better than one: The two views of binocular vision. *Journal of Experimental Psychology: Human Perception and Performance, 7,* 30–40.

Judge, S. J., & Bradford, C. M. (1988). Adaptation to telestereoscopic viewing measured by one-handed ball-catching performance. *Perception, 17,* 783–802.

Lee, D. N. (1976). A theory of visual control of braking based on information about time-to-collision. *Perception, 5,* 437–459.

Lee, D. N. (1980). The optic flow field: The foundation of vision. *Philosophical Transactions of the Royal Society of London, B290,* 169–179.

Lee, D. N., Lishman, J. A., & Thomson, J. A. (1982). Visual regulation of gait in long jumping. *Journal of Experimental Psychology: Human Perception and Performance, 8*, 448–459.

Mark, L. S. (1987). Eyeheight scaled information about affordances: A study of sitting and stair climbing. *Journal of Experimental Psychology: Human Perception and Performance, 13*, 360–370.

McLeod, P., McLaughlin, C., & Nimmo-Smith, I. (1985). Information encapsulation and automaticity: Evidence from the visual control of finely timed actions (pp. 391–400). *Attention & performance XI*. Hillsdale, NJ: Erlbaum.

Spottiswoode, R. (1969). *The focal encyclopedia of film and television techniques.* New York: Hastings House.

Todd, J. T. (1981). Visual information about moving objects. *Journal of Experimental Psychology: Human Perception and Performance, 7*, 795–810.

Warren, W. H., & Hannon, D. J. (1990). Eye movements and optical flow. *Journal of the Optical Society of America, A7*, 160–169.

Warren, W. H., Young, D. S., & Lee, D. N. (1986). Visual control of step length during running over irregular terrain. *Journal of Experimental Psychology: Human Perception and Performance, 12*, 259–266.

Watson, J. S., Banks, M. S., Hofsten, C. von, & Royden, C. S. (1992). Gravity as a monocular cue for absolute distance and/or absolute size. *Perception, 21*, 69–76.

Woodworth, R. S., & Schlosberg, H. (1954). *Experimental psychology.* New York: Holt.

Yonas, A., Pettersen, L., & Granrud, C. E. (1982). Infants' sensitivity to familiar size as information for distance. *Child Development, 53*, 1285–1290.

Optic Sphere Theory

On the Optic Sphere Theory and the Nature of Visual Information

James T. Todd

Ohio State University

Abstract: This paper examines the optic sphere theory recently proposed by Johansson and Börjesson (1989) to account for the perception of surface slant under wide angle viewing. It is argued that although polar perspective is necessary to cope with wide angle conditions, there is no intrinsic advantage of spheres over other types of projection surfaces for the analysis of optical motion. Also considered are several different types of optical deformation, which may require an even more radical departure from traditional theory.

In his long and distinguished career, Gunnar Johansson has made numerous contributions to our understanding of human motion perception. His most recent research in collaboration with Erik Börjesson (Johansson & Börjesson, 1989) has focused on the importance of wide angle stimulation in the perceptual analysis of optical flow. Many other contemporary theorists have attempted to model the optic array as if it were a picture plane, but Johansson and Börjesson believe that this approach is fundamentally misguided. Because the human eye is spherical, they argue, the picture plane approximation is only valid for small visual angles, and cannot therefore provide an adequate account of the potential information in wide angle viewing arising from the effects of perspective.

In contrast to these picture plane models of the optic array, Johansson and Börjesson have proposed a new alternative, which they refer to as the optic sphere theory. Their model consists of two components: a spherical projection surface independent of the retina that is used to characterize the array of light reflected from the environment at the nodal point of the eye; and a neurophysiological processor that is able to measure the structure of this array and to determine its relative orientation with respect to the eye and the direction of gravity. In developing this model Johansson and Börjesson have identified a simple invariant within the changing structure of the optic sphere that provides potential information about the slants of observed surfaces under wide angle conditions. They have also obtained empirical support for the psychological validity of this analysis by showing that the accuracy and reliability of observers' slant judgments of moving surfaces are enhanced by wide angle viewing.

Although I believe these are important contributions, in the present essay I will adopt the role of critic in an effort to facilitate a continuing debate on the fundamental issues of visual space perception and the nature of optical information. My specific goals are twofold: First I will argue that some of Johansson and Börjesson's criticisms of traditional models are unfounded and that their "new" alternative is in fact quite compatible with many other existing analyses. Second, I will then go on to describe a number of issues involving how we characterize the nature of optical motion that I believe will require a much more radical departure from current approaches.

What Is the Optic Array?

In order to avoid the metaphor of pictures or retinal images, Gibson (1979) described the optic array at a point of observation as a cone of visual solid angles. In performing a mathematical analysis, however, it is often useful to describe the structure of this cone of light at its intersection with some hypothetical projection surface. Although almost all existing analyses of visual information employ this technique, there are important distinctions among different theories involving the shape of the projection surface and the relative orientations of the intersecting light rays.

Consider first the issue of shape. For many theorists, including Johansson and Börjesson (1989), the most logical way of analyzing visual information is to adopt a hemispherical projection surface, because that is the approximate shape of the human retina. It is important to keep in mind, however, that the structure of light does not depend on the specific anatomical structure of the human eye and could be analyzed just as easily using some other form of projection surface such as a plane (e.g., Todd, 1981) or a cylinder (e.g., Lee, 1974). For the purposes of a formal analysis, the choice of a projection surface is purely a matter of mathematical convenience, since a description of visual information in terms of one projection surface can always be uniquely transformed into a description in terms of any other. It is for this reason that Johansson and Börjesson's criticism of the picture plane approach seems overly strong. While there may be aspects of optical structure that are most conveniently described using spherical coordinates, there is no intrinsic advantage to this particular coordinate framework for dealing with the effects of perspective in wide angle viewing (e.g., see Todd, 1981; Lee, 1974).

A more important distinction among existing theories involves the relative orientations of the incoming light rays as they intersect the projection surface. Some models, including the optic sphere theory, use a polar or central projection where the incoming light rays intersect the projection surface at oblique angles to one another as they converge on the point of observation. Other models employ an orthographic or parallel projection where it is assumed that the light rays are all parallel to one another. Although a perfect parallel projection can never be achieved under natural viewing conditions, it is closely approximated for objects that subtend small visual angles and may therefore be useful for modeling human vision when an observed object is relatively small or viewed from a relatively long distance. Analyses based on polar projection have no restrictions on viewing distance from a purely mathematical point of view. However, any model that specifically requires measurable effects of perspective (e.g., Longuet-Higgins, 1981) may only be useful in practice for objects that are relatively large or a small distance from the point of observation. There is an overwhelming amount of evidence that human observers can perceive the layout of the environment under either parallel or polar projection, but a theoretical explanation for this high degree of flexibility remains a mystery.

What Is Optical Motion?

One important limitation of the optic sphere theory in its current state of development concerns the range of possible events for which it is applicable. Like most other theorists who have considered the problem of motion perception, Johansson and Börjesson have restricted their analysis to the projected motions of identifiable feature points, such as the vertices of a polyhedron or small inhomogeneities of reflectance on a smoothly curved surface. A fundamental property of identifiable feature points in three-dimensional space is that they can be mapped one-to-one onto a corresponding set of identifiable feature points within a two-dimensional optical projection, which can retain their identities over a sequence of multiple views. I shall refer to this viewpoint invariant mapping as the property of projective correspondence (see Todd, 1985). Its defining characteristic is that multiple views of an identifiable image feature must all correspond to the same physical point in three-dimensional space. A similar projective correspondence can also be defined for multiple images of identifiable space curves. However, because of the aperture problem, it may be difficult in that case to track the trajectory of any specific point (e.g., see Hildreth, 1984; Mingolla, Todd, & Norman, 1992).

Projective correspondence of identifiable feature points over multiple views is a necessary condition for virtually all computational models for determining structure from motion or stereopsis, but there are several other types of optical deformation that do not satisfy this condition (cf. Gibson, 1979). Consider, for example, the projected motion of a solid object that is bounded by a smooth homogeneous surface. At each point on the object we can define two vectors: one that is normal to the surface, and another that is oriented toward the point of observation. The optical contour that bounds the object's projection will correspond to the locus of points for which these vectors are perpendicular (i.e., the contour is formed by the visual rays that just graze the object's surface). If the object moves or is viewed stereoscopically this optical contour will be deformed, but the locus of surface points to which it corresponds will also be continuously changing (e.g., imagine a head viewed frontally and in profile). Analyses that assume projective correspondence are of little use with this type of optical deformation - even as a local approximation. Indeed, it is often the case that the optical motion of the bounding contour will be in one direction while the projected motion of any identifiable point on that contour is in the opposite direction. Although the optical deformations of smooth occlusion contours are theoretically anomalous for models that assume projective correspondence, there is a growing amount of evidence that such deformations provide perceptually salient information for actual human observers (Todd, 1985; Loomis & Eby, 1988; Cortese & Andersen, 1991; Pollick, 1989; Norman, Todd, & Fukuda, 1992), and there have also been a few attempts to develop alternative computational models of how this information could potentially be analyzed (Giblin & Weiss, 1987; Blake & Cipolla, 1989; Siebert & Waxman, 1991).

Another type of optical deformation that can violate the assumption of projective correspondence is produced by the motions of cast shadows. Shadow deformations can be subdivided into two distinct categories: (1) those produced by an observer's motion with respect to a fixed scene, and (2) those produced by the motions of other objects or their sources of illumination. Let us first consider the case where a fixed scene is viewed from multiple vantage points (e.g., as in binocular vision), such that all visible objects maintain a constant relation with all sources of illumination. When an observer moves within a static environment, shadow borders remain bound to fixed positions in three-dimensional space, which satisfies the condition of projective correspondence. Thus, they can be analyzed using existing algorithms to determine the three-dimensional structures of the background surfaces on which they are cast. A very different pattern of deformation occurs, however, when an object moves relative to the light source. A shadow of a moving object will itself move over the background surface, which violates the assumption of projective correspondence. Nevertheless, Norman, Todd, and Fukuda (1992) have recently demonstrated that human observers can successfully analyze this type of deformation to distinguish between rigid and nonrigid motions of an otherwise invisible object.

Gradations of shading on a smoothly curved surface are another important property of optical structure for which object motion and observer motion produce distinctly different patterns of deformation. To better appreciate the structure of image shading, it is useful to consider a set of points on a surface that all have the same luminance. For a smoothly curved surface with homogeneous reflectance, these points will be aligned along continuous space curves, which are called isoluminance contours or isophotes (Koenderink & van Doorn, 1976, 1980, 1982). There are several different factors that can influence how these isophotes deform over time within a visual image. Most previous analyses of shading deformations have focused exclusively on observer motion relative to matte (Lambertian) surfaces, which maintain a fixed relation with their sources of illumination (e.g., see Horn & Shunk, 1979; Nagel, 1981, 1987). The optical deformations of the isophotes in that case satisfy the condition of projective correspondence and can therefore be analyzed using existing algorithms to determine a surface's three-dimensional structure from motion or stereopsis. Existing analyses of three-dimensional structure from intensity-based motion or stereo will not work, however, when an object moves relative to the light source or for surfaces that contain specular highlights, because the isoluminance contours under those conditions will move over an object's surface thus destroying the property of projective correspondence. Although there have been several demonstrations reported in the literature that human observers can perceptually interpret all of these different types of shading deformations (Blake & Bulthoff, 1990, 1991; Bulthoff & Mallot, 1988; Todd, 1985), the precise mechanisms by which this is accomplished have yet to be revealed.

Still another type of optical motion that can violate the condition of projective correspondence involves the systematic deformations over time of higher order field structures such as texture fields. Consider a surface that is covered with a stochastically regular distribution of small blotches. In the optical projection of such a surface, the projected size of a blotch in any given region is determined by the slant of the surface in that region relative to the observer's direction of gaze. To describe the overall organization of these projected blotches it is useful to consider the isoarea contours in the image along which all of the depicted surface points have the same slant (see Todd & Mingolla, 1984). If a textured surface is viewed stereoscopically or in motion, the individual texture elements satisfy the condition of projective correspondence (i.e., each blotch remains fixed at a particular surface location), but this is not the case for the isoarea contours that define the pattern of texture gradients. When an object moves relative to the observer, the points that project to a given isoarea contour will slide over its surface, thus violating the condition of projective correspondence. In order to examine these latter deformations in isolation, it is possible to eliminate the coherent displacements of individual elements by creating a different random distribution of texture for each frame of a stereogram or an apparent motion sequence so that they are completely uncorrelated across the multiple views. If such a display is viewed stereoscopically it does not produce a compelling impression of a smoothly curved surface. If, however, the same pair of images is presented over time as part of an apparent motion sequence then the structure of the surface is perceived quite clearly as a scintillating object rotating rigidly in depth (see Todd, 1985).

It is interesting to note when considering this phenomenon that the deformations of isoarea texture contours are closely related to the deformations of isointensity contours when an object moves relative to the light source (see Todd & Mingolla, 1984). The isoarea contours are determined by the surface slant relative to the direction of gaze, while the isointensity contours (for a matte Lam-

Table 1.

Categories of Optical Deformation

	Observer Motion	Object Motion
Reflectance Contours		
Cast Shadows		
Lambertian Isophotes		
Isotexture Contours		
Smooth Occlusions		
Specular Isophotes		

bertian surface) are determined by the surface slant relative to the direction of illumination. Under some circumstances when both of these directions are the same (e.g., when a sequence of images is produced with a flash camera), the patterns of deformations for shading and texture will be formally identical in all respects. It seems reasonable to speculate, therefore, that the mechanisms involved in their perceptual analysis might be closely related as well.

Table 1 provides a summary of all of the different categories of optical deformation described above. The rows of this table represent different types of optical contours while the columns are used to distinguish observer motion from object motion. Note that some of the borders between cells in this table have been removed. These open areas combine classes of deformation that are formally equivalent. For example, the deformations of reflectance contours, shadow contours and isointensity contours caused by observer motion, and the deformations of reflectance contours caused by object motion are all formally equivalent in that they satisfy the condition of projective correspondence.

It would of course be unfair to single out Johansson and Börjesson for failing to deal with the many different types of optical deformation described in Table 1. Indeed, a fundamental limitation of all existing analyses of visual information is that they are only appropriate for specific types of optical deformation, and cannot function effectively in other contexts. This does not seem to be the case, however, for actual human vision. Although a specialized analysis can be theoretically useful in order to explain perceptual performance for a limited domain of experimental displays, one should not lose sight of the richness and variety of optical structure that occurs in natural vision. To accommodate this variety in a single theoretical analysis is likely to require something far more radical than anything that has been proposed to date.

References

Blake, A., & Bulthoff, H. H. (1990). Does the brain know the physics of specular reflection? *Nature, 343*, 165–168.

Blake, A., & Bulthoff, H. H. (1991). Shape from specularities: Computation and psychophysics. *Philosophical Transactions of the Royal Society London B, 331*, 237–252.

Blake, A., & Cipolla, R. (1989). *Robust estimation of surface curvature from deformation of apparent contours.* (Technical report OUEL 1278/89). University of Oxford, England.

Bulthoff, H. H., & Mallot, H. A. (1988). Integration of depth modules: Stereo and shading. *Journal of the Optical Society of America, 5*, 1749–1758.

Cortese, J. M., & Andersen, G. J. (1991). Recovery of 3-D shape from deforming contours. *Perception & Psychophysics, 49*, 315–327.

Giblin, P., & Weiss, R. (1987). Reconstruction of surfaces from profiles. In *Proceedings of the IEEE First International Conference on Computer Vision*, (pp. 136–144). Washington, DC: IEEE.

Gibson, J. J. (1979). *The ecological approach to visual perception.* Boston: Houghton Mifflin.

Hildreth, E. C. (1984). *The measurement of visual motion.* Cambridge, MA: MIT Press.

Horn, B. K. P., & Schunk, B. G. (1981). Determining optical flow. *Artificial Intelligence, 17*, 185–203.

Johansson, G., & Börjesson, E. (1989). Toward a new theory of vision in wide-angle space perception. *Ecological Psychology, 1*, 301–332. [Chapter 10, this volume.]

Koenderink, J. J., & van Doorn, A. J. (1976). The singularities of the visual mapping. *Biological Cybernetics, 24*, 51–59.

Koenderink, J. J., & van Doorn, A. J. (1980). Photometric invariants related to solid shape. *Optica Acta, 27*, 981–996.

Koenderink, J. J., & van Doorn, A. J. (1982). Perception of solid shape and spatial layout through photometric invariants. In R. Trappl (Ed.), *Cybernetics and systems research* (pp. 943–948). Amsterdam: North-Holland.

Lee, D. N. (1974). Visual information during locomotion. In R. B. MacLeod & H. Pick (Eds.), *Perception: Essays in honor of James Gibson*. Ithaca, NY: Cornell University Press.

Longuet-Higgins, H. C. (1981). A computer algorithm for reconstructing a scene from two projections. *Nature, 293*, 133–135.

Loomis, J. M., & Eby, D. W. (1988). Perceiving structure from motion: Failure of shape constancy. In *Proceedings from the Second International Conference on Computer Vision* (pp. 383–391). Washington, DC: IEEE.

Mingolla, E., Todd, J. T., & Norman, J. F. (1992). The perception of globally coherent motion. *Vision Research, 32*, 1015–1032.

Norman, J. F., Todd, J. T., & Fukuda, H. (1992) The visual perception of 3-dimensional structure from the deformation of shadows and occlusion contours. *Investigative Ophthalmology and Visual Science, 33*, 315.

Nagel, H. H. (1981). On the derivation of 3D rigid point configurations from image sequences. *Proceedings of the IEEE Conference on Pattern Recognition and Image Processing* (pp. 103–108). New York: IEEE Computer Society Press.

Nagel, H. H. (1987). On the estimation of optical flow: Relations between different approaches and some new results. *Artificial Intelligence, 33*, 299–324.

Pollick, F. E. (1989). Shape perception from dynamic occluding contours. *Investigative Ophthalmology and Visual Science, 30*, 264.

Siebert, M., & Waxman, A. M. (1991). Adaptive 3D-object recognition from multiple views. *IEEE Transactions on Pattern Analysis and Machine Intelligence*.

Todd, J. T. (1981). Visual information about moving objects. *Journal of Experimental Psychology: Human Perception & Performance, 7*, 795–810.

Todd, J. T. (1985). Perception of structure from motion: Is projective correspondence of moving elements a necessary condition? *Journal of Experimental Psychology: Human Perception & Performance, 11*, 689–710.

Todd, J. T., & Mingolla, E. (1984). The simulation of curved surfaces from patterns of optical texture. *Journal of Experimental Psychology: Human Perception and Performance, 10*, 734–739.

The Optic Sphere Theory as a
Slant Determining Mechanism[†]

Erik Börjesson

Uppsala University

Abstract: The optic sphere theory as a smart mechanism for determining slant was discussed. The mechanism involves an extrapolation of a projected arc to a great circle on the optic sphere and a location of the points of no change on that great circle. It was pointed out that this formulation restricts the theory to determination of slant of non-rotating distal lines. A general theory requires a new mechanism that analyzes the rotation of a great circle into component rotations. In an experiment a prediction from the theory was tested, namely that a long extrapolation from the projected arc to the point of no change should make slant judgment less accurate than a short extrapolation. Using only two pairs of dots defining the end points of two rods, the subjects had to decide which rod tilted most in depth. The results that supported the prediction were discussed in relation to alternative interpretations.

One of the most important aspects of the optic sphere theory as proposed by Johansson and Börjesson (1989) is the smart mechanism (Runeson, 1977) it provides for determination of slant. Figure 1 demonstrates this.

As a distal line L moves from L1 to L2 the projected arc of a great circle moves from B1 to B2. The arc defines a great circle that then rotates around the axis RA. This axis intersects the optic sphere in the two S-points. The two axes RA and L are constrained by a common plane defined by the great circle. This means that RA and L are parallel. The visual system can take advantage of this fact. First, the projected arc has to be extrapolated and second, the points of no change on the rotating great circle, the S-points, have to be located. With located S-points, the RA-axis is determined and also the orientation of L. In this way the visual system can easily without extensive computations determine distal slant from motion of a projected arc on the retina.

There are two comments on information with regard to the optic sphere and a distal line as described so far I would like to make. First, there is still more in-

---

[†] I gratefully acknowledge the assistance of Lars Eriksson in the data collection.

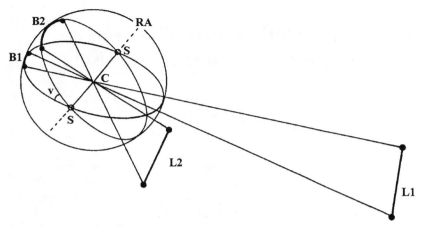

Fig. 1. The optic sphere and a moving distal line.

formation to be used and second there is still too little information to determine distal slant unless some additional constraint(s) is/are applied. Concerning the first issue, it should be noted that the optic sphere theory does not take into account any other characteristics of the projected arc than those needed to specify a great circle. There are especially two characteristics that are not taken into account and which certainly carry information about what is going on outside the sphere. They are the change of length of the arc and the gliding of the arc along the extrapolated great circle. None of these characteristics affects the great circle. However, they will be commented on below as a means for deciding translation and rotation. The second issue concerns correspondence between the orientation of RA and L. The optic sphere theory states that the points of no change on the extrapolated great circle are searched for. A prerequisite for this is that the great circle rotates around a *stationary* axis *on* the great circle. However, this is a special case. In a general case the stationary axis is not confined to the plane of the great circle. In Fig. 2, Column 1, the two situations are shown. The circles in Fig. 2 represent the optic sphere and the two ellipses in each circle represent two positions of a rotating great circle.

Rotation A shows a rotation around a stationary axis on the great circle and Rotation B shows a rotation around a stationary axis that is not on the great circle. In this latter case there are no points of no change on the great circle. As formulated above the optic sphere theory can not handle Rotation B since there are no points of no change on the great circle in this type of rotation. According to the optic sphere theory, the axis of rotation is parallel to a distal line. Further, the distal line is projected as the arc that specifies the great circle on the optic sphere. It follows that the axis of rotation must lie *on* the great circle. As a consequence, Rotation B has to be described as a rotation around an axis *on* the great circle. Since there is no such stationary axis we have to look for a *rotating*

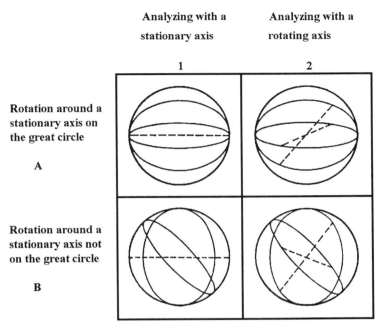

Fig. 2. Two different rotations (A and B) of a great circle analyzed with a stationary axis (1) and with a rotating axis (2). The axes are shown as dotted lines.

axis on the great circle. Any uniform rotation can be analyzed into two rotation components: One component is the rotation of the great circle around an axis on the great circle and the other component is the rotation of that axis itself. The Rotations A and B in Fig. 2 are analyzed in this way in Column 2. As noted above, the optic sphere theory analyzes Rotation A according to Column 1 with a stationary axis on the great circle. Rotation B should be analyzed according to Column 2 with a rotating axis on the great circle. However, there is an infinite number of such combinations of rotation components and the optic sphere theory does not tell how to select one of these combinations. Obviously, some kind of constraint is needed. One constraint would be to select the axis with the smallest angular velocity of rotation. This constraint can be considered to generalize the notion of locating the points of no change (angular velocity equals zero) that is the working principle with Rotation A. Another constraint would be to select a rotating axis that lies in the horizontal plane. In one of the experiments reported by Johansson and Börjesson (1989) it was found that when the number of dots carrying information of slant was reduced, there was an increasing tendency to perceive horizontal slant. This suggests a constraint of horizontal slant.

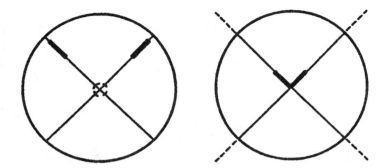

Fig. 3. Rotation of a great circle analyzed with a stationary axis (left) and with a rotating axis (right).

An ingenious mechanical model constructed by Johansson (1988, personal communication) mainly for educational reasons uses this horizontal constraint to solve the ambiguity. Due to technical circumstances the axis of rotation was locked to the horizontal plane. As a consequence, the motion of a distal line always produces in the mechanical model an axis of rotation that is horizontal. Rotations and translations of the distal line are correctly represented as long as the distal line stays in the horizontal plane. When the distal line deviates from the horizontal plane the mechanical model does not work.

Finally, an important special case will be considered in which characteristics of the projected arc might determine the selection of axis of rotation. As noted above, the arc's changes in size and position on the great circle do not affect the great circle as such and were not discussed by Johansson and Börjesson (1989). However, it seems plausible that characteristics of the arc should be included in the optic sphere theory. In Fig. 3 the circles represent the optic sphere and the two diameters in each circle represent two positions of a rotating great circle. The thick parts of the diameters show the projected arc. The motion of the great circle is the same in the left and the right sphere. In the left sphere the rotation of the great circle is analyzed as a rotation around a stationary axis on the great circle. The axis lies along the line of sight in the center of the small dotted circle. In the right sphere the rotation of the great circle is analyzed as a rotation of an axis of rotation (in this special case the rotation of the great circle around its axis equals zero). The rotating axis is perpendicular to the line of sight and shown as dotted lines. According to the principle of no change, the rotation of the great circle should be analyzed with a stationary axis as is the rotation in the left sphere in Fig. 3. Such an axis corresponds to a distal line parallel to the line of sight and translating from left to right or vice versa depending on the direction of rotation. Johansson (1991) has however suggested that when the arc is on the stationary axis a rotating axis is selected. In the right sphere in Fig. 3 this case is shown. One end of the arc lies on the stationary axis (along the line of sight on the center of the sphere) and the analysis is made with a rotating axis as the two positions of the rotating axis show. This axis corresponds to a distal line perpendicular to the line of sight rotating in a fronto-parallel plane. In addition to the position of the arc it seems plausible that changes of the arc's length might affect selection of axis of rotation for instance by application of the constraint of constant distal line length. For instance, given this constraint, the rotation of the great circle in Fig. 3 would always, irrespective of the position of the arc, be analyzed with a rotating axis if the arc had a constant length throughout the motion. The only way to maintain a constant distal length in this case is to locate the distal motion (that is rotation) in a fronto-parallel plane. Applications of distal constraints might in this way resolve the problem of selection of axis of rotation. But, do these constraints violate the computational free quality of the optic sphere theory?

To summarize, any uniform rotation of a great circle can be considered as the sum of two component rotations; a rotation of the great circle around an axis on the great circle and a rotation of this axis itself. The rotation of the great circle around its axis corresponds to a translation of a distal line slanted in depth and the rotation of the axis itself corresponds to a rotation of the distal line. The optic sphere theory as described by Johansson and Börjesson (1989) suggests a constraint that states that a stationary axis of rotation is selected. This means that only translating, non-rotating distal lines can be analyzed. In order to include distal lines that translate and rotate, the visual system has to do what it is good at as shown by Johansson (1950, 1964) since the 1950s: to analyze motions into components. Taking for granted that a rotation can be analyzed into a combination of rotation components some constraint(s) is/are needed to decide which combination is selected. These constraints might deal with the angular velocity or the plane of the rotating axis. Two additional possible constraints are position of the arc relative to the stationary axis and constant distal line length. The latter distal constraint puts some computational load on the theory.

Experiment

As has been noted above, the visual system according to the optic sphere theory extrapolates the projected arc to a great circle and locates the place(s) where there is/are no change. An extrapolation has a certain degree of precision that might be affected by different factors. For instance, Johansson and Börjesson (1990) found that slant judgments were less accurate when the patterns subtended a small visual angle than when they subtended a large angle. Patterns subtending small angles required a longer extrapolation than did patterns subtending a large angle. In the present experiment two questions were addressed. First, is it possible to discriminate slant that is represented by only two moving

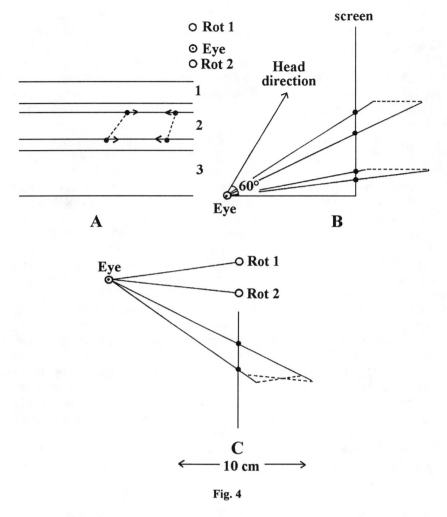

Fig. 4

A. Front view showing three "windows" (1–3), two pairs of dots that have passed a quarter of their motion path, and the location of the eye.

B. Top view showing two pairs of dots and the simulated lines (dotted) to the right of the picture plane.

C. Rear view showing two pairs of dots (behind each other) and two simulated lines (dotted) parallel to the Eye-Rot 2 lines, respectively.

dots? If so, does the distance of extrapolation affect the precision of judged slant? It is predicted that slant can be discriminated from only two dots, and second, it is predicted that the shorter the extrapolation, the better will be the precision of discrimination of slant.

Method

Stimuli. Each stimulus pattern consisted of two pairs of dots that moved back and forth in horizontal motion paths. Each pair of dots defined a virtual line representing a distal line, with a specific slant, moving translatorily behind a "window" with horizontal edges. The situation with a stimulus pattern consisting of two pairs of dots is shown in Fig. 4. The front view (A) shows the three "windows" or pairs of motion paths (1–3) used in the experiment and the position of the eye. The dotted lines (not present in the experiment) connect the dots of a pair. The arrows show the direction and relative velocity of the dots. The top view, Fig. 4B, shows the dots on the screen and, as dotted lines, the simulated lines to the right and, from the subject's point of view, behind the screen. Finally, the rear view, Fig. 4C, shows, as dotted lines, the simulated lines to the right of the screen. Further, the simulated slants are shown as parallel to the lines connecting the Eye and Rot 1 and Rot 2 respectively. This will be more commented on below.

The different pairs of dots used in the experiment are shown as front views in Figs. 5 and 6. Each figure shows three "windows" (1–3), each consisting of an upper and a lower motion path.

Three different pairs of dots were used in each "window". All pairs had their right end positions under the Eye as indicated by the dots connected by the dotted vertical lines. The three pairs had, however, different left end points as shown by P1–P3. Each stimulus pattern consisted of two different pairs (P1–P2; P2–P3; P1–P3) of dots appearing at opposite ends of their respective motion paths and then moving back and forth with the same frequency and with a phase difference of 180°. In this way three stimulus patterns were constructed in each of the three "windows" making a total of nine stimulus patterns for each of the Figs. 5 and 6. The vertical separation between the dots of a pair subtended a visual angle of 9° when the dots appeared in their right most position. The horizontal motion for each pair is given as the mean of the two dots' distances. The horizontal motions in Fig. 5 subtended in "window" 1 for P1, P2, and P3 visual angles of 26.0°, 17.3°, and 12.6°, respectively. Corresponding values were for "window" 2 33.8°, 29.6°, and 27.1° and for window 3 39.8°, 38.6° and 38.1°. It should be noted that there are relatively great differences between the pairs in "window" 1 and small differences between the pairs in "window" 3. In Fig. 6 all horizontal motions for a given "window" subtended the same visual angle; in "window" 1 subtending a visual angle of 38.6°, in "window" 2 35.6° and in "window" 3 30.6°. The dots moved continuously back and forth without pauses at the end positions. The motion from one end to the other lasted for 3 sec, thus one cycle was completed in 6 sec. In order to make it easier for the subject to report which pair of dots tilted most, the dots of one pair in each stimulus pattern

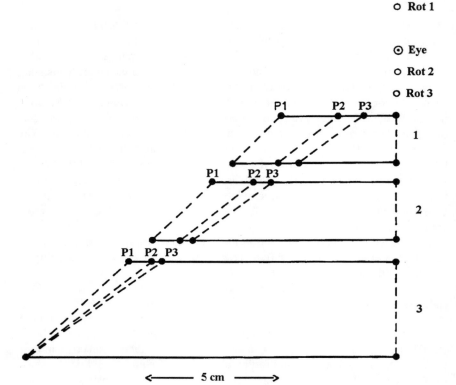

Fig. 5. Stimulus patterns used in the experiment.

were made of two illuminated pixels and the dots of the other pair of three illuminated pixels. This difference was balanced in the experiment.

Considerations behind construction of stimuli. The three different pairs (P1–P3 in Figs. 5 and 6) of dots simulated three different slants. Consider for instance P1 moving back and forth. The virtual (dotted) line connecting the dots rotates around the point Rot 1 (not present in the display). Rot 1 is the projection on the picture plane of the point at infinity of the simulated line. This means that a line from the eye to Rot 1 is parallel to the simulated line as shown in Fig. 4C. As seen by the ideal subject, the line is slanted upwards with the farther end higher than the closer, deviating 9.5° from the horizontal. The P2- and P3-pairs rotate around Rot 2 and Rot 3, respectively. P2 simulates a line that is tilted downwards deviating 4.8° from the horizontal, and P3 simulates a line that is til-

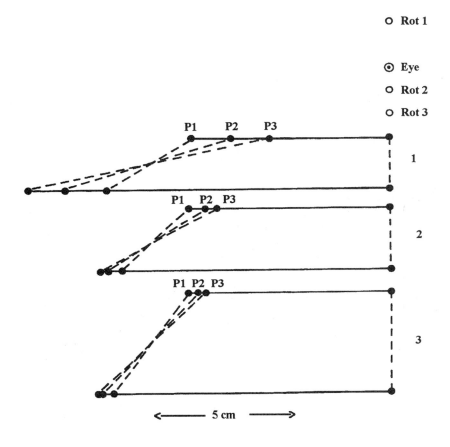

Fig. 6. Stimulus patterns used in the experiment.

ted downwards deviating 9.5° from the horizontal. It should be noted that it is the position of Rot 1–3 relative to the eye that determines simulated slant. Since these relative positions are held constant in Figs. 5 and 6 and for all "windows" all P1-pairs simulate the same slant irrespective of in which pattern they appear in the experiment. The same of course is true for the P2- and P3-pairs.

Three different "windows" (1–3 in Figs. 5 and 6) were used in the experiment. They are situated at different distances from the rotation points (Rot 1–3). In terms of the optic sphere theory it can be said that a "window" determines the motions of the dots that, as projected, define an arc of a great circle on the optic sphere. Further, the rotation point (Rot) corresponds to a point of no change (S in Fig. 1) on the extrapolated great circle. It follows that the projections of dots from different "windows" are located at different distances from the point of no change, S. For instance dot projections from "window" 3 require a longer extrapolation to reach S than those from "window" 2 do, which in turn require a longer extrapolation to S than those from "window" 1 do. The three "windows" are three levels on the main independent variable. According to the prediction the precision in slant judgments increases when the distance from the projected arc to the point of no change decreases.

Finally, two sets (Fig. 5 and 6) of nine stimulus patterns each were used in an effort to control the same proximal parameters. It is important that the dot patterns from different "windows" differ in only one respect, that is distance from Rot. It is not possible to achieve this. In Fig. 5, the P1 has the same slant across all "windows." This is also true for P2 and P3. However, in "window" 1, there is a substantial difference (26.0°–12.6°) between the Ps concerning length of motion path whereas this difference is small (39.8°–38.1°) in "window" 3. Thus it might be stated that a difference in precision of slant judgments between "windows" is due to this difference rather than to distance to Rot. In order to keep length of motion path constant the stimulus patterns in Fig. 6 were added. For any "window" all Ps have the same length of motion path. On the other hand it was not possible to keep the slant of each P constant across "windows" as was the case in Figure 5.

Viewing conditions. The subjects looked with their right eye at the computer screen onto which a green film was attached in order to eliminate visible traces from the moving dots. The head and eye position at a distance of 10 cm from the screen was controlled by a combined chin and forehead support. During the stimulus presentations the room was darkened.

Procedure. The subjects were told that four moving dots would appear on the screen and that it would be possible to perceive them as the endpoints of two rods oriented in depth. The subjects were asked to report which pair of dots slanted most downwards and to report them as equal if they could not make a decision. Finally the subjects were told that no limit was set for inspection time. Two stimulus patterns, not to appear in the experiment, were presented to test the ability to perceive depth and slant. If depth and the general orientation of slant of the simulated lines were reported the subjects passed the test and the 18 stimulus patterns were presented once in randomized order. When the subjects had given their reports the room was lighted, the report noted, and thereafter the next stimulus pattern was presented.

Subjects. Eighteen subjects participated in the experiment. Participation was part of course requirements.

Table 1

Frequencies of different categories of reports for the different "windows" summarized over subjects and stimulus patterns (N = 16).

Stimulus condition		Report category		
		Correct	Equal	Reverse
"Window" 1	Fig. 5	34	4	10
	Fig. 6	41	2	5
"Window" 2	Fig. 5	32	6	10
	Fig. 6	33	6	9
"Window" 3	Fig. 5	21	15	12
	Fig. 6	29	13	6
		190	46	52

Results and Conclusions

Two subjects were excluded from the data treatment; one did not pass the introductory test and the other gave such odd reports that it was taken for granted that the instruction had been misunderstood.

The reports were divided into three categories: "correct," "equal," and "reverse." A "reverse" report meant that the subject reported the wrong pair as the one slanting most and an "equal" report indicated that the subject could not tell which pair seemed to slant most. The results are presented in Table 1.

The first question concerned whether it was possible to make judgments of slant from only two dots moving in horizontal motion paths. As shown in Table 1, it is obvious that this is the case. Out of 288 judgments, 190 (66%) are correct.

According to the second prediction, the precision in the judgments should increase when the distance from the "window" to Rot decreases. This was also the case. "Window" 1, being closest to Rot, yielded 78% correct reports, "window" 2, 68% correct reports, and "window" 3, most distant from Rot, 52% correct reports. The decrease in number of correct responses was balanced by an increase in equal responses, whereas the number of reverse responses was about the same for all "windows."

The trend toward more correct responses with shorter distances between "window" and Rot was tested with Page's L trend test. Since each subject judged a total of six stimulus patterns for each "window" a subject could get a score from 0 to 6 of correct responses for each "window." These scores were tested and a significant trend was found $L = 206.5$, $p < .01$. It is concluded that it is possible to make judgments of slant from two moving dots and that the precision of slant judgments increases when the distance between the "window" and Rot decreases.

Discussion

The results were in accordance with the predictions. Although the optic sphere theory was supported, the data do not rule out other interpretations of the mechanisms behind perception of slant. The critical length of extrapolation along a great circle on the optic sphere has been the basis for the experiment. However, there is in the experiment a proximal covariation to this length (distance "window" to Rot). Therefore the results can be accounted for in terms of a conventional two-dimensional proximal analysis although such an analysis requires other types of constraints.

There were greater proximal differences between the pairs of dots in "window" 1 than in "window" 2 that had greater such differences than "window" 3. In Fig. 5 the differences concerned motion distance, and in Fig. 6 the differences concerned proximal slant. Proximal differences might affect detectability of differences between pairs but do not necessarily affect number of correct answers. It should be kept in mind that simulated slant (distance Rot–Eye) was constant between "windows." Not only did the "equal" answers decrease but there was also an increase in correct answers when the distance "window"–Rot decreased. It is not probable that the naive subjects guided only by discrimination of proximal changes could make a deduction regarding simulated slant. It is therefore taken for granted that the reports were mediated by a real impression of slant in depth based on the relative position Rot–Eye.

In terms of the optic sphere theory the subjects in this experiment had to locate an axis of rotation by applying the constraint of no change on the great circle. Obviously the subjects could do that since most reports were correct. One question is whether this constraint is always applied when it is possible. Another way to put this question is: Does the visual system always perceive a translation if this is sufficient to account for the proximal change? Are translations preferred to rotations? These questions remain to be answered.

Another problem is what happens when there is no point of no change on the great circle. The visual system then has to analyze rotations into rotation components yielded by constraints that in a natural way take advantage of the spherical shape of the projection surface. Experiments with simulated translating and rotating lines may help to explore these questions.

References

Johansson, G. (1950). *Configurations in event perception.* Uppsala: Almqvist & Wiksell. [Chapter 2, this volume.]

Johansson, G. (1964). Perception of motion and changing form. *Scandinavian Journal of Psychology, 5*, 181–208. [Chapter 4, this volume.]

Johansson, G., & Börjesson, E. (1989). Towards a new theory of vision. Studies in wide-angle space perception. *Ecological Psychology, 1*, 301–331. [Chapter 10, this volume]

Johansson, G., & Börjesson, E. (1990). Experiments on the optic sphere theory. Slant perception from central stimulation (Uppsala Psychological Reports, No. 424). Uppsala University, Department of Psychology.

Runeson, S. (1977). On the possibility of "smart" perceptual mechanisms. *Scandinavian Journal of Psychology, 18*, 172–179.

Concluding Remarks

Personal Comments

Gunnar Johansson

Uppsala University

The editors invited me to comment on the participants' contributions to the symposium. I will do so, and according to the subjects discussed, my comments have been grouped under the following headings:
Broad theoretical questions
Vector analysis and biological motion
Wide angle stimulation
Optic sphere theory
Traffic safety research

Broad Theoretical Questions

Braunstein. Braunstein concentrates on the concept "decoding principles" and analyzes the theoretical implications of this concept from a number of theoretical aspects. I find that he, in a rather congenial way, has grasped my underlying intentions. The article is of a great theoretical interest.

Hochberg. Since the 1950s Julian Hochberg and I have in common an engagement in studies on perceptual vector analysis, what Hochberg now baptizes "The Johansson effect." Julian is one of the most sophisticated investigators in this field and I have found his present chapter of great interest.

When reading this chapter I found that Julian and I in our latest publications, more distinctly than earlier, have moved in different directions (both hopefully important). Since my 1964 paper, my interest in the broad biological aspect of visual perception has led me to seek a type of theory applicable to the primitive visual systems from which the human one has descended. With the optic sphere approach (Johansson & Börjesson, 1989) and my present chapter on relations between this theory and the theory of perceptual vector analysis (chapter 10, this volume), I have built up the basic structure of such a theory. Julian, as he describes in his present chapter under the jocular heading "On daring to say 'mental structure' in Uppsala" (p. 424 in this volume), has moved in the opposite direction. As Julian surely knows, for me such a "swearing in the church" not only is accepted but, if seriously innovative, very welcome. However, I think that it is correct to state that at present Julian and I represent two clearly different branches of research on visual event perception.

The theoretical structure I am constructing takes into consideration the evolution of visual processing, common to all types of the chambered eye, even the most primitive one. This processing is the result of sensory communication of information between mainly the visual, vestibular, and kinesthetic sense organs. This cooperation between sense channels is regarded as being of a fundamental importance for a correct understanding of the sensory processes underlying visual space perception. It is characterized by its mechanical, automatic, and in this meaning "direct" nature. However, we must also observe that this system, in a so far not satisfactorily clarified way, is controlled by the perceiving organism's immediate need and intentions. This holds true also for primitive organisms.

Julian's current research concerns "mental structure" and "cognitive perception," thus vision in connection with known or supposed capacities of the human brain for *interpreting, evaluating,* and *changing* the outcome of the optical stimulation. (This aspect of animal life is outside the optic sphere theory in its present form.) He anchors his research in this field in experimental studies of the "Johansson effect" of type 1950, studies showing that in these cases the perceptual vector analysis should not be regarded as an exclusively mechanical process.

Typical for Julian's analyses is that he searches for indications of conscious cognitive control of the perceptual output. From this follows that it differs from my initial vector theory which was intended to cover also vision of other vertebrates, as well as from the optic sphere theory. Still, just this search for possible human cognitive selection or even manipulating of the information in the optic flow is of a special interest also for me, partly because it touches at the well-known and theoretically interesting satiation effects (from my point of view probably not mainly stemming from the *optical* component of the stimulation).

Surely, Julian has noticed that accepting the optic sphere theory implies a drastic reduction of what earlier has been treated as perceptual effects of cognitive processes. For instance, the automatic mechanical interpretation of perspective projection, the components in the optic flow stemming from eye movements and body movements, are in the optic sphere theory explained as mechanical, non-cognitive effects. It must also be observed, however, that while the perceptual recording and processing of these effects can be explained by the optic sphere theory, explaining the intentional character of the observer's (man or animal) movements determining the wide angle character of this flow is outside the range of the optic sphere theory. Here future studies of "mental structures" of higher order, controlling the self-motion components in the optic flow, will be of great interest. And it seems to me that Julian Hochberg is moving in this direction. Julian's positive comments to the optic sphere theory show that he, like myself, has not found any decisive conflicts between our theoretical structures.

Lappin. Reading Lappin's paper "Seeing Structures in Space-Time" gave me a strong feeling of satisfaction. There I found a confirmation of my own earlier tentative conclusion about a basic relationship between the principles of the perceptual vector analysis approach and the outstanding research on visual space and motion perception going on at Lappin's laboratory.

Lappin here documents a profound understanding of the theoretical foundation on which the vector analysis approach is built in my dissertation and my later studies in this field. His classifications of the theoretical structures of the studies of event perception in theories of an intrinsic versus an extrinsic character, when it is a question of reference system, is very instructive. In this connection he also points out the complications and constructional troubles (and even invalidity) inherent in the extrinsic approaches.

After sketching the basic structure of the perceptual vector analysis and its consequences, Lappin proceeds to discuss the following important questions: *"How might such a vector analysis be accomplished? How is information about global structure and motion obtained from the local motions of individual points? Could such global information be associated with local properties, as Johansson (1976) suggested?"* In fact, these questions are good formulations of the basic (not solved) problems evoked especially by the multisensory experiments described in Johansson (1950). These questions remain in the forefront of my thinking on visual processing of optical stimulation.

Vector Analysis

Bergström. The vector analysis approach to visual perception is programmatically relational. It is Bergström's merit to have transferred this basic principle in the perceptual vector analysis approach to the study of perception of color and illumination. His paper gives a clear view of this long-term project in a fruitful state of progress.

Personally I am very interested in this work. I regard it as a defect in my own research on visual perception that I myself, after some early contributions (Johansson, 1950, 1951) where I touched on these problems, never was active in this field. From that time, however (and probably due to influences from David Katz), I have fully recognized that the study of visual space perception comprises two important aspects, namely recording of spatial change over time and recording of the "qualitative" characteristics of stimulation (color, illumination effects, etc.) that vary with the spatial ones. As long as we students of space perception limit ourselves to the study of the *form* aspect as such, we can hardly reach a full understanding of everyday visual space perception. Therefore, my hope is that the branch of visual research in which Bergström is one of the pioneers will be given high priority in the coming decades.

Koenderink. Both from a theoretical and methodological point of view Koenderink's paper is of great interest for me (and, I hope, for all other readers). The mathematician Koenderink analyzes my concept perceptual vector analysis and constructs in a most elegant way a simple algorithm covering this theoretical approach and its experimental results in Johansson (1950, 1964). His final conclusion is important because it ought to stimulate to future applications.

Runeson. Runeson's paper concerns both perception of biological motion and visual perception of dynamics. Initially I introduced the studies of biological motion as a test of the applicability of the vector analysis model to highly complicated patterns of change. Therefore, in spite of the fact that Runeson's paper basically concerns perception of dynamics, I prefer to comment on this paper under the present heading.

Runeson's contribution to the book forms an interesting counterpart to Koenderink's. While Koenderink applies a computational approach, Runeson is profoundly engaged in the mechanics of visual perception. Runeson has earlier supplemented the kinematic specification of optical stimulation with its dynamic aspect, thus perception of physical forces. Runeson's and Frykholm's (1981, 1983) compelling demonstrations of the capacity of the visual system when it is a question of recording exertion of forces in an active human body, as presented in the biological motion way, always has fascinated me. I myself touched at this aspect of perception in Johansson (1978, pp. 700–702). Theoretically the Runeson and Frykholm approach is of a crucial importance. In the present paper Runeson adds still more convincing arguments for his position.

Wide Angle Stimulation

Held and Leibowitz. Two of our most prominent investigators of visual perception, both with special competence in the field of vection, discuss the theoretical consequences of my (Johansson, 1977a) studies of vection, evoked from extremely impoverished peripheral stimulation. The authors' assessment of the theoretical value of this investigation makes me mention a second study of mine in this field, a study which seems to me to have still higher relevance in the present context. Regrettably, however, this study was never officially published. Waiting for a planned but never performed second step, I described the experiment only in a prepublication report (Johansson, 1977b).

In this experiment I presented one moving dot to the periphery of each of the S's eyes (75° from the fovea). The dots moved in a vertical pendulum motion with amplitudes between 2.7° and 22°, and the subjects' task was to report the amplitude of the perceived self-motion. The results indicated that stimulation by just one such vertically moving bright spot in each eye brought about distinct saturated vection and also that the amplitudes of the perceived self-motion, recorded in millimeter measures, corresponded to the amplitudes of the moving dots.

The authors discuss and explain the vection effects in a highly interesting and theoretically important way. In the section "The Ubiquitous Self" (pp. 452) they bring to the fore "the presence of the observer as a platform for the distance senses." I very much appreciate this statement, especially since in my studies on vection such an anchorage of visual perception of the environment in simultaneous recordings of the own body has played a crucial role in my theorizing on visual perception. From own experience during my pilot studies and when serving as a subject in the two experimental studies mentioned, I found that sparse linear motion stimulation on the extreme periphery of the retina (80°–100° from the optic axis) was not perceived. Nevertheless, this stimulation evoked visual perception of corresponding linear motion of myself and the laboratory. Applied to everyday perception this use of the optical stimulation, though not consciously recorded, seems to indicate that the peripheral parts of the own face and other body parts act as an ultimate frame of reference for behaviorally veridical perception of the environment. As the authors point out, this effect, if accepted, indicates that distances in the visual environment can be recorded in behavioral units. This assumption is one of the basic conditions for the validity of the optic sphere theory.

Optic Sphere Theory

Börjesson. Erik Börjesson is my collaborator in the optic sphere project. Thus, I leave his article without comments.

Jansson. Gunnar Jansson has contributed in an important way to the Uppsala research on event perception and especially on perception of changing form. In his present paper he analyzes the relations between these early studies on perception of changing form and the optic sphere theory. The experimental studies on wide angle perception of waves in the optic sphere framework going on at the Uppsala laboratory (Johansson, Börjesson, & Vedeler, 1993) are in a direct way both theoretically and experimentally related to these studies.

Lee and von Hofsten. These authors have chosen to penetrate the validity of the optic sphere theory and they have fulfilled this intention in a highly enjoyable but also very instructive way.

They decide to discuss one of the most important components of this theory, namely the possibility of explaining perceptual recording of specific distance. While keeping close contact with the structure of the optic sphere theory they specify in an elegant step-by-step procedure an analogous specification of distance perception in computational terms, using an approach mainly borrowed from Lee's famous studies on the visual recording of time to contact.

The authors hesitate about accepting the basic principle in the optic sphere theory about interaction between visual and kinesthetic perception. Their argument in this respect is that this only means transferring the problem to another sense modality. If I had taken part in the conversation, my comment at that point would have been that the supposed interaction or "overhearing" implies a combination of spatial and optical sensory information and that this intersensory communication of spatial information implies a process yielding enrichment of information in both channels. Probably I would also have called attention to the fact that, for explaining space perception, a combination of reactions to muscular and retinal stimulation traditionally is regarded as necessary. We have been taught that in this respect there exist two categories of visual information: pictorial (optical) cues and physiological (kinesthetical) cues.

However, when proceeding, the discussants find that some kind of computational algorithm must stand in for the assumption of sensory interaction in the optic sphere theory. They explore Lee's tau margin and agree that a scaling factor related to measures in the perceiver's body will do the job. Distance between the eyes, convergence angles, eye height, and body size are discussed and proposed as yielding possible scaling units.

From my point of view this analysis finally results in a nice, complete parallelism between my mechanical and Lee and von Hofsten's computational approach to specific distance. Both achieve a behaviorally relevant visual recording of distance by a sensory combination of optical and kinesthetic event recordings. It goes without saying that I welcome this qualified verification of the relevance of my non-computational, mechanical alternative as specified in the optic sphere theory.

Todd. Todd starts his examination of the optic sphere theory by declaring that he will "adopt the role of a critic." This is the correct attitude when it is a question of evaluating a proposed new theory, and I appreciate it. It is also satisfying to find that Todd has not found any technical deficiencies in the construction of the theory worth being mentioned. Less satisfying for me personally is his statement that the theory mostly has to be regarded as iterations of what already has been established in current computational models. It goes without saying that I am of another opinion. If not, the theory would never have been published. Therefore, I will proceed with an attempt to find the reasons for our different standpoints in this respect.

My main point is that Todd has not taken into consideration my motive for constructing the optic sphere theory: my intentions to construct a biologically relevant theory built on an optical/mechanical model, applicable also to wide angle stimulation.

The optic sphere theory (as well as my earlier contributions to the study of visual perception) in a programmatic way concerns how vertebrate vision works as a biological system. I tried to construct a theory which as closely as possible will instantiate an analogy to known optical and mechanical functions in connection with vertebrate vision. The solution worked out was my optical/mechanical model constituted of two parts, a neurophysiological and a geometrical one.

The current computational approaches differ from such a biological approach in the respect that they basically are designed for constructing *mathematical* analogies to the optical information about objects and space, analogies valid also when it is a question of artificial vision.

In his statement that "their 'new' alternative in fact is compatible with many other existing analyses," Todd evidently has disregarded the decisive role of the processor part of the theory and left this part outside his analysis. He has limited his comments to stressing the projective equivalence between projection on a sphere and on a plane. In this respect there exists of course no disagreement between us. The optic sphere theory, as well as the experimental method described, is built on the geometrical characteristic mentioned. The main difference between the approaches instead concerns the theoretical and experimental wide angle applications of this characteristic in the optic sphere theory.

The optic sphere construction with its processor was worked out as a continuation of the theoretical approach in Johansson (1964). To my knowledge, the rigidity constraint (together with the 3D preference) as a specific concept was first brought forward in this paper (with Wallach and Gibson as important forerunners). Later Ullman (1979), referring to my paper (Johansson, 1964), introduced this assumption as a key assumption for specifying one-to-one relations in his computational theory. Thus this theory also has a "processor" component, and, like my 1964 initial attempt, this component is lacking a relevant biological anchorage.

From the above it should be clear that from my point of view the geometrical part of the optic sphere theory is not a theory about perception per se and should not be treated as such. It is an anatomic-geometric model relevant for my purpose and nothing more. At first the combination of the processor, including also the kinesthetic and vestibular components, and the optic sphere model, yields an analogy to *visual* information processing.

In this connection I am anxious to declare that I have in no way intended to criticize the computational approach, for which I have a great admiration, not least because of its opening of ways toward computer-aided artificial vision. My own field, however, is biological vision and my long-term search for an adequate model fitting that objective has resulted in my present mechanical model, intended to be computation-free and therefore appropriate as an analogy to the information processing in vertebrates.

I will limit my comments on Todd's paper to these viewpoints, together with a declaration of full agreement with Todd when it is a question of the necessity of expanding our domain of research to include effects of brightness, color, and illumination. This aspect was mentioned in Johansson (1991) and is emphasized above also in my comments to Bergström's present paper.

Traffic Safety Research

Leibowitz. In his paper in this section Leibowitz comments on my combining of basic and applied research and what he calls my originality in theoretical respects. Hersch's assumption is that my independence of current theoretical positions partly is a result of my rather exceptional background as a student of visual perception with mostly private studies during the lengthy time-out between the elementary school and the beginning of my university studies at the age of 29.

In an attempt to retrospect I find that Hersch's supposition probably is correct. When beginning the university studies I brought with me a limited basis from my homemade studies in philosophy. In a similar way, during a pause in my academical studies of about 3 years of practical work after my graduation in philosophy, I was strongly engaged in spare-time reading of the psychology of perception, especially vision. As Hersch guesses, these preparatory studies of perceptual psychology at matured age gave me a good and totally independent overview of the current theories of perception. In the books and papers penetrated, however, I found that in this material, with few exceptions, the experimental studies concerned perceptual information in static pictures, seen by a stationary observer. This fact made me astonished—and critical. From own everyday experience I knew, of course, that all active space perception was perception of change over time and I considered it as self-evident that studies of this aspect should be regarded as the most essential field of research on space perception. This nearly total lack of studies of perception of ongoing events, found during my prepatory spare-time studies, was my main reason for choosing motion perception as the general theme for my dissertation.

Hersch's next supposition is that my experience of interaction with the real world during all the years of professional practical work before my studies of perception has made me open to research in perception of everyday type. I agree. This holds true for both basic and applied research.

Rumar. Kåre Rumar acted as my right hand in my traffic safety research and he has great merit concerning the quality of this work. He received a highly meritorious doctor degree for his contributions in this field and later a chair as a professor. Rumar's continued traffic safety research has resulted in a leading position in the Swedish traffic safety research and an advanced international position.

References

Johansson, G. (1950). *Configurations in event perception.* Uppsala: Almqvist & Wiksell. [Chapter 2, this volume.]

Johansson, G. (1951). The effect of uniform and continuous chromatic changes. In *Essays in psychology: Dedicated to David Katz* (pp. 139–160). Uppsala: Almqvist & Wiksell.

Johansson, G. (1964). Perception of motion and changing form. *Scandinavian Journal of Psychology, 5,* 181–208. [Chapter 4, this volume.]

Johansson, G. (1976). Spatio-temporal differentiation and integration in visual motion perception. *Psychological Research, 38,* 379–393. [Chapter 8, this volume.]

Johansson, G. (1977a). Studies on visual perception of locomotion. *Perception, 6,* 365–376. [Chapter 9, this volume.]

Johansson, G. (1977b). *Visual perception of locomotion, elicited and controlled by a bright spot moving in the periphery of the visual field* (Report No. 210). Uppsala: Uppsala University, Department of Psychology.

Johansson, G. (1978). Visual event perception. In R. Held, H. W. Leibowitz, & H.-L. Teuber (Eds.), *Handbook of sensory physiology, Vol. VIII. Perception* (pp. 675–711). Berlin: Springer.

Johansson, G. (1991). *Elaborating the optic sphere theory.* Preliminary manuscript. Uppsala University, Department of Psychology.

Johansson, G., & Börjesson, E. (1989). Toward a new theory of vision. Studies in wide-angle space perception. *Ecological Psychology, 1,* 301–331. [Chapter 10, this volume]

Johansson, G., Börjesson, E., & Vedeler, G. (1993). *On perception of waves. A study of monocular wide angle space perception.* Manuscript. Uppsala: Uppsala University, Department of Psychology.

Runeson, S., & Frykholm, G. (1981). Visual perception of lifted weight. *Journal of Experimental Psychology: Human perception and Performance, 7,* 733–740.

Runeson, S., & Frykholm, G. (1983). Kinematic specification of dynamics as an informational basis for person and action perception: Expectations, gender recognition, and deceptive intention. *Journal of Experimental Psychology: General, 112,* 585–615.

Ullman, S. (1979). *The interpretation of visual motion.* Cambridge, MA: MIT Press.

Bibliography 1950–1993

Gunnar Johansson

Uppsala University

Johansson, G. (1950). *Configurations in event perception.* Uppsala: Almqvist & Wiksell.

Johansson, G. (1950). Configurations in the perception of velocity. *Acta Psychologica, 7,* 25–79.

Johansson, G. (1951). Demonstrations of some phenomena in motion perception. *Thirteenth International Congress of Psychology held at the University of Stockholm under the presidency of Professor David Katz: Proceedings and papers.* Stockholm: Nordiska bokhandeln.

Johansson, G. (1951). The effect of uniform and continuous chromatic changes. In *Essays in psychology: Dedicated to David Katz* (pp. 117–160). Uppsala: Almqvist & Wiksell.

Johansson, G. (1955). *A note on differences in motion track enlargements between male and female subjects* (Report No. 24). Stockholm University, Department of Psychology.

Johansson, G., Dureman, I., & Sälde, H. (1955). Motion perception and personality. *Acta Psychologica, 11,* 289–296.

Johansson, G. (1956). The velocity of the motion after-effect. *Acta Psychologica, 12,* 19–24.

Johansson, G., Backlund, F., & Bergström, S.-S. (1957). *Studies on motion thresholds I* (Report No. 1). Uppsala University, Department of Psychology.

Johansson, G., Backlund, F., & Bergström, S.-S. (1957). *Studies on motion thresholds II* (Report No. 2). Uppsala University, Department of Psychology.

Johansson, G., Dureman, I., & Sälde, H. (1957). Motion perception and personality II and III. *Acta Psychologica, 13,* 61–67.

Johansson, G. (1958). Rigidity, stability, and motion in perceptual space. *Acta Psychologica, 14,* 359–370.

Johansson, G., Backlund, F., & Bergström, S.-S. (1958). *Experimentell prövning av olika instrumentpanelers läsbarhet* (Experimental examination of the readability of different instrument panels). Mimeographed. Uppsala University, Department of Psychology.

Johansson, G., Backlund, F., & Bergström, S.-S. (1958). *Undersökning av ögonomställningsvårigheter enligt beställning Nr E 7 - 16973* (Examination of eye adjustment difficulties according to order No. E 7 - 16973). Mimeographed. Uppsala University, Department of Psychology.

Johansson, G., Backlund, F., & Bergström, S.-S. (1959). *Luminance changes and visual acuity* (Report No. 5). Uppsala University, Department of Psychology.

Johansson, G., Backlund, F., & Bergström, S.-S. (1959). *Läsbarhet hos horisontindikatorer* (Readability of horisont indicators). Mimeographed. Uppsala University, Department of Psychology.

Johansson, G., Backlund, F., & Bergström, S.-S. (1959). *Studier av rörelsetrösklar III* (Studies of motion thresholds III). Mimeographed. Uppsala University, Department of Psychology.

Johansson, G., Backlund, F., & Bergström, S.-S. (1959). *Styrningsprecision som funktion av hastigheten hos den förflyttning, som skall kompenseras* (Steering precision as a function of the speed of the motion to be compensated). Mimeographed. Uppsala University, Department of Psychology.

Johansson, G. (1960). Bewegungsnachbild nach Einzelreizung (Motion aftereffect from non-iterated stimulus motion). *Psychologische Beiträge, 5*, 81–92.

Johansson, G. (1960). Binocular interaction in motion perception. *Scandinavian Journal of Psychology, 1*, 65–68.

Johansson, G. (1960). *Människan som feldetektor* (Man as a fault detector). Paper given at courses arranged by IVA:s kommitté för oförstörande provning and Kontrollingenjörernas Förening in Getå, Sweden, 7–8 November, 1959, and 6–7 February, 1960. Mimeographed. Uppsala University, Department of Psychology.

Johansson, G., & Backlund, F. (1960). A versatile eye-movement recorder. *Scandinavian Journal of Psychology, 1*, 181–186.

Johansson, G., & co-workers (1960). *Bilförare och trafiksignaler. Del 1* (Drivers and road signs. Part 1). Mimeographed. Uppsala University, Department of Psychology.

Johansson, G., & Backlund, F. (1961). *Bilförare och trafiksignaler. Del 2* (Drivers and road signs. Part 2). Mimeographed. Uppsala University, Department of Psychology.

Johansson, G., & Backlund, F. (1961). *Bilförare och trafiksignaler. Del 3* (Drivers and road signs. Part 3). Mimeographed. Uppsala University, Department of Psychology.

Johansson, G., Backlund, F., & Bergström, S.-S. (1961). *Inverkan av indikatorbildens storlek på sannolikheten för målupptäckt* (Effect of the size of the indicator picture on the probability of goal detection). Mimeographed. Uppsala University, Department of Psychology.

Johansson, G. (1962). Perceptual overestimation of small motion tracks. *Psychologische Beiträge, 6*, 570–580.

Johansson, G. (1963). Perceptionsforskning (Perception research). *Nordisk psykologi, 15*, 133–140.

Johansson, G., Bergström, S. S., Jansson, G., Ottander, C., Rumar, K., & Örnberg, G. (1963). Visible distances in simulated night driving conditions with full and dipped headlights. *Ergonomics, 6*, 171–179.

Johansson, G., & Rumar, K. (1963). *Available braking distances in night driving* (Report No. 13). Uppsala University, Department of Psychology.

Johansson, G. (1964). Perception of motion and changing form. *Scandinavian Journal of Psychology, 5*, 181–208.

Johansson, G., & Jansson, G. (1964). Smoking and night driving. *Scandinavian Journal of Psychology, 5*, 124–128.

Johansson, G., & Ottander, C. (1964). Recovery time after glare. An experimental investigation of glare after-effect under night driving conditions. *Scandinavian Journal of Psychology, 5*, 17–25.

Rumar, K., & Johansson, G. (1965). *Siktsträckor under mörkertrafik vid möte med felinställt halvljus* (Visibility distances in night driving with misaligned meeting dipped headlights) (Report No. S 13). Uppsala University, Department of Psychology.

Dureman, I., Johansson, G., & Sälde, H. (1965). *Köns- och åldersskillnader vid visuell bedömning av rörelsebanelängd* (Sex and age differences in visual judgements of the length of motion paths) (Report No. S 17). Uppsala University, Department of Psychology.

Johansson, G. (1966). Geschehenswahrnehmung (Event perception). In W. Metzger (Ed.), *Handbuch der Psychologie, Band 1, Wahrnehmung und Bewusstsein* (pp. 745–775). Berlin: Springer.

Johansson, G., & Rumar, K. (1966). Drivers and road signs: A preliminary investigation of the capacity of car drivers to get information from road signs. *Ergonomics, 9*, 57–62.

Johansson, G., & Jansson, G. (1967). *The perception of free fall.* Seminar paper. Uppsala University, Department of Psychology.

Johansson, G., & Rumar, K. (1967). Visible distances and safe speeds for night driving car meetings. *CIE*, Washington.

Johansson, G. (1968). *En mörkermötessimulator för utveckling av polariserat billjus* (A night driving simulator for the development of polarized headlight) (Report No. S 34). Uppsala University, Department of Psychology.

Johansson, G. (1968). Space perception from continuously changing stimulus patterns. In *Rezumatele comunicarilor. Conferinta Nationala de Psihologie, Bucuresti, 21–23 octombrie 1968* (pp. 24–25). Bucharest, Romania: Asociatia psihologilor din Republica Socialista România.

Johansson, G. (1968). Vision without contours: Study of visual information from ordinal stimulation. *Perceptual and Motor Skills, 26*, 335–351.

Epstein, W., Jansson, G., & Johansson, G. (1968). Perceived angle of oscillatory motion. *Perception & Psychophysics, 3*, 12–16.

Johansson, G., & Jansson, G. (1968). Perceived rotary motion from changes in a straight line. *Perception & Psychophysics, 4*, 165–170.

508 · GUNNAR JOHANSSON

Johansson, G., & Rumar, K. (1968). *A new system with polarized headlights* (Report No. 64). Uppsala University, Department of Psychology.

Johansson, G., & Rumar, K. (1968). Visible distances and safe approach speeds for night driving. *Ergonomics, 11*, 275–282.

Johansson, G. (1969). Ergonomi och människa-teknikproblem. Något om ett aktuellt forskningsområde inom psykologin (Ergonomics and man-machine problems. Notes on a research area of current interest within psychology). *Acta Universitatis Upsaliensis, Studia Psychologica Upsaliensa*, No. 1.

Johansson, G. (1969). Varseblivningspsykologi (Perception psychology). In A. Attman, Å. Bruhn-Möller, H. Hessler, & L. Kebbon (Eds.), *20 års samhällsforskning* (pp. 198–204). Stockholm: P.A. Norstedt & Söner.

Johansson, G. (1969). Visuell förändring. Något om problem-, metod- och teoriutveckling vid studiet av perception av rörelse och formförändring (Visual change. Notes on problem, method, and theory development when studying the perception of motion and change of form). In *Universitetet och forskningen, Acta Universitatis Upsaliensis, Skrifter rörande Uppsala Universitet 17* (pp. 189–206).

Johansson, G., Backlund, F., & Bergström, S. S. (1969). Shortest perceptible length of motion track as a function of stimulus velocity. In A. Lehtovaara et al. (Eds.), *Contemporary research in psychology of perception. In honorem Kai von Fieandt sexagenarii* (pp. 71–86). Porvoo, Finland: Söderström.

Johansson, G., Rumar, K., Forsgren, J.-B., & Snöborgs, M. (1969). *Experimentella studier av polariserat mötesljus I. Siktsträcka som funktion av polarisatortyp* (Experimental studies of polarized headlight I. Visibility distances as a function of type of polarizer) (Report No. S 37). Uppsala University, Department of Psychology.

Johansson, G., Rumar, K., Forsgren, J.-B., & Snöborgs, M. (1969). *Experimentella studier av polariserat mötesljus II. Siktsträcka som funktion av strålkastar-intensitet under olika atmosfärförhållanden* (Experimental studies of polarized headlight II. Visibility distance as a function of headlight intensity under different atmospheric conditions) (Report No. S 38). Uppsala University, Department of Psychology.

Johansson, G., Rumar, K., Forsgren, J.-B., & Snöborgs, M. (1969). *Experimentella studier av polariserat mötesljus III. Siktsträcka som funktion av visortyp* (Experimental studies of polarized headlight III. Visibility distance as a function of type of visor) (Report No. S 39). Uppsala University, Department of Psychology.

Johansson, G., Rumar, K., Forsgren, J.-B., & Snöborgs, M. (1969). *Experimentella studier av polariserat mötesljus IV. Siktsträcka vid möten mellan konventionellt halvljus och polariserat mötesljus* (Experimental studies of polarized headlight IV. Visibility distance during meetings between conventional dipped light and polarized meeting light) (Report No. S 40). Uppsala University, Department of Psychology.

Johansson, G. (1970). On theories for visual space perception. A letter to Gibson. *Scandinavian Journal of Psychology*, *11*, 67–79.

Johansson, G., & Backlund, F. (1970). Drivers and road signs. *Ergonomics*, *13*, 749–759.

Johansson, G., & Rumar, K. (1970). A new polarized headlight system. *Lighting Research and Technology*, *2*, 28–32.

Johansson, G., Rumar, K., Forsgren, J.-B., & Snöborgs, M. (1970). *Experimental studies of a polarized headlight system V. Visibility distances obtained with some laminated and tempered windshields* (Report No. 87). University of Uppsala, Department of Psychology.

Johansson, G. (1970). *Visual motion perception. A model for visual motion and space perception from changing proximal stimulation* (Report No. 98). Uppsala University, Department of Psychology.

Maas, J. B., Johansson, G., Jansson, G., & Runeson, S. (1970). *Motion perception, Part I.* (Film). Boston: Houghton Mifflin.

Maas, J. B., Johansson, G., Jansson, G., & Runeson, S. (1971). *Motion perception, Part II.* (Film). Boston: Houghton Mifflin.

Johansson, G., & Rumar, K. (1971). Drivers' brake reaction times. *Human Factors*, *13*, 23–27.

Johansson, G., & Rumar, K. (1971). Silhouette effects in night driving. *Scandinavian Journal of Psychology*, *12*, 80–89.

Rumar, K., Forsgren, J-B., Thorell, M., & Johansson, G. (1971). Polarized headlight systems: The effect of laminated and toughened windscreens on visibility distance. *Lighting Research and Technology*, *3*, 158–161.

Johansson, G. (1972). Perceptual psychology. In A. Attman, Å. Bruhn-Möller, H. Hessler, & L. Kebbon (Eds.), *Social science research in Sweden* (pp. 171–177). Stockholm: The Swedish Council for Social Science Research.

Johansson, G. (1972). Toward a theory for kinetic space perception. In *Abstract guide of the XXth International Congress of Psychology* (p. 157). Sciences Council of Japan.

Johansson, G. (1973). Monocular movement parallax and near-space perception. *Perception*, *2*, 135–146.

Johansson, G. (1973). Visual perception of biological motion and a model for its analysis. *Perception & Psychophysics, 14*, 201–211.

Jansson, G., & Johansson, G. (1973). Visual perception of bending motion. *Perception*, *2*, 321–326.

Johansson, G. (1974). Huvudlinjer i den empiriska psykologins utveckling och problematik (Main lines in the development and the problems of empirical psychology). In J. Ullenhag (Ed), *Samhällsvetenskap på 70-talet* (pp. 48–59). Stockholm: Aldus.

Johansson, G. (1974). Projective transformations as determining visual space perception. In R. B. MacLeod & H. L. Pick (Eds.), *Perception: Essays in honor of J. J. Gibson* (pp. 117–138), Ithaca, NY: Cornell University Press.

Johansson, G. (1974). Vector analysis in visual perception of rolling motion. A quantitative approach. *Psychologische Forschung, 36,* 311–319.

Johansson, G. (1974). Visual perception of rotary motion as transformations of conic sections—A contribution to the theory of visual space perception. *Psychologia—An International Journal of Psychology in the Orient, 17,* 226–237.

Johansson, G. (1975). Visual motion perception. *Scientific American, 232* (6), pp. 76–88.

Johansson, G. (1976). Spatio-temporal differentiation and integration in visual motion perception. *Psychological Research, 38,* 379–393.

Johansson, G. (1977) About the geometry underlying spontaneous visual decoding of the optical message. In E. L. J. Leeuwenberg & H. F. J. Buffart (Eds.), *Formal theories of visual perception* (pp. 265–276). New York: Wiley.

Johansson, G. (1977). Spatial constancy and motion in visual perception. In W. Epstein (Ed.), *Stability and constancy in visual perception. Mechanisms & processes* (pp. 375–419). New York: Wiley.

Johansson, G. (1977). Studies on visual perception of locomotion. *Perception, 6,* 365–376.

Johansson, G. (1977). Synperceptionsforskning med Uppsala-signatur (Visual perception research with Uppsala signature). *Läkartidningen, 74,* 3416–3418.

Johansson, G. (1977). *Visual perception of locomotion, elicited and controlled by a bright spot moving in the periphery of the visual field* (Report No. 210). Uppsala University, Department of Psychology.

Johansson, G. (1978). Visual event perception. In R. Held, H. W. Leibowitz, & H.-L. Teuber (Eds.), *Handbook of sensory physiology, Vol. VIII. Perception* (pp. 675–711). Berlin: Springer.

Johansson, G. (1979). *Metrics, motion perception and neural processing in vision* (Report No. 250). Uppsala University, Department of Psychology.

Johansson, G. (1979). *A misleading test of the theory of perceptual vector analysis* (Report No. 266). Uppsala University, Department of Psychology.

Johansson, G. (1979). Memory functions in visual event perception. In L.-G. Nilsson (Ed.), *Perspectives in memory research* (pp. 93–103). Hillsdale, NJ: Erlbaum.

Johansson, G. (1980). *About perspective transformation induced by motion and the theory of visual space perception* (Report No. 278). Uppsala University, Department of Psychology.

Johansson, G., Hofsten, C. von, & Jansson, G. (1980). Event perception. *Annual Review of Psychology, 31,* 27–63.

Johansson, G., Hofsten, C. von, & Jansson, G. (1980). Direct perception and perceptual processes. *The Behavioral and Brain Sciences, 3,* 388.

Johansson, G. (1980). Visual space through motion. In A. H. Wertheim, W. A. Waagenaar, & H. W. Leibowitz (Eds.), *Tutorials on motion perception* (pp. 19–39). New York: Plenum.

Johansson, G. (1983). Optic flow, icons, and memory. *The Behavioral and Brain Sciences, 6,* 23–24.

Johansson, G. (1985). About visual event perception. In W. H. Warren & R. E. Shaw (Eds.), *Persistence and change: Proceedings of the First International Conference on Event Perception* (pp. 29–45). Hillsdale, NJ: Erlbaum.

Johansson, G. (1985). Vector analysis and process combinations in motion perception: A reply to Wallach, Becklen, and Nitzberg. *Journal of Experimental Psychology: Human Perception and Performance, 11,* 367–371.

Johansson, G. (1986). Relational invariance and visual space perception: On perceptual vector analysis of the optic flow. *Acta Psychologica, 63,* 89–101.

Johansson, G., & Börjesson, E. (1989). Toward a new theory of vision. Studies in wide-angle space perception. *Ecological Psychology, 1,* 301–331.

Johansson, G., & Börjesson, E. (1990). *Experiments on the optic sphere theory. Slant perception from central stimulation* (Uppsala Psychological Reports, No. 424). Uppsala University, Department of Psychology.

Johansson, G. (1991). *Elaborating the optic sphere theory.* Preliminary manuscript. Uppsala University, Department of Psychology.

Johansson, G., Börjesson, E., & Vedeler, G. (1993). *On perception of waves. A study of monocular wide angle space perception.* Manuscript. Uppsala University, Department of Psychology.

Name Index

Subject index